ROTHMANS RUGBY LEAGUE YEARBOOK 1994-95

Raymond Fletcher
and David Howes

C000155418

ROTHMANS

HEADLINE

© Rothmans Publications Ltd 1994

First published in 1994
by HEADLINE BOOK PUBLISHING

10 9 8 7 6 5 4 3 2 1

COVER PHOTOGRAPHS

Front Cover: Wigan's teenage second row man Andrew Farrell in action for Great Britain in the John Smith's Test against France at Carcassonne in March 1994, having become the youngest forward to play for the Lions, against New Zealand at Leeds the previous November.

Back Cover: Castleford skipper Lee Crooks, who led the Tigers to Regal Trophy success in January 1994 and was recalled by Great Britain against France in March 1994 after a two-year absence.

ACKNOWLEDGEMENTS
The compilers would like to acknowledge the assistance of the Rugby League Record Keepers' Club, club secretaries and individuals in providing material as a further source of reference for accuracy.

PHOTOGRAPHS
Modern day domestic photographs in this *Rothmans Rugby League Yearbook* are mainly from the files of the *Rugby Leaguer.* The compilers acknowledge the co-operation of Chief Photographer Gerald Webster and his staff.
The colour photographs on the front and back covers, plus a significant number of black-and-white contributions, are by freelance photographer Andrew Varley.

British Library Cataloguing in Publication Data
Rothmans Rugby League Yearbook — 1994-95
  1. Rugby football — Great Britain —
  Periodicals
  796.33.3.0941 GV945.9.G7

ISBN 0 7472 7851 2

Photoset by TTX LTD, London

Reproduced, printed and bound in Great Britain by
The Bath Press, Avon

HEADLINE BOOK PUBLISHING
A division of Hodder Headline PLC
338 Euston Road
London NW1 3BH

Rothmans Rugby League Yearbook 1994-95

CONTENTS

1. **Editorial Preface**   5

2. **Coaches' Select XIII**   6

3. **Memories**   9
   1993-94 Headlines   10
   June 1993 to May 1994   13

4. **Clubs**   21
   Honours, records, coaching registers, Great Britain registers, 1993-94 signings registers, players' summaries and match analyses

5. **Records**   145
   Leading scorers 1993-94   146
   Outstanding scoring feats 1993-94   146
   Record-breaking feats 1993-94   147
   Milestones 1993-94   152
   Leading scorers 1895-1993   161
   All-time records   167

6. **Charts**   171
   Most tries, goals and points in a match   172
   Most tries, goals and points in a season   175
   Most tries, goals and points in a career   178
   Most appearances in a career   180

7. **Cups**   181
   Challenge Cup   182
   Regal Trophy   205
   Premiership Trophies   221
   Lancashire Cup   237
   Yorkshire Cup   241
   Charity Shield   246
   World Club Challenge   248
   BBC-2 Floodlit Trophy   250
   Captain Morgan Trophy   252

8. **League**   253
   1993-94 Championship   254
   Divisional review   257
   Divisional records   260
   Championship play-off finals   263

9. **Coaches**   265
   Index of coaches 1974-94   266
   Dossier of coaches 1993-94   270

10. **Australia**   275
    Test review   276
    Teams 1974-93   280
    Register 1974-93   290
    Tours of Britain 1908-90   296
    Kangaroo Tour records   313
    Tours of France, New Zealand and Papua New Guinea   313
    Test and World Cup records   314

11. **1993 Kiwis**   315
    Tour review   316
    Tour data   318
    Match by match   322

12.	**Down Under**	335
	1993 Sydney Grand Final	336
	British players in Grand	
	Finals	338
	1993 State of Origin series	339
	New Zealand v. Australia	
	1993	343
13.	**Great Britain**	345
	1993-94 Test review	346
	Test results and records	348
	Teams 1974-94	354
	Register	364
	Tour summaries	374
	Tour squads	376
	World Cup data	382
	All-time scoring charts	386
14.	**Under-21s**	389
	1993-94 review	390
	Under-21 results	391
	Under-21 register	391
	Under-21 records	394
	Under-24 results	394
	Under-24 register	394
15.	**England and Wales**	395
	1993-94 review	396
	European Championship	398
	1975 World Championship	399
	Other International matches	400
	England records	401
	Wales records	402
	England teams	404
	England register	407
	Wales teams	409
	Wales register	413
16.	**Transfers**	415
	Review 1993-94	416
	Overseas register 1993-94	417
	Record transfers	419

17.	**Awards**	421
	Man of Steel 1994	422
	Teams of the Month	
	1993-94	426
	Entertainer of the	
	Month 1993-94	426
	Top scorers 1993-94	426
18.	**Referees**	427
	Honours 1993-94	427
	Senior referees 1994-95	427
19.	**Alliance**	429
	Final tables and results	
	1993-94	429
20.	**Pot Pourri**	431
	Diary of landmarks 1895-94	431
	Disciplinary review 1993-94	433
	Sponsorship review 1993-94	435
	Queen's honours	436
21.	**Attendances**	437
	Club review	437
	Competition review	439
	20,000-plus crowds	
	since 1985	439
	Analysis 1993-94	440
22.	**Fixtures**	443
	Stones Bitter	
	Championship 1994-95	443
	Second Division 1994-95	445
	Principal dates 1994-95	448

EDITORIAL PREFACE

One of the joys of record keeping is to compile a long list of statistics. Thus the drawing up of ten such factual charts for a new chapter in this 1994-95 *Rothmans Rugby League Yearbook* has been particularly satisfying.

Our first-ever display of the top scorers in a match, season and career, plus leading appearance makers, on the British Rugby League scene provides an accurate review of impressive facts and figures. But we like to think that the stark black-and-white type will evoke colourful memories of great players who have graced the domestic game, contributing masses of tries, goals and points to the annals of Rugby League history. As for the record number of appearances – a chart of 650 or more games reaching a pinnacle at 928 matches – longevity of performance is indeed an attribute of greatness.

As fellow *aficionados* of international Rugby League, it has been a pleasure to extend the *Yearbook's* deadline by 24 hours to include details of Wigan's incredible triumph over Australian premiers Brisbane Broncos in the 1994 World Club Challenge. The Riversiders' world title success also heightened anticipation for the 1994 John Smith's Test series between Great Britain and Australia, with Malcolm Reilly's charges superbly placed to go one better than their one-Test victories in the 1988, 1990 and 1992 series. We look forward to being able to chronicle the Lions' first Ashes success since 1970 in the next *Yearbook*!

We offer our traditional thanks to all those who have supplied data as part of the mammoth statistical verification process, particularly fellow members of the RL Record Keepers' Club – whose research has been particularly useful when dealing with records from more than 50 years ago – club secretaries and staff at the Rugby Football League.

The annual repetition of thanks to our better halves for being *Rothmans* widows does not dilute its sincerity. Also to Ian Marshall at Headline for his continued support and guidance. Last, but certainly not least, to our media colleagues and members of the public who have cared enough about the essential recording of our beloved game's statistics to offer encouragement and welcome constructive criticism.

● Facts and figures in this *Rothmans Rugby League Yearbook* as at 1 June 1994.

RAYMOND FLETCHER, of the *Yorkshire Post*

DAVID HOWES, Managing Director of *David Howes and Associates*

COACHES' SELECT XIII

The 1993-94 Coaches' Select XIII, an exclusive feature of the *Rothmans Rugby League Yearbook*, includes six debutants ... Bradford Northern duo Dave Watson and Paul Newlove, Castleford pair St. John Ellis and Lee Crooks, Warrington's Stones Bitter Man of Steel Jonathan Davies and youngest-ever Great Britain forward Andrew Farrell.

For the sixth successive year, the coaches in the Stones Bitter Championship were invited to select their form team of the season, not including members of their own club sides, basing their choice on opposition performances during the 1993-94 campaign, while taking general form into account. It is based on individual form and does not necessarily represent their best team.

Of the 16 coaches in the First Division, only Bradford Northern's Peter Fox declined the invitation to select a form XIII.

Wigan again dominated the final line-up, providing six players including Test winger Martin Offiah, who extended his record of being the only player to feature in all six Coaches' Select XIIIs since the introduction of this *Yearbook* feature. Only Hull K.R., Leigh and Salford did not have a First Division club nomination.

A total of 56 players were nominated with the widest spread of candidates being six for full back, six for each half back position, 11 for second row and 10 for prop forward.

For the third time in the six annual polls, no player received 100 per cent support, the most popular choices being Newlove with 13 votes out of a possible 15, Davies with 12 and Martin Dermott, Shaun Edwards, Ellis and Offiah with 10.

Two overseas imports gained inclusion in the form line-up, full back Watson and stand off Frano Botica, both of whom appeared for New Zealand in the 1993 John Smith's Tests against Great Britain.

Of the remaining 11 Britons selected, all but Ellery Hanley turned out for Great Britain during 1993-94, the Leeds skipper having announced his retirement from international

football. Hanley's return to the Coaches' Select XIII was his fourth selection in six years.

Six players were named for more than one position. Davies and Wigan's Gary Connolly were nominated for both full back and centre; Edwards for stand off and scrum half; Bradford's Karl Fairbank for prop and second row; and, as with 1992-93, Phil Clarke and Tawera Nikau for both second row and loose forward.

To comply with the wishes of some coaches who did not want their team published it was agreed to abandon this practice and replace it with a summary of nominations for each position.

The Coaches' Select XIII poll produced the following nominees:

Full back

Bradford Northern's Kiwi Dave Watson was the clear winner, polling more than twice as many votes as fellow candidates Gary Connolly (Wigan), Jonathan Davies (Warrington), Henry Paul (Wakefield T.), Graham Steadman (Castleford) and Alan Tait (Leeds), the previous season's choice.

Wingers

Only four players were nominated, all of whom represented Great Britain during 1993-94. Castleford's St. John Ellis, second top try scorer in the League, and Martin Offiah (Wigan) shared top billing just ahead of John Bentley (Halifax), with Jason Robinson (Wigan) gaining support in his Test debut campaign.

Centres

Paul Newlove (Bradford N.) and First Division Player of the Year Jonathan Davies dominated the voting with nominal support for Richard Blackmore (Castleford), Gary Connolly (Wigan), Graeme Hallas (Halifax) and Barrie-Jon Mather (Wigan).

Stand off

New Zealand Test winger Frano Botica topped the voting, ahead of Sheffield Eagles skipper Daryl Powell, a Great Britain 1993-94 ever-present as substitute. Support was also forthcoming for Shaun Edwards (Wigan), Tony Kemp (Castleford), Martin Pearson (Featherstone R.) and Kelly Shelford (Warrington).

Scrum half

Wigan captain Shaun Edwards dominated the poll for his fifth selection in six years. Each of the other five candidates received only one vote ... Mark Aston (Sheffield E.), Deryck Fox (Bradford N.), Bobby Goulding (Widnes), Des Hasler (Hull) and Greg Mackey (Warrington).

Props

Great Britain and Wigan prop Kelvin Skerrett received more than twice as many votes as fellow choice Lee Crooks (Castleford). Wigan's Andy Platt, in his final campaign before joining Auckland Warriors, was also well supported with votes being cast for Gary Chambers (Warrington), Karl Fairbank (Bradford N.), Karl Harrison (Halifax), Harvey Howard (Leeds), Steve Molloy (Featherstone R.), Rowland Phillips (Warrington) and Tim Street (Hull).

Hooker

For the second successive year, Wigan's Test hooker Martin Dermott polled 66 per cent of the votes, ahead of John Clarke (Oldham), Bernard Dwyer (St. Helens) and Lee Jackson (Sheffield E.).

Coaches' Select XIII debutant Dave Watson, the Bradford Northern and New Zealand full back.

Second row

Wigan's teenage prodigy Andrew Farrell crowned his 1993-94 appearances for Great Britain at Test, Under-21 and Academy levels by being a clear winner in the 11-man poll. Bradford Northern's Karl Fairbank figured in the Coaches' Select XIII for the second time, just edging out French Test packman Daniel Divet (Hull), Chris Joynt (St. Helens) and Gary Mercer (Leeds), with votes also being cast for Denis Betts (Wigan), Paul Carr (Sheffield E.), Phil Clarke (Wigan), Esene Faimalo (Widnes), George Mann (St. Helens) and Tawera Nikau (Castleford).

Loose forward

Leeds captain Ellery Hanley edged his way back into the Select XIII ahead of close contenders Phil Clarke (Wigan) and Tawera Nikau (Castleford), both of whom figured in the previous season's final line-up.

Youngest-ever Great Britain forward Andrew Farrell.

COACHES' SELECT XIII

1. **Dave Watson** (Bradford N.)
2. **St. John Ellis** (Castleford)
3. **Jonathan Davies** (Warrington)
4. **Paul Newlove** (Bradford N.)
5. **Martin Offiah** (Wigan)
6. **Frano Botica** (Wigan)
7. **Shaun Edwards** (Wigan)
8. **Kelvin Skerrett** (Wigan)
9. **Martin Dermott** (Wigan)
10. **Lee Crooks** (Castleford)
11. **Andrew Farrell** (Wigan)
12. **Karl Fairbank** (Bradford N.)
13. **Ellery Hanley** (Leeds)

Wigan's Test forward Kelvin Skerrett, who dominated the props' poll.

Coaches' Select XIII newcomer and 1994 Stones Bitter Man of Steel, Jonathan Davies.

Newlove quits in sevens bust-up

Cup chance for amateur clubs

Tuigamala settles in at Wigan

Broncos take over London Crusaders

Hanley calls a close to Britain career

Double winner Davies

Kiwi whitewash fires warning to the Aussies

MEMORIES

1993-94 HEADLINES
Behind the scoring feats and records of the 1993-94 season were a number of stories which made the headlines:

INGA THE WINGER ARRIVES
Wigan pulled off one of the biggest Rugby Union conversion coups of all time when they signed All Black winger Va'aiga Tuigamala.

The big Western Samoan had become New Zealand's best known rugby player as he led the national side in their *haka* or pre-match war dance and was used prominently in their promotional campaigns.

He had just toured England with the 1993 All Blacks when the many rumours of his switching codes became fact. Wigan were hoping to announce their capture at their Boxing Day match but the news leaked out and hit the headlines in Britain on 23 December.

It was reported that Tuigamala (24) had signed a four-year contract worth £350,000, equalling the world record sum John Gallagher — another former All Black — had negotiated with Leeds in May 1990.

Tuigamala had totalled five tries in 19 Test matches for New Zealand.

He arrived early in the New Year but it was not until 4 February that he made a surprise debut in a Stones Bitter Championship match at Widnes.

The public had been led to believe that *Inga the Winger* would make his debut at home 12 days later, but coach John Dorahy fooled everyone by not announcing his selection until about 20 minutes before the kick-off.

Dorahy explained later that he did not want to put Tuigamala under undue pressure. A crowd of only 5,629 saw his unheralded appearance which he crowned with a last-minute try in the 27-12 victory.

Tuigamala was left out of Wigan's next match – a Silk Cut Challenge Cup-tie at Hull – and he made his home debut in a midweek League match on 16 February when Wakefield Trinity spoiled the occasion with a shock 20-13

win. The attendance of 13,165 was 3,000 more than attended the corresponding midweek fixture a year earlier.

Tuigamala took a little more time to settle and gain a regular place but he played in Wigan's last three League matches to clinch a place in their Silk Cut Challenge Cup final line-up at Wembley ahead of Great Britain winger Jason Robinson.

CUP REVOLUTION
The Silk Cut Challenge Cup and Regal Trophy both underwent revolutionary changes with a massive influx of amateur clubs into the competitions.

A total of 64 amateur clubs, including all 32 from the newly-formed National Conference League, competed in the Challenge Cup which exempted professional teams until the third round. Then the remaining amateurs were compulsorily drawn away against Division Two opposition.

The 16 Division One clubs entered for an open fourth round draw by which time all the amateur clubs had been knocked out.

The Regal Trophy started with a new-style first round consisting of the 16 professional Division Two clubs, two from France as in the previous season, the three former professional clubs and Hemel Hempstead plus 10 amateurs.

The professional clubs had automatic home advantage against the French and non-League opponents before the Division One sides appeared in a random round two draw.

The revolutionary changes signified a major move towards greater harmony between the professional and amateur organisations.

It was only the previous season that the long tradition of amateurs competing in the professional tournaments was ended by the Rugby Football League as the dispute with BARLA hotted up.

But even during more peaceful times, just three or four amateur clubs were granted entry and then only in an unpopular small preliminary round.

HOWES DEPARTS

Rothmans co-editor David Howes (42) made his own headlines when he shook the game with his sudden resignation as the Rugby Football League's Public Affairs Executive.

The announcement came on 18 January, followed 10 days later by the equally surprising decision to appoint radio and television personality Harry Gration as his successor.

Howes became the League's first Public Relations Officer in October 1974 when the game was at its lowest ebb. But his drive and enthusiasm made an immediate impact as, along with newly-appointed RL Secretary David Oxley, he helped to give Rugby League a bright, new image.

He left office on 25 February to fulfil a long-held ambition to form his own public relations and sponsorship agency.

Gration (43) took over immediately to end 15 years with radio and television, including 10 as co-presenter of BBC-TV's *Look North* programme.

SEVENS ROW REVIVED

The World Sevens in Sydney caused controversy in England for a third successive season. In an attempt to avoid a repeat of previous years, when Wigan's inclusion caused fixture complications and then their expulsion from the Sevens for naming a weakened squad, the League decided to send a Great Britain squad for the first time.

They also restricted selection to no more than two players from one club but still ran into trouble when three players withdrew from the squad.

Paul Newlove, of Bradford Northern, plus Wigan's Shaun Edwards and Martin Offiah then faced a charge of bringing the game into disrepute.

Edwards, who had been named as captain, was cleared after the League's Board of Directors accepted his explanation that he withdrew because of a shoulder injury.

Offiah was also cleared as the League became enmeshed in a complicated insurance wrangle.

But the Newlove affair dragged on. Newlove, who withdrew because he was moving house and disliked flying, announced his retirement from international rugby because of the disrepute charge.

Although that charge was dropped, he then faced the lesser charge of misconduct which was quietly shelved as he agreed to withdraw his international retirement threat and flew with Great Britain to France for the John Smith's Test at Carcassonne.

Britain's original Sevens squad was: John Bentley (Halifax), Jonathan Davies (Warrington), John Devereux (Widnes), Shaun Edwards (Wigan, capt.), Chris Joynt (St. Helens), Paul Newlove (Bradford N.), Martin Offiah (Wigan), Alan Tait (Leeds), Lee Jackson and Daryl Powell (Sheffield E.).

In addition to the three charged players, Devereux and Powell withdrew because of injuries. The five replacements were: Paul Medley (Bradford N.), Martin Pearson (Featherstone R.), Phil Clarke (Wigan), St. John Ellis and Graham Steadman (Castleford). Davies was the new captain.

Britain were knocked out of the major tournament in the first round but won the Plate consolation series.

Manly beat St. George 44-12 in the final of an event that attracted a total of nearly 90,000 fans over three days.

CENTENARY PLANS

Plans for Rugby League's 1995 Centenary celebrations were announced on 24 January. They included confirmation of a World Cup tournament and an issue of commemorative stamps by the Royal Mail.

More than £1m was pledged in Centenary premiums by the League's three main sponsors – Silk Cut, Regal and Stones Bitter. In addition, John Smith's would sponsor England and Wales in the World Cup as part of their £1.3m package.

11

The Centenary plans were announced at the George Hotel, Huddersfield, where the famous breakaway meeting by Northern Rugby Union clubs took place in 1895. TV personality Michael Parkinson was invited to make the announcement.

The following month, the 10 entries for the World Cup were confirmed as: England, Wales, Australia, New Zealand, France, Papua New Guinea, South Africa, Western Samoa, Fiji and Tonga.

RECORD FINES FOR LEEDS

Leeds were twice fined record amounts for fielding weakened teams as they prepared for the Silk Cut Challenge Cup final at Wembley.

They were first fined £8,000 for fielding a virtual reserve team in a League match at St. Helens on 13 April when they lost 68-0. Forwards Marcus Vassilakopoulos and Mike O'Neill were the only ones to play at St. Helens and Wembley, both making substitute appearances in the Cup final.

Leeds were then fined £12,000 – half suspended for 12 months – for fielding a weakened team at home to Bradford Northern a week before playing at Wembley.

Bradford won this match 52-10 against a Leeds side that began with only four of their Wembley starting line-up – backs Jim Fallon, Kevin Iro, Craig Innes and Graham Holroyd. Vassilakopoulos and O'Neill, the Wembley substitutes, also began the game against Bradford.

It was the last League match of the season for both clubs and there was a strong protest feeling that Leeds had "gifted" title-chasing Bradford two points.

In both cases Leeds pleaded that the players left out were all injured or, in the case of the younger players, had played too much rugby.

They backed up their argument with medical evidence but were found guilty of breaching the by-law which stated: "Each club shall play its full strength in all matches, unless some satisfactory reason be given."

WIGAN SACK DORAHY

Wigan sacked Australian coach John Dorahy on 4 May, just four days after they had completed a Cup and Championship trophy double by winning at Wembley.

Although Dorahy's departure had been speculated for several months, the timing of it came as some surprise as Wigan had insisted they would not review the situation until after their World Club Challenge match in Brisbane on 1 June.

The exact reason for Dorahy's dismissal after only one season was clouded in mystery as he said he had been told it was for "gross misconduct", while Wigan referred to "unhappy differences".

Unconfirmed reports told of players rebelling and Dorahy's clash with club chairman Jack Robinson after he omitted to mention the coach in his post-Wembley victory speech.

A few weeks earlier, Dorahy's authority had been undermined when the club appointed centre Dean Bell as his assistant.

Dorahy threatened legal action over his dismissal as he claimed he had a three-year contract. Wigan counter-claimed that the contract was for one year with a two-year option.

The two parties later issued a statement which said that the dispute had been settled "amicably and honourably".

Meanwhile, reserve team coach Graeme West had been appointed caretaker coach and steered Wigan to the Stones Bitter Premiership and World Club Challenge trophies. West was later given the job full-time.

Dorahy was always going to have a tough job matching the success of his predecessor John Monie, who had gained the respect of players and officials alike during a highly successful four years as coach.

In a troubled season for Dorahy, he had also been fined £250 by the League for his criticism of referee Robin Whitfield following the shock home defeat by Wakefield Trinity.

LONDON BRONCOS ARRIVE

London Crusaders were to become London Broncos from the start of the 1994-95 season following a takeover by the hugely successful Australian club Brisbane Broncos.

Brisbane officials stepped in at a time when the Crusaders, formerly Fulham, were in danger of folding after being taken over by the Rugby Football League and being subject to a rival bid from a consortium headed by the son of former England soccer manager Bobby Robson.

JUNE

Ground crisis club Leigh offered a 12-month reprieve to stay at Hilton Park .... Hunslet sign Kenyan winger Bramwell Mwololo, a soccer and Rugby Union international .... Hull K.R. offer scrum half Gary Chatfield at £85,000 .... Hull forward Steve McNamara joins Sydney club St. George on a summer contract .... Hull list international packmen Andy Dannatt at £150,000 and Ian Marlow at £80,000 .... The International Board confirm eight entrants for the 1995 Centenary World Cup: Australia, France, Great Britain, New Zealand and Papua New Guinea, plus associate members Fiji, Tonga and Western Samoa .... Leeds put eight players up for sale, headed by hooker Colin Maskill at £30,000 and prop Shaun Wane at £25,000 .... Wigan winger Martin Offiah forced to return home after an exploratory operation on a shoulder injury sustained after only 54 minutes of his debut for summer contract Sydney club Eastern Suburbs .... Jim Mills quits as Welsh manager in protest at Wales not being considered for entry into the Centenary World Cup .... Suspended Richard Eyres joins Australian club Canberra to clear a six-match ban and prepare for the new British season .... Dewsbury hand over £27,500 for Widnes and Great Britain loose forward Les Holliday .... Highfield appoint Mike Peers as coach .... Wakefield Trinity list six players headed by Phil Eden at £18,000, while reducing the asking price on Mark Conway and Paul Lord .... Wigan appoint John Dorahy

as coach, the assistant coach at Australian club Newcastle Knights having previously played for Leigh and Hull K.R. and been player-coach of Halifax .... Hull make seven more players available for transfer, led by loose forward Jon Sharp at £90,000 .... Hull coach Royce Simmons runs five marathons to raise money for Australian imports .... Warrington list 13 players at a total asking price of £340,000 after offering lower contract payments .... Wigan full back Steve Hampson, listed at £15,000, offers to take a wage cut and play for match fees only .... Wigan respond by giving him a free transfer .... The line-up for the first-ever National Conference League is named as demoted professional trio Blackpool Gladiators, Chorley Borough and Nottingham City, former Younger's Alliance side Hemel Hempstead, plus BARLA nominees Saddleworth, Egremont, Wigan St. Patricks, Woolston, Leigh Miners, Dudley Hill, West Hull and Askam .... Rochdale Hornets record points-scorer Steve Gartland listed at £50,000 .... Bob Ashby steps down as the League's longest-serving Chairman after six years .... St. Helens grant veteran scrum half Neil Holding a free transfer, allowing him to take an assistant coach role at Bradford Northern .... Newcastle Knights prop Rodney Howe signs for Widnes en route to joining Winfield Cup newcomers Perth Reds .... Wakefield Trinity Chairman Rodney Walker is appointed Chairman of the League .... Oldham skipper Richard Russell listed at £75,000 .... Barrow put three players on offer for disciplinary reasons, Mike Kavanagh at £25,000, Stuart Rhodes at £50,000 and Paul Crarey at £20,000 .... Huddersfield assistant coach Terry Flanagan resigns due to the pressure of business .... The International Board decides that the World Club Challenge is to be staged in Australia for the first time in June 1994 .... London Crusaders move from Crystal Palace Sports Centre to the Copthall Sports Stadium at Barnet .... Leigh ask £100,000 for scrum half Jason Donohue .... Wigan's Test prop Ian Lucas forced to retire at 25 because of a neck injury sustained on the 1992 tour Down Under .... Featherstone Rovers list Test centre Paul Newlove at world record £750,000.

JULY

Halifax sign Wigan's Steve Hampson .... Wigan outbid Castleford and Halifax at over £140,000 for Wakefield Trinity's Under-21 stand off Nigel Wright .... Salford sack coach Kevin Tamati .... Warrington take over Widnes's contract with Jonathan Davies, paying no transfer fee and beating off the late challenge of Wakefield Trinity .... London Crusaders sign Leeds utility back John Gallagher .... Sheffield Eagles appoint Brisbane Broncos assistant coach Bill Gardner as coach .... Halifax recruit former All Black RU centre John Schuster from Australian club Newcastle Knights .... Richard Eyres returns from Canberra without being registered as a player, his six-match ban remaining unchanged .... Rochdale Hornets list Cliff Eccles at £70,000, Karl Marriott and Ian Gormley at £35,000 each and Paul Reynolds at £10,000 .... Keighley Cougars sign Kevin Marr, formerly with Australian duo North Sydney and Gold Coast .... Halifax sign Newcastle Knights skipper Michael Hagan .... Hull recruit Australian duo Des Hasler from Manly and Jeff Doyle from North Sydney .... Halifax second row man Peter Bell joins Dewsbury .... Featherstone Rovers sign New Zealand Test prop Gavin Hill .... Leeds Test prop Paul Dixon moves to Bradford Northern .... Halifax sign a third Newcastle Knights player, forward David Boyd .... Sheffield Eagles full back Garry Jack is appointed player-coach of Salford .... Halifax offer Australian forward Greg Pearce at £9,000 .... Hussain M'Barki appointed as the first-ever development officer for Morocco .... St. Helens want-away Test centre Gary Connolly chased by Wigan and Australian duo Manly and Canterbury-Bankstown .... Bradford Northern swoop to sign Featherstone Rovers centre Paul Newlove .... Widnes put asking price of £350,000 on Test forward Richard Eyres .... Leeds sign Ian Scott from Workington Town

in exchange for Shaun Wane plus £10,000 .... St. Helens agree £250,000 transfer of Gary Connolly to arch-rivals Wigan .... Halifax sign Wakefield Trinity's Test forward Michael Jackson for around £90,000 .... Castleford sign New Zealand Test stand off Tony Kemp from Australian club Newcastle Knights .... Rochdale Hornets' Kiwi forward Mike Kuiti joins Oldham .... Want-away Oldham stand off Tommy Martyn priced at £125,000 .... Widnes recruit prop Jon Grieve from Australian club Manly .... League Tribunal instructs Bradford Northern to pay £245,000 for Paul Newlove and £70,000 for Paul Dixon .... Oldham sign Jason Fogerty from Huddersfield, while brother Adam moves from Halifax to St. Helens.

AUGUST

Halifax offer seven players at a total of £140,000, headed by prop John Fieldhouse at £40,000 .... Wakefield Trinity recruit prop Mark Sheals from Oldham .... St. Helens hand over cash and hooker Paul Groves for Oldham stand off Tommy Martyn .... London Crusaders sign winger Abi Ekoku, brother of Norwich City's Efan .... Leeds win the race to sign Warrington's Neil Harmon .... Featherstone Rovers recruit Leeds Test prop Steve Molloy .... Leigh hooker Andy Ruane moves to Barrow .... Wakefield Trinity sign Matt Fuller from Australian club South Sydney .... French Test back David Fraisse moves from Carpentras to Sheffield Eagles .... Wigan refuse to release five players for a Great Britain Under-21 residential camp at Lilleshall .... Newly appointed Sheffield Eagles coach Bill Gardner accepts the coaching role at new Australian club Queensland Crushers .... Oldham tempt Leigh full back Paul Topping out of retirement .... Featherstone Rovers hand over a club record £150,000 for Widnes centre Andy Currier .... Salford sign Michael Neil from Australian club Illawarra .... Wigan skipper Dean Bell announces his move to newcomers Auckland Warriors in 1994 .... Warrington half back Robert Turner joins Doncaster .... Australian prop Craig Teitzel moves from

Illawarra to Warrington .... Hunslet sign Castleford centre Giles Boothroyd .... Leeds recruit Test man Richard Eyres from Widnes .... Stones Bitter announce a First Division record winner's purse of £56,000 .... Wakefield Trinity's Gary Price pulls out of a move to Oldham and signs for Featherstone Rovers .... Andy Goodway leaves Leeds to join Oldham for £15,000 .... Castleford sign Featherstone Rovers tourist Ian Smales .... League Tribunal prices Neil Harmon's move from Warrington to Leeds at £75,000, and Steve Molloy's transfer from Leeds to Featherstone Rovers at £95,000 .... Wakefield Trinity agree terms with Hull for Test prop Andy Dannatt but fail to tempt the player .... Hull sign winger Paul Sterling from Bradford and Bingley RU .... Leeds sell Carl Gibson to Featherstone Rovers for £15,000 .... Oldham's Sean Tyrer joins Whitehaven in exchange for Charlie McAlister and cash.

SEPTEMBER
Wakefield Trinity recruit Gary Christie from Oldham .... Bradford Northern's former Great Britain Under-21 prop Craig Richards moves to Oldham .... Brewers Courage sponsor Great Britain under the John Smith's banner in a £1.3m three-year deal .... St. Helens make an offer to Wales RU centre Scott Gibbs .... Hull reduce the asking price on Test hooker Lee Jackson from £400,000 to £250,000 .... St. Helens lose patience with Scott Gibbs and pull out of £250,000 deal .... Leeds sign Featherstone Rovers forward Gary Rose .... Welsh international packman Ian Marlow moves from Hull to Wakefield Trinity .... Leeds deputation flies to France to talk to Test scrum half Patrick Entat .... The League invites more than 70 amateur clubs to take part in new-style formats for the Regal Trophy and the Silk Cut Challenge Cup .... Wakefield Trinity pay £20,000 to Wigan for Great Britain Under-21 forward Mike Forshaw .... Former international forward Mike Nicholas appointed manager of Wales .... Oldham sign scrum half Martin Crompton from Wigan for around £30,000 .... Rochdale Hornets

centre Matt Calland moves to Featherstone Rovers .... Widnes angry at £350,000-rated Richard Eyres being priced at £135,000 for a move to Leeds by the League Tribunal .... Warrington teenage back Iestyn Harris, still to play in the first team, called into the Wales preparation squad for the international with New Zealand .... Huddersfield sign hooker Seamus McCallion from Leeds .... Featherstone Rovers' £150,000 capture Andy Currier ruled out for the rest of the season with a knee injury .... Doncaster fined £1,000 and Hunslet £500 for brawling at Elland Road, Doncaster's substitutes coming off the bench to join in .... Hull's Test forward Mark Jones fined £200 for making obscene gestures .... Bramley appoint Ray Ashton as coach in succession to Maurice Bamford .... Fit-again Mike Gregory, of Warrington, included in a 30-man Great Britain train-on squad .... Hull hooker Lee Jackson joins Sheffield Eagles .... Halifax recruit prop Paul Anderson from Leeds .... Ellery Hanley retires from Test football .... St. Helens sign Hull's Test prop Andy Dannatt .... Salford sign Wales RU flanker Richard Webster .... Wales admitted into the Centenary World Cup .... League Tribunal rates Matt Calland's move from Rochdale Hornets to Featherstone Rovers at £30,000.

OCTOBER
New Zealand open their 13th tour of Britain with a 24-19 victory over Wales at Swansea .... Kiwi coach Howie Tamati fails to tempt Wigan centre Dean Bell out of international retirement .... Bradford Northern beat the New Zealanders 17-10 .... The Kiwis record a 25-18 success at Wigan .... Castleford inflict a second successive midweek defeat on the New Zealanders by 16-4 .... Jonathan Davies selected at full back for Great Britain for the first Kiwi Test .... Two-try Jason Robinson is a Test debutant hero of Britain's 17-0 victory over New Zealand at Wembley in front of more than 36,000 fans .... Junior Kiwis beat Great Britain Academy 30-22 in a first-ever meeting as a curtain-raiser to the Wembley Test .... Dislocated elbow rules

Wigan hooker Martin Dermott out of the rest of the John Smith's Test series .... Bradford Northern turn down a Kiwi request for the release of Dave Watson for a tour fixture .... The New Zealanders beat St. Helens 14-8 .... Warrington send assistant coach Clive Griffiths on a scouting trip to South Africa .... Several British clubs approach Junior Kiwis coach Frank Endacott .... First-ever international trial by video results in no action being taken against New Zealand forward Steve Kearney and Great Britain skipper Garry Schofield .... League Tribunal orders Sheffield Eagles to pay £83,000 to Hull for hooker Lee Jackson .... New Zealand hammer Leeds 35-6 .... Great Britain Under-21s fall to the Kiwis 37-24 at Workington .... Sonny Nickle's second cap against the Kiwis earns Sheffield Eagles a £25,000 bonus from St. Helens as part of the League Tribunal's payment ruling .... Featherstone Rovers list stay-away full back Chris Bibb at £90,000 .... Kiwi coach Howie Tamati accuses Great Britain scrum half Shaun Edwards of cheating in the John Smith's Test .... Great Britain clinch the John Smith's series with a 29-12 second Test victory at Wigan.

NOVEMBER

Wigan's teenage sensation Andrew Farrell called up for a third Test debut as New Zealand axe skipper Gary Freeman .... Hull sign Leigh skipper Tim Street in a near-£100,000 deal .... New Zealand beat Widnes 18-10 .... Bramley list winger Norman Francis at £10,000 .... Featherstone Rovers release Kiwi Test prop Gavin Hill after only six weeks .... New Zealand Test centre Iva Ropati agrees to join Featherstone Rovers at the end of the Kiwi tour of France .... Great Britain complete a home Test whitewash, their first for 42 years, with a 29-10 victory over New Zealand at Leeds .... Wigan drop Test backs Martin Offiah and Shaun Edwards as a disciplinary measure .... Leeds scrum half Andy Gregory decides to join Salford instead of Wakefield Trinity .... Brisbane Broncos propose setting up a club base in London .... Widnes receive a transfer request from half back Chris

Kelly, the 1993 Younger's Alliance Player of the Year .... Castleford offer hooker Chris Watson at £20,000 .... Hull sign Welsh RU winger Marcus Bernard .... Leeds take Leigh scrum half Jason Donohue on loan .... London Crusaders introduce a 20 per cent wage cut as cash crisis looms .... Centenary World Cup plans put in jeopardy as Rugby Union hint at switching their 1995 World Cup from South Africa to be in direct competition .... The League seek Government assistance to cover the cost of ground improvements .... Widnes anger over prop Harvey Howard staying away amid plans to join Australian club Eastern Suburbs.

DECEMBER

Bramley threatened with extinction as local council refuses planning permission for redevelopment of their McLaren Field ground .... The Rugby League Academy boosted by backing of £135,000 from sponsors JJB Sports and a Government grant .... Sheffield Eagles coach Bill Gardner leaves after serving only five months of a two-year contract, club chairman Gary Hetherington returning to the coaching role .... Salford list winger Tex Evans at £85,000 .... Referees given a League reminder about speeding up the play-the-ball and stamping out high tackles .... Oldham deny reports of a £100,000 bid for Welsh RU winger and former Olympic hurdler Nigel Walker .... Rochdale Hornets ask £50,000 for utility back Steve Warburton .... The League offer to help London Crusaders find additional, or possibly replacement, directors .... St. Helens coach Mike McClennan apologises for pouring a glass of beer over a fan's head during the home defeat by Warrington in the Regal Trophy .... Widnes put Harvey Howard on offer at £130,000 .... Bradford Northern succeed in retaining home advantage in the Regal Trophy tie with Halifax after being ordered by the League to play the weather-hit tie at Leeds .... Mike McClennan resigns as coach of St. Helens for family reasons .... Oldham's Martin Strett goes to Rochdale

Hornets in exchange for winger Adrian Belle and back row man David Chrimes .... Wigan sign New Zealand All Black RU winger Va'aiga Tuigamala .... St. Helens appoint Academy coach Eric Hughes as first team supremo .... Wigan protest about Auckland Warriors bidding to sign contracted players .... Leigh recruit Mark Meadows from Oldham .... St. Helens part company with assistant coach Frank Barrow .... Wigan Test forward Andy Platt agrees to join Auckland Warriors at the end of the season .... Paul Daley quits as coach of Hunslet.

JANUARY
St. Helens utility back Tea Ropati decides to join Sydney Premiership newcomers Auckland Warriors .... Leeds sign Widnes prop Harvey Howard in £110,000 deal .... Wakefield Trinity football chairman Stuart Farrar fined £100 by the League for verbal abuse of referee Russell Smith .... The League fine Dewsbury £500 for refusing to play their Boxing Day Second Division fixture at Batley .... Widnes join St. Helens in the chase for Keighley Cougars centre Greg Austin .... Leeds deny interest in Wigan's Test winger Martin Offiah .... Bradford Northern stage clear-out on eve of the Silk Cut Challenge Cup deadline, granting free transfers to veteran front row men David Hobbs and Brian Noble, while placing a fee of £40,000 on centre Steve McGowan and £15,000 on Welsh winger Gerald Cordle .... Widnes recruit ex-New Zealand Test three-quarter Mark Elia and Australian second row man Tim Russell .... Halifax fail in bid to sign Wigan's Under-21 star Nigel Wright .... Paul Round's move from Wakefield Trinity to Halifax is the only cash deal on the day of the Silk Cut Challenge Cup deadline .... St. Helens sign the brother-in-law of Wigan's Va'aiga Tuigamala, forward Peauafi Leuila .... Wigan demand a fee from Auckland Warriors for skipper Dean Bell after originally granting a free transfer .... The League name Wembley, Old Trafford, Manchester, and Elland Road, Leeds, as the venues for the three John Smith's

Tests between Great Britain and Australia in autumn 1994 .... New Zealand sack Test coach Howie Tamati after the whitewash by Great Britain .... The League back St. Helens and Oldham in their demands for transfer fees from Auckland Warriors for Tea Ropati and Tiny Solomona respectively .... Rugby League Public Affairs Executive David Howes quits after 20-year service to establish an independent PR and sponsorship consultancy .... Carlisle coach Cameron Bell announces his intention to return to New Zealand at the end of the season .... Bramley plan to leave McLaren Field at the end of the season to share the ground of Northern Premier League soccer club Farsley Celtic .... Australian champions Brisbane Broncos take over London Crusaders .... Newly departed Hunslet coach Paul Daley joins the coaching staff at Sheffield Eagles .... Castleford lift the Regal Trophy with a record-breaking 33-2 victory over holders Wigan .... The League launch the logo for the 1995-96 Centenary season .... Highfield fined £1,000 for playing three unregistered players in a Silk Cut Challenge Cup tie, plus one misidentified player .... Leigh full back Duncan Platt retires due to pressure of business .... Bradford Northern centre Paul Newlove pulls out of the Great Britain World Sevens squad because of a move of house .... Featherstone Rovers successfully appeal against South African Andre Stoop playing for London Crusaders in the Silk Cut Challenge Cup after not being registered in time .... Broadcaster Harry Gration appointed as the new Public Affairs Executive for the League.

FEBRUARY
Jonathan Davies appointed skipper of the Great Britain World Sevens squad as Wigan duo Martin Offiah and Shaun Edwards withdraw on the eve of departure to be replaced by clubmate Phil Clarke and Featherstone Rovers' Martin Pearson .... Australian half back Mike Neil, released by Salford, turns down offer from Hull K.R. .... The Rugby League

Council calls for an inquiry to consider whether the withdrawal from the World Sevens by Paul Newlove, Martin Offiah and Shaun Edwards had brought the game into disrepute .... Hunslet forward David Croft listed at £15,000 after asking for a move .... Bradford Northern centre Paul Newlove quits international Rugby League .... Va'aiga Tuigamala scores a try on his shock debut for Wigan in the Stones Bitter Championship fixture at Widnes .... Great Britain Sevens squad defeated by Western Samoa and Canberra in the main competition but win the consolation plate by defeating Japan, South Sydney and Balmain .... Former Wales and British Lions forward Richard Webster included in the Welsh squad to meet France at Ninian Park, Cardiff, in March .... June's World Club Challenge between Brisbane Broncos and the newly crowned British League Champions to be sponsored by MMI Insurance for £125,000 .... Great Britain Academy beat their French counterparts 22-6 at Ryedale-York .... Hull K.R.'s New Zealand Test half back Dean Clark returns home because of domestic problems .... The International Board decide that the Centenary World Cup should be staged in Britain in the autumn of 1995 even if the Rugby Union World Cup moves from South Africa to become a head-on clash .... South Africa admitted to the Centenary World Cup as a 10th competitor, the tournament to be staged in three qualifying groups with semi-finals and a final .... Hong Kong earmarked as a future venue for the World Club Challenge .... Peter Tunks quits as coach of Oldham, replaced to the end of the season by fellow Australian Bob Lindner .... The League accept explanations for World Sevens withdrawal from Wigan duo Shaun Edwards and Martin Offiah, and reduce pending charge on Paul Newlove from disrepute to misconduct .... Wigan asked to assure the League that insurance wrangle which affected Martin Offiah's selection for the World Sevens would not hinder his future Test appearances .... St. Helens halve the asking price for winger Les Quirk to £15,000 .... Hull K.R.'s Australian back David Liddiard returns home with a serious ankle injury .... Bradford Northern sign Doncaster centre Carl Hall .... David Creasser makes a comeback with Keighley Cougars two years after packing in at Leeds with a shoulder injury .... Sheffield Eagles list scrum half Tim Lumb at £25,000 .... Warrington offer Welsh second row man Rowland Phillips at £110,000 .... International Board Tribunal orders Sheffield Eagles to pay Australian club Canterbury-Bankstown £15,000 for former Test forward Bruce McGuire .... On-offer Hunslet forward David Croft turns down a move to Hull K.R. .... The League's former controller of referees, Fred Lindop, switches to taking control of Rugby Union matches .... Wigan coach John Dorahy fined £250 for making public criticism of Widnes referee Robin Whitfield .... Australian Steve Martin agrees a new one-year contract with Featherstone Rovers.

MARCH

Keighley Cougars' Australian centre Greg Austin joins Salford for a second time .... Wigan and Featherstone Rovers each fined £500, half suspended for 12 months, for brawling .... The League suspend Bruce McGuire after Sheffield Eagles refuse to pay an international transfer fee .... Wakefield Trinity recruit Hull K.R. winger Bright Sodje on loan .... Batley announce the go-ahead for a new £500,000 stand .... Wales snatch a last minute 13-12 victory over France at Cardiff City's Ninian Park .... Sheffield Eagles' forward Bruce McGuire freed to continue playing after obtaining a High Court injunction for restraint of trade .... Bradford Northern centre Paul Newlove withdraws his threat to quit international football after a meeting with Great Britain coach Malcolm Reilly and is selected to face France .... Wigan's annual accounts show a players' wage bill of over £2m .... St. Helens object to the postponement of a lucrative home televised fixture with Leeds due to Academy international call-ups .... St. Helens appoint former Test forward Brian Case as assistant coach .... Workington Town sign loose forward Neil Shaw on loan from Barrow .... Widnes centre John Devereux ruled out for the rest of the season with a prolonged back injury .... Utility back Craig Booth pays £500 to secure his own transfer from Featherstone Rovers to Oldham .... Australian coach Royce Simmons announces his departure from Hull at the end of the season .... The League abandon an experiment to allow touch judges to police the 10-metre rule after only one match .... Great Britain struggle to beat France 12-4 in Carcassonne .... Bramley offer hooker Gary Barnett at £5,000 .... The British and French League decide to revive the European Championship involving England, Wales and France, with the long term possibility of Moldova and Russia being added .... Former Test forward Hugh Waddell appointed to take over as coach of Carlisle when Kiwi Cameron Bell returns home at the end of the season .... The Administrator in charge at Huddersfield invites offers for any British player .... Salford player-coach Garry Jack decides to quit playing at the end of the season .... Oldham offer forwards Paul Groves and Craig Richards .... Cardiff councillors offer to support the League in a bid to hire Rugby Union's Cardiff Arms Park for the proposed autumn John Smith's Tour fixture between Wales and Australia .... Bruce McGuire gains High Court ruling to continue playing for Sheffield Eagles until the end of the season .... Leeds centre Craig Innes turns down a summer contract from Australian club Canterbury-Bankstown .... Wigan appoint club skipper Dean Bell as co-ordinator and motivator .... Carlisle fail in a bid to exchange Gary Murdock for Whitehaven's Clayton Friend.

APRIL
Peter Roe quits as coach of Keighley Cougars .... Hull Australian Des Hasler warns that Antipodean player supply will be curtailed by the emergence of four new Sydney Premiership clubs .... Leeds announce a 10-year £2.3m sponsorship deal with brewers Tetley .... The Rugby League Council back an International Tribunal ruling that Sheffield Eagles must pay a £15,000 fee for Australian import Bruce McGuire .... Swinton sign Rochdale Hornets centre Steve Warburton .... Leeds and Sheffield Eagles run up the highest-ever draw of 46-46 .... Leeds face a League inquiry after fielding a complete reserve side for the Stones Bitter Championship fixture at St. Helens, crashing to a 68-0 defeat .... Castleford list top scoring winger St. John Ellis at £130,000 .... The League consider a BSkyB proposal to screen three separate matches over three days as the three-horse Stones Bitter Championship title race reaches a climax .... Featherstone Rovers' Kiwi centre Iva Ropati joins Sydney club Parramatta for the summer .... Leeds fined a record-equalling £8,000 for fielding a weakened side at St. Helens .... Bradford Northern chairman Chris Caisley resigns from the League's Board of Directors over a conflict of interests including the League's switch of day for his club's final Championship fixture at Leeds .... Keighley and Batley each fined £600, half suspended for 12 months, for brawling .... Wales RU centre Scott Gibbs signs for St. Helens in a five-year deal worth nearly £200,000 .... Huddersfield skipper Phil Hellewell quits after being dropped .... Hunslet list Richard Francis at £8,000 .... Featherstone Rovers capture Hull's French international second row man Daniel Divet .... Halifax winger John Bentley signs a summer contract with Sydney club Balmain .... Leigh list Andy Collier at £50,000 .... Wigan seal their fifth consecutive Stones Bitter Championship title with victory at Oldham in the last match of the campaign .... Workington Town clinch the Second Division Championship Bowl in Bramley's last match at McClaren Field .... The runners-up spot is clinched by Doncaster with a 10-5 victory at Batley .... Leigh reduce the asking price for

scrum half Jason Donohue from £100,000 to £30,000 .... David Topliss resigns as coach of Wakefield Trinity after a seven-year spell .... Wigan refuse to discuss an extension to John Dorahy's coaching contract until after the World Club Challenge in Brisbane on 1 June .... Wigan beat Leeds 26-16 to lift the Silk Cut Challenge Cup for a seventh successive season, completing a League and Cup double for a fifth consecutive time .... Two-try hero Martin Offiah is awarded the Lance Todd Trophy as Man of the Match.

MAY

Wakefield Trinity appoint David Hobbs as coach .... The League dispute proposed BBC TV dates for the 1994-95 Regal Trophy, alleging preference being given to England Rugby Union internationals with Canada and Romania .... Bob Lindner resigns as coach of Oldham .... Wigan sack coach John Dorahy days after clinching the Cup and League double, alleging "gross misconduct" .... Tony Gordon steps down as coach of London Crusaders to be replaced by Gary Grienke, current coach of Brisbane Wests .... The receiver in charge at Huddersfield sacks team manager Alex Murphy and the rest of the backroom staff .... Welsh RU reject notion of the League hiring Cardiff Arms Park for the Wales v. Australia John Smith's International .... George Fairbairn quits as coach of Hull K.R. .... Jonathan Davies turns down a contract with new Australian club Western Reds in Perth and agrees to play for Warrington until season 1995-96 .... Australian skipper Mal Meninga rules out a return to St. Helens after the 1994 Australian season .... Bradford Northern full back Dave Watson signs a summer contract with Australian club Cronulla .... Phil Larder quits as coach of Widnes .... Jonathan Davies named as Stones Bitter Man of Steel and First Division Player of the Year .... Leeds fined a record £12,000, half suspended for 12 months,

for fielding a weakened side in the last League match at home to title contenders Bradford Northern .... Keighley Cougars appoint Phil Larder as coach .... Wigan prop forward Andy Platt refuses to play in the World Club Challenge in Brisbane and is dropped for the Stones Bitter Premiership final at Old Trafford ..... Warrington sign Featherstone Rovers stand off Francis Maloney for £60,000 .... Oldham appoint Andy Goodway as coach .... Bradford Northern recruit French centre David Fraisse from Sheffield Eagles .... Wigan lift the Stones Bitter Premiership Trophy with a 24-20 success over Castleford .... Workington Town complete a Second Division League-Premiership double with a 30-22 victory over London Crusaders .... Warrington sign Sheffield Eagles second row man Bruce McGuire .... Oldham prop forward Barrie McDermott joins Wigan .... Halifax offer utility back Warren Wilson at £15,000 .... Doncaster sign Hull K.R. prop forward Wayne Jackson .... Leeds pay £4,000 to French club Avignon for Test scrum half and skipper Patrick Entat .... Wigan and John Dorahy reach an "amicable and honourable" settlement .... The League refer to the Disciplinary Committee a blow by Dean Sampson on Kelvin Skerrett in the Stones Bitter Premiership final .... Steve Crooks leaves Ryedale-York to take up the coaching role at former club Hull K.R. .... Newly-crowned National Conference League champions Woolston Rovers fail in their bid to be promoted to the Second Division in place of bottom club Highfield .... Wigan centre Sam Panapa, winner of the 1994 Harry Sunderland Trophy, joins Salford for £20,000 .... Ged Dunn resigns from Hull K.R. after 22 years' service as player and assistant coach .... Widnes appoint newly-retired player Tony Myler as coach .... Hull appoint Tony Gordon as coach .... Sheffield Eagles list scrum half Mark Aston at £250,000 .... Wigan's Billy McGinty joins Workington Town.

Sheffield Eagles hooker Lee Jackson, a September 1993 recruit from Hull, prepares to off-load over the top of St. Helens skipper Shane Cooper.

CLUBS

The following is a focus on last season's 32 professional Rugby League clubs, the section providing each club with a profile and an analysis of their 1993-94 campaign on a match-by-match basis with a summary for each first team player.

KEY

In the individual club profiles the following headings are featured:

First season refers to when the club gained senior league status. In some instances clubs have disbanded and re-formed, sometimes under different titles. For record purposes these changes are ignored except where there has been a break of more than one full season.

Honours. Until they were scrapped in 1970, the Yorkshire and Lancashire Leagues were among the honours in the professional game. Before 1903 they operated under the title of the Lancashire and Yorkshire Senior Competitions. Winners of these competitions are included under the Lancashire and Yorkshire League Champions. The pre-1903 Yorkshire Senior Competition should not be confused with the league operating for A-teams in Yorkshire which had the same title.

Regal Trophy is the current title for the John Player/Player's No. 6 Trophy competition.

Coaches. The clubs' individual coaching register is from the start of the 1974-75 season.

Attendances. Crowds in brackets are at neutral venues.

Appearances. Players' totals are based on official teamsheets submitted to the League after each first team match. + indicates playing substitute appearance.

Great Britain Register. The figure in brackets after a player's name is the number of Great Britain appearances he made while serving the club under whose entry he is listed, and the number after the + sign indicates playing substitute. This is followed by the time-span between his first and last British cap while at that club.

Signings Register. * Indicates where clubs have agreed to a player being signed 'on loan', a temporary transfer, the Rugby Football League prohibiting a subsequent transfer within 28 days. Where a player on loan has not been retained, his return to his original club is also marked *.

Date of Birth: The dates are supplied in good faith by the Rugby Football League from their registration of players. This also applies to dates of signing and previous club.

In the match-by-match review for each club the following abbreviations are used:

SBC	—	Stones Bitter Championship	L	—	Lost
SD	—	Second Division	D	—	Drawn
RT	—	Regal Trophy	dg	—	Drop goal
CC	—	Challenge Cup	Fr	—	France
PT	—	Premiership Trophy	Aus	—	Australia
SDP	—	Second Division Premiership	NZ	—	New Zealand
P	—	Preliminary Round	PNG	—	Papua New Guinea
H	—	Home	SA	—	South Africa
A	—	Away	Pr	—	Probationer
W	—	Won			

BARROW

Ground: Craven Park (0229-820273)
First Season: 1900-01
Nickname: Braves
Chairman: Steve Johnson
Secretary: Karen Heighton
Honours: **Division Two** Champions, 1975-76, 1983-84
Challenge Cup Winners, 1954-55
Beaten finalists, 1937-38, 1950-51, 1956-57, 1966-67
Regal Trophy Beaten finalists, 1980-81
Lancashire Cup Winners, 1954-55, 1983-84
Beaten finalists, 1937-38

RECORDS

Match
Goals: 12 by Frank French v. Maryport, 19 Feb 1938
Willie Horne v. Cardiff, 8 Sep 1951
Steve Tickle v. Kent Invicta, 8 Apr 1984
Mike Kavanagh v. Blackpool G., 21 Mar 1993
Tries: 6 by Val Cumberbatch v. Batley, 21 Nov 1936
Jim Thornburrow v. Maryport, 19 Feb 1938
Frank Castle v. York, 29 Sep 1951
Steve Rowan at Nottingham C., 15 Nov 1992
Points: 28 by Keith Jarrett v. Doncaster, 25 Aug 1970
Steve Tickle v. Kent Invicta, 8 Apr 1984
Dean Marwood at Runcorn H., 16 Apr 1989
Mike Kavanagh v. Blackpool G., 21 Mar 1993

Season
Goals: 135 by Joe Ball, 1956-57
Tries: 50 by Jim Lewthwaite, 1956-57
Points: 305 by Ian Ball, 1979-80

Career
Goals: 741 by Willie Horne, 1943-58
Tries: 352 by Jim Lewthwaite, 1943-57
Points: 1,818 by Willie Horne, 1943-58
Appearances: 500 by Jim Lewthwaite, 1943-57
Highest score: 83-3 v. Maryport, 19 Feb 1938
Highest against: 90-0 at Leeds, 11 Feb 1990
Attendance: 21,651 v. Salford (League), 15 Apr 1938

COACHING REGISTER
● **Since 1974-75**

Frank Foster	May 73 - Apr 83
Tommy Dawes	May 83 - Feb 85
Tommy Bishop	Feb 85 - Apr 85
Ivor Kelland	May 85 - Feb 87
Dennis Jackson	Feb 87 - Nov 87
Rod Reddy	Nov 87 - Nov 89
Dennis Jackson	Nov 89 - Apr 90
Steve Norton	May 90 - Feb 91
Paul Kavanagh	Feb 91 - July 92
Geoff Worrall	July 92 - Apr 93
Denis Ramsdale	May 93 -

GREAT BRITAIN REGISTER
(19 players)

Bill Burgess	(16)	1924-29
Bill Burgess	(13)	1962-68
David Cairns	(2)	1984
Chris Camilleri	(2)	1980
Charlie Carr	(7)	1924-26
Frank Castle	(4)	1952-54
Roy Francis	(1)	1947
Harry Gifford	(2)	1908
Dennis Goodwin	(5)	1957-58
Jack Grundy	(12)	1955-57
Phil Hogan	(4+1)	1977-78
Willie Horne	(8)	1946-52
Phil Jackson	(27)	1954-58
Joe Jones	(1)	1946
Bryn Knowelden	(1)	1946
Eddie Szymala	(1+1)	1981
Ted Toohey	(3)	1952
Alec Troup	(2)	1936
Jack Woods	(1)	1933

1993-94 SIGNINGS REGISTER

Signed	Player	Club From
16.6.93	Heslop, Stephen	Holker P. ARL
16.6.93	Smith, Jamie	Roose ARL
22.6.93	Bent, Peers	Blackpool G.
24.6.93	Atkinson, Phil	Ulverston ARL
24.6.93	Neale, Steve	Holker P. ARL
24.6.93	Norman, Colin	Askam ARL
3.8.93	Thexton, John	Roose ARL
5.8.93	Brennan, Paul	Walney C. ARL
10.8.93	Howarth, Stuart	Ulverston ARL
10.8.93	Whalley, Andrew	Ulverston ARL
12.8.93	Creary, Richard	Askam ARL
13.8.93	Ruane, Andy	Widnes
17.8.93	Coulson, Mark	Askam ARL
27.8.93	Bradbury, Paul	Swillington M. W. ARL
27.8.93	Hulston, Tony	Marsh H. ARL
27.8.93	Smedley, Gary	Ulverston ARL
3.9.93	Wallis, Lee	Roose ARL
10.9.93	Singleton, Tony	Manly, Aus.
23.9.93	Eaton, Mark	Railway ARL
28.9.93	Jones, Wayne	Askam ARL
4.10.93	Hansen, Sam	Tonga
7.10.93	Regan, Craig	ARL
4.11.93	Atkinson, Neil	Ulverston ARL
9.12.93	*Ashcroft, Steve	Chorley B.
8.1.94	Foster, Steve	ARL
8.1.94	Robinson, Glyn	Millom ARL
10.1.94	*Blakeley, Michael	Leigh
21.1.94	Shaw, Steve	Ulverston ARL
29.1.94	Hulston, Simon	Marsh H. ARL
14.2.94	*McTigue, Mick	Chorley B.
18.3.94	Clark, Darren	Roose ARL
18.3.94	Whinfield, Thomas	Ulverston ARL
26.3.94	Henderson, Paul	Walney C. ARL

*Teenager Phil Everett, a Barrow debutant in 1993-94 as a 17-year-old, confronts London Crusaders at Craven Park.
Photo: North-West Evening Mail.*

BARROW 1993-94 PLAYERS' SUMMARY

	(Date of Birth)	App	T	G	D	Pts	Previous club	Signed
Ashcroft, Steve	(29.12.69)	17	2	—	—	8	Chorley B.	9.12.93
Atkinson, Phil	(25.9.74)	27+3	7	—	1	29	Ulverston ARL	24.6.93
Bent, Peers	(28.12.70)	30+3	—	—	—	—	Blackpool G.	22.6.93
Blakeley, Mike	(22.11.70)	3	—	1	—	2	Leigh	10.1.94
Brown, Dave	(25.10.67)	1+1	—	—	—	—	ARL	21.12.93
Casson, Neil	(13.6.67)	1+2	—	—	—	—	Dalton ARL	5.1.93
Chapman, Martin	(12.3.71)	1	—	—	—	—	Ulverston ARL	22.1.94
Coulson, Mark	(13.11.70)	3+12	—	—	—	—	Askam ARL	17.8.93
Creary, Richard	(21.6.69)	12	8	—	—	32	Askam ARL	12.8.93
Dolan, Shaun	(1.1.70)	7	2	—	—	8	Highfield	27.1.94
Eccles, Bob	(10.7.57)	31+3	18	—	4	76	Blackpool G.	11.1.93
Everett, Phil	(23.4.76)	32+1	11	—	—	44	Barrow Island ARL	24.5.93
Hadley, Derek	(6.6.54)	6+2	1	—	—	4	ARL	26.8.73
Hansen, Sam	(23.7.68)	16+2	1	—	—	4	Tonga	4.10.93
Honey, Chris	(25.1.68)	31+2	13	—	—	52	Thatto Heath ARL	26.9.91
Howarth, Stuart	(2.9.74)	3+4	—	—	—	—	Ulverston ARL	10.8.93
Jackson, Wayne	(17.9.66)	4+4	2	—	—	8	Dalton ARL	6.9.90
Kavanagh, Mike	(5.2.71)	34	12	94	—	236	Carlisle	17.10.92
McMurty, John	(22.3.67)	7+1	1	—	—	4	Hemel Hempstead	4.9.93
Middleton, Glen	(3.9.68)	1+1	—	—	—	—	Barrow Island ARL	2.9.88
Morrow, Shaun	(31.12.63)	11	1	—	—	4	Walney I. ARL	3.7.91
Neale, Steve	(24.4.68)	9+13	1	—	—	4	Holker Pioneers ARL	24.6.93
Norman, Colin	(27.6.63)	0+1	—	—	—	—	Askam ARL	24.6.93
Petcher, Graeme	(24.3.72)	14	1	—	—	4	Barrow Island ARL	26.6.91
Rhodes, Stuart	(16.1.72)	31	10	—	—	40	Askam ARL	6.9.90
Robinson, Roy	(18.1.65)	23+2	7	—	—	28	Millom ARL	10.8.92
Ruane, Andy	(6.9.62)	25	6	4	8	40	Widnes	13.8.93
Shaw, Steve	(29.9.71)	5+3	—	—	—	—	Ulverston ARL	21.1.94
Singleton, Anthony	(25.3.69)	30	11	—	—	44	Australia	10.9.93
Thexton, John	(3.12.75)	0+1	—	—	—	—	Roose ARL	3.8.93
Trainor, Pat	(8.4.64)	17	7	—	—	28	Walney C. ARL	20.10.87
Westwood, Gary	(15.2.69)	5+1	—	—	—	—	Barrow Island ARL	17.6.91
Whalley, Andy	(4.3.75)	5+3	2	—	—	8	Ulverston ARL	10.8.93
TOTALS								
33 players			124	99	13	707		

BARROW 1993-94 MATCH ANALYSIS

Date	Competition	H/A	Opponent	Rlt	Score	Tries	Goals	Attendance	Referee
29.8.93	SD	H	Keighley C.	L	22-30	Kavanagh, Rhodes, Ruane, Trainor	Kavanagh (3)	2341	Carter
5.9.93	SD	A	Swinton	W	28-22	Jackson (2), Eccles, Honey	Kavanagh (4), Ruane (1,2dg)	—	—
12.9.93	SD	H	Highfield	W	44-22	Everett (3), Eccles, Hadley, Honey, Ruane, Kavanagh	Kavanagh (6)	1017	Gilmour
19.9.93	SD	A	Doncaster	L	16-27	Atkinson, Eccles, Everett	Kavanagh (2)	—	—
26.9.93	SD	H	Huddersfield	L	25-30	Singleton (2), Robinson, Trainor	Kavanagh (4), Ruane (dg)	1470	Asquith
3.10.93	SD	H	London C.	W	37-12	Atkinson, Everett, Honey, Kavanagh, Robinson, Trainor	Kavanagh (6), Eccles (dg)	1229	Redfearn
10.10.93	SD	A	Hunslet	W	15-12	Honey (2), Eccles	Kavanagh, Ruane (dg)	—	—
24.10.93	SD	H	Bramley	W	24-16	Atkinson, Honey, Kavanagh, Robinson	Kavanagh (4)	1374	Volante
31.10.93	RT(1)	H	Leigh M.W.	W	54-12	Trainor (3), Atkinson, Eccles, Honey, Kavanagh, Petcher, Rhodes, Singleton	Kavanagh (5), Ruane (2)	1140	Cross
7.11.93	SD	A	Dewsbury	L	12-56	Kavanagh, Singleton	Kavanagh (2)	—	—
14.11.93	RT(2)	H	Bradford N.	L	8-28	McMurty, Robinson	—	2796	Nicholson
21.11.93	SD	H	Rochdale H.	W	28-14	Atkinson, Everett, Hansen, Kavanagh, Singleton	Kavanagh (3), Ruane	1192	Presley
28.11.93	SD	A	Ryedale-York	L	10-29	Honey, Whalley	Kavanagh	—	—
5.12.93	SD	A	Batley	L	6-14	Trainor	Kavanagh	—	—
12.12.93	SD	H	Whitehaven	W	20-8	Eccles (2), Ruane, Whalley	Kavanagh (2)	1115	Tennant
28.12.93	SD	H	Carlisle	W	26-14	Rhodes (2), Everett, Ruane	Kavanagh (4), Ruane (2dg)	1310	Nicholson
2.1.94	SD	A	Workington T.	L	6-50	Singleton	Kavanagh	—	—
9.1.94	SD	H	Swinton	L	12-20	Honey, Singleton	Kavanagh (2)	1045	Whitelam
16.1.94	CC(3)	H	East Leeds	W	34-10	Eccles (3), Dolan, Everett, Kavanagh	Kavanagh (5)	729	Nicholson
19.1.94	SD	A	Keighley C.	L	4-68	Neale	—	—	—
23.1.94	SD	A	Highfield	D	8-8	Kavanagh	Blakeley, Kavanagh	—	—
30.1.94	CC(4)	H	Bradford N.	L	30-58	Eccles, Everett, Honey, Rhodes, Singleton	Kavanagh (5)	2260	Asquith
6.2.94	SD	H	Doncaster	W	23-21	Dolan, Eccles, Honey, Singleton	Kavanagh (3), Eccles (dg)	1067	Gilmour
20.2.94	SD	A	Huddersfield	L	17-20	Atkinson, Honey, Kavanagh	Kavanagh (2), Ruane (dg)	—	—
27.2.94	SD	A	London C.	L	14-52	Creary, Eccles	Kavanagh (3)	—	—
6.3.94	SD	H	Hunslet	W	16-10	Creary (2), Rhodes	Kavanagh (2)	889	Gilmour
13.3.94	SD	A	Bramley	W	34-15	Creary, Kavanagh, Morrow, Rhodes, Robinson, Ruane	Kavanagh (5)	—	—
20.3.94	SD	H	Dewsbury	W	23-16	Creary, Eccles, Honey, Rhodes	Kavanagh (3), Atkinson (dg)	1040	Morris
27.3.94	SD	A	Rochdale H.	L	14-24	Eccles, Singleton	Kavanagh (3)	—	—
1.4.94	SD	A	Carlisle	L	24-29	Eccles (2), Rhodes, Robinson, Ruane	Kavanagh (2)	—	—
4.4.94	SD	H	Workington T.	L	14-26	Ashcroft, Everett, Robinson	Kavanagh	2557	Galtress
10.4.94	SD	A	Whitehaven	L	17-36	Creary, Rhodes, Singleton	Kavanagh (2), Eccles (dg)	—	—
17.4.94	SD	H	Batley	L	7-20	Creary	Kavanagh, Eccles (dg)	1304	Carter
24.4.94	SD	H	Ryedale-York	W	35-22	Ashcroft, Atkinson, Creary, Eccles, Everett, Kavanagh	Kavanagh (5), Ruane (dg)	819	Cross

BATLEY

Ground: Mount Pleasant (0924-472208)
First Season: 1895-96
Nickname: Gallant Youths
Chairman: Stephen Ball
Secretary: Richard Illingworth
Honours: **Championship** Winners, 1923-24
              Challenge Cup Winners, 1896-97,
              1897-98, 1900-01
              Yorkshire Cup Winners, 1912-13
              Beaten finalists, 1909-10, 1922-23,
              1924-25, 1952-53
              Yorkshire League Winners,
              1898-99, 1923-24

RECORDS
Match
Goals: 10 by Steve Parrish at Nottingham C.,
        10 Nov 1991
Tries: 5 by Joe Oakland v. Bramley,
        19 Dec 1908
        Tommy Brannan v. Swinton,
        17 Jan 1920
        Jim Wale v. Bramley, 4 Dec 1926
        Jim Wale v. Cottingham,
        12 Feb 1927
        Tommy Oldroyd at Highfield,
        6 Mar 1994
Points: 26 by Jack Perry v. Liverpool C.,
        16 Sep 1951

Season
Goals: 120 by Stan Thompson, 1958-59
Tries: 29 by Jack Tindall, 1912-13
Points: 281 by Jack Perry, 1950-51
Career
Goals: 463 by Wharton "Wattie" Davies,
            1897-1912
Tries: 123 by Wharton "Wattie" Davies,
            1897-1912
Points: 1,297 by Wharton "Wattie" Davies,
            1897-1912
Appearances: 421 by Wharton "Wattie" Davies,
            1897-1912

Highest score: 64-0 at Nottingham C.,
              10 Nov 1991
              64-1 v. Queens,
              31 Oct 1993
Highest against: 78-9 at Wakefield T.,
              26 Aug 1967
Attendance: 23,989 v. Leeds (RL Cup),
              14 Mar 1925

COACHING REGISTER
● **Since 1974-75**

Don Fox	Nov 72 - Oct 74
Alan Hepworth	Nov 74 - Apr 75
Dave Cox	May 75 - June 75
Trevor Walker	June 75 - June 77
Albert Fearnley	June 77 - Oct 77
Dave Stockwell	Oct 77 - June 79
*Tommy Smales	June 79 - Oct 81
Trevor Lowe	Oct 81 - May 82
Terry Crook	June 82 - Nov 84
George Pieniazek	Nov 84 - Nov 85
Brian Lockwood	Nov 85 - May 87
Paul Daley	July 87 - Apr 90
Keith Rayne	May 90 - Apr 91
David Ward	May 91 -

Ex-forward

GREAT BRITAIN REGISTER
(4 players)

Norman Field	(1)	1963
Frank Gallagher	(8)	1924-26
Carl Gibson	(+1)	1985
Joe Oliver	(4)	1928

1993-94 SIGNINGS REGISTER

Signed	Player	Club From
1.7.93	Hunter, Richard	B.R.K. ARL
1.7.93	Middleton, Graham	Leeds
1.8.93	Moxon, Darren	Bradford N.
16.8.93	Pastre, Regis	Villeneuve, Fr.
19.8.93	Kiss, Jeff	Caboolture, Aus.
7.9.93	Brook, Richard	Hunslet
1.10.93	Walton, Tony	Doncaster

BATLEY 1993-94 PLAYERS' SUMMARY

	(Date of Birth)	App	T	G	D	Pts	Previous club	Signed
Booth, Michael	(20.3.60)	32	9	—	—	36	Australia	20.8.90
Bownass, Mark	(1.6.66)	1	—	—	—	—	Dewsbury Colts	2.8.90
Brook, Richard	(18.2.70)	23+5	2	—	—	8	Hunslet	7.9.93
Cameron, Mick	(19.12.67)	33	7	—	—	28	Australia	8.9.92
Cass, Mark	(17.11.71)	10+3	3	—	—	12	Hull	29.2.92
Child, Darren	(30.10.66)	8+10	1	—	—	4	Morley RU	13.9.90
Dyson, Jeremy	(15.2.72)	17	5	41	—	102	Thornhill ARL	29.8.91
Grayshon, Jeff	(4.3.49)	14+18	—	—	—	—	Featherstone R.	11.8.91
Heron, Wayne	(5.5.61)	19+9	—	—	—	—	Bradford N.	22.2.90
Holmes, Philip	(25.7.74)	6	3	22	—	56	East Leeds ARL	13.1.93
Irvine, Jimmy	(28.4.60)	30+1	7	—	—	28	Halifax	2.10.92
Marshall, Paul	(17.4.65)	2+1	—	—	—	—	Shaws ARL	17.3.89
Middleton, Graham	(2.11.70)	14	1	—	—	4	Leeds	1.7.93
Moxon, Darren	(17.9.70)	35	27	—	—	108	Bradford N.	11.12.92
Oldroyd, Tommy	(30.12.69)	7+3	5	—	—	20	Hunslet	30.9.92
Parkinson, Andrew	(8.7.65)	37	6	—	—	24	Dewsbury	2.1.90
Pastre, Regis	(23.3.70)	3+13	2	—	—	8	France	16.8.93
Scott, Mark	(30.1.65)	23+3	5	—	—	20	Batley Boys ARL	9.5.84
Thornton, Gary	(9.3.63)	29+1	17	—	—	68	Wakefield T.	24.8.90
Tomlinson, Glen	(18.3.70)	35	21	—	1	85	Australia	29.8.91
Walker, Steve	(8.11.69)	17	14	1	—	58	Dudley Hill ARL	17.12.92
Walton, Tony	(20.12.63)	33+1	8	—	—	32	Doncaster	22.6.92
Whittaker, Gary	(29.7.69)	0+2	—	—	—	—	Shaw Cross ARL	14.3.93
Wilkinson, Shaun	(23.9.63)	17+1	8	—	—	32	Hunslet	1.7.92
Wilson, Simon	(22.10.67)	36	10	55	2	152	Batley Boys ARL	16.11.84
TOTALS								
25 players			161	119	3	885		

Batley's Australian scrum half Glen Tomlinson, runner-up for the 1994 Stones Bitter Second Division Player of the Year award, feeds the scrum against Hunslet.

BATLEY 1993-94 MATCH ANALYSIS

Date	Com-petition	H/A	Opponent	Rlt	Score	Tries	Goals	Atten-dance	Referee
27.8.93	SD	A	London C.	L	6-40	Middleton	Wilson	—	—
5.9.93	SD	H	Workington T.	L	4-24	Moxon	—	1239	R. Connolly
12.9.93	SD	A	Ryedale-York	W	22-19	Wilkinson (3), Dyson	Dyson (3)	—	—
19.9.93	SD	H	Rochdale H.	W	26-17	Cass (2), Cameron, Holmes, Moxon	Holmes (3)	1003	Kendrew
26.9.93	SD	H	Whitehaven	W	28-16	Irvine (2), Cass, Moxon, Parkinson	Holmes (4)	769	Carter
3.10.93	SD	A	Huddersfield	L	12-37	Tomlinson (2)	Holmes (2)	—	—
10.10.93	SD	H	Highfield	W	58-16	Tomlinson (3), Holmes (2), Wilson (2), Cameron, Scott, Thornton, Walton	Holmes (7)	548	Cross
24.10.93	SD	A	Carlisle	W	20-10	Walton, Wilkinson, Wilson	Holmes (4)	—	—
31.10.93	RT(1)	H	Queens	W	64-1	Moxon (4), Cameron (3), Dyson (2), Brook, Parkinson, Thornton, Wilson	Dyson (6)	608	Cummings
7.11.93	SD	A	Swinton	W	22-16	Tomlinson (2), Irvine, Thornton	Dyson (3)	—	—
14.11.93	RT(2)	H	Sheffield E.	W	8-6	Tomlinson (2)	—	1278	Gilmour
21.11.93	SD	H	Keighley C.	W	8-16	Tomlinson	Holmes (2)	1789	Redfearn
28.11.93	SD	A	Doncaster	L	6-16	Wilson	Dyson	—	—
5.12.93	SD	H	Barrow	W	14-6	Booth, Irvine, Moxon	Dyson	467	Kendrew
14.12.93	RT(3)	H	Salford	L	8-12	Tomlinson	Dyson (2)	809	Atkin
29.12.93	SD	H	Dewsbury	W	16-2	Dyson, Irvine, Scott	Dyson (2)	1812	Atkin
2.1.94	SD	A	Bramley	W	32-8	Thornton (3), Moxon (2), Tomlinson, Wilson	Dyson (2)	—	—
9.1.94	SD	A	Workington T.	L	6-28	Dyson	Dyson	—	—
15.1.94	CC(3)	H	Dewsbury C.	W	58-2	Moxon (3), Walker (3), Irvine, Parkinson, Thornton, Walton	Dyson (9)	1235	Presley
18.1.94	SD	A	Hunslet	D	14-14	Thornton, Tomlinson	Wilson (3)	—	—
23.1.94	SD	H	Ryedale-York	W	21-14	Booth, Cameron, Moxon, Thornton	Dyson (2), Wilson (dg)	707	McGregor
30.1.94	CC(4)	H	Keighley C.	L	8-29	Wilson	Dyson (2)	2409	Carter
6.2.94	SD	A	Rochdale H.	L	12-24	Parkinson, Scott	Dyson (2)	—	—
13.2.94	SD	H	London C.	W	29-18	Booth, Child, Irvine, Moxon, Walton	Wilson (4), Tomlinson (dg)	608	Presley
20.2.94	SD	A	Whitehaven	W	26-16	Walton (2), Parkinson, Moxon	Dyson (5)	—	—
2.3.94	SD	H	Huddersfield	W	28-16	Tomlinson (2), Booth (2), Thornton	Wilson (4)	1509	Nicholson
6.3.94	SD	A	Highfield	W	50-0	Oldroyd (5), Moxon (2), Pastre, Tomlinson	Wilson (7)	—	—
13.3.94	SD	H	Carlisle	W	56-6	Thornton (3), Walker (3), Moxon (2), Parkinson, Scott	Wilson (8)	519	Wood
20.3.94	SD	H	Swinton	W	32-8	Walker (3), Moxon, Thornton, Tomlinson	Wilson (4)	828	Bates
27.3.94	SD	A	Keighley C.	W	22-6	Tomlinson (2), Walker, Walton	Wilson (3)	—	—
1.4.94	SD	A	Dewsbury	W	34-8	Booth (2), Walker (2), Tomlinson, Walton	Wilson (5)	—	—
4.4.94	SD	H	Bramley	W	50-0	Thornton (3), Moxon (2), Brook, Wilkinson (2), Pastre, Walker	Wilson (5)	1003	Nicholson
10.4.94	SD	H	Hunslet	W	28-8	Wilson (2), Cameron, Moxon, Wilkinson	Wilson (3), Walker	1127	Gilmour
17.4.94	SD	A	Barrow	W	20-7	Moxon, Scott, Wilkinson	Wilson (4)	—	—
24.4.94	SD	H	Doncaster	L	5-10	Tomlinson	Wilson (dg)	4500	Gilmour
8.5.94	SDP(1)	H	Huddersfield	W	28-17	Booth (2), Moxon, Walker, Wilson	Wilson (4)	1459	Gilmour
15.5.94	SDP(SF)	A	Workington T.	L	4-19	Moxon	—	—	—

BRADFORD NORTHERN

Ground: Odsal Stadium (0274-733899)
First Season: 1895-96 as "Bradford". Disbanded and became Bradford Northern in 1907-08. Disbanded during 1963-64 and re-formed for start of 1964-65
Nickname: Northern
Chairman: Chris Caisley
Secretary: Gary Tasker
Honours: **Championship** Beaten finalists, 1947-48, 1951-52
War Emergency League Championship winners, 1939-40, 1940-41, 1944-45
Beaten finalists, 1941-42
Division One Champions, 1903-04, 1979-80, 1980-81
Division Two Champions, 1973-74
Challenge Cup Winners, 1905-06, 1943-44, 1946-47, 1948-49
Beaten finalists, 1897-98, 1944-45, 1947-48, 1972-73
Regal Trophy Winners, 1974-75, 1979-80
Beaten finalists, 1990-91, 1992-93
Premiership Winners, 1977-78
Beaten finalists, 1978-79, 1979-80, 1989-90
Yorkshire Cup Winners, 1906-07, 1940-41, 1941-42, 1943-44, 1945-46, 1948-49, 1949-50, 1953-54, 1965-66, 1978-79, 1987-88, 1989-90
Beaten finalists, 1913-14, 1981-82, 1982-83, 1991-92
Yorkshire League Winners, 1899-1900, 1900-01, 1939-40, 1940-41, 1947-48

RECORDS
Match
Goals: 14 by Joe Phillips v. Batley, 6 Sep 1952
Tries: 7 by Joe Dechan v. Bramley, 13 Oct 1906
Points: 36 by John Woods v. Swinton, 13 Oct 1985

Season
Goals: 173 by Eddie Tees, 1971-72
Tries: 63 by Jack McLean, 1951-52
Points: 364 by Eddie Tees, 1971-72
Career
Goals: 779 by Keith Mumby, 1973-90 & 1992-93
Tries: 261 by Jack McLean, 1950-56
Points: 1,828 by Keith Mumby, 1973-90 & 1992-93
Appearances: 580+8 by Keith Mumby, 1973-90 & 1992-93
Highest score: 76-0 v. Leigh East, 17 Nov 1991
Highest against: 75-18 at Leeds, 14 Sep 1931
Attendance: 102,569 Warrington v. Halifax (RL Cup final replay), 5 May 1954
Home match: 69,429 v. Huddersfield (RL Cup), 14 Mar 1953

COACHING REGISTER
● **Since 1974-75**

Ian Brooke	Jan 73 - Sep 75
Roy Francis	Oct 75 - Apr 77
Peter Fox	Apr 77 - May 85
Barry Seabourne	May 85 - Sep 89
Ron Willey	Oct 89 - Mar 90
David Hobbs	Mar 90 - Oct 91
Peter Fox	Oct 91 -

Neil Summers, scorer of 21 tries in 39 appearances in 1993-94.

GREAT BRITAIN REGISTER
(33 players)

David Barends	(2)	1979
Eric Batten	(4)	1946-47
Ian Brooke	(5)	1966
Len Casey	(5)	1979
Gerald Cordle	(1)	1990
Willie Davies	(3)	1946-47
Karl Fairbank	(10+6)	1987-94
Tony Fisher	(8)	1970-78
Phil Ford	(7)	1987-88
Trevor Foster	(3)	1946-48
Deryck Fox	(1)	1992
Jeff Grayshon	(11)	1979-82
Ellery Hanley	(10+1)	1984-85
David Hobbs	(1+1)	1989
Dick Jasiewicz	(1)	1984
Jack Kitching	(1)	1946
Arthur Mann	(2)	1908
Keith Mumby	(11)	1982-84
Paul Newlove	(4)	1993-94
Brian Noble	(11)	1982-84
Terry Price	(1)	1970
Johnny Rae	(1)	1965
Bill Ramsey	(+1)	1974
Alan Rathbone	(4+1)	1982-85
Alan Redfearn	(1)	1979
David Redfearn	(6+1)	1972-74
Kelvin Skerrett	(8)	1989-90
Tommy Smales	(3)	1965
Bert Smith	(2)	1926
Jimmy Thompson	(1)	1978
Ken Traill	(8)	1950-54
Ernest Ward	(20)	1946-52
Frank Whitcombe	(2)	1946

1993-94 SIGNINGS REGISTER

Signed	Player	Club From
1.7.93	Holding, Neil	St. Helens
13.7.93	Newlove, Paul	Featherstone R.
1.8.93	Dixon, Paul	Leeds
10.8.93	Hepworth, Phil	Dudley Hill ARL
9.9.93	Winterburn, Carl	Birkenshaw ARL
25.11.93	Afoa, Faasu	Northcote T., NZ
14.2.94	Hall, Carl	Doncaster
28.2.94	Clegg, Jason	ARL

Welsh international winger Gerald Cordle, 14 touchdowns in 21 games for Northern in 1993-94.

Veteran Dave Heron, who passed his 36th birthday during the 1993-94 campaign, making 31 appearances.

BRADFORD NORTHERN 1993-94 PLAYERS' SUMMARY

	(Date of Birth)	App	T	G	D	Pts	Previous club	Signed
Afoa, Faasu	(29.9.69)	1	—	—	—	—	New Zealand	25.11.93
Austerfield, Shaun	(11.9.75)	1	—	—	—	—	Oulton ARL	23.11.92
Boothroyd, Alan	(19.6.66)	0+2	—	—	—	—	Huddersfield	22.9.92
Clark, Trevor	(28.5.62)	36+4	8	—	—	32	Featherstone R.	13.8.92
Cordle, Gerald	(29.9.60)	22	14	—	—	56	Cardiff RU	12.7.89
Darkes, Richard	(5.10.68)	7	1	—	—	4	Huddersfield	22.9.92
Dixon, Paul	(28.10.62)	35+2	7	—	—	28	Leeds	1.8.93
Fairbank, Karl	(1.6.63)	35	13	—	—	52	Elland ARL	24.7.86
Fox, Deryck	(17.9.64)	39	8	137	11	317	Featherstone R.	9.9.92
Grayshon, Paul	(11.7.67)	21+6	—	—	—	—	Bradford N. Colts	2.12.85
Greenwood, Adam	(26.5.67)	7+5	1	—	—	4	Calder Valley ARL	27.1.92
Hall, Carl	(10.8.69)	13	9	—	—	36	Doncaster	14.2.94
Hamer, Jon	(23.2.66)	27+13	—	—	—	—	Elland ARL	29.8.84
Heron, David	(1.3.58)	19+12	6	—	—	24	Leeds	27.7.92
Hobbs, David	(13.9.58)	9	—	1	—	2	Oldham	1.4.87
Holding, Neil	(15.12.60)	0+5	1	—	—	4	St. Helens	1.7.93
Kebbie, Brimah	(21.9.65)	27	16	—	—	64	Huddersfield	19.8.92
McDermott, Brian	(16.3.70)	0+1	—	—	—	—	Eastmoor ARL	22.9.92
McGowan, Steve	(25.2.64)	13+5	5	—	—	20	Leeds Colts	31.5.83
Marchant, Tony	(22.12.62)	2+1	—	—	—	—	Castleford	21.12.89
Medley, Paul	(21.9.66)	23+6	9	—	—	36	Halifax	31.8.89
Mumby, Keith	(21.2.57)	1+1	—	—	—	—	Sheffield E.	11.12.92
Newlove, Paul	(10.8.71)	34+2	35	—	—	140	Featherstone R.	13.7.93
Noble, Brian	(14.2.61)	2	—	—	—	—	Queensbury ARL	16.5.78
Powell, Daio	(9.3.73)	10+4	4	—	—	16	Middleton ARL	3.7.90
Powell, Roy	(30.4.65)	38+3	3	—	—	12	Leeds	28.2.92
Shelford, Darrall	(29.7.62)	32	9	—	—	36	New Zealand	20.7.90
Simpson, Roger	(27.8.67)	4+4	—	—	—	—	Moldgreen ARL	17.1.85
Summers, Neil	(10.10.68)	39	21	4	—	92	Headingley RU	4.6.90
Turpin, David	(21.1.73)	1	—	—	—	—	Dudley Hill ARL	13.8.91
Watson, Dave	(24.5.66)	35	15	—	—	60	Halifax	19.8.92
Winterburn, Carl	(8.9.70)	0+5	1	—	—	4	Birkenshaw ARL	9.9.93

TOTALS

			T	G	D	Pts		
32 players			186	142	11	1,039		

Representative appearances 1993-94

Cordle — Wales (2, 2t); Newlove — Britain (4, 2t); D. Powell — Wales (+1), GB Under-21s (2, 1t); Watson — New Zealand (3, 1t); Fairbank — Britain (4, 1t).

BRADFORD NORTHERN 1993-94 MATCH ANALYSIS

Date	Competition	H/A	Opponent	Rlt	Score	Tries	Goals	Attendance	Referee
29.8.93	SBC	H	Widnes	W	32-18	Medley (2), Kebbie, Newlove, Summers, Watson	Fox (4)	6921	Holdsworth
3.9.93	SBC	A	Oldham	W	24-20	Summers (2), McGowan, Watson	Fox (3), Hobbs	—	—
12.9.93	SBC	H	Sheffield E.	W	36-26	Newlove (2), Clark, Dixon, R. Powell, Watson	Fox (6)	5017	Whitfield
19.9.93	SBC	A	Wakefield T.	W	13-8	Fox, Kebbie	Fox (2,1dg)	—	—
26.9.93	SBC	H	Featherstone R.	W	31-16	Dixon, Fairbank, Kebbie, Newlove, Summers	Fox (5,1dg)	7044	J. Connolly
3.10.93	SBC	A	Hull K.R.	L	12-16	Kebbie, Summers	Fox (2)	—	—

Date	Competition	H/A	Opponent	Rlt	Score	Tries	Goals	Attendance	Referee
6.10.93	Tour	H	New Zealand	W	17-10	Cordle, Kebbie	Fox (4,1dg)	4945	R. Smith
10.10.93	SBC	H	Warrington	W	47-16	Cordle (2), Kebbie (2), Greenwood, Newlove, Shelford, Watson	Fox (7,1dg)	6723	Holdsworth
24.10.93	SBC	A	Leigh	W	42-16	Newlove (2), Clark, Cordle, Shelford, Summers, Watson	Fox (7)	—	—
31.10.93	SBC	H	Salford	W	44-24	Watson (2), Clark, Dixon, Kebbie, Newlove, Shelford, Summers, Winterburn	Fox (4)	5609	Holdsworth
7.11.93	SBC	A	St. Helens	L	3-54	—	Fox (1,1dg)	—	—
14.11.93	RT(2)	A	Barrow	W	28-8	Clark, Darkes, Kebbie, Shelford, Watson	Summers (4)	—	—
19.11.93	SBC	H	Wigan	Ab. 13m.	4-2	Cordle	—	7138	R. Smith
28.11.93	SBC	H[1]	Leeds	W	36-28	Summers (2), Cordle, Dixon, R. Powell, Shelford	Fox (6)	7538	J. Smith
5.12.93	SBC	A	Castleford	W	13-6	Cordle, Newlove	Fox (2,1dg)	—	—
16.12.93	RT(3)	H	Halifax	W	16-8	Fairbank, McGowan, Newlove	Fox (2)	5057	J. Connolly
19.12.93	RT(4)	A	London C.	W	22-10	Newlove (2), Cordle, Fairbank	Fox (3)	—	—
26.12.93	SBC	H	Halifax	W	26-18	McGowan (3), Dixon, Summers	Fox (3)	11,385	R. Smith
1.1.94	RT(SF)	H	Castleford	L	10-23	Kebbie (2)	Fox	8351	J. Connolly
5.1.94	SBC	A	Hull	L	4-20	Newlove	—	—	—
9.1.94	SBC	H	Oldham	W	48-16	Fox (2), Clark, Fairbank, Medley, Newlove, D. Powell, Watson	Fox (8)	5119	Holdsworth
12.1.94	SBC	A	Widnes	W	28-8	Fairbank (2), Heron (2), Newlove, Summers	Fox (2)	—	—
16.1.94	SBC	A	Sheffield E.	W	29-28	Kebbie (3), Clark, Dixon	Fox (4,1dg)	—	—
21.1.94	SBC	H	Wakefield T.	W	28-10	Newlove, Heron, Medley, Shelford, Summers	Fox (4)	4571	J. Connolly
30.1.94	CC(4)	A	Barrow	W	58-30	Newlove (4), Fox (2), Dixon, Heron, Medley, Shelford, Summers	Fox (7)	—	—
6.2.94	SBC	A	Featherstone R.	W	13-11	Shelford, Watson	Fox (2,1dg)	—	—
13.2.94	CC(5)	A	Workington T.	W	32-0	Fairbank (2), Kebbie (2), R. Powell, Summers	Fox (4)	—	—
20.2.94	SBC	H	Hull K.R.	W	54-8	Fox (3), Summers (2), Hall, Medley, Newlove, D. Powell, Watson	Fox (7)	4854	Holdsworth
27.2.94	CC(6)	A	Leeds	L	10-33	Clark, Newlove	Fox	—	—
6.3.94	SBC	A	Warrington	W	27-10	Hall (2), Heron, Newlove, Watson	Fox (2,3dg)	—	—
13.3.94	SBC	H	Leigh	L	14-24	Fairbank, Hall, Newlove	Fox	4152	Whitfield
18.3.94	SBC	A	Salford	W	14-6	Heron, Medley, Summers	Fox	—	—
1.4.94	SBC	A	Halifax	L	18-27	Newlove (2), Medley	Fox (3)	—	—
4.4.94	SBC	H	Hull	L	30-32	Cordle (4), Hall (2), Clark	Fox	4647	R. Connolly
8.4.94	SBC	H	Castleford	W	24-16	Newlove, Summers, Cordle, D. Powell	Fox (4)	4295	Campbell
12.4.94	SBC	H	Wigan	W	10-6	Fairbank, Hall	Fox	14,043	Cummings
15.4.94	SBC	A	Wigan	L	14-41	D. Powell, Medley	Fox (3)	—	—
19.4.94	SBC	H	St. Helens	W	18-16	Fairbank, Hall, Newlove	Fox (3)	5782	Holdsworth
23.4.94	SBC	A	Leeds	W	52-10	Newlove (3), Watson (2), Cordle, Hall, Holding, Summers	Fox (8)	—	—
8.5.94	PT(1)	H	Leeds	W	42-16	Newlove (3), Fairbank, Shelford, Summers, Watson	Fox (7)	10,244	R. Connolly
15.5.94	PT(SF)	H	Castleford	L	16-24	Fairbank, Newlove, Summers	Fox (2)	7914	J. Connolly

H[1] Bradford C. FC

BRAMLEY

Ground: McLaren Field (0532-564842)
First Season: 1896-97
Nickname: Villagers
Chairman: Jeff Wine
Secretary: Anthony Sugare
Honours: **BBC-2 Floodlit Trophy** Winners, 1973-74

RECORDS
Match
Goals: 11 by Bernard Ward v. Doncaster, 1 Sep 1974
Tries: 7 by Joe Sedgewick v. Normanton, 16 Apr 1906
Points: 28 by Bernard Ward v. Doncaster, 1 Sep 1974
Season
Goals: 138 by Steve Carroll, 1991-92
Tries: 34 by Peter Lister, 1985-86
Points: 288 by Steve Carroll, 1991-92
Career
Goals: 926 by John Wilson, 1953-64
Tries: 140 by Peter Lister, 1982-91
Points: 1,903 by John Wilson, 1953-64
Appearances: 406+4 by John Wolford, 1962-76
Highest score: 62-14 v. Dewsbury, 30 Oct 1988
Highest against: 92-7 v. Australia, 9 Nov 1921
Attendance: 12,600 v. Leeds (League), 7 May 1947 — at Barley Mow
7,500 v. Bradford N. (RL Cup), 17 Feb 1972 — at McLaren Field

COACHING REGISTER
● **Since 1974-75**

Arthur Keegan	May 73 - Sep 76
Peter Fox	Sep 76 - Apr 77
*Tommy Smales	May 77 - Dec 77
Les Pearce	Jan 78 - Oct 78
Don Robinson	Oct 78 - May 79
Dave Stockwell	June 79 - June 80
Keith Hepworth	June 80 - May 82
Maurice Bamford	May 82 - Oct 83
Peter Jarvis	Oct 83 - Apr 85
Ken Loxton	Apr 85 - Dec 85
Allan Agar	Dec 85 - Apr 87
Chris Forster	June 87 - Nov 87
Tony Fisher	Nov 87 - Feb 89
Barry Johnson	Mar 89 - Dec 90
John Kear	Dec 90 - Jan 91
Roy Dickinson	Jan 91 - Apr 92
Maurice Bamford	Apr 92 - Sep 93
Ray Ashton	Sep 93 -

Ex-forward

1993-94 SIGNINGS REGISTER

Signed	Player	Club From
17.6.93	Long, Gordon	Westgate ARL
15.8.93	Hall, Dean	Dewsbury
30.9.93	Garrett, Paul	Saddleworth R. ARL
30.9.93	Mort, Craig	Oldham
6.10.93	Ashton, Ray	Workington T.
26.10.93	Danes, David	Bilambil, Aus.
11.11.93	*Summerscales, Damian	Keighley C.
12.11.93	*Paver, Ian	Ryedale-York
16.11.93	Wigglesworth, Iain	Ryedale-York
29.12.93	Middleton, Roger	Nottingham C.
7.1.94	*Burke, Tony	Leigh
17.2.94	*Ashton, Lee	Widnes
18.3.94	Clark, Nathan	Oldham
31.3.94	Eaves, Chris	ARL
12.4.94	Hudson, Shaun	Normanton ARL
17.4.94	Tighe, Kevin	Waterhead ARL
21.4.94	Bradshaw, Michael	Waterhead ARL
21.4.94	Crowther, Graham	Higginshaw ARL
21.4.94	Dawson, William	Knottingley RU
21.4.94	Sillers, Jonathan	Moortown RU

BRAMLEY 1993-94 PLAYERS' SUMMARY

	(Date of Birth)	App	T	G	D	Pts	Previous club	Signed
Agar, Andy	(27.5.73)	0+2	—	—	—	—	Pudsey ARL	4.6.91
Ashton, Lee	(29.9.72)	4	2	—	—	8	Widnes	17.2.94
Ashton, Ray	(26.10.60)	26	2	—	4	12	Workington ARL	6.10.93
Barnett, Gary	(25.3.71)	20+4	5	—	—	20	Stanningley ARL	8.12.89
Bell, Kevin	(13.10.64)	23	8	—	—	32	Wakefield R. ARL	2.7.91
Blankley, Dean	(28.10.68)	33	7	—	3	31	Castleford	2.11.90
Brier, Simon	(10.2.68)	1	—	—	—	—	Milford ARL	1.7.92
Briscoe, Carl	(22.2.62)	3	—	—	—	—	Chorley B.	
Burke, Tony	(25.8.61)	2	—	—	—	—	Leigh	7.1.94
Cain, Mick	(7.1.72)	1+2	—	—	—	—	Normanton ARL	3.9.91
Clark, Nathan	(26.12.72)	6+1	1	—	—	4	Oldham	18.3.94
Costello, Dave	(3.11.70)	0+1	—	—	—	—	Waterhead ARL	23.9.92
Creasser, Dean	(18.8.70)	14	1	—	—	4	Bison S. ARL	17.12.91
Danes, David	(1.1.72)	1+5	1	—	—	4	Australia	26.10.93
Eaves, Chris	(27.6.72)	2+1	—	—	—	—	ARL	31.3.94
Fisher, Julian	(4.10.70)	3+1	1	—	—	4	Normanton ARL	15.12.92
Francis, Norman	(2.10.64)	16+1	7	—	—	28	Oldham	11.10.91
Fraser, Paul	(19.6.70)	3+1	—	—	—	—	—	22.5.89
Freeman, Glen	(9.4.72)	16+2	3	—	—	12	Pudsey ARL	4.6.91
Freeman, Wayne	(30.4.74)	21+2	8	—	—	32	Pudsey ARL	27.8.91
Gardner, Chris	(27.4.74)	0+1	—	—	—	—	Stanningley ARL	10.3.94
Garrett, Paul	(29.9.72)	14+2	3	—	—	12	Saddleworth R. ARL	30.9.93
Hall, Dean	(5.6.69)	22	5	—	—	20	Dewsbury	15.8.93
Hall, Gary	(11.11.64)	13+8	4	—	—	16	Featherstone R.	30.8.91
Harker, Keith	(27.9.72)	13+2	1	—	—	4	Ryedale-York	4.3.91
Harwood, Dean	(8.5.71)	0+5	—	—	—	—	Eastmoor ARL	5.4.90
Hester, Terry	(21.1.65)	1	—	—	—	—	Fitton Hill ARL	29.7.92
Holt, Richard	(24.10.71)	1+1	—	—	—	—	Heworth ARL	26.8.93
Hudson, Shaun	(19.10.65)	0+1	—	—	—	—	Normanton ARL	12.4.94
Jewitt, Roy	(26.2.72)	17+2	2	—	—	8	Waterhead ARL	18.5.93
Laws, Mark	(26.4.71)	8	1	—	—	4	Ryedale-York	3.3.94
Lee, Darren	(22.9.72)	1+5	—	—	—	—	Bradford N.	2.2.94
Long, Gordon	(5.1.70)	34	12	41	—	130	Westgate ARL	17.6.93
Lyons, Paddy	(23.1.63)	8+4	3	—	—	12	Hunslet	12.8.91
Maltby, Mark	(17.9.73)	1+5	1	—	—	4	—	27.8.93
Marson, Andy	(19.5.65)	30	5	—	—	20	Hunslet	12.8.91
Morris, Dean	(19.5.71)	0+1	—	—	—	—	Australia	9.9.93
Morse, Ian	(19.4.69)	2	—	—	—	—	Normanton ARL	27.9.92
Mort, Craig	(21.9.72)	8+2	1	—	—	4	Oldham	30.9.93
Nickle, Vince	(3.5.67)	3	—	—	—	—	W. Yorks Fire ARL	6.1.92
Paver, Ian	(8.3.63)	15	1	—	—	4	Ryedale-York	12.11.93
Perks, John		21+1	—	5	—	10	—	
Quinlan, Brian		1	—	—	—	—	—	—
Ryan, Joe	(1.2.67)	0+2	—	—	—	—	New Zealand	1.10.93
Sharp, Ian		5+1	—	—	—	—	—	—
Sharp, Ron	(6.10.64)	10	1	—	—	4		16.3.88
Stansfield, Ivan	(7.12.67)	1	—	—	—	—	Blackpool G.	15.3.93
Stead, Richard	(22.3.70)	15+2	1	5	—	14	Normanton ARL	15.12.92
Whitehead, Craig	(3.2.63)	1	—	—	—	—	Dewsbury	24.12.91
Wigglesworth, Iain	(25.4.67)	11	2	—	—	8	Ryedale-York	24.9.92
*TOTALS								
50 players			89	51	7	465		

*These totals include two trialists, who made 2 + 1 appearances between them.

BRAMLEY 1993-94 MATCH ANALYSIS

Date	Competition	H/A	Opponent	Rlt	Score	Tries	Goals	Attendance	Referee
29.8.93	SD	H	Whitehaven	L	4-20	W. Freeman	—	621	Kershaw
5.9.93	SD	A	Doncaster	L	10-20	Blankley, D. Hall	Stead	—	—
12.9.93	SD	H	Carlisle	L	2-16	—	Stead	380	Asquith
19.9.93	SD	A	Swinton	L	22-36	D. Hall (2), W. Freeman, Harker, Long	Long	—	—
26.9.93	SD	H	Highfield	L	13-16	Bell, Francis	Long (2), Blankley (dg)	373	Crashley
3.10.93	SD	A	Dewsbury	L	10-52	Long, R. Sharp	Long	—	—
10.10.93	SD	H	Rochdale H.	L	10-28	Barnett, Blankley	Perks	750	Cummings
24.10.93	SD	A	Barrow	L	16-24	Barnett, Maltby, Marson	Perks (2)	—	—
31.10.93	RT(1)	H	Woolston R.	W	17-8	Danes, G. Hall	Long (4), R. Ashton (dg)	510	Atkin
7.11.93	SD	H	Ryedale-York	L	20-32	R. Ashton, Bell, Garrett, Long	Long (2)	—	McGregor
14.11.93	RT(2)	A	Rochdale H.	W	11-10	Marson (2)	Perks, Blankley (dg)	—	—
28.11.93	SD	A	Workington T.	L	24-34	R. Ashton, Bell, W. Freeman, G. Hall	Long (4)	—	—
1.12.93	SD	H	London C.	L	18-30	W. Freeman, Mort, G. Freeman	Long (3)	367	Whitelam
5.12.93	SD	A	Huddersfield	L	6-20	Bell	Long	—	—
12.12.93	RT(3)	A	Carlisle	L	4-34	W. Freeman	—	—	—
19.12.93	SD	A	Whitehaven	L	14-34	Creasser, Fisher	Long (3)	—	—
26.12.93	SD	A	Hunslet	W	18-4	Long (2), Francis	Long (2), R. Ashton (2 dg)	—	—
2.1.94	SD	H	Batley	L	8-32	W. Freeman, G. Hall	—	1025	Tennant
9.1.94	SD	H	Doncaster	L	12-19	Bell, Long	Long (2)	738	Redfearn
16.1.94	CC(3)	H	Redhill	W	46-20	Barnett (2), Bell (2), Blankley, Francis, W. Freeman, Garrett, Long	Long (5)	535	Galtress
23.1.94	SD	A	Carlisle	L	16-20	Wigglesworth (2), G. Hall	Long (2)	—	—
30.1.94	CC(4)	H	Widnes	L	11-20	Barnett, G. Freeman	Long, R. Ashton (dg)	1179	Atkin
6.2.94	SD	H	Swinton	L	14-18	Bell, Garrett, Marson	Long	505	Kendrew
20.2.94	SD	A	Highfield	W	28-6	Blankley (2), L. Ashton, Francis, G. Freeman, D. Hall	Long (2)	—	—
27.2.94	SD	H	Dewsbury	L	6-22	Blankley	Long	694	Wood
6.3.94	SD	A	Rochdale H.	L	10-54	D. Hall, Paver	Long	—	—
9.3.94	SD	H	Keighley C.	L	24-48	Long (3), Jewitt, Stead	Long (2)	1201	Carter
13.3.94	SD	H	Barrow	L	15-34	L. Ashton, Jewitt, Long	Long, Blankley (dg)	—	McGregor
20.3.94	SD	A	Ryedale-York	L	0-50	—	—	—	—
27.3.94	SD	A	London C.	L	0-64	—	—	—	—
1.4.94	SD	H	Hunslet	W	18-16	Clark, Francis, Laws, Long	Perks	500	Ollerton
4.4.94	SD	A	Batley	L	0-50	—	—	—	—
10.4.94	SD	A	Keighley C.	L	10-76	Lyons, Marson	Stead	—	—
17.4.94	SD	H	Huddersfield	L	20-30	Lyons (2), Blankley, Francis	Stead (2)	837	Galtress
24.4.94	SD	H	Workington T.	L	8-52	Francis, W. Freeman	—	2000	Morris

Action from Bramley's final league match of the 1993-94 season, against Workington Town who clinched the Second Division title with a 52-8 success.

CARLISLE

Ground: Gillford Park (0228-401212)
First Season: 1981-82. Carlisle City entered the
               League in 1928-29 but withdrew
               after 10 matches
Chairman: Alan Tucker
Secretary: Doug Fisher

RECORDS

Match
Goals: 10 by Barry Vickers at Nottingham C.,
         11 Mar 1990
Tries: 4 by Gary Peacham v. Workington T.,
         25 Jan 1987
         Kevin Pape v. Rochdale H.,
         11 Feb 1987
Points: 24 by Barry Vickers at Nottingham C.,
         11 Mar 1990

Season
Goals: 113 by Steve Ferres, 1981-82
Tries: 25 by Mick Morgan, 1981-82
         Gary Peacham, 1984-85
Points: 242 by Steve Ferres, 1981-82

Career
Goals: 352 by Barry Vickers, 1988-92
Tries: 184 by Kevin Pape, 1984-
Points: 736 by Kevin Pape, 1984-
Appearances: 317 by Kevin Pape, 1984-
Highest score: 60-0 v. Nottingham C.,
         11 Mar 1990
Highest against: 112-0 at St. Helens, 14 Sep 1986
Attendance: 5,903 v. Workington T. (League),
         6 Sep 1981 — at Brunton Park
         2,042 v. Workington T. (RL Cup),
         30 Jan 1994 — at Gillford Park

COACHING REGISTER
● **Since formation in 1981**

Allan Agar	May 81 - June 82
Mick Morgan	July 82 - Feb 83
John Atkinson	Feb 83 - Feb 86
Alan Kellett	Feb 86 - May 86
Roy Lester	June 86 - Nov 88
Tommy Dawes	Dec 88 - Jan 90
Cameron Bell	Feb 90 - Apr 94
Hugh Waddell	Apr 94 -

1993-94 SIGNINGS REGISTER

Signed	Player	Club From
27.7.93	Chorley, Mark	Egremont ARL
27.7.93	Henderson, Carl	Egremont ARL
27.7.93	Sharpley, Spencer	Dalston ARL
17.8.93	Dalton, Sid	Dalston ARL
17.8.93	McManus, Geoff	Dalston ARL
17.8.93	McManus, Chris	Dalston ARL
17.8.93	McManus, Ian	Dalston ARL
17.8.93	Smith, Shaun	Dalston ARL
17.8.93	Wilson, Mark	Glasson R. ARL
17.8.93	Wilson, Andrew	Dalston ARL
18.8.93	Weber, Gareth	Carlisle U-17s ARL
18.8.93	Mason, Philip	Dalston ARL
19.8.93	Blake, Paul	Wigton RU
19.8.93	Semple, Dale	Broughton R.R. ARL
23.8.93	Russell, Danny	Manly, Aus.
17.9.93	Bertoli, Adam	Manly, Aus.
1.10.93	*Ryan, Mark	Whitehaven
3.10.93	McMullen, Alan	Workington T.
19.11.93	*McCartney, Duncan	Whitehaven
30.11.93	Richardson, Willie	Whitehaven
2.1.94	*Crarey, Paul	Barrow
2.1.94	*Westwood, Gary	Barrow
9.1.94	Waddell, Hugh	Sheffield E.

*Much travelled Test prop Hugh Waddell, appointed coach at
Carlisle in May 1994.*

CARLISLE 1993-94 PLAYERS' SUMMARY

	(Date of Birth)	App	T	G	D	Pts	Previous club	Signed
Armstrong, Derek	(2.11.66)	13+11	1	—	—	4	Hawick RU	20.4.92
Armstrong, Ian	(13.3.70)	5+1	—	—	—	—	Cockermouth RU	8.1.90
Bertoli, Adam	(7.12.71)	25	8	—	—	32	Australia	17.9.93
Bethwaite, Kevin	(11.4.68)	7+3	6	—	—	24	Aspatria RU	31.12.92
Blake, Paul	(17.11.70)	31+4	7	—	—	28	Wigton RU	19.8.93
Boucher, Philip	(8.10.70)	1	—	—	—	—	Swinton	23.8.93
Brierley, Steve	(30.3.61)	24+2	—	—	—	—	ARL	22.8.83
Charlton, Gary	(5.3.67)	19+2	5	—	—	20	Whitehaven	27.11.90
Chorley, Mark	(31.8.70)	2+7	—	—	—	—	Egremont ARL	27.7.93
Coffey, Anthony	(12.10.71)	19	9	—	—	36	Australia	23.8.93
Crarey, Paul	(4.1.66)	15	5	—	—	20	Barrow	2.1.94
Fox, Kevin	(16.2.69)	9+1	4	—	—	16	Salford	27.8.92
Graham, George	(19.1.66)	24+1	9	—	—	36	Stirling C. RU	22.10.91
Harris, Grant	(23.12.67)	0+3	—	—	—	—	Hawick RU	28.9.92
Henderson, Carl	(12.6.69)	7+2	—	—	—	—	Egremont ARL	27.7.93
Knox, Simon	(14.10.72)	27+3	9	—	—	36	Hensingham ARL	1.12.91
McCartney, Duncan	(28.5.65)	4	—	—	—	—	Whitehaven	19.11.93
McManus, Geoff	(26.2.58)	0+1	—	—	—	—	Dalston ARL	17.8.93
McMullen, Alan	(1.8.62)	25	2	—	—	8	Workington T.	3.10.93
Manning, Phil	(23.2.62)	0+1	—	—	—	—	Ayr RU	13.8.90
Murdock, Gary	(6.1.68)	11	2	—	—	8	ARL	15.6.87
Pape, Kevin	(17.12.61)	36	24	—	—	96	Glasson R. ARL	29.7.84
Paxton, Colin	(19.6.71)	7	4	—	—	16	Hawick RU	3.1.92
Richardson, Willie	(6.10.60)	36	3	99	—	210	Whitehaven	11.12.92
Russell, Danny	(24.12.69)	36	10	—	—	40	Australia	23.8.93
Ryan, Mark	(31.7.64)	3	—	—	2	2	Whitehaven	1.10.93
Scott, Tony	(17.5.62)	16+6	—	—	—	—	Horse & Farrier ARL	9.4.84
Thomason, Malcolm	(24.9.64)	18	1	—	—	4	Broughton ARL	30.9.85
Waddell, Hugh	(1.9.59)	17	5	—	—	20	Sheffield E.	9.1.94
Westwood, Gary	(15.2.69)	8	—	—	—	—	Barrow	2.1.94
White, Nigel	(31.10.65)	3	—	—	—	—	New Zealand	6.8.90
Wilkinson, Les	(9.4.70)	0+1	—	—	—	—	Aspatria H. ARL	9.1.93
Williams, Barry	(15.5.71)	5+17	7	—	4	32	Broughton ARL	6.9.89
*TOTALS								
33 players			123	99	6	696		

Representative appearances 1993-94
Williams — Wales (2).

*These totals include eight trialists, who played 15 + 3 matches between them, scoring two tries for eight points.

CARLISLE 1993-94 MATCH ANALYSIS

Date	Competition	H/A	Opponent	Rlt	Score	Tries	Goals	Attendance	Referee
29.8.93	SD	A	Dewsbury	L	6-48	Graham	Richardson	—	—
5.9.93	SD	H	Hunslet	W	24-20	Bethwaite (2), Blake, Knox	Richardson (4)	448	Burke
12.9.93	SD	A	Bramley	W	16-2	Bethwaite, Blake, Russell	Richardson (2)	—	—
19.9.93	SD	H	Workington T.	L	12-28	Bertoli, Bethwaite	Richardson (2)	1923	Redfearn
26.9.93	SD	H	Swinton	W	29-20	Coffey, Knox, Murdock, Pape, Richardson	Richardson (4), Williams (dg)	466	McGregor
3.10.93	SD	A	Highfield	W	27-19	Coffey (2), Pape (2), Bertoli	Richardson (3), Ryan (dg)	—	—
10.10.93	SD	A	Doncaster	L	22-27	Bertoli, Pape, Williams	Richardson (4), Ryan (dg), Williams (dg)	—	—
24.10.93	SD	H	Batley	L	10-20	Coffey, Pape	Richardson	488	Whitelam
31.10.93	RT(1)	H	Carcassonne	W	36-24	Knox (2), Williams (2), Bertoli, Blake, Graham	Richardson (4)	593	Kendrew
7.11.93	SD	H	Keighley C.	W	26-24	Williams (2), Bertoli, Charlton, Knox	Richardson (3)	1092	R. Connolly
14.11.93	RT(2)	H	Wakefield T.	W	28-12	Charlton, Coffey, Knox, Pape	Richardson (6)	746	Morris
21.11.93	SD	A	Huddersfield	L	16-42	Knox, Williams	Richardson (4)	—	—
28.11.93	SD	A	London C.	L	24-38	Graham (2), Coffey, Thomason	Richardson (4)	—	—
5.12.93	SD	H	Ryedale-York	L	26-32	Pape (2), Charlton (2), Graham	Richardson (3)	461	Galtress
12.12.93	RT(3)	H	Bramley	W	34-4	Graham (3), Pape (2), Coffey, Russell	Richardson (3)	516	Presley
19.12.93	RT(4)	A	Castleford	L	4-44	McMullen	—	—	—
28.12.93	SD	H	Barrow	L	14-26	Coffey, Pape	Richardson (3)	—	—
2.1.94	SD	H	Whitehaven	L	12-34	Blake, Pape	Richardson (2)	937	Carter
5.1.94	SD	A	Rochdale H.	L	18-34	Pape (2), Blake, Crarey	Richardson	—	—
9.1.94	SD	A	Hunslet	W	18-16	D. Armstrong, Knox, Richardson, Russell	Richardson	—	—
16.1.94	CC(3)	H	Askam	W	42-8	Russell (2), Coffey, Crarey, Murdock, Pape, Richardson, Williams	Richardson (5)	521	McGregor
23.1.94	SD	H	Bramley	W	20-16	Blake, Crarey, Pape	Richardson (4)	329	Presley
30.1.94	CC(4)	H	Workington T.	L	12-13	Crarey, Russell	Richardson (2)	2042	Tennant
6.2.94	SD	A	Workington T.	L	16-23	Bertoli (2)	Richardson (4)	—	—
13.2.94	SD	H	Dewsbury	L	18-40	Knox, Pape, Waddell	Richardson (3)	480	Burke
20.2.94	SD	A	Swinton	L	6-38	Waddell	Richardson	—	—
27.2.94	SD	H	Highfield	W	36-8	Pape (2), Russell (2), Bertoli, McMullen, Waddell	Richardson (4)	275	Galtress
6.3.94	SD	H	Doncaster	L	20-34	Fox, Pape, Paxton, Waddell	Richardson (2)	443	Redfearn
13.3.94	SD	A	Batley	L	6-56	Crarey	Richardson	—	—
20.3.94	SD	A	Keighley C.	L	12-50	Pape (2)	Richardson (2)	—	—
27.3.94	SD	H	Huddersfield	L	14-21	Charlton, Fox, Waddell	Richardson	600	Burke
1.4.94	SD	H	Barrow	W	29-24	Paxton (3), Blake, Russell	Richardson (4), Williams (dg)	398	Kendrew
4.4.94	SD	A	Whitehaven	L	4-46	—	Richardson (2)	—	—
10.4.94	SD	H	Rochdale H.	L	25-32	Pape (2), Russell, Trialist	Richardson (4), Williams (dg)	393	Wood
17.4.94	SD	A	Ryedale-York	L	22-34	Bethwaite (2), Fox, Trialist	Richardson (3)	—	—
24.4.94	SD	H	London C.	L	12-26	Fox, Graham	Richardson (2)	411	Galtress

CASTLEFORD

Ground: Wheldon Road (0977-552674)
First Season: 1926-27. There was also a
Castleford team from 1896-97 to
1905-06 inclusive
Nickname: Tigers
Chairman: Eddie Ashton
Secretary: Denise Cackett
Honours: **Championship** Beaten finalists,
1938-39, 1968-69
Challenge Cup Winners, 1934-35,
1968-69, 1969-70, 1985-86
Beaten finalists, 1991-92
Regal Trophy Winners, 1976-77,
1993-94
Premiership Beaten finalists,
1983-84, 1993-94
Yorkshire Cup Winners, 1977-78,
1981-82, 1986-87, 1990-91, 1991-92
Beaten finalists, 1948-49, 1950-51,
1968-69, 1971-72, 1983-84,
1985-86, 1987-88, 1988-89
Yorkshire League Winners,
1932-33, 1938-39, 1964-65
Eastern Division Championship
Beaten finalists, 1963-64
Charity Shield Beaten finalists,
1986-87
BBC-2 Floodlit Trophy Winners,
1965-66, 1966-67, 1967-68, 1976-77

RECORDS

Match
Goals: 17 by Geoff "Sammy" Lloyd v. Millom,
16 Sep 1973
Tries: 5 by Derek Foster v. Hunslet,
10 Nov 1972
John Joyner v. Millom, 16 Sep 1973
Steve Fenton v. Dewsbury,
27 Jan 1978
Ian French v. Hunslet, 9 Feb 1986
St. John Ellis at Whitehaven,
10 Dec 1989
Points: 43 by Geoff "Sammy" Lloyd v. Millom,
16 Sep 1973

Season
Goals: 158 by Geoff "Sammy" Lloyd, 1976-77
Tries: 40 by St. John Ellis, 1993-94
Points: 334 by Bob Beardmore, 1983-84

Career
Goals: 875 by Albert Lunn, 1951-63
Tries: 206 by Alan Hardisty, 1958-71
Points: 1,870 by Albert Lunn, 1951-63
Appearances: 585+28 by John Joyner, 1973-92
Highest score: 94-12 v. Huddersfield,
18 Sep 1988
Highest against: 62-12 at St. Helens,
16 Apr 1986
Attendance: 25,449 v. Hunslet (RL Cup),
9 Mar 1935

COACHING REGISTER
● **Since 1974-75**

Dave Cox	Apr 74 - Nov 74
*Malcolm Reilly	Dec 74 - May 87
Dave Sampson	May 87 - Apr 88
Darryl Van de Velde	July 88 - May 93
John Joyner	May 93 -

*Shortly after his appointment Reilly returned
to Australia to fulfil his contract before
resuming at Castleford early the next season.*

GREAT BRITAIN REGISTER
(28 players)

Arthur Atkinson	(11)	1929-36
Kevin Beardmore	(13+1)	1984-90
Bill Bryant	(4+1)	1964-67
Lee Crooks	(5)	1992-94
Jim Croston	(1)	1937
Bernard Cunniffe	(1)	1937
Billy Davies	(1)	1933
Derek Edwards	(3+2)	1968-71
St. John Ellis	(+3)	1991-94
Keith England	(6+5)	1987-91
Mike Ford	(+2)	1993
Alan Hardisty	(12)	1964-70
Dennis Hartley	(9)	1968-70
Keith Hepworth	(11)	1967-70
Shaun Irwin	(+4)	1990
John Joyner	(14+2)	1978-84
Brian Lockwood	(7)	1972-74
Tony Marchant	(3)	1986
Roger Millward	(1)	1966
Steve Norton	(2+1)	1974

David Plange	(1)	1988
Malcolm Reilly	(9)	1970
Peter Small	(1)	1962
Graham Steadman	(8+1)	1990-94
Gary Stephens	(5)	1979
Doug Walton	(1)	1965
Johnny Ward	(3)	1963-64
Kevin Ward	(14)	1984-89

1993-94 SIGNINGS REGISTER

Signed	Player	Club From
25.7.93	Kemp, Tony	Newcastle K., Aus.
13.8.93	Russell, Richard	Oldham
18.8.93	*Daniel, Alan	Hunslet
21.8.93	Smales, Ian	Featherstone R.
18.11.93	Hill, Stephen	Redhill ARL
17.1.94	Burns, Peter	Redhill ARL
17.1.94	Flowers, Stuart	Fryston ARL
9.2.94	Coventry, James	Castleford Ac'y.

CASTLEFORD 1993-94 PLAYERS' SUMMARY

	(Date of Birth)	App	T	G	D	Pts	Previous club	Signed
Anderson, Grant	(21.2.69)	32+2	15	—	—	60	Castleford Colts	23.2.87
Blackmore, Richard	(2.7.69)	34+1	20	—	—	80	New Zealand	17.7.91
Crooks, Lee	(18.9.63)	39	2	135	1	279	Leeds	8.1.90
Ellis, St. John	(3.10.64)	41	40	4	—	168	York	15.9.89
England, Keith	(27.2.64)	2+13	—	—	—	—	Castleford Colts	22.6.81
Fisher, Andy	(17.11.67)	4+3	1	—	—	4	Featherstone R.	11.1.93
Flowers, Jason	(30.1.75)	3+4	1	—	—	4	Redhill ARL	12.5.93
Ford, Mike	(18.11.65)	43	22	—	2	90	Oldham	24.6.91
Hay, Andy	(5.11.73)	15+18	7	—	—	28	Redhill ARL	12.11.90
Kemp, Tony	(18.1.68)	27	9	—	1	37	Australia	25.7.93
Ketteridge, Martin	(2.10.64)	33+7	3	18	—	48	Moorends ARL	22.6.83
Middleton, Simon	(2.2.66)	42	21	—	—	84	Knottingley RU	20.4.91
Morrison, Tony	(17.12.65)	30+2	10	—	—	40	Swinton	27.5.92
Nelson, David	(8.9.62)	4+1	—	—	—	—	Sheffield E.	27.8.91
Nikau, Tawera	(1.1.67)	42	6	—	—	24	Ryedale-York	19.8.91
Russell, Richard	(24.11.67)	42	9	—	—	36	Oldham	13.8.93
Sampson, Dean	(27.6.67)	19+12	6	—	—	24	Stanley R. ARL	1.9.86
Smales, Ian	(26.9.68)	36+6	10	—	—	40	Featherstone R.	21.8.93
Smith, Chris	(31.10.71)	4+2	3	—	—	12	Redhill ARL	28.1.92
Smith, Tony	(16.7.70)	23+7	6	—	—	24	Wheldale ARL	25.1.88
Steadman, Graham	(8.12.61)	40	16	7	1	79	Featherstone R.	23.8.89
Sykes, Nathan	(8.9.74)	0+6	1	—	—	4	Moldgreen ARL	14.9.91
Watson, Chris	(9.9.67)	1	—	—	—	—	Cutsyke ARL	15.11.91
Wray, Jon	(19.5.70)	3	1	—	—	4	Morley RU	24.10.90
TOTALS								
24 players		209	164	5		1,169		

Representative appearances 1993-94
Steadman — Britain (1); Crooks — Britain (1, 1g); Ellis — Britain (+1);
Nikau — New Zealand (1); Kemp — New Zealand (3); Blackmore — New Zealand (+1);
Sykes — GB Under-21s (1).

CASTLEFORD 1993-94 MATCH ANALYSIS

Date	Com-petition	H/A	Opponent	Rlt	Score	Tries	Goals	Atten-dance	Referee
27.8.93	SBC	H	Leeds	L	12-21	Anderson, Ellis	Crooks (2)	8578	J. Connolly
5.9.93	SBC	A	Sheffield E.	W	20-11	Fisher, Smales, T. Smith, Steadman	Crooks, Ketteridge	—	—
12.9.93	SBC	H	Hull	W	12-4	Ford	Crooks (4)	5753	Ollerton
17.9.93	SBC	A	Widnes	W	37-12	Blackmore (2), Ellis (2), Hay, Russell	Crooks (6), Ford (dg)	—	—
26.9.93	SBC	H	St. Helens	L	18-35	Ellis, Ford, T. Smith	Crooks (3)	6479	Campbell
3.10.93	SBC	A	Leigh	D	15-15	Blackmore, Ford, T. Smith	Crooks, Ford (dg)	—	—
10.10.93	SBC	H	Hull K.R.	W	54-18	Blackmore (3), Ellis (3), Middleton (2), Nikau, Steadman	Crooks (7)	4492	Nicholson
12.10.93	Tour	H	New Zealand	W	16-4	Ellis (3), Middleton	—	5113	Campbell
24.10.93	SBC	A	Salford	W	34-0	Blackmore, Ford, Kemp, Smales, Wray, Steadman	Crooks (5)	—	—
31.10.93	SBC	H	Wigan	W	46-0	Ellis (3), Middleton (2), Anderson, Blackmore, Ford	Crooks (7)	7745	Whitfield
7.11.93	SBC	A	Halifax	W	35-10	Ellis (2), Steadman (2), Anderson, Kemp, Middleton	Steadman (3, 1dg)	—	—
15.11.93	RT(2)	A	Hull K.R.	W	16-12	Middleton, Morrison, Steadman	Crooks (2)	—	—
21.11.93	SBC	A	Warrington	L	10-20	Ford	Crooks (3)	—	—
28.11.93	SBC	H	Wakefield T.	W	34-10	Ellis (2), Anderson, Blackmore, Flowers, Kemp, Smales	Crooks (3)	5244	R. Connolly
5.12.93	SBC	H	Bradford N.	L	6-13	Ford	Crooks	7000	Campbell
13.12.93	RT(3)	H	Leigh	W	54-14	Middleton (3), Ellis (2), Ford, Smales, Morrison, T. Smith, Steadman	Crooks (4), Ketteridge (2), Steadman	2116	J. Smith
19.12.93	RT(4)	H	Carlisle	W	44-4	Steadman (2), Anderson, Ellis, Hay, Kemp, Sampson, Smales	Ketteridge (6)	2624	Cummings
26.12.93	SBC	A	Featherstone R.	W	28-18	Ellis (2), Sampson, Smales, T. Smith	Crooks (4)	—	—
1.1.94	RT(SF)	A	Bradford N.	W	23-10	Ford, Russell, T. Smith, Steadman	Crooks (3,1dg)	—	—
5.1.94	SBC	A	Leeds	L	4-8	—	Crooks (2)	—	—
9.1.94	SBC	H	Sheffield E.	W	20-18	Ford (2), Hay	Crooks (4)	4279	J. Smith
12.1.94	SBC	H	Oldham	W	34-16	Anderson, Ellis, Hay, Middleton, Morrison, Russell	Crooks (5)	3828	Nicholson
16.1.94	SBC	A	Hull	W	24-22	Anderson, Blackmore, Ford, Kemp, Morrison	Crooks (2)	—	—
22.1.94	RT(F)	N[1]	Wigan	W	33-2	Ketteridge (2), Anderson, Crooks, Nikau	Crooks (6), Kemp (dg)	(15,626)	Campbell
30.1.94	CC(4)	H	Salford	W	36-4	Anderson (3), Ellis, Russell, Smales	Crooks (5), Ketteridge	5662	R. Connolly
6.2.94	SBC	A	St. Helens	L	12-33	Anderson, Middleton	Crooks (2)	—	—
13.2.94	CC(5)	A	Keighley C.	W	52-14	Middleton (2), Anderson, Blackmore, Ellis, Kemp, Morrison, Nikau, Smales, Steadman	Crooks (6)	—	—
20.2.94	SBC	H	Leigh	W	70-6	Ellis (3), Ford (2), Kemp (2), Anderson, Blackmore, Hay, Nikau, Sampson, Smales	Ketteridge (5), Ellis (4)	4005	R. Connolly
26.2.94	CC(6)	H	Widnes	W	30-6	Morrison (2), Ford (2), Steadman	Crooks (5)	6062	J. Connolly
2.3.94	SBC	H	Widnes	W	42-6	Morrison (2), Anderson, Blackmore, Ellis, Middleton, Russell, Steadman	Crooks (3), Ketteridge (2)	3938	J. Smith

Date	Competition	H/A	Opponent	Rlt	Score	Tries	Goals	Attendance	Referee
6.3.94	SBC	A	Hull K.R.	W	44-24	Ford (3), Blackmore (2), Ellis (2), Middleton	Crooks (6)	—	—
12.3.94	CC(SF)	N[1]	Wigan	L	6-20	Kemp	Crooks	(17,049)	Cummings
23.3.94	SBC	H	Salford	W	22-14	Blackmore, Ellis, Middleton, Nikau, Sampson	Steadman	3639	Atkin
27.3.94	SBC	H	Halifax	L	18-26	Hay, Sampson, Steadman	Crooks (3)	6090	J. Connolly
1.4.94	SBC	H	Featherstone R.	W	26-6	Blackmore (2), Ellis, Ford, Middleton	Crooks (3)	6247	J. Connolly
4.4.94	SBC	A	Oldham	W	28-10	Ellis, Ford, Ketteridge, Morrison, Russell	Crooks (3), Ketteridge	—	—
8.4.94	SBC	A	Bradford N.	L	16-24	Russell, Smales, Ellis	Crooks (2)	—	—
17.4.94	SBC	H	Warrington	L	16-21	Crooks, Hay	Crooks (4)	6021	J. Connolly
20.4.94	SBC	A	Wigan	L	12-21	Ellis, Russell	Crooks (2)	—	—
24.4.94	SBC	A	Wakefield T.	W	38-24	Ellis (2), C. Smith (2), Nikau, Russell	Crooks (7)	—	—
6.5.94	PT(1)	H	Halifax	W	28-23	Blackmore (2), Ellis (2), Steadman	Crooks (4)	4617	Campbell
15.5.94	PT(SF)	A	Bradford N.	W	24-16	Middleton (3), Ford, C. Smith	Crooks (2)	—	—
22.5.94	PT(F)	N[2]	Wigan	L	20-24	Sampson, Steadman, Sykes	Crooks (2), Steadman (2)	(35,644)	Cummings

N[1] Leeds
N[2] Manchester U. FC

Castleford's New Zealand Test centre Richard Blackmore takes a low profile in evading Wigan's Barrie-Jon Mather.

DEWSBURY

Ground: Mount Pleasant, Batley; Crown Flatt, Owl Lane, from 1994-95
First Season: 1901-02
Chairman: Ken Davies
Secretary: Ian Clough
Honours: **Championship** Winners, 1972-73
Beaten finalists, 1946-47
War Emergency League Winners, 1941-42 (1942-43 won final but championship declared null and void because Dewsbury played an ineligible player.) Beaten finalists, 1943-44
Division Two Champions, 1904-05
Challenge Cup Winners, 1911-12, 1942-43
Beaten finalists, 1928-29
Yorkshire Cup Winners, 1925-26, 1927-28, 1942-43
Beaten finalists, 1918-19, 1921-22, 1940-41, 1972-73
Yorkshire League Winners, 1946-47
BBC-2 Floodlit Trophy Beaten finalists, 1975-76

Dewsbury's Paul Crook, a 1993-94 debutant from Stanley Rangers ARL.

Highest score: 90-5 at Blackpool G., 4 Apr 1993
Highest against: 82-0 at Widnes, 30 Nov 1986
Attendance: 26,584 v. Halifax (Yorks Cup), 30 Oct 1920 — at Crown Flatt

RECORDS

Match
Goals: 13 by Greg Pearce at Blackpool G., 4 Apr 1993
Tries: 8 by Dai Thomas v. Liverpool C., 13 Apr 1907
Points: 29 by Joe Lyman v. Hull, 22 Apr 1919

Season
Goals: 145 by Nigel Stephenson, 1972-73
Tries: 40 by Dai Thomas, 1906-07
Points: 368 by Nigel Stephenson, 1972-73

Career
Goals: 863 by Nigel Stephenson, 1967-78 & 1984-86
Tries: 144 by Joe Lyman, 1913-31
Points: 2,082 by Nigel Stephenson, 1967-78 & 1984-86
Appearances: 454 by Joe Lyman, 1913-31

COACHING REGISTER
● **Since 1974-75**

Maurice Bamford	June 74 - Oct 74
Alan Hardisty	Oct 74 - June 75
Dave Cox	June 75 - July 77
Ron Hill	July 77 - Dec 77
Lewis Jones	Dec 77 - Apr 78
Jeff Grayshon	May 78 - Oct 78
Alan Lockwood	Oct 78 - Oct 80
Bernard Watson	Oct 80 - Oct 82
Ray Abbey	Nov 82 - Apr 83
*Tommy Smales	May 83 - Feb 84
Jack Addy	Feb 84 - Jan 87
Dave Busfield	Jan 87 - Apr 87
Terry Crook	Apr 87 - Dec 88
Maurice Bamford	Dec 88 - Dec 90
Jack Addy	Dec 90 - Aug 93
Norman Smith	Aug 93 -

*Ex-forward

GREAT BRITAIN REGISTER

(6 players)

Alan Bates	(2+2)	1974
Frank Gallagher	(4)	1920-21
Jim Ledgard	(2)	1947
Roy Pollard	(1)	1950
Mick Stephenson	(5+1)	1971-72
Harry Street	(4)	1950

1993-94 SIGNINGS REGISTER

Signed	Player	Club From
1.6.93	Wilcock, Gilbert	Dewsbury Moor ARL
14.6.93	Holliday, Les	Widnes
22.6.93	Conway, Mark	Wakefield T.
1.7.93	Longo, Davide	Stanley R. ARL
9.7.93	Bell, Peter	Halifax
26.8.93	Agar, Richard	Travellers Sts ARL
13.9.93	Hoyle, Adam	Dewsbury Moor ARL
23.9.93	Johnson, Errol	Bradford N.
13.1.94	Marchant, Tony	Bradford N.
27.4.94	North, Chris	—

DEWSBURY 1993-94 PLAYERS' SUMMARY

	(Date of Birth)	App	T	G	D	Pts	Previous club	Signed
Agar, Richard	(20.1.72)	19+5	7	9	1	47	Travellers Sts ARL	26.8.93
Bailey, Dennis	(15.2.66)	14	10	—	—	40	Queenswood ARL	12.12.85
Bell, Glen	(23.6.65)	17+2	4	—	—	16	New Zealand	10.8.91
Bell, Peter	(29.6.62)	12	2	—	—	8	Halifax	9.7.93
Charles, Marquis	(5.12.66)	27+2	18	—	—	72	Bramley	24.12.91
Cocks, Gary	(7.6.61)	22+2	6	—	—	24	Wakefield T.	7.9.87
Conway, Mark	(31.1.64)	33	16	129	1	323	Wakefield T.	22.6.93
Cornforth, Phil	(16.11.69)	2+1	—	—	—	—	Bradford N.	1.6.92
Coughlan, Glen	(3.2.63)	13+15	5	—	—	20	Dewsbury Moor ARL	10.12.89
Crook, Paul	(12.2.74)	2+1	—	—	—	—	Stanley R. ARL	31.5.91
Delaney, Paul	(18.10.68)	15	4	—	—	16	Leeds	21.5.91
Dickinson, Andy	(26.8.61)	14+14	5	—	—	20	Huddersfield	1.7.90
Fleary, Darren	(2.12.72)	22+1	—	—	—	—	Moldgreen ARL	19.9.91
Graham, Nathan	(23.11.71)	34	16	—	—	64	Dewsbury Colts	23.11.89
Haigh, Mark	(24.1.70)	1+9	—	—	—	—	Hanging Heaton ARL	26.7.89
Holliday, Les	(8.8.62)	28	4	3	—	22	Widnes	14.6.93
Holliday, Mike	(14.1.65)	0+1	—	—	—	—	Folly Lane ARL	22.10.93
Johnson, Erroll	(17.1.67)	23	7	—	—	28	Bradford N.	23.9.93
Jordan, Trent	(31.7.69)	2+4	—	—	—	—	Highfield	2.3.94
Kelly, Neil	(10.5.62)	28	7	—	—	28	Wakefield T.	31.10.88
Longo, Davide	(9.12.75)	9	5	—	—	20	Stanley R. ARL	1.7.93
McRae, Ian	(13.12.71)	12+4	1	—	—	4	Wigan	11.2.93
Marchant, Tony	(22.12.62)	15	4	—	—	16	Bradford N.	13.1.94
Rogers, Darren	(6.5.74)	18	10	—	—	40	Stanley R. ARL	31.5.91
Rombo, Eddie	(19.3.67)	34	20	—	—	80	Leeds	28.11.91
Williams, Shane	(20.10.71)	9+6	3	—	—	12	Dewsbury C. ARL	1.6.92
Worthy, Paul	(14.5.68)	30+1	4	—	—	16	Leeds	21.5.91
TOTALS								
27 players			158	141	2	916		

DEWSBURY 1993-94 MATCH ANALYSIS

Date	Com-petition	H/A	Opponent	Rlt	Score	Tries	Goals	Atten-dance	Referee
29.8.93	SD	H	Carlisle	W	48-6	Charles (3), G. Bell, Conway, Graham, Kelly, Rogers, Rombo	Conway (6)	936	Presley
5.9.93	SD	A	Highfield	W	62-8	Bailey (4), P. Bell, G. Bell, Charles, Delaney, Graham, L. Holliday, Kelly, Rombo	Conway (4), Agar (2), L. Holliday	—	—
12.9.93	SD	H	Whitehaven	D	16-16	Kelly, Rogers	Conway (3), L. Holliday	1058	Cross
19.9.93	SD	A	Keighley C.	L	9-30	Graham	Agar (2,1dg)	—	—
26.9.93	SD	A	London C.	W	42-17	Bailey, Charles, Conway, L. Holliday, Johnson, Rombo, Worthy	Conway (7)	—	—
3.10.93	SD	H	Bramley	W	52-10	Johnson (2), Kelly (2), G. Bell, Charles, Conway, Graham, McRae	Conway (8)	1099	Gilmour
10.10.93	SD	A	Workington T.	L	14-30	Bailey, Charles	Conway (3)	—	—
24.10.93	SD	H	Rochdale H.	L	20-26	Conway, Graham, Rogers	Conway (4)	1293	Kershaw
29.10.93	RT(1)	H	West Bowling	W	56-10	Conway (3), Rombo (2), Bailey, Charles, Delaney, Graham, Rogers	Conway (7), Agar	616	McGregor
7.11.93	SD	H	Barrow	W	56-12	Conway (3), Williams (3), Rombo (2), Delaney, Johnson	Conway (8)	989	Cummings
12.11.93	RT(2)	H	St. Helens	L	6-20	Bailey	Conway	2272	Wood
21.11.93	SD	A	Ryedale-York	W	27-10	Charles, Delaney, Graham, Rombo	Conway (5,1dg)	—	—
28.11.93	SD	H	Huddersfield	W	28-6	Charles (2), Conway (2), Bailey	Conway (4)	2789	Cummings
5.12.93	SD	A	Swinton	W	28-6	Bailey, Dickinson, Graham, Kelly	Conway (5), L. Holliday	—	—
29.12.93	SD	A	Batley	L	2-16	—	Agar	—	—
9.1.94	SD	H	Highfield	W	38-0	Charles (2), Graham (2), Conway, Coughlan, Dickinson, Worthy	Conway (3)	691	Tennant
16.1.94	CC(3)	H	Hensingham	W	64-6	Johnson (3), Coughlan (2), L. Holliday (2), Agar, Charles, Cocks, Graham	Conway (10)	729	J. Smith
23.1.94	SD	A	Whitehaven	W	10-6	Conway	Conway (2), Agar	—	—
30.1.94	CC(4)	A	Doncaster	L	6-18	Rombo	Conway	—	—
2.2.94	SD	H	Hunslet	W	48-8	Worthy (2), G. Bell, Charles, Cocks, Dickinson, Graham, Kelly, Rogers	Conway (6)	867	Presley
6.2.94	SD	H	Keighley C.	W	12-6	Cocks, Rombo	Conway (2)	2873	Redfearn
13.2.94	SD	A	Carlisle	W	40-18	Graham (2), Rombo (2), Cocks, Conway	Conway (8)	—	—
20.2.94	SD	H	London C.	L	16-30	Graham, Rogers, Rombo	Conway (2)	992	Smith
27.2.94	SD	A	Bramley	W	22-6	Agar, Cocks, Marchant, Rombo	Conway (3)	—	—
6.3.94	SD	H	Workington T.	L	10-21	Graham, Rogers	Conway	1725	Presley
9.3.94	SD	H	Doncaster	L	12-18	Charles (2)	Conway (2)	1396	Tennant
13.3.94	SD	A	Rochdale H.	W	20-12	Agar (2), Rombo (2)	Conway (2)	—	—
20.3.94	SD	A	Barrow	L	16-23	Marchant (2), Coughlan	Conway (2)	—	—
27.3.94	SD	H	Ryedale-York	L	12-16	Rombo	Conway (4)	909	Bates
1.4.94	SD	H	Batley	L	8-34	Cocks	Conway (2)	2154	Atkin
4.4.94	SD	A	Hunslet	W	36-6	Longo (2), Agar, Conway, Marchant, Rogers	Conway (6)	—	—
10.4.94	SD	A	Doncaster	L	12-29	Longo (2)	Agar, Conway	—	—
17.4.94	SD	H	Swinton	W	22-10	Agar (2), P. Bell, Rombo	Conway (3)	725	Redfearn
21.4.94	SD	A	Huddersfield	W	28-12	Coughlan, Dickinson, Longo, Rogers, Rombo	Conway (3), Agar	—	—
8.5.94	SDP(1)	A	Doncaster	L	18-48	Charles, Dickinson, Rogers, Rombo	Conway	—	—

DONCASTER

Ground: Tattersfield (0302-390150)
First Season: 1951-52
Nickname: Dons
Chairman: John Desmond
Secretary: Ray Green

RECORDS

Match

Goals: 12 by Tony Zelei v. Nottingham C.,
1 Sep 1991
Robert Turner v. Highfield,
20 Mar 1994
Tries: 5 by Carl Hall v. Mysons,
31 Oct 1993
Points: 32 by Tony Zelei v. Nottingham C.,
1 Sep 1991

Season

Goals: 123 by Robert Turner, 1993-94
Tries: 21 by Mark Roache, 1989-90
Points: 272 by Robert Turner, 1993-94

Career

Goals: 850 by David Noble, 1976-77, 1980-89
& 1992
Tries: 104 by Mark Roache, 1985-
Points: 1,751 by David Noble, 1976-77, 1980-89
& 1992
Appearances: 305+15 by David Noble, 1976-77,
1980-89 & 1992
Highest score: 96-0 v. Highfield, 20 Mar 1994
Highest against: 75-3 v. Leigh, 28 Mar 1976
Attendance: 5,274 v. Wigan (RL Cup),
29 Jan 1989 — at Tattersfield
10,000 v. Bradford N. (RL Cup),
16 Feb 1952 - at York Road Stadium

COACHING REGISTER

● **Since 1974-75**

Ted Strawbridge	Feb 73 - Apr 75
Derek Edwards	July 75 - Nov 76
Don Robson	Nov 76 - Sep 77
Trevor Lowe	Sep 77 - Apr 79
*Tommy Smales	Feb 78 - Apr 79
Billy Yates	Apr 79 - May 79
Don Vines	Sep 79 - Jan 80
Bill Kenny	June 80 - May 81
Alan Rhodes	Aug 81 - Mar 83
Clive Sullivan	Mar 83 - May 84
John Sheridan	June 84 - Nov 87
Graham Heptinstall	Nov 87 - Jan 88
John Sheridan	Jan 88 - Apr 89
Dave Sampson	May 89 - Jan 92
Geoff Morris	Jan 92 - Nov 92
Tony Fisher	Nov 92 -

*Ex-forward, who shared the coaching post
with Trevor Lowe for just over a year.*

1993-94 SIGNINGS REGISTER

Signed	Player	Club From
1.7.93	Hall, Carl	NZ
14.7.93	Whakarau, Sonny	NZ
21.7.93	Hudson, Justin	ARL
28.7.93	Gascoigne, Andy	Keighley C.
13.8.93	Eaton, Barry	ARL
26.8.93	*Reeves, Mark	Wakefield T.
1.9.93	Ellis, John	ARL
1.9.93	Clarke, Andy	Castleford
1.9.93	Bloem, Jamie	Oldham
1.10.93	Tomlinson, Maxwell	Moortown RU
25.11.93	Carlyle, Brendan	—
1.12.93	Matautia, Vila	NZ
4.1.94	*McTigue, Mick	Chorley B.
4.1.94	Rothwell, Andy	Moorends ARL
18.1.94	Bailey, Mark	ARL
14.2.94	*Burke, Tony	Leigh
14.2.94	*McDermott, Brian	Bradford N.
1.4.94	*Eden, Phil	Wakefield T.

DONCASTER 1993-94 PLAYERS' SUMMARY

	(Date of Birth)	App	T	G	D	Pts	Previous club	Signed
Battye, Neil	(11.8.63)	3	1	—	—	4	Castleford	9.11.93
Bellis, Craig		0+1	—	—	—	—	Beverley ARL	—
Bloem, Jamie	(26.5.71)	31+3	8	4	—	40	Oldham	1.9.93
Bowes, Tony	(14.6.70)	16+3	3	—	—	12	Walnut Warriors ARL	3.1.92
Carlyle, Brendan	(25.12.68)	21+3	7	—	—	28	—	25.11.93
Carr, Alan	(4.1.66)	2+3	—	—	—	—	Askern W. ARL	18.1.86
Clarke, Andy	(27.7.64)	10+2	1	—	—	4	Castleford	28.11.92
Eaton, Barry	(30.9.73)	2+1	1	—	—	4	ARL	13.8.93
Eden, Phil	(13.12.63)	5	1	—	—	4	Wakefield T.	1.4.94
Ellis, John	(12.11.66)	9	2	—	—	8	ARL	1.9.93
Evans, David	(17.6.69)	24+2	13	—	—	52	Staffs. Poly ARL	3.1.92
Evans, John	(22.7.62)	14+7	1	—	—	4	Bentley ARL	25.8.87
Fletcher, Ian	(4.3.65)	10+2	2	—	—	8	York	28.3.89
Gascoigne, Andy	(2.4.62)	28+1	9	—	1	37	Keighley C.	8.4.93
Green, Alex	(9.2.71)	24+5	8	4	—	40	Bradford N.	10.2.93
Hall, Carl	(10.8.69)	19	18	—	—	72	New Zealand	1.7.93
Hayes, Brad	(22.4.67)	10+1	3	—	—	12	Australia	4.9.92
Lingard, Glynn	(1.1.69)	22+4	1	—	—	4	Scarborough P.	15.9.92
McDermott, Brian	(16.3.70)	5	3	—	—	12	Bradford N.	14.2.94
McTigue, Mick	(13.12.59)	0+5	—	—	—	—	Chorley B.	4.1.94
Matautia, Vila	(31.8.69)	21	14	—	1	57	New Zealand	1.12.93
Miller, Tony	(30.3.68)	32	3	—	—	12	Oldham	14.2.91
Pell, Richard	(17.10.66)	14+5	—	—	—	—	Cutsyke ARL	3.1.92
Pennant, Audley	(26.2.63)	30+7	13	—	—	52	Bradford N.	24.9.85
Roache, Mark	(24.10.62)	18	14	—	—	56	Castleford	2.9.85
Robson, Steve	(13.3.70)	2	—	—	—	—	Hull K.R.	27.8.93
Rothwell, Andy	(5.9.67)	1	—	—	—	—	Moorends ARL	4.1.94
Rowse, Martin	(8.3.69)	2+1	—	—	—	—	Leeds	3.1.92
Thornton, Wayne	(31.8.66)	7+3	—	—	—	—	Castleford	13.8.92
Tomlinson, Maxwell	(12.4.70)	24	16	—	—	64	Moortown RU	1.10.93
Turner, Robert	(14.3.69)	35	9	113	10	272	Warrington	8.8.93
Whakarau, Sonny	(13.1.66)	35	8	—	—	32	Bramley	14.7.93
Youngs, Mark		2+5	—	—	—	—	—	—
Zelei, Tony	(5.1.68)	16+10	10	1	—	42	Wakefield T.	23.3.90
TOTALS								
34 players			169	122	12	932		

DONCASTER 1993-94 MATCH ANALYSIS

Date	Com-petition	H/A	Opponent	Rlt	Score	Tries	Goals	Atten-dance	Referee
1.9.93	SD	A	Hunslet	W	32-28	Roache (2), Zelei (2), Ellis	Turner (6)	—	—
5.9.93	SD	H	Bramley	W	20-10	Bloem, Green, Turner, Whakarau	Turner (2)	1182	Redfearn
10.9.93	SD	A	London C.	L	18-38	Roache, Fletcher, Green	Turner (3)	—	—
19.9.93	SD	H	Barrow	W	27-16	Clarke, Green, Hall, Roache, Turner	Turner (3,1dg)	1022	Crashley

Date	Com-petition	H/A	Opponent	Rlt	Score	Tries	Goals	Atten-dance	Referee
26.9.93	SD	A	Workington T.	L	13-32	Hall, Miller	Turner (2,1dg)	—	—
3.10.93	SD	H	Keighley C.	L	20-30	Battye, Bloem, Roache	Turner (4)	2359	Presley
10.10.93	SD	H	Carlisle	W	27-22	Hall, Hayes, Roache, Zelei	Turner (5,1dg)	1042	R. Connolly
24.10.93	SD	A	Whitehaven	L	12-34	Green, Hall	Turner (2)	—	—
31.10.93	RT(1)	H	Mysons	W	62-4	Hall (5), Gascoigne (2), D. Evans, Green, Roache, Turner, Zelei	Turner (7)	858	Asquith
7.11.93	SD	A	Highfield	W	34-14	Hayes (2), Fletcher, Tomlinson, Turner, Whakarau	Turner (5)	—	—
14.11.93	RT(2)	A	Widnes	L	4-24	D. Evans	—	—	—
21.11.93	SD	A	Swinton	L	20-40	Hall, Eaton, Whakarau, Zelei	Turner (2)	—	—
28.11.93	SD	H	Batley	W	16-6	Hall (2), Gascoigne	Turner (2)	1040	Galtress
5.12.93	SD	H	Rochdale H.	W	34-12	Carlyle, J. Evans, D. Evans, Hall, Turner, Zelei	Turner (5)	1048	Atkin
19.12.93	SD	H	Hunslet	W	22-12	Gascoigne, Green, Pennant, Whakarau	Turner (3)	940	Kendrew
1.1.94	SD	A	Huddersfield	W	34-18	Carlyle, Gascoigne, Hall, Lingard, Matautia, Roache	Turner (4,1dg), Gascoigne (dg)	—	—
9.1.94	SD	A	Bramley	W	19-12	D. Evans, Hall, Matautia	Turner (3,1dg)	—	—
16.1.94	CC(3)	H	Wigan St. Patricks	W	36-4	D. Evans (3), Tomlinson (2), Hall, Matautia	Green (4)	927	Wood
19.1.94	SD	H	Ryedale-York	W	20-8	Gascoigne (3), Hall, Matautia	—	1098	Cross
23.1.94	SD	H	London C.	W	20-10	Pennant (2), Tomlinson, Turner	Turner (2)	1448	Tennant
30.1.94	CC(4)	H	Dewsbury	W	18-6	Tomlinson (2), D. Evans, Matautia	Turner	1733	Steele
6.2.94	SD	A	Barrow	L	21-23	Tomlinson (2), D. Evans, Hall	Turner (2,1dg)	—	—
13.2.94	CC(5)	H	Oldham	W	20-0	Pennant (2), D. Evans, Tomlinson	Bloem (2)	2872	Holdsworth
20.2.94	SD	H	Workington T.	W	15-11	Bowes, Tomlinson	Turner (3,1dg)	1946	McGregor
27.2.94	CC(6)	A	St. Helens	L	9-40	Ellis	Turner (2), Matautia (dg)	—	—
2.3.94	SD	A	Keighley C.	D	12-12	Eden, Whakarau	Bloem (2)	—	—
6.3.94	SD	A	Carlisle	W	34-20	McDermott (3), Bloem, Tomlinson, Turner	Turner (5)	—	—
9.3.94	SD	A	Dewsbury	W	18-12	Gascoigne, Whakarau, Bloem	Turner (3)	—	—
13.3.94	SD	H	Whitehaven	W	20-6	Matautia (2), Pennant, Roache	Turner (2)	1473	Kershaw
20.3.94	SD	H	Highfield	W	96-0	Pennant (3), Roache (3), Bloem (2), Bowes (2), Tomlinson (2), Whakarau (2), Zelei (2), Matautia, Miller	Turner (12)	1483	Galtress
27.3.94	SD	H	Swinton	W	42-0	Green (2), Carlyle, Matautia, Pennant, Roache, Turner, Zelei	Turner (4), Zelei	1708	Carter
1.4.94	SD	A	Ryedale-York	W	23-16	Bloem, Carlyle, Miller, Roache	Turner (3,1dg)	—	—
4.4.94	SD	H	Huddersfield	W	19-7	Carlyle, Matautia, Tomlinson	Turner (3,1dg)	4208	Tennant
10.4.94	SD	H	Dewsbury	W	29-12	Matautia (2), Carlyle, D. Evans, Pennant	Turner (4,1dg)	2723	Cross
17.4.94	SD	A	Rochdale H.	L	2-20	—	Turner	—	—
24.4.94	SD	A	Batley	W	10-5	Carlyle, Turner	Turner	—	—
8.5.94	SDP(1)	H	Dewsbury	W	48-18	Matautia (2), Pennant (2), Tomlinson (2), Bloem, D.Evans, Zelei	Turner (6)	2706	Wood
15.5.94	SDP(SF)	H	London C.	L	6-16	D. Evans	Turner	3238	R. Smith

49

FEATHERSTONE ROVERS

Ground: Post Office Road (0977-702386)
First Season: 1921-22
Nickname: Colliers
Chairman: Steve Wagner
Secretary: Terry Jones
Honours: **Championship** Beaten finalists,
              1927-28
              Division One Champions, 1976-77
              Division Two Champions, 1979-80,
              1992-93
              Challenge Cup Winners, 1966-67,
              1972-73, 1982-83
              Beaten finalists, 1951-52, 1973-74
              **Second Division/Divisional
              Premiership** Winners, 1992-93
              Beaten finalists, 1987-88
              Yorkshire Cup Winners, 1939-40,
              1959-60
              Beaten finalists, 1928-29, 1963-64,
              1966-67, 1969-70, 1970-71,
              1976-77, 1977-78, 1989-90
              Captain Morgan Trophy Beaten
              finalists, 1973-74

RECORDS

Match
Goals: 13 by Mark Knapper v. Keighley,
        17 Sep 1989
Tries: 6 by Mike Smith v. Doncaster,
        13 Apr 1968
        Chris Bibb v. Keighley, 17 Sep 1989
Points: 30 by Mark Knapper v. Keighley,
        17 Sep 1989

Season
Goals: 163 by Steve Quinn, 1979-80
Tries: 48 by Paul Newlove, 1992-93
Points: 391 by Martin Pearson, 1992-93

Career
Goals: 1,210 by Steve Quinn, 1975-88
Tries: 162 by Don Fox, 1953-66
Points: 2,654 by Steve Quinn, 1975-88
Appearances: 440 by Jim Denton, 1921-34

Highest score: 86-18 v. Keighley, 17 Sep 1989
Highest against: 70-2 at Halifax, 14 Apr 1941
Attendance: 17,531 v. St. Helens (RL Cup),
             21 Mar 1959

COACHING REGISTER
● **Since 1974-75**

*Tommy Smales	July 74 - Sep 74
Keith Goulding	Sep 74 - Jan 76
†Tommy Smales	Feb 76 - May 76
Keith Cotton	June 76 - Dec 77
Keith Goulding	Dec 77 - May 78
Terry Clawson	July 78 - Nov 78
†Tommy Smales	Nov 78 - Apr 79
Paul Daley	May 79 - Jan 81
Vince Farrar	Feb 81 - Nov 82
Allan Agar	Dec 82 - Oct 85
George Pieniazek	Nov 85 - Nov 86
Paul Daley	Nov 86 - Apr 87
Peter Fox	May 87 - Oct 91
Allan Agar	Oct 91 - Aug 92
Steve Martin	Sep 92 -

Ex-forward
†Ex-scrum half*

Former Oldham prop Leo Casey, 32 appearances in 1993-94.

GREAT BRITAIN REGISTER
(16 players)

Tommy Askin	(6)	1928
Chris Bibb	(1)	1990
John "Keith" Bridges	(3)	1974
Terry Clawson	(2)	1962
Malcolm Dixon	(2)	1962-64
Steve Evans	(5+3)	1979-80
Deryck Fox	(9+4)	1985-92
Don Fox	(1)	1963
David Hobbs	(7+1)	1984
Gary Jordan	(2)	1964-67
Steve Molloy	(1)	1994
Arnold Morgan	(4)	1968
Steve Nash	(16)	1971-74
Paul Newlove	(7+3)	1989-93
Peter Smith	(1+5)	1977-84
Jimmy Thompson	(19+1)	1970-77

1993-94 SIGNINGS REGISTER

Signed	Player	Club From
11.8.93	Currier, Andy	Widnes
20.8.93	Price, Gary H.	Wakefield T.
25.8.93	Gibson, Carl	Leeds
2.9.93	Hughes, Darren	Leeds
8.9.93	Calland, Matt	Rochdale H.
30.9.93	Jackson, Craig	Isberg C. ARL
3.11.93	Molloy, Steve	Leeds
4.11.93	Ropati, Iva	NZ
16.12.93	Southernwood, Graham	Castleford
4.3.94	*Richards, Craig	Oldham
26.3.94	*Ellis, Mark	Hunslet

Martin Pearson, Featherstone Rovers' top scorer in 1993-94 with a 267-point haul.

Double tourist Carl Gibson, an August 1993 Post Office Road capture from Leeds.

FEATHERSTONE ROVERS 1993-94 PLAYERS' SUMMARY

	(Date of Birth)	App	T	G	D	Pts	Previous club	Signed
Bibb, Chris	(3.6.68)	9	1	—	—	4	Lock Lane ARL	21.6.85
Bonson, Paul	(18.10.71)	0+3	—	—	—	—	Featherstone MW ARL	21.10.88
Burton, Chris	(5.10.56)	2+1	—	—	—	—	Hull K.R.	8.1.89
Butt, Ikram	(25.10.68)	32	12	—	—	48	Leeds	9.8.90
Calland, Matt	(20.8.71)	11+3	6	—	—	24	Rochdale H.	8.9.93
Casey, Leo	(17.9.65)	32	1	—	—	4	Oldham	26.7.90
Daunt, Brett	(8.10.65)	32	5	—	—	20	Australia	24.9.92
Ellis, Mark	(23.5.67)	1+2	—	—	—	—	Hunslet	26.3.94
Gibson, Carl	(23.4.63)	34	17	—	—	68	Leeds	25.8.93
Gunn, Richard	(25.2.67)	32+2	3	—	—	12	Leeds	24.9.92
Hill, Gavin	(11.12.65)	0+4	—	—	—	—	New Zealand	28.9.93
Hughes, Darren	(19.6.74)	0+1	—	—	—	—	Leeds	2.9.93
Maloney, Francis	(26.5.73)	17	6	19	2	64	Leeds	12.11.92
Manning, Terry	(4.12.65)	23+6	7	—	—	28	Keighley	17.10.89
Molloy, Steve	(11.3.69)	31+1	2	—	—	8	Leeds	3.11.93
O'Brien, Richard	(25.10.71)	3+2	—	—	—	—	West Hull ARL	27.4.93
Pearson, Martin	(24.10.71)	31+1	21	91	1	267	Travellers Sts ARL	16.11.88
Price, Gary H.	(28.10.69)	28+6	8	—	—	32	Wakefield T.	20.8.93
Price, Gary S.	(9.3.61)	23+5	—	—	—	—	Leeds	4.8.89
Richards, Craig	(27.1.70)	0+1	—	—	—	—	Oldham	4.3.94
Richardson, Sean	(28.8.73)	0+1	—	—	—	—	Prince of Wales ARL	1.11.92
Roebuck, Neil	(4.10.69)	13+17	4	—	—	16	Castleford	13.1.93
Ropati, Iva	(18.7.68)	20+1	14	—	—	56	New Zealand	4.11.93
Simpson, Owen	(12.9.65)	28	14	—	—	56	Keighley	9.11.90
Southernwood, Graham	(5.11.71)	7+3	—	—	—	—	Castleford	16.12.93
Tuuta, Brendon	(29.4.65)	32	7	—	—	28	Australia	14.9.90
Wilson, Mark	(3.10.65)	1+4	—	—	—	—	Bradford N.	22.7.91

TOTALS
27 players 128 110 3 735

Representative appearances 1993-94
Maloney — GB Under-21s (2, 1t); Molloy — Britain (1).

Stand off Francis Maloney, scorer of 64 points in 17 appearances in 1993-94.

FEATHERSTONE ROVERS 1993-94 MATCH ANALYSIS

Date	Com-petition	H/A	Opponent	Rlt	Score	Tries	Goals	Atten-dance	Referee
29.8.93	SBC	A	Leigh	W	26-12	Tuuta (2), Butt, Pearson, Simpson	Pearson (3)	—	—
5.9.93	SBC	H	Hull K.R.	W	30-20	Butt, Maloney, Manning, Simpson, Tuuta	Maloney (4), Pearson	3751	Nicholson
12.9.93	SBC	A	Halifax	L	8-32	Manning	Pearson (2)	—	—
19.9.93	SBC	H	Wigan	W	35-22	Maloney (2), Butt, Manning, G.H. Price, Roebuck, Tuuta	Pearson, Maloney (2,1dg)	5572	J. Smith
26.9.93	SBC	A	Bradford N.	L	16-31	Gibson (2), Manning	Maloney (2)	—	—
1.10.93	SBC	H	St. Helens	L	16-37	Butt, Roebuck	Pearson (4)	3671	Ollerton
10.10.93	SBC	A	Sheffield E.	D	18-18	Daunt, Maloney, Pearson	Pearson (3)	—	—
19.10.93	SBC	H	Leeds	W	22-20	Butt, Pearson, Roebuck	Pearson (5)	4829	McCallum (Aus)
31.10.93	SBC	A	Widnes	L	12-24	Gibson, Simpson	Pearson (2)	—	—
7.11.93	SBC	H	Oldham	W	30-24	Butt (2), Pearson (2), Manning, Simpson	Pearson (2), Maloney	3719	Campbell
14.11.93	RT(2)	A	London C.	L	12-26	Calland, Maloney	Maloney (2)	—	—
21.11.93	SBC	H	Hull	W	21-10	Simpson (2), Gibson	Pearson (4, 1dg)	3301	Morris
28.11.93	SBC	A	Salford	L	24-34	Simpson (2), Daunt, Gunn	Maloney (4)	—	—
5.12.93	SBC	A	Warrington	L	14-30	Daunt, Pearson	Pearson (3)	—	—
19.12.93	SBC	H	Leigh	W	36-0	Ropati (3), Gibson (2), Maloney, G.H. Price, Simpson	Maloney, Pearson	2521	J. Connolly
26.12.93	SBC	H	Castleford	L	18-28	Molloy, Ropati, Simpson	Pearson (3)	6854	Whitfield
2.1.94	SBC	A	Wakefield T.	W	24-10	Gibson (3), Pearson, Ropati	Pearson (2)	—	—
9.1.94	SBC	A	Hull K.R.	W	14-10	Calland, G.H. Price, Simpson	Pearson	—	—
16.1.94	SBC	H	Halifax	W	20-16	Butt, Pearson, G.H. Price	Pearson (4)	4753	Ollerton
30.1.94	CC(4)	A	London C.	W	28-14	Pearson (2), Butt, Calland, Tuuta	Pearson (4)	—	—
6.2.94	SBC	H	Bradford N.	L	11-13	Butt	Maloney (3, 1dg)	4659	R. Connolly
13.2.94	CC(5)	A	Hull K.R.	W	30-8	Pearson (2), Butt, Calland, Molloy	Pearson (5)	—	—
20.2.94	SBC	A	St. Helens	L	18-27	G.H. Price, Ropati, Simpson, Tuuta	Pearson	—	—
27.2.94	CC(6)	A	Wigan	L	14-32	Calland, Gibson, Ropati	Pearson	—	—
2.3.94	SBC	A	Wigan	L	10-28	Manning, G.H. Price	Pearson	—	—
6.3.94	SBC	H	Sheffield E.	L	28-38	Ropati (2), Gibson, Manning, Pearson	Pearson (4)	3481	J. Smith
13.3.94	SBC	A	Leeds	W	36-10	Butt, Calland, Gibson, Gunn, G.H. Price, Ropati	Pearson (6)	—	—
20.3.94	SBC	H	Widnes	L	22-29	Bibb, Gibson, Ropati, Pearson	Pearson (3)	3200	Atkin
27.3.94	SBC	A	Oldham	L	8-22	Ropati	Pearson (2)	—	—
1.4.94	SBC	A	Castleford	L	6-26	Pearson	Pearson	—	—
4.4.94	SBC	H	Wakefield T.	W	42-22	Daunt (2), Gibson, Pearson, G.H. Price, Roebuck, Ropati	Pearson (7)	3784	Whitfield
10.4.94	SBC	H	Warrington	L	24-27	Pearson (2), Casey, Gibson	Pearson (4)	3401	Campbell
17.4.94	SBC	A	Hull	L	16-37	Pearson, Ropati, Simpson	Pearson (2)	—	—
24.4.94	SBC	H	Salford	W	46-24	Gibson (2), Pearson (2), Gunn, Simpson, Tuuta	Pearson (9)	2958	Campbell

HALIFAX

Ground: Thrum Hall (0422-361026)
First Season: 1895-96
Nickname: Thrum Hallers
Chairman: Tony Gartland
Secretary: David Fleming
Honours: **Championship** Winners, 1906-07, 1964-65
Beaten finalists, 1952-53, 1953-54, 1955-56, 1965-66
War Emergency League Beaten finalists, 1942-43, 1944-45
Division One Champions, 1902-03, 1985-86
Challenge Cup Winners, 1902-03, 1903-04, 1930-31, 1938-39, 1986-87
Beaten finalists, 1920-21, 1940-41, 1941-42, 1948-49, 1953-54, 1955-56, 1987-88
Regal Trophy Winners, 1971-72
Beaten finalists, 1989-90
Premiership Trophy Beaten finalists, 1985-86
Second Division Premiership Beaten finalists, 1990-91
Yorkshire Cup Winners, 1908-09, 1944-45, 1954-55, 1955-56, 1963-64
Beaten finalists, 1905-06, 1907-08, 1941-42, 1979-80
Yorkshire League Winners, 1908-09, 1920-21, 1952-53, 1953-54, 1955-56, 1957-58
Eastern Division Championship Winners, 1963-64
Charity Shield Winners, 1986-87
Beaten finalists, 1987-88

RECORDS

Match
Goals: 14 by Bruce Burton v. Hunslet, 27 Aug 1972
Tries: 8 by Keith Williams v. Dewsbury, 9 Nov 1957
Points: 31 by Bruce Burton v. Hunslet, 27 Aug 1972

Season
Goals: 147 by Tysul Griffiths, 1955-56
Tries: 48 by Johnny Freeman, 1956-57
Points: 298 by Colin Whitfield, 1986-87

Career
Goals: 1,028 by Ron James, 1960-72
Tries: 290 by Johnny Freeman, 1954-67
Points: 2,191 by Ron James, 1960-72
Appearances: 481 by Stan Kielty, 1946-58
Highest score: 82-8 v. Runcorn H., 14 Oct 1990
Highest against: 64-0 at Wigan, 7 Mar 1923
Attendance: 29,153 v. Wigan (RL Cup), 21 Mar 1959

COACHING REGISTER
● Since 1974-75

Derek Hallas	Aug 74 - Oct 74
Les Pearce	Oct 74 - Apr 76
Alan Kellett	May 76 - Apr 77
Jim Crellin	June 77 - Oct 77
Harry Fox	Oct 77 - Feb 78
Maurice Bamford	Feb 78 - May 80
Mick Blacker	June 80 - June 82
Ken Roberts	June 82 - Sep 82
Colin Dixon	Sep 82 - Nov 84
Chris Anderson	Nov 84 - May 88
Graham Eadie	May 88 - Aug 88
Ross Strudwick	Aug 88 - Feb 89
Alan Hardisty	Feb 89 - Apr 89
John Dorahy	June 89 - Aug 90
Peter Roe	Aug 90 - May 91
Roger Millward	May 91 - Dec 92
Malcolm Reilly	Jan 93 -

Alan Kellett, Halifax coach in season 1976-77.

GREAT BRITAIN REGISTER
(32 players)

Alvin Ackerley	(2)	1952-58
Arthur Bassett	(2)	1946
Jack Beames	(2)	1921
Nat Bentham	(2)	1929
John Bentley	(1)	1994
Harry Beverley	(2)	1937
Oliver Burgham	(1)	1911
Arthur Daniels	(3)	1952-55
Will Davies	(1)	1911
Colin Dixon	(1)	1968
Paul Dixon	(3+3)	1987-88
Percy Eccles	(1)	1907
Terry Fogerty	(+1)	1966
Tony Halmshaw	(1)	1971
Karl Harrison	(5+3)	1991-93
Michael Jackson	(+2)	1993
Neil James	(1)	1986
Robbie Lloyd	(1)	1920
Alf Milnes	(2)	1920
Stuart Prosser	(1)	1914
Dai Rees	(1)	1926
Charlie Renilson	(7+1)	1965-68
Joe Riley	(1)	1910
Ken Roberts	(10)	1963-66
Asa Robinson	(3)	1907-08
Derrick Schofield	(1)	1955
John Shaw	(5)	1960-62
Cyril Stacey	(1)	1920
John Thorley	(4)	1954
Jack Wilkinson	(6)	1954-55
Frank Williams	(2)	1914
David Willicombe	(1)	1974

1993-94 SIGNINGS REGISTER

Signed	Player	Club From
14.6.93	Marshall, Richard	St. Helens Academy
1.7.93	Dean, Craig	Leigh East ARL
2.7.93	Hampson, Steve	Wigan
13.7.93	Jackson, Michael	Wakefield T.
1.8.93	Lay, Steve	Hunslet
2.8.93	Highton, Paul	Waterhead ARL
3.8.93	Topliss, Matthew	Siddal ARL
5.8.93	Waite, Tony	Siddal ARL
5.8.93	Martindale, Michael	Saddleworth R. ARL
5.8.93	Burton, Daniel	Oulton ARL
18.8.93	Fairhurst, John	Dewsbury Moor ARL
18.8.93	Simpson, Nick	Dudley Hill ARL
20.8.93	Harland, Lee	Leeds
22.8.93	Schuster, John	Newcastle K., Aus.
2.9.93	Boyd, David	Newcastle K., Aus.
2.9.93	Hagan, Michael	Newcastle K., Aus.
16.9.93	Anderson, Paul	Leeds
27.9.93	Render, Nick	Leeds
27.9.93	Smithson, Martyn	Leeds
27.9.93	Arundel, Stuart	Leeds
1.10.93	*James, Neil	Sheffield E.
7.12.93	*Roadnight, John	Batley
10.1.94	Round, Paul	Wakefield T.
17.2.94	Sucker, George	Waterhead ARL
11.3.94	Denton, Lee	Oulton ARL
11.3.94	Mayall, Michael	Halifax Academy
11.3.94	Radford, Chris	Stanningley ARL
15.4.94	McAndrew, Phil	—

August 1993 overseas recruit John Schuster, scorer of 198 Halifax points.

55

HALIFAX 1993-94 PLAYERS' SUMMARY

	(Date of Birth)	App	T	G	D	Pts	Previous club	Signed
Anderson, Paul ....(25.10.71).....		0+7	—	—	—	—	Leeds	16.9.93
Bailey, Mark ....(5.5.68)........		2+3	1	—	—	4	St. Helens	4.3.92
Bentley, John ....(5.9.66)........		32	25	—	—	100	Leeds	21.8.92
Bishop, Paul ....(5.7.67)........		23	6	41	5	111	St. Helens	13.8.92
Boyd, David ....(13.5.66)......		20+4	1	—	—	4	Australia	2.9.93
Divorty, Gary ....(28.1.66)......		34	14	—	—	56	Leeds	21.8.92
Fieldhouse, John ....(28.6.62)......		19+2	1	—	—	4	Oldham	17.10.91
Hagan, Michael...........(12.8.64)......		33	9	—	—	36	Australia	2.9.93
Hallas, Graeme ....(27.2.71)......		27	11	—	—	44	Hull K.R.	29.10.92
Hampson, Steve ....(14.8.61)......		14+1	2	—	1	9	Wigan	2.7.93
Hancock, Andy...........(11.6.69)......		0+3	—	—	—	—	—	17.5.88
Harland, Lee...............(4.9.73)........		6+10	1	—	—	4	Leeds	20.8.93
Harrison, Karl ....(20.2.64)......		24	1	—	—	4	Hull	8.8.91
Jackson, Michael ....(11.10.69).....		17+1	3	—	—	12	Wakefield T.	13.7.93
Lawless, Johnny ....(3.11.74)......		4	—	—	—	—	Siddal ARL	1.6.92
Lay, Steve ....(28.3.68)......		21+5	4	—	—	16	Hunslet	1.8.93
Lord, Gary ....(6.7.66)........		24+9	3	—	—	12	Leeds	15.10.91
Perrett, Mark ....(18.7.73)......		16+9	2	—	—	8	Ovenden ARL	18.9.91
Preston, Mark ....(3.4.67)........		32	18	—	—	72	Wigan	11.6.91
Robinson, Chris ....(2.9.70)........		11	3	—	—	12	Dudley Hill ARL	27.11.90
Round, Paul ....(24.9.63)......		10+1	4	—	—	16	Wakefield T.	10.1.94
Schuster, John ....(17.1.64)......		33	17	65	—	198	Australia	22.8.93
Sharp, Henry ....(17.9.66)......		8+4	4	—	—	16	Dudley Hill ARL	18.2.91
Smith, Richard ....(18.6.73)......		1	—	—	—	—	Siddal ARL	18.5.92
Smithson, Martyn........(5.10.68)......		0+1	—	—	—	—	Leeds	27.9.93
Southernwood, Roy ......(23.6.68)......		30	3	—	—	12	Castleford	24.8.90
Wilson, Warren ....(3.5.63)........		1+5	—	—	—	—	Leeds	13.9.90
TOTALS								
27 players			133	106	6	750		

Representative appearances 1993-94
Bentley — Britain (1); Harland — GB Under-21s (+1); Harrison — Britain (2); Jackson — Britain (+2); Perrett — Wales (1), GB Under-21s (1).

Three tries in 33 games for forward Gary Lord.

Hooker Roy Southernwood, scorer of three tries in 30 games.

HALIFAX 1993-94 MATCH ANALYSIS

Date	Competition	H/A	Opponent	Rlt	Score	Tries	Goals	Attendance	Referee
29.8.93	SBC	H	Oldham	W	26-12	Bailey, Bentley, Divorty, Preston, Schuster	Bishop (3)	7340	Campbell
5.9.93	SBC	A	Hull	D	18-18	Divorty, Preston, Schuster	Bishop (3)	—	—
12.9.93	SBC	H	Featherstone R.	W	32-8	Preston (2), Bishop, Divorty, Hallas, Perrett	Bishop (3), Schuster	7152	Steele
19.9.93	SBC	A	Sheffield E.	W	40-14	Hagan (2), Bentley, Harland, Harrison, Lay, Preston	Bishop (6)	—	—
26.9.93	SBC	H	Leigh	W	27-26	Bishop, Divorty, Hallas, Preston, Sharp	Bishop (3,1dg)	6019	Nicholson
8.10.93	SBC	H	Salford	W	20-12	Bishop, Lay, Schuster	Bishop (4)	5096	Ollerton
18.10.93	SBC	A	Warrington	L	7-15	Bentley	Bishop (1,1dg)	—	—
24.10.93	SBC	H	Wigan	L	22-31	Jackson (2), Preston	Bishop (5)	9820	Campbell
31.10.93	SBC	A	Hull K.R.	W	28-18	Bentley, Divorty, Hallas, Lord, Preston	Bishop (4)	—	—
7.11.93	SBC	H	Castleford	L	10-35	Hallas (2)	Bishop	8084	Steele
14.11.93	RT(2)	H	Keighley C.	W	19-10	Bentley (2), Hallas	Bishop (3,1dg)	7321	Ollerton
21.11.93	SBC	A	Wakefield T.	W	12-2	Bentley, Hallas, Robinson	—	—	—
26.11.93	SBC	A	St. Helens	D	16-16	Preston (2), Robinson	Schuster (2)	—	—
5.12.93	SBC	H	Widnes	W	20-12	Bentley (2), Divorty	Schuster (4)	5717	Holdsworth
16.12.93	RT(3)	A	Bradford N.	L	8-16	Bentley, Lay	—	—	—
19.12.93	SBC	A	Oldham	W	28-11	Schuster (2), Bentley, Hagan, Lord	Schuster (4)	—	—
26.12.93	SBC	A	Bradford N.	L	18-26	Bentley, Divorty, Southernwood	Schuster (3)	—	—
2.1.94	SBC	H	Leeds	L	12-18	Bentley, Preston	Schuster (2)	9429	R. Connolly
9.1.94	SBC	H	Hull	W	24-10	Bentley, Boyd, Hagan, Schuster	Schuster (4)	5598	Asquith
16.1.94	SBC	A	Featherstone R.	L	16-20	Round, Schuster, Southernwood	Schuster (2)	—	—
23.1.94	SBC	H	Sheffield E.	L	20-26	Bentley, Robinson, Round	Schuster (4)	5336	Holdsworth
29.1.94	CC(4)	H	Warrington	L	18-22	Hallas, Bentley, Bishop	Schuster (2), Bishop	4775	J. Connolly
6.2.94	SBC	A	Leigh	W	32-10	Divorty, Fieldhouse, Hallas, Lay, Perrett, Schuster	Schuster (4)	—	—
18.2.94	SBC	H	Warrington	W	22-7	Bishop, Bentley, Schuster, Hagan	Schuster (3)	4202	Campbell
27.2.94	SBC	A	Salford	L	14-34	Hagan, Hampson, Round	Bishop	—	—
20.3.94	SBC	H	Hull K.R.	W	42-26	Hallas (2), Schuster (2), Divorty, Preston, Round, Southernwood	Schuster (5)	4689	Whitfield
27.3.94	SBC	A	Castleford	W	26-18	Divorty, Hagan, Preston, Schuster	Schuster (5)	—	—
1.4.94	SBC	H	Bradford N.	W	27-18	Schuster (2), Bentley, Bishop, Preston	Schuster (3), Bishop (dg)	9205	Campbell
4.4.94	SBC	A	Leeds	L	16-26	Bentley (2), Schuster	Schuster (2)	—	—
7.4.94	SBC	A	Wigan	L	0-38	—	—	—	—
10.4.94	SBC	A	Widnes	L	16-28	Bentley, Divorty	Schuster (4)	—	—
17.4.94	SBC	H	Wakefield T.	W	54-16	Bentley (3), Hagan (2), Preston (2), Divorty, Jackson, Sharp	Schuster (7)	5221	R. Smith
24.4.94	SBC	H	St. Helens	W	37-30	Bentley, Divorty, Hampson, Lord, Preston, Schuster, Sharp	Schuster (4), Hampson (dg)	6212	R. Connolly
6.5.94	PT(1)	A	Castleford	L	23-28	Divorty, Preston, Schuster, Sharp	Bishop (3,1dg)	—	—

HIGHFIELD

Ground: Hoghton Road; Prescot AFC
from 1994-95
First Season: 1922-23 as Wigan Highfield.
Became London Highfield in
1933-34. Became Liverpool Stanley
in 1934-35 and changed to
Liverpool City in 1951-52. Became
Huyton in 1968-69 and changed to
Runcorn Highfield in 1984-85.
Became Highfield in 1991-92.
Chairman: Geoff Fletcher
Secretary: Brian Morris
Honours: **Lancashire League** Winners,
1935-36

RECORDS
Match
Goals: 11 by Peter Wood v. Batley, 21 Oct 1984
Tries: 5 by John Maloney v. Bramley,
25 Apr 1931
Points: 30 by Norman Barrow v. Keighley,
31 Mar 1991
Season
Goals: 126 by Peter Wood, 1984-85
Tries: 28 by John Maloney, 1930-31
Points: 240 by Peter Wood, 1984-85
Career
Goals: 304 by Wilf Hunt, 1955-66
Tries: 204 by John Maloney, 1926-45
Points: 731 by Wilf Hunt, 1955-66
Appearances: 413 by John Maloney, 1926-45
Highest score: 59-11 v. Bramley, 4 May 1934
Highest against: 96-0 at Doncaster,
20 Mar 1994
Attendance: 18,000 v. Wigan (League),
2 Sep 1922 — at Tunstall Lane,
Pemberton
1,600 v. Halifax (League),
6 Jan 1991 — at Hoghton Road

COACHING REGISTER
● Since 1974-75

Terry Gorman	Aug 74 - May 77
Geoff Fletcher	Aug 77 - June 86
Frank Wilson	July 86 - Nov 86
Arthur Daley	
Paul Woods	} Nov 86 - Apr 87

Bill Ashurst	Apr 87 - Jan 89
John Cogger	Jan 89 - Feb 89
Geoff Fletcher	Feb 89 - Apr 89
Dave Chisnall	June 89 - Oct 90
Alan Bishop	Oct 90 - Apr 91
Chris Arkwright	Apr 91 - Aug 91
Willie Johnson	Aug 91 - Apr 93
Mike Peers	Apr 93 -

GREAT BRITAIN REGISTER
(4 players)

Ray Ashby	(1)	1964
Billy Belshaw	(6)	1936-37
Nat Bentham	(6)	1928
Harry Woods	(5)	1936

1993-94 SIGNINGS REGISTER

Signed	Player	Club From
5.8.93	Durnin, Paul	Woolston R. ARL
10.8.93	Barnes, David	—
10.8.93	Forber, Gary	ARL
16.8.93	Potter, Ian	Bramley
16.8.93	Morris, Graham	Nutgrove ARL
16.8.93	Drinkwater, Matthew	Woolston R. ARL
16.8.93	Connor, Cavan	Simms Cross ARL
24.8.93	Brown, David	Whitehaven
24.8.93	Pilat, Stewart	Woolston R. ARL
27.8.93	*Ashall, Barry	Swinton
1.9.93	*Stewart, Mike	Rochdale H.
9.9.93	Brown, Tim	RU
25.9.93	Jordan, Trent	Mullambimby, Aus.
30.9.93	Idle, Graham	Nottingham C.
30.9.93	Cartwright, Phil	Roundhill ARL
6.10.93	Denning, Mike	—
6.10.93	Flannery, Steve	Blackpool G.
6.10.93	Raines, Tony	RU
27.10.93	Mudge, Scott	Leigh East ARL
6.1.94	*Evans, Andrew	Chorley B.
7.1.94	*Crook, Lee	Chorley B.
9.1.94	*Clayton, Richard	Chorley B.
3.2.94	*Crehan, Andy	Swinton
2.3.94	Garforth, Chris	Saddleworth R. ARL
18.3.94	Hester, Terry	
25.3.94	Ogburn, John	Simms Cross ARL
25.3.94	Worthington, Peter	Simms Cross ARL

HIGHFIELD 1993-94 PLAYERS' SUMMARY

	(Date of Birth)	App	T	G	D	Pts	Previous club	Signed
Ashall, Barry	(1.9.71)	4	—	—	—	—	Swinton	27.8.93
Bamber, Simon	(3.2.63)	5	—	—	—	—	Rochdale H.	—
Barnes, Dave	(21.10.73)	14+12	1	—	—	4	Wigan St. Judes ARL	7.11.92
Barrow, Shaun	(8.11.67)	27	5	—	—	20	St. Helens	24.8.89
Brown, Dave	(17.2.65)	19+8	3	—	—	12	Whitehaven	24.8.93
Brown, Tim	(1.1.72)	10+6	—	—	—	—	RU	9.9.93
Carr, Mike	(14.11.64)	22+3	1	—	—	4	Pilkington ARL	11.8.92
Cartwright, Phil	(14.1.61)	3	1	—	—	4	Roundhill ARL	30.9.93
Clayton, Richard	(24.2.70)	4	1	—	—	4	Chorley B.	9.1.94
Connor, Cavan	(10.6.72)	1	—	—	—	—	Simms Cross ARL	16.8.93
Crehan, Andy	(27.11.67)	12	—	—	—	—	Swinton	3.2.94
Crook, Lee	(15.2.71)	2+2	1	—	—	4	Chorley B.	7.1.94
Denning, Mike	(11.1.65)	7	2	—	—	8	Pilkington ARL	22.9.92
Dolan, Shaun	(1.1.70)	22	7	—	—	28	Blackbrook ARL	24.8.89
Drinkwater, Matt	(18.4.75)	10+3	2	—	—	8	Woolston R. ARL	16.8.93
Durnin, Paul	(5.11.60)	2	—	—	—	—	Bramley	11.8.92
Evans, Andy	(19.4.70)	9+1	4	—	—	16	Chorley B.	7.1.93
Flannery, Steve	(3.2.71)	5	—	—	—	—	Blackpool G.	6.10.93
Forber, Gary	(22.1.68)	21	8	—	1	33	Swinton	28.2.91
Garforth, Chris	(5.6.73)	5+4	—	—	1	1	Saddleworth R. ARL	2.3.94
Garritty, Brian		2	—	—	—	—	Rochdale H.	1.1.94
Grady, Mick	(1.11.69)	2+2	—	—	—	—	—	8.1.90
Griffiths, David	(9.4.69)	10+1	1	—	—	4	—	21.1.94
Hester, Terry	(21.1.65)	2	—	—	—	—	Bramley	12.3.93
Hine, David	(5.3.67)	8+2	—	—	—	—	Ruskin Park RU	1.9.89
Idle, Graham	(10.3.50)	2+1	—	—	—	—	Nottingham C.	30.9.93
Johnson, Chris	(29.5.60)	33	2	50	2	110	Blackpool G.	16.3.93
Johnson, Willie	(26.10.60)	26	2	—	—	8	Dewsbury	25.1.91
Jordan, Trent	(31.7.69)	18	—	—	—	—	Australia	25.9.93
Littler, Paul	(25.8.66)	19+5	1	—	—	4	Thatto Heath ARL	3.2.91
Mudge, Scott	(27.8.73)	6+1	—	—	—	—	Leigh East ARL	27.10.93
Ogburn, John	(3.10.64)	1	—	—	—	—	Simms Cross ARL	25.3.94
Pemberton, Tony	(26.5.64)	29+1	2	—	—	8	Blackpool G.	12.3.93
Pilat, Stewart	(25.10.73)	1+6	—	—	—	—	Woolston R. ARL	24.8.93
Potter, Ian	(6.8.58)	22+3	1	—	—	4	Bramley	13.11.92
Raines, Tony	(25.3.71)	1	—	—	—	—	RU	6.10.93
Rippon, Andy	(10.2.65)	26+1	3	4	—	20	Blackpool G.	—
Stephenson, Colin	(4.2.70)	10	1	—	—	4	Crosfields ARL	21.3.93
Stewart, Mike	(16.1.66)	4	1	—	—	4	Rochdale H.	1.9.93
Viller, Mark	(25.10.65)	1	—	—	—	—	Blackpool G.	12.3.93
Wood, David		14	3	—	1	13	—	—
Worthington, Peter	(9.12.64)	1	—	—	—	—	Simms Cross ARL	25.3.94
TOTALS								
42 players			53	54	5	325		

HIGHFIELD 1993-94 MATCH ANALYSIS

Date	Com-petition	H/A	Opponent	Rlt	Score	Tries	Goals	Atten-dance	Referee
29.8.93	SD	A	Rochdale H.	L	8-64	Carr	C. Johnson (2)	—	—
5.9.93	SD	H	Dewsbury	L	8-62	Littler	C. Johnson (2)	609	Asquith
12.9.93	SD	A	Barrow	L	22-44	Forber (2), Barrow, Dolan	C. Johnson (2), Rippon	—	—
19.9.93	SD	H	Ryedale-York	L	10-24	Dolan	C. Johnson (3)	316	Whitelam
26.9.93	SD	A	Bramley	W	16-13	W. Johnson, Potter, Stewart	C. Johnson (2)	—	—
3.10.93	SD	H	Carlisle	L	19-27	Cartwright, Dolan, Forber, Wood	C. Johnson, Wood (dg)	363	Volante
10.10.93	SD	A	Batley	L	16-58	D. Brown, Forber, Stephenson	C. Johnson (2)	—	—
17.10.93	SD	A	London C.	L	6-62	Wood	C. Johnson	—	—
24.10.93	SD	A	Huddersfield	L	20-60	D. Brown, Forber, Wood	C. Johnson (4)	—	—
31.10.93	RT(1)	H	Ellenborough	W	30-22	Forber (2), C. Johnson (2), Denning	C. Johnson (5)	227	Galtress
7.11.93	SD	H	Doncaster	L	14-34	Forber, Rippon	Rippon (3)	284	Cross
14.11.93	RT(2)	H	Oldham	L	8-26	Denning, Rippon	—	880	Crashley
21.11.93	SD	A	Whitehaven	L	1-32	—	Forber (dg)	—	—
28.11.93	SD	A	Keighley C.	L	6-44	Rippon	C. Johnson	—	—
5.12.93	SD	H	Hunslet	L	16-30	Dolan (2), W. Johnson	C. Johnson (2)	325	Burke
12.12.93	SD	A	Workington T.	L	4-26	—	C. Johnson (2)	—	—
19.12.93	SD	H	Rochdale H.	L	6-22	—	C. Johnson (3)	326	Kershaw
9.1.94	SD	A	Dewsbury	L	0-38	—	—	—	—
16.1.94	CC(3)	H	Saddleworth R.	W	16-13	Crook, Evans, Pemberton	C. Johnson (2)	277	Gilmour
23.1.94	SD	H	Barrow	D	8-8	Clayton	C. Johnson (2)	200	Bates
30.1.94	CC(4)	H	Whitehaven	L	4-15	Evans	—	316	Burke
6.2.94	SD	A	Ryedale-York	L	16-40	Evans (2), Barrow	C. Johnson (2)	—	—
13.2.94	SD	H	Swinton	L	0-10	—	—	363	Steele
20.2.94	SD	H	Bramley	L	6-28	Barrow	C. Johnson	219	Nicholson
27.2.94	SD	A	Carlisle	L	8-36	Pemberton	C. Johnson (2)	—	—
6.3.94	SD	H	Batley	L	0-50	—	—	365	McGregor
13.3.94	SD	H	Huddersfield	L	12-36	Dolan, Griffiths	C. Johnson (2)	595	Burke
20.3.94	SD	A	Doncaster	L	0-96	—	—	—	—
27.3.94	SD	H	Whitehaven	L	12-46	Barrow, Drinkwater	C. Johnson (2)	235	Lee
1.4.94	SD	H[1]	London C.	L	6-58	Barnes	C. Johnson	339	Kershaw
4.4.94	SD	A	Swinton	L	10-26	Drinkwater	C. Johnson (2,2dg)	—	—
10.4.94	SD	H[1]	Workington T.	L	1-40	—	Garforth (dg)	736	Kendrew
19.4.94	SD	A	Hunslet	L	8-44	Dolan	C. Johnson (2)	—	—
24.4.94	SD	H[1]	Keighley C.	L	8-76	Barrow, D. Brown	—	784	Bates

H[1] Prescot AFC

Andy Rippon, scorer of three tries and four goals.

Packman Ian Potter, one touchdown in 25 appearances.

HUDDERSFIELD

Ground: Leeds Road; Kirklees Stadium from 1994-95
First Season: 1895-96; added Barracudas to title from 1984-85 to 1987-88 inclusive
Nickname: Fartowners
Chairman: Bob Scott
General Manager: Les Coulter
Honours: **Championship** Winners, 1911-12, 1912-13, 1914-15, 1928-29, 1929-30, 1948-49, 1961-62
Beaten finalists, 1913-14, 1919-20, 1922-23, 1931-32, 1945-46, 1949-50
Division Two Champions, 1974-75
Division Three Champions, 1991-92
Challenge Cup Winners, 1912-13, 1914-15, 1919-20, 1932-33, 1944-45, 1952-53
Beaten finalists, 1934-35, 1961-62
Yorkshire Cup Winners, 1909-10, 1911-12, 1913-14, 1914-15, 1918-19, 1919-20, 1926-27, 1931-32, 1938-39, 1950-51, 1952-53, 1957-58
Beaten finalists, 1910-11, 1923-24, 1925-26, 1930-31, 1937-38, 1942-43, 1949-50, 1960-61
Yorkshire League Winners, 1911-12, 1912-13, 1913-14, 1914-15, 1919-20, 1921-22, 1928-29, 1929-30, 1948-49, 1949-50, 1951-52
Eastern Division Beaten finalists, 1962-63

RECORDS

Match
Goals: 18 by Major Holland v. Swinton Park, 28 Feb 1914
Tries: 10 by Lionel Cooper v. Keighley, 17 Nov 1951
Points: 39 by Major Holland v. Swinton Park, 28 Feb 1914

Season
Goals: 147 by Ben Gronow, 1919-20
Tries: 80 by Albert Rosenfeld, 1913-14
Points: 332 by Pat Devery, 1952-53

Career
Goals: 958 by Frank Dyson, 1950-63
Tries: 420 by Lionel Cooper, 1947-55
Points: 2,072 by Frank Dyson, 1950-63
Appearances: 485 by Doug Clark, 1909-29
Highest score: 119-2 v. Swinton Park, 28 Feb 1914
Highest against: 94-12 at Castleford, 18 Sep 1988
Attendance: 35,136 Leeds v. Wakefield T. (RL Cup SF), 19 Apr 1947
Home match: 32,912 v. Wigan (League), 4 Mar 1950

COACHING REGISTER
● **Since 1974-75**

Brian Smith	Jan 73 - Mar 76
Keith Goulding	Mar 76 - Dec 76
Bob Tomlinson	Jan 77 - May 77
Neil Fox	June 77 - Feb 78
*Roy Francis	-
Keith Goulding	May 78 - July 79
Ian Brooke	July 79 - Mar 80
Maurice Bamford	May 80 - May 81
Les Sheard	June 81 - Nov 82
Dave Mortimer	Nov 82 - Aug 83
Mel Bedford	Aug 83 - Nov 83
Brian Lockwood	Nov 83 - Feb 85
Chris Forster	Feb 85 - Dec 86
Jack Addy	Jan 87 - Mar 88
Allen Jones Neil Whittaker	Mar 88 - Nov 88
Nigel Stephenson	Nov 88 - Mar 90
Barry Seabourne	Mar 90 - Feb 91
Mick Blacker Francis Jarvis	Feb 91 - Sep 91
Alex Murphy	Sep 91 - Apr 94

*Although Roy Francis was appointed he was unable to take over and Dave Heppleston stood in until the next appointment.

GREAT BRITAIN REGISTER
(24 players)

Jim Bowden	(3)	1954
Ken Bowman	(3)	1962-63
Brian Briggs	(1)	1954
Stan Brogden	(9)	1929-33
Jack Chilcott	(3)	1914
Doug Clark	(11)	1911-20
Don Close	(1)	1967
Dick Cracknell	(2)	1951
Jim Davies	(2)	1911
Frank Dyson	(1)	1959
Ben Gronow	(7)	1911-20
Fred Longstaff	(2)	1914
Ken Loxton	(1)	1971
Stan Moorhouse	(2)	1914
Bob Nicholson	(3)	1946-48
Johnny Rogers	(7)	1914-21
Ken Senior	(2)	1965-67
Tommy Smales	(5)	1962-64
Mick Sullivan	(16)	1954-57
Gwyn Thomas	(8)	1920-21
Dave Valentine	(15)	1948-54
Rob Valentine	(1)	1967
Harold Wagstaff	(12)	1911-21
Harold Young	(1)	1929

1993-94 SIGNINGS REGISTER

Signed	Player	Club From
17.6.93	Morris, Nigel	Thatto Heath ARL
1.7.93	Barton, Ben	ARL
28.7.93	Oates, David	—
11.8.93	Pickles, Damien	Halifax
20.8.93	Corion, Rudolph	ARL
20.8.93	Medcalf, Richard	Wyke ARL
24.8.93	Jammes, Pierre	Limoux, Fr.
24.8.93	Lucchese, Laurent	Tarn Sud, Fr.
25.8.93	King, David	London C.
27.8.93	Reynolds, Simon	Moldgreen ARL
27.8.93	Richards, Basil	Warrington
3.9.93	*Bimson, Jeff	Chorley B.
3.9.93	*Cosgrove, David	St. Helens
10.9.93	*Harrison, Paul	Hull
10.9.93	*McCallion, Seamus	Leeds
15.9.93	Pearce, Greg	Halifax
1.11.93	White, Brendan	Keighley C.
6.1.94	*Vasey, Chris	Dewsbury
1.3.94	Salmon, Robert	Moldgreen ARL
4.3.94	Feather, Steve	Hull
15.3.94	Seal, Daniel	Greetland ARL

Seven tries in 34 games in 1993-94 for utility forward Joe Naidole.

HUDDERSFIELD 1993-94 PLAYERS' SUMMARY

	(Date of Birth)	App	T	G	D	Pts	Previous club	Signed
Barnett, Steve	(8.10.68)	31+1	2	—	—	8	Bradford N.	22.9.92
Barton, Ben	(4.12.74)	2	—	—	—	—	ARL	1.7.93
Bimson, Jeff	(15.1.67)	3	—	—	—	—	Chorley B.	3.9.93
Blacker, Brian	(20.3.63)	17+13	6	—	—	24	Hull	20.8.92
Chapman, Chris	(14.4.66)	11	3	—	—	12	Castleford	11.6.90
Cosgrove, David	(29.1.68)	2+4	—	—	—	—	St. Helens	3.9.93
Coulter, Gary	(12.7.69)	16+4	6	—	—	24	Doncaster	17.1.92
Davis, Brad	(13.3.68)	30	12	—	1	49	Nottingham C.	8.10.92
Flanagan, Neil	(11.6.70)	27+1	6	—	2	26	Oldham	21.8.92
Harrison, Paul	(24.9.70)	3	—	—	—	—	Hull	10.9.93
Hellewell, Phil	(23.4.67)	32	10	46	—	132	Bradford N.	22.9.92
Jammes, Pierre	(13.12.72)	2	—	—	—	—	France	24.8.93
King, David	(6.9.67)	34+1	11	—	—	44	London C.	25.8.93
Laurence, Jason	(23.1.70)	30+2	19	—	—	76	Nottingham C.	8.10.92
Lucchese, Laurent	(4.4.73)	16+1	2	—	—	8	France	24.8.93
Maders, Martin	(29.6.73)	10+5	1	—	—	4	Saddleworth R.ARL	30.1.92
Meillam, Paul	(30.8.70)	7+1	3	—	—	12	York All Blacks ARL	24.8.90
Naidole, Joe	(23.12.67)	27+7	7	—	—	28	Deighton W. ARL	8.1.90
Needham, David	(25.10.64)	8+1	—	—	—	—	Workington T.	27.11.92
Pearce, Greg	(2.9.67)	22+3	7	71	1	171	Halifax	15.9.93
Pearson, Richard	(9.10.74)	3+1	1	—	—	4	Ovenden ARL	31.10.91
Pickles, Damien	(2.12.70)	28	12	—	—	48	Halifax	11.8.93
Pucill, Andy	(19.11.67)	34	3	—	—	12	Swinton	21.8.92
Reynolds, Simon	(10.3.73)	3	1	—	—	4	Moldgreen ARL	27.8.93
Richards, Basil	(9.7.65)	13+7	1	—	—	4	Warrington	27.8.93
Scholes, Damon	(5.7.66)	0+2	—	—	—	—	Paddock ARL	24.8.90
Senior, Gary	(11.9.62)	7+10	—	—	—	—	Hunslet	21.8.89
Sewell, Andy	(5.4.69)	0+1	—	—	—	—	Moldgreen ARL	2.8.89
St. Hilaire, Lee	(15.2.67)	2	—	—	—	—	ARL	30.12.92
Simpson, Andy	(16.3.66)	2+1	1	—	—	4		4.8.92
Slater, Lee	(8.9.74)	1+1	—	3	—	6	Ovenden ARL	12.8.92
Thomas, Ian	(6.11.64)	31	21	—	—	84		3.6.83
Vasey, Chris	(28.2.63)	1	—	—	—	—	Dewsbury	6.1.94
TOTALS								
33 players			135	120	4	784		

Representative appearance 1993-94
Lucchese – France Under-21s (1).

HUDDERSFIELD 1993-94 MATCH ANALYSIS

Date	Competition	H/A	Opponent	Rlt	Score	Tries	Goals	Attendance	Referee
29.8.93	SD	A	Workington T.	W	10-9	Simpson	Hellewell (3)	—	—
5.9.93	SD	H	Rochdale H.	W	30-8	Naidole (2), Davis, Flanagan, Hellewell, Pickles	Hellewell (3)	2000	Gilmour
12.9.93	SD	A	Hunslet	W	34-4	Thomas (3), Davis, Hellewell, Lucchese, Pickles	Hellewell (3)	—	—
19.9.93	SD	H	London C.	W	34-10	Barnett, Blacker, Laurence, Naidole, Thomas	Hellewell (7)	2949	R. Connolly
26.9.93	SD	A	Barrow	W	30-25	Flanagan, Hellewell, King, Laurence, Pickles, Thomas	Hellewell (3)	—	—
3.10.93	SD	H	Batley	W	37-12	Thomas (3), Blacker, Hellewell, Laurence	Hellewell (6), Flanagan (dg)	3324	Kershaw
10.10.93	SD	A	Swinton	W	24-18	Coulter, Davis, Laurence, Pickles, Thomas	Pearce (2)	—	—
24.10.93	SD	H	Highfield	W	60-20	Davis (2), Thomas (2), Blacker, King, Laurence, Meillam, Naidole, Pearce, Pickles	Hellewell (4), Pearce (4)	2010	Carter
31.10.93	RT(1)	H	Irlam H.	W	36-8	Thomas (2), Blacker, Flanagan, King, Naidole, Pickles	Hellewell (2), Pearce (2)	1705	Presley
7.11.93	SD	H	Whitehaven	W	14-9	Hellewell, Meillam	Pearce (3)	2180	Kendrew
14.11.93	RT(2)	A	Leigh	L	12-20	Davis (2), Thomas	—	—	—
21.11.93	SD	H	Carlisle	W	42-16	Pickles (2), Davis, Hellewell, King, Meillam, Thomas	Pearce (4), Hellewell (3)	1922	Kershaw
28.11.93	SD	A	Dewsbury	L	6-28	Thomas	Hellewell	—	—
5.12.93	SD	H	Bramley	W	20-6	Naidole (2), Blacker, Maders	Hellewell (2)	1755	Gilmour
8.12.93	SD	A	Ryedale-York	W	8-0	Hellewell	Hellewell (2)	—	—
19.12.93	SD	H	Workington T.	L	4-20	—	Hellewell (2)	3310	Atkin
1.1.94	SD	H	Doncaster	L	18-34	Barnett, Laurence, Pearson	Hellewell (3)	2286	Kershaw
9.1.94	SD	A	Rochdale H.	L	8-42	Davis	Hellewell (2)	—	—
16.1.94	CC(3)	H	Woolston R.	W	42-6	Pickles (2), Blacker, Hellewell, King, Pearce, Pucill, Thomas	Pearce (5)	1376	Burke
23.1.94	SD	H	Hunslet	W	40-24	Laurence (2), Davis, King, Pearce, Pickles, Thomas	Pearce (6)	1659	Cross
30.1.94	CC(4)	H	St. Helens	L	16-23	Flanagan, Hellewell, Pucill	Pearce (2)	5155	R. Smith
2.2.94	SD	A	Keighley C.	L	10-35	Flanagan, King	Pearce	—	—
6.2.94	SD	A	London C.	W	24-10	Chapman, Hellewell, King, Laurence	Pearce (4)	—	—
20.2.94	SD	H	Barrow	W	20-17	Chapman, Laurence, King	Pearce (4)	1669	Presley
2.3.94	SD	A	Batley	L	16-28	Pearce (2)	Pearce (4)	—	—
6.3.94	SD	H	Swinton	W	18-8	King, Pearce	Pearce (5)	1737	Tennant
13.3.94	SD	A	Highfield	W	36-12	Laurence (3), Davis, Pearce, Richards	Pearce (6)	—	—
20.3.94	SD	A	Whitehaven	L	4-9	—	Pearce (2)	—	—
27.3.94	SD	A	Carlisle	W	21-14	Coulter, Laurence, Thomas	Pearce (4), Flanagan (dg)	—	—
31.3.94	SD	H	Keighley C.	W	32-10	Coulter (2), Flanagan, Lucchese, Thomas	Pearce (6)	3539	Asquith
4.4.94	SD	A	Doncaster	L	7-19	Chapman	Pearce (1,1dg)	—	—
10.4.94	SD	H	Ryedale-York	L	12-23	King, Laurence	Pearce (2)	1415	Steele
17.4.94	SD	A	Bramley	W	30-20	Laurence (4), Coulter, Pucill	Slater (3)	—	—
21.4.94	SD	H	Dewsbury	L	12-28	Davis, Pickles	Pearce (2)	1650	Asquith
8.5.94	SDP(1)	A	Batley	L	17-28	Coulter, Reynolds, Thomas	Pearce (2), Davis (dg)	—	—

HULL

Ground: The Boulevard (0482-29040)
First Season: 1895-96
Nickname: Airlie Birds
Chairman: David Latham
Secretary: Brian Johnson
Honours: **Championship** Winners, 1919-20,
               1920-21, 1935-36, 1955-56, 1957-58
               Beaten finalists, 1956-57
               Division One Champions, 1982-83
               Division Two Champions, 1976-77,
               1978-79
               Challenge Cup Winners, 1913-14,
               1981-82
               Beaten finalists, 1907-08, 1908-09,
               1909-10, 1921-22, 1922-23, 1958-59,
               1959-60, 1979-80, 1982-83, 1984-85
               Regal Trophy Winners, 1981-82
               Beaten finalists, 1975-76, 1984-85
               Premiership Winners, 1990-91
               Beaten finalists, 1980-81, 1981-82,
               1982-83, 1988-89
               Yorkshire Cup Winners, 1923-24,
               1969-70, 1982-83, 1983-84, 1984-85
               Beaten finalists, 1912-13, 1914-15,
               1920-21, 1927-28, 1938-39, 1946-47,
               1953-54, 1954-55, 1955-56, 1959-60,
               1967-68, 1986-87
               Yorkshire League Winners,
               1918-19, 1922-23, 1926-27, 1935-36
               Charity Shield Beaten finalists,
               1991-92
               BBC-2 Floodlit Trophy Winners,
               1979-80

RECORDS
Match
Goals: 14 by Jim Kennedy v. Rochdale H.,
            7 Apr 1921
        Geoff "Sammy" Lloyd v. Oldham,
            10 Sep 1978
Tries: 7 by Clive Sullivan at Doncaster,
            15 Apr 1968
Points: 36 by Jim Kennedy v. Keighley,
            29 Jan 1921

Season
Goals: 170 by Geoff "Sammy" Lloyd, 1978-79
Tries: 52 by Jack Harrison, 1914-15
Points: 369 by Geoff "Sammy" Lloyd, 1978-79

Career
Goals: 687 by Joe Oliver, 1928-37 & 1943-45
Tries: 250 by Clive Sullivan, 1961-74 &
            1981-85
Points: 1,842 by Joe Oliver, 1928-37 & 1943-45
Appearances: 501 by Edward Rogers, 1906-25
Highest score: 86-0 v. Elland, 1 Apr 1899
Highest against: 64-2 at St. Helens, 17 Feb 1988
Attendance: 28,798 v. Leeds (RL Cup),
            7 Mar 1936

COACHING REGISTER
● **Since 1974-75**

David Doyle-Davidson	May 74 - Dec 77
Arthur Bunting	Jan 78 - Dec 85
Kenny Foulkes	Dec 85 - May 86
Len Casey	June 86 - Mar 88
Tony Dean ⎫	Mar 88 - Apr 88
Keith Hepworth ⎭	
*Brian Smith	July 88 - Jan 91
*Noel Cleal	Sep 90 - Apr 92
Royce Simmons	May 92 - Apr 94
Tony Gordon	May 94 -

Joint coaches Sep 90 - Jan 91.

Len Casey, Hull coach from June 1986 to March 1988.

GREAT BRITAIN REGISTER
(35 players)

Billy Batten	(1)	1921
Harold Bowman	(8)	1924-29
Frank Boylen	(1)	1908
Robin Coverdale	(4)	1954
Mick Crane	(1)	1982
Lee Crooks	(11+2)	1982-87
Andy Dannatt	(3)	1985-91
Gary Divorty	(2)	1985
Jim Drake	(1)	1960
Bill Drake	(1)	1962
Paul Eastwood	(13)	1990-92
Steve Evans	(2)	1982
Vince Farrar	(1)	1978
Dick Gemmell	(2)	1968-69
Emlyn Gwynne	(3)	1928-29
Tommy Harris	(25)	1954-60
Karl Harrison	(3)	1990
Mick Harrison	(7)	1967-73
Billy Holder	(1)	1907
Lee Jackson	(11)	1990-92
Mark Jones	(+1)	1992
Arthur Keegan	(9)	1966-69
Steve McNamara	(+2)	1992-93
Edgar Morgan	(2)	1921
Steve Norton	(9)	1978-82
Wayne Proctor	(+1)	1984
Paul Rose	(1)	1982
Garry Schofield	(15)	1984-87
Trevor Skerrett	(6)	1980-82
Billy Stone	(8)	1920-21
Clive Sullivan	(17)	1967-73
Harry Taylor	(3)	1907
Bob Taylor	(2)	1921-26
David Topliss	(1)	1982
Johnny Whiteley	(15)	1957-62

1993-94 SIGNINGS REGISTER

Signed	Player	Club From
16.6.93	Aston, Jon	Hull K.R.
5.7.93	Doyle, Jeff	North Sydney, Aus.
19.8.93	Windley, Johan	Isberg C. ARL
19.8.93	Sterling, Paul	Bradford & Bingley RU
9.9.93	Hasler, Des	Manly, Aus.
2.11.93	Foster, Shane	Hull Academy
2.11.93	Thompson, James	Northern Dairies ARL
7.11.93	Mitchell, Philip	Northern Dairies ARL
9.11.93	Roberts, Paul	Minehead ARL
18.11.93	Smith, Kevin	Isberg C. ARL
25.11.93	Bernard, Marcus	Pontypool RU
29.11.93	Street, Tim	Leigh
4.3.94	*Pearson, Richard	Huddersfield
15.3.94	Salter, Andrew	Northern Dairies ARL
1.4.94	Sagar, Paul	ARL
1.4.94	Harris, Wayne	Mysons ARL

Australian centre James Grant, scorer of 18 tries in 33 games in 1993-94.

HULL 1993-94 PLAYERS' SUMMARY

	(Date of Birth)	App	T	G	D	Pts	Previous club	Signed
Boulter, Lee	(13.12.73)	0+1	—	—	—	—	Northern Dairies ARL	5.11.91
Busby, Dean	(1.12.73)	9+3	—	—	—	—	Bransholme ARL	1.2.90
Cassidy, Jez	(30.3.74)	2+7	—	—	—	—	—	31.10.92
Danby, Rob	(30.8.74)	19+4	—	—	—	—	Hull Boys ARL	30.8.91
Dearlove, Andrew	(19.9.72)	1	—	—	—	—	British Gas ARL	14.8.90
Divet, Daniel	(11.12.66)	28+5	3	—	—	12	France	6.9.93
Dixon, Mike	(6.4.71)	32	2	—	—	8	East Park ARL	29.8.89
Doyle, Jeff	(1.10.67)	30	9	—	—	36	Australia	5.7.93
Eastwood, Paul	(3.12.65)	29	8	68	—	168	Hullensians RU	21.1.85
Gay, Richard	(9.3.69)	32	17	—	—	68	Hull Boys ARL	13.9.89
Grant, James	(22.5.64)	33	18	—	—	72	Australia	27.7.92
Gray, Kevin	(10.12.75)	1	—	—	—	—	Minehead ARL	1.7.92
Greenwood, Brandon	(28.4.72)	5+5	4	—	—	16	Ovenden ARL	16.3.93
Hasler, Des	(16.2.61)	28	10	—	—	40	Australia	9.9.93
Hewitt, Mark	(17.3.74)	12	2	22	1	53	Hull Academy	9.3.93
Jackson, Anthony	(20.11.69)	15+12	2	—	—	8	Greatfield ARL	8.7.88
Jones, Mark	(22.6.65)	13+6	2	—	—	8	Neath RU	12.10.90
McNamara, Steve	(18.9.71)	21+4	2	2	4	16	Skirlaugh ARL	15.6.89
Nolan, Gary	(31.5.66)	21+1	11	—	—	44	Hull Dockers ARL	2.4.91
Nolan, Rob	(2.10.68)	19+6	6	3	—	30	Hull Colts	1.1.88
Sharp, Jon	(8.3.67)	32+1	1	—	—	4	Travellers Sts ARL	12.3.84
Sterling, Paul	(2.8.64)	27	7	—	—	28	Bradford & Bingley RU	19.8.93
Street, Tim	(29.6.68)	23	2	—	—	8	Leigh	29.11.93
Walker, Russ	(1.9.62)	16+11	1	—	—	4	Barrow	8.1.90
Wilson, Rob	(31.8.72)	7+3	1	—	—	4	West Hull ARL	13.8.91
TOTALS								
25 players			108	95	5	627		

Representative appearances 1993-94

Cassidy — GB Under-21s (+2); Danby — GB Under-21s (2, 1t); Jones — Wales (2); Divet — France (2).

A 168-point tally for Paul Eastwood.   *Australian Jeff Doyle, scorer of nine tries.*

HULL 1993-94 MATCH ANALYSIS

Date	Com-petition	H/A	Opponent	Rlt	Score	Tries	Goals	Atten-dance	Referee
29.8.93	SBC	A	Wigan	L	8-16	Gay	Eastwood (2)	—	—
5.9.93	SBC	H	Halifax	D	18-18	Gay, R. Nolan	Eastwood (5)	5339	Wood
12.9.93	SBC	A	Castleford	L	4-12	Gay	—	—	—
19.9.93	SBC	H	Salford	W	28-12	Eastwood, Gay, Jones, Sterling	Eastwood (6)	3982	Steele
26.9.93	SBC	H	Warrington	L	6-19	Sterling	Eastwood	4292	Morris
3.10.93	SBC	A	Leeds	D	22-22	Grant (2), A. Jackson, R. Nolan	R. Nolan (3)	—	—
10.10.93	SBC	H	Widnes	W	20-14	Divet, Eastwood, Grant, Hasler	Eastwood (2)	4369	Steele
24.10.93	SBC	H	Oldham	L	8-33	Eastwood	Eastwood (2)	4553	R. Smith
31.10.93	SBC	A	Sheffield E.	L	15-18	Gay, McNamara	Eastwood (3), McNamara (dg)	—	—
7.11.93	SBC	H	Wakefield T.	W	16-8	Gay, Grant, Sterling	Eastwood (2)	3828	Galtress
14.11.93	RT(2)	A	Swinton	W	36-14	Doyle, Gay, Hasler, Jones, Sterling, Street, Walker	Eastwood (4)	—	—
21.11.93	SBC	A	Featherstone R.	L	10-21	Grant	Eastwood (3)	—	—
28.11.93	SBC	A	Leigh	W	22-7	Doyle, Gay, Sterling	Eastwood (5)	—	—
3.12.93	SBC	H	St. Helens	W	18-14	Grant (2), Hasler (2)	Eastwood	2733	J. Connolly
12.12.93	RT(3)	H	Widnes	W	10-6	G. Nolan, R. Nolan	Eastwood	3412	Ollerton
19.12.93	RT(4)	A	Salford	L	6-26	Hasler	Eastwood	—	—
26.12.93	SBC	A	Hull K.R.	L	6-14	Eastwood	Eastwood	—	—
5.1.94	SBC	H	Bradford N.	W	20-4	G. Nolan (2), Gay, A. Jackson	Eastwood (2)	3580	Whitfield
9.1.94	SBC	A	Halifax	L	10-24	Hasler, G. Nolan	Eastwood	—	—
16.1.94	SBC	H	Castleford	L	22-24	Doyle, Eastwood, Gay, Grant	Eastwood (3)	4620	Campbell
23.1.94	SBC	A	Salford	W	22-11	Gay, Grant, Greenwood, G. Nolan	Eastwood (3)	—	—
30.1.94	CC(4)	A	Swinton	W	18-12	Greenwood (2), Eastwood	Eastwood (3)	—	—
6.2.94	SBC	A	Warrington	L	8-22	Hasler	Eastwood (2)	—	—
13.2.94	CC(5)	H	Wigan	L	21-22	Divet, Hasler, Sharp	Eastwood (4), McNamara (dg)	10,517	Campbell
20.2.94	SBC	H	Leeds	W	21-14	R. Nolan (2), Grant, G. Nolan	Eastwood (2), Hewitt (dg)	5424	J. Connolly
6.3.94	SBC	A	Widnes	L	6-28	R. Nolan	Eastwood	—	—
13.3.94	SBC	A	Oldham	L	12-19	Dixon, Street	Hewitt (2)	—	—
23.3.94	SBC	H	Wigan	W	18-4	Dixon, Doyle, Gay	Hewitt (3)	4374	Campbell
27.3.94	SBC	A	Wakefield T.	L	8-10	G. Nolan	Hewitt (2)	—	—
1.4.94	SBC	H	Hull K.R.	W	14-6	Grant, McNamara, Sterling	Eastwood	7213	Whitfield
4.4.94	SBC	A	Bradford N.	W	32-30	Gay (2), Grant, G. Nolan, Sterling, Wilson	Eastwood (4)	—	—
10.4.94	SBC	A	St. Helens	L	10-52	Hasler (2)	Eastwood	—	—
13.4.94	SBC	H	Sheffield E.	W	25-22	Eastwood (2), Doyle, G. Nolan	Eastwood (2), McNamara (2,1dg)	2748	Holdsworth
17.4.94	SBC	H	Featherstone R.	W	37-16	Hewitt (2), Gay, Grant, Greenwood, G. Nolan	Hewitt (6), McNamara (dg)	3484	J. Smith
24.4.94	SBC	H	Leigh	W	70-16	Grant (5), Doyle (4), Gay (2), Divet, G. Nolan	Hewitt (9)	4000	Holdsworth

HULL KINGSTON ROVERS

Ground: Craven Park (0482-74648)
First Season: 1899-1900
Nickname: Robins
Chairman: Phil Lowe
Secretary: Ron Turner
Honours: **Championship** Winners, 1922-23, 1924-25
Beaten finalists, 1920-21, 1967-68
Division One Champions, 1978-79, 1983-84, 1984-85
Division Two Champions, 1989-90
Challenge Cup Winners, 1979-80
Beaten finalists, 1904-05, 1924-25, 1963-64, 1980-81, 1985-86
Regal Trophy Winners, 1984-85
Beaten finalists, 1981-82, 1985-86
Premiership Winners, 1980-81, 1983-84
Beaten finalists, 1984-85
Second Division Premiership
Beaten finalists, 1989-90
Yorkshire Cup Winners, 1920-21, 1929-30, 1966-67, 1967-68, 1971-72, 1974-75, 1985-86
Beaten finalists, 1906-07, 1911-12, 1933-34, 1962-63, 1975-76, 1980-81, 1984-85
Yorkshire League Winners, 1924-25, 1925-26
Eastern Division Championship Winners, 1962-63
Charity Shield Beaten finalists, 1985-86
BBC-2 Floodlit Trophy Winners, 1977-78
Beaten finalists, 1979-80

RECORDS

Match
Goals: 14 by Alf Carmichael v. Merthyr Tydfil, 8 Oct 1910
Mike Fletcher v. Whitehaven, 18 Mar 1990
Colin Armstrong v. Nottingham C. (at Doncaster), 19 Aug 1990
Tries: 11 by George West v. Brookland R., 4 Mar 1905
Points: 53 by George West v. Brookland R., 4 Mar 1905

Season
Goals: 199 by Mike Fletcher, 1989-90
Tries: 45 by Gary Prohm, 1984-85
Points: 450 by Mike Fletcher, 1989-90

Career
Goals: 1,192 by Cyril Kellett, 1956-67
Tries: 207 by Roger Millward, 1966-80
Points: 2,489 by Cyril Kellett, 1956-67
Appearances: 481+8 by Mike Smith, 1974-91
Highest score: 100-6 v. Nottingham C. (at Doncaster), 19 Aug 1990
Highest against: 76-8 at Halifax, 20 Oct 1991
Attendance: 27,670 v. Hull (League), 3 Apr 1953 — at Boothferry Park, Hull C. AFC
8,557 v. Hull (League), 1 Jan 1991 — at new Craven Park

COACHING REGISTER
● **Since 1974-75**

Arthur Bunting	Feb 72 - Nov 75
Harry Poole	Dec 75 - Mar 77
Roger Millward	Mar 77 - May 91
George Fairbairn	May 91 - May 94
Steve Crooks	May 94 -

Full back Mike Fletcher, top goals and points scorer in a season.

69

GREAT BRITAIN REGISTER
(26 players)

David Bishop	(+1)	1990
Chris Burton	(8+1)	1982-87
Alan Burwell	(7+1)	1967-69
Len Casey	(7+2)	1977-83
Garry Clark	(3)	1984-85
Alec Dockar	(1)	1947
George Fairbairn	(3)	1981-82
Jack Feetham	(1)	1929
Peter Flanagan	(14)	1962-70
Frank Foster	(1)	1967
David Hall	(2)	1984
Paul Harkin	(+1)	1985
Steve Hartley	(3)	1980-81
Phil Hogan	(2+2)	1979
Roy Holdstock	(2)	1980
Bill Holliday	(8+1)	1964-67
David Laws	(1)	1986
Brian Lockwood	(1+1)	1978-79
Phil Lowe	(12)	1970-78
Roger Millward	(27+1)	1967-78
Harry Poole	(1)	1964
Paul Rose	(1+3)	1974-78
Mike Smith	(10+1)	1979-84
Brian Tyson	(3)	1963-67
David Watkinson	(12+1)	1979-86
Chris Young	(5)	1967-68

1993-94 SIGNINGS REGISTER

Signed	Player	Club From
8.6.93	Charlesworth, Adam	Hull University ARL
19.6.93	Feeney, Carl	Isberg C. ARL
1.7.93	Whitaker, Sam	Hull Boys ARL
9.7.93	Carroll, Peter	Embassy ARL
23.7.93	Scott, Paul	Hull Academy
9.8.93	Everitt, Christian	Hull K.R. Academy
11.8.93	*Holderness, Kevin	London C.
11.8.93	Halafihi, Nick	London C.
16.8.93	Bateman, Karl	Hull Boys ARL
28.8.93	Batty, Chris	Minehead ARL
6.9.93	Bristow, Carl	Hull Boys ARL
17.9.93	Hosking, David	Manly, Aus.
20.9.93	*Rhoades, Simon	Sheffield E.
13.10.93	Coult, Mick	Scunthorpe RU
20.10.93	Swales, Edward	Hull Boys ARL
26.11.93	Oliver, Richard	Hull RU
2.2.94	Charles, Chris	Hull Boys ARL
28.2.94	*Glancy, John	Wakefield T.

Hooker Peter Flanagan, capped 14 times for Great Britain.

Half back Wayne Parker, Hull K.R. skipper in 1993-94.

HULL KINGSTON ROVERS 1993-94 PLAYERS' SUMMARY

	(Date of Birth)	App	T	G	D	Pts	Previous club	Signed
Barkworth, Julian	(10.4.69)	30	9	4	—	44	Ionians RU	11.9.91
Bibby, Mike	(23.10.70)	20+2	4	—	—	16	East Park ARL	21.6.89
Brown, Gary	(5.9.74)	4	1	—	—	4	Embassy ARL	16.9.92
Chamberlain, Richard	(1.4.73)	32	6	—	—	24	Greatfield ARL	1.6.91
Charles, Chris	(7.3.76)	0+3	—	—	1	1	Hull Boys ARL	2.2.94
Charlesworth, Adam	(8.6.73)	12+2	1	—	—	4	Hull University ARL	8.6.93
Chatfield, Gary	(26.7.67)	10+4	4	—	2	18	Eureka ARL	24.8.90
Clark, Dean	(6.1.68)	17+5	3	—	—	12	New Zealand	10.12.92
Coult, Mick	(14.10.69)	4+1	1	—	—	4	Scunthorpe RU	13.10.93
Crane, Mike	(11.2.71)	8+9	2	—	1	9	Greatfield ARL	14.7.90
Fletcher, Mike	(14.4.67)	32	3	90	—	192	Hull K.R. Colts	28.9.85
Fletcher, Paul	(17.3.70)	26+2	5	—	—	20	Eureka ARL	1.9.87
Glancy, John	(14.4.62)	7+1	—	—	—	—	Wakefield T.	28.2.94
Hadi, Steve	(26.2.68)	4	—	—	—	—	Scarborough P.	15.8.93
Halafihi, Nick	(23.12.67)	8+9	2	—	—	8	London C.	11.8.93
Hardy, Craig	(24.8.73)	1+3	—	—	—	—	Hull K.R. Academy	11.12.92
Harrison, Chris	(28.9.67)	28+1	4	—	—	16	Eureka ARL	23.9.91
Harrison, Des	(10.10.64)	3	—	—	—	—	Hull K.R. Colts	16.4.85
Hoe, Sean	(3.12.70)	10+2	1	—	—	4	ARL	14.7.90
Hosking, David	(15.9.69)	15+1	1	—	—	4	Australia	17.9.93
Hutchinson, Rob	(20.9.68)	21+1	6	—	—	24	Halifax	29.10.92
Jackson, Wayne	(19.9.67)	26+1	1	—	—	4	West Hull ARL	28.9.90
Leighton, Jamie	(5.9.73)	9+7	2	—	—	8	Crown Malet ARL	22.7.91
Liddiard, David	(24.2.61)	11	3	—	—	12	Australia	3.12.92
Lyman, Paul	(24.5.65)	1+1	—	—	—	—	Featherstone R.	8.1.89
O'Brien, Craig	(4.4.69)	16+6	5	—	—	20	West Hull ARL	28.9.88
Oliver, Richard	(15.1.72)	7	1	—	—	4	Hull RU	26.11.93
Parker, Wayne	(2.4.67)	31	8	—	1	33	ARL	8.9.86
Richardson, Steve	(5.10.68)	4+1	—	—	—	—	Greatfield ARL	9.8.91
Sodje, Bright	(21.4.66)	20	9	—	—	36	Blackheath RU	20.8.90
Thompson, Andy	(29.6.68)	8	2	—	—	8	Hull K.R. Colts	24.8.87
Wardrobe, Neil	(12.9.72)	4+2	—	—	—	—	Beverley RU	30.9.92
TOTALS								
32 players			84	94	5	529		

Representative appearances 1993-94
Chamberlain — GB Under-21s (1).

HULL KINGSTON ROVERS 1993-94 MATCH ANALYSIS

Date	Com-petition	H/A	Opponent	Rlt	Score	Tries	Goals	Atten-dance	Referee
29.8.93	SBC	H	St. Helens	W	16-10	Liddiard, Parker, Sodje	Barkworth (2)	4504	Morris
5.9.93	SBC	A	Featherstone R.	L	20-30	C. Harrison, Liddiard, Thompson	M. Fletcher (4)	—	—
12.9.93	SBC	H	Oldham	L	14-28	Hutchinson, Liddiard	M. Fletcher (3)	3832	Wood
19.9.93	SBC	A	Leeds	L	6-42	Sodje	Barkworth	—	—
26.9.93	SBC	A	Wakefield T.	W	34-24	Leighton, Sodje (2), Barkworth, C. Harrison, Chamberlain	M. Fletcher (5)	—	—
3.10.93	SBC	H	Bradford N.	W	16-12	Barkworth, C. Harrison, Thompson	M. Fletcher (2)	4356	J. Smith
10.10.93	SBC	A	Castleford	L	18-54	Barkworth, Clark, O'Brien	M. Fletcher (3)	—	—
24.10.93	SBC	A	Warrington	L	10-24	Bibby	M. Fletcher (3)	—	—
31.10.93	SBC	H	Halifax	L	18-28	Bibby, Clark, Parker	M. Fletcher (3)	4240	J. Connolly
7.11.93	SBC	A	Leigh	W	22-17	Bibby, C. Harrison, Hosking, Sodje	M. Fletcher (3)	—	—
15.11.93	RT(2)	H	Castleford	L	12-16	Chatfield, P. Fletcher	M. Fletcher (2)	2724	Campbell
21.11.93	SBC	H	Salford	L	6-10	Chatfield	M. Fletcher	2529	Steele
28.11.93	SBC	H	Widnes	L	10-32	Chatfield, Leighton	M. Fletcher	2566	Asquith
5.12.93	SBC	A	Wigan	L	16-54	P. Fletcher (2), Chamberlain	M. Fletcher (2)	—	—
17.12.93	SBC	A	St. Helens	L	22-23	Barkworth (2), M. Fletcher	M. Fletcher (5)	—	—
26.12.93	SBC	H	Hull	W	14-6	Clark, P. Fletcher	M. Fletcher (3)	6245	R. Connolly
2.1.94	SBC	A	Sheffield E.	L	17-30	Halafihi, Parker, Sodje	M. Fletcher (2), Chatfield (dg)	—	—
9.1.94	SBC	H	Featherstone R.	L	10-14	M. Fletcher, O'Brien	M. Fletcher	3005	Steele
16.1.94	SBC	A	Oldham	W	17-16	Chamberlain, Parker	M. Fletcher (3), Barkworth, Chatfield (dg)	—	—
23.1.94	SBC	H	Leeds	L	4-24	—	M. Fletcher (2)	4087	R. Smith
30.1.94	CC(4)	H	Ryedale-York	W	16-6	Bibby, Brown, Parker	M. Fletcher (2)	1886	Morris
6.2.94	SBC	H	Wakefield T.	L	20-28	Sodje (2), Chatfield	M. Fletcher (4)	3020	Campbell
13.2.94	CC(5)	A	Featherstone R.	L	8-30	Sodje	M. Fletcher (2)	3076	Whitfield
20.2.94	SBC	A	Bradford N.	L	8-54	P. Fletcher, Hutchinson	—	—	—
6.3.94	SBC	H	Castleford	L	24-44	O'Brien (2), Parker	M. Fletcher (6)	2736	Ollerton
13.3.94	SBC	H	Warrington	L	10-26	Barkworth, O'Brien	M. Fletcher	1868	R. Smith
20.3.94	SBC	A	Halifax	L	26-42	Barkworth, Chamberlain, M. Fletcher, Halafihi, Hutchinson	M. Fletcher (3)	—	—
25.3.94	SBC	H	Leigh	W	40-16	Hutchinson (2), Hoe, Jackson, Oliver	M. Fletcher (10)	1720	R. Smith
1.4.94	SBC	A	Hull	L	6-14	Crane	M. Fletcher	—	—
4.4.94	SBC	H	Sheffield E.	L	23-30	Chamberlain, Hutchinson, Parker	M. Fletcher (5), Charles (dg)	1848	R. Smith
10.4.94	SBC	H	Wigan	W	21-10	Barkworth (2), Chamberlain	M. Fletcher (4), Crane (dg)	3026	J. Smith
17.4.94	SBC	A	Salford	L	12-30	Charlesworth, Coult	M. Fletcher (2)	—	—
24.4.94	SBC	A	Widnes	W	13-10	Crane, Parker	M. Fletcher (2), Parker (dg)	—	—

Hooker Richard Chamberlain.

Prop Wayne Jackson.

HUNSLET

Ground: Elland Road (0532-711675);
McLaren Field, Bramley, from 1994-95
First Season: 1895-96. Disbanded at end of
1972-73. Re-formed as New
Hunslet in 1973-74. Retitled
Hunslet from start of 1979-80
Chairman: Graham Liles
Secretary: Derek Blackman
Honours: **Championship** Winners, 1907-08,
1937-38
Beaten finalists, 1958-59
Division Two Champions, 1962-63,
1986-87
Challenge Cup Winners, 1907-08,
1933-34
Beaten finalists, 1898-99, 1964-65
Second Division Premiership
Beaten finalists, 1986-87
Yorkshire Cup Winners, 1905-06,
1907-08, 1962-63
Beaten finalists, 1908-09, 1929-30,
1931-32, 1944-45, 1956-57, 1965-66
Yorkshire League Winners,
1897-98, 1907-08, 1931-32

RECORDS

Match
Goals: 12 by Billy Langton v. Keighley,
18 Aug 1959
Tries: 7 by George Dennis v. Bradford N.,
20 Jan 1934
Points: 28 by Tim Lumb v. Runcorn H.,
7 Oct 1990

Season
Goals: 181 by Billy Langton, 1958-59
Tries: 34 by Alan Snowden, 1956-57
Points: 380 by Billy Langton, 1958-59

Career
Goals: 1,044 by Billy Langton, 1955-66
Tries: 154 by Fred Williamson, 1943-55
Points: 2,202 by Billy Langton, 1955-66
Appearances: 569+10 by Geoff Gunney, 1951-73
572 by Jack Walkington, 1927-48

Highest score: 76-4 at Nottingham C.,
21 Feb 1993
Highest against: 76-8 v. Halifax, 27 Aug 1972
Attendance: 54,112 v. Leeds (Championship
final), 30 Apr 1938
Home match: 14,004 v. Castleford
(RL Cup), 13 Mar 1983

COACHING REGISTER
● **Since 1974-75**

Paul Daley	Apr 74 - Aug 78
Bill Ramsey	Aug 78 - Dec 79
Drew Broatch	Dec 79 - Apr 81
Paul Daley	Apr 81 - Nov 85
*Peter Jarvis	Nov 85 - Apr 88
*David Ward	July 86 - Apr 88
Nigel Stephenson	June 88 - Oct 88
Jack Austin	}Oct 88 - Jan 89
John Wolford	
David Ward	Jan 89 - May 89
Graeme Jennings	Sep 89 - Apr 90
Paul Daley	May 90 - Dec 93
Steve Ferres	Jan 94 -

Joint coaches from July 1986.

GREAT BRITAIN REGISTER
(23 players)

Billy Batten	(9)	1907-11
Harry Beverley	(4)	1936-37
Alf Burnell	(3)	1951-54
Hector Crowther	(1)	1929
Jack Evans	(4)	1951-52
Ken Eyre	(1)	1965
Brian Gabbitas	(1)	1959
Geoff Gunney	(11)	1954-65
Dennis Hartley	(2)	1964
John Higson	(2)	1908
Dai Jenkins	(1)	1929
Albert Jenkinson	(2)	1911
Bill Jukes	(6)	1908-10
Bernard Prior	(1)	1966
Bill Ramsey	(7)	1965-66
Brian Shaw	(5)	1956-60
Geoff Shelton	(7)	1964-66
Fred Smith	(9)	1910-14
Sam Smith	(4)	1954
Cecil Thompson	(2)	1951
Les White	(7)	1932-33
Dicky Williams	(3)	1954
Harry Wilson	(3)	1907

1993-94 SIGNINGS REGISTER

Signed	Player	Club From	Signed	Player	Club From
30.6.93	McElhatton, Craig	Wakefield T.	29.10.93	*Vasey, Chris	Dewsbury
7.8.93	*Cooper, David	Halifax	26.1.94	Longstaff, Jason	Oulton ARL
17.8.93	Boothroyd, Giles	Castleford	2.2.94	*Rhoades, Simon	Sheffield E.
26.8.93	*Lay, Steve	Halifax	14.2.94	*Dixon, Keith	Keighley C.
6.9.93	Jowitt, Warren	Stanley R. ARL	18.2.94	*Pell, Richard	Doncaster
7.9.93	Mwololo, Bramwell	Barclays Bank RU	18.2.94	*Rowse, Martin	Dewsbury
8.9.93	Hughes, Paul	Dewsbury	15.3.94	*Armstrong, Mick	Doncaster
15.9.93	Beath, Paul	Aus.	23.3.94	*Johnson, Marc	Bradford N.
23.9.93	*Milner, Richard	Halifax	25.3.94	*Limb, Scott	Featherstone R.
21.10.93	Clark, Brett	Rochdale H.	5.4.94	*Close, David	Ryedale-York
21.10.93	*Moore, Jonathan	Huddersfield	5.4.94	*Kellett, Neil	Batley

Hunslet's Kenyan winger Eric Kibe, scorer of 15 tries in 1993-94, in action against Batley.

HUNSLET 1993-94 PLAYERS' SUMMARY

	(Date of Birth)	App	T	G	D	Pts	Previous club	Signed
Armstrong, Mick	(21.1.72)	3	—	—	—	—	Doncaster	15.3.94
Bartliff, Andrew	(10.7.64)	17+1	4	15	—	46	Queenswood ARL	9.10.91
Beath, Paul	(17.1.68)	25+1	9	—	—	36	Australia	2.9.92
Bennett, Mike		2	—	—	—	—	Australia	—
Boothroyd, Giles	(17.3.69)	33	8	—	—	32	Castleford	17.8.93
Brook, David	(4.2.71)	18+5	6	—	—	24	Middleton ARL	4.6.90
Burrow, Paul	(8.5.64)	26+2	12	—	—	48	—	18.4.89
Clark, Brett	(1.11.61)	24+1	8	—	—	32	Rochdale H.	21.10.93
Close, David	(7.5.66)	3	1	—	—	4	Ryedale-York	5.4.94
Cooper, David	(29.3.64)	4	1	—	—	4	Halifax	7.8.93
Coyle, Michael	(5.3.71)	8+1	—	—	—	—	Middleton ARL	18.7.90
Croft, David	(2.8.69)	9	—	—	—	—	Bradford N.	16.10.92
Currie, Eugene	(25.2.65)	13+9	1	—	—	4	—	16.9.92
Daniel, Alan	(1.2.69)	8	1	—	—	4	Queens ARL	6.1.91
Dixon, Keith	(16.9.66)	3	1	5	1	15	Keighley C.	14.2.94
Ellis, Mark	(23.5.67)	12+1	3	—	—	12	Doncaster	21.2.93
Francis, Richard	(10.9.64)	20+1	5	—	—	20	Bradford N.	18.8.92
Harkin, Paul	(8.3.58)	17	2	—	—	8	Halifax	30.9.92
Hughes, Paul	(25.6.63)	32	2	—	—	8	Dewsbury	8.9.93
Jowitt, Warren	(9.9.74)	1	—	—	—	—	Stanley R. ARL	6.9.93
Kellett, Neil	(20.12.61)	0+2	1	—	—	4	Batley	5.4.94
Kibe, Eric	(23.3.71)	27	15	—	—	60	Dewsbury	23.4.93
Langton, Steve	(24.3.64)	1	—	—	—	—	Batley	3.10.89
Lee, Neil	(23.8.75)	2	—	—	—	—	Middleton ARL	17.8.93
Liles, Richard	(5.12.69)	0+6	1	—	—	4	Oulton ARL	26.3.90
Limb, Scott	(15.6.73)	4+1	1	4	—	12	Featherstone R.	25.3.94
Longstaff, Jason	(8.2.71)	2+5	—	—	—	—	Oulton ARL	26.1.94
McElhatton, Craig	(24.2.70)	1+3	—	—	—	—	Wakefield T.	18.12.92
McKelvie, Danny	(19.8.67)	4+2	1	—	—	4	Australia	2.9.92
Marks, Warren	(3.2.66)	11	3	—	—	12	Bradford N.	11.2.94
Marsh, David		1	—	—	—	—	Australia	—
Milner, Richard	(2.5.65)	1	—	—	—	—	Halifax	23.9.93
Mwololo, Bramwell	(17.7.65)	5	2	—	—	8	Kenya RU	7.9.93
Pell, Richard	(17.10.66)	4	—	1	—	2	Doncaster	18.2.94
Petch, Andrew	(3.9.66)	3	2	—	—	8	Middleton ARL	26.3.90
Precious, Andrew	(10.10.70)	27+3	1	32	—	68	York All Blacks ARL	27.9.90
Rhoades, Simon	(5.10.72)	2	—	—	—	—	Sheffield E.	2.2.94
Rose, Ian	(24.10.66)	2	—	—	—	—	Ossett T. ARL	14.7.92
Rowse, Martin	(8.3.69)	2	—	—	—	—	Doncaster	18.2.94
Sampson, Lee	(11.4.66)	1+2	—	—	—	—	Nottingham C.	16.12.92
Sampson, Roy	(28.11.61)	30	11	—	—	44	Dewsbury	17.2.87
Seabourne, Peter	(19.7.70)	0+1	—	—	—	—	Bradford N.	26.8.92
Snee, Gavin	(6.1.71)	9+6	—	—	—	—	Bradford N.	14.10.92
Sowerby, Gary	(5.5.69)	2+2	—	—	—	—	—	16.9.92
Vasey, Chris	(28.2.63)	8	—	17	—	34	Dewsbury	29.10.93
Walsh, David	(..)	1	—	—	—	—	—	—
White, Paul	(5.11.64)	2	—	—	—	—	Ryedale-York	5.3.91
Wilson, Sean	(13.3.72)	2+5	3	—	—	12	Hunslet Parkside ARL	28.3.91
Wright, Jason	(14.3.73)	0+2	—	—	—	—	—	6.12.90
TOTALS								
49 players			105	74	1	569		

HUNSLET 1993-94 MATCH ANALYSIS

Date	Com- petition	H/A	Opponent	Rlt	Score	Tries	Goals	Atten- dance	Referee
1.9.93	SD	H	Doncaster	L	28-32	R. Sampson (2), Brook, Francis, Petch	Precious (4)	948	Whitelam
5.9.93	SD	A	Carlisle	L	20-24	Boothroyd, Cooper, Petch	Precious (4)	—	—
12.9.93	SD	H	Huddersfield	L	4-34	Boothroyd	—	1456	Presley
19.9.93	SD	A	Whitehaven	L	10-26	Beath, Mwololo	Precious	—	—
26.9.93	SD	H	Keighley C.	L	12-36	Francis, Harkin	Precious (2)	1898	Cummings
3.10.93	SD	A	Ryedale-York	L	12-36	Bartliff, McKelvie	Precious (2)	—	—
10.10.93	SD	H	Barrow	L	12-15	Beath, Burrow	Precious (2)	499	McGregor
24.10.93	SD	A	London C.	L	12-48	Boothroyd, Francis	Precious (2)	—	—
31.10.93	RT(1)	H	Chorley B.	W	30-19	Burrow (2), Bartliff, Clark, Kibe, R. Sampson	Vasey (3)	299	Gilmour
7.11.93	SD	A	Rochdale H.	W	20-15	Burrow (4)	Vasey (2)	—	—
14.11.93	RT(2)	A	Warrington	L	16-58	Clark, Precious, R. Sampson	Vasey (2)	—	—
21.11.93	SD	H	Workington T.	L	6-10	Kibe	Vasey	667	McGregor
28.11.93	SD	H	Swinton	L	12-22	Kibe, R. Sampson	Vasey (2)	572	Cross
5.12.93	SD	A	Highfield	W	30-16	Beath, Clark, Harkin, Kibe, R. Sampson	Vasey (5)	—	—
19.12.93	SD	A	Doncaster	L	12-22	Boothroyd, Hughes	Vasey (2)	—	—
26.12.93	SD	H	Bramley	L	4-18	Kibe	—	—	McGregor
9.1.94	SD	H	Carlisle	L	16-18	Francis, Liles, R. Sampson	Bartliff (2)	351	Morris
16.1.94	CC(3)	H	Barrow I.	W	58-2	Kibe (4), R. Sampson (2), Bartliff, Boothroyd, Burrow, Clark, Ellis, Francis	Precious (4), Bartliff	498	Atkin
18.1.94	SD	H	Batley	D	14-14	Boothroyd, Clark, Kibe	Precious	735	Burke
23.1.94	SD	A	Huddersfield	L	24-40	Burrow (2), Ellis (2)	Precious (4)	—	—
30.1.94	CC(4)	H	Oldham	L	20-30	Beath, Burrow, Daniel, Mwololo	Bartliff (2)	1257	Wood
2.2.94	SD	A	Dewsbury	L	8-48	Bartliff	Bartliff (2)	—	—
6.2.94	SD	H	Whitehaven	L	12-38	Beath, Boothroyd, Clark	—	459	Galtress
20.2.94	SD	A	Keighley C.	L	10-30	Beath (2)	Bartliff	—	—
27.2.94	SD	H	Ryedale-York	L	13-23	Dixon, Kibe	Dixon (2,1dg)	520	Redfearn
6.3.94	SD	A	Barrow	L	10-16	Hughes, Kibe	Dixon	—	—
13.3.94	SD	H	London C.	L	22-46	Clark, Kibe, Marks, R. Sampson	Dixon (2), Pell	399	Carter
20.3.94	SD	H	Rochdale H.	L	10-33	Burrow, Marks	Precious	722	Presley
27.3.94	SD	A	Workington T.	L	4-24	Brook	—	—	—
1.4.94	SD	A	Bramley	L	16-18	Brook, Kibe	Precious (4)	—	—
4.4.94	SD	H	Dewsbury	L	6-36	Wilson	Precious	686	Steele
10.4.94	SD	A	Batley	L	8-28	Kibe	Bartliff (2)	—	—
19.4.94	SD	H	Highfield	W	44-8	Beath (2), Boothroyd, Clark, Close, Currie, Kellett, Limb, Marks	Limb (4)	426	Morris
24.4.94	SD	A	Swinton	L	34-40	Brook (3), Wilson (2), R. Sampson	Bartliff (5)	—	—

Veteran scrum half Paul Harkin.

1993-94 beneficiary Roy Sampson.

KEIGHLEY COUGARS

Ground: Cougar Park (0535-602602), previously titled Lawkholme Park until the 1992-93 season.
First Season: 1901-02. Added Cougars to title at start of 1991-92.
Nickname: Cougars
Chairman: Mike O'Neill
Secretary: Jack Wainwright
Honours: **Division Two** Champions, 1902-03
Division Three Champions, 1992-93
Challenge Cup Beaten finalists, 1936-37
Yorkshire Cup Beaten finalists, 1943-44, 1951-52

RECORDS

Match
Goals: 15 by John Wasyliw v. Nottingham C., 1 Nov 1992
Tries: 5 by Ike Jagger v. Castleford, 13 Jan 1906
Sam Stacey v. Liverpool C., 9 Mar 1907
Points: 36 by John Wasyliw v. Nottingham C., 31 Oct 1993

Season
Goals: 187 by John Wasyliw, 1992-93
Tries: 31 by Nick Pinkney, 1993-94
Points: 490 by John Wasyliw, 1992-93

Career
Goals: 967 by Brian Jefferson, 1965-77
Tries: 155 by Sam Stacey, 1904-20
Points: 2,116 by Brian Jefferson, 1965-77
Appearances: 372 by Hartley Tempest, 1902-15
David McGoun, 1925-38
Highest score: 86-0 v. Nottingham C., 1 Nov 1992
86-0 v. Highfield, 31 Jan 1993
Highest against: 92-2 at Leigh, 30 Apr 1986
Attendance: 14,500 v. Halifax (RL Cup), 3 Mar 1951

COACHING REGISTER
● Since 1974-75

Alan Kellett	Jan 73 - May 75
Roy Sabine	Aug 75 - Oct 77
Barry Seabourne	Nov 77 - Mar 79
Albert Fearnley (Mgr)	Apr 79 - Aug 79
Alan Kellett	Apr 79 - Apr 80
Albert Fearnley	May 80 - Feb 81
Bakary Diabira	Feb 81 - Sep 82
Lee Greenwood	Sep 82 - Oct 83
Geoff Peggs	Nov 83 - Sep 85
Peter Roe	Sep 85 - July 86
Colin Dixon	July 86 - June 89
Les Coulter	July 89 - Apr 90
Tony Fisher	June 90 - Sep 91
Peter Roe	Sep 91 - Apr 94
Phil Larder	May 94 -

GREAT BRITAIN REGISTER
(1 player)

Terry Hollindrake	(1)	1955

1993-94 SIGNINGS REGISTER

Signed	Player	Club From
27.7.93	Delaney, Andrew	Dewsbury Moor ARL
1.9.93	*Tanner, Dave	Leigh
2.9.93	Wartley, Phil	Stanningley ARL
2.9.93	Adams, Marc	Newcastle Univ. ARL
2.9.93	Berry, Joe	ARL
2.9.93	Burks, Jake	Elland ARL
2.9.93	Caine, Parris	Milford ARL
2.9.93	Casey, Ashley	London C.
2.9.93	Hannah, Chris	Keighley Celtic ARL
9.9.93	Pounder, Jason	Dudley Hill ARL
10.9.93	Hill, Brendan	Halifax
4.11.93	Marr, Kevin	Woy Woy, Aus.
11.1.94	Galtress, Matthew	Keighley C. Academy
11.1.94	Hogg, Chris	Keighley C. Academy
11.1.94	Senior, Andrew	Keighley C. Academy
11.1.94	Ward, James	Keighley C. Academy
11.1.94	Wheeler, Stuart	Keighley C. Academy
3.2.94	Kelly, Lee	Keighley C. Academy
3.2.94	Lister, Jason	Keighley C. Academy
3.2.94	Hewitt, Richard	ARL
4.2.94	Creasser, David	Leeds
21.2.94	*Francis, Richard	Hunslet
24.2.94	Atkinson, Keith	Oldham
3.3.94	*Bateman, Andy	St. Helens
15.3.94	Gibson, Chris	Featherstone R. Academy
24.3.94	Shaw, Andrew	Bradford N.

KEIGHLEY COUGARS 1993-94 PLAYERS' SUMMARY

	(Date of Birth)	App	T	G	D	Pts	Previous club	Signed
Appleby, Darren	(14.6.67)	12+3	5	—	—	20	Featherstone R.	18.9.92
Austin, Greg	(14.6.63)	15	19	—	—	76	Halifax	8.5.93
Bateman, Andy	(26.6.65)	2+3	—	—	—	—	St. Helens	3.3.94
Berry, Joe	(7.5.74)	4+8	1	—	—	4	ARL	2.9.93
Brooke-Cowden, Mark	(12.6.63)	21	7	—	—	28	Halifax	12.12.91
Butterfield, Jeff	(13.8.64)	9+2	3	—	—	12	—	10.8.91
Creasser, David	(18.6.65)	8+2	3	2	—	16	Leeds	4.2.94
Dixon, Keith	(16.9.66)	14+6	3	8	—	28	Keighley Albion ARL	28.8.84
Eyres, Andy	(1.10.68)	31+4	16	—	2	66	Widnes	24.3.91
Farrell, Carlton	(23.6.66)	14+7	—	—	—	—	Deighton W. ARL	2.8.90
Francis, Richard	(10.9.64)	4	2	—	—	8	Hunslet	21.2.94
Gately, Ian	(21.3.66)	32	3	—	—	12	Australia	18.8.92
Gibson, Chris	(9.10.75)	0+1	1	—	—	4	Featherstone R. Ac'y	15.3.94
Grima, Joe	(18.9.60)	7+4	—	—	—	—	Widnes	22.6.92
Hall, Steve	(7.9.67)	25+10	8	—	—	32	Dudley Hill ARL	13.7.91
Hill, Brendan	(15.9.64)	26+1	17	—	—	68	Halifax	10.9.93
Marr, Kevin	(22.4.65)	22+2	4	—	—	16	Australia	4.11.93
Milner, Mark	(21.6.66)	16	8	1	—	34	Featherstone R.	8.1.93
Moses, Paul	(21.8.63)	10+3	3	—	—	12	Halifax	2.1.85
Pinkney, Nick	(6.12.70)	31	31	—	—	124	Ryedale-York	13.5.93
Pounder, Jason	(16.2.75)	1	—	—	—	—	Dudley Hill ARL	9.9.93
Race, Wayne	(17.4.66)	22	9	—	—	36	Doncaster	13.8.91
Ramshaw, Jason	(23.7.69)	26+1	9	—	4	40	Halifax	27.7.92
Reeves, Bob	(16.5.70)	0+1	—	—	—	—	Mayfield ARL	6.2.92
Rose, Kevin	(28.9.67)	2+1	—	—	—	—	Yew Tree ARL	3.1.89
Stephenson, Andy	(28.8.67)	19+2	5	—	—	20	Clayton ARL	19.3.91
Stephenson, Phil	(17.6.72)	15+8	3	—	—	12	Clayton ARL	19.3.91
Tanner, David	(29.9.65)	11+1	1	20	—	44	Leigh	1.9.93
Walker, John	(27.12.68)	19+1	9	35	—	106	Otley RU	29.10.91
Wasyliw, John	(23.10.67)	17	11	61	—	166	Halifax RU	5.3.91
Wood, Martin	(24.6.70)	33+1	19	—	1	77	Scarborough P.	17.1.92
TOTALS								
31 players			200	127	7	1,061		

KEIGHLEY COUGARS 1993-94 MATCH ANALYSIS

Date	Competition	H/A	Opponent	Rlt	Score	Tries	Goals	Attendance	Referee
29.8.93	SD	A	Barrow	W	30-22	Appleby, Brooke-Cowden, Pinkney, Ramshaw, Wasyliw	Wasyliw (5)	—	—
5.9.93	SD	H	London C.	L	14-17	Wasyliw (2), Appleby	Wasyliw	3240	Cummings
12.9.93	SD	A	Rochdale H.	W	16-14	Austin (2), Wood	Tanner (2)	—	—
19.9.93	SD	H	Dewsbury	W	30-9	Pinkney (2), Eyres, Hill, Wood	Wasyliw (5)	3246	Atkin
26.9.93	SD	A	Hunslet	W	36-12	Austin (3), Wood (2), Hill	Wasyliw (4), Tanner, Eyres (dg), Wood (dg)	—	—

Date	Com-petition	H/A	Opponent	Rlt	Score	Tries	Goals	Atten-dance	Referee
3.10.93	SD	A	Doncaster	W	30-20	Austin (2), Hill (2), Eyres	Wasyliw (5)	—	—
10.10.93	SD	H	Whitehaven	W	40-12	Austin (3), Hill (2), Pinkney (2), Wasyliw	Wasyliw (4)	3124	Burke
24.10.93	SD	H	Swinton	W	51-16	Austin (4), Pinkney (4), Hill, Wasyliw, Wood	Wasyliw (3), Eyres (dg)	3099	Gilmour
31.10.93	RT(1)	H	Nottingham C.	W	72-12	Wasyliw (4), Austin (3), Pinkney (2), Dixon, Eyres, Moses, Race	Wasyliw (10)	2283	Crashley
7.11.93	SD	A	Carlisle	L	24-26	Appleby, Eyres, Pinkney, Race	Wasyliw (4)	—	—
14.11.93	RT(2)	A	Halifax	L	10-19	Austin, Ramshaw	Wasyliw	—	—
21.11.93	SD	A	Batley	W	16-8	Hill, Pinkney, Walker	Walker (2)	—	—
28.11.93	SD	H	Highfield	W	44-6	Hill (3), Austin, Eyres, Race, P. Stephenson, Walker, Wasyliw	Walker (3), Wasyliw	2859	Whitelam
5.12.93	SD	H	Workington T.	L	4-16	Milner	—	3728	Presley
2.1.94	SD	A	Ryedale-York	L	4-11	—	Walker (2)	—	—
16.1.94	CC(3)	H	Oulton	W	68-0	Pinkney (4), Milner (3), Race (2), Brooke-Cowden, Eyres, Hall, Ramshaw, Wood	Walker (5), Milner	2210	Tennant
19.1.94	SD	H	Barrow	W	68-4	Ramshaw (3), Pinkney (2), Butterfield, Milner, Gately, Hill, Race, Moses, Walker, Wood	Walker (8)	2044	Morris
23.1.94	SD	H	Rochdale H.	W	40-12	Pinkney (2), Brooke-Cowden, Butterfield, Gately, Hill, Race, Wood	Walker (4)	3090	Nicholson
30.1.94	CC(4)	A	Batley	W	29-8	Gately, Hall, Marr, Race, Walker	Walker (3), Ramshaw (3dg)	—	—
2.2.94	SD	H	Huddersfield	W	35-10	Hall (3), Wood (2), Ramshaw	Walker (5), Ramshaw (dg)	5260	Atkin
6.2.94	SD	A	Dewsbury	L	6-12	Eyres	Walker	—	—
13.2.94	CC(5)	H	Castleford	L	14-52	Brooke-Cowden, Eyres, Hall	Walker	5860	Morris
16.2.94	SD	A	London C.	L	10-13	Brooke-Cowden, Wood	Walker	—	—
20.2.94	SD	H	Hunslet	W	30-10	Wood (2), Brooke-Cowden, Hill, Marr, Race	Wasyliw (3)	2563	Bates
2.3.94	SD	H	Doncaster	D	12-12	Ramshaw, Tanner	Tanner (2)	3000	Steele
6.3.94	SD	A	Whitehaven	L	10-16	Hall, Pinkney	Tanner	—	—
9.3.94	SD	A	Bramley	W	48-24	Eyres (2), A. Stephenson (2), Brooke-Cowden, Pinkney, Wood, Francis, Hill	Tanner (6)	—	—
13.3.94	SD	A	Swinton	W	20-16	Eyres, Pinkney, A. Stephenson, Wood	Tanner (2)	—	—
20.3.94	SD	H	Carlisle	W	50-12	Wood (2), Hill (2), Eyres, Francis, Hall, Marr, Pinkney, A. Stephenson	Tanner (5)	2719	Carter
27.3.94	SD	H	Batley	L	6-22	A. Stephenson	Tanner	3108	Asquith
31.3.94	SD	A	Huddersfield	L	10-32	Pinkney, Ramshaw	Wasyliw	—	—
4.4.94	SD	H	Ryedale-York	W	18-16	Appleby (2), Milner	Wasyliw (3)	2167	Redfearn
10.4.94	SD	H	Bramley	W	76-10	Creasser (3), Eyres (2), Wood (2), Marr, Milner, Moses, Pinkney, P. Stephenson, Walker, Wasyliw	Wasyliw (10)	2233	Carter
17.4.94	SD	A	Workington T.	L	2-54	—	Wasyliw	—	—
24.4.94	SD	A	Highfield	W	76-8	Walker (4), Pinkney (3), Dixon (2), Berry, Butterfield, Eyres, Gibson, Milner, P. Stephenson	Dixon (8)	—	—
8.5.94	SDP(1)	A	London C.	L	12-66	Eyres, Pinkney	Creasser (2)	—	—

79

LEEDS

Ground: Headingley (0532-786181)
First Season: 1895-96
Nickname: Loiners
Chairman: Dennis Greenwood
Chief Exec: Alf Davies
Honours: **Championship** Winners, 1960-61, 1968-69, 1971-72
Beaten finalists, 1914-15, 1928-29, 1929-30, 1930-31, 1937-38, 1969-70, 1972-73
League Leaders Trophy Winners, 1966-67, 1967-68, 1968-69, 1969-70, 1971-72
Challenge Cup Winners, 1909-10, 1922-23, 1931-32, 1935-36, 1940-41, 1941-42, 1956-57, 1967-68, 1976-77, 1977-78
Beaten finalists, 1942-43, 1946-47, 1970-71, 1971-72, 1993-94
Regal Trophy Winners, 1972-73, 1983-84
Beaten finalists, 1982-83, 1987-88, 1991-92
Premiership Winners, 1974-75, 1978-79
Yorkshire Cup Winners, 1921-22, 1928-29, 1930-31, 1932-33, 1934-35, 1935-36, 1937-38, 1958-59, 1968-69, 1970-71, 1972-73, 1973-74, 1975-76, 1976-77, 1979-80, 1980-81, 1988-89
Beaten finalists, 1919-20, 1947-48, 1961-62, 1964-65
Yorkshire League Winners, 1901-02, 1927-28, 1930-31, 1933-34, 1934-35, 1936-37, 1937-38, 1950-51, 1954-55, 1956-57, 1960-61, 1966-67, 1967-68, 1968-69, 1969-70
BBC-2 Floodlit Trophy Winners, 1970-71

RECORDS

Match
Goals: 13 by Lewis Jones v. Blackpool B., 19 Aug 1957
Tries: 8 by Fred Webster v. Coventry, 12 Apr 1913
Eric Harris v. Bradford N., 14 Sep 1931
Points: 31 by Lewis Jones v. Bradford N., 22 Aug 1956

Season
Goals: 166 by Lewis Jones, 1956-57
Tries: 63 by Eric Harris, 1935-36
Points: 431 by Lewis Jones, 1956-57

Career
Goals: 1,244 by Lewis Jones, 1952-64
Tries: 391 by Eric Harris, 1930-39
Points: 2,920 by Lewis Jones, 1952-64
Appearances: 608+18 by John Holmes, 1968-89
Highest score: 102-0 v. Coventry, 12 Apr 1913
Highest against: 74-6 at Wigan, 10 May 1992
Attendance: 40,175 v. Bradford N. (League), 21 May 1947

COACHING REGISTER
● **Since 1974-75**

Roy Francis	June 74 - May 75
Syd Hynes	June 75 - Apr 81
Robin Dewhurst	June 81 - Oct 83
Maurice Bamford	Nov 83 - Feb 85
Malcolm Clift	Feb 85 - May 85
Peter Fox	May 85 - Dec 86
Maurice Bamford	Dec 86 - Apr 88
Malcolm Reilly	Aug 88 - Sep 89
David Ward	Sep 89 - May 91
Doug Laughton	May 91 -

Syd Hynes, coach of Leeds from June 1975 to April 1981.

GREAT BRITAIN REGISTER
(74 players)

Les Adams	(1)	1932
John Atkinson	(26)	1968-80
Jim Bacon	(11)	1920-26
Ray Batten	(3)	1969-73
John Bentley	(1)	1992
Jim Birch	(1)	1907
Stan Brogden	(7)	1936-37
Jim Brough	(5)	1928-36
Gordon Brown	(6)	1954-55
Mick Clark	(5)	1968
Terry Clawson	(3)	1972
David Creasser	(2+2)	1985-88
Lee Crooks	(1)	1989
Willie Davies	(2)	1914
Kevin Dick	(2)	1980
Roy Dickinson	(2)	1985
Paul Dixon	(8+1)	1990-92
Les Dyl	(11)	1974-82
Richard Eyres	(+2)	1993
Tony Fisher	(3)	1970-71
Phil Ford	(5)	1989
Dick Gemmell	(1)	1964
Carl Gibson	(10)	1990-91
Bobby Goulding	(1)	1992
Jeff Grayshon	(2)	1985
Bob Haigh	(3+1)	1970-71
Derek Hallas	(2)	1961
Ellery Hanley	(2)	1992-93
Fred Harrison	(3)	1911
David Heron	(1+1)	1982
John Holmes	(14+6)	1971-82
Syd Hynes	(12+1)	1970-73
Billy Jarman	(2)	1914
David Jeanes	(3)	1972
Dai Jenkins	(1)	1947
Lewis Jones	(15)	1954-57
Ken Jubb	(2)	1937
John Lowe	(1)	1932
Paul Medley	(3+1)	1987-88
Steve Molloy	(1)	1993
Ike Owens	(4)	1946
Steve Pitchford	(4)	1977
Harry Poole	(2)	1966
Roy Powell	(13+6)	1985-91
Dai Prosser	(1)	1937
Keith Rayne	(4)	1984
Kevin Rayne	(1)	1986
Bev Risman	(5)	1968
Don Robinson	(5)	1956-60
David Rose	(4)	1954
Garry Schofield	(29)	1988-94
Barry Seabourne	(1)	1970
Brian Shaw	(1)	1961
Mick Shoebottom	(10+2)	1968-71
Barry Simms	(1)	1962
Alan Smith	(10)	1970-73
Stanley Smith	(10)	1929-33
David Stephenson	(4+1)	1988
Jeff Stevenson	(15)	1955-58
Squire Stockwell	(3)	1920-21
Alan Tait	(1+4)	1992-93
Abe Terry	(1)	1962
Arthur "Ginger" Thomas	(4)	1926-29
Phil Thomas	(1)	1907
Joe Thompson	(12)	1924-32
Andrew Turnbull	(1)	1951
Hugh Waddell	(1)	1989
Billy Ward	(1)	1910
David Ward	(12)	1977-82
Fred Webster	(3)	1910
Dicky Williams	(9)	1948-51
Harry Woods	(1)	1937
Geoff Wriglesworth	(5)	1965-66
Frank Young	(1)	1908

Garry Schofield, Leeds's most capped player with 29 Great Britain appearances while serving at Headingley.

81

1993-94 SIGNINGS REGISTER

Signed	Player	Club From
21.6.93	Parrish, Steve	Batley
14.7.93	Scott, Ian	Workington T.
27.7.93	Fozzard, Nick	Shaw Cross ARL
10.8.93	Gibbons, Anthony	East Leeds ARL
10.8.93	Gibbons, David	East Leeds ARL
10.8.93	Hassan, Phil	St. Pauls ARL
19.8.93	Marquez-Laynez, Lorenzo	Hull Boys ARL
24.8.93	Harmon, Neil	Warrington
1.9.93	Maher, Lee	ARL
2.9.93	Rose, Gary	Featherstone R.
7.9.93	Leatham, Jim	Leeds Academy
16.9.93	Eyres, Richard	Widnes
17.9.93	Handley, Patrick	ARL
20.9.93	Vassilakopoulos, Marcus	Hull ARL
22.9.93	Field, Jamie	ARL
30.9.93	Grigg, Carl	Canning, Aus.
12.10.93	Cummins, Francis	St. John Fisher ARL
1.11.93	Wright, Ricky	ARL
8.11.93	Law, Martin	Eastmoor ARL
8.11.93	Hirst, Andrew	East Leeds ARL
8.11.93	Osborne, Wayne	East Leeds ARL
9.11.93	Kennedy, Matthew	ARL
19.11.93	Battye, Neil	Doncaster
22.11.93	Hughes, Adam	Milford ARL
26.11.93	*Donohue, Jason	Leigh
1.12.93	Gleadhill, Paul	Leeds Academy
22.12.93	Golden, Marvin	Hunslet Parkside ARL
4.1.94	Howard, Harvey	Widnes
30.3.94	Riley, John	Blackbrook ARL
10.5.94	Morley, Adrian	Eccles ARL

Leeds centre Kevin Iro, recalled by New Zealand for Test duty in autumn 1993.

LEEDS 1993-94 PLAYERS' SUMMARY

	(Date of Birth)	App	T	G	D	Pts	Previous club	Signed
Barratt, Anthony	(26.10.73)	1	—	—	—	—	Middleton ARL	17.6.91
Battye, Neil	(11.8.63)	0+1	—	—	—	—	Doncaster	19.11.93
Cook, Paul	(23.7.76)	9+1	6	—	—	24	Hull ARL	1.12.92
Cummins, Francis	(12.10.76)	23+2	17	1	—	70	St. John Fisher ARL	12.10.93
Donohue, Jason	(18.4.72)	8+4	—	—	—	—	Leigh	26.11.93
Eyres, Richard	(7.12.64)	29	8	—	—	32	Widnes	16.9.93
Fallon, Jim	(27.3.65)	34	16	—	—	64	Bath RU	6.7.92
Fawcett, Vince	(13.11.70)	2	—	—	—	—	Middleton ARL	13.11.87
Fozzard, Nick	(22.7.77)	0+1	—	—	—	—	Shaw Cross ARL	27.7.93
Gregory, Andy	(10.8.61)	2+1	—	—	—	—	Wigan	19.8.92
Hanley, Ellery	(27.3.61)	29+1	25	—	1	101	Wigan	6.9.91
Harmon, Neil	(9.1.69)	25+4	1	—	—	4	Warrington	24.8.93
Hassan, Phil	(18.8.74)	2+2	—	—	—	—	St. Pauls ARL	10.8.93
Holroyd, Graham	(25.10.75)	29+6	7	100	3	231	Siddal ARL	24.9.92
Howard, Harvey	(29.8.68)	17+1	1	—	—	4	Widnes	4.1.94
Innes, Craig	(10.9.69)	24+1	11	—	—	44	New Zealand RU	4.1.92
Iro, Kevin	(25.5.68)	33	14	—	—	56	Australia	29.10.92
Irving, Simon	(22.3.67)	14+4	2	23	—	54	Headingley RU	30.1.90
Leatham, Jim	(10.10.74)	0+1	—	—	—	—	Leeds Academy	7.9.93
Lowes, James	(11.10.69)	35	6	—	—	24	Hunslet	30.9.92
Maher, Lee	(29.10.75)	1	—	—	—	—	ARL	1.9.93
Maskill, Colin	(15.3.64)	4+1	—	—	—	—	Wakefield T.	21.1.85
Mercer, Gary	(22.6.66)	33	8	—	—	32	Warrington	5.8.92
O'Neill, Mike	(29.11.60)	13+4	—	—	—	—	Rochdale H.	21.8.91
Parrish, Steve	(15.3.65)	0+2	—	—	—	—	Batley	21.6.93
Pearson, Carl	(1.2.75)	1+1	—	—	—	—	BP Chemicals ARL	24.2.92
Pickles, Steve	(2.11.73)	2	—	—	—	—	Middleton ARL	20.6.91
Rose, Gary	(25.7.65)	15+13	1	—	—	4	Featherstone R.	2.9.93
Scales, Jonathan	(28.7.74)	12	1	—	—	4	Gosforth RU	28.3.93
Scott, Ian	(20.4.69)	17+3	1	—	—	4	Workington T.	14.7.93
Schofield, Garry	(1.7.65)	24+1	9	2	2	42	Hull	23.10.87
Schultz, Matthew	(9.8.75)	3+3	—	—	—	—	—	9.8.92
Shaw, Matt	(3.10.72)	1	—	—	—	—	Ryedale-York	4.2.92
Stephens, Gareth	(15.4.74)	13+1	2	—	—	8	Lock Lane ARL	21.9.90
Tait, Alan	(2.7.64)	34	11	—	—	44	Widnes	14.8.92
Vassilakopoulos, Marcus	(19.9.76)	5+16	2	—	—	8	Hull ARL	20.9.93
TOTALS								
36 players			149	126	6	854		

Representative appearances 1993-94

Eyres — Britain (+2); Holroyd — GB Under-21s (+1); Iro — New Zealand (4, 2t); Mercer — New Zealand (+1); Schofield — Britain (4, 1t, 1dg); Stephens — GB Under-21s (2); Tait — Britain (+3).

LEEDS 1993-94 MATCH ANALYSIS

Date	Competition	H/A	Opponent	Rlt	Score	Tries	Goals	Attendance	Referee
27.8.93	SBC	A	Castleford	W	21-12	Hanley (2), Holroyd, Innes	Irving (2), Hanley (dg)	—	—
5.9.93	SBC	H	Warrington	W	21-19	Schofield (2), Fallon, Irving	Irving (2), Schofield (dg)	11,188	R. Smith
10.9.93	SBC	A	Wigan	L	18-32	Hanley (2)	Irving (5)	—	—
19.9.93	SBC	H	Hull K.R.	W	42-6	Hanley (3), Cummins (2), Cook, Schofield	Holroyd (7)	9224	Campbell
26.9.93	SBC	A	Salford	L	18-23	Innes (2), Iro, Tait	Holroyd	—	—
3.10.93	SBC	H	Hull	D	22-22	Eyres, Lowes, Mercer, Schofield	Irving (3)	10,336	Whitfield
10.10.93	SBC	A	Oldham	L	6-21	Stephens	Irving	—	—
19.10.93	SBC	A	Featherstone R.	L	20-22	Eyres, Scales, Tait	Irving (4)	—	—
24.10.93	Tour	H	New Zealand	L	6-35	Iro	Irving	6898	Holdsworth
13.11.93	RT(2)	A	Salford	L	12-21	Iro, Tait	Irving (2)	—	—
17.11.93	SBC	H	St. Helens	L	18-21	Holroyd, Tait, Vassilakopoulos	Irving (3)	7170	R. Smith
21.11.93	SBC	H	Leigh	W	27-18	Tait (2), Cummins, Holroyd, Irving	Holroyd (3,1dg)	6620	Campbell
28.11.93	SBC	A[1]	Bradford N.	L	28-36	Iro (2), Fallon, Tait	Holroyd (6)	—	—
1.12.93	SBC	A	Widnes	L	6-8	Iro	Cummins	—	—
5.12.93	SBC	A	Sheffield E.	W	31-8	Fallon, Hanley, Mercer, Rose, Stephens	Holroyd (5,1dg)	—	—
26.12.93	SBC	H	Wakefield T.	W	20-16	Cummins, Fallon, Schofield, Tait	Holroyd (2)	14,455	Morris
2.1.94	SBC	A	Halifax	W	18-12	Cummins (2), Hanley, Mercer	Holroyd	—	—
5.1.94	SBC	H	Castleford	W	8-4	—	Holroyd (4)	10,830	Ollerton
9.1.94	SBC	A	Warrington	L	18-37	Cummins, Eyres, Tait	Holroyd (3)	—	—
14.1.94	SBC	H	Wigan	L	14-26	Cummins, Iro	Holroyd (3)	12,096	Cummings
23.1.94	SBC	A	Hull K.R.	W	24-4	Cummins, Fallon, Hanley, Lowes	Holroyd (4)	—	—
30.1.94	CC(4)	A	Rochdale H.	W	40-18	Fallon (2), Cummins, Eyres, Hanley, Innes, Lowes, Tait	Holroyd (4)	—	—
6.2.94	SBC	H	Salford	W	22-16	Cook, Hanley, Iro, Mercer	Holroyd (3)	8315	Ollerton
12.2.94	CC(5)	H	Warrington	W	38-4	Fallon (2), Innes (2), Hanley, Iro, Schofield	Holroyd (5)	9713	Cummings
20.2.94	SBC	A	Hull	L	14-21	Iro, Vassilakopoulos	Holroyd (3)	—	—
27.2.94	CC(6)	H	Bradford N.	W	33-10	Hanley (2), Cummins, Fallon, Holroyd, Lowes	Holroyd (4,1dg)	22,615	Campbell
6.3.94	SBC	H	Oldham	W	26-22	Cook (2), Hanley (2), Harmon	Holroyd (3)	8635	Atkin
13.3.94	SBC	H	Featherstone R.	L	10-36	Fallon (2)	Holroyd	7910	R. Connolly
26.3.94	CC(SF)	N[1]	St. Helens	W	20-8	Hanley (2), Eyres	Holroyd (4)	(20,771)	Holdsworth
1.4.94	SBC	A	Wakefield T.	W	29-20	Cummins, Fallon, Hanley, Iro, Lowes	Holroyd (2), Schofield (2,1dg)	—	—
4.4.94	SBC	H	Halifax	W	26-16	Iro (2), Cook, Fallon	Holroyd (5)	11,650	Holdsworth
10.4.94	SBC	H	Sheffield E.	D	46-46	Cummins (2), Innes (2), Hanley, Holroyd, Howard, Mercer	Holroyd (7)	8236	Whitfield
13.4.94	SBC	A	St. Helens	L	0-68	—	—	—	—
17.4.94	SBC	A	Leigh	W	52-20	Hanley (3), Eyres (2), Cummins, Fallon, Iro, Lowes, Mercer	Holroyd (6)	—	—
20.4.94	SBC	H	Widnes	W	58-16	Innes (2), Mercer (2), Cummins, Eyres, Hanley, Holroyd, Schofield, Tait	Holroyd (9)	7735	J. Smith
23.4.94	SBC	H	Bradford N.	L	10-52	Cook, Scott	Holroyd	9014	J. Connolly
30.4.94	CC(F)	N[2]	Wigan	L	16-26	Schofield, Fallon, Cummins	Holroyd (2)	(78,348)	Campbell
8.5.94	PT(1)	A	Bradford N.	L	16-42	Holroyd, Innes, Schofield	Holroyd (2)	—	—

A[1] Bradford C. FC; N[1] Wigan; N[2] Wembley

LEIGH

Ground: Hilton Park (0942-674437)
First Season: 1895-96
Chairman: Mick Higgins
General
  Manager: Wendy Stott
Honours: **Championship** Winners, 1905-06
Division One Champions, 1981-82
Division Two Champions, 1977-78,
1985-86, 1988-89
Challenge Cup Winners, 1920-21,
1970-71
Lancashire Cup Winners, 1952-53,
1955-56, 1970-71, 1981-82
Beaten finalists, 1905-06, 1909-10,
1920-21, 1922-23, 1949-50, 1951-52,
1963-64, 1969-70
BBC2 Floodlit Trophy Winners,
1969-70, 1972-73
Beaten finalists, 1967-68, 1976-77

RECORDS

Match
Goals: 15 by Mick Stacey v. Doncaster,
28 Mar 1976
Tries: 6 by Jack Wood v. York, 4 Oct 1947
Points: 38 by John Woods v. Blackpool B.,
11 Sep 1977
John Woods v. Ryedale-York,
12 Jan 1992

Season
Goals: 173 by Chris Johnson, 1985-86
Tries: 49 by Steve Halliwell, 1985-86
Points: 400 by Chris Johnson, 1985-86

Career
Goals: 1,043 by Jim Ledgard, 1948-58
Tries: 189 by Mick Martyn, 1954-67
Points: 2,492 by John Woods, 1976-85 & 1990-92
Appearances: 503 by Albert Worrall, 1921-35 &
1936-38
Highest score: 92-2 v. Keighley, 30 Apr 1986
Highest against: 70-6 at Castleford, 20 Feb 1994
70-16 at Hull, 24 Apr 1994
Attendance: 31,324 v. St. Helens (RL Cup),
14 Mar 1953

COACHING REGISTER
● **Since 1974-75**

Eddie Cheetham	May 74 - Mar 75
Kevin Ashcroft	June 75 - Jan 77
Bill Kindon	Jan 77 - Apr 77
John Mantle	Apr 77 - Nov 78
Tom Grainey	Nov 78 - Dec 80
*Alex Murphy	Nov 80 - June 82
*Colin Clarke	June 82 - Dec 82
Peter Smethurst	Dec 82 - Apr 83
Tommy Bishop	June 83 - June 84
John Woods	June 84 - May 85
Alex Murphy	Feb 85 - Nov 85
Tommy Dickens	Nov 85 - Dec 86
Billy Benyon	Dec 86 - Mar 90
Alex Murphy	Mar 90 - Aug 91
Kevin Ashcroft	Sep 91 - June 92
Jim Crellin	June 92 - Sep 92
Steve Simms	Nov 92 -

*From Dec 80 to June 82 Clarke was
officially appointed coach and Murphy
manager.*

*John Woods, top scorer in Leigh's history and
club coach in 1984-85.*

GREAT BRITAIN REGISTER
(19 players)

Kevin Ashcroft	(5)	1968-70
Joe Cartwright	(7)	1920-21
Dave Chisnall	(2)	1970
Joe Darwell	(5)	1924
Steve Donlan	(+2)	1984
Des Drummond	(22)	1980-86
Peter Foster	(3)	1955
Chris Johnson	(1)	1985
Frank Kitchen	(2)	1954
Jim Ledgard	(9)	1948-54
Gordon Lewis	(1)	1965
Mick Martyn	(2)	1958-59
Walter Mooney	(2)	1924
Stan Owen	(1)	1958
Charlie Pawsey	(7)	1952-54
Bill Robinson	(2)	1963
Joe Walsh	(1)	1971
Billy Winstanley	(2)	1910
John Woods	(7+3)	1979-83

Hooker Kevin Ashcroft, five Test caps between 1968-70.

1993-94 SIGNINGS REGISTER

Signed	Player	Club From
7.6.93	Jones, Simon	Leigh Academy
24.6.93	Winstanley, Paul	Wigan St. Patricks ARL
3.8.93	Aspinall, Scott	Warrington Academy
18.8.93	Jones, Carl	Leigh Miners ARL
18.8.93	Daniel, Paul	Leigh Miners ARL
19.8.93	Hall, Tony	Leigh Harriers ARL
19.8.93	Hall, Barry	Leigh Harriers ARL
19.8.93	Purtill, Dean	Wigan St. Patricks ARL
26.8.93	Heaton, William	—
16.9.93	Maloney, Sean	—
19.9.93	Horrabin, Andrew	Leigh Academy
24.9.93	Sarsfield, Mark	Widnes
4.10.93	Cawley, Steve	Leigh Miners ARL
29.10.93	*Fletcher, Darren	Chorley B.
11.11.93	Davies, Glyn	St. Helens
26.11.93	*Hudspith, Mark	Oldham
9.12.93	Cheetham, Andrew	Orrell St. James ARL
17.12.93	Warburton, Steve	Rochdale H.
21.12.93	Meadows, Mark	Oldham
19.1.94	*Neale, Mike	Wigan
24.1.94	*Marsh, Paul	St. Helens
10.2.94	Macaree, James	Leigh East ARL
17.2.94	Harrison, Neil	Eccles ARL
24.2.94	*Westwood, Lee	Warrington
10.3.94	Verdon, Paul	Eccles ARL
26.3.94	Wright, David	Wigan
31.3.94	Jukes, Neil	Rosebridge ARL

Winger Des Drummond, called up 22 times by Great Britain while serving Leigh.

LEIGH 1993-94 PLAYERS' SUMMARY

	(Date of Birth)	App	T	G	D	Pts	Previous club	Signed
Aspinall, Scott	(26.4.75)	0+1	—	—	—	—	Warrington Academy	3.8.93
Baldwin, Simon	(31.3.75)	21+6	7	11	—	50	Leigh East ARL	31.3.92
Blakeley, Mike	(22.11.70)	2+4	—	6	—	12	Leigh Miners ARL	16.7.90
Booth, Simon	(9.12.71)	15+4	1	—	—	4	Leigh Miners ARL	16.7.90
Bridge, Russ	(8.10.64)	1	—	—	—	—	Fulham	12.10.90
Burke, Tony	(25.8.61)	2+1	—	—	—	—	Warrington	10.8.92
Cawley, Steve	(10.6.71)	12+3	—	—	—	—	Leigh Miners ARL	4.10.93
Cheetham, Andrew	(25.1.75)	13+1	4	—	—	16	Orrell St. James ARL	9.12.93
Clarke, Troy	(19.4.67)	12+1	3	26	—	64	Carlisle	1.2.93
Collier, Andy	(3.6.68)	29+1	3	—	—	12	—	30.4.86
Costello, John	(10.3.70)	23+2	2	—	—	8	Leigh Miners ARL	6.9.91
Daniel, Paul	(16.3.74)	12+9	3	—	—	12	Leigh Miners ARL	18.8.93
Davies, Glyn	(3.12.74)	7+1	2	6	—	20	St. Helens	11.11.93
Donohue, Jason	(18.4.72)	6+1	—	—	1	1	Golborne ARL	24.3.88
Fanning, Sean	(16.6.62)	1+3	—	—	—	—	Hare & Hounds ARL	5.4.92
Fletcher, Darren	(25.10.73)	0+2	—	—	—	—	Chorley B.	26.3.93
Gunning, John	(30.3.69)	22+2	—	10	2	22	Leigh East ARL	10.1.93
Hall, Tony	(31.8.70)	2+1	1	—	—	4	Leigh Harriers ARL	19.8.93
Hanger, Dean	(24.2.70)	29+1	14	—	—	56	Australia	1.2.93
Hansen, Lee	(3.7.68)	17	—	—	—	—	New Zealand	1.7.92
Hill, David	(4.9.68)	5+2	1	—	—	4	Blackbrook ARL	5.10.88
Jones, Simon	(13.11.74)	0+2	—	—	—	—	Leigh Academy	7.6.93
Maloney, Sean	(15.11.93)	6+2	—	—	—	—	—	16.9.93
Marsh, Paul	(18.6.74)	2+2	—	—	—	—	St. Helens	24.1.94
Martin, Scott	(29.12.74)	26	4	—	—	16	Leigh East ARL	29.12.91
Meadows, Mark	(9.5.65)	16	1	—	—	4	Oldham	21.12.93
Neale, Mike	(4.9.73)	4+2	—	—	—	—	Wigan	19.1.94
Pendlebury, John	(18.4.61)	25+1	1	—	—	4	Bradford N.	18.7.92
Platt, Duncan	(19.7.65)	8+3	—	4	—	8	Oldham	14.8.92
Pratt, Gareth	(23.8.69)	18+2	2	—	—	8	Mayfield ARL	5.9.92
Pugsley, Stuart	(14.11.67)	9+2	1	—	—	4	Whitehaven	1.9.92
Purtill, Dean	(4.1.75)	1	—	—	—	—	Wigan St. Patricks ARL	19.8.93
Robinshaw, Alan	(8.3.74)	2+1	—	—	—	—	Leigh East ARL	10.12.92
Rowley, Paul	(12.3.75)	32	8	—	—	32	Leigh Miners ARL	29.3.92
Sarsfield, Mark	(22.3.71)	19	9	—	1	37	Widnes	24.9.93
Street, Tim	(29.6.68)	9	1	—	—	4	Oldham	14.8.92
Warburton, Steve	(6.2.69)	8	2	—	—	8	Rochdale H.	17.12.93
Webster, David	(20.10.68)	5	1	—	—	4	Rochdale H.	2.3.94
Winstanley, Paul	(9.5.74)	5+2	—	—	—	—	Wigan St. Patricks ARL	24.6.93
Wright, David	(13.10.74)	3	—	—	—	—	Wigan	26.3.94
TOTALS								
40 players			71	63	4	414		

Representative appearances 1993-94

Martin — GB Under-21s (+2).

LEIGH 1993-94 MATCH ANALYSIS

Date	Competition	H/A	Opponent	Rlt	Score	Tries	Goals	Attendance	Referee
29.8.93	SBC	H	Featherstone R.	L	12-26	Hanger	Blakeley (3), Platt	3526	Wood
5.9.93	SBC	A	Widnes	L	10-34	Baldwin	Platt (3)	—	—
12.9.93	SBC	H	Wakefield T.	L	4-10	—	Clarke (2)	3015	Galtress
19.9.93	SBC	A	St. Helens	L	16-34	Collier, Hanger, Martin	Clarke (2)	—	—
26.9.93	SBC	A	Halifax	L	26-27	Sarsfield (2), Hall, Martin	Clarke (5)	—	—
3.10.93	SBC	H	Castleford	D	15-15	Clarke, Rowley, Sarsfield	Clarke, Donohue (dg)	3019	Galtress
19.10.93	SBC	A	Wigan	L	12-38	Clarke, Sarsfield	Clarke (2)	—	—
24.10.93	SBC	H	Bradford N.	L	16-42	Baldwin, Clarke, Street	Clarke (2)	4206	Morris
29.10.93	SBC	A	Warrington	L	6-24	Rowley	Clarke	—	—
7.11.93	SBC	H	Hull K.R.	L	17-22	Costello, Hanger	Clarke (4), Gunning (dg)	2318	Wood
14.11.93	RT(2)	H	Huddersfield	W	20-12	Baldwin, Booth, Pratt, Rowley	Clarke (2)	3407	Asquith
21.11.93	SBC	A	Leeds	L	18-27	Hanger (2), Baldwin	Clarke (3)	—	—
28.11.93	SBC	H	Hull	L	7-22	Pugsley	Clarke, Gunning (dg)	2581	Whitfield
5.12.93	SBC	A	Oldham	L	6-42	Martin	Clarke	—	—
13.12.93	RT(3)	A	Castleford	L	14-54	Davies, Hanger	Davies (3)	—	—
19.12.93	SBC	A	Featherstone R.	L	0-36	—	—	—	—
28.12.93	SBC	H	Sheffield E.	L	14-24	Davies, Hanger, Warburton	Davies	1985	Ollerton
2.1.94	SBC	A	Salford	L	10-23	Cheetham, Hanger	Davies	—	—
7.1.94	SBC	H	Widnes	L	14-25	Cheetham, Hanger, Pratt	Davies	2242	R. Connolly
16.1.94	SBC	A	Wakefield T.	L	10-18	Cheetham, Rowley	Baldwin	—	—
23.1.94	SBC	H	St. Helens	W	21-4	Collier, Martin, Warburton	Gunning (4), Sarsfield (dg)	4160	J. Smith
30.1.94	CC(4)	A	Sheffield E.	L	10-42	Rowley, Sarsfield	Gunning	—	—
6.2.94	SBC	H	Halifax	L	10-32	Baldwin, Hill	Baldwin	3371	Morris
20.2.94	SBC	A	Castleford	L	6-70	Daniel	Baldwin	—	—
6.3.94	SBC	H	Wigan	L	8-26	Cheetham, Sarsfield	—	7292	Asquith
13.3.94	SBC	A	Bradford N.	W	24-14	Hanger (2), Meadows, Pendlebury	Gunning (4)	—	—
22.3.94	SBC	H	Warrington	L	6-14	Webster	Gunning	4684	Cross
25.3.94	SBC	A	Hull K.R.	L	16-40	Costello, Hanger, Rowley	Baldwin, Blakeley	—	—
1.4.94	SBC	A	Sheffield E.	L	4-48	Baldwin	—	—	—
4.4.94	SBC	H	Salford	L	18-19	Baldwin, Daniel, Sarsfield	Baldwin (3)	2833	Atkin
10.4.94	SBC	H	Oldham	L	8-34	Hanger	Baldwin (2)	2750	J. Connolly
17.4.94	SBC	H	Leeds	L	20-52	Rowley (2), Collier, Sarsfield	Baldwin (2)	2793	Whitfield
24.4.94	SBC	A	Hull	L	16-70	Daniel, Hanger, Sarsfield	Blakeley (2)	—	—

Dean Hanger, Leigh's top try scorer in 1993-94.

Long serving forward Andy Collier.

LONDON CRUSADERS

Ground: Barnet Copthall (081-203 4211)
First Season: 1980-81. Began as Fulham.
Became London Crusaders at start of 1991-92 and changed to London Broncos in 1994-95.

General
Manager: Robbie Moore

Honours: **Division Two** Champions, 1982-83
Second Division Premiership Beaten finalists, 1993-94

RECORDS

Match

Goals: 11 by Steve Guyett v. Huddersfield, 23 Oct 1988
Greg Pearce v. Runcorn H., 26 Aug 1990

Tries: 4 by Mark Riley v. Highfield, 17 Oct 1993
Mark Johnson at Highfield, 1 Apr 1994

Points: 24 by John Gallagher v. Bramley, 27 Mar 1994

Season

Goals: 159 by John Gallagher, 1993-94
Tries: 43 by Mark Johnson, 1993-94
Points: 384 by John Gallagher, 1993-94

Career

Goals: 309 by Steve Diamond, 1981-84
Tries: 74 by Hussain M'Barki, 1981-84 & 1988-91
Points: 691 by Steve Diamond, 1981-84
Appearances: 148+14 by Hussain M'Barki, 1981-84 & 1988-91

Highest score: 66-12 v. Keighley C., 8 May 1994
Highest against: 72-6 v. Whitehaven, 14 Sep 1986
Attendance: 2,324 v. Hull (John Player Trophy), 18 Nov 1984 — at Crystal Palace
15,013 v. Wakefield T. (RL Cup), 15 Feb 1981 — at Craven Cottage
1,878 v. Bradford N. (Regal Trophy), 19 Dec 1993 — at Barnet Copthall

COACHING REGISTER

● **Since formation in 1980**

Reg Bowden	July 80 - June 84
Roy Lester	June 84 - Apr 86
Bill Goodwin	Apr 86 - May 88
*Bev Risman	May 88 - Feb 89
Phil Sullivan	Feb 89 - Mar 89
Bill Goodwin	Mar 89 - Apr 89
Ross Strudwick	June 89 - Feb 93
Tony Gordon	Feb 93 - May 94
Gary Grienke	May 94 -

Team manager

GREAT BRITAIN REGISTER

(1 player)

John Dalgreen (1) 1982

1993-94 SIGNINGS REGISTER

Signed	Player	Club From
1.7.93	Gallagher, John	Leeds
29.7.93	Ekoku, Abi	St. Marys ARL
11.8.93	Johnson, Mark	Harlequins RU
13.8.93	Walker, Jason	Rotorua, NZ
17.8.93	Stewart, Sam	Charlestown, NZ
17.8.93	Perryment, Ian	Loughborough Univ. ARL
17.8.93	Matautia, Ben	NZ
17.8.93	Lofthouse, Norman	Mill Hill RU
17.8.93	Chambers, Paul	Rosslyn Park RU
18.8.93	McIvor, Dixon	South London ARL
19.8.93	Luxon, Geoff	Crystal Palace ARL
19.8.93	Laxon, Lee	Crystal Palace ARL
1.9.93	Carter, Scott	—
2.9.93	Fitzsimmons, Peter	La Reole, Fr.
15.9.93	Spencer, Adrian	Cambridge Univ. ARL
5.10.93	Irish, Vincent	Saracens RU
5.10.93	Ratti, William	Croydon RU
29.10.93	*Clark, Nathan	Oldham
5.1.94	Stoop, Andre	Wigan
10.1.94	Campbell, Logan	Newcastle K., Aus.
14.1.94	Carroll, Bernard	South London ARL
28.1.94	Timms, Victor	Brisbane B., Aus.
8.2.94	Dynevor, Leo	Brisbane B., Aus.
24.3.94	Helg, Albert	Surrey Heath ARL
24.3.94	Wilkinson, Richard	Surrey Heath ARL

LONDON CRUSADERS 1993-94 PLAYERS' SUMMARY

	(Date of Birth)	App	T	G	D	Pts	Previous club	Signed
Aiyede, Bola	(21.8.63)	0+1	—	—	—	—	America	27.7.92
Blackman, Richard	(29.3.70)	5+1	2	—	—	8	Oldham	14.8.92
Campbell, Logan	(23.5.71)	18+1	15	—	—	60	Australia	10.1.94
Carter, Scott	(14.7.67)	31+1	5	—	1	21	—	1.9.93
Chambers, Paul	(21.6.68)	1+1	—	—	—	—	Rosslyn Park RU	17.8.93
Dynevor, Leo	(13.2.74)	13	7	—	—	28	Australia	8.2.94
Ekoku, Abi	(13.4.66)	16	8	—	—	32	St. Marys ARL	29.7.93
Gallagher, John	(29.1.64)	39	17	157	2	384	Leeds	1.7.93
Johnson, Mark	(28.2.69)	37	43	—	—	172	South Africa	18.3.93
Luxon, Geoff	(2.6.71)	1+8	1	—	—	4	Crystal Palace ARL	19.8.93
McIvor, Dixon	(30.1.68)	16+11	4	—	—	16	South London ARL	18.8.93
Matautia, Ben	(12.12.67)	0+1	—	—	—	—	New Zealand	17.8.93
Michalski, Darren	(17.11.68)	16+11	2	—	—	8	Australia	12.2.93
Mulkerin, Danny	(19.11.68)	17+1	1	—	—	4	Australia	20.8.92
Perryment, Ian	(28.11.72)	2+2	2	—	—	8	Loughborough Univ. ARL	17.8.93
Ramsey, Neville	(7.4.63)	38	12	—	1	49	New Zealand	11.3.93
Riley, Mark	(16.6.67)	37	30	—	—	120	Peckham ARL	6.10.92
Roskell, Scott	(25.4.69)	33	21	—	—	84	Australia	27.8.92
Rosolen, Steve	(16.11.68)	39	5	—	—	20	Australia	2.1.92
Rotheram, Dave	(16.8.68)	19+16	—	—	—	—	W. London Inst. ARL	28.8.90
Rugless, Troy	(18.11.70)	15	4	—	—	16	Australia	8.10.93
Smith, Kris	(8.8.66)	10+9	1	—	—	4	Twickenham RU	30.8.91
Spencer, Adrian	(3.3.73)	2	—	—	—	—	Cambridge Univ. ARL	22.3.93
Stewart, Sam	(5.12.62)	37	4	—	—	16	New Zealand	17.8.93
Stoop, Andre	(8.10.66)	15	9	—	—	36	Wigan	5.1.94
Timms, Victor	(22.5.71)	8+5	3	—	—	12	Australia	28.1.94
Walker, Jason	(20.7.71)	17	6	—	—	24	New Zealand	13.8.93
Whiteley, Chris	(31.1.67)	25+6	—	—	—	—	Salford	27.8.92
TOTALS								
28 players			202	157	4	1,126		

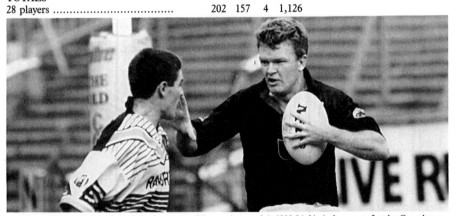

Former All Black RU star John Gallagher, creator of three scoring records in 1993-94, his single season at London Crusaders.

LONDON CRUSADERS 1993-94 MATCH ANALYSIS

Date	Com-petition	H/A	Opponent	Rlt	Score	Tries	Goals	Atten-dance	Referee
27.8.93	SD	H	Batley	W	40-6	McIvor (2), Perryment (2), Johnson, Ramsey, Riley	Gallagher (6)	790	Asquith
5.9.93	SD	A	Keighley C.	W	17-14	Gallagher (2), Riley	Gallagher (2), Carter (dg)	—	—
10.9.93	SD	H	Doncaster	W	38-18	Johnson (3), Mulkerin, Walker, Gallagher	Gallagher (7)	690	McGregor
19.9.93	SD	A	Huddersfield	L	10-34	Carter, Riley	Gallagher	—	—
26.9.93	SD	H	Dewsbury	L	17-42	Riley (2)	Gallagher (4,1dg)	840	Burke
3.10.93	SD	A	Barrow	L	12-37	Johnson (2), Ramsey	—	—	—
10.10.93	SD	H	Ryedale-York	W	24-20	Carter, Ekoku, Johnson, Riley	Gallagher (4)	593	Crashley
17.10.93	SD	H	Highfield	W	62-6	Riley (4), Stewart (3), Ekoku (2), Johnson, Rosolen, Walker	Gallagher (7)	648	Cummings
24.10.93	SD	H	Hunslet	W	48-12	Johnson (2), Roskell (2), Michalski, Riley, Ramsey, Rosolen, Walker	Gallagher (6)	493	Atkin
31.10.93	RT(1)	H	St. Esteve	W	48-16	Carter (2), Johnson (2), Riley (2), Ekoku, Michalski	Gallagher (8)	746	R. Connolly
7.11.93	SD	A	Workington T.	W	13-12	Johnson (2), Gallagher	Gallagher (dg)	—	—
14.11.93	RT(2)	H	Featherstone R.	W	26-12	Ekoku, Johnson, Ramsey, Carter, Rosolen	Gallagher (3)	981	Burke
28.11.93	SD	H	Carlisle	W	38-24	Ekoku (2), Johnson (2), Gallagher, Ramsey, Riley	Gallagher (5)	554	McGregor
1.12.93	SD	A	Bramley	W	30-18	Rugless (2), Blackman, Riley, Walker	Gallagher (5)	—	—
5.12.93	SD	A	Whitehaven	D	16-16	Gallagher, Ramsey, Riley	Gallagher (2)	—	—
12.12.93	RT(3)	A	Ryedale-York	W	42-10	Roskell (3), Riley (2), Ekoku, Rosolen, Rugless	Gallagher (5)	—	—
19.12.93	RT(4)	H	Bradford N.	L	10-22	Roskell (2)	Gallagher	1878	Holdsworth
29.12.93	SD	H	Swinton	W	22-12	Walker (2), Johnson, Riley	Gallagher (3)	602	Cummings
2.1.94	SD	A	Rochdale H.	L	8-15	Johnson	Gallagher (2)	—	—
16.1.94	CC(3)	H	Shaw Cross	W	40-14	Gallagher (2), Roskell (2), Campbell, Johnson, Smith, Stewart	Gallagher (4)	551	Cross
23.1.94	SD	A	Doncaster	L	10-20	McIvor, Rugless	Gallagher	—	—
30.1.94	CC(4)	H	Featherstone R.	L	14-28	Roskell (2)	Gallagher (3)	1557	Whitfield
6.2.94	SD	H	Huddersfield	L	10-24	Blackman, Ramsey	Gallagher	1036	Wood
13.2.94	SD	A	Batley	L	18-29	Riley (3), Ramsey	Gallagher	—	—
16.2.94	SD	H	Keighley C.	W	13-10	Campbell, Johnson	Gallagher (2), Ramsey (dg)	672	Gilmour
20.2.94	SD	A	Dewsbury	W	30-16	Campbell, Gallagher, McIvor, Roskell, Stoop	Gallagher (5)	—	—
27.2.94	SD	H	Barrow	W	52-14	Johnson (3), Gallagher (3), Gallagher, Ramsey, Riley	Gallagher (8)	605	Kershaw
6.3.94	SD	A	Ryedale-York	W	22-14	Campbell (2), Johnson, Stoop	Gallagher (3)	—	—
13.3.94	SD	A	Hunslet	W	46-22	Dynevor (2), Gallagher (2), Campbell, Ramsey, Riley, Roskell, Stoop	Gallagher (5)	—	—
20.3.94	SD	H	Workington T.	D	20-20	Dynevor, Johnson	Gallagher (6)	1479	Tennant
27.3.94	SD	H	Bramley	W	64-0	Gallagher (2), Johnson (2), Riley (2), Roskell (2), Stoop (2), Dynevor, Rosolen	Gallagher (8)	514	J. Smith
1.4.94	SD	A	Highfield	W	58-6	Johnson (4), Dynevor (2), Timms (2), Gallagher, Riley	Gallagher (9)	—	—
4.4.94	SD	H	Rochdale H.	W	28-10	Stoop (2), Campbell, Johnson, Roskell	Gallagher (4)	661	Morris
12.4.94	SD	A	Swinton	W	20-18	Gallagher (2), Ramsey, Roskell	Gallagher (2)	—	—
17.4.94	SD	H	Whitehaven	W	30-21	Roskell (2), Campbell, Johnson, Riley	Gallagher (5)	836	Wood

Date	Com-petition	H/A	Opponent	Rlt	Score	Tries	Goals	Atten-dance	Referee
24.4.94	SD	A	Carlisle	W	26-12	Johnson (2), Dynevor, Timms	Gallagher (5)	—	—
8.5.94	SDP(1)	H	Keighley C.	W	66-12	Johnson (3), Campbell (2), Riley (2), Stoop (2), Luxon, Ramsey, Roskell	Gallagher (9)	1247	Cross
15.5.94	SDP(SF)	A	Doncaster	W	16-6	Campbell, Johnson, Roskell	Gallagher (2)	—	—
22.5.94	SDP(F)	N[1]	Workington T.	L	22-30	Johnson (3), Campbell	Gallagher (3)	—	J. Connolly

N[1] Manchester U. FC

Twelve tries in 38 appearances in 1993-94 for New Zealander Neville Ramsey.

OLDHAM

Ground: Watersheddings (061-624-4865)
First Season: 1895-96
Nickname: Roughyeds
Chairman: Jim Quinn
Secretary: Karen Scott
Honours: **Championship** Winners, 1909-10,
1910-11, 1956-57
Beaten finalists, 1906-07, 1907-08,
1908-09, 1921-22, 1954-55
Division One Champions, 1904-05
Division Two Champions, 1963-64,
1981-82, 1987-88
Challenge Cup Winners, 1898-99,
1924-25, 1926-27
Beaten finalists, 1906-07, 1911-12,
1923-24, 1925-26
**Second Division/Divisional
Premiership** Winners, 1987-88,
1989-90
Beaten finalists, 1991-92
Lancashire Cup Winners, 1907-08,
1910-11, 1913-14, 1919-20, 1924-25,
1933-34, 1956-57, 1957-58, 1958-59
Beaten finalists, 1908-09, 1911-12,
1918-19, 1921-22, 1954-55, 1966-67,
1968-69, 1986-87, 1989-90
Lancashire League Winners,
1897-98, 1900-01, 1907-08, 1909-10,
1921-22, 1956-57, 1957-58

RECORDS

Match
Goals: 14 by Bernard Ganley v. Liverpool C.,
4 Apr 1959
Tries: 7 by James Miller v. Barry, 31 Oct 1908
Points: 30 by Abe Johnson v. Widnes, 9 Apr 1928

Season
Goals: 200 by Bernard Ganley, 1957-58
Tries: 49 by R. Farrar, 1921-22
Points: 412 by Bernard Ganley, 1957-58

Career
Goals: 1,365 by Bernard Ganley, 1951-61
Tries: 173 by Alan Davies, 1950-61
Points: 2,775 by Bernard Ganley, 1951-61
Appearances: 626 by Joe Ferguson, 1899-1923

Highest score: 67-6 v. Liverpool C., 4 Apr 1959
Highest against: 67-11 at Hull K.R., 24 Sep 1978
Attendance: 28,000 v. Huddersfield (League),
24 Feb 1912

COACHING REGISTER
● **Since 1974-75**

Jim Challinor	Aug 74 - Dec 76
Terry Ramshaw	Jan 77 - Feb 77
Dave Cox	July 77 - Dec 78
Graham Starkey (Mgr)	Jan 79 - May 81
Bill Francis	June 79 - Dec 80
Frank Myler	May 81 - Apr 83
Peter Smethurst	Apr 83 - Feb 84
Frank Barrow	Feb 84 - Feb 84
Brian Gartland	Mar 84 - June 84
Frank Myler	June 84 - Apr 87
*Eric Fitzsimons	June 87 - Nov 88
*Mal Graham	June 87 - Apr 88
Tony Barrow	Nov 88 - Jan 91
John Fieldhouse	Jan 91 - Apr 91
Peter Tunks	Apr 91 - Feb 94
Bob Lindner	Feb 94 - Apr 94
Andy Goodway	May 94 -

Joint coaches June 87 - Apr 88

1993-94 SIGNINGS REGISTER

Signed	Player	Club From
10.6.93	Goulbourne, Alf	Isberg C. ARL
14.6.93	Holden, Martin	Wigan St. Patricks ARL
5.8.93	Groves, Paul	St. Helens
11.8.93	Irwin, Shaun	Castleford
11.8.93	Kuiti, Mike	Rochdale H.
13.8.93	Jones, David	Wakefield T.
25.8.93	McAlister, Charlie	Whitehaven
25.8.93	Green, Iyan	—
1.9.93	Richards, Craig	Bradford N.
7.9.93	Crompton, Martin	Wigan
20.9.93	Goodway, Andy	Leeds
27.9.93	Topping, Paul	Leigh
19.10.93	Parr, Chris	Swinton
22.10.93	Belle, Adrian	Rochdale H.
30.10.93	Booth, Craig	Featherstone R.
7.12.93	Ainge, Damian	Tweedheads, Aus.
20.12.93	Burns, Gary	—
22.12.93	Chrimes, David	Rochdale H.
4.2.94	Liddiard, Glen	North Sydney, Aus.
8.2.94	Leaff, James	Ashton-on-Mersey RU
1.3.94	Prescott, Michael	Wigan St. Judes ARL

GREAT BRITAIN REGISTER
(40 players)

Albert Avery	(4)	1910-11
Charlie Bott	(1)	1966
Albert Brough	(2)	1924
Terry Clawson	(9)	1973-74
Alan Davies	(20)	1955-60
Evan Davies	(3)	1920
Terry Flanagan	(4)	1983-84
Des Foy	(3)	1984-85
Bernard Ganley	(3)	1957-58
Andy Goodway	(11)	1983-85
Billy Hall	(4)	1914
Herman Hilton	(7)	1920-21
David Hobbs	(2)	1987
Dave Holland	(4)	1914
Bob Irving	(8+3)	1967-72
Ken Jackson	(2)	1957
Ernest Knapman	(1)	1924
Syd Little	(10)	1956-58
Tom Llewellyn	(2)	1907
Jim Lomas	(2)	1911
Bill Longworth	(3)	1908
Les McIntyre	(1)	1963
Terry O'Grady	(5)	1954
Jack Oster	(1)	1929
Dave Parker	(2)	1964
Doug Phillips	(3)	1946
Frank Pitchford	(2)	1958-62
Tom Rees	(1)	1929
Sid Rix	(9)	1924-26
Bob Sloman	(5)	1928
Arthur Smith	(6)	1907-08
Ike Southward	(7)	1959-62
Les Thomas	(1)	1947
Derek Turner	(11)	1956-58
George Tyson	(4)	1907-08
Hugh Waddell	(4)	1988
Tommy White	(1)	1907
Charlie Winslade	(1)	1959
Alf Wood	(4)	1911-14
Mick Worrall	(3)	1984

Half back Martin Crompton, signed by Oldham from Wigan in September 1993, scoring eight tries in 21 appearances.

OLDHAM 1993-94 PLAYERS' SUMMARY

	(Date of Birth)	App	T	G	D	Pts	Previous club	Signed
Abram, Darren	(27.9.67)	30	20	11	—	102	Rochdale H.	19.2.93
Belle, Adrian	(23.11.70)	1	—	—	—	—	Rochdale H.	22.10.93
Bradbury, David	(16.3.72)	5+7	—	—	—	—	Leigh Miners ARL	15.8.91
Clarke, John	(3.3.74)	22	3	—	—	12	East Leeds ARL	1.5.93
Crompton, Martin	(29.9.69)	20+1	8	—	3	35	Wigan	7.9.93
Gibson, Wally	(5.4.67)	27+1	8	—	1	33	Huddersfield	25.9.92
Goodway, Andy	(2.6.61)	27+3	1	—	—	4	Leeds	20.9.93
Goulbourne, Alf	(23.6.75)	1	—	—	—	—	Isberg C. ARL	10.6.93
Green, Iyan	(21.4.72)	4+9	2	—	—	8	—	25.8.93
Groves, Paul	(27.5.65)	6	2	—	—	8	St. Helens	5.8.93
Heslop, Nigel	(4.12.63)	21+2	7	—	—	28	Orrell RU	18.2.93
Holden, Martin	(23.6.69)	1+1	—	—	—	—	Wigan St. Patricks ARL	14.6.93
Irwin, Shaun	(8.12.68)	26	8	—	—	32	Castleford	11.8.93
Jones, David	(7.12.67)	25+2	5	—	—	20	Wakefield T.	13.8.93
Kerry, Steve	(10.3.66)	14+5	2	12	3	35	Salford	2.10.92
Kuiti, Mike	(18.3.63)	32+1	5	—	—	20	Rochdale H.	11.8.93
Liddiard, Glen	(28.11.65)	10+1	4	4	1	25	Australia	4.2.94
Lindner, Bob	(10.11.62)	28+2	10	—	—	40	Australia	2.9.93
McAlister, Charlie	(17.3.63)	8+7	2	—	—	8	Whitehaven	1.9.93
McDermott, Barrie	(22.7.72)	10+1	1	—	—	4	Waterhead ARL	15.8.91
Meadows, Mark	(9.5.65)	2	—	—	—	—	Blackpool G.	14.8.92
Mitchell, Patrick	(26.1.73)	4	1	—	—	4	Saddleworth R. ARL	24.1.90
Olsen, Ben	(17.3.65)	1	—	—	—	—	London C.	14.8.92
Parr, Chris	(31.5.71)	4+1	—	—	—	—	Swinton	19.10.93
Ranson, Scott	(20.9.67)	29	12	—	—	48	Swinton	6.2.92
Richards, Craig	(27.1.70)	3+5	2	—	—	8	Bradford N.	1.9.93
Sherratt, Ian	(9.8.65)	29	—	—	—	—	Salford	8.11.91
Solomona, Se'e	(9.3.65)	10+3	1	—	—	4	Widnes	31.3.92
Stephenson, David	(6.10.72)	5	—	—	—	—	Queens Park ARL	3.2.92
Strett, Martin	(4.4.68)	5+1	1	8	—	20	Orrell RU	26.11.92
Topping, Paul	(18.9.65)	17+9	2	55	—	118	Leigh	27.9.93
Tupaea, Shane	(24.12.63)	15+6	—	—	—	—	Swinton	13.9.91
TOTALS								
32 players			107	90	8	616		

Representative appearances 1993-94
Solomona — New Zealand (2).

OLDHAM 1993-94 MATCH ANALYSIS

Date	Com-petition	H/A	Opponent	Rlt	Score	Tries	Goals	Atten-dance	Referee
29.8.93	SBC	A	Halifax	L	12-26	Groves, Heslop	Kerry, Topping	—	—
3.9.93	SBC	H	Bradford N.	L	20-24	Richards (2), Solomona	Strett (4)	4054	Ollerton
12.9.93	SBC	A	Hull K.R.	W	28-14	Irwin (2), Abram, Crompton, Groves	Topping (4)	—	—
19.9.93	SBC	H	Warrington	L	12-18	Crompton	Topping (4)	5755	Nicholson
26.9.93	SBC	H	Sheffield E.	L	15-22	Gibson, Lindner	Topping (3), Crompton (dg)	3476	Steele
3.10.93	SBC	A	Widnes	L	12-14	Clarke, Irwin	Strett (2)	—	—
10.10.93	SBC	H	Leeds	W	21-6	Kerry, McAlister, Ranson	Topping (3), Kerry (1,1dg)	5079	Morris
24.10.93	SBC	A	Hull	W	33-8	Abram, Kerry, Kuiti, Lindner, Ranson	Topping (6), Kerry (dg)	—	—
31.10.93	SBC	A	Wakefield T.	L	21-22	Ranson, Lindner, Topping	Topping (4), Kerry (dg)	—	—
7.11.93	SBC	A	Featherstone R.	L	24-30	Clarke, Gibson, Goodway, Irwin	Topping (4)	—	—
14.11.93	RT(2)	A	Highfield	W	26-8	Abram (2), Heslop, Kuiti, Strett	Topping (3)	—	—
21.11.93	SBC	H	St. Helens	L	2-12	—	Topping	5621	Whitfield
28.11.93	SBC	A	Wigan	L	12-38	Lindner, McAlister	Strett (2)	—	—
5.12.93	SBC	H	Leigh	W	42-6	Abram (4), Green (2), Kuiti, Ranson	Topping (5)	3316	Asquith
12.12.93	RT(3)	H	Wigan	L	8-16	McDermott	Topping (2)	6342	Holdsworth
19.12.93	SBC	H	Halifax	L	11-28	Abram, Jones	Topping, Crompton (dg)	4001	Whitfield
26.12.93	SBC	H	Salford	L	8-20	Jones	Topping (2)	4576	J. Smith
9.1.94	SBC	A	Bradford N.	L	16-48	Lindner (2), Gibson	Topping (2)	—	—
12.1.94	SBC	A	Castleford	L	16-34	Abram, Crompton, Ranson	Abram (2)	—	—
16.1.94	SBC	H	Hull K.R.	L	16-17	Gibson, Jones, Ranson	Abram (2)	2889	Whitfield
23.1.94	SBC	A	Warrington	L	6-23	Abram	Kerry	—	—
30.1.94	CC(4)	A	Hunslet	W	30-20	Heslop (2), Jones, Mitchell, Ranson	Kerry (5)	—	—
6.2.94	SBC	A	Sheffield E.	L	14-28	Abram (2), Liddiard	Kerry	—	—
13.2.94	CC(5)	A	Doncaster	L	0-20	—	—	—	—
20.2.94	SBC	H	Widnes	W	22-12	Abram, Irwin, Jones, Ranson	Liddiard (3)	2962	Ollerton
6.3.94	SBC	A	Leeds	L	22-26	Abram, Crompton, Irwin, Lindner, Topping	Abram	—	—
13.3.94	SBC	H	Hull	W	19-12	Crompton (2), Kuiti, Ranson	Topping, Crompton (dg)	2749	Morris
20.3.94	SBC	H	Wakefield T.	D	20-20	Clarke, Crompton, Kuiti, Liddiard	Abram, Liddiard	3718	Cummings
27.3.94	SBC	H	Featherstone R.	W	22-8	Abram, Gibson, Lindner, Ranson	Topping (3)	3893	Morris
1.4.94	SBC	A	Salford	W	26-23	Liddiard (2), Ranson (2), Lindner	Topping (3)	—	—
4.4.94	SBC	H	Castleford	L	10-28	Abram	Kerry (2), Abram	4139	J. Smith
10.4.94	SBC	A	Leigh	W	34-8	Gibson (3), Abram, Crompton, Heslop, Irwin	Abram (3)	—	—
17.4.94	SBC	A	St. Helens	W	30-26	Heslop (2), Abram, Irwin, Lindner	Topping (3), Kerry, Gibson (dg), Liddiard (dg)	—	—
24.4.94	SBC	H	Wigan	L	6-50	Abram	Abram	8187	Atkin

ROCHDALE HORNETS

Australian Peter Regan, sacked as Hornets' coach in October 1993 after a 10-month stint.

Ground: Spotland (0706-48004)
First Season: 1895-96
Nickname: Hornets
Chairman: Peter Rush
Secretary: Linda Connolly
Honours: **Challenge Cup** Winners, 1921-22
Regal Trophy Beaten finalists, 1973-74
Lancashire Cup Winners, 1911-12, 1914-15, 1918-19
Beaten finalists, 1912-13, 1919-20, 1965-66, 1991-92
Lancashire League Winners, 1918-19
BBC-2 Floodlit Trophy Beaten finalists, 1971-72

RECORDS

Match

Goals: 14 by Steve Turner v. Runcorn H., 5 Nov 1989
Tries: 5 by Jack Corsi v. Barrow, 31 Dec 1921
Jack Corsi v. Broughton Moor, 25 Feb 1922
Jack Williams v. St. Helens, 4 Apr 1933
Norman Brelsford v. Whitehaven, 3 Sep 1972
Points: 32 by Steve Turner v. Runcorn H., 5 Nov 1989
Steve Turner v. Blackpool G., 31 Oct 1993

Season

Goals: 115 by Kevin Harcombe, 1985-86
Tries: 30 by Jack Williams, 1934-35
Points: 276 by Steve Gartland, 1992-93

Career

Goals: 741 by Walter Gowers, 1922-46
Tries: 103 by Jack Williams, 1931-37
Points: 1,497 by Walter Gowers, 1922-46
Appearances: 456 by Walter Gowers, 1922-46

Highest score: 92-0 v. Runcorn H., 5 Nov 1989
Highest against: 79-2 at Hull, 7 Apr 1921
Attendance: 8,150 v. Oldham (Div. 2), 26 Dec 1989 — at Spotland
26,664 v. Oldham (RL Cup), 25 Mar 1922 — at Athletic Grounds

COACHING REGISTER

● **Since 1974-75**

Frank Myler	May 71 - Oct 74
Graham Starkey	Oct 74 - Nov 75
Henry Delooze	Nov 75 - Nov 76
Kel Coslett	Nov 76 - Aug 79
Paul Longstaff	Sep 79 - May 81
Terry Fogerty	May 81 - Jan 82
Dick Bonser	Jan 82 - May 82
Bill Kirkbride	June 82 - Sep 84
Charlie Birdsall	Sep 84 - Apr 86
Eric Fitzsimons	June 86 - June 87
Eric Hughes	June 87 - June 88
Jim Crellin	June 88 - June 89
Allan Agar	July 89 - Jan 91
Neil Holding	Jan 91 - Apr 91
Stan Gittins	Apr 91 - Jan 93
Peter Regan	Jan 93 - Oct 93
Steve Gibson	Oct 93 -

GREAT BRITAIN REGISTER

(8 players)

Johnie Baxter	(1)	1907
Jack Bennett	(6)	1924
Joe Bowers	(1)	1920
Terry Fogerty	(1)	1974
Ernest Jones	(4)	1920
Malcolm Price	(2)	1967
Jack Robinson	(2)	1914
Tommy Woods	(2)	1911

1993-94 SIGNINGS REGISTER

Signed	Player	Club From
22.7.93	Harte, Joseph	Heywood ARL
22.7.93	Seabrook, Tony	U.G.B. ARL
26.7.93	Partington, Carl	Swinton
29.7.93	Bates, Ian	Oldham
29.7.93	Hourigan, Paul	Oldham
12.8.93	Pitt, Darren	ARL
13.8.93	Diggle, Craig	Mayfield ARL
13.8.93	Heaton, Graham	Milnrow ARL
27.8.93	*Booth, John	Highfield
3.9.93	Cullen, Brett	Wests, Aus.
3.9.93	Harmer, David	Wentworthville, Aus.
13.9.93	*Clark, Nathan	Oldham
16.9.93	Smith, Michael	ARL
24.9.93	Oldham, Michael	ARL
5.10.93	Gibson, Steve	Salford
5.10.93	Cassidy, Frank	Salford
11.10.93	Cannon, Glen	Aus.
24.11.93	*Waddell, Hugh	Sheffield E.
30.11.93	Ratu, Michael	Smallbridge ARL
17.12.93	Pugsley, Stuart	Whitehaven
17.12.93	Strett, Martin	Oldham
7.1.94	Miller, Vincent	Fitton Hill ARL
28.1.94	Fell, David	Salford
24.3.94	Shuttleworth, Ian	Waterhead ARL
1.4.94	Churm, Chris	Oldham St. A. ARL

Rochdale Hornets' Australian forward Cavill Heugh powers into the heart of the Dewsbury defence in the 1993-94 clash at Spotland.
Photo: Rochdale Observer.

ROCHDALE HORNETS 1993-94 PLAYERS' SUMMARY

	(Date of Birth)	App	T	G	D	Pts	Previous club	Signed
Bamber, Simon	(3.2.63)	13+1	—	—	—	—	Trafford B.	8.12.88
Bates, Ian	(2.3.68)	18+11	7	—	—	28	Oldham	29.7.93
Brown, Colin	(17.6.71)	9+1	1	—	2	6	Skirlaugh ARL	11.6.92
Cannon, Glen	(8.12.71)	14+3		—	—	16	Australia	11.10.93
Cassidy, Frank	(10.6.66)	2+1	—	—	—	—	Salford	5.10.93
Chrimes, David	(16.12.69)	6+2	1	—	—	4	Mayfield ARL	10.3.93
Churm, Chris	(20.9.66)	1+1	—	—	—	—	Oldham St. Annes ARL	1.4.94
Cullen, Brett	(25.4.70)	17+1	6	—	—	24	Australia	3.9.93
Eccles, Cliff	(4.9.67)	28+3	6	—	—	24	Trafford B.	19.9.91
Fell, David	(25.4.66)	17+2	4	—	—	16	Salford	28.1.94
Gartland, Steve	(3.10.70)	26+2	18	20	5	117	Oldham St. Annes ARL	17.8.90
Gibson, Steve	(23.11.62)	26	11	—	—	44	Salford	5.10.93
Gotts, Richard	(25.3.71)	0+1	—	—	—	—	Skirlaugh ARL	11.6.92
Green, Jason	(19.1.72)	32	15	—	—	60	Wigan St. Patricks ARL	23.9.92
Hall, Robert	(13.5.71)	16+4	2	—	—	8	Oldham St. Annes ARL	8.1.90
Harmer, David	(15.10.71)	13+5	1	—	—	4	Australia	3.9.93
Heugh, Cavill	(31.8.62)	31+1	6	—	—	24	Leeds	25.8.92
Hourigan, Paul	(15.10.71)	6	2	21	—	50	Oldham	29.7.93
Marriott, Karl	(21.11.69)	24+4	7	—	1	29	Mayfield ARL	17.8.89
Miller, Vincent	(1.3.64)	14+5	10	—	—	40	Fitton Hill ARL	7.1.94
O'Keefe, Paul	(28.6.71)	31+1	19	—	—	76	—	15.12.91
Pachniuk, Richard	(24.3.71)	35	6	3	—	30	Oldham	19.2.93
Partington, Carl	(1.8.65)	2	—	—	—	—	Swinton	26.7.93
Pitt, Darren	(14.5.71)	3+2	—	—	—	—	Widnes Tigers ARL	17.4.90
Pugsley, Stuart	(14.11.67)	14+1	1	—	—	4	Leigh	17.12.93
Ratu, Emon	(30.10.65)	15+10	6	1	—	26	Swinton	27.7.93
Reddican, Mal	(21.11.68)	3+1	—	—	—	—	Langworthy ARL	26.12.91
Stewart, Mike	(16.1.66)	7+1	2	—	—	8	Blackpool G.	29.7.92
Strett, Martin	(4.4.68)	16	9	53	—	142	Oldham	18.1.93
Turner, Steve	(5.12.61)	8+4	3	22	2	58	Swinton	22.2.88
Waddell, Hugh	(1.9.59)	3	—	—	—	—	Sheffield E.	24.11.93
Warburton, Steve	(6.2.69)	5	2	—	—	8	Oldham	19.3.93
Webster, David	(20.10.68)	1	—	—	—	—	Widnes St. Maries ARL	20.4.91
Worrall, Mick	(22.3.62)	9+3	1	—	—	4	Leeds	26.3.93
TOTALS								
34 players			150	120	10	850		

ROCHDALE HORNETS 1993-94 MATCH ANALYSIS

Date	Com-petition	H/A	Opponent	Rlt	Score	Tries	Goals	Atten-dance	Referee
29.8.93	SD	H	Highfield	W	64-8	Green (3), Heugh (2), O'Keefe (2), Hall (2), Bates, Brown, Ratu	Hourigan (8)	900	McGregor
5.9.93	SD	A	Huddersfield	L	8-30	Turner	Hourigan (2)	—	—
12.9.93	SD	H	Keighley C.	L	14-16	Heugh (2)	Hourigan (2), Brown (2dg)	1888	R. Connolly
19.9.93	SD	A	Batley	L	17-26	Cullen, Green, Pachniuk	Turner (2,1dg)	—	—
26.9.93	SD	H	Ryedale-York	L	18-26	Green (2), Ratu	Hourigan (2), Turner	900	Cross
3.10.93	SD	H	Workington T.	L	22-28	Green (2), Hourigan (2)	Hourigan (3)	1240	Atkin
10.10.93	SD	A	Bramley	W	28-10	Bates, Cullen, Gartland, Gibson, O'Keefe	Hourigan (4)	—	—
24.10.93	SD	A	Dewsbury	W	26-20	Bates (2), Gibson (2), Cannon	Pachniuk (3)	—	—
31.10.93	RT(1)	H	Blackpool G.	W	80-10	Eccles (3), Gibson (2), Turner (2), Warburton (2), Chrimes, Green, Marriott, O'Keefe, Pachniuk	Turner (12)	863	Whitelam
7.11.93	SD	H	Hunslet	L	15-20	Cullen, Green, O'Keefe	Turner (1,1dg)	751	Crashley
14.11.93	RT(2)	H	Bramley	L	10-11	O'Keefe, Ratu	Turner	730	Steele
21.11.93	SD	A	Barrow	L	14-28	Cannon, Gibson, Ratu	Ratu	—	—
28.11.93	SD	H	Whitehaven	W	18-14	Gartland, Green, Ratu	Gartland (3)	926	Wood
5.12.93	SD	A	Doncaster	L	12-34	Gibson, O'Keefe	Gartland (2)	—	—
19.12.93	SD	A	Highfield	W	22-6	Marriott (3), Strett	Strett (3)	—	—
2.1.94	SD	H	London C.	W	15-8	Marriott, Stewart, Strett	Strett, Gartland (dg)	891	Atkin
5.1.94	SD	H	Carlisle	W	34-18	Gartland (2), Strett (2), Gibson	Strett (7)	656	Cross
9.1.94	SD	H	Huddersfield	W	42-8	Gartland (2), O'Keefe (2), Gibson, Ratu, Strett	Strett (7)	1296	Cummings
16.1.94	CC(3)	H	Millom	W	32-0	Bates, Cannon, Miller, O'Keefe, Pachniuk, Worrall	Strett (4)	710	Carter
19.1.94	SD	A	Swinton	W	13-8	Green, O'Keefe	Strett (2), Gartland (dg)	—	—
23.1.94	SD	A	Keighley C.	L	12-40	Bates, Strett	Strett (2)	—	—
30.1.94	CC(4)	H	Leeds	L	18-40	O'Keefe (3), Miller	Gartland	3435	Holdsworth
6.2.94	SD	H	Batley	W	24-12	Heugh, Marriott, Strett	Strett (6)	912	Burke
27.2.94	SD	A	Workington T.	W	37-12	Gartland (2), Bates, Heugh, Miller, Pachniuk	Strett (6), Gartland (dg)	—	—
6.3.94	SD	H	Bramley	W	54-10	Gartland (3), O'Keefe (3), Cannon, Eccles, Marriott, Strett	Strett (7)	640	Bates
13.3.94	SD	H	Dewsbury	L	12-20	Eccles, Miller, Pugsley	—	1088	Gilmour
16.3.94	SD	A	Ryedale-York	L	8-20	Strett	Strett (2)	—	—
20.3.94	SD	A	Hunslet	W	33-10	Miller (3), Fell (2), Harmer	Strett (2), Turner (2), Marriott (dg)	—	—
27.3.94	SD	H	Barrow	W	24-14	Green (2), Gartland Miller	Turner (3), Gartland	1008	Oddy
1.4.94	SD	H	Swinton	W	38-26	Fell (2), Cullen, Eccles, Gartland, Green, Miller	Gartland (5)	1014	Presley
4.4.94	SD	A	London C.	L	10-28	Gartland, Miller	Gartland	—	—
10.4.94	SD	A	Carlisle	W	32-25	Gartland (2), Gibson (2), Cullen, Pachniuk	Gartland (4)	—	—
17.4.94	SD	H	Doncaster	W	20-2	Gartland, O'Keefe, Stewart	Gartland (3,2dg)	1991	Bates
24.4.94	SD	A	Whitehaven	W	18-5	Gartland, O'Keefe, Pachniuk	Strett (3)	—	—
8.5.94	SDP(1)	A	Workington T.	L	6-50	Cullen	Strett	—	—

RYEDALE-YORK

Ground: Ryedale Stadium (0904-634636)
First Season: 1901-02 as York. Moved and became
Ryedale-York at start of 1989-90
Nickname: Wasps
Chairman: John Stabler
Honours: **Division Two** Champions, 1980-81
Challenge Cup Beaten finalists,
1930-31
Yorkshire Cup Winners, 1922-23,
1933-34, 1936-37
Beaten finalists, 1935-36, 1957-58,
1978-79

RECORDS
Match
Goals: 12 by Gary Pearce at Nottingham C.,
4 Oct 1992
Tries: 6 by Roy Hardgrave v. Bramley,
5 Jan 1935
David Kettlestring at Keighley,
11 Mar 1990
Points: 28 by Gary Pearce at Nottingham C.,
4 Oct 1992
Season
Goals: 146 by Vic Yorke, 1957-58
Tries: 35 by John Crossley, 1980-81
Points: 318 by Graham Steadman, 1984-85
Career
Goals: 1,060 by Vic Yorke, 1954-67
Tries: 167 by Peter Foster, 1955-67
Points: 2,159 by Vic Yorke, 1954-67
Appearances: 449 by Willie Hargreaves, 1952-65
Highest score: 84-0 at Nottingham C., 4 Oct 1992
Highest against: 75-3 at Warrington, 23 Sep 1950
Attendance: 14,689 v. Swinton (RL Cup),
10 Feb 1934 — at Clarence Street
4,977 v. Halifax (Div. 2),
5 Jan 1990 — at Ryedale Stadium

COACHING REGISTER
● **Since 1974-75**
Keith Goulding	Nov 73 - Sep 74
Gary Cooper	Dec 74 - Sep 76
Mal Dixon	Sep 76 - Dec 78
Paul Daley	Jan 79 - May 79
David Doyle-Davidson	July 79 - July 80

Bill Kirkbride	Aug 80 - Apr 82
Alan Hardisty	May 82 - Jan 83
Phil Lowe	Mar 83 - Mar 87
Danny Sheehan	Mar 87 - Apr 88
Gary Stephens	Apr 88 - June 91
Derek Foster	July 91 - Nov 92
Steve Crooks	Nov 92 - May 94

GREAT BRITAIN REGISTER
(7 players)
Edgar Dawson	(1)	1956
Harry Field	(3)	1936
Geoff Smith	(3)	1963-64
Jeff Stevenson	(4)	1959-60
Mick Sullivan	(1)	1963
Basil Watts	(5)	1954-55
Les White	(4)	1946

1993-94 SIGNINGS REGISTER
Signed	Player	Club From
30.6.93	Sharp, Tim	Featherstone R.
1.7.93	Tichener, Lee	Bramley
9.8.93	Deakin, Leigh	Leeds
19.8.93	*Pagdin, Wayne	Castleford
20.8.93	Marsden, Lee	Hull
26.8.93	Thomas, Dean	Liverpool St. Helens RU
6.10.93	*Jackson, Darryl	Nottingham C.
6.10.93	*Simpson, Anthony	Sheffield E.
20.10.93	Wade, Cameron	St. George, Aus.
28.10.93	Lyons, Mark	St. George, Aus.
22.11.93	*Brook, David	Hunslet
10.12.93	Hayes, Brad	Doncaster
3.2.94	Brown, Colin	Rochdale H.
31.3.94	*Mowthorpe, Lee	Sheffield E.
5.4.94	*Precious, Andrew	Hunslet

Steve Crooks, coach at Ryedale Stadium
from November 1992 to May 1994.

RYEDALE-YORK 1993-94 PLAYERS' SUMMARY

	(Date of Birth)	App	T	G	D	Pts	Previous club	Signed
Atkins, Gary	(12.10.66)	34	16	—	—	64	Castleford	31.7.92
Brook, David	(4.2.71)	1	—	—	—	—	Hunslet	22.11.93
Brown, Colin	(17.6.71)	0+1	—	—	—	—	Rochdale H.	3.2.94
Close, David	(7.5.66)	16	4	—	5	21	Sheffield E.	20.6.92
Craven, Steve	(9.4.72)	34	8	—	—	32	York All Blacks ARL	28.2.90
Crooks, Steve	(10.5.58)	5	—	—	1	1	Hull	28.8.93
Deakin, Leigh	(27.12.72)	10+2	11	—	—	44	Leeds	9.8.93
Dobson, Steve	(27.4.63)	19	3	—	5	17	Sheffield E.	23.7.90
Fellows, Darren	(26.9.72)	0+2	—	—	—	—	Middleton ARL	23.7.90
Hammerton, Chris	(21.11.63)	0+1	—	—	—	—	Heworth ARL	28.8.87
Hayes, Brad	(22.4.67)	0+1	—	—	—	—	Doncaster	10.12.93
Hayes, Richard	(21.2.70)	33	—	—	—	—	York All Blacks ARL	13.1.89
Hopcutt, Chris	(6.12.69)	15+1	6	—	1	25	Scarborough P.	12.11.91
Horton, Stuart	(10.9.63)	35	3	—	1	13	Castleford	27.8.87
Hutchinson, Darren	(13.10.67)	13+5	5	—	—	20	—	—
Hutchinson, Paul	(13.1.71)	29+2	10	—	—	40	Redhill ARL	19.5.89
Jackson, Darryl	(6.2.71)	12+9	—	—	—	—	Nottingham C.	6.10.93
Judge, Chris	(7.11.72)	1+1	—	—	—	—	Heworth ARL	11.9.92
Kettlestring, David	(18.11.67)	34	16	—	—	64	York All Blacks ARL	8.1.90
Laws, Mark	(26.4.71)	0+1	1	—	—	4	Newland ARL	27.3.90
Lockwood, Peter	(15.1.64)	9+4	2	22	—	52	Acorn ARL	14.1.92
Lydiat, John	(10.1.60)	0+2	—	—	—	—	Hull K.R.	30.7.92
Lyons, Mark	(31.3.65)	8+5	6	—	—	24	Australia	28.10.93
McKelvie, Danny	(10.10.69)	8	—	—	—	—	Hunslet	—
Marsden, Lee	(28.1.68)	19+3	2	—	—	8	Hull	20.8.93
Pallister, Alan	(4.12.70)	0+3	—	—	—	—	York All Blacks ARL	1.11.90
Paver, Ian	(8.3.63)	0+1	—	—	—	—	Heworth ARL	2.11.90
Pearce, Gary	(11.11.60)	0+1	—	—	—	—	Scarborough P.	9.6.92
Precious, Andrew	(10.10.70)	2+1	1	6	—	16	Hunslet	5.4.94
Pryce, Steve	(12.5.69)	5+1	1	—	—	4	West Bowling ARL	23.7.90
Ramsden, Mick	(13.11.71)	17+9	8	—	—	32	York Civil Serv. ARL	1.6.91
Sharp, Tim	(20.2.70)	29	13	—	—	52	Featherstone R.	30.6.93
Simpson, Anthony	(12.3.69)	11	2	—	—	8	Sheffield E.	6.10.93
Sullivan, Graham	(27.1.67)	21+4	10	69	—	178	Punch Bowl ARL	27.7.87
Thomas, Dean	(10.5.66)	9+2	—	—	—	—	Liverpool St. H. RU	26.8.93
Tichener, Lee	(5.8.71)	0+1	—	—	—	—	Bramley	1.7.93
Wade, Cameron	(28.9.69)	26+2	16	12	1	89	Australia	20.10.93
White, Paul	(5.11.64)	0+3	—	—	—	—	—	6.11.86
TOTALS								
38 players			144	109	14	808		

RYEDALE-YORK 1993-94 MATCH ANALYSIS

Date	Com-petition	H/A	Opponent	Rlt	Score	Tries	Goals	Atten-dance	Referee
29.8.93	SD	H	Swinton	W	28-14	Atkins, Hopcutt, Kettlestring, Ramsden	Sullivan (6)	1327	Atkin
5.9.93	SD	A	Whitehaven	D	14-14	Deakin, Sharp	Sullivan (3)	—	—
12.9.93	SD	H	Batley	L	19-22	Hopcutt (2), P. Hutchinson	Sullivan (3), Close (dg)	1383	Cummings
19.9.93	SD	A	Highfield	W	24-10	Deakin (2), Close, Craven, Sullivan	Sullivan (2)	—	
26.9.93	SD	A	Rochdale H.	W	26-18	Sharp (2), Deakin, Hopcutt, Kettlestring	Sullivan (3)	—	—
3.10.93	SD	H	Hunslet	W	36-12	Deakin (3), Atkins (2), P. Hutchinson	Sullivan (5), Close (dg), Crooks (dg)	1366	Carter
10.10.93	SD	A	London C.	L	20-24	Atkins (2), D. Hutchinson, Sharp	Sullivan (2)	—	—
24.10.93	SD	H	Workington T.	W	29-12	Ramsden (3), Deakin, P. Hutchinson	Sullivan (3), Wade, Close (dg)	1897	Presley
31.10.93	RT(1)	H	Hemel Hempstead	W	66-14	Sharp (3), Deakin (2), P. Hutchinson (2), Close, Kettlestring, Laws, Pryce, Sullivan	Sullivan (9)	835	Burke
7.11.93	SD	A	Bramley	W	32-20	Craven, Horton, Lyons, Ramsden, Wade	Sullivan (6)	—	—
14.11.93	RT(2)	H	Workington T.	W	12-11	Sharp	Sullivan (3), Close (2dg)	1456	Atkin
21.11.93	SD	H	Dewsbury	L	10-27	Sullivan, Wade	Sullivan	1423	Gilmour
28.11.93	SD	H	Barrow	W	29-10	Atkins (2), Horton, Ramsden, Sharp	Sullivan (4), Wade (dg)	1017	Carter
5.12.93	SD	A	Carlisle	W	32-26	Wade (2), Sharp (2), Close, Marsden	Sullivan (4)	—	—
8.12.93	SD	H	Huddersfield	L	0-8	—	—	1271	Wood
12.12.93	RT(3)	H	London C.	L	10-42	Atkins, Close	Sullivan	741	Asquith
19.12.93	SD	A	Swinton	L	10-29	Sullivan, Wade	Sullivan	—	—
2.1.94	SD	H	Keighley C.	W	11-4	Hopcutt, Lockwood	Dobson (dg), Hopcutt (dg), Horton (dg)	2451	Galtress
9.1.94	SD	H	Whitehaven	W	34-4	Atkins, Craven, Hopcutt, P. Hutchinson, Kettlestring, Lyons	Lockwood (5)	1162	Atkin
16.1.94	CC(3)	H	Leigh M.W.	W	52-2	Atkins (2), Kettlestring (2), Wade (2), Dobson, P. Hutchinson, Lyons, Sullivan	Lockwood (4), Sullivan, Wade	718	Redfearn
19.1.94	SD	A	Doncaster	L	8-20	Atkins, Kettlestring	—	—	—
23.1.94	SD	A	Batley	L	14-21	Craven, Lyons, Wade	Lockwood	—	—
30.1.94	CC(4)	A	Hull K.R.	L	6-16	Wade	Lockwood	—	—
6.2.94	SD	H	Highfield	W	40-16	P. Hutchinson (2), Horton, Kettlestring, Marsden, Sharp, Wade	Lockwood (6)	916	Carter
27.2.94	SD	A	Hunslet	W	23-13	Dobson, Kettlestring, Simpson	Lockwood (5), Dobson (dg)	—	—
6.3.94	SD	H	London C.	L	14-22	Lyons, Wade	Sullivan (2), Wade	1023	Steele
13.3.94	SD	A	Workington T.	L	12-40	Atkins, Lockwood, Lyons	—	—	—
16.3.94	SD	H	Rochdale H.	W	20-8	D. Hutchinson, Kettlestring, Dobson, Craven	Wade, Dobson (2dg)	622	McGregor
20.3.94	SD	H	Bramley	W	50-0	Atkins (3), Kettlestring (2), Craven, Simpson, Sullivan, Wade	Wade (7)	836	Gilmour
27.3.94	SD	A	Dewsbury	W	16-12	P. Hutchinson, D. Hutchinson, Kettlestring	Sullivan, Wade	—	—
1.4.94	SD	H	Doncaster	L	16-23	Craven (2), Wade	Sullivan (2)	2037	Tennant

(Continued)

103

CLUBS

Date	Competition	H/A	Opponent	Rlt	Score	Tries	Goals	Attendance	Referee
4.4.94	SD	A	Keighley C.	L	16-18	Wade (2), Kettlestring	Sullivan (2)	—	—
10.4.94	SD	A	Huddersfield	W	23-12	Sullivan (2), Kettlestring, Sharp	Sullivan (3), Dobson (dg)	—	—
17.4.94	SD	H	Carlisle	W	34-22	D. Hutchinson (2), Sullivan (2), Kettlestring, Ramsden	Precious (3), Sullivan (2)	948	Presley
24.4.94	SD	A	Barrow	L	22-35	Deakin, Precious, Ramsden, Wade	Precious (3)	—	—

Ripping time at Ryedale Stadium as Ryedale-York's Richard Hayes and Leigh Deakin (right) tackle Swinton's Welsh international Paul Kennett during their August 1993 clash. Photo: Yorkshire Evening Press.

ST. HELENS

Ground: Knowsley Road (0744-23697)
First Season: 1895-96
Nickname: Saints
Chairman: Eric Ashton
Secretary: Geoff Sutcliffe
Honours: **Championship** Winners, 1931-32, 1952-53, 1958-59, 1965-66, 1969-70, 1970-71
Beaten finalists, 1964-65, 1966-67, 1971-72
League Leaders Trophy Winners, 1964-65, 1965-66
Club Championship (Merit Table) Beaten finalists, 1973-74
Division One Champions, 1974-75
Challenge Cup Winners, 1955-56, 1960-61, 1965-66, 1971-72, 1975-76
Beaten finalists, 1896-97, 1914-15, 1929-30, 1952-53, 1977-78, 1986-87, 1988-89, 1990-91
Regal Trophy Winners, 1987-88
Premiership Winners, 1975-76, 1976-77, 1984-85, 1992-93
Beaten finalists, 1974-75, 1987-88, 1991-92
Lancashire Cup Winners, 1926-27, 1953-54, 1960-61, 1961-62, 1962-63, 1963-64, 1964-65, 1967-68, 1968-69, 1984-85, 1991-92
Beaten finalists, 1932-33, 1952-53, 1956-57, 1958-59, 1959-60, 1970-71, 1982-83, 1992-93
Lancashire League Winners, 1929-30, 1931-32, 1952-53, 1959-60, 1964-65, 1965-66, 1966-67, 1968-69
Western Division Championship Winners, 1963-64
Charity Shield Winners, 1992-93
BBC-2 Floodlit Trophy Winners, 1971-72, 1975-76
Beaten finalists, 1965-66, 1968-69, 1970-71, 1977-78, 1978-79

RECORDS

Match

Goals: 16 by Paul Loughlin v. Carlisle, 14 Sep 1986
Tries: 6 by Alf Ellaby v. Barrow, 5 Mar 1932
         Steve Llewellyn v. Castleford, 3 Mar 1956
         Steve Llewellyn v. Liverpool C., 20 Aug 1956
         Tom Van Vollenhoven v. Wakefield T., 21 Dec 1957
         Tom Van Vollenhoven v. Blackpool B., 23 Apr 1962
         Frank Myler v. Maryport, 1 Sep 1969
         Shane Cooper v. Hull, 17 Feb 1988
Points: 40 by Paul Loughlin v. Carlisle, 14 Sep 1986

Season

Goals: 214 by Kel Coslett, 1971-72
Tries: 62 by Tom Van Vollenhoven, 1958-59
Points: 452 by Kel Coslett, 1971-72

Career

Goals: 1,639 by Kel Coslett, 1961-76
Tries: 392 by Tom Van Vollenhoven, 1957-68
Points: 3,413 by Kel Coslett, 1961-76
Appearances: 519+12 by Kel Coslett, 1961-76
Highest score: 112-0 v. Carlisle, 14 Sep 1986
Highest against: 78-3 at Warrington, 12 Apr 1909
Attendance: 35,695 v. Wigan (League), 26 Dec 1949

COACHING REGISTER
● **Since 1974-75**

Eric Ashton	May 74 - May 80
Kel Coslett	June 80 - May 82
Billy Benyon	May 82 - Nov 85
Alex Murphy	Nov 85 - Jan 90
Mike McClennan	Feb 90 - Dec 93
Eric Hughes	Jan 94 -

GREAT BRITAIN REGISTER
(53 players)

Chris Arkwright	(+2)	1985
Len Aston	(3)	1947
Billy Benyon	(5+1)	1971-72
Tommy Bishop	(15)	1966-69
Frank Carlton	(1)	1958
Eric Chisnall	(4)	1974
Gary Connolly	(7+3)	1991-93
Eddie Cunningham	(1)	1978
Rob Dagnall	(4)	1961-65
David Eckersley	(2+2)	1973-74
Alf Ellaby	(13)	1928-33
Les Fairclough	(6)	1926-29
John Fieldhouse	(1)	1986
Alec Fildes	(4)	1932
Alf Frodsham	(3)	1928-29
Peter Gorley	(2+1)	1980-81
Doug Greenall	(6)	1951-54
Jonathan Griffiths	(1)	1992
Paul Groves	(1)	1987
Roy Haggerty	(2)	1987
Mervyn Hicks	(1)	1965
Neil Holding	(4)	1984
Dick Huddart	(12)	1959-63
Alan Hunte	(4)	1992-93
Les Jones	(1)	1971
Chris Joynt	(4+1)	1993-94
Tony Karalius	(4+1)	1971-72
Vince Karalius	(10)	1958-61
Ken Kelly	(2)	1972
Barry Ledger	(2)	1985-86
Paul Loughlin	(14+1)	1988-92
Stan McCormick	(1)	1948
Tom McKinney	(1)	1957
John Mantle	(13)	1966-73
Roy Mathias	(1)	1979
Glyn Moses	(9)	1955-57
Alex Murphy	(26)	1958-66
Frank Myler	(9)	1970
George Nicholls	(22)	1973-79
Sonny Nickle	(1+4)	1992-93
Harry Pinner	(5+1)	1980-86
Andy Platt	(4+3)	1985-88
Alan Prescott	(28)	1951-58
Austin Rhodes	(4)	1957-61
Jim Stott	(1)	1947
Anthony Sullivan	(1)	1991
Mick Sullivan	(10)	1961-62
Jim Tembey	(2)	1963-64
Abe Terry	(10)	1958-61
John Walsh	(4+1)	1972
Kevin Ward	(1+2)	1990-92
John Warlow	(3+1)	1964-68
Cliff Watson	(29+1)	1963-71

1993-94 SIGNINGS REGISTER

Signed	Player	Club From
23.6.93	Poynton, Philip	Thatto Heath ARL
1.7.93	Arkwright, James	Leigh Miners ARL
29.7.93	Fogerty, Adam	Halifax
2.8.93	Martyn, Tommy	Oldham
10.8.93	Pickavance, Ian	Swinton
10.8.93	Haigh, Andrew	Crosfields ARL
27.8.93	Devine, Nicholas	Crosfields ARL
23.9.93	Dannatt, Andy	Hull
28.10.93	Cunningham, Keiron	—
10.11.93	*Hill, David	Leigh
1.12.93	Newall, Chris	Wigan St. Patricks ARL
7.12.93	Walker, Martin	Leigh Miners ARL
7.12.93	Waring, Philip	Eccles ARL
7.12.93	Bateman, Matthew	Leigh Miners ARL
8.1.94	Mathison, Paul	St. Helens Academy
9.1.94	Leuila, Peaufai	Tonga RU
26.3.94	O'Loughlin, Kevin	—
30.3.94	Leatham, Andrew	Crosfields ARL
31.3.94	*Marsh, Paul	Leigh
2.4.94	Anderson, Paul	St. Helens Academy
15.4.94	Arnold, Danny	St. Helens Academy
18.4.94	Gibbs, Scott	Swansea RU

Heroic Alan Prescott, capped 28 times for Great Britain during a seven-year Test career with St. Helens.

ST. HELENS 1993-94 PLAYERS' SUMMARY

	(Date of Birth)	App	T	G	D	Pts	Previous club	Signed
Atherton, Peter	(29.12.70)	0+2	—	—	—	—	Widnes Tigers ARL	12.7.89
Casey, Sean	(9.12.71)	3+2	3	—	—	12	Blackbrook ARL	16.12.91
Connor, Ian	(21.3.70)	0+1	—	—	—	—	Swinton	15.12.89
Cooper, Shane	(26.5.60)	35+3	5	—	—	20	New Zealand	13.10.87
Dannatt, Andy	(20.11.65)	27+3	2	—	—	8	Hull	23.9.93
Dwyer, Bernard	(20.4.67)	30+1	10	12	—	64	Hare & Hounds ARL	22.5.84
Fenlon, Tony	(2.2.72)	0+1	—	—	—	—	Widnes Tigers ARL	16.12.91
Fogerty, Adam	(6.3.69)	6+6	—	—	—	—	Halifax	29.7.93
Griffiths, Jonathan	(23.8.64)	24+2	7	—	—	28	Llanelli RU	22.5.89
Haigh, Andrew	(3.9.75)	5+2	—	—	—	—	Crosfields ARL	10.8.93
Harrison, John	(10.3.65)	5+4	—	—	—	—	Parkside ARL	30.12.87
Hodgkinson, Tommy	(15.4.70)	11+2	3	—	—	12	Blackbrook ARL	1.2.89
Hunte, Alan	(11.7.70)	24+1	16	—	—	64	Wakefield T.	3.3.89
Joynt, Chris	(7.12.71)	35+1	14	—	—	56	Oldham	2.9.92
Leuila, Peaufai	(24.10.69)	1+1	2	—	—	8	Tonga RU	9.1.94
Loughlin, Paul	(28.7.66)	29	3	58	—	128	St. Helens Colts	8.8.83
Lyon, David	(3.9.65)	20	8	3	—	38	Warrington	23.9.92
McAtee, John	(11.11.75)	2+1	—	—	—	—	Eccles ARL	9.10.92
Mann, George	(31.7.65)	24	6	—	—	24	New Zealand	31.7.89
Martyn, Tommy	(4.6.71)	22	16	28	9	129	Oldham	2.8.93
Morley, Chris	(22.9.73)	2+2	1	—	—	4	Woolston R. ARL	16.12.91
Neill, Jonathan	(19.12.68)	16+1	—	—	1	1	Kells ARL	27.7.87
Nickle, Sonny	(4.5.69)	19	4	—	—	16	Sheffield E.	3.7.91
O'Donnell, Gus	(11.12.70)	10+11	1	—	11	15	Wigan	1.7.92
Pickavance, Ian	(20.9.68)	21+4	6	—	—	24	Swinton	10.8.93
Prescott, Steve	(26.12.73)	13+2	3	29	—	70	Nutgrove ARL	3.11.92
Quirk, Les	(6.3.65)	4+2	—	—	—	—	Barrow	5.10.87
Riley, Mike	(20.11.70)	27+5	5	—	—	20	Widnes Tigers ARL	5.1.90
Roach, Jason	(2.5.71)	1+3	—	—	—	—	St. Helens Academy	22.5.89
Ropati, Tea	(7.9.65)	20+2	7	—	—	28	New Zealand	25.8.90
Sullivan, Anthony	(23.11.68)	31	23	—	—	92	Hull K.R.	29.4.91
Veivers, Phil	(25.5.64)	27+6	3	—	—	12	Australia	18.9.84
TOTALS								
32 players			148	130	21	873		

Representative appearances 1993-94

Joynt — Britain (4); Nickle — Britain (1+2); Sullivan — Wales (2); Griffiths — Wales (2, 1dg).

ST. HELENS 1993-94 MATCH ANALYSIS

Date	Com-petition	H/A	Opponent	Rlt	Score	Tries	Goals	Atten-dance	Referee
29.8.93	SBC	A	Hull K.R.	L	10-16	Ropati	Loughlin (2), O'Donnell (2dg)	—	—
5.9.93	SBC	H	Salford	W	22-14	Dwyer, Joynt, Sullivan	Martyn (4), Loughlin	7587	Whitfield
12.9.93	SBC	A	Warrington	L	10-17	Sullivan	Lyon, Martyn (1,2dg)	—	—
19.9.93	SBC	H	Leigh	W	34-16	Lyon (2), Griffiths, Nickle, Riley, Ropati	Martyn (5)	6372	Holdsworth
26.9.93	SBC	A	Castleford	W	35-18	Dwyer, Joynt, Mann, Nickle, Ropati, Veivers	Loughlin (5), O'Donnell (dg)	—	—
1.10.93	SBC	A	Featherstone R.	W	37-16	Hunte (3), Mann (2), Joynt, Lyon	Loughlin (4), O'Donnell (dg)	—	—
10.10.93	SBC	H	Wakefield T.	W	36-10	Lyon (2), Dwyer, Hunte, Loughlin, Veivers	Loughlin (6)	7660	J. Smith
20.10.93	Tour	H	New Zealand	L	8-14	Hunte, Riley	—	8165	J. Connolly
24.10.93	SBC	H	Sheffield E.	L	12-19	Lyon (2)	Lyon (2)	6199	Steele
7.11.93	SBC	H	Bradford N.	W	54-3	Sullivan (4), Cooper (2), Dwyer, Hunte, Joynt, O'Donnell	Loughlin (7)	8459	Ollerton
12.11.93	RT(2)	A	Dewsbury	W	20-6	Mann, Martyn, Sullivan	Loughlin (3), Martyn (dg), O'Donnell (dg)	—	—
17.11.93	SBC	A	Leeds	W	21-18	Dannatt, Riley, Sullivan	Martyn (4), O'Donnell (dg)	—	—
21.11.93	SBC	A	Oldham	W	12-2	Dannatt, Griffiths	Prescott, O'Donnell (2dg)	—	—
26.11.93	SBC	H	Halifax	D	16-16	Dwyer (2)	Prescott (4)	5614	Campbell
3.12.93	SBC	A	Hull	L	14-18	Prescott, Joynt	Prescott (3)	—	—
11.12.93	RT(3)	H	Warrington	L	8-16	Cooper, Nickle	—	5366	R. Smith
17.12.93	SBC	H	Hull K.R.	W	23-22	Griffiths, Joynt, Loughlin	Prescott (5), O'Donnell (dg)	3239	Nicholson
26.12.93	SBC	A	Wigan	L	8-40	Prescott	Prescott (2)	—	—
2.1.94	SBC	H	Widnes	W	24-16	Joynt, Lyon, Nickle	Loughlin (3), Prescott (2), Neill (dg), O'Donnell (dg)	10,219	Ollerton
12.1.94	SBC	A	Salford	L	2-34	—	Loughlin	—	—
16.1.94	SBC	H	Warrington	L	11-21	Casey (2)	Loughlin, O'Donnell (dg)	8762	J. Connolly
23.1.94	SBC	A	Leigh	L	4-21	Casey	—	—	—
30.1.94	CC(4)	A	Huddersfield	W	23-16	Griffiths, Joynt, Martyn, Sullivan	Loughlin (3), Martyn (dg)	—	—
6.2.94	SBC	H	Castleford	W	33-12	Griffiths (2), Martyn, Pickavance, Sullivan, Veivers	Loughlin (4), Martyn (dg)	7605	Cummings
13.2.94	CC(5)	A	Whitehaven	W	46-4	Joynt (3), Cooper, Hunte, Martyn, Pickavance, Riley, Ropati	Loughlin (5)	—	—
20.2.94	SBC	H	Featherstone R.	W	27-18	Hodgkinson (2), Joynt, Sullivan	Loughlin (5), Martyn (dg)	6902	Atkin
27.2.94	CC(6)	H	Doncaster	W	40-9	Martyn (2), Cooper, Griffiths, Hunte, Joynt, Sullivan	Loughlin (6)	8695	R. Smith
6.3.94	SBC	A	Wakefield T.	W	35-22	Sullivan (3), Hunte (2), Hodgkinson	Martyn (4,1dg), Loughlin	—	—
11.3.94	SBC	A	Sheffield E.	L	6-18	Loughlin	Loughlin	—	—
26.3.94	CC(SF)	N[1]	Leeds	L	8-20	Martyn	Martyn (2)	(20,771)	Holdsworth
1.4.94	SBC	H	Wigan	L	9-15	Dwyer	Martyn (2,1dg)	12,114	R. Smith
4.4.94	SBC	A	Widnes	L	17-20	Martyn (2), Sullivan	Martyn (2,1dg)	—	—
10.4.94	SBC	H	Hull	W	52-10	Martyn (3), Dwyer (2), Leuila (2), Mann, Sullivan	Prescott (7), Martyn	5199	Cummings
13.4.94	SBC	H	Leeds	W	68-0	Pickavance (3), Hunte (2), Ropati (2), Prescott, Martyn, Sullivan, Joynt, Riley, Mann	Prescott (5), Dwyer (3)	6106	R. Connolly
17.4.94	SBC	H	Oldham	L	26-30	Martyn (2), Dwyer, Hunte, Sullivan	Martyn (3)	6937	Cummings

Date	Com-petition	H/A	Opponent	Rlt	Score	Tries	Goals	Atten-dance	Referee
19.4.94	SBC	A	Bradford N.	L	16-18	Sullivan (2), Morley	Dwyer (2)	—	—
24.4.94	SBC	A	Halifax	L	30-37	Hunte (2), Sullivan (2), Ropati	Dwyer (5)	—	—
8.5.94	PT(1)	A	Wigan	L	16-34	Hunte, Martyn, Pickavance	Dwyer (2)	—	—

N[1] Wigan

St. Helens skipper Shane Cooper, 38 appearances in his seventh season at Knowsley Road.

SALFORD

Ground: The Willows (061-737-6363)
First Season: 1896-97
Nickname: Red Devils
Chairman: John Wilkinson
Chief
 Executive: Dave Tarry
Honours: **Championship** Winners, 1913-14,
 1932-33, 1936-37, 1938-39
 Beaten finalists, 1933-34
 Division One Champions, 1973-74,
 1975-76
 Division Two Champions, 1990-91
 Challenge Cup Winners, 1937-38
 Beaten finalists, 1899-1900,
 1901-02, 1902-03, 1905-06, 1938-39,
 1968-69
 Regal Trophy Beaten finalists,
 1972-73
 Premiership Beaten finalists,
 1975-76
 Second Division Premiership
 Winners, 1990-91
 Lancashire Cup Winners, 1931-32,
 1934-35, 1935-36, 1936-37, 1972-73
 Beaten finalists, 1929-30, 1938-39,
 1973-74, 1974-75, 1975-76, 1988-89,
 1990-91
 Lancashire League Winners,
 1932-33, 1933-34, 1934-35, 1936-37,
 1938-39
 BBC-2 Floodlit Trophy Winners,
 1974-75

RECORDS
Match
Goals: 13 by Gus Risman v. Bramley, 5 Apr 1933
 Gus Risman v. Broughton R.,
 18 May 1940
 David Watkins v. Keighley,
 7 Jan 1972
 Steve Rule v. Doncaster, 4 Sep 1981
Tries: 6 by Frank Miles v. Leeds, 5 Mar 1898
 Ernest Bone v. Goole, 29 Mar 1902
 Jack Hilton v. Leigh, 7 Oct 1939
Points: 39 by Jim Lomas v. Liverpool C.,
 2 Feb 1907

Season
Goals: 221 by David Watkins, 1972-73
Tries: 46 by Keith Fielding, 1973-74
Points: 493 by David Watkins, 1972-73
Career
Goals: 1,241 by David Watkins, 1967-79
Tries: 297 by Maurice Richards, 1969-83
Points: 2,907 by David Watkins, 1967-79
Appearances: 496+2 by Maurice Richards,
 1969-83
Highest score: 78-0 v. Liverpool C., 2 Feb 1907
Highest against: 70-6 at Wigan, 14 Mar 1993
Attendance: 26,470 v. Warrington (RL Cup),
 13 Feb 1937

COACHING REGISTER
● **Since 1974-75**

Les Bettinson	Dec 73 - Mar 77
Colin Dixon	Mar 77 - Jan 78
Stan McCormick	Feb 78 - Mar 78
Alex Murphy	May 78 - Nov 80
Kevin Ashcroft	Nov 80 - Mar 82
Alan McInnes	Mar 82 - May 82
Malcolm Aspey	May 82 - Oct 83
Mike Coulman	Oct 83 - May 84
Kevin Ashcroft	May 84 - Oct 89
Kevin Tamati	Oct 89 - July 93
Garry Jack	July 93 -

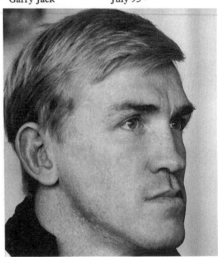

Former Australian Test full back Garry Jack, appointed coach of Salford in July 1993.

GREAT BRITAIN REGISTER

(28 players)

Bill Burgess	(1)	1969
Paul Charlton	(17+1)	1970-74
Mike Coulman	(2+1)	1971
George Curran	(6)	1946-48
Eddie Curzon	(1)	1910
Tom Danby	(3)	1950
Colin Dixon	(11+2)	1969-74
Alan Edwards	(7)	1936-37
Jack Feetham	(7)	1932-33
Keith Fielding	(3)	1974-77
Ken Gill	(5+2)	1974-77
Jack Gore	(1)	1926
Chris Hesketh	(21+2)	1970-74
Barney Hudson	(8)	1932-37
Emlyn Jenkins	(9)	1933-37
Jim Lomas	(5)	1908-10
Tom McKinney	(7)	1951-54
Alf Middleton	(1)	1929
Steve Nash	(8)	1977-82
Maurice Richards	(2)	1974
Gus Risman	(17)	1932-46
Jack Spencer	(1)	1907
Johnny Ward	(1)	1970
Silas Warwick	(2)	1907
Billy Watkins	(7)	1933-37
David Watkins	(2+4)	1971-74
Billy Williams	(2)	1929-32
Peter Williams	(1+1)	1989

1993-94 SIGNINGS REGISTER

Signed	Player	Club From
30.7.93	Naylor, Scott	Wigan
25.8.93	Jack, Garry	Sheffield E.
29.9.93	Webster, Richard	Swansea RU
7.10.93	Marsden, Bob	Rochdale H.
21.10.93	Tauro, Chris	Manly, Aus.
16.11.93	Gregory, Andy	Leeds
14.12.93	Arden, Chris	—
8.2.94	McAvoy, Nathan	Eccles ARL
8.3.94	Austin, Greg	Keighley C.

Two substitute appearances in 1993-94 for Darren Betts.

Paul Forber, a nine-try tally in 30 games in 1993-94.

SALFORD 1993-94 PLAYERS' SUMMARY

	(Date of Birth)	App	T	G	D	Pts	Previous club	Signed
Austin, Greg	(14.6.63)	3	—	—	—	—	Keighley C.	8.3.94
Betts, Darren	(21.8.70)	0+2	—	—	—	—	Langworthy ARL	5.4.90
Birkett, Martin	(16.9.65)	11+1	—	6	—	12	Frizington ARL	7.12.89
Blakeley, Steve	(17.10.72)	27+5	7	70	1	169	Wigan	19.11.92
Blease, Ian	(1.1.65)	16+1	3	—	—	12	Folly Lane ARL	13.3.85
Brookfield, Keri	(17.3.73)	2	—	—	—	—	Wigan St. Patricks ARL	11.6.92
Brown, Shaun	(19.10.69)	14+5	2	11	1	31	Leigh East ARL	3.8.89
Burgess, Andy	(1.4.70)	31	4	—	—	16	Irlam H. ARL	1.4.87
Critchley, Jason	(7.12.70)	35	25	—	—	100	Widnes	4.8.92
Evans, Tex	(25.1.64)	15	3	—	—	12	Swinton	17.8.88
Forber, Paul	(29.4.64)	29+1	9	—	—	36	St. Helens	11.1.93
Ford, Phil	(16.3.61)	29	12	—	—	48	Leeds	28.8.92
Gilfillan, John	(11.3.65)	4+3	—	—	—	—	Wigan	13.9.90
Gregory, Andy	(10.8.61)	17+1	3	1	1	15	Leeds	16.11.93
Hansen, Shane	(5.12.60)	1	—	—	—	—	New Zealand	20.9.90
Howard, Tony	(9.11.68)	0+1	—	—	—	—	Army RU	18.1.90
Jack, Garry	(14.3.61)	34	10	—	—	40	Sheffield E.	30.6.93
Lee, Mark	(27.3.68)	33	5	—	4	24	St. Helens	8.1.90
McAvoy, Nathan	(31.12.76)	0+1	—	—	—	—	Eccles ARL	8.2.94
Marsden, Bob	(28.2.66)	8+17	4	—	—	16	Rochdale H.	7.10.93
Naylor, Scott	(2.2.72)	5+1	1	—	—	4	Wigan	30.7.93
Neil, Michael	(26.4.64)	8+1	1	—	—	4	Australia	26.8.93
O'Connor, Terry	(13.10.71)	27+4	3	—	—	12	Widnes Tigers ARL	5.8.91
O'Neill, Paul	(21.7.70)	7	2	—	—	8	Leigh Miners ARL	18.10.89
Potts, Ian	(5.1.69)	1+2	—	—	—	—	—	23.4.87
Randall, Craig	(22.9.72)	3+2	—	—	—	—	Leigh Miners ARL	21.5.91
Reid, Wayne	(15.12.69)	3+4	—	—	—	—	Wigan	28.8.91
Smith, Paul	(22.9.74)	1	—	—	—	—	Eccles ARL	29.4.92
Southern, Paul	(18.3.76)	0+1	—	—	—	—	Salford Academy	22.4.93
Stazicker, Ged	(2.1.68)	7+4	—	—	—	—	Wigan	8.7.91
Swift, Phil	(10.1.72)	3	2	—	—	8	Saddleworth R. ARL	19.10.90
Tauro, Chris	(4.1.70)	17+5	3	—	—	12	Australia	21.10.93
Tyrer, Gary	(1.2.71)	1+1	2	—	—	8	Orrell RU	1.12.92
Webster, Richard	(9.7.68)	1+4	1	—	—	4	Swansea RU	29.9.93
Williams, Peter	(14.12.58)	28+1	6	—	—	24	Orrell RU	22.3.88
Wynne, Steve	(9.12.71)	1	—	—	—	—	Widnes	4.8.92
Young, David	(26.7.67)	33	3	1	—	14	Leeds	25.4.91
TOTALS								
37 players			111	89	7	629		

Representative appearances 1993-94

Ford — Wales (2); Young — Wales (2); Webster — Wales (+1, 1t)

SALFORD 1993-94 MATCH ANALYSIS

Date	Com-petition	H/A	Opponent	Rlt	Score	Tries	Goals	Atten-dance	Referee
29.8.93	SBC	H	Sheffield E.	L	20-32	Blakeley, Burgess, Forber	Blakeley (4)	3119	Nicholson
5.9.93	SBC	A	St. Helens	L	14-22	Blease, Jack	Blakeley (3)	—	—
12.9.93	SBC	H	Widnes	W	33-19	Critchley (2), Blease, Ford, Jack	Blakeley (6), Lee (dg)	4293	J. Smith
19.9.93	SBC	A	Hull	L	12-28	Forber, Ford	Blakeley (2)	—	—
26.9.93	SBC	H	Leeds	W	23-18	Critchley (2), Neil	Blakeley (5,1dg)	4943	Galtress
3.10.93	SBC	H	Wigan	L	2-24	—	Blakeley	8765	Wood
8.10.93	SBC	A	Halifax	L	12-20	Blakeley, Ford	Blakeley (2)	—	—
24.10.93	SBC	H	Castleford	L	0-34	—	—	3769	J. Smith
31.10.93	SBC	A	Bradford N.	L	24-44	Critchley (2), Burgess, Evans	Blakeley (4)	—	—
5.11.93	SBC	H	Warrington	L	6-20	Critchley	Blakeley	2746	Morris
13.11.93	RT(2)	H	Leeds	W	21-12	Lee (2), Critchley, Forber	Birkett (2), Brown (dg)	1799	Whitfield
21.11.93	SBC	A	Hull K.R.	W	10-6	Jack, Williams	Birkett	—	—
28.11.93	SBC	H	Featherstone R.	W	34-24	Critchley (2), Jack (2), Brown, Ford, Lee	Birkett (3)	3526	Nicholson
5.12.93	SBC	H	Wakefield T.	W	22-8	Critchley (2), Forber, Ford, Jack	Brown	3525	R. Smith
14.12.93	RT(3)	A	Batley	W	12-8	Gregory, O'Connor	Blakeley (2)	—	—
19.12.93	RT(4)	H	Hull	W	26-6	Gregory (2), Forber, Marsden, Tauro	Brown (3)	3207	R. Smith
22.12.93	SBC	A	Sheffield E.	L	22-28	Forber (2), Jack, Webster	Brown (2), Blakeley	—	—
26.12.93	SBC	A	Oldham	W	20-8	Ford, Marsden, Williams	Blakeley (4)	—	—
2.1.94	SBC	H	Leigh	W	23-10	Burgess, Forber, Ford, Williams	Blakeley (3), Gregory (dg)	4338	Steele
8.1.94	RT(SF)	H	Wigan	L	12-18	Ford, Marsden	Blakeley (2)	7483	R. Smith
12.1.94	SBC	H	St. Helens	W	34-2	Critchley, Forber, O'Connor, O'Neill, Tauro, Young	Brown (4), Blakeley	4439	R. Smith
16.1.94	SBC	A	Widnes	L	22-30	Critchley (3), Jack, O'Neill	Brown	—	—
23.1.94	SBC	H	Hull	L	11-22	Critchley, Ford	Young, Lee (dg)	3459	Cummings
30.1.94	CC(4)	A	Castleford	L	4-36	Blakeley	—	—	—
6.2.94	SBC	A	Leeds	L	16-22	Critchley, Marsden	Blakeley (4)	—	—
20.2.94	SBC	A	Wigan	L	12-34	Jack, Young	Blakeley (2)	—	—
27.2.94	SBC	H	Halifax	W	34-14	Critchley (2), Burgess, Forber, Ford, Young	Blakeley (5)	4304	R. Connolly
18.3.94	SBC	H	Bradford N.	L	6-14	Lee	Blakeley	3189	R. Smith
23.3.94	SBC	A	Castleford	L	14-22	Blakeley, Critchley, Williams	Blakeley	—	—
27.3.94	SBC	A	Warrington	L	14-18	Blease, Critchley, Evans	Blakeley	—	—
1.4.94	SBC	H	Oldham	L	23-26	Ford, Lee, Naylor, O'Connor	Blakeley (3), Lee (dg)	4317	Wood
4.4.94	SBC	A	Leigh	W	19-18	Blakeley, Brown, Williams	Blakeley (3), Lee (dg)	—	—
10.4.94	SBC	A	Wakefield T.	L	18-25	Critchley (2), Swift	Blakeley (3)	—	—
17.4.94	SBC	H	Hull K.R.	W	30-12	Tyrer (2), Blakeley, Jack, Swift, Tauro	Blakeley (3)	2871	R. Connolly
24.4.94	SBC	A	Featherstone R.	L	24-46	Blakeley, Critchley, Evans, Williams	Blakeley (3), Gregory	—	—

113

SHEFFIELD EAGLES

Ground: Don Valley Stadium (0742-610326)
First Season: 1984-85
Nickname: Eagles
Chairman: Gary Hetherington
Secretary: Julie Bush
Honours: **Division Two** Champions, 1991-92
Second Division/Divisional Premiership Winners, 1988-89, 1991-92
Yorkshire Cup Beaten finalists, 1992-93

RECORDS

Match
Goals: 12 by Roy Rafferty at Fulham, 21 Sep 1986
Mark Aston v. Keighley C., 25 Apr 1992
Tries: 5 by Daryl Powell at Mansfield M., 2 Jan 1989
Points: 32 by Roy Rafferty at Fulham, 21 Sep 1986

Season
Goals: 148 by Mark Aston, 1988-89
Tries: 30 by Iva Ropati, 1991-92
Points: 307 by Mark Aston, 1988-89

Career
Goals: 622 by Mark Aston, 1986-
Tries: 108 by Daryl Powell, 1984-
Points: 1,370 by Mark Aston, 1986-
Appearances: 287+4 by Daryl Powell, 1984-
Highest score: 80-8 v. Wigan St. Patricks, 13 Nov 1988
Highest against: 62-11 at Warrington, 9 Feb 1986
Attendance: 8,000 v. Wakefield T. (Div. 1), 26 Sep 1990 — at Don Valley
8,636 v. Widnes (Div. 1), 8 Oct 1989 — at Bramall Lane, Sheffield U. FC

Gary Hetherington, who took the Sheffield coaching reins for a second time in December 1993.

COACHING REGISTER
● **Since formation in 1984**

Alan Rhodes	Apr 84 - May 86
Gary Hetherington	July 86 - Apr 93
Bill Gardner	May 93 - Dec 93
Gary Hetherington	Dec 93 -

GREAT BRITAIN REGISTER
(3 players)

Mark Aston	(+1)	1991
Lee Jackson	(3)	1993-94
Daryl Powell	(17+8)	1990-94

1993-94 SIGNINGS REGISTER

Signed	Player	Club From
27.6.93	Chapman, Richard	Dewsbury Moor ARL
27.7.93	Stockdale, Ian	Sheffield E. Academy
3.8.93	Fraisse, David	Carpentras, Fr.
9.9.93	McKenna, Chris	Brisbane B., Aus.
17.9.93	Jackson, Lee	Hull
8.11.93	Summerill, Darren	Rossington ARL
1.12.93	*Webster, David	Rochdale H.
20.12.93	Armswood, Richard	ARL
11.3.94	Hayes, Brad	Ryedale-York
8.4.94	*Pearson, Richard	Huddersfield
21.4.94	Brier, Ben	Leicester RU

SHEFFIELD EAGLES 1993-94 PLAYERS' SUMMARY

	(Date of Birth)	App	T	G	D	Pts	Previous club	Signed
Armswood, Richard	(20.1.75)	2	—	—	—	—	ARL	20.12.93
Aston, Mark	(27.9.67)	35	14	118	5	297	Gaffers ARL	25.11.86
Brier, Ben	(6.10.70)	0+1	—	—	—	—	Leicester RU	21.4.94
Broadbent, Paul	(24.5.68)	27	3	—	—	12	Lock Lane ARL	26.10.87
Cain, Alex	(2.9.73)	0+2	—	—	—	—	—	—
Carr, Paul	(13.5.67)	26+1	12	—	—	48	Hunslet	1.7.92
Cook, Michael	(1.8.61)	25+2	3	—	—	12	Hunslet Jct. ARL	28.2.87
Farrell, Anthony	(17.1.69)	26+1	5	—	—	20	Huddersfield	1.11.89
Fraisse, David	(20.12.68)	26+5	23	2	—	96	France	3.8.93
Gamson, Mark	(17.8.65)	31	8	—	—	32	Crigglestone ARL	27.7.84
Grimoldby, Nick	(31.1.62)	7+5	1	—	—	4	Fulham	9.1.89
Hayes, Brad	(22.4.67)	6+1	1	—	—	4	Ryedale-York	11.3.94
Hughes, Ian	(13.3.72)	17+15	8	—	—	32	East Leeds ARL	1.7.91
Jackson, Lee	(12.3.69)	24+2	4	—	—	16	Hull	17.9.93
Laughton, Dale	(10.10.70)	12+4	—	—	—	—	Dodworth ARL	3.9.89
Lumb, Tim	(19.2.70)	1+2	—	—	3	3	Hunslet	2.3.92
McGuire, Bruce	(31.1.62)	30+2	2	—	—	8	Australia	1.9.92
McKenna, Chris	(29.10.74)	4	—	—	—	—	Australia	9.9.93
Mann, David	(28.10.69)	7+2	1	—	—	4	Dodworth ARL	20.8.92
Mycoe, David	(1.5.72)	2	—	—	—	—	Crigglestone ARL	31.7.89
Picksley, Richard	(29.12.70)	12	2	—	—	8	Lock Lane ARL	31.7.89
Plange, David	(24.7.65)	18	5	—	—	20	Castleford	27.8.91
Powell, Daryl	(21.7.65)	24+1	10	—	—	40	Redhill ARL	27.7.84
Price, Richard	(26.6.70)	35	16	—	—	64	Hull	19.3.91
Randall, Karl	(22.12.71)	2+5	—	—	—	—	Dodworth ARL	20.8.92
Sheridan, Ryan	(24.5.75)	17+9	8	—	—	32	Dewsbury Moor ARL	10.7.91
Stott, Lynton	(9.5.71)	28+1	13	—	—	52	Halifax	19.12.92
Summerill, Darren	(26.4.73)	0+1	—	—	—	—	Rossington ARL	8.11.93
Summers, Jamie	(25.3.73)	1+1	—	—	—	—	Leeds	24.2.94
Thompson, Alex	(29.7.74)	9+1	1	—	—	4	Crown Malet ARL	1.7.91
Turner, Darren	(13.10.73)	1+3	—	—	—	—	Leeds Academy	1.1.92
Webster, David	(20.10.68)	0+1	—	—	—	—	Rochdale H.	1.12.93
TOTALS								
32 players			140	120	8	808		

Representative appearances 1993-94

Powell — Britain (+4); Jackson — Britain (3); Thompson — GB Under-21s (1); Fraisse — France (2).

SHEFFIELD EAGLES 1993-94 MATCH ANALYSIS

Date	Competition	H/A	Opponent	Rlt	Score	Tries	Goals	Attendance	Referee
29.8.93	SBC	A	Salford	W	32-20	Aston, Fraisse, Powell, Price, Stott	Aston (5,2dg)	—	—
5.9.93	SBC	H	Castleford	L	11-20	Price	Aston (3,1dg)	3046	J. Smith
12.9.93	SBC	A	Bradford N.	L	26-36	Sheridan (2), Carr, Plange, Stott	Aston (3)	—	—
19.9.93	SBC	H	Halifax	L	14-40	Gamson, Plange, Stott	Aston	4005	Galtress
26.9.93	SBC	A	Oldham	W	22-15	Sheridan (2), Carr, Price	Aston (3)	—	—
3.10.93	SBC	H	Wakefield T.	L	20-30	Carr, Gamson, Price	Aston (4)	3096	Morris
10.10.93	SBC	H	Featherstone R.	D	18-18	Aston (2), Price	Aston (3)	3059	Wood
24.10.93	SBC	A	St. Helens	W	19-12	Aston, Fraisse, Picksley	Aston (3,1dg)	—	—
31.10.93	SBC	H	Hull	W	18-15	Aston, Gamson, Stott	Aston (2), Lumb (2dg)	2244	Nicholson
14.11.93	RT(2)	A	Batley	L	6-8	Mann	Aston	—	—
21.11.93	SBC	A	Widnes	L	28-32	Farrell (2), Hughes (2), Stott	Aston (4)	—	—
24.11.93	SBC	A	Wigan	L	10-40	Hughes, Stott	Aston	—	—
28.11.93	SBC	H	Warrington	L	22-36	Aston, Farrell, Fraisse, Powell	Aston (3)	3284	Morris
5.12.93	SBC	H	Leeds	L	8-31	Fraisse, Jackson	—	3521	R. Connolly
22.12.93	SBC	H	Salford	W	28-22	Aston (2), Fraisse (2)	Aston (6)	1605	J. Connolly
28.12.93	SBC	A	Leigh	W	24-14	Fraisse, Plange, Powell, Price, Stott	Aston (2)	—	—
2.1.94	SBC	H	Hull K.R.	W	30-17	Jackson (2), Carr, Powell, Stott	Aston (5)	2151	Holdsworth
9.1.94	SBC	A	Castleford	L	18-20	Aston, Cook, Jackson	Aston (2), Fraisse	—	—
16.1.94	SBC	H	Bradford N.	L	28-29	Fraisse (2), Gamson (2), Price	Aston (4)	3544	Morris
23.1.94	SBC	A	Halifax	W	26-20	Carr (2), Farrell, Price, Thompson	Aston (3)	—	—
30.1.94	CC(4)	H	Leigh	W	42-10	Aston, Carr, Hughes, Plange, Price, Sheridan	Aston (9)	1676	Campbell
6.2.94	SBC	H	Oldham	W	28-14	Fraisse (2), McGuire, Sheridan	Aston (6)	2400	R. Smith
13.2.94	CC(5)	A	Widnes	L	6-22	Fraisse	Aston	—	—
20.2.94	SBC	A	Wakefield T.	W	23-11	Aston, Broadbent, Fraisse, Stott	Aston (3), Lumb (dg)	—	—
6.3.94	SBC	A	Featherstone R.	W	38-28	Broadbent, Cook, Hughes, McGuire, Powell, Price, Stott	Aston (5)	—	—
11.3.94	SBC	H	St. Helens	W	18-6	Gamson (2), Fraisse	Aston (3)	2729	Campbell
27.3.94	SBC	H	Wigan	W	10-5	Aston	Aston (3)	5465	Atkin
1.4.94	SBC	H	Leigh	W	48-4	Carr (2), Fraisse (2), Price (2), Hughes, Picksley, Powell	Aston (6)	1720	Cross
4.4.94	SBC	A	Hull K.R.	W	30-23	Fraisse (2), Stott (2), Aston, Gamson	Aston (3)	—	—
10.4.94	SBC	A	Leeds	D	46-46	Carr (2), Aston, Cook, Farrell, Fraisse, Powell, Sheridan	Aston (7)	—	—
13.4.94	SBC	A	Hull	L	22-25	Price (2), Broadbent, Sheridan	Aston (3)	—	—
17.4.94	SBC	H	Widnes	W	21-6	Powell (2), Carr, Fraisse	Aston (2,1dg)	2831	Tennant
22.4.94	SBC	A	Warrington	L	18-36	Grimoldby, Price, Stott	Aston (3)	—	—
8.5.94	PT(1)	A	Warrington	W	32-16	Fraisse (2), Hughes, Plange, Powell, Price	Aston (4)	—	—
13.5.94	PT(SF)	A	Wigan	L	18-52	Fraisse, Hayes, Hughes	Aston (2), Fraisse	—	—

SWINTON

Ground: Gigg Lane, Bury (061-761-2328)
First Season: 1896-97
Nickname: Lions
Chairman: Malcolm White
General
  Manager: Tony Barrow
Honours: **Championship** Winners, 1926-27,
1927-28, 1930-31, 1934-35
Beaten finalists, 1924-25, 1932-33
War Emergency League Beaten
finalists, 1939-40
Division One Champions, 1962-63,
1963-64
Division Two Champions, 1984-85
Challenge Cup Winners,
1899-1900, 1925-26, 1927-28
Beaten finalists, 1926-27, 1931-32
Second Division Premiership
Winners, 1986-87
Beaten finalists, 1988-89
Lancashire Cup Winners, 1925-26,
1927-28, 1939-40, 1969-70
Beaten finalists, 1910-11, 1923-24,
1931-32, 1960-61, 1961-62, 1962-63,
1964-65, 1972-73
Lancashire League Winners,
1924-25, 1927-28, 1928-29, 1930-31,
1960-61
Lancashire War League Winners,
1939-40
Western Division Championship
Beaten finalists, 1963-64
BBC-2 Floodlit Trophy
Beaten finalists, 1966-67

RECORDS

Match
Goals: 12 by Ken Gowers v. Liverpool C.,
3 Oct 1959
Tries: 5 by Morgan Bevan v. Morecambe,
10 Sep 1898
Billy Wallwork v. Widnes,
15 Dec 1900

Jack Evans v. Bradford N.,
30 Sep 1922
Hector Halsall v. St. Helens,
24 Jan 1925
Dick Cracknell v. Whitehaven Rec.,
11 Feb 1928
Randall Lewis v. Keighley,
12 Jan 1946
John Stopford v. Bramley,
22 Dec 1962
Alan Buckley v. Salford, 8 Apr 1964
Joe Ropati v. Nottingham C.,
21 Jan 1990
Points: 29 by Bernard McMahon v. Dewsbury,
15 Aug 1959

Season
Goals: 128 by Albert Blan, 1960-61
Tries: 42 by John Stopford, 1963-64
Points: 283 by Albert Blan, 1960-61

Career
Goals: 970 by Ken Gowers, 1954-73
Tries: 197 by Frank Evans, 1921-31
Points: 2,105 by Ken Gowers, 1954-73
Appearances: 593+8 by Ken Gowers, 1954-73
Highest score: 76-4 v. Pontefract, 8 Sep 1906
Highest against: 78-0 v. Wigan, 29 Sep 1992
Attendance: 44,621 Wigan v. Warrington
(RL Cup SF), 7 Apr 1951
Home match: 26,891 v. Wigan
(RL Cup), 12 Feb 1964

COACHING REGISTER
● **Since 1974-75**

Austin Rhodes	June 74 - Nov 75
Bob Fleet	Nov 75 - Nov 76
John Stopford	Nov 76 - Apr 77
Terry Gorman	June 77 - Nov 78
Ken Halliwell	Nov 78 - Dec 79
Frank Myler	Jan 80 - May 81
Tom Grainey	May 81 - Oct 83
Jim Crellin	Nov 83 - May 86
Bill Holliday Mike Peers	} June 86 - Oct 87
Frank Barrow	Oct 87 - June 89
Jim Crellin	July 89 - July 91
Chris O'Sullivan	July 91 - Dec 91
Tony Barrow	Jan 92 -

GREAT BRITAIN REGISTER
(15 players)

Tom Armitt	(8)	1933-37
Alan Buckley	(7)	1963-66
Fred Butters	(2)	1929
Billy Davies	(1)	1968
Bryn Evans	(10)	1926-33
Frank Evans	(4)	1924
Jack Evans	(3)	1926
Ken Gowers	(14)	1962-66
Hector Halsall	(1)	1929
Martin Hodgson	(16)	1929-37
Ron Morgan	(2)	1963
Billo Rees	(11)	1926-29
Dave Robinson	(12)	1965-67
John Stopford	(12)	1961-66
Joe Wright	(1)	1932

1993-94 SIGNINGS REGISTER

Signed	Player	Club From
8.6.93	Ashurst, Chris	Widnes
8.6.93	Mikhail, Andrew	Blackbrook ARL
1.7.93	Allison, Stephen	Salford Academy
9.7.93	Gartland, Paul	Wigan
30.7.93	Turner, Stuart	Wigan
1.9.93	Meadowcroft, Neil	Pilkington Recs ARL
1.9.93	Robinson, Colin	Folly Lane ARL
1.9.93	Elliott, Paul	Salford Juniors ARL
1.9.93	Bateman, Andrew	Langworthy ARL
1.9.93	Baines, Vincent	—
3.9.93	*Bridge, Russell	Leigh
16.9.93	Maxwell, John	Oldham
20.9.93	Hansen, Shane	Salford
22.9.93	Lord, Paul	Wakefield T.
18.10.93	*Harthill, David	Warrington
6.11.93	*Painter, Trevor	Chorley B.
19.11.93	Ellis, Steve	Batley
21.11.93	Danes, Paul	St. George, Aus.
18.2.94	*Clayton, Richard	Chorley B.
19.2.94	*Tinsley, Eddie	Highfield
29.3.94	Atkinson, Keith	Keighley C.

Swinton threequarter Alan Buckley, capped seven times for Great Britain.

Bill Holliday, Lions' coach from June 1986 to October 1987, in a joint role with Mike Peers.

SWINTON 1993-94 PLAYERS' SUMMARY

	(Date of Birth)	App	T	G	D	Pts	Previous club	Signed
Allison, Steve	(22.5.74)	0+3	—	—	—	—	Salford Academy	1.7.93
Ashcroft, Simon	(27.6.70)	34	20	—	—	80	Highfield	3.6.92
Ashall, Barry	(1.9.71)	2+1	1	—	—	4	Thatto Heath ARL	21.2.89
Ashurst, Chris	(24.7.65)	15+2	1	—	—	4	Widnes	8.6.93
Atkinson, Keith	(15.12.64)	2	—	—	—	—	Keighley C.	29.3.94
Baines, Vincent	(18.11.73)	0+1	1	—	—	4	—	1.9.93
Barrow, Paul	(20.10.74)	3+1	1	—	—	4	—	15.3.93
Barrow, Tony	(19.10.71)	25	3	—	—	12	Oldham	6.2.92
Best, Brian	(26.9.69)	2	—	—	—	—	Oldham St. Annes ARL	14.1.91
Cooper, Carl	(21.9.69)	0+1	—	—	—	—	St. Helens	23.1.92
Clayton, Richard	(24.2.70)	5+1	2	—	—	8	Chorley B.	18.2.94
Danes, Paul	(15.9.66)	24+1	4	—	—	16	Australia	21.11.93
Earner, Adrian	(19.11.66)	3+1	—	—	—	—	Leigh	3.11.92
Ellis, Steve	(10.1.71)	1	—	2	—	4	Batley	19.11.93
Errington, Craig	(17.8.72)	21+2	7	43	4	118	Folly Lane ARL	8.9.92
Garrett, Colin	(7.6.61)	0+1	—	—	—	—	—	—
Gartland, Paul	(2.11.72)	23+4	8	35	—	102	Wigan	9.7.93
Hansen, Shane	(5.12.60)	24	4	—	—	16	Salford	20.9.93
Harthill, David	(19.4.74)	0+2	—	—	—	—	Warrington	18.10.93
Humphries, Tony	(3.9.63)	27+3	3	—	—	12	Rochdale H.	25.3.93
Kay, Paul	(30.11.68)	0+2	—	—	—	—	Batley	28.2.92
Kennett, Paul	(7.1.71)	21+4	5	—	—	20	Tondu RU	22.10.90
Ledger, Barry	(19.6.62)	28+3	7	7	—	42	Leigh	25.4.93
Lord, Paul	(22.12.67)	28	8	—	—	32	Wakefield T.	22.9.93
Marsh, David	(8.10.68)	31+1	—	—	—	—	Widnes	20.5.93
Maxwell, John	(14.9.69)	4+1	2	—	—	8	Oldham	16.9.93
Melling, Alex	(12.8.64)	9	1	—	—	4	Leigh	10.4.88
O'Bryan, Shaun	(17.10.68)	19+1	3	2	2	18	Australia	22.9.93
Prince, Glen	(8.4.67)	13+9	—	—	—	—	Langworthy ARL	9.5.91
Skeech, Ian	(4.2.67)	23+6	13	—	—	52	Newton-le-Willows RU	24.11.87
Tinsley, Eddie	(31.7.63)	0+2	—	—	—	—	Highfield	19.2.94
Turner, Stuart	(13.11.69)	19	8	—	—	32	Wigan	30.7.93
Warburton, Steve	(6.2.69)	1	—	—	—	—	Rochdale H.	..
Welsby, Mark	(17.9.71)	25	4	—	—	16	Thatto Heath ARL	25.2.93
Whittle, Danny	(18.7.70)	10+9	—	—	—	—	Nutgrove ARL	12.3.92
TOTALS								
35 players			106	89	6	608		

SWINTON 1993-94 MATCH ANALYSIS

Date	Com-petition	H/A	Opponent	Rlt	Score	Tries	Goals	Atten-dance	Referee
29.8.93	SD	A	Ryedale-York	L	14-28	Gartland (2), Turner	Errington	—	—
5.9.93	SD	H	Barrow	L	22-28	Ashurst, P. Barrow, Errington, Kennett	Errington (3)	685	Cross
12.9.93	SD	A	Workington T.	L	6-52	Skeech	Errington	—	—
19.9.93	SD	H	Bramley	W	36-22	Skeech (2), Errington, Gartland, Maxwell, Welsby	Errington (4), Gartland (2)	498	Burke
26.9.93	SD	A	Carlisle	L	20-29	Welsby (2), Ashcroft, Ledger	Errington (2)	—	—
3.10.93	SD	A	Whitehaven	L	0-20	—	—	—	—
10.10.93	SD	H	Huddersfield	L	18-24	T. Barrow, Ledger, Turner	Errington (2), O'Bryan	1790	Asquith
24.10.93	SD	A	Keighley C.	L	16-51	Hansen, Lord, Turner	Errington (2)	—	—
31.10.93	RT(1)	H	Saddleworth R.	W	24-13	T. Barrow, Kennett, Lord, O'Bryan, Welsby	Gartland (2)	468	Redfearn
7.11.93	SD	H	Batley	L	16-22	Hansen, Maxwell, Skeech	Errington, Ledger	707	Burke
14.11.93	RT(2)	H	Hull	L	14-36	Errington (2), Ashcroft	Errington	851	McGregor
21.11.93	SD	H	Doncaster	W	40-20	Ledger (2), Skeech (2), Ashcroft, Hansen, O'Bryan, Turner	Ledger (3), Errington	645	Carter
28.11.93	SD	A	Hunslet	W	22-12	Ashcroft, Melling, O'Bryan, Turner	Errington (2,2dg)	—	—
5.12.93	SD	H	Dewsbury	L	6-28	Ashcroft	Errington	962	Kershaw
19.12.93	SD	H	Ryedale-York	W	29-10	Humphries (2), Errington, Ashcroft, Lord	Errington (4), O'Bryan (dg)	530	Gilmour
29.12.93	SD	A	London C.	L	12-22	Danes, Skeech	Errington (2)	—	—
9.1.94	SD	A	Barrow	W	20-12	Errington, Skeech, Turner	Errington (3,2dg)	—	—
16.1.94	CC(3)	H	Irlam H.	W	30-0	Turner (2), Ashcroft, Errington, Skeech	Errington (5)	710	Bates
19.1.94	SD	H	Rochdale H.	L	8-13	Gartland	Errington, O'Bryan	1003	Refearn
23.1.94	SD	H	Workington T.	L	8-22	Ashcroft	Errington (2)	1200	Galtress
30.1.94	CC(4)	H	Hull	L	12-18	T. Barrow	Gartland (4)	926	Ollerton
6.2.94	SD	A	Bramley	W	18-14	Ashcroft, Danes, Gartland	Gartland (3)	—	—
13.2.94	SD	A	Highfield	W	10-0	Kennett, Skeech	Gartland	—	—
20.2.94	SD	H	Carlisle	W	38-6	Ashcroft (3), Lord (2), Gartland, Skeech	Gartland (5)	513	Cross
27.2.94	SD	H	Whitehaven	W	17-10	Humphries, Kennett	Gartland (4), O'Bryan (dg)	640	Burke
6.3.94	SD	A	Huddersfield	L	8-18	Skeech, Lord	—	—	—
13.3.94	SD	H	Keighley C.	L	16-20	Ashcroft (2), Ashall	Gartland (2)	1304	Nicholson
20.3.94	SD	A	Batley	L	8-32	Lord	Ellis (2)	—	—
27.3.94	SD	A	Doncaster	L	0-42	—	—	—	—
1.4.94	SD	A	Rochdale H.	L	26-38	Ledger (2), Ashcroft, Danes, Skeech	Errington (3)	—	—
4.4.94	SD	H	Highfield	W	26-10	Ashcroft, Danes, Gartland, Kennett	Gartland (3), Errington (2)	371	Kirkpatrick
12.4.94	SD	H	London C.	W	18-20	Ashcroft, Hansen, Ledger	Gartland (3)	340	Nicholson
17.4.94	SD	A	Dewsbury	L	10-22	Ashcroft, Lord	Gartland	—	—
24.4.94	SD	H	Hunslet	W	40-34	Ashcroft (2), Clayton (2), Baines, Gartland	Gartland (5), Ledger (3)	596	Kershaw

WAKEFIELD TRINITY

Ground: Belle Vue (0924-372445)
First Season: 1895-96
Nickname: Dreadnoughts
Chairman: Ted Richardson
Honours: **Championship** Winners, 1966-67, 1967-68
Beaten finalists, 1959-60, 1961-62
Division Two Champions, 1903-04
Challenge Cup Winners, 1908-09, 1945-46, 1959-60, 1961-62, 1962-63
Beaten finalists, 1913-14, 1967-68, 1978-79
Regal Trophy Beaten finalists, 1971-72
Yorkshire Cup Winners, 1910-11, 1924-25, 1946-47, 1947-48, 1951-52, 1956-57, 1960-61, 1961-62, 1964-65, 1992-93
Beaten finalists, 1926-27, 1932-33, 1934-35, 1936-37, 1939-40, 1945-46, 1958-59, 1973-74, 1974-75, 1990-91
Yorkshire League Winners, 1909-10, 1910-11, 1945-46, 1958-59, 1959-60, 1961-62, 1965-66

RECORDS

Match
Goals: 13 by Mark Conway v. Highfield, 27 Oct 1992
Tries: 7 by Fred Smith v. Keighley, 25 Apr 1959
Keith Slater v. Hunslet, 6 Feb 1971
Points: 34 by Mark Conway v. Highfield, 27 Oct 1992

Season
Goals: 163 by Neil Fox, 1961-62
Tries: 38 by Fred Smith, 1959-60
David Smith, 1973-74
Points: 407 by Neil Fox, 1961-62

Career
Goals: 1,836 by Neil Fox, 1956-69 & 1970-74
Tries: 272 by Neil Fox, 1956-69 & 1970-74
Points: 4,488 by Neil Fox, 1956-69 & 1970-74
Appearances: 605 by Harry Wilkinson, 1930-49

Highest score: 90-12 v. Highfield, 27 Oct 1992
Highest against: 72-6 v. Wigan, 29 Mar 1987
Attendance: 37,906 Leeds v. Huddersfield (RL Cup SF), 21 Mar 1936
Home match: 30,676 v. Huddersfield (RL Cup), 26 Feb 1921

COACHING REGISTER
● **Since 1974-75**

Peter Fox	June 74 - May 76
Geoff Gunney	June 76 - Nov 76
Brian Lockwood	Nov 76 - Jan 78
Ian Brooke	Jan 78 - Jan 79
Bill Kirkbride	Jan 79 - Apr 80
Ray Batten	Apr 80 - May 81
Bill Ashurst	June 81 - Apr 82
Ray Batten	May 82 - July 83
Derek Turner	July 83 - Feb 84
Bob Haigh	Feb 84 - May 84
Geoff Wraith	May 84 - Oct 84
David Lamming	Oct 84 - Apr 85
Len Casey	Apr 85 - June 86
Tony Dean	June 86 - Dec 86
Trevor Bailey	Dec 86 - Apr 87
David Topliss	May 87 - Apr 94
David Hobbs	May 94 -

Tony Dean, Trinity coach for seven months in 1986.

GREAT BRITAIN REGISTER
(24 players)

Ian Brooke	(8)	1967-68
Neil Fox	(29)	1959-69
Bob Haigh	(2)	1968-70
Bill Horton	(14)	1928-33
Michael Jackson	(2+2)	1991-92
David Jeanes	(5)	1971-72
Berwyn Jones	(3)	1964-66
Herbert Kershaw	(2)	1910
Frank Mortimer	(2)	1956
Harry Murphy	(1)	1950
Tommy Newbould	(1)	1910
Jonty Parkin	(17)	1920-29
Charlie Pollard	(1)	1924
Ernest Pollard	(2)	1932
Harold Poynton	(3)	1962
Gary Price	(+1)	1991
Don Robinson	(5)	1954-55
Gerry Round	(8)	1959-62
Trevor Skerrett	(4)	1979
Stanley Smith	(1)	1929
David Topliss	(3)	1973-79
Derek Turner	(13)	1959-62
Don Vines	(3)	1959
Jack Wilkinson	(7)	1959-62

1993-94 SIGNINGS REGISTER

Signed	Player	Club From
29.6.93	Raw, Andy	Hunslet
14.7.93	Flynn, Wayne	Dewsbury Moor ARL
14.7.93	Stephenson, Francis	Dewsbury Moor ARL
2.8.93	Hanlan, Lee	Batley
5.8.93	Hanlan, Mark	Batley
18.8.93	Christie, Gary	Oldham
18.8.93	Sheals, Mark	Oldham
26.8.93	*Waddell, Hugh	Sheffield E.
28.8.93	Longstaff, Simon	Swinton
1.9.93	Durham, Steve	Hull
2.9.93	Woods, David	Canberra R., Aus.
3.9.93	Marlow, Ian	Hull
8.9.93	Forshaw, Mike	Wigan
10.9.93	Child, Lee	Leeds
18.9.93	Fuller, Matt	Canterbury, Aus.
1.10.93	Brown, Paul	Walnut Warriors ARL
7.10.93	*McCartney, Duncan	Whitehaven
20.10.93	*Longstaff, Spencer	Featherstone R.
4.11.93	Martin, Kevin	Ryedale-York
2.12.93	Paul, Henry	Te Atatu, NZ
3.12.93	*Bibb, Chris	Featherstone R.
3.2.94	Hobbs, David	Bradford N.
3.3.94	*Sodje, Bright	Hull K.R.

Trinity centre Richard Goddard, capped twice for Great Britain Under-21s in 1993-94.

Welsh international Ian Marlow, a September 1993 Trinity recruit from Hull.

WAKEFIELD TRINITY 1993-94 PLAYERS' SUMMARY

	(Date of Birth)	App	T	G	D	Pts	Previous club	Signed
Allen, Kieran	(21.11.75)	2+1	—	—	—	—	Wakefield Academy	21.11.92
Bagnall, Geoff	(4.11.65)	8	—	—	—	—	Australia	3.8.92
Bell, Nigel	(4.11.62)	25+2	2	—	—	8	Eastmoor ARL	1.9.83
Bibb, Chris	(3.6.68)	0+1	—	—	—	—	Featherstone R.	3.12.93
Brown, Paul	(20.1.70)	7+3	4	—	—	16	Walnut Warriors ARL	1.10.93
Child, Lee	(28.9.74)	5+3	2	—	—	8	Leeds	10.9.93
Christie, Gary	(23.1.72)	16+1	1	—	—	4	Oldham	18.8.93
Conway, Billy	(31.1.67)	21+4	3	13	—	38	Wakefield Colts	30.8.84
Durham, Steve	(12.10.63)	19+2	1	—	—	4	Hull	1.9.93
Eden, Phil	(13.12.63)	1+1	—	—	—	—	ARL	21.10.82
Flynn, Adrian	(9.9.74)	15+6	3	—	—	12	Dewsbury Moor ARL	4.1.92
Forshaw, Mike	(5.1.70)	19	5	—	—	20	Wigan	8.9.93
Fuller, Matt	(31.1.70)	20+2	3	—	—	12	Australia	18.9.93
Glancy, John	(14.4.62)	1	—	—	—	—	Sheffield E.	9.8.88
Goddard, Richard	(28.4.74)	19+3	6	17	—	58	Stanley R. ARL	31.12.90
Hanlan, Lee	(6.10.71)	22+5	4	—	—	16	Batley	2.8.93
Hicks, Simon	(30.8.73)	1	—	—	—	—	—	—
Hirst, John	(18.12.70)	2+1	1	—	—	4	Stanley R. ARL	15.8.89
Hobbs, David	(13.9.58)	7+3	—	1	1	3	Bradford N.	3.2.94
Knighton, Adam	(18.9.73)	0+2	—	—	—	—	Crigglestone ARL	8.4.92
Longstaff, Simon	(2.1.70)	3+2	—	—	—	—	Swinton	28.8.93
McDonald, Wayne	(3.9.75)	0+3	—	—	—	—	Middleton ARL	6.4.93
Marlow, Ian	(18.1.63)	23+1	—	—	—	—	Hull	3.9.93
Mason, Andy	(10.11.62)	32	16	—	—	64	Leeds	3.8.87
Morris, Lynton	(18.5.72)	7	—	—	—	—	Oulton ARL	4.8.89
Mosley, James	(30.9.74)	5+2	1	—	—	4	Moldgreen ARL	24.1.92
Myers, David	(20.7.72)	0+1	—	—	—	—	Middleton ARL	14.11.91
Paul, Henry	(10.2.74)	19	7	41	1	111	New Zealand	2.12.93
Raw, Andy	(15.9.67)	1+1	—	—	—	—	Hunslet	29.6.93
Round, Paul	(24.9.63)	10+5	—	—	—	—	Oldham	17.10.91
Sheals, Mark	(26.11.63)	0+1	—	—	—	—	Oldham	18.8.93
Slater, Richard	(29.8.70)	13+3	1	—	—	4	Normanton ARL	4.8.88
Sodje, Bright	(21.4.66)	9	4	—	—	16	Hull K.R.	3.3.94
Spencer, Gary	(16.9.66)	29+1	6	—	—	24	Leeds	16.1.91
Stephenson, Francis	(20.1.76)	0+3	—	—	—	—	Dewsbury Moor ARL	14.7.93
Thompson, John	(3.5.59)	3	—	—	—	—	Eastmoor ARL	1.7.78
Waddell, Hugh	(1.9.59)	5	—	—	—	—	Sheffield E.	26.8.93
Webster, Mark	(23.6.70)	5	—	—	—	—	St. Helens	23.8.90
Wilson, Andy	(5.10.63)	24+1	9	—	—	36	Queens Park ARL	8.11.88
Woods, David	(6.3.66)	18	6	—	—	24	Australia	2.9.93
TOTALS								
40 players			85	72	2	486		

Representative appearances 1993-94

Goddard — GB Under-21s (2); Marlow — Wales (1+1).

WAKEFIELD TRINITY 1993-94 MATCH ANALYSIS

Date	Competition	H/A	Opponent	Rlt	Score	Tries	Goals	Attendance	Referee
29.8.93	SBC	A	Warrington	L	14-32	Christie, Mason	Conway (3)	—	—
5.9.93	SBC	H	Wigan	L	16-40	Fuller, Mason, Woods	Conway (2)	6685	Campbell
12.9.93	SBC	A	Leigh	W	10-4	Goddard, Woods	Conway	—	—
19.9.93	SBC	H	Bradford N.	L	8-13	Goddard	Goddard (2)	5388	Ollerton
26.9.93	SBC	H	Hull K.R.	L	24-34	Forshaw (2), Goddard, Hanlan, Wilson	Goddard (2)	2942	Whitfield
3.10.93	SBC	A	Sheffield E.	W	30-20	Brown (2), Bell, Mason, Slater	Goddard (5)	—	—
10.10.93	SBC	A	St. Helens	L	10-36	Durham	Goddard (3)	—	—
22.10.93	SBC	H	Widnes	L	0-10	—	—	2772	McCallum (Aus)
31.10.93	SBC	H	Oldham	W	22-21	Forshaw, Goddard, Hanlan, Mason, Spencer	Goddard	3832	Wood
7.11.93	SBC	A	Hull	L	8-16	Mason	Goddard (2)	—	—
14.11.93	RT(2)	A	Carlisle	L	12-28	Child, Mason	Conway (2)	—	—
21.11.93	SBC	H	Halifax	L	2-12	—	Goddard	3900	Nicholson
28.11.93	SBC	A	Castleford	L	10-34	Hirst, Mason	Goddard	—	—
5.12.93	SBC	A	Salford	L	8-22	Child	Conway, Paul	—	—
22.12.93	SBC	H	Warrington	W	12-10	Paul, Wilson	Paul (2)	2371	J. Smith
26.12.93	SBC	A	Leeds	L	16-20	Bell, Woods	Conway (4)	—	—
2.1.94	SBC	H	Featherstone R.	L	10-24	Conway, Mason	Paul	5069	Asquith
16.1.94	SBC	H	Leigh	W	18-10	Mason, Spencer, Woods	Paul (3)	2549	R. Smith
21.1.94	SBC	A	Bradford N.	L	10-28	Paul, Woods	Paul	—	—
30.1.94	CC(4)	A	Wigan	L	16-24	Mason (2), Wilson	Paul (2)	—	—
6.2.94	SBC	A	Hull K.R.	W	28-20	Fuller (2), Conway, Spencer, Woods	Paul (4)	—	—
16.2.94	SBC	A	Wigan	W	20-13	Forshaw, Paul, Spencer	Paul (4)	—	—
20.2.94	SBC	H	Sheffield E.	L	11-23	Flynn, Hanlan	Paul, Hobbs (dg)	3058	Whitfield
6.3.94	SBC	A	St. Helens	L	22-35	Brown (2), Paul, Spencer	Paul (3)	4056	Holdsworth
13.3.94	SBC	A	Widnes	L	12-22	Conway, Goddard	Paul (2)	—	—
20.3.94	SBC	A	Oldham	D	20-20	Paul (2), Sodje, Wilson	Paul (2)	—	—
27.3.94	SBC	H	Hull	W	10-8	Sodje, Wilson	Paul	2986	Campbell
1.4.94	SBC	H	Leeds	L	20-29	Flynn, Mason, Sodje, Wilson	Paul (2)	4807	R. Connolly
4.4.94	SBC	A	Featherstone R.	L	22-42	Flynn, Mason, Mosley, Wilson	Paul (3)	—	—
10.4.94	SBC	H	Salford	W	25-18	Hanlan, Mason, Spencer, Wilson	Paul (3,1dg), Hobbs	2685	Holdsworth
17.4.94	SBC	A	Halifax	L	16-54	Goddard, Mason, Wilson	Paul (2)	—	—
24.4.94	SBC	H	Castleford	L	24-38	Forshaw, Mason, Paul, Sodje	Paul (4)	4235	Cummings

Fifteen Trinity 1993-94 appearances for Paul Round before joining Halifax.

August 1993 recruit Mark Sheals, restricted to one substitute appearance by a broken leg.

WARRINGTON

Ground: Wilderspool (0925-35338)
First Season: 1895-96
Nickname: Wire
Chairman: Peter Higham
General
Manager: Ron Close
Honours: **Championship** Winners, 1947-48, 1953-54, 1954-55
Beaten finalists, 1925-26, 1934-35, 1936-37, 1948-49, 1950-51, 1960-61
League Leaders Trophy Winners, 1972-73
Club Championship (Merit Table) Winners, 1973-74
Challenge Cup Winners, 1904-05, 1906-07, 1949-50, 1953-54, 1973-74
Beaten finalists, 1900-01, 1903-04, 1912-13, 1927-28, 1932-33, 1935-36, 1974-75, 1989-90
Regal Trophy Winners, 1973-74, 1977-78, 1980-81, 1990-91
Beaten finalists, 1978-79, 1986-87
Premiership Trophy Winners, 1985-86
Beaten finalists, 1976-77, 1986-87
Lancashire Cup Winners, 1921-22, 1929-30, 1932-33, 1937-38, 1959-60, 1965-66, 1980-81, 1982-83, 1989-90
Beaten finalists, 1906-07, 1948-49, 1950-51, 1967-68, 1985-86, 1987-88
Lancashire League Winners, 1937-38, 1947-48, 1948-49, 1950-51, 1953-54, 1954-55, 1955-56, 1967-68
BBC-2 Floodlit Trophy Beaten finalists, 1974-75
Captain Morgan Trophy Winners, 1973-74

RECORDS

Match
Goals: 14 by Harold Palin v. Liverpool C., 13 Sep 1950
Tries: 7 by Brian Bevan v. Leigh, 29 Mar 1948
Brian Bevan v. Bramley, 22 Apr 1953
Points: 33 by George Thomas v. St. Helens, 12 Apr 1909

Season
Goals: 170 by Steve Hesford, 1978-79
Tries: 66 by Brian Bevan, 1952-53
Points: 363 by Harry Bath, 1952-53

Career
Goals: 1,159 by Steve Hesford, 1975-85
Tries: 740 by Brian Bevan, 1945-62
Points: 2,416 by Steve Hesford, 1975-85
Appearances: 620 by Brian Bevan, 1945-62
Highest score: 78-3 v. St. Helens, 12 Apr 1909
Highest against: 68-14 at Hunslet, 10 Apr 1928
Attendance: 34,304 v. Wigan (League), 22 Jan 1949

COACHING REGISTER
● **Since 1974-75**

Alex Murphy	May 71 - May 78
Billy Benyon	June 78 - Mar 82
Kevin Ashcroft	Mar 82 - May 84
Reg Bowden	June 84 - Mar 86
Tony Barrow	Mar 86 - Nov 88
Brian Johnson	Nov 88 -

Warrington's Welsh international centre Allan Bateman, scorer of 41 points for the Wire in 1993-94.

GREAT BRITAIN REGISTER
(46 players)

Jack Arkwright	(6)	1936-37
Kevin Ashcroft	(+1)	1974
Willie Aspinall	(1)	1966
Allan Bateman	(1+1)	1992-93
Billy Belshaw	(2)	1937
Nat Bentham	(2)	1929
John Bevan	(6)	1974-78
Tom Blinkhorn	(1)	1929
Ernie Brooks	(3)	1908
Jim Challinor	(3)	1958-60
Neil Courtney	(+1)	1982
Billy Cunliffe	(11)	1920-26
Jonathan Davies	(3)	1993
George Dickenson	(1)	1908
Billy Dingsdale	(3)	1929-33
Des Drummond	(2)	1987-88
Ronnie Duane	(3)	1983-84
Bob Eccles	(1)	1982
Kevin Ellis	(+1)	1991
Jim Featherstone	(6)	1948-52
Mark Forster	(2)	1987
Eric Fraser	(16)	1958-61
Laurie Gilfedder	(5)	1962-63
Bobby Greenough	(1)	1960
Andy Gregory	(1)	1986
Mike Gregory	(19+1)	1987-90
Gerry Helme	(12)	1948-54
Keith Holden	(1)	1963
Albert Johnson	(6)	1946-47
Ken Kelly	(2)	1980-82
Tom McKinney	(3)	1955
Joe Miller	(6)	1933-36
Alex Murphy	(1)	1971
Albert Naughton	(2)	1954
Terry O'Grady	(1)	1961
Harold Palin	(2)	1947
Ken Parr	(1)	1968
Albert Pimblett	(3)	1948
Ray Price	(9)	1954-57
Bob Ryan	(5)	1950-52
Ron Ryder	(1)	1952
Frank Shugars	(1)	1910
George Skelhorne	(7)	1920-21
George Thomas	(1)	1907
Derek Whitehead	(3)	1971
John Woods	(+1)	1987

1993-94 SIGNINGS REGISTER

Signed	Player	Club From
1.6.93	Eckersley, Chris	Warrington Academy
4.6.93	Foster, Paul	Warrington Academy
14.6.93	Harthill, David	Warrington Academy
1.7.93	Appleby, Craig	Eccles ARL
6.7.93	Davies, Jonathan	Widnes
2.8.93	Harris, Iestyn	Oldham St. Annes ARL
16.8.93	Teitzel, Craig	Illawarra, Aus.
10.10.93	Knott, Ian	—
5.11.93	Holden, Chris	Orrell St. James ARL
25.11.93	Whitter, Damien	Wigan St. Patricks ARL
2.12.93	Hough, John	Warrington Academy
27.3.94	Price, Anthony	Warrington Academy
28.4.94	Lee, Jason	Dudley Hill ARL
8.5.94	Close, Graeme	Warrington Academy

Former Test captain Mike Gregory, capped 20 times between 1987 and 1990.

WARRINGTON 1993-94 PLAYERS' SUMMARY

	(Date of Birth)	App	T	G	D	Pts	Previous club	Signed
Bateman, Allan	(6.3.65)	30	10	—	1	41	Neath RU	28.9.90
Bennett, Andrew	(23.7.73)	0+5	2	—	—	8	Woolston R. ARL	10.8.90
Chambers, Gary	(5.1.70)	16+2	2	—	—	8	Kells ARL	15.2.88
Cullen, Paul	(4.3.63)	19	2	—	—	8	Crosfields ARL	25.11.80
Darbyshire, Paul	(3.12.69)	12+11	2	—	—	8	Wigan St. Patricks ARL	16.12.88
Davies, Jonathan	(24.10.62)	30	21	99	11	293	Widnes	6.7.93
Elliott, David	(23.2.71)	11+6	1	—	—	4	Kells ARL	21.5.90
Ellis, Kevin	(29.5.65)	32+3	5	—	—	20	Bridgend RU	18.6.90
Forster, Mark	(25.11.64)	32	12	—	—	48	Woolston R. ARL	27.11.81
Gregory, Mike	(20.5.64)	12+5	2	—	—	8	—	8.6.82
Harris, Iestyn	(25.6.76)	10	4	19	—	54	Oldham St. Annes ARL	2.8.93
Hilton, Mark	(31.3.75)	1+13	1	—	—	4	Warrington Academy	13.8.92
Hodkinson, Colin	(26.3.74)	2+2	—	—	—	—	Leigh Miners ARL	7.4.91
Jackson, Bob	(13.8.60)	15+1	5	—	—	20	Australia	15.8.89
Mackey, Greg	(20.10.61)	36	4	—	2	18	Hull	18.8.92
Myler, Robert	(4.3.70)	26	17	1	—	70	Widnes St. Maries ARL	2.10.89
Penny, Lee	(24.9.74)	33	9	—	—	36	Orrell St. James ARL	15.10.91
Phillips, Rowland	(28.7.65)	17+8	4	—	—	16	Neath RU	28.9.90
Roper, Jonathan	(5.5.76)	4	2	—	—	8	Hensingham ARL	5.5.93
Rudd, Chris	(17.12.69)	7+1	1	—	—	4	Kells ARL	15.2.88
Sanderson, Gary	(21.2.67)	17+3	1	—	—	4	Thatto Heath ARL	30.12.85
Shelford, Kelly	(4.5.66)	34	13	—	2	54	New Zealand	5.10.91
Tees, Gary	(25.7.67)	10+3	—	—	—	—	Barrow	5.12.90
Teitzel, Craig	(26.12.63)	22+5	4	—	—	16	Australia	16.8.93
Thorniley, Tony	(10.10.66)	2	1	—	—	4	Woolston R. ARL	1.4.86
Thursfield, John	(22.10.69)	32	—	—	—	—	—	9.9.86
Williamson, Paul	(27.11.69)	6	—	—	—	—	Woolston R. ARL	9.11.87
TOTALS								
27 players			125	119	16	754		

Representative appearances 1993-94

Bateman — Wales (2); Davies — Britain (3, 1t, 10g, 2dg), Wales (2, 9g, 1dg); Ellis — Wales (2); Harris — GB Under-21s (2, 1t, 8g); Penny — GB Under-21s (2); Phillips — Wales (2).

Wire skipper Greg Mackey.

Long serving Paul Cullen.

WARRINGTON 1993-94 MATCH ANALYSIS

Date	Com-petition	H/A	Opponent	Rlt	Score	Tries	Goals	Atten-dance	Referee
29.8.93	SBC	H	Wakefield T.	W	32-14	Bateman (3), Jackson, Shelford	Davies (6)	5237	Steele
5.9.93	SBC	A	Leeds	L	19-21	Davies, Myler, Penny	Davies (3), Shelford (dg)	—	—
12.9.93	SBC	H	St. Helens	W	17-10	Sanderson, Shelford	Davies (4,1dg)	7805	J. Connolly
19.9.93	SBC	A	Oldham	W	18-12	Davies (2), Shelford	Davies (3)	—	—
26.9.93	SBC	A	Hull	W	19-6	Davies, Phillips, Shelford	Davies (3), Shelford (dg)	—	—
10.10.93	SBC	A	Bradford N.	L	16-47	Davies, Jackson, Shelford	Davies (2)	—	—
18.10.93	SBC	H	Halifax	W	15-7	Davies, Phillips	Davies (3,1dg)	6361	R. Smith
24.10.93	SBC	H	Hull K.R.	W	24-10	Chambers, Davies, Ellis, Shelford	Davies (4)	4764	Galtress
29.10.93	SBC	H	Leigh	W	24-6	Chambers, Darbyshire, Ellis, Thorniley	Harris (4)	3975	J. Smith
5.11.93	SBC	A	Salford	W	20-6	Bateman, Shelford, Teitzel	Harris (4)	—	—
14.11.93	RT(2)	H	Hunslet	W	58-16	Harris (3), Penny (3), Myler (2), Davies, Mackey, Shelford	Davies (6), Harris	3037	Redfearn
21.11.93	SBC	H	Castleford	W	20-10	Myler (2), Cullen	Davies (3,2dg)	5775	J. Smith
28.11.93	SBC	A	Sheffield E.	W	36-22	Davies (2), Myler, Rudd, Shelford, Teitzel	Davies (6)	—	—
5.12.93	SBC	H	Featherstone R.	W	30-14	Myler (2), Cullen, Davies, Elliott	Davies (5)	5626	Whitfield
11.12.93	RT(3)	A	St. Helens	W	16-8	Shelford, Myler	Davies (4)	—	—
18.12.93	RT(4)	H	Wigan	L	10-27	Myler	Davies (3)	7321	Campbell
22.12.93	SBC	A	Wakefield T.	L	10-12	Ellis, Phillips	Davies	—	—
28.12.93	SBC	A	Widnes	W	18-10	Forster, Gregory, Shelford	Davies (3)	—	—
2.1.94	SBC	H	Wigan	L	6-8	Forster	Davies	11,397	R. Smith
9.1.94	SBC	H	Leeds	W	37-18	Forster (3), Myler (2), Davies, Penny	Davies (4,1dg)	6664	Campbell
16.1.94	SBC	A	St. Helens	W	21-11	Gregory, Myler, Penny	Davies (4,1dg)	—	—
23.1.94	SBC	H	Oldham	W	23-6	Davies, Ellis, Myler, Teitzel	Davies (2,1dg), Myler	5875	Atkin
29.1.94	CC(4)	A	Halifax	W	22-18	Myler, Davies (2)	Davies (5)	—	—
6.2.94	SBC	H	Hull	W	22-8	Darbyshire, Forster, Mackey, Penny	Harris (3)	5361	J. Smith
12.2.94	CC(5)	A	Leeds	L	4-38	Myler	—	—	—
18.2.94	SBC	A	Halifax	L	7-22	Bateman	Davies, Mackey (dg)	—	—
6.3.94	SBC	H	Bradford N.	L	10-27	Mackey	Harris (3)	5775	J. Connolly
13.3.94	SBC	A	Hull K.R.	W	26-10	Bateman (2), Forster, Jackson, Penny	Harris (3)	—	—
22.3.94	SBC	A	Leigh	W	14-6	Davies (2)	Davies (3)	—	—
27.3.94	SBC	H	Salford	W	18-14	Ellis, Myler	Davies (5)	4587	Cummings
1.4.94	SBC	H	Widnes	W	28-14	Jackson (2), Davies, Forster, Shelford	Davies (3,2dg)	6720	Holdsworth
4.4.94	SBC	A	Wigan	L	14-21	Forster (2), Bennett	Harris	—	—
10.4.94	SBC	A	Featherstone R.	W	27-24	Bateman, Bennett, Hilton, Penny, Teitzel	Davies (3,1dg)	—	—
17.4.94	SBC	A	Castleford	W	21-16	Forster (2), Davies, Roper	Davies (2,1dg)	—	—
22.4.94	SBC	H	Sheffield E.	W	36-18	Bateman, Davies, Harris, Mackey, Phillips, Roper	Davies (5), Bateman (dg), Mackey (dg)	6031	Whitfield
8.5.94	PT(1)	H	Sheffield E.	L	16-32	Bateman, Davies, Shelford	Davies (2)	5031	Holdsworth

WHITEHAVEN

Ground: Recreation Ground (0946-692915)
First Season: 1948-49
Nickname: Warriors
Chairman: Derek Mossop
Secretary: Bill Madine

RECORDS

Match
Goals: 12 by Steve Maguire v. Nottingham C.,
12 Apr 1992
Tries: 6 by Vince Gribbin v. Doncaster,
18 Nov 1984
Points: 28 by Steve Maguire v. Highfield,
28 Feb 1993

Season
Goals: 141 by John McKeown, 1956-57
Tries: 31 by Vince Gribbin, 1991-92
Points: 291 by John McKeown, 1956-57

Career
Goals: 1,050 by John McKeown, 1948-61
Tries: 148 by Bill Smith, 1950-62
Points: 2,133 by John McKeown, 1948-61
Appearances: 417 by John McKeown, 1948-61
Highest score: 80-6 v. Nottingham C.,
12 Apr 1992
Highest against: 92-10 at Hull K.R., 18 Mar 1990
Attendance: 18,500 v. Wakefield T. (RL Cup),
19 Mar 1960

*Frank Foster, coach of Whitehaven for two years
from June 1983.*

COACHING REGISTER
● **Since 1974-75**

Jeff Bawden	May 72 - May 75
Ike Southward	Aug 75 - June 76
Bill Smith	Aug 76 - Oct 78
Ray Dutton	Oct 78 - Oct 79
Phil Kitchin	Oct 79 - Jan 82
Arnold Walker	Jan 82 - May 82
Tommy Dawes	June 82 - May 83
Frank Foster	June 83 - June 85
Phil Kitchin	June 85 - Oct 87
John McFarlane	Oct 87 - May 88
Barry Smith	July 88 - Sep 89
Eric Fitzsimons	Oct 89 - Mar 90
Norman Turley	June 90 - Apr 91
Jackie Davidson	May 91 - June 92
Gordon Cottier	June 92 - May 93
Kurt Sorensen	May 93 -

GREAT BRITAIN REGISTER
(5 players)

Vince Gribbin	(1)	1985
Bill Holliday	(1)	1964
Dick Huddart	(4)	1958
Phil Kitchin	(1)	1965
Arnold Walker	(1)	1980

1993-94 SIGNINGS REGISTER

Signed	Player	Club From
23.6.93	Sorensen, Kurt	Widnes
6.8.93	Chambers, Craig	Kells ARL
6.8.93	Morton, Graeme	Kells ARL
24.8.93	Tyrer, Sean	Oldham
29.8.93	Pechey, Michael	Aus.
7.9.93	Seeds, David	Kells ARL
10.9.93	Lewthwaite, Graeme	Hensingham ARL
16.9.93	Morgan, Damien	Kells ARL
18.9.93	Kiddie, Lee	Kells ARL
23.9.93	*Creary, Richard	Barrow
17.12.93	Burney, Stephen	—
10.1.94	Anderson, Scott	Wath Brow H. ARL
17.2.94	*Wear, Steve	Workington T.

WHITEHAVEN 1993-94 PLAYERS' SUMMARY

	(Date of Birth)	App	T	G	D	Pts	Previous club	Signed
Anderson, Scott	(9.12.70)	13+2	2	—	—	8	Wath Brow H. ARL	10.1.94
Beckwith, Mark	(7.8.64)	14+2	1	—	—	4	Barrow	11.1.91
Blaney, Ged	(17.6.65)	9+2	2	—	—	8	Mirehouse ARL	8.1.89
Branthwaite, Steve	(25.12.61)	7+6	—	—	—	—	Gosforth RU	28.3.88
Burney, Steve	(7.6.63)	0+1	—	—	—	—	—	17.12.93
Chambers, Craig	(25.4.73)	22+1	4	—	—	16	Kells ARL	6.8.93
Crarey, Paul	(4.1.66)	3	—	—	—	—	Barrow	5.2.93
Davidson, Alan	(9.12.64)	2	—	—	—	—	Kells ARL	12.8.88
Dover, Peter	(9.12.65)	10	4	—	—	16	Flimby ARL	1.7.89
Dunn, Reg	(23.5.68)	31+1	1	—	—	4	Barrow	28.1.92
Fisher, Billy	(27.10.62)	25+1	6	—	—	24	St. Benedicts RU	20.7.81
Friend, Clayton	(22.3.62)	30	8	1	2	38	Carlisle	24.9.92
Gribbin, Vince	(15.3.65)	29+1	16	—	—	64	Hensingham ARL	23.7.82
Hetherington, Gary	(5.7.65)	8+16	3	—	—	12	Kells ARL	26.7.85
Kendall, Dave	(7.6.63)	14+4	—	—	—	—	Barrow	2.10.92
Kiddie, Lee	(2.1.75)	12+2	4	3	4	26	Kells ARL	18.9.93
Lewthwaite, Graeme	(5.7.72)	12+8	14	—	—	56	Hensingham ARL	10.9.93
Lightfoot, David	(24.6.63)	22+1	3	—	—	12	Hull K.R.	28.2.92
McCartney, Duncan	(28.5.65)	4+7	—	—	—	—	—	26.7.85
Maguire, Steve	(12.8.63)	28	3	66	—	144	Barrow	11.1.91
Morton, Graeme	(15.1.73)	19+3	2	—	—	8	Kells ARL	6.8.93
Mounsey, Gary	(21.8.61)	8	1	—	—	4	Glasson R. ARL	30.6.87
Pechey, Mick	(16.12.68)	31	16	—	—	64	Australia	29.8.93
Routledge, John	(7.2.65)	19	5	—	—	20	Egremont RU	24.8.90
Ryan, Mark	(31.7.64)	4+7	1	1	—	6	Mirehouse ARL	10.11.87
Sanders, Kevin	(21.3.62)	2	—	—	—	—	Hensingham ARL	29.8.91
Seeds, David	(23.6.74)	27	17	—	—	68	Kells ARL	7.9.93
Sorensen, Kurt	(8.11.56)	27+1	3	—	—	12	Widnes	23.6.93
Tyrer, Sean	(2.3.70)	19	10	13	—	62	Oldham	24.8.93
Wear, Steve	(13.12.70)	4	—	5	—	10	Workington T.	17.2.94
TOTALS								
30 players			126	89	6	688		

WHITEHAVEN 1993-94 MATCH ANALYSIS

Date	Competition	H/A	Opponent	Rlt	Score	Tries	Goals	Attendance	Referee
29.8.93	SD	A	Bramley	W	20-4	Beckwith, Fisher, Gribbin, Pechey	Maguire (2)	–	–
5.9.93	SD	H	Ryedale-York	D	14-14	Gribbin (2), Blaney	Maguire	1121	Crashley
12.9.93	SD	A	Dewsbury	D	16-16	Lewthwaite (2), Mounsey	Tyrer (2)	–	–
19.9.93	SD	H	Hunslet	W	26-10	Friend, Hetherington, Kiddie, Seeds, Tyrer	Tyrer (3)	1023	Volante
26.9.93	SD	A	Batley	L	16-28	Gribbin, Seeds, Sorensen	Friend, Tyrer	–	–
3.10.93	SD	H	Swinton	W	20-0	Kiddie (2), Friend, Tyrer	Tyrer (2)	1155	Whitelam
10.10.93	SD	A	Keighley C.	L	12-40	Seeds, Tyrer	Tyrer (2)	–	–
24.10.93	SD	H	Doncaster	W	34-12	Routledge (2), Lewthwaite, Morton, Pechey, Seeds, Tyrer	Tyrer (3)	1140	Redfearn
31.10.93	RT(1)	H	Egremont	W	46-0	Tyrer (3), Fisher (2), Friend, Gribbin, Lewthwaite, Lightfoot, Routledge	Maguire (3)	1480	Campbell
7.11.93	SD	A	Huddersfield	L	9-14	Seeds	Maguire (2), Friend (dg)	–	–
14.11.93	RT(2)	H	Wigan	L	8-22	Seeds	Maguire (2)	5185	Kershaw
21.11.93	SD	H	Highfield	W	32-1	Lightfoot (2), Pechey (2), Gribbin, Seeds	Maguire (3), Ryan	887	Atkin
28.11.93	SD	A	Rochdale H.	L	14-18	Fisher, Gribbin	Maguire (3)	–	–
5.12.93	SD	H	London C.	D	16-16	Morton, Seeds	Maguire (4)	913	Redfearn
12.12.93	SD	A	Barrow	L	8-20	Friend	Maguire (2)	–	–
19.12.93	SD	H	Bramley	W	34-14	Lewthwaite (3), Dover (2), Pechey, Seeds	Maguire (3)	691	Crashley
28.12.93	SD	H	Workington T.	D	0-0	–	–	4311	Cummings
2.1.94	SD	A	Carlisle	W	34-12	Pechey (2), Seeds (2), Chambers, Gribbin	Maguire (5)	–	–
9.1.94	SD	A	Ryedale-York	L	4-34	Friend	–	–	–
16.1.94	CC(3)	H	West Hull	W	44-4	Lewthwaite (2), Tyrer (2), Dover, Dunn, Hetherington, Maguire	Maguire (6)	718	R. Connolly
23.1.94	SD	H	Dewsbury	L	6-10	Lewthwaite	Maguire	1054	Steele
30.1.94	CC(4)	A	Highfield	W	15-4	Gribbin, Lewthwaite	Maguire (3), Friend (dg)	–	–
6.2.94	SD	A	Hunslet	W	38-12	Lewthwaite (3), Friend, Gribbin, Ryan, Tyrer	Maguire (5)	–	–
13.2.94	CC(5)	H	St. Helens	L	4-46	Fisher	–	4161	R. Connolly
20.2.94	SD	H	Batley	L	16-26	Dover, Gribbin, Pechey	Wear (2)	901	Carter
27.2.94	SD	A	Swinton	L	10-17	Kiddie, Pechey	Wear	–	–
6.3.94	SD	H	Keighley C.	W	16-10	Fisher, Pechey, Routledge	Wear (2)	1437	Kendrew
13.3.94	SD	A	Doncaster	L	6-20	Sorensen	Kiddie	–	–
20.3.94	SD	H	Huddersfield	W	9-4	Gribbin	Kiddie (2, 1dg)	901	Ollerton
27.3.94	SD	A	Highfield	W	46-12	Seeds (3), Gribbin (2), Chambers, Friend, Pechey, Routledge	Maguire (5)	–	–
1.4.94	SD	A	Workington T.	W	7-4	Seeds	Maguire, Kiddie (dg)	–	–
4.4.94	SD	H	Carlisle	W	46-4	Chambers (2), Gribbin (2), Maguire (2), Blaney, Hetherington, Pechey	Maguire (5)	1043	McGregor
10.4.94	SD	H	Barrow	W	36-17	Pechey (2), Anderson, Friend, Seeds, Sorensen	Maguire (6)	1068	Burke
17.4.94	SD	A	London C.	L	21-30	Pechey (2), Seeds	Maguire (4), Kiddie (dg)	–	–
24.4.94	SD	H	Rochdale H.	L	5-18	Anderson	Kiddie (dg)	991	Redfearn

131

WIDNES

Ground: Naughton Park (051-495-2250)
First Season: 1895-96
Nickname: Chemics
Chairman: Jim Mills
General
  Manager: Frank Myler
Honours: **Championship** Beaten finalists,
1935-36
Division One Champions, 1977-78,
1987-88, 1988-89
Challenge Cup Winners, 1929-30,
1936-37, 1963-64, 1974-75, 1978-79,
1980-81, 1983-84
Beaten finalists, 1933-34, 1949-50,
1975-76, 1976-77, 1981-82, 1992-93
Regal Trophy Winners, 1975-76,
1978-79, 1991-92
Beaten finalists, 1974-75, 1977-78,
1979-80, 1983-84, 1988-89
Premiership Winners, 1979-80,
1981-82, 1982-83, 1987-88, 1988-89,
1989-90
Beaten finalists, 1977-78, 1990-91
Lancashire Cup Winners, 1945-46,
1974-75, 1975-76, 1976-77, 1978-79,
1979-80, 1990-91
Beaten finalists, 1928-29, 1939-40,
1955-56, 1971-72, 1981-82, 1983-84
Lancashire League Winners,
1919-20
Western Division Championship
Beaten finalists, 1962-63
Charity Shield Winners, 1988-89,
1989-90, 1990-91
World Club Challenge Winners,
1989-90
BBC-2 Floodlit Trophy Winners,
1978-79
Beaten finalists, 1972-73, 1973-74

RECORDS

Match

Goals: 11 by Robin Whitfield v. Oldham,
        28 Oct 1965
Tries: 5 by Eddie Cunningham v. Doncaster,
        15 Feb 1981
        John Basnett at Hunslet,
        17 Oct 1981
        John Basnett v. Hull K.R.,
        2 Nov 1986
        David Hulme v. Dewsbury,
        30 Nov 1986
        Andy Currier v. Featherstone R.,
        25 Sep 1988
        Martin Offiah v. Warrington,
        15 Mar 1989
Points: 34 by Andy Currier v. Featherstone R.,
        25 Sep 1988
        Jonathan Davies v. Whitehaven,
        26 Aug 1990

Season

Goals: 140 by Mick Burke, 1978-79
Tries: 58 by Martin Offiah, 1988-89
Points: 342 by Jonathan Davies, 1990-91

Career

Goals: 1,083 by Ray Dutton, 1966-78
Tries: 234 by Mal Aspey, 1964-80
Points: 2,195 by Ray Dutton, 1966-78
Appearances: 587+4 by Keith Elwell, 1970-86
Highest score: 82-0 v. Dewsbury, 30 Nov 1986
Highest against: 60-5 at Oldham, 9 Apr 1928
Attendance: 24,205 v. St. Helens (RL Cup),
                16 Feb 1961

COACHING REGISTER

● **Since 1974-75**

Vince Karalius	Jan 72 - May 75
Frank Myler	May 75 - May 78
Doug Laughton	May 78 - Mar 83
Harry Dawson Colin Tyrer }	Mar 83 - May 83
*Vince Karalius Harry Dawson }	May 83 - May 84
Eric Hughes	June 84 - Jan 86
Doug Laughton	Jan 86 - May 91
Frank Myler	June 91 - May 92
Phil Larder	May 92 - May 94
Tony Myler	May 94 -

*Dawson quit as coach in Mar 1984 with
Karalius continuing as team manager.*

GREAT BRITAIN REGISTER

(46 players)

Mick Adams	(11+2)	1979-84
John Basnett	(2)	1984-86
Keith Bentley	(1)	1980
Mick Burke	(14+1)	1980-86
Frank Collier	(1)	1964
Andy Currier	(2)	1989-93
Jonathan Davies	(8+1)	1990-93
John Devereux	(6+2)	1992-93
Ray Dutton	(6)	1970
Keith Elwell	(3)	1977-80
Richard Eyres	(3+4)	1989-93
John Fieldhouse	(6)	1985-86
Ray French	(4)	1968
Les Gorley	(4+1)	1980-82
Andy Gregory	(8+1)	1981-84
Ian Hare	(1)	1967
Fred Higgins	(6)	1950-51
Harold Higgins	(2)	1937
Les Holliday	(3)	1991-92
Eric Hughes	(8)	1978-82
David Hulme	(7+1)	1988-89
Paul Hulme	(3+5)	1988-92
Albert Johnson	(4)	1914-20
Vince Karalius	(2)	1963
George Kemel	(2)	1965
Doug Laughton	(4)	1973-79
Joe Lydon	(9+1)	1983-85
Tommy McCue	(6)	1936-46
Steve McCurrie	(1)	1993
Jim Measures	(2)	1963
Jim Mills	(6)	1974-79
Paul Moriarty	(1+1)	1991-94
Frank Myler	(14+1)	1960-67
Tony Myler	(14)	1983-86
George Nicholls	(7)	1971-72
Martin Offiah	(20)	1988-91
Dennis O'Neill	(2+1)	1971-72
Mike O'Neill	(3)	1982-83
Harry Pinner	(1)	1986
Glyn Shaw	(1)	1980
Nat Silcock	(12)	1932-37
Stuart Spruce	(1)	1993
Alan Tait	(9)	1989-92
John Warlow	(3)	1971
Darren Wright	(+1)	1988
Stuart Wright	(7)	1977-78

1993-94 SIGNINGS REGISTER

Signed	Player	Club From
1.8.93	Barrow, Stephen	—
2.9.93	*Reynolds, Paul	Rochdale H.
13.9.93	Hunter, Jason	Blackbrook ARL
16.9.93	Ruane, David	Leigh
1.10.93	Ruane, Nicky	Simms Cross ARL
26.11.93	Boscoe, Stephen	Widnes St. Maries ARL
6.1.94	Elia, Mark	Northcote T., NZ
6.1.94	Mellor, Terry	Widnes St. Bedes ARL
7.1.94	Russell, Tim	Easts, Aus.
13.2.94	*Knox, Simon	Carlisle
20.2.94	Owen, Barry	Widnes Academy
8.3.94	Clarke, Philip	Widnes Academy
7.4.94	Owen, Lee	Golborne ARL

Bobby Goulding, scorer of 176 points in 1993-94, his second season at Naughton Park.

WIDNES 1993-94 PLAYERS' SUMMARY

	(Date of Birth)	App	T	G	D	Pts	Previous club	Signed
Barrow, Steve	(8.12.75)	0+1	—	—	—	—	—	23.1.93
Davidson, Paul	(1.8.69)	5+6	1	—	—	4	Hensingham ARL	29.11.90
Devereux, John	(30.3.66)	15	3	5	—	22	Bridgend RU	10.10.89
Elia, Mark	(25.12.62)	3+1	—	—	—	—	New Zealand	6.1.94
Faimalo, Esene	(11.10.66)	32+1	3	—	—	12	New Zealand	17.10.90
Goulding, Bobby	(4.2.72)	34	6	75	2	176	Leeds	14.8.92
Grieve, Jon	(29.9.70)	6+1	—	—	—	—	Australia	17.9.93
Hadley, Adrian	(1.3.63)	28	9	—	—	36	Salford	4.8.92
Halliwell, Adrian	(25.8.72)	1+1	1	—	—	4	—	8.1.90
Hammond, Karl	(25.4.74)	28+6	10	—	—	40	—	23.7.90
Harris, Paul	(18.4.74)	1+1	—	—	—	—	Widnes St. Maries ARL	13.8.92
Holden, Graham	(3.1.74)	0+1	—	—	—	—	Blackbrook ARL	28.6.91
Howard, Harvey	(29.8.68)	4	—	—	—	—	Waterloo RU	23.3.90
Howe, Rodney	(31.1.73)	10	1	—	—	4	Australia	
Hulme, David	(6.2.64)	26+1	4	—	—	16	Halton H. ARL	4.8.80
Hulme, Paul	(19.4.66)	26	4	—	—	16	Halton H. ARL	5.7.83
Hunter, Jason	(27.8.71)	2+4	—	—	—	—	Blackbrook ARL	13.9.93
Ireland, Andy	(6.12.71)	31+1	1	—	—	4	Golborne ARL	24.7.91
Kelly, Chris	(29.8.73)	1	—	—	—	—	—	23.7.90
Koloto, Emosi	(23.1.65)	8+3	2	—	—	8	New Zealand RU	21.10.88
McCurrie, Steve	(2.7.73)	33	11	—	1	45	Hensingham ARL	23.7.90
Makin, Craig	(13.4.73)	1+6	—	—	—	—	Orrell St. James ARL	10.1.92
Moriarty, Paul	(16.7.64)	14+5	7	—	—	28	Swansea RU	3.4.89
Myers, Dave	(31.7.71)	33+1	8	—	—	32	Wigan	8.10.92
O'Reilly, Steve		1+2	—	5	—	10	Blackbrook ARL	25.4.93
Reynolds, Paul	(1.4.68)	1	—	—	—	—	Rochdale H.	2.9.93
Ruane, David	(24.9.63)	24+2	9	—	—	36	Leigh	16.9.93
Ruane, Nicky	(22.12.73)	2	—	—	—	—	Simms Cross ARL	1.10.93
Russell, Tim	(7.10.69)	11+2	—	—	—	—	Australia	7.1.94
Sarsfield, Mark	(22.3.71)	0+2	1	—	—	4	Leigh Miners ARL	14.12.89
Smith, David	(15.3.68)	23+9	2	—	—	8	—	5.6.87
Smith, Peter	(1.9.73)	10	2	—	—	8	Widnes Tigers ARL	6.9.91
Spruce, Stuart	(3.1.71)	31	11	7	—	58	Widnes Tigers ARL	8.1.90
Tyrer, Christian	(19.12.73)	16+8	6	6	—	36	Leigh Rangers ARL	23.7.90
Wright, Darren	(17.1.68)	7+1	1	—	—	4	Leigh Miners ARL	23.3.85
TOTALS								
35 players			103	98	3	611		

Representative appearances 1993-94

Devereux — Britain (3, 3t), Wales (1); Hadley — Wales (+1); McCurrie — GB Under-21s (2, 2t); Makin — GB Under-21s (+1); Moriarty — Britain (+1), Wales (1).

WIDNES 1993-94 MATCH ANALYSIS

Date	Com-petition	H/A	Opponent	Rlt	Score	Tries	Goals	Atten-dance	Referee
29.8.93	SBC	A	Bradford N.	L	18-32	D. Hulme, Myers, Spruce	Goulding (3)	—	—
5.9.93	SBC	H	Leigh	W	34-10	Spruce (4), Halliwell	Goulding (7)	4785	Morris
12.9.93	SBC	A	Salford	L	19-33	Koloto (2), D. Hulme	Goulding (3), McCurrie (dg)	—	—
17.9.93	SBC	H	Castleford	L	12-37	McCurrie, Spruce	Goulding (2)	3494	J. Connolly
24.9.93	SBC	A	Wigan	L	2-32	—	Spruce	—	—
3.10.93	SBC	H	Oldham	W	14-12	McCurrie, Spruce	Spruce (3)	4752	Holdsworth
10.10.93	SBC	A	Hull	L	14-20	Myers, D. Ruane	Spruce (3)	—	—
22.10.93	SBC	A	Wakefield T.	W	10-0	Goulding, Hadley	Devereux	—	—
31.10.93	SBC	H	Featherstone R.	W	24-12	Faimalo, Howe, D. Hulme, P. Hulme	Devereux (4)	4464	Morris
2.11.93	Tour	H	New Zealand	L	10-18	Myers, Tyrer	Tyrer	5646	Ollerton
14.11.93	RT(2)	H	Doncaster	W	24-4	Goulding, Hadley, Hammond, Spruce	Goulding (4)	3075	Presley
21.11.93	SBC	H	Sheffield E.	W	32-28	Faimalo, Goulding, Hadley, McCurrie, Myers	Goulding (6)	3511	Ollerton
28.11.93	SBC	A	Hull K.R.	W	32-10	Spruce (2), Devereux, Goulding, Moriarty, Myers	Goulding (4)	—	—
1.12.93	SBC	H	Leeds	W	8-6	Devereux	Goulding (2)	4773	J. Connolly
5.12.93	SBC	A	Halifax	L	12-20	Devereux, Myers	Goulding (2)	—	—
12.12.93	RT(3)	A	Hull	L	6-10	McCurrie	Goulding	—	—
28.12.93	SBC	H	Warrington	L	10-18	Hadley, Tyrer	Goulding	7686	J. Connolly
2.1.94	SBC	A	St. Helens	L	16-24	Faimalo, Sarsfield	Goulding (2), Tyrer (2)	—	—
7.1.94	SBC	A	Leigh	W	25-14	McCurrie (2), Hadley, Hammond, Moriarty	Goulding (1,1dg), Tyrer	—	—
12.1.94	SBC	H	Bradford N.	L	8-28	D. Smith, P. Smith	—	4023	Morris
16.1.94	SBC	H	Salford	W	30-22	Davidson, Hadley, Hammond, D. Ruane, Tyrer	O'Reilly (5)	4589	Asquith
30.1.94	CC(4)	A	Bramley	W	20-11	Hammond (2), Hadley, Myers	Goulding (2)	—	—
4.2.94	SBC	H	Wigan	L	12-27	Hammond, D. Ruane	Goulding (2)	5722	Holdsworth
13.2.94	CC(5)	H	Sheffield E.	W	22-6	Hammond, P. Hulme, McCurrie	Goulding (5)	4631	J. Connolly
20.2.94	SBC	A	Oldham	L	12-22	Hammond, McCurrie	Goulding (2)	—	—
26.2.94	CC(6)	A	Castleford	L	6-30	Moriarty	Goulding	—	—
2.3.94	SBC	A	Castleford	L	6-42	Hammond	Goulding	—	—
6.3.94	SBC	H	Hull	W	28-6	P. Hulme (2), D. Ruane, Spruce, Myers	Goulding (4)	3389	R. Smith
13.3.94	SBC	H	Wakefield T.	W	22-12	Goulding, Hammond, McCurrie, D. Ruane	Goulding (3)	3271	Asquith
20.3.94	SBC	A	Featherstone R.	W	29-22	D. Ruane (2), Tyrer, Wright	Goulding (6,1dg)	—	—
1.4.94	SBC	A	Warrington	L	14-28	Moriarty, D.Ruane	Goulding (3)	—	—
4.4.94	SBC	H	St. Helens	W	20-17	Goulding, Hadley, Ireland, D. Smith	Goulding (2)	5901	J. Connolly
10.4.94	SBC	H	Halifax	W	28-16	Moriarty (2), Hadley, McCurrie, Tyrer	Goulding (4)	4468	Morris
17.4.94	SBC	A	Sheffield E.	L	6-21	McCurrie	Tyrer	—	—
20.4.94	SBC	A	Leeds	L	16-58	D. Hulme, Moriarty, Tyrer	Goulding, Tyrer	—	—
24.4.94	SBC	H	Hull K.R.	L	10-13	D. Ruane, P. Smith	Goulding	3052	R. Smith

WIGAN

Ground: Central Park (0942-31321)
First Season: 1895-96
Nickname: Riversiders
Chairman: Jack Robinson
Secretary: Mary Charnock
Honours: **Championship** Winners, 1908-09,
1921-22, 1925-26, 1933-34, 1945-46,
1946-47, 1949-50, 1951-52, 1959-60
Beaten finalists, 1909-10, 1910-11,
1911-12, 1912-13, 1923-24, 1970-71
War Emergency League
Winners, 1943-44
Beaten finalists, 1940-41
League Leaders Trophy Winners,
1970-71
Division One Champions, 1986-87,
1989-90, 1990-91, 1991-92, 1992-93,
1993-94
Challenge Cup Winners, 1923-24,
1928-29, 1947-48, 1950-51, 1957-58,
1958-59, 1964-65, 1984-85, 1987-88,
1988-89, 1989-90, 1990-91, 1991-92,
1992-93, 1993-94
Beaten finalists, 1910-11, 1919-20,
1943-44, 1945-46, 1960-61, 1962-63,
1965-66, 1969-70, 1983-84
Regal Trophy Winners, 1982-83,
1985-86, 1986-87, 1988-89, 1989-90,
1992-93
Beaten finalists, 1993-94
Premiership Winners, 1986-87,
1991-92, 1993-94
Beaten finalists, 1992-93
Lancashire Cup Winners, 1905-06,
1908-09, 1909-10, 1912-13, 1922-23,
1928-29, 1938-39, 1946-47, 1947-48,
1948-49, 1949-50, 1950-51, 1951-52,
1966-67, 1971-72, 1973-74, 1985-86,
1986-87, 1987-88, 1988-89, 1992-93
Beaten finalists, 1913-14, 1914-15,
1925-26, 1927-28, 1930-31, 1934-35,
1935-36, 1936-37, 1945-46, 1953-54,
1957-58, 1977-78, 1980-81, 1984-85
Lancashire League Winners,
1901-02, 1908-09, 1910-11, 1911-12,
1912-13, 1913-14, 1914-15, 1920-21,
1922-23, 1923-24, 1925-26, 1945-46,
1946-47, 1949-50, 1951-52, 1958-59,
1961-62, 1969-70

Lancashire War League Winners,
1940-41
Charity Shield Winners, 1985-86,
1987-88, 1991-92
Beaten finalists, 1988-89, 1989-90,
1990-91, 1992-93
World Club Challenge Winners,
1987-88, 1991-92, 1993-94
Beaten finalists, 1992-93
BBC-2 Floodlit Trophy Winners,
1968-69
Beaten finalists, 1969-70

RECORDS
Match
Goals: 22 by Jim Sullivan v. Flimby & Fothergill,
14 Feb 1925
Tries: 10 by Martin Offiah v. Leeds,
10 May 1992
Shaun Edwards at Swinton,
29 Sep 1992
Points: 44 by Jim Sullivan v. Flimby & Fothergill,
14 Feb 1925

Season
Goals: 184 by Frano Botica, 1992-93
Tries: 62 by Johnny Ring, 1925-26
Points: 423 by Frano Botica, 1992-93

Career
Goals: 2,317 by Jim Sullivan, 1921-46
Tries: 478 by Billy Boston, 1953-68
Points: 4,883 by Jim Sullivan, 1921-46
Appearances: 774 by Jim Sullivan, 1921-46
Highest score: 116-0 v. Flimby & Fothergill,
14 Feb 1925
Highest against: 58-3 at Leeds, 14 Oct 1972
Attendance: 47,747 v. St. Helens (League),
27 Mar 1959

COACHING REGISTER ● Since 1974-75

Ted Toohey	May 74 - Jan 75
Joe Coan	Jan 75 - Sep 76
Vince Karalius	Sep 76 - Sep 79
Kel Coslett	Oct 79 - Apr 80
George Fairbairn	Apr 80 - May 81
Maurice Bamford	May 81 - May 82
Alex Murphy	June 82 - Aug 84
Colin Clarke	
Alan McInnes	} Aug 84 - May 86
Graham Lowe	Aug 86 - June 89
John Monie	Sep 89 - May 93
John Dorahy	June 93 - May 94
Graeme West	May 94 -

GREAT BRITAIN REGISTER
(86 players)

Ray Ashby	(1)	1965
Ernest Ashcroft	(11)	1947-54
Eric Ashton	(26)	1957-63
Bill Ashurst	(3)	1971-72
Frank Barton	(1)	1951
John Barton	(2)	1960-61
Jack Bennett	(1)	1926
Denis Betts	(21+1)	1990-93
Dai Bevan	(1)	1952
Billy Blan	(3)	1951
Dave Bolton	(23)	1957-63
Billy Boston	(31)	1954-63
Tommy Bradshaw	(6)	1947-50
Frank Carlton	(1)	1962
Brian Case	(6+1)	1984-88
Norman Cherrington	(1)	1960
Colin Clarke	(7)	1965-73
Phil Clarke	(12+1)	1990-93
Percy Coldrick	(4)	1914
Frank Collier	(1)	1963
Gary Connolly	(4)	1993-94
Neil Cowie	(1)	1993
Jack Cunliffe	(4)	1950-54
Martin Dermott	(11)	1990-93
Shaun Edwards	(30+4)	1985-94
Joe Egan	(14)	1946-50
Roy Evans	(4)	1961-62
George Fairbairn	(14)	1977-80
Andrew Farrell	(2)	1993-94
Terry Fogerty	(1)	1967
Phil Ford	(1)	1985
Bill Francis	(4)	1967-77
Danny Gardiner	(1)	1965
Ken Gee	(17)	1946-51
Henderson Gill	(14+1)	1981-88
Andy Goodway	(12)	1985-90
Bobby Goulding	(5)	1990
John Gray	(5+3)	1974
Andy Gregory	(16)	1987-92
Steve Hampson	(11+1)	1987-92
Ellery Hanley	(23)	1985-91
Cliff Hill	(1)	1966
David Hill	(1)	1971
Jack Hilton	(4)	1950
Tommy Howley	(6)	1924
Bill Hudson	(1)	1948
Danny Hurcombe	(8)	1920-24
Bert Jenkins	(12)	1907-14
Ken Jones	(2)	1970
Roy Kinnear	(1)	1929
Nicky Kiss	(1)	1985
Doug Laughton	(11)	1970-71
Johnny Lawrenson	(3)	1948
Jim Leytham	(5)	1907-10
Ian Lucas	(1+1)	1991-92
Joe Lydon	(14+6)	1986-92
Billy McGinty	(4)	1992
Brian McTigue	(25)	1958-63
Barrie-Jon Mather	(+1)	1994
Joe Miller	(1)	1911
Jack Morley	(2)	1936-37
Martin Offiah	(10)	1992-94
Andy Platt	(17+1)	1989-93
Ian Potter	(7+1)	1985-86
Jack Price	(4)	1924
Dick Ramsdale	(8)	1910-14
Gordon Ratcliffe	(3)	1947-50
Johnny Ring	(2)	1924-26
Dave Robinson	(1)	1970
Jason Robinson	(1)	1993
Martin Ryan	(4)	1947-50
Billy Sayer	(7)	1961-63
Jim Sharrock	(4)	1910-11
Nat Silcock	(3)	1954
Dick Silcock	(1)	1908
Kelvin Skerrett	(6+2)	1992-93
David Stephenson	(5)	1982-87
Jim Sullivan	(25)	1924-33
Mick Sullivan	(19)	1957-60
Gwyn Thomas	(1)	1914
Johnny Thomas	(8)	1907-11
Shaun Wane	(2)	1985-86
Edward Ward	(3)	1946-47
Les White	(2)	1947
David Willicombe	(2)	1974
Billy Winstanley	(3)	1911

1993-94 SIGNINGS REGISTER

Signed	Player	Club From
22.6.93	Riley, David	Wigan Academy
1.7.93	Wright, Nigel	Wakefield T.
1.8.93	Connolly, Gary	St. Helens
3.8.93	Roberts, Stephen	Blackbrook ARL
9.8.93	Cantillon, Philip	Wigan Academy
19.8.93	Murdock, Craig	Hensingham ARL
27.8.93	Barr, Brendan	—
3.9.93	Barrow, Warren	Orrell St. James ARL
22.9.93	Whittle, David	Wigan St. Patricks ARL
24.9.93	Long, Sean	Wigan St. Judes ARL

1.10.93	Brent, Andrew	Stanningley ARL
7.10.93	Taylor, Stephen	Blackbrook ARL
1.11.93	Craig, Andrew	Wigan Academy
12.11.93	Hammill, David	East Leeds ARL
8.1.94	Tuigamala, Va'aiga	Ponsonby RU, NZ

16.2.94	Doherty, John	Wigan St. Patricks ARL
22.2.94	Prest, Lee	Hensingham ARL
22.2.94	Smyth, Robert	Rose Bridge ARL

WIGAN 1993-94 PLAYERS' SUMMARY

	(Date of Birth)	App	T	G	D	Pts	Previous club	Signed
Atcheson, Paul	(17.5.73)	16+1	3	—	—	12	Widnes	8.10.92
Bell, Dean	(29.4.62)	13+3	—	—	—	—	Australia	24.10.86
Betts, Denis	(14.9.69)	18+5	9	—	—	36	Leigh Rangers ARL	6.10.86
Botica, Frano	(3.8.63)	42	13	177	6	412	New Zealand RU	15.6.90
Cassidy, Mick	(3.7.73)	20+15	4	—	—	16	Wigan St. Judes ARL	24.5.90
Clarke, Phil	(16.5.71)	29	7	—	—	28	Wigan St. Pat's ARL	26.10.87
Connolly, Gary	(22.6.71)	41	10	—	—	40	St. Helens	1.8.93
Cowie, Neil	(16.1.67)	33+4	6	—	—	24	Rochdale H.	3.9.91
Craig, Andrew	(16.3.76)	2	1	—	—	4	Wigan Academy	1.11.93
Crompton, Martin	(29.9.69)	0+1	—	—	—	—	Warrington	27.7.92
Dermott, Martin	(25.9.67)	22+4	1	—	—	4	Wigan St. Pat's ARL	7.11.84
Edwards, Shaun	(17.10.66)	35+2	19	—	—	76	Wigan St. Pat's ARL	18.10.83
Ellison, Danny	(16.12.72)	11	2	—	—	8	Golborne ARL	29.12.91
Farrell, Andrew	(30.5.75)	34+7	9	4	1	45	Orrell St. James ARL	19.10.92
Gildart, Ian	(14.10.69)	12+6	—	—	—	—	Wigan Colts	24.10.86
Hall, Martin	(5.12.68)	22+2	2	—	—	8	Rochdale H.	11.1.93
Haughton, Simon	(10.11.75)	0+3	1	—	—	4	Dudley Hill ARL	10.11.92
Lydon, Joe	(26.11.63)	19+10	—	4	—	8	Widnes	20.1.86
McGinty, Billy	(6.12.64)	4+5	—	—	—	—	Warrington	29.8.91
Mather, Barrie-Jon	(15.1.73)	32	20	—	—	80	—	14.8.91
Murdock, Craig	(24.10.73)	3	—	—	—	—	Hensingham ARL	19.8.93
Offiah, Martin	(29.12.66)	34	35	—	1	141	Widnes	3.1.92
Panapa, Sam	(14.5.62)	34+9	21	—	—	84	Sheffield E.	30.8.91
Platt, Andy	(9.10.63)	30+1	2	—	—	8	St. Helens	7.9.88
Radlinski, Kris	(9.4.76)	0+1	—	—	—	—	Wigan Academy	25.5.93
Robinson, Jason	(30.7.74)	29+1	11	—	—	44	Hunslet P. ARL	31.7.91
Skerrett, Kelvin	(22.5.66)	35+1	3	—	—	12	Bradford N.	13.8.90
Stevens, Paul	(7.10.74)	2+3	2	—	—	8	Orrell St. James ARL	31.10.91
Tuigamala, Va'aiga	(4.9.69)	10+1	4	—	—	16	New Zealand RU	8.1.94
Williams, Darren	(27.4.74)	1	1	—	—	4	Woolston R. ARL	20.8.91
Wright, Nigel	(8.11.73)	15+1	4	—	1	17	Wakefield T.	1.7.93

TOTALS
31 players 190 185 9 1139

Representative appearances 1993-94
Robinson — Britain (1, 2t); Cassidy — GB Under-21s (2); Connolly — Britain (4); Edwards — Britain (4, 1t); Dermott — Britain (1); Betts — Britain (1); Clarke — Britain (3, 1t); Offiah — Britain (3, 2t); Skerrett — Britain (1); Farrell — Britain (2, 1t, 1g), GB Under-21s (1, 2t); Mather — Britain (+1), GB Under-21s (2, 1t); Botica — New Zealand (2, 5g); Wright — GB Under-21s (+1).

WIGAN 1993-94 MATCH ANALYSIS

Date	Com-petition	H/A	Opponent	Rlt	Score	Tries	Goals	Atten-dance	Referee
29.8.93	SBC	H	Hull	W	16-8	Mather, Robinson	Botica (4)	13,707	R. Smith
5.9.93	SBC	A	Wakefield T.	W	40-16	Mather (2), Betts, Botica, Ellison, Robinson, Skerrett	Botica (6)	—	—
10.9.93	SBC	H	Leeds	W	32-18	Robinson (2), Edwards, Mather, Wright	Botica (6)	14,229	Holdsworth
19.9.93	SBC	A	Featherstone R.	L	22-35	Betts, Mather, Robinson, Skerrett	Botica (2), Lydon	—	—
24.9.93	SBC	H	Widnes	W	32-2	Botica, Connolly, Edwards, Mather	Botica (8)	12,879	R. Smith
3.10.93	SBC	A	Salford	W	24-2	Botica (2), Connolly, Panapa	Botica (4)	—	—
10.10.93	Tour	H	New Zealand	L	18-25	Cowie, Edwards, Hall	Botica (3)	13,669	Whitfield
19.10.93	SBC	H	Leigh	W	38-12	Connolly, Edwards, Farrell, Hall, Offiah	Botica (9)	12,394	Nicholson
24.10.93	SBC	A	Halifax	W	31-22	Clarke (2), Offiah (2), Edwards, Robinson	Botica (3,1dg)	—	—
31.10.93	SBC	A	Castleford	L	0-46	—	—	—	—
14.11.93	RT(2)	A	Whitehaven	W	22-8	Cowie, Haughton, Panapa, Williams	Botica (3)	—	—
19.11.93	SBC	A	Bradford N.	Ab. 13min.	2-4	—	Botica	—	—
24.11.93	SBC	H	Sheffield E.	W	40-10	Cassidy (2), Offiah (2), Panapa (2), Ellison, Farrell	Botica (4)	7658	Holdsworth
28.11.93	SBC	H	Oldham	W	38-12	Offiah (3), Clarke (2), Cowie, Mather	Botica (5)	11,509	Steele
5.12.93	SBC	H	Hull K.R.	W	54-16	Betts (2), Offiah (2), Clarke, Connolly, Craig, Mather, Panapa, Stevens	Botica (7)	10,533	Morris
12.12.93	RT(3)	A	Oldham	W	16-8	Connolly, Panapa, Robinson	Botica (2)	—	—
18.12.93	RT(4)	A	Warrington	W	27-10	Robinson (2), Mather, Skerrett, Stevens	Botica (3, 1dg)	—	—
26.12.93	SBC	H	St. Helens	W	40-8	Clarke, Cowie, Dermott, Edwards, Farrell, Offiah, Panapa	Botica (3), Lydon (3)	29,100	Holdsworth
2.1.94	SBC	A	Warrington	W	8-6	Offiah	Botica (2)	—	—
8.1.94	RT(SF)	A	Salford	W	18-12	Edwards, Mather, Offiah	Farrell (3)	—	—
14.1.94	SBC	A	Leeds	W	26-14	Edwards, Farrell, Mather, Offiah	Botica (5)	—	—
22.1.94	RT(F)	N[1]	Castleford	L	2-33	—	Botica	(15,626)	Campbell
30.1.94	CC(4)	H	Wakefield T.	W	24-16	Connolly, Panapa, Wright	Botica (6)	12,171	Cummings
4.2.94	SBC	A	Widnes	W	27-12	Atcheson, Connolly, Panapa, Platt, Tuigamala	Botica (3,1dg)	—	—
13.2.94	CC(5)	A	Hull	W	22-21	Mather (2), Farrell, Panapa	Botica (3)	—	—
16.2.94	SBC	H	Wakefield T.	L	13-20	Atcheson, Mather, Panapa	Wright (dg)	12,965	Whitfield
20.2.94	SBC	H	Salford	W	34-12	Panapa (2), Mather, Offiah, Wright	Botica (7)	11,911	Morris
27.2.94	CC(6)	H	Featherstone R.	W	32-14	Mather (2), Botica, Connolly, Panapa	Botica (6)	16,019	Cummings
2.3.94	SBC	H	Featherstone R.	W	28-10	Cowie, Mather, Offiah, Panapa	Botica (6)	10,655	Campbell
6.3.94	SBC	A	Leigh	W	26-8	Offiah (2), Botica, Panapa	Botica (5)	—	—
12.3.94	CC(SF)	N[1]	Castleford	W	20-6	Atcheson, Botica, Offiah	Botica (4)	(17,049)	Cummings
23.3.94	SBC	A	Hull	W	4-18	Robinson	—	—	—
27.3.94	SBC	A	Sheffield E.	L	5-10	Connolly	Botica (dg)	—	—
1.4.94	SBC	A	St. Helens	W	15-9	Edwards, Platt	Botica (3), Offiah (dg)	—	—
4.4.94	SBC	H	Warrington	W	21-14	Cassidy, Edwards, Panapa	Botica (4,1dg)	19,045	Campbell
7.4.94	SBC	H	Halifax	W	38-0	Offiah (3), Botica, Clarke, Cowie, Edwards	Botica (5)	14,061	Holdsworth
10.4.94	SBC	A	Hull K.R.	L	10-21	Farrell, Wright	Farrell	—	—
12.4.94	SBC	A	Bradford N.	L	6-10	Edwards	Botica	—	—
15.4.94	SBC	H	Bradford N.	W	41-14	Offiah (3), Edwards (2), Panapa, Farrell	Botica (6,1dg)	17,781	Holdsworth

(Continued)

Date	Com-petition	H/A	Opponent	Rlt	Score	Tries	Goals	Atten-dance	Referee
20.4.94	SBC	H	Castleford	W	21-12	Edwards, Offiah, Tuigamala	Botica (4), Farrell (dg)	19,706	Holdsworth
24.4.94	SBC	A	Oldham	W	50-6	Botica (2), Offiah (2), Mather, Edwards (2), Connolly, Panapa	Botica (7)	—	—
30.4.94	CC(F)	N^2	Leeds	W	26-16	Offiah (2), Farrell, Panapa	Botica (5)	(78,348)	Campbell
8.5.94	PT(1)	H	St. Helens	W	34-16	Edwards (2), Offiah (2), Betts, Cassidy	Botica (5)	17,367	R. Smith
13.5.94	PT(SF)	H	Sheffield E.	W	52-18	Offiah (3), Betts (2), Botica (2), Tuigamala (2)	Botica (8)	11,340	Campbell
22.5.94	PT(F)	N^3	Castleford	W	24-20	Farrell, Panapa, Botica, Betts	Botica (4)	(35,644)	Cummings
1.6.94	WCC	A	Brisbane B.	W	20-14	Robinson, Mather, Betts	Botica (4)	(54,220)	McCallum

^{1} Leeds;   N^2 Wembley;   N^3 Manchester U. FC

Winger Jason Robinson, scorer of 11 tries in 30 games in 1993-94.

WORKINGTON TOWN

Ground: Derwent Park (0900-603609)
First Season: 1945-46
Nickname: Town
Chairman: Kevan Gorge
Secretary: John Bell
Honours: **Championship** Winners, 1950-51
Beaten finalists, 1957-58
Division Two Champions, 1993-94
Challenge Cup Winners, 1951-52
Beaten finalists, 1954-55, 1957-58
Second Division/Divisional Premiership Winners, 1993-94
Beaten finalists, 1992-93
Lancashire Cup Winners, 1977-78
Beaten finalists, 1976-77, 1978-79, 1979-80
Western Division Championship Winners, 1962-63

RECORDS

Match
Goals: 13 by Dean Marwood v. Highfield, 1 Nov 1992
Tries: 7 by Ike Southward v. Blackpool B., 17 Sep 1955
Points: 42 by Dean Marwood v. Highfield, 1 Nov 1992

Season
Goals: 186 by Lyn Hopkins, 1981-82
Tries: 49 by Johnny Lawrenson, 1951-52
Points: 438 by Lyn Hopkins, 1981-82

Career
Goals: 809 by Iain MacCorquodale, 1972-80
Tries: 274 by Ike Southward, 1952-59 & 1960-68
Points: 1,800 by Iain MacCorquodale, 1972-80
Appearances: 415+4 Paul Charlton, 1961-69 & 1975-80
Highest score: 78-0 v. Highfield, 1 Nov 1992
78-12 at Blackpool G., 28 Feb 1993
Highest against: 68-0 at Wigan, 18 Jan 1987
68-6 at Leigh, 8 Mar 1992
Attendance: 17,741 v. Wigan (RL Cup), 3 Mar 1965 — at Derwent Park

20,403 v. St. Helens (RL Cup), 8 Mar 1952 — at Borough Park

COACHING REGISTER
● **Since 1974-75**

Ike Southward	Aug 73 - June 75
Paul Charlton	June 75 - June 76
Ike Southward	June 76 - Feb 78
Sol Roper	Feb 78 - Apr 80
Keith Irving	Aug 80 - Oct 80
Tommy Bishop	Nov 80 - June 82
Paul Charlton	July 82 - Dec 82
Dave Cox	Mar 83 - Mar 83
Harry Archer/Bill Smith	May 83 - June 84
Bill Smith	June 84 - Apr 85
Jackie Davidson	Apr 85 - Jan 86
Keith Davies	Feb 86 - Mar 87
Norman Turley	Mar 87 - Apr 88
Maurice Bamford	July 88 - Dec 88
Phil Kitchin	Dec 88 - May 90
Ray Ashton	June 90 - Dec 91
Dean Williams	Dec 91 - Apr 92
Peter Walsh	May 92 -

GREAT BRITAIN REGISTER
(9 players)

Eddie Bowman	(4)	1977
Paul Charlton	(1)	1965
Brian Edgar	(11)	1958-66
Norman Herbert	(6)	1961-62
Vince McKeating	(2)	1951
Billy Martin	(1)	1962
Albert Pepperell	(2)	1950-51
Ike Southward	(4)	1958
George Wilson	(3)	1951

1993-94 SIGNINGS REGISTER

Signed	Player	Club From
21.6.93	Moore, Jason	Ellenborough R. ARL
19.7.93	Gorley, Jonathan	Ellenborough R. ARL
2.8.93	Wane, Shaun	Leeds
10.8.93	Dawson, Peter	Great Clifton ARL
24.8.93	Chilton, Lee	Ellenborough R. ARL
25.8.93	Nicholson, Tony	Workington RU
27.8.93	Cocker, Stuart	Oldham
14.9.93	Neill, Justin	Kells ARL
18.10.93	Fryer, Stephen	—
3.12.93	Barker, Craig	—
4.2.94	*Richards, Craig	Oldham
4.3.94	*Shaw, Neil	Barrow
27.3.94	Smith, Leigh	Hensingham ARL

141

WORKINGTON TOWN 1993-94 PLAYERS' SUMMARY

	(Date of Birth)	App	T	G	D	Pts	Previous club	Signed
Armstrong, Colin	(26.1.63)	35+1	1	—	—	4	Hull K.R.	3.10.90
Buglass, Barry	(9.2.72)	6+9	—	—	—	—	Cockermouth ARL	19.8.91
Burns, Paul	(9.2.67)	25+1	10	—	—	40	Barrow	16.8.92
Byrne, Ged	(14.6.62)	33+1	7	—	—	28	Oldham	12.2.93
Carter, Darren	(8.1.72)	2+2	—	—	—	—	Millom ARL	31.10.92
Chilton, Lee	(29.9.72)	1	2	—	—	8	Ellenborough R. ARL	24.8.93
Cocker, Stuart	(8.5.66)	37	35	—	—	140	Oldham	27.8.93
Drummond, Des	(17.6.58)	35	17	—	—	68	Warrington	19.3.93
Gorley, Jonathan	(21.7.71)	4+1	1	—	—	4	Ellenborough R. ARL	19.7.93
Hepi, Brad	(11.2.68)	29+3	10	—	—	40	Carlisle	1.5.92
Kay, Tony	(16.4.64)	36	19	—	—	76	Barrow	2.10.92
Kitchin, Wayne	(26.11.70)	29	13	43	5	143	Kells ARL	26.9.89
McGuirk, Gary	(26.9.71)	5+12	1	—	—	4	British Steel ARL	18.6.90
McKenzie, Phil	(13.6.63)	34	4	—	—	16	Widnes	4.2.93
McLean, Ian	(20.5.65)	6	2	—	—	8	Oldham St. Annes ARL	24.8.90
Marwood, Dean	(22.2.70)	27	4	99	1	215	Barrow	23.12.91
Moore, Jason	(27.12.70)	0+13	3	—	—	12	Ellenborough R. ARL	21.6.93
Mulligan, Mark	(6.3.70)	38	24	1	1	99	Australia	17.9.92
Nicholson, Tony	(12.3.66)	6	2	—	—	8	Workington RU	25.8.93
Oglanby, Martin	(22.7.64)	23+2	5	—	—	20	Glasson R. ARL	24.7.90
Penrice, Paul	(27.2.66)	12+4	3	—	—	12	Gt. Clifton ARL	30.7.87
Pickering, James	(11.12.66)	24+3	3	—	—	12	New Zealand	5.11.92
Richards, Craig	(27.1.70)	3	—	—	—	—	Oldham	4.2.94
Riley, Peter	(1.3.68)	10+14	—	—	—	—	Gt. Clifton ARL	30.7.87
Schubert, Gary	(18.9.66)	21+6	3	—	—	12	Carlisle	9.8.91
Shaw, Neil	(29.9.68)	6+1	1	—	—	4	Barrow	4.3.94
Smith, Garry	(2.10.62)	1	—	—	—	—	Egremont ARL	3.9.84
Wane, Shaun	(14.9.64)	6+2	2	—	—	8	Leeds	2.8.93
TOTALS								
28 players			172	143	7	981		

Celebrations at Old Trafford for 1994 Stones Bitter Second Division Premiership victors, Workington Town.

WORKINGTON TOWN 1993-94 MATCH ANALYSIS

Date	Com-petition	H/A	Opponent	Rlt	Score	Tries	Goals	Atten-dance	Referee
29.8.93	SD	H	Huddersfield	L	9-10	Schubert	Kitchin (2,1dg)	2665	Cummings
5.9.93	SD	A	Batley	W	24-4	Mulligan (2), Drummond, Kay	Kitchin (4)	—	—
12.9.93	SD	H	Swinton	W	52-6	Drummond (2), Kitchin (2), Byrne, Cocker, Hepi, Kay, Moore, Nicholson	Kitchin (6)	2259	Kershaw
19.9.93	SD	A	Carlisle	W	28-12	Cocker (2), Kay, Kitchin	Kitchin (6)	—	—
26.9.93	SD	H	Doncaster	W	32-13	Cocker (2), Hepi, Kitchin, Mulligan, Nicholson	Kitchin (4)	2253	Volante
3.10.93	SD	A	Rochdale H.	W	28-22	Cocker, Drummond, Kay, Kitchin, Oglanby, Pickering	Kitchin (2)	—	—
10.10.93	SD	H	Dewsbury	W	30-14	Armstrong, Cocker, Drummond, Kitchin, McLean	Kitchin (5)	2698	Kendrew
24.10.93	SD	A	Ryedale-York	L	12-29	Hepi, Mulligan	Kitchin (2)	—	—
31.10.93	RT(1)	H	Wigan St. Patricks	W	74-6	Mulligan (3), Cocker (2), Hepi (2), Kay (2), Kitchin (2), Wane (2), Drummond	Kitchin (9)	1464	Carter
7.11.93	SD	H	London C.	L	12-13	Hepi, McKenzie	Kitchin (2)	2054	Asquith
14.11.93	RT(2)	A	Ryedale-York	L	11-12	McLean, Mulligan	Kitchin (1,1dg)	—	—
21.11.93	SD	A	Hunslet	W	10-6	Mulligan	Marwood (3)	—	—
28.11.93	SD	H	Bramley	W	34-24	Kay (2), Cocker, Kitchin, McKenzie	Marwood (7)	1777	Crashley
5.12.93	SD	A	Keighley C.	W	16-4	Cocker, Gorley	Marwood (4)	—	—
12.12.93	SD	H	Highfield	W	26-4	Cocker (2), Drummond, Kitchin	Marwood (5)	1467	Galtress
19.12.93	SD	A	Huddersfield	W	20-4	Cocker, Kay, Kitchin, Pickering	Marwood (2)	—	—
28.12.93	SD	A	Whitehaven	D	0-0	—	—	—	—
2.1.94	SD	H	Barrow	W	50-6	Cocker (5), Drummond, Hepi, Kitchin, Schubert	Marwood (7)	3237	Burke
9.1.94	SD	H	Batley	W	28-6	Cocker (2), Mulligan, Pickering, Schubert	Marwood (4)	2342	Wood
16.1.94	CC(3)	H	Beverley	W	24-10	Burns, Kitchin, Marwood, Mulligan	Marwood (4)	1277	Steele
23.1.94	SD	A	Swinton	W	22-8	Hepi (2), Cocker	Marwood (5)	—	—
30.1.94	CC(4)	A	Carlisle	W	13-12	Cocker, Drummond	Marwood (2), Kitchin (dg)	—	—
6.2.94	SD	H	Carlisle	W	23-16	Burns, Cocker, McGuirk	Marwood (5), Kitchin (dg)	2686	Kershaw
13.2.94	CC(5)	H	Bradford N.	L	0-32	—	—	5294	R. Smith
20.2.94	SD	A	Doncaster	L	11-15	Burns, Mulligan	Marwood (1,1dg)	—	—
27.2.94	SD	H	Rochdale H.	L	12-37	Byrne, Oglanby	Marwood, Mulligan	2230	Cross
6.3.94	SD	A	Dewsbury	W	21-10	Burns, Cocker, Mulligan	Marwood (4), Mulligan (dg)	—	—
13.3.94	SD	H	Ryedale-York	W	40-12	Kay (2), Mulligan (2), Oglanby (2), Cocker, Penrice	Marwood (4)	2090	Tennant
20.3.94	SD	A	London C.	D	20-20	Cocker (2), Drummond, Penrice	Marwood (2)	—	—
27.3.94	SD	H	Hunslet	W	24-4	Chilton (2), Burns, Kay, Mulligan	Marwood (2)	2130	Wood
1.4.94	SD	H	Whitehaven	L	4-7	Burns	—	5404	J. Smith
4.4.94	SD	A	Barrow	W	26-14	Mulligan (2), Cocker, Penrice	Marwood (5)	—	—
10.4.94	SD	A	Highfield	W	40-1	Drummond (2), Kay (2), Burns, Cocker, Marwood, Shaw	Marwood (4)	—	—
17.4.94	SD	H	Keighley C.	W	54-2	Drummond (3), Burns (2), Byrne, Kay, Marwood, McKenzie, Mulligan	Marwood (7)	3760	Ollerton

(Continued)

Date	Competition	H/A	Opponent	Rlt	Score	Tries	Goals	Attendance	Referee
24.4.94	SD	A	Bramley	W	52-8	Byrne (2), Kay (2), Cocker, Drummond, Hepi, Moore, Mulligan	Marwood (8)	—	—
8.5.94	SDP(1)	H	Rochdale H.	W	50-6	Mulligan (2), Burns, Byrne, Cocker, Kay, McKenzie, Moore, Oglanby	Marwood (7)	3448	Presley
15.5.94	SDP(SF)	H	Batley	W	19-4	Cocker, Marwood, Mulligan	Marwood (3), Kitchin (dg)	3659	Cummings
22.5.94	SDP(F)	N[1]	London C.	W	30-22	Byrne, Kay, Cocker (2), Drummond, Mulligan	Marwood (3)	—	J. Connolly

N[1] Manchester U. FC

Workington Town scrum half Dean Marwood shows off the Tom Bergin Trophy as Second Division Premiership Man of the Match.

Jonathan Davies, who scored his 100th career try during the 1993-94 campaign, finishing as the League's top drop goal kicker.

RECORDS

RECORDS

LEADING SCORERS FOR 1993-94

TOP TEN TRIES

1. Mark Johnson (London C.)........................... 43
2. St. John Ellis (Castleford)........................... 40
3. Paul Newlove (Bradford N.) 37
   Martin Offiah (Wigan) 37
5. Stuart Cocker (Workington T.) 35
6. Nick Pinkney (Keighley C.)......................... 31
7. Mark Riley (London C.) 30
8. Carl Hall (Bradford N.) 27
   Darren Moxon (Batley) 27
10. Jason Critchley (Salford) 25
    John Bentley (Halifax).............................. 25
    Ellery Hanley (Leeds) 25

● Others with 20 or more: Mark Mulligan (Workington T.), Kevin Pape (Carlisle) 24; David Fraisse (Sheffield E.), Anthony Sullivan (St. Helens) 23; Jonathan Davies (Warrington), Mike Ford (Castleford) 22; Barrie-Jon Mather (Wigan), Simon Middleton (Castleford), Sam Panapa (Wigan), Martin Pearson (Featherstone R.), Scott Roskell (London C.), Neil Summers (Bradford N.), Ian Thomas (Huddersfield), Glen Tomlinson (Batley) 21; Darren Abram (Oldham), Simon Ashcroft (Swinton), Richard Blackmore (Castleford), Shaun Edwards (Wigan), Eddie Rombo (Dewsbury) 20.

TOP TEN GOALS
(Including drop goals)

1. Frano Botica (Wigan) 188
2. John Gallagher (London C.)......................... 159
3. Deryck Fox (Bradford N.).......................... 148
4. Lee Crooks (Castleford) 137
5. Jonathan Davies (Warrington) 132
6. Mark Conway (Dewsbury) 130
7. Robert Turner (Doncaster) 123
   Mark Aston (Sheffield E.) 123
9. Graham Holroyd (Leeds) 103
10. Dean Marwood (Workington T.) 100

TOP FIVE DROP GOALS

1. Jonathan Davies (Warrington) 14
2. Deryck Fox (Bradford N.).......................... 11
   Gus O'Donnell (St. Helens) 11
4. Robert Turner (Doncaster) 10
5. Tommy Martyn (St. Helens)........................ 9

TOP TEN POINTS

	T	G	DG	Pts
1. Frano Botica (Wigan)	13	182	6	422
2. John Gallagher (London C.)	17	157	2	384
3. Jonathan Davies (Warrington)................	22	118	14	338
4. Mark Conway (Dewsbury)..	16	129	1	323
5. Deryck Fox (Bradford N.)..	8	137	11	317
6. Mark Aston (Sheffield E.).	14	118	5	297

7. Lee Crooks (Castleford)	2	136	1	281
8. Robert Turner (Doncaster)..	9	113	10	272
9. Martin Pearson (Featherstone R.)	21	91	1	267
10. Graham Holroyd (Leeds) ...	7	100	3	231

Key:
SBC .... Stones Bitter Championship
SD .... Second Division
PT .... Premiership Trophy
SDP .... Second Division Premiership
RT .... Regal Trophy
CC .... Challenge Cup
WCC .... World Club Challenge
NA .... Non-appearance

OUTSTANDING SCORING FEATS IN 1993-94
INDIVIDUAL

Most tries in a match:
5 by Carl Hall (Bradford N.) v. Mysons .... RT
  Stuart Cocker (Workington T.) v. Barrow ... SD
  Tommy Oldroyd (Batley) at Highfield .... SD
  James Grant (Hull) v. Leigh .... SBC

Most goals in a match:
12 by Steve Turner (Rochdale H.) v. Blackpool G. . RT
  Robert Turner (Doncaster) v. Highfield ...... SD
10 by John Wasyliw (Keighley C.) v.
  Nottingham C. .... RT
  John Wasyliw (Keighley C.) v. Bramley ...... SD
  Mark Conway (Dewsbury) v. Hensingham .. CC
  Mike Fletcher (Hull K.R.) v. Leigh .... SBC

Most points in a match:
36 by John Wasyliw (Keighley C.) v.
  Nottingham C. .... RT
32 by Steve Turner (Rochdale H.) v. Blackpool G. . RT

Paul Newlove, joint third top try scorer in his first season with Bradford Northern.

TEAM

Highest score:

Doncaster 96 v. Highfield 0 .... SD

● There was a total of 57 matches in which a team scored 50 points or more, compared with 73 in the previous season, a record since the try was increased from three to four points in 1983. The other 60-plus scores in 1993-94 were:

Home:

Rochdale H. 80 v. Blackpool G. 10	RT
Keighley C. 76 v. Bramley 10	SD
Workington T. 74 v. Wigan St. Patricks 6	RT
Keighley C. 72 v. Nottingham C. 12	SD
Castleford 70 v. Leigh 6	SBC
Hull 70 v. Leigh 16	SBC
Keighley C. 68 v. Oulton 0	CC
St. Helens 68 v. Leeds 0	SBC
London C. 66 v. Keighley C. 12	SDP
Ryedale-York 66 v. Hemel Hempstead 14	RT
Batley 64 v. Queens 1	RT
London C. 64 v. Bramley 0	SD
Rochdale H. 64 v. Highfield 8	SD
Dewsbury 64 v. Hensingham 6	CC
Doncaster 62 v. Mysons 4	RT
London C. 62 v. Highfield 6	SD
Huddersfield 60 v. Highfield 20	SD

Away:

Highfield 8 v. Keighley C. 76	SD
Highfield 8 v. Dewsbury 62	SD

Highest score by a losing team:

Swinton 40 v. Hunslet 34 .... SD

● There was a record total of 86 matches in which a team scored 20 points or more and lost. The previous record since the increase of a try from three to four points in 1983 was 64 matches, set in 1988-89 and 1992-93.

High-scoring draws:

Leeds 46 v. Sheffield E. 46	SBC
Oldham 20 v. Wakefield T. 20	SBC
London C. 20 v. Workington T. 20	SD

Scoreless draw:

Whitehaven 0 v. Workington T. 0 .... SD

● From the start of the 1983-84 season, the value of a try was raised from three to four points. It was decided officially that records for most points in a match, season or career would subsequently include the four-point try and that no attempt would be made to adjust existing records featuring the three-point try.
● Substitute appearances do not count towards players' full appearance records.
● Points and appearances in abandoned matches are included in records, except in League matches which are replayed. Although the abandoned League match points and appearances are included in players' overall totals they do not count towards League records.

RECORD FEATS IN 1993-94

AT A GLANCE

ST. JOHN ELLIS of Castleford scored a club record 40 tries in a season.

NICK PINKNEY of Keighley Cougars scored a club record 31 tries in a season.

ROBERT TURNER of Doncaster achieved three club records: 123 goals and 272 points in a season, plus 12 goals in a match.

MARK JOHNSON of London Crusaders scored a club record 43 tries in a season and equalled the match record of four touchdowns.

JOHN GALLAGHER of London Crusaders broke three club records: 159 goals and 384 points in a season, plus 24 points in a match.

TOMMY OLDROYD of Batley equalled a club record of five tries in a match, which is believed also to be the best by any hooker.

CARL HALL of Doncaster broke a club match record with five tries.

MARK RILEY of London Crusaders scored a club record four tries in a match.

JOHN WASYLIW of Keighley Cougars notched up a club record 36 points in a match.

STEVE TURNER of Rochdale Hornets equalled the club points in a match record with 32.

LEE CROOKS of Castleford beat the Regal Trophy final record with 16 points, including a record-equalling six goals.

DONCASTER ran up a club and Division Two record score with a 96-0 defeat of Highfield.

BATLEY equalled their highest score with a 64-1 victory over amateur club Queens.

LONDON CRUSADERS three times broke the club's record score with a 62-6 defeat of Highfield, followed by a 64-0 win over Bramley and a 66-12 scoreline against Keighley Cougars.

CASTLEFORD achieved a record Regal Trophy final score and winning margin with their 33-2 defeat of Wigan.

LEIGH twice conceded a club record 70 points. They lost 70-6 at Castleford and 70-16 at Hull.

HIGHFIELD suffered a club record defeat of 96-0 to Doncaster.

LEEDS and SHEFFIELD EAGLES were involved in a record 46-46 draw.

HUNSLET equalled the Division Two record score for a losing team when they lost 40-34 at Swinton.

WHITEHAVEN and WORKINGTON TOWN produced only the second scoreless Division Two match.

NEW RECORDS IN DETAIL . . .

ST. JOHN ELLIS of Castleford scored a club record 40 tries in a season, beating the 36 by winger Keith Howe in 1963-64.

Ellis's total came in 41 matches, missing only two games. He played 34 on the right wing, two in the centre and the last five at full back when he scored five of his tries.

He was at full back when he broke the record with the first of two tries in a 38-24 Division One win at Wakefield Trinity on 24 April. His total included four hat-tricks and he also kicked four goals.

Howe played in 38 of Castleford's 45 matches in 1963-64, all on the wing, mostly on the right. His total included two hat-tricks.

Ellis's record also took the former York player's career total past 100 (as detailed in MILESTONES).

His match-by-match record-breaking season went as follows:

Leeds	(H)	1
Sheffield E.	(A)	0
Hull	(H)	0
Widnes	(A)	2
St. Helens	(H)	1
Leigh	(A)	0
Hull K.R.	(H)	3
New Zealand (Tour)	(H)	3
Salford	(A)	NA
Wigan	(H)	3
Halifax	(A)	2
Hull K.R. (RT)	(A)	0
Warrington	(A)	0
Wakefield T.	(H)	2
Bradford N.	(H)	0
Leigh (RT)	(H)	2
Carlisle (RT)	(H)	1
Featherstone R.	(A)	2
Bradford N. (RT)	(A)	0
Leeds	(A)	0
Sheffield E.	(H)	0
Oldham	(H)	1
Hull	(A)	0
Wigan (RT)	(N[1])	0
Salford (CC)	(H)	1
St. Helens	(A)	NA
Keighley C. (CC)	(A)	1
Leigh	(H)	3
Widnes (CC)	(H)	0
Widnes	(H)	1
Hull K.R.	(A)	2
Wigan (CC)	(N[1])	0
Salford	(H)	1
Halifax	(H)	0
Featherstone R.	(H)	1
Oldham	(A)	1
Bradford N.	(A)	1
Warrington	(H)	0
Wigan	(A)	1
Wakefield T.	(A)	2
Halifax (PT)	(H)	2
Bradford N. (PT)	(A)	0
Wigan (PT)	(N[2])	0

Totals

41 appearances		**40**

(N[1]) at Leeds
(N[2]) at Manchester U. FC

NICK PINKNEY of Keighley Cougars scored a club record 31 tries in his first season after signing from Ryedale-York.

The centre broke the record in the last match of the season with a try in the 66-12 Division Two Premiership first round defeat at London Crusaders on 8 May.

Joe Sherburn had set the record with 30 tries in 1934-35 when he played in all but two of Keighley's 43 matches, 40 on the wing and one at centre.

Pinkney played 31 matches, two at stand off and 29 in the centre, missing five.

Pinkney's match-by-match record was as follows:

Barrow	(A)	1
London C.	(H)	0
Rochdale H.	(A)	0
Dewsbury	(H)	2
Hunslet	(A)	0
Doncaster	(A)	0
Whitehaven	(H)	2
Swinton	(H)	4
Nottingham C. ... (RT)	(H)	2
Carlisle	(A)	1
Halifax (RT)	(A)	0
Batley	(A)	1
Highfield	(H)	0
Workington T.	(H)	0
Ryedale-York	(A)	0
Oulton (CC)	(H)	4
Barrow	(H)	2
Rochdale H.	(H)	2
Batley (CC)	(A)	0
Huddersfield	(H)	NA
Dewsbury	(A)	NA
Castleford (CC)	(H)	NA
London C.	(A)	NA
Hunslet	(H)	NA
Doncaster	(H)	0
Whitehaven	(A)	1
Bramley	(A)	1
Swinton	(A)	1
Carlisle	(H)	1
Batley	(H)	0
Huddersfield	(A)	1
Ryedale-York	(H)	0
Bramley	(H)	1
Workington T.	(A)	0
Highfield	(A)	3
London C. (SDP)	(A)	1

Totals

31 appearances		**31**

ROBERT TURNER of Doncaster broke three club records in his first season after signing from Warrington. The stand off's 123 goals and 272 points were both records for a season and included a match best-equalling 12 goals.

Turner's 123 goals, including 10 drop goals, beat the 118 in 37 matches plus two substitute appearances by David Noble in 1985-86, which included six drop goals.

Noble set the old points record with 250 in 1986-87 when he played and scored in all 33 of Doncaster's matches, the forward notching 114 goals, including two drop goals, and six tries.

Turner played in 35 of Doncaster's 38 matches last season, 21 at stand off, eight centre and six loose forward. His points total included nine tries.

He passed the points in a season record with the first of five goals in the 29-12 Division Two home defeat of Dewsbury on 10 April. The season goals record went with the third of six in a 48-18 Division Two Premiership first round home defeat of Dewsbury on 8 May.

Turner had equalled the 12 goals in a match record in the 96-0 Division Two home defeat of Highfield on 20 March. Tony Zelei also kicked 12 in the 88-6 Division Three home defeat of Nottingham City on 1 September 1991.

Turner's match-by-match figures last season were:

		T	G	Pts
Hunslet	(A)	0	6	12
Bramley	(H)	1	2	8
London C.	(A)	0	3	6
Barrow	(H)	1	4(1)	11
Workington T.	(A)	0	3(1)	5
Keighley C.	(H)	0	4	8
Carlisle	(H)	0	6(1)	11
Whitehaven	(A)	0	2	4
Mysons (RT)	(H)	1	7	18
Highfield	(A)	1	5	14
Widnes (RT)	(A)	0	0	0
Swinton	(A)	0	2	4
Batley	(H)	0	2	4
Rochdale H.	(H)	1	5	14
Hunslet	(H)	0	3	6
Huddersfield	(A)	0	5(1)	9
Bramley	(A)	0	4(1)	7
Wigan St. Patricks (CC)	(H)	NA		
Ryedale-York	(H)	0	0	0
London C.	(H)	1	2	8
Dewsbury (CC)	(H)	0	1	2
Barrow	(A)	0	3(1)	5
Oldham (CC)	(H)	NA		
Workington T.	(H)	0	4(1)	7
St. Helens (CC)	(A)	0	2	4
Keighley C.	(A)	NA		
Carlisle	(A)	1	5	14
Dewsbury	(A)	0	3	6
Whitehaven	(H)	0	2	4
Highfield	(H)	0	12	24
Swinton	(H)	1	4	12
Ryedale-York	(A)	0	4(1)	7

Huddersfield	(H)	0	4(1)	7
Dewsbury	(H)	0	5(1)	9
Rochdale H.	(A)	0	1	2
Batley	(A)	1	1	6
Dewsbury (SDP)	(H)	0	6	12
London C. (SDP)	(H)	0	1	2
Totals				
35 appearances		**9**	**123(10)**	**272**

() denotes drop goals included in total.

MARK JOHNSON of London Crusaders scored a club record 43 tries in the season and also equalled the best match feat of four tries. The South African winger played in all but two of London's 39 matches.

The previous record of 27 in a season was set by stand off John Crossley in 1982-83 when the club was still Fulham. Crossley also played in all but two of 39 matches.

Johnson broke the record with two tries in the 64-0 Division Two home defeat of Bramley on 27 March. He equalled the match record with four tries in a 58-6 Division Two away win against Highfield on 1 April. The record had been set earlier in the season by scrum half Mark Riley in a 62-6 home defeat of Highfield.

Johnson scored three tries in London's 22-30 Division Two Premiership final defeat by Workington Town at Old Trafford to finish as the season's top try scorer with 43.

Johnson's match-by-match try scoring figures were as follows:

Batley	(H)	1
Keighley C.	(A)	0
Doncaster	(H)	3
Huddersfield	(A)	0
Dewsbury	(H)	0
Barrow	(A)	2
Ryedale-York	(H)	1
Highfield	(H)	1
Hunslet	(H)	2
St. Esteve (RT)	(H)	2
Workington T.	(H)	2
Featherstone R. (RT)	(H)	1
Carlisle	(H)	2
Bramley	(A)	0
Whitehaven	(A)	0
Ryedale-York (RT)	(A)	0
Bradford N. (RT)	(H)	0
Swinton	(H)	1
Rochdale H.	(A)	1
Shaw Cross (CC)	(H)	1
Doncaster	(A)	0
Featherstone R. (CC)	(H)	NA
Huddersfield	(H)	NA
Batley	(A)	0
Keighley C.	(H)	1
Dewsbury	(A)	0
Barrow	(H)	3

Ryedale-York	(H)	1
Hunslet	(A)	0
Workington T.	(H)	1
Bramley	(H)	2
Highfield	(A)	4
Rochdale H.	(H)	1
Swinton	(A)	0
Whitehaven	(H)	1
Carlisle	(A)	2
Keighley C. (SDP)	(H)	3
Doncaster (SDP)	(A)	1
Workington T. (SDP)	(N)	3
Totals		
37 appearances		43

(N) at Manchester U. FC

JOHN GALLAGHER of London Crusaders broke three club records in his first season after joining them from Leeds. The former New Zealand Rugby Union international full back set records of 159 goals, including two drop goals, and 384 points in a season plus a match best of 24 points.

Centre Steve Diamond held the old records of 136 goals and 308 points in a season in 1982-83 when he played in all 39 matches.

Gallagher was also an ever-present in 39 matches, 22 at full back, two in the centre and the last 15 on the wing.

He was on the wing when he scored a club record 24 points with eight goals and two tries in the 64-0 Division Two home defeat of Bramley on 27 March.

The previous record of 22 was shared by two players: second row Alan Platt scored seven goals and two tries in a 43-20 Division Two home defeat of Mansfield Marksman on 10 May 1986; and full back Greg Pearce kicked 11 goals in a 50-0 Lancashire Cup first round home defeat of Runcorn Highfield on 26 August 1990.

Gallagher passed the points in a season record with 22 in a 58-6 Division Two win at Highfield on 1 April.

The goals record went on 17 April in a 30-21 Division Two home defeat of Whitehaven.

His match-by-match record was:

		T	G	Pts
Batley	(H)	0	6	12
Keighley C.	(A)	2	2	12
Doncaster	(H)	1	7	18
Huddersfield	(A)	0	1	2
Dewsbury	(H)	0	5(1)	9
Barrow	(A)	0	0	0
Ryedale-York	(H)	0	4	8
Highfield	(H)	0	7	14
Hunslet	(H)	0	6	12
St. Esteve (RT)	(H)	0	8	16
Workington T.	(A)	1	1(1)	5
Featherstone R. (RT)	(H)	0	3	6
Carlisle	(H)	1	5	14

Bramley	(A)	0	5	10
Whitehaven	(A)	1	2	8
Ryedale-York (RT)	(A)	0	5	10
Bradford N. (RT)	(H)	0	1	2
Swinton	(H)	0	3	6
Rochdale H.	(A)	0	2	4
Shaw Cross (CC)	(H)	2	4	16
Doncaster	(A)	0	1	2
Featherstone R. (CC)	(H)	0	3	6
Huddersfield	(H)	0	1	2
Batley	(A)	0	1	2
Keighley C.	(H)	0	2	4
Dewsbury	(A)	1	5	14
Barrow	(H)	1	8	20
Ryedale-York	(A)	0	3	6
Hunslet	(A)	2	5	18
Workington T.	(H)	0	6	12
Bramley	(H)	2	8	24
Highfield	(A)	1	9	22
Rochdale H.	(H)	0	4	8
Swinton	(A)	2	2	12
Whitehaven	(H)	0	5	10
Carlisle	(A)	0	5	10
Keighley C. (SDP)	(H)	0	9	18
Doncaster (SDP)	(A)	0	2	4
Workington T. (SDP)	(N)	0	3	6
Totals				
39 appearances		17	159(2)	384

() denotes drop goals included in total.
(N) at Manchester U. FC

TOMMY OLDROYD of Batley equalled a club record with five tries in the 50-0 Division Two win at Highfield on 6 March. It is believed also to be a record by a hooker in any match.

Oldroyd had not scored in five previous appearances during the season, including one as substitute, and totalled only four tries in 16 matches, including one as substitute, in 1992-93 – his first season after signing from Hunslet.

Others to have scored five tries in a match for Batley are: Joe Oakland (scrum half) v. Bramley on 19 December 1908; Tommy Brannan (winger) v. Swinton on 17 January 1920; Jim Wale (winger) v. Bramley on 4 December 1926 and v. Cottingham on 12 February 1927.

CARL HALL of Doncaster scored a club match record five tries in the 62-4 Regal Trophy first round home defeat of Hull amateurs Mysons on 31 October.

The centre's feat was one better than the previous record shared by Vernon Grace (1952), Brian Tasker (1963), John Buckton (1981), Tony Kemp (1986), Neil Turner (1989) and Mark Roache (1991).

MARK RILEY and MARK JOHNSON of London Crusaders both scored a club record four tries in different matches against Highfield.

Scrum half Riley became the first player to score more than three tries in a match for London since they began as Fulham in 1980. He did it with four in the club's then record 62-6 Division Two home defeat of Highfield on 17 October.

Winger Johnson equalled the record with four tries in the 58-6 Division Two win at Highfield on Good Friday, 1 April.

JOHN WASYLIW of Keighley Cougars broke the club points in a match record he already held when scoring half the points in a 72-12 Regal Trophy first round home defeat of Nottingham City on 31 October.

The winger's 36 points were made up of 10 goals and four tries to beat his 34 points from a try and club record 15 goals in the 86-0 Division Three home defeat of Nottingham on 1 November 1992.

STEVE TURNER of Rochdale Hornets equalled a club match points record he already held with 32 in the 80-10 Regal Trophy first round home defeat of non-League side Blackpool Gladiators on 31 October.

The stand off's total was made up of 12 goals and two tries. He had set the record with 14 goals and a try playing loose forward in the 92-0 Division Two home defeat of Runcorn Highfield on 5 November 1989.

LEE CROOKS of Castleford achieved two Regal Trophy final records in the 33-2 defeat of Wigan at Headingley.

The Castleford prop and captain's 16 points beat the 15 by Warrington full back Derek Whitehead in the 27-16 defeat of Rochdale Hornets at Wigan in 1973-74. Both kicked a trophy final best six goals, with the extra point for a try giving Crooks the points record.

DONCASTER scored a club and Division Two record victory with their 96-0 home defeat of Highfield on 20 March.

The 18-try romp beat the club record 88-6 Division Three home defeat of Nottingham City on 1 September 1991 when they scored 16 tries. It also surpassed the Division Two record shared by: Leigh 92 v. Keighley 2 (30 April 1986), Hull K.R. 92 v. Whitehaven 10 (18 March 1990), Rochdale H. 92 v. Runcorn H. 0 (5 November 1989).

Doncaster's 96-0 victory was also the biggest in a League match since the reintroduction of divisional rugby in 1973. But the record score in any League match remains Leeds's 102-0 home defeat of Coventry on 12 April 1913 in the old one-league days.

BATLEY equalled their highest score with a 64-1 Regal Trophy first round home defeat of Leeds amateur side Queens on 31 October. They scored 13 tries compared with the 11 when winning 64-0 at Nottingham City in a Division Three match on 10 November 1991.

Batley's previous highest home win was the 58-16 Division Two defeat of Highfield on 10 October 1993 when they scored 11 tries.

LONDON CRUSADERS broke the club's record score three times during the season. First, with a 62-6 Division Two home defeat of Highfield on 17 October.

Their previous highest score was the 61-22 Division Two home defeat of Huddersfield on 23 October 1988 when they scored 10 tries compared with 12 against Highfield.

London broke the record again with a 64-0 Division Two home defeat of Bramley on 27 March when they scored 12 tries.

The present record was achieved with a 12-try 66-12 home defeat of Keighley Cougars in a Division Two Premiership first round game on 8 May.

CASTLEFORD achieved a Regal Trophy final record score and winning margin with their five-try 33-2 defeat of Wigan at Headingley.

The previous highest score came in Warrington's five-try 27-16 defeat of Rochdale Hornets at Wigan in 1973-74.

Widnes had held the widest winning margin with a four-try 24-0 defeat of Leeds at Wigan in 1991-92.

LEIGH twice conceded a club record 70 points during the season. They conceded 13 tries in a 70-6 Division One defeat at Castleford on 20 February.

Then they lost 70-16 in a League match at Hull on 24 April, again conceding 13 tries.

Before last season, the previous highest score against Leigh was a 64-9 Division One defeat at St. Helens on 6 January 1993 when they conceded 12 tries.

HIGHFIELD went down to a club record defeat with their 96-0 Division Two loss at Doncaster on 20 March. The 18-try defeat surpassed the 92-2 John Player Special Trophy defeat at Wigan, who also scored 18 tries on 13 November 1988, and Rochdale Hornets' 92-0 Division Two 16-try win on 5 November 1989.

LEEDS and SHEFFIELD EAGLES produced the highest scoring draw in the game's history with a 46-46 scoreline at Headingley on 10 April, when both teams scored eight tries.

HUNSLET equalled the record Division Two score for a losing team when they lost 40-34 at Swinton on 24 April after scoring six tries.

The other record scores are: Dewsbury 36 v. Rochdale Hornets 34 on 9 October 1988, and Oldham 50 v. Keighley 34 on 12 November 1989. Each time the losers scored six tries.

WHITEHAVEN and WORKINGTON TOWN produced only the second 0-0 Division Two result on 28 December. The other scoreless draw was between Dewsbury and Rochdale Hornets on 30 January 1983.

MILESTONES . . .

MARTIN OFFIAH of Wigan scored the 300th try of his career with the second of two in the 54-16 Division One home defeat of Hull Kingston Rovers on 5 December.

The winger's 325 total at the end of the season consisted of 95 for Wigan, 181 for Widnes and 49 in representative matches, including 26 in Test and World Cup matches for Great Britain. His tries have come in a total of only 278 club and representative matches, including three substitute appearances.

Offiah holds the Widnes record for most tries in a season with 58 in 1988-89, having set the record with 42 the previous term – his first in Rugby League. He is also the joint holder of the Widnes match record with five against Warrington on 15 March 1989, and shares the Wigan match record of 10 tries in a Stones Bitter Premiership home semi-final against Leeds on 10 May 1992. He holds the Great Britain Test match record with five tries against France at Headingley on 16 February 1991.

The Test winger raced to the fastest century of Division One tries, reaching the milestone in his 70th match. No other player has scored a century in fewer than 100 matches. He was the top try scorer in each of his first four seasons and has never finished outside the top ten.

His total of 35 hat-tricks includes 10 in a match, five on five occasions, plus eight four-try feats.

The former Rosslyn Park RU winger made his Rugby League debut for Widnes at home to Halifax on 30 August 1987 when he failed to score in a 28-6 Division One victory. He moved to Wigan for a world record £440,000 fee and made another non-tryscoring debut in a 20-2 Division One home defeat of Wakefield Trinity on 5 January 1992.

His season-by-season try totals are as follows (not including matches with Australian clubs):

	App.	Tries	
Widnes			
1987-88	35	42	+1 GB, 1 RL XIII
1988-89	41	58	+2 GB
			(Inc 1 non-Test)
1989-90	32	40	+5 GB
1990-91	37	41	+8 GB
Wigan			
1991-92	15+1	30	
1992-93	38	30	+2 England
1993-94	34	35	+2 GB
Totals			
Widnes	145	181	
Wigan	87+1	95	
Britain	31*	27*	Inc. 1 in non-Test
Tours	9+2	19	Not inc. Tests
England...............	1	2	
RL XIII	1	1	
Lancashire	1	0	
GRAND TOTALS	**275+3**	**325**	

GREG AUSTIN scored the 200th try of his career with one for Keighley Cougars in the 44-6 Division Two home defeat of Highfield on 28 November – his last match for the club before returning to Salford.

The Australian centre did not add to his total at Salford and his 200 tries are made up of 19 for Keighley, 11 Rochdale Hornets, 25 Salford, 45 Hull Kingston Rovers and 100 Halifax.

Austin is the joint holder of the Division Two match record with six tries for Halifax in a 66-26 home defeat of Trafford Borough on 7 April 1991. He also scored six in a match for Hull K.R. and his total of hat-tricks includes two five-try feats and four touchdowns on three occasions.

Austin has finished in the top ten try chart four times, being second to Martin Offiah twice.

A former Manly player, he began his British career with Rochdale, making a substitute debut in a 52-13 Division Two home defeat of Doncaster on 22 September 1985. His full debut followed seven days later when he scored a try in a 25-16 League victory at Keighley.

He moved to Salford the next season and scored two goals on his debut at Wigan on 31 August 1986 in a 42-12 Division One defeat. Austin had two seasons at Salford, returned to Australia for a year then signed for Hull K.R., for whom he made a two-try debut in a 54-12 Yorkshire Cup first round victory at Bramley on 17 September 1989.

He stayed at Rovers for just over a season before they released him from their overseas quota to make way for New Zealand international forward James Goulding. Halifax snapped him up and he made another tryscoring debut as a substitute at Bramley in a 56-8 Division Two win on 23 September 1990. A week later he was in the centre for a 26-18 League victory at home to Ryedale-York.

A move to Keighley Cougars saw him make his debut in the 30-22 Division Two win at Barrow on 29 August 1993. But he stayed for only 15 matches before returning to Salford and making his debut in a 6-14 Division One home defeat by Bradford Northern on 18 March 1994.

Austin has also totalled 28 goals, including two drop goals, for a total of 854 points. His season-by-season try totals are as follows:

	App.	Tries
Rochdale H.		
1985-86	20+2	11
Salford		
1986-87	31+1	17
1987-88	16	8
1993-94	3	0
Hull K.R.		
1989-90	34	38
1990-91	4	7
Halifax		
1990-91	29+1	40
1991-92	33	33
1992-93	26	27

Keighley C.

1993-94	15	19
Totals		
Rochdale H.	20+2	11
Salford	50+1	25
Hull K.R.	38	45
Halifax................	88+1	100
Keighley C.	15	19
GRAND TOTALS	**211+4**	**200**

GRAHAM STEADMAN of Castleford scored the 200th try of his career with the first of two in a 35-10 Division One win at Halifax on 8 November.

The Great Britain back's total at the end of the season was 212 with 94 for Castleford, 63 York, 48 Featherstone Rovers and seven in representative matches, including three in Test matches. His tries have come in 373 matches with 13 hat-tricks, including a best match feat of four touchdowns.

An amateur with Knottingley Welfare, Steadman also played for Knottingley Rugby Union club. He made his senior professional debut for York at Hull Kingston Rovers as an unnamed trialist stand off on 24 March 1982. York lost the Division One match 36-7, but Steadman played in their next match before being signed.

Steadman was transferred to Featherstone Rovers in 1986 for a then record for both clubs of £50,000. He made his debut for Rovers at Leeds on 16 February 1986 when he scored their try and goal in a 44-6 Division One defeat.

He moved to Castleford for the start of the 1989-90 season in a then world record deal, set by a transfer tribunal, of £145,000 plus £25,000 when he played in a Test for Britain. Steadman made his debut for Castleford at stand off in a 20-22 home defeat by Featherstone on 3 September 1989.

He switched to full back on a regular basis in 1991-92 when he finished fifth in the try chart with his best tally of 31, including two for Britain. He has also finished in the top ten on two other occasions.

Steadman has also kicked 517 goals, including 26 drop goals, for a total of 1,846 points. His season-by-season try totals are as follows:

	App.	Tries
York		
1981-82	5	1
1982-83	16	9
1983-84	28	25
1984-85	29	20
1985-86	19	8
Featherstone Rovers		
1985-86	11	5
1986-87	28	12
1987-88	30+1	17
1988-89	26	14

Castleford

1989-90	26	17	+2 Yorkshire
1990-91	32+1	23	
1991-92	35+1	29	+2 GB
1992-93	24+1	9	
1993-94	40	16	
Totals			
York	97	63	
Featherstone R.	95+1	48	
Castleford	157+3	94	
Britain	8+1	3	
Tours	5+2	2	Not inc. Tests
Yorkshire	1+3	2	
GRAND TOTALS	**363+10**	**212**	

MARK CONWAY of Dewsbury scored the 100th try of his career with the first of three in the 56-12 Division Two home defeat of Barrow on 7 November.

The scrum half's end-of-season total of 108 is made up of 16 for Dewsbury, 54 Wakefield Trinity, 37 Leeds and one for Great Britain Under-21s. He has made 321 appearances, including 29 as substitute.

A former Stanley Rangers (Wakefield) amateur player, Conway made his senior professional debut with Leeds as a substitute in a 33-10 Yorkshire Cup first round victory at Castleford on 5 September 1982. He made three more substitute appearances before his full debut at stand off in the 33-5 Division One defeat at Hull on 13 October 1982.

Conway moved to Wakefield in a six-player exchange deal and made his debut for them with two tries as a scrum half in a 56-8 Division Two home defeat of Carlisle on 30 August 1987. The half back's first season at Wakefield was also his most prolific as he finished in the top ten try list for the only time with 20 in 10th place.

He was transferred to Dewsbury for the start of last season. Playing scrum half, Conway scored a try and six goals on his debut in a 48-6 Division Two home defeat of Carlisle on 29 August.

Conway has scored only two hat-tricks, in successive matches for Dewsbury last season. He has also scored 583 goals, including 10 drop goals, for a points total of 1,582.

Conway's season-by-season tryscoring figures are as follows:

	App.	Tries	
Leeds			
1982-83	15+7	6	
1983-84	16+1	3	
1984-85	18+6	10	+1 GB Under-21s
1985-86	20+7	8	
1986-87	17+5	10	

Wakefield Trinity	App.	Tries
1987-88	35	20
1988-89	31+2	10
1989-90	31+1	6
1990-91	34	6
1991-92	30	6
1992-93	11	6
Dewsbury		
1993-94	33	16
Totals		
Leeds.................	86+26	37
Wakefield T.	172+3	54
Dewsbury.............	33	16
GB Under-21s.......	1	1
GRAND TOTALS	**292+29**	**108**

Widnes	App.	Tries	
1988-89	12+4	7	
1989-90	29+1	16	
1990-91	32+2	30	
1991-92	24	13	+2 Wales
1992-93	29+1	14	
Warrington			
1993-94	30	21	+1 GB
Totals			
Widnes................	126+8	80	
Warrington	30	21	
Britain	11+1	3	
Wales	4	2	
1990 tour	5+1	4	Not inc. 2t in 5 Tests
GRAND TOTALS.	**176+10**	**110**	

JONATHAN DAVIES of Warrington scored the 100th try of his career with one in the 30-14 Division One home defeat of Featherstone Rovers on 5 December.

The former Welsh Rugby Union international's total at the end of the season was 110 made up of 80 for Widnes, 21 Warrington and nine in representative matches, including three in Tests for Great Britain. He has played a total of 186 first class matches, including 10 as a substitute.

The former Llanelli Rugby Union fly half signed for Widnes on 5 January 1989 on a four-year contract officially reported at £150,000. He made his debut as a substitute in a 50-8 Division One home defeat of Salford on 15 January 1989. One other substitute appearance followed before he started at stand off and scored a try plus five goals in a 38-14 home League defeat of Oldham on 5 February.

Warrington took over his new contract for the start of last season with no transfer fee involved. He made his debut for Warrington at centre in the 32-14 Division One home defeat of Wakefield Trinity on 29 August 1993.

Davies has finished in the top ten try scorers once, when he was fifth with 30 in 1990-91 playing in a variety of positions. They helped him to a Widnes record of 342 points in a season.

He has scored four tries in a match twice plus two other hat-tricks, all for Widnes. He added nine goals to his four tries against Whitehaven on 26 August 1990 for a club record-equalling 34 points.

At Widnes, Davies began 47 matches in the centre, 42 stand off, 23 full back and 14 wing, plus eight as a substitute. He has played 28 matches at centre and two at full back for Warrington, and is one of the few players to have begun a Test match for Great Britain in four different positions: full back, wing, centre and stand off, plus a substitute appearance.

Davies has also scored 639 goals, including 19 drop goals, for a total of 1,699 points. His season-by-season try totals are as follows:

JOHN DEVEREUX of Widnes scored the 100th try of his career with the first of two in Great Britain's 29-12 second John Smith's Test win at Wigan on 30 October.

The threequarter's total of 104 at the end of the season came from 92 for Widnes and 12 in representative matches, including six tries in Tests for Great Britain.

A former Bridgend, Wales and British Lions Rugby Union player, Devereux made his senior Rugby League debut as a Widnes substitute in a 28-6 Lancashire Cup semi-final defeat at Warrington on 10 October 1989. He made one other substitute appearance before playing on the left wing in a 16-18 Division One home defeat against Leigh on 12 November 1989.

Devereux, who has played mostly on the wing but occasionally at centre, has scored five hat-tricks including two four-try feats. His most prolific season was 1991-92 when he totalled 35 tries, including one each for Wales and Great Britain, to finish second in the try chart. He also finished in the top ten with 23 in 1990-91.

His season-by-season totals are as follows:

Widnes	App.	Tries	
1989-90	23+2	12	
1990-91	37	23	
1991-92	27	33	+1 GB, 1 Wales
1992-93	33	21	+2 GB, 1 Wales
1993-94	15	3	+3 GB
Totals			
Widnes................	135+2	92	
Britain	6+2	6	
Wales	5	2	
Tours	12+1	4	Not inc. 1 Test sub app.
GRAND TOTALS	**158+5**	**104**	

ST. JOHN ELLIS of Castleford scored the 100th try of his career with the first of three in a 46-0 Division One home defeat of Wigan on 31 October.

The winger's total of 129 at the end of the season was made up of 97 in 175 appearances for Castleford and 32 tries in 75 matches at York. He has also made three substitute appearances for Great Britain without scoring.

Ellis's 40 tries during the season beat the club record of 36 set by Keith Howe in 1963-64 (see RECORDS). He is also the joint holder of the Castleford tries in a match record with five in a 62-2 Regal Trophy second round win at Whitehaven on 10 December 1989. He has scored five other hat-tricks for Castleford and another for York.

A former Southlands (York) ARL player, Ellis made his senior debut on the wing for York and scored two goals in an 18-16 Division Two defeat at Fulham on 21 December 1986. He moved to Castleford in exchange for Dean Mountain plus £10,000 and made his debut on the wing against New Zealand on 3 October 1989, scoring four goals.

He has finished in the top ten try chart twice, including last season when he was second with 40. He has also kicked 142 goals for Castleford and York for a total of 700 points.

His season-by-season try figures are as follows:

	App.	Tries
York		
1986-87	14	9
1987-88	29	12
1988-89	29	10
1989-90	3	1
Castleford		
1989-90	26	23
1990-91	31+1	8
1991-92	39+1	15
1992-93	36	11
1993-94	41	40
Totals		
York	75	32
Castleford	173+2	97
Britain	0+3	0
GRAND TOTALS	248+5	129

MARK FORSTER of Warrington scored his 100th try for the club with one in the 22-8 Division One home defeat of Hull on 6 February. The winger's total at the end of the season was 106 in 279 matches, including 15 as substitute.

His hat-trick in the 37-18 Division One home defeat of Leeds on 9 January took him past a century in all games, as he has also scored one try each for Great Britain and the Under-21s. It was only the third hat-trick of Forster's career. The others included his best match tally of four tries in a John Player Trophy tie against Barrow on 1 December 1985.

The former Woolston Rovers amateur player made his senior debut for Warrington in the centre when they lost 17-10 in a Division One match at Barrow on 16 January 1983. His best season's tally for Warrington was 16 in 1984-85.

He has also kicked three goals for Warrington and season-by-season try totals are as follows:

	App.	Tries	
Warrington			
1982-83	2	1	
1983-84	21	8	
1984-85	27+1	16	
1985-86	34+6	14	+1 GB U-21s
1986-87	27+1	10	+1 GB
1987-88	22+1	8	
1988-89	16	5	
1989-90	35+1	15	
1990-91	15	6	
1991-92	9+1	5	
1992-93	24+4	6	
1993-94	32	12	
Totals			
Warrington	264+15	106	
Britain	2	1	
GB U-21s	3	1	
Lancashire	2	0	
GRAND TOTALS	271+15	108	

DAVID HERON of Bradford Northern scored the 100th try of his career with one in the 58-30 win at Barrow in the Silk Cut Challenge Cup fourth round on 30 January.

Heron's total at the end of the season was 102 made up of 94 for Leeds, seven for Bradford and one for Yorkshire. He has made 477 club and representative appearances, including 67 as substitute. His best season's total was 16 tries for Leeds in 1979-80 and he has scored only one hat-trick, against Halifax on 22 August 1982.

A former Hunslet Under-18 player and BARLA's first Youth Player of the Year, Heron signed for Leeds in April 1976 for a then club record fee for a junior of £1,800. He made his senior debut as a substitute in a 40-6 RL Challenge Cup home defeat of Batley on 12 February 1977. His full debut came in Leeds's next match six days later when he scored a try as a second row in a 13-12 Division One win at Castleford.

Heron made 400 appearances for Leeds, including 46 as substitute, before moving to Bradford for about £15,000. He made his Northern debut at loose forward in a 16-10 Yorkshire Cup preliminary round win at Castleford on 23 August 1992.

His season-by-season totals are as follows:

	App.	Tries
Leeds		
1976-77	3+8	2
1977-78	3+4	2
1978-79	1+1	0
1979-80	31+1	16
1980-81	31+1	14
1981-82	34+2	14

RECORDS

	App.	Tries	
1982-83	31+2	12	
1983-84	22+3	4	
1984-85	32+4	5	
1985-86	33+2	6	+1 Yorkshire
1986-87	31	5	
1987-88	33+1	3	
1988-89	33+1	4	
1989-90	23+1	5	
1990-91	8+8	1	
1991-92	5+7	1	
Bradford Northern			
1992-93	34+4	1	
1993-94	19+12	6	
Totals			
Leeds	354+46	94	
Bradford N.	53+16	7	
Britain	1+1	0	
Yorkshire	2+4	1	
GRAND TOTALS	**410+67**	**102**	

ANDY MASON of Wakefield Trinity scored his 100th career try for the club with one in the 34-10 Division One defeat at Castleford on 28 November. The centre's total of 109 tries at the end of the season came in 216 appearances for Trinity, including one as a substitute.

A former Roundhay (Leeds) RU player, Mason began his senior Rugby League career with Bramley in January 1985 before moving to Leeds in October 1986. He moved on to Wakefield Trinity in one of the most remarkable player-exchange deals of all time, joining Trinity along with Mark Conway, Phil Fox and Keith Rayne, while Gary Spencer and John Lyons signed for Leeds. The deal was estimated at £120,000.

Mason made a two-try debut for Trinity in the centre when they beat Carlisle 56-8 in a Division Two home match on 30 August 1987.

His best season's tally was 22 for Trinity in 1992-93 and he has scored four hat-tricks for the club. He totalled 32 tries with Bramley, five at Leeds and two for Yorkshire for an overall career total of 148.

Mason's season-by-season try totals for Wakefield are as follows:

	App.	Tries
1987-88	31	14
1988-89	27	14
1989-90	31	17
1990-91	35	16
1991-92	30	10
1992-93	29+1	22
1993-94	32	16
Totals	**215+1**	**109**

DARYL POWELL of Sheffield Eagles became the first player to score a century of tries for the club when he touched down in the 22-36 Division One home defeat by Warrington on 28 November. His total at the end of the season stood at 108 in a club record 326 appearances, including 13 as substitute.

The former Redhill (Castleford) Under-19 amateur was the first player to sign for Sheffield when they were formed in 1984. He made his debut at centre in their first match when they beat Rochdale Hornets 29-10 on 2 September 1984.

Powell has remained a regular first team player at centre, stand off and loose forward. He also holds the club record of most tries in a match, with five against Mansfield Marksman on 2 January 1989. He has scored three other hat-tricks.

Powell's best season's tally for Sheffield is 28 in 1988-89, which was a club record until broken by Iva Ropati's 30 in 1991-92.

Powell has also scored 14 drop goals for Sheffield and three tries for Great Britain. His season-by-season try totals for Sheffield are as follows:

	App.	Tries
1984-85	29	5
1985-86	31	9
1986-87	28+1	8
1987-88	32	9
1988-89	30	28
1989-90	33	16
1990-91	29+1	7
1991-92	26+1	13
1992-93	25	3
1993-94	24+1	10
Totals	**287+4**	**108**

SCOTT RANSON of Oldham scored the 100th try of his career with the first of two in the 26-23 Division One defeat at Salford on 1 April. The winger's end of season total of 101 was made up of 32 in 62 appearances for Oldham, plus 69 in 129 matches at Swinton.

His best season's total was 22 for Swinton in 1989-90 and he has never finished in the top ten. Ranson has scored four tries in a match three times (twice for Swinton) and no other hat-tricks.

A former Thatto Heath (St. Helens) player and Great Britain amateur international, Ranson made his senior professional debut for Swinton in a 52-12 Division One home defeat by Widnes on 13 December 1987.

He moved to Oldham in February 1992 in exchange for Simon Longstaff, Richard Irving and Tony Barrow, and made his debut for the club on 24 February 1992 in a 30-6 Division Two home defeat of Ryedale-York.

His season-by-season scoring figures are as follows:

	App.	Tries
Swinton		
1987-88	17	10
1988-89	32	16
1989-90	34	22
1990-91	31	15
1991-92	15	6
Oldham		
1991-92	9	8
1992-93	24	12
1993-94	29	12
Totals		
Swinton...............	129	69
Oldham...............	62	32
GRAND TOTALS	**191**	**101**

MARK ROACHE of Doncaster became the first player to total 100 career tries for the club with the first of three in a 96-0 Division Two home defeat of Highfield on 20 March.

His Doncaster total at the end of the season was 104 from 239 matches, including 10 as substitute. The winger had also scored five in 20 appearances for Castleford, reaching his overall century of tries in Doncaster's 20-30 Division Two home defeat against Keighley Cougars on 3 October.

The winger also holds the Doncaster record for most tries in a season with 21 in 1989-90, and had held the match record, with four in an 88-6 Third Division home defeat of Nottingham City on 1 September 1991, until it was beaten by Carl Hall's five last season. He has scored only one other hat-trick.

A former Rossington Hornets amateur, Roache began his professional career with Castleford. He made his debut for them on the right wing in a 21-7 First Division home defeat of Leigh on 19 December 1982. He moved to Doncaster in an exchange deal involving David Plange and made his debut while on loan, playing right wing in a 17-14 Second Division win at Southend Invicta on 3 March 1985.

Roache had a spell in the centre before settling back on the wing. His season-by-season totals are as follows:

	App.	Tries
Castleford		
1982-83	2	1
1983-84	0	0
1984-85	18	4
Doncaster		
1984-85	10	4
1985-86	29+1	3
1986-87	14+3	6
1987-88	32	8
1988-89	31+1	14
1989-90	32+1	21
1990-91	32+1	15

	App.	Tries
1991-92	20+3	12
1992-93	11	7
1993-94	18	14
Totals		
Castleford	20	5
Doncaster	229+10	104
GRAND TOTALS	**249+10**	**109**

ANTHONY SULLIVAN of St. Helens scored the 100th try of his career with the second of three in a 35-22 Division One win at Wakefield Trinity on 6 March. The winger's total at the end of the season was 109 made up of 44 for St. Helens, 61 for Hull Kingston Rovers and four in representative matches, including one for Great Britain. He has played in 166 matches overall, including four as substitute.

Sullivan's best season's total was 35 in 1989-90, when he achieved his only top ten finish of third. His eight hat-tricks include two five-try feats for Hull K.R. and a four for St. Helens.

The son of former Great Britain captain Clive Sullivan, Anthony made his senior debut for Hull K.R. at Swinton on 29 November 1987. Signed from Rovers' Colts, he played on the left wing and scored a try in the 26-18 Division One win six days after his 19th birthday.

Sullivan left his father's old club when he signed for St. Helens in April 1991 for a then record fee for a winger of about £100,000. He made his debut for St. Helens at another of his father's old clubs, Hull, on 1 September 1991, playing on the left wing in a 31-10 Division One win.

Sullivan went on Great Britain's 1990 tour of Papua New Guinea and New Zealand but was injured and returned home without playing. His season-by-season scoring facts are as follows:

	App.	Tries	
Hull K.R.			
1987-88	2	1	
1988-89	13	4	
1989-90	28	34	+1 GB Under-21s
1990-91	29	22	
St. Helens			
1991-92	27+1	13	+1 GB, 2 Wales
1992-93	24+3	8	
1993-94	31	23	
Totals			
Hull K.R.	72	61	
St. Helens............	82+4	44	
Britain	1	1	
Wales	6	2	
GB Under-21s.......	1	1	
GRAND TOTALS	**162+4**	**109**	

MARK ASTON of Sheffield Eagles became the first player to total 500 goals for the club with the first of seven in a 33-20 Stones Bitter Championship win at Salford on 29 August. His total at the end of the season stood at 622, including 34 drop goals in 228 full appearances plus four as substitute.

The half back and occasional loose forward holds a number of other Sheffield records, most of them set in 1988-89 when he became one of the few players to score in every match in a season. He finished that season with club records of 148 goals and 307 points, including 13 drop goals and six tries.

Aston shares with Roy Rafferty the Eagles' goals in a match record with 12 in a 72-14 Divisional Premiership second round home defeat of Keighley Cougars on 25 April 1992.

Signed from Selby pub team *The Gaffers*, Aston made his Sheffield debut at scrum half in a 36-6 Division Two home defeat of Huddersfield Barracudas on 30 March 1986.

He had a two-match loan spell with Bramley in 1987-88, without scoring, and has since been a regular in Sheffield's team. He has registered 40 tries for the club for a total of 1,370 points.

His season-by-season goals record for Sheffield is as follows:

	App.	Goals
1985-86	7	0
1986-87	22	26
1987-88	16+2	0
1988-89	36	148(13)
1989-90	29	99(5)
1990-91	22	60(2)
1991-92	31+1	104(6)
1992-93	30+1	62(3)
1993-94	35	123(5)
Totals	**228+4**	**622(34)**

() denotes drop goals included in total.

FRANO BOTICA of Wigan kicked the 500th goal of his British-based career with the third of four in a 24-2 Division One home win at Salford on 3 October. The New Zealander's total at the end of the season stood at 659 including 13 drop goals in a total of 148 club and representative matches. Five of his goals came in two Test match appearances for New Zealand.

The utility back kicked a Wigan record 184 goals in 1992-93, which also helped him to the club points in a season record of 423.

A former All Black Rugby Union international, Botica made his debut for Wigan at stand off in the CIS Insurance Charity Shield match at Swansea on 19 August 1990, when he scored all their points with two goals and a try in the 24-8 defeat by Widnes. He finished second in the goals chart that 1990-91 season with 126, first with 161 the following year, second again in 1992-93 with 184, and top last season with 188.

Botica has also been the top Division One kicker in the past three seasons with 86, 107 and 124 League goals. His best match feat is 12 goals and he has also kicked 11 in a match, plus a Premiership final record of 10 against St. Helens in 1992.

He has also scored 57 tries for a Wigan career points total of 1,523, including the British record for the fastest 1,000 in 93 matches. His season-by-season goals totals are:

	App.	Goals
1990-91	30	126
1991-92	34	161(2)
1992-93	40	184(5)
1993-94	42	183(6)+5 New Zealand
Totals		
Wigan	146	654(13)
New Zealand	2	5
GRAND TOTALS	**148**	**659(13)**

() denotes drop goals included in total.
NB: Not including goals scored in New Zealand.

LEE CROOKS of Castleford scored the 2,000th point of his career with four goals and a try in the 16-21 Division One home defeat by Warrington on 17 April. The Great Britain forward's end of season total of 2,045 is made up of 923 for Castleford, 947 Hull, 104 Leeds and 71 in representative matches, including 35 in Tests. He has played in 449 matches overall, including 22 as substitute.

Crooks turned professional with Hull on his 17th birthday, 18 September 1980, and made his debut in the second row when they won 15-10 in a Division One home game against Salford on 30 November. He made just five appearances that season, including two as a substitute, but established himself the following season when he played 42 matches and scored 254 points.

Hull's financial problems forced them to sell Crooks to Leeds in June 1987 for a then world record £150,000. He made his debut for Leeds with two goals and a try in the second row in a 38-12 Division One home defeat of Leigh on 30 August 1987.

Crooks was transferred to Castleford, also for £150,000, over three years later and made his debut at prop in a 39-12 RL Challenge Cup preliminary round defeat at St. Helens on 14 January 1990.

His best match points tally remains the 23 from three tries and seven goals for Hull against Leeds in 1982. His season-by-season totals are as follows:

	App.	T	G	Pts	
Hull					
1980-81	3+2	0	0	0	
1981-82	35+7	7	118(3)	254	
1982-83	41	11	115(2)	261	+4g, 1dg GB
1983-84	19+1	6	36	96	+2g GB
1984-85	33	4	27	70	
1985-86	30	9	53(1)	141	+8g GB
1986-87	35+2	7	51(5)	125	+1g GB

Leeds

1987-88	14+1	4	30(2)	74
1988-89	32	7	1	30
1989-90	9	0	0	0

Castleford

1989-90	6+1	1	14	32
1990-91	31+1	4	61	138
1991-92	31+1	5	111	242 +2g Yorkshire
1992-93	34	2	112	232 +1t,4g England
1993-94	39	2	136(1)	279 +1g GB

Totals

Hull	196+12	44	400(11)	947
Leeds.....................	55+1	11	31(2)	104
Castleford	141+3	14	434(1)	923
Britain	17+2	0	18(1)	35
Tours (3)..............	14+4	1	8	20 Not inc. 1g in 4 Tests
England...............	1	1	4	12
Yorkshire	3	0	2	4
GRAND TOTALS	427+22	71	897(15)	2,045

PAUL LOUGHLIN of St. Helens passed the 2,000 career points mark with four goals in the 37-16 Division One home defeat of Featherstone Rovers on 1 October. The Great Britain centre's total of 2,110 at the end of the season came from 1,936 for St. Helens and 174 in representative matches, including 70 in Test matches.

Loughlin holds two club match records with 16 goals and 40 points in a 112-0 Lancashire Cup first round home defeat of Carlisle on 14 September 1986. His most prolific season

was 1986-87, when he headed two scoring charts with 190 goals and 424 points.

Signed from St. Helens Colts, Loughlin made his senior debut as a substitute and kicked a goal in the 31-20 Division One home win against Oldham on 1 April 1984. He made one other substitute appearance before making his full debut in the centre 22 days later, kicking another goal in a 28-28 League draw at Widnes.

His season-by-season totals are as follows:

	App.	T	G	Pts
St. Helens				
1983-84	1+2	0	2	4
1984-85	2+2	0	5	10
1985-86	24+3	4	43	102
1986-87	39	9	178	392 +2t,12g GB U-21s
1987-88	37+1	8	111	254 +3g GB
1988-89	33	5	109	238 +3g GB, 1g Lancs
1989-90	32	17	135	338 +8g GB, 2g Lancs
1990-91	27	8	94	220 +1t GB
1991-92	11	5	40	100
1992-93	19+1	5	65	150
1993-94	29	3	58	128
Totals				
St. Helens.............	254+9	64	840	1,936
Britain	*15+1	2	31	70
Tours (2)..............	8+3	0	33	66 Not inc. Tests
GB Under-21s.......	2	2	12	32
Lancashire	2	0	3	6
GRAND TOTALS	281+13	68	919	2,110

*Including match against World XIII which was not a Test.

Castleford skipper Lee Crooks, who passed his 2,000-point career landmark in April 1994.

SHAUN EDWARDS of Wigan scored the 1,000th point of his career with a try in the 26-14 Division One win at Leeds on 14 January. The half back's total for Wigan and in representative matches at the end of the season was 1,051 from 252 tries and 22 goals, including one drop goal. He has played in 434 matches, including 15 as substitute.

Edwards shares the Wigan record of tries in a match with 10 in a 78-0 Lancashire Cup second round away win against Swinton on 29 September 1992. It was also a County Cup record and, playing at scrum half, the most by a non-winger in any match.

In addition, Edwards has thrice scored four tries in a match for Wigan and five other hat-tricks. He was the game's top try scorer in 1991-92 with 40, second in 1992-93 with 46, and has finished in the top ten on three other occasions.

The former schoolboy international signed for Wigan on his 17th birthday, 17 October 1983, and made his debut at stand off in a 30-13 John Player Special Trophy first round home defeat of York on 6 November 1983.

Edwards's season-by-season totals are as follows:

A career milestone of 1,000 points for Wigan's Shaun Edwards in January 1994.

	App.	T	G	Pts
Wigan				
1983-84	24	6	1	26
1984-85	34	11	1	46
1985-86	33+3	14	0	56 +1t GB U-21s
1986-87	41	24	6	108 +2t GB
1987-88	32+2	17	0	68 +2t GB, 2t Lancs
1988-89	31+1	15	0	60 +3tGB*
1989-90	32+1	25	10	120 +1t GB
1990-91	33+1	16	1	66 +3t GB
1991-92	37	40	2	164
1992-93	44	43	1(1)	173 +3t GB
1993-94	35+2	19	0	76 +1t GB
Totals				
Wigan	376+10	230	22(1)	963
Britain	*31+4	16	0	64
1992 Tour	4	3	0	12 Not inc. 1t in 5+1 Tests
GB Under-21s.......	4	1	0	4
Chairman's XIII	1	0	0	0
Lancashire	3+1	2	0	8
GRAND TOTALS	**419+15**	**252**	**22(1)**	**1,051**

() denotes drop goal included in total.

* Including one try in match against World XIII which was not a Test.

• 1988 tour: played in only one match, the Test against Papua New Guinea, which is included in his Great Britain total.

LEADING SCORERS 1895-1975

	TRIES	GOALS	POINTS
1895-96	Hurst (Oldham) 28	Lorimer (Manningham).....35	Cooper (Bradford).......... 106
			Lorimer (Manningham)... 106
1896-97	Hannah (Hunslet)............19	Goldthorpe (Hunslet)........26	Rigg (Halifax)............... 112
		Sharpe (Liversedge)..........26	
1897-98	Hoskins (Salford).............30	Goldthorpe (Hunslet)........66	Goldthorpe (Hunslet)...... 135
1898-99	Williams (Oldham) 39	Goldthorpe (Hunslet)........67	Jaques (Hull)................ 169
1899-00	Williams (Oldham) 36	Cooper (Bradford)............39	Williams (Oldham) 108
1900-01	Williams (Oldham) 47	Goldthorpe (Hunslet)........44	Williams (Oldham) 141
1901-02	Wilson (Broughton R.) 38	James (Broughton R.)........75	Lomas (Salford) 172
1902-03	Evans (Leeds)..................27	Goldthorpe (Hunslet)........48	Davies (Batley) 136
1903-04	Hogg (Broughton R.) 34	Lomas (Salford) 66	Lomas (Salford) 222
1904-05	Dechan (Bradford)...........31	Ferguson (Oldham)...........50	Lomas (Salford) 146
1905-06	Leytham (Wigan) 40	Ferguson (Oldham)...........49	Leytham (Wigan) 160
1906-07	Eccles (Halifax)...............41	Lomas (Salford) 86	Lomas (Salford) 280
1907-08	Leytham (Wigan) 44	Goldthorpe (Hunslet)...... 101	Goldthorpe (Hunslet)...... 217
1908-09	Miller (Wigan) 49	Lomas (Salford) 88	Lomas (Salford) 272
	Williams (Halifax) 49		
1909-10	Leytham (Wigan) 48	Carmichael (Hull K.R.) 78	Leytham (Wigan) 232
1910-11	Kitchen (Huddersfield) 40	Carmichael (Hull K.R.) .. 129	Carmichael (Hull K.R.) .. 261
	Rosenfeld (Huddersfield) 40		
	Miller (Wigan) 40		
1911-12	Rosenfeld (Huddersfield) 78	Carmichael (Hull K.R.) .. 127	Carmichael (Hull K.R.) .. 254
1912-13	Rosenfeld (Huddersfield) 56	Carmichael (Hull K.R.) 93	Thomas (Wigan)............ 198
1913-14	Rosenfeld (Huddersfield) 80	Holland (Huddersfield) ... 131	Holland (Huddersfield) ... 268
1914-15	Rosenfeld (Huddersfield) 56	Gronow (Huddersfield) 136	Gronow (Huddersfield) 284

● Competitive matches suspended during war years

	TRIES	GOALS	POINTS
1918-19	Francis (Hull)...................25	Kennedy (Hull) 54	Kennedy (Hull) 135
1919-20	Moorhouse (Huddersfield)....39	Gronow (Huddersfield) 148	Gronow (Huddersfield) 332
1920-21	Stone (Hull) 41	Kennedy (Hull) 108	Kennedy (Hull) 264
1921-22	Farrar (Oldham)...............49	Sullivan (Wigan)............ 100	Farrar (Oldham)............. 213
1922-23	Ring (Wigan) 41	Sullivan (Wigan)............ 161	Sullivan (Wigan)............ 349
1923-24	Ring (Wigan) 49	Sullivan (Wigan)............ 158	Sullivan (Wigan)............ 319
1924-25	Ring (Wigan) 54	Sullivan (Wigan)............ 138	Sullivan (Wigan)............ 282
1925-26	Ring (Wigan) 63	Sullivan (Wigan)............ 131	Sullivan (Wigan)............ 274
1926-27	Ellaby (St. Helens)...........55	Sullivan (Wigan)............ 149	Sullivan (Wigan)............ 322
1927-28	Ellaby (St. Helens)...........37	Thompson (Leeds)......... 106	Thompson (Leeds)......... 233
1928-29	Brown (Wigan) 44	Sullivan (Wigan)............ 107	Sullivan (Wigan)............ 226
	Mills (Huddersfield)........44		
1929-30	Ellaby (St. Helens)...........39	Thompson (Leeds)......... 111	Thompson (Leeds)......... 243
1930-31	Harris, E. (Leeds) 58	Sullivan (Wigan)............ 133	Sullivan (Wigan)............ 278
1931-32	Mills (Huddersfield)........50	Sullivan (Wigan)............ 117	Sullivan (Wigan)............ 249
1932-33	Harris, E. (Leeds) 57	Sullivan (Wigan)............ 146	Sullivan (Wigan)............ 307
1933-34	Brown (Salford) 45	Sullivan (Wigan)............ 194	Sullivan (Wigan)............ 406
1934-35	Morley (Wigan) 49	Sullivan (Wigan)............ 165	Sullivan (Wigan)............ 348
1935-36	Harris, E. (Leeds) 63	Sullivan (Wigan)............ 117	Sullivan (Wigan)............ 246
1936-37	Harris, E. (Leeds) 40	Sullivan (Wigan)............ 120	Sullivan (Wigan)............ 258
1937-38	Harris, E. (Leeds) 45	Sullivan (Wigan)............ 135	Sullivan (Wigan)............ 285

	TRIES	GOALS	POINTS
1938-39	Markham (Huddersfield) 39	Sullivan (Wigan)............ 124	Risman (Salford) 267

● For the next six seasons emergency war-time competitions resulted in a reduction of matches and players were allowed to "guest" for other clubs

	TRIES	GOALS	POINTS
1939-40	Batten (Hunslet)..............38	Hodgson (Swinton) 98	Hodgson (Swinton) 208
1940-41	Walters (Bradford N.)........32	Lockwood (Halifax) 70	Belshaw (Warrington)...... 174
1941-42	Francis (Barrow) 30	Lockwood (Halifax) 91	Lockwood (Halifax) 185
1942-43	Batten (Hunslet)..............24	Lockwood (Halifax) 65	Lockwood (Halifax) 136
1943-44	Lawrenson (Wigan)...........21	Horne (Barrow)...............57	Horne (Barrow).............. 144
1944-45	Batten (Bradford N.)........41	Stott (Wakefield T.) 51	Stott (Wakefield T.) 129

● Normal peace-time rugby resumed

	TRIES	GOALS	POINTS
1945-46	Batten (Bradford N.)........35	Ledgard (Dewsbury).........89	Bawden (Huddersfield) 239
1946-47	Bevan (Warrington)...........48	Miller (Hull)................. 103	Bawden (Huddersfield) 243
1947-48	Bevan (Warrington)...........57	Ward (Wigan)................ 141	Ward (Wigan)................ 312
1948-49	Cooper (Huddersfield) 60	Ward (Wigan)................ 155	Ward (Wigan)................ 361
1949-50	Nordgren (Wigan)............57	Gee (Wigan) 133	Palin (Warrington) 290
		Palin (Warrington) 133	
1950-51	Bevan (Warrington)...........68	Cook (Leeds)................. 155	Cook (Leeds)................. 332
1951-52	Cooper (Huddersfield) 71	Ledgard (Leigh)............. 142	Horne (Barrow).............. 313
1952-53	Bevan (Warrington)...........72	Bath (Warrington) 170	Bath (Warrington) 379
1953-54	Bevan (Warrington)...........67	Metcalfe (St. Helens)...... 153	Metcalfe (St. Helens)...... 369
		Bath (Warrington) 153	
1954-55	Cooper (Huddersfield) 66	Ledgard (Leigh)............. 178	Ledgard (Leigh)............. 374
1955-56	McLean (Bradford N.)......61	Ledgard (Leigh)............. 155	Bath (Warrington) 344
1956-57	Boston (Wigan) 60	Jones (Leeds)................ 194	Jones (Leeds)................ 496
1957-58	Sullivan (Wigan)..............50	Ganley (Oldham)........... 219	Ganley (Oldham)............ 453
1958-59	Vollenhoven (St. Helens) 62	Ganley (Oldham)........... 190	Griffiths (Wigan) 394
1959-60	Vollenhoven (St. Helens) 54	Rhodes (St. Helens) 171	Fox (Wakefield T.).......... 453
		Fox (Wakefield T.).......... 171	
1960-61	Vollenhoven (St. Helens) 59	Rhodes (St. Helens) 145	Rhodes (St. Helens) 338
1961-62	Boston (Wigan) 51	Fox (Wakefield T.).......... 183	Fox (Wakefield T.).......... 456
1962-63	Glastonbury (Work'ton T.) ...41	Coslett (St. Helens)........ 156	Coslett (St. Helens)........ 321
1963-64	Stopford (Swinton)...........45	Coslett (St. Helens)........ 138	Fox (Wakefield T.).......... 313
1964-65	Lake (Wigan)..................40	Kellett (Hull K.R.) 150	Killeen (St. Helens) 360
1965-66	Killeen (St. Helens) 32	Killeen (St. Helens) 120	Killeen (St. Helens) 336
	Lake (Wigan)..................32		
1966-67	Young (Hull K.R.) 34	Risman (Leeds)............. 163	Killeen (St. Helens) 353
	Howe (Castleford).............34		
1967-68	Millward (Hull K.R.)........38	Risman (Leeds)............. 154	Risman (Leeds)............. 332
1968-69	Francis (Wigan) 40	Risman (Leeds)............. 165	Risman (Leeds)............. 345
1969-70	Atkinson (Leeds)..............38	Tyrer (Wigan) 167	Tyrer (Wigan) 385
1970-71	Haigh (Leeds)..................40	Coslett (St. Helens)........ 193	Coslett (St. Helens)........ 395
	Jones (St. Helens)............40		
1971-72	Atkinson (Leeds)..............36	Coslett (St. Helens)........ 214	Watkins (Salford) 473
	Lamb (Bradford N.)........36		
1972-73	Atkinson (Leeds).............39	Watkins (Salford) 221	Watkins (Salford) 493
1973-74	Fielding (Salford) 49	Watkins (Salford) 183	Watkins (Salford) 438
1974-75	Dunn (Hull K.R.) 42	Fox (Hull K.R.).............. 146	Fox (Hull K.R.).............. 333
1975-76	Richards (Salford)............37	Watkins (Salford) 175	Watkins (Salford) 385

LEADING SCORERS 1976-93

TRIES

1976-77

Stuart Wright (Widnes)	31
Bruce Burton (Castleford)	29
David Smith (Leeds)	28
Keith Fielding (Salford)	27
Ged Dunn (Hull K.R.)	26
Eddie Cunningham (St. Helens)	26
David Topliss (Wakefield T.)	24
Maurice Richards (Salford)	23
Roy Mathias (St. Helens)	23
David Barends (York)	22

1977-78

Stuart Wright (Widnes)	33
Keith Fielding (Salford)	31
Eddie Cunningham (St. Helens)	30
John Bevan (Warrington)	30
Steve Fenton (Castleford)	30
Green Vigo (Wigan)	29
Peter Glynn (St. Helens)	28
David Smith (Leeds)	28
Terry Morgan (York)	27
Bruce Burton (Castleford)	27

1978-79

Steve Hartley (Hull K.R.)	35
Stuart Wright (Widnes)	28
David Barends (Bradford N.)	25
Phil Lowe (Hull K.R.)	25
Paul Prendiville (Hull)	25
Keith Fielding (Salford)	24
David Redfearn (Bradford N.)	23
Roy Mathias (St. Helens)	22
Graham Bray (Hull)	21
Keiron O'Loughlin (Wigan)	21
Clive Sullivan (Hull K.R.)	21

1979-80

Keith Fielding (Salford)	30
Steve Hubbard (Hull K.R.)	30
Geoff Munro (Oldham)	29
Ian Ball (Barrow)	27
Keith Bentley (Widnes)	27
Peter Glynn (St. Helens)	27
Roy Mathias (St. Helens)	27
John Bevan (Warrington)	26
David Redfearn (Bradford N.)	26
David Smith (Leeds)	24

1980-81

John Crossley (York)	35
Terry Richardson (Castleford)	28
Steve Hubbard (Hull K.R.)	25
Steve Hartley (Hull K.R.)	23
Paul McDermott (York)	23

Ian Slater (Huddersfield)	23
Des Drummond (Leigh)	20
Ian Ball (Barrow)	19
John Bevan (Warrington)	19
Peter Cramp (Huddersfield)	19
Gary Hyde (Castleford)	19
Denis Ramsdale (Wigan)	19

1981-82

John Jones (Workington T.)	31
Des Drummond (Leigh)	26
John Basnett (Widnes)	26
Ray Ashton (Oldham)	26
Mick Morgan (Carlisle)	25
Steve Hartley (Hull K.R.)	23
Lyn Hopkins (Workington T.)	23
Terry Day (Hull)	23
Steve Evans (Hull)	22
David Hobbs (Featherstone R.)	21
David Moll (Keighley)	21

1982-83

Bob Eccles (Warrington)	37
Steve Evans (Hull)	28
John Crossley (Fulham)	27
Tommy David (Cardiff C.)	26
David Topliss (Hull)	24
Hussain M'Barki (Fulham)	23
Gary Hyde (Castleford)	22
Paul McDermott (York)	22
James Leuluai (Hull)	21
Phil Ford (Warrington)	20
Garry Clark (Hull K.R.)	20

1983-84

Garry Schofield (Hull)	38
Joe Lydon (Widnes)	28
Graham King (Hunslet)	28
John Woods (Leigh)	27
John Basnett (Widnes)	26
Carl Gibson (Batley)	26
Steve Herbert (Barrow)	25
Graham Steadman (York)	25
Gary Prohm (Hull K.R.)	25
Garry Clark (Hull K.R.)	24

1984-85

Ellery Hanley (Bradford N.)	55
Gary Prohm (Hull K.R.)	45
Henderson Gill (Wigan)	34
Barry Ledger (St. Helens)	30
Mal Meninga (St. Helens)	28
Vince Gribbin (Whitehaven)	27
Carl Gibson (Batley)	26
Gary Peacham (Carlisle)	25
Ged Byrne (Salford)	25
Steve Evans (Hull)	24
John Ferguson (Wigan)	24

163

1985-86
Steve Halliwell (Leigh) 49
Ellery Hanley (Wigan)......................................38
Peter Lister (Bramley).....................................34
John Henderson (Leigh) 31
Tommy Frodsham (Blackpool B.)..............................30
Phil Fox (Leigh)...29
Stewart Williams (Barrow)..................................27
Brian Garrity (Runcorn H.) 24
Carl Gibson (Leeds)..23
David Beck (Workington T.) 23

1986-87
Ellery Hanley (Wigan)......................................63
Garry Schofield (Hull).....................................37
Henderson Gill (Wigan).....................................32
Derek Bate (Swinton).......................................31
Phil Ford (Bradford N.)....................................30
John Henderson (Leigh) 27
Shaun Edwards (Wigan) 26
Brian Johnson (Warrington) 25
Joe Lydon (Wigan)..24
Brian Dunn (Rochdale H.) 23
Barry Ledger (St. Helens) 23
Kevin McCormack (St. Helens) 23

1987-88
Martin Offiah (Widnes) 44
Ellery Hanley (Wigan)......................................36
Garry Schofield (Leeds)....................................25
Carl Gibson (Leeds)..24
Andy Goodway (Wigan).......................................23
Kevin Pape (Carlisle) 23
Shaun Edwards (Wigan) 21
Des Foy (Oldham) 21
Peter Smith (Featherstone R.) 21
Chris Bibb (Featherstone R.)...............................20
Mark Conway (Wakefield T.) 20
Mark Elia (St. Helens) 20
Les Quirk (St. Helens) 20

1988-89
Martin Offiah (Widnes) 60
Barry Ledger (Leigh).......................................34
Derek Bate (Swinton).......................................32
Ellery Hanley (Wigan)......................................29
Peter Lister (Bramley).....................................28
Daryl Powell (Sheffield E.) 28
Peter Lewis (Bramley)......................................26
Les Quirk (St. Helens) 24
Grant Anderson (Castleford) 24
Paul Burns (Barrow) 24

1989-90
Martin Offiah (Widnes) 45
Greg Austin (Hull K.R.)....................................38
Anthony Sullivan (Hull K.R.) 35
Mark Preston (Wigan).......................................33
Gerald Cordle (Bradford N.) 32
Steve Larder (Castleford) 29
Paul Lord (Oldham) 29

Shaun Edwards (Wigan) 26
Andy Goodway (Wigan).......................................26
John Cogger (Oldham) 24
St. John Ellis (Castleford) 24
Wilf George (Halifax)......................................24
Mark Lord (Rochdale H.)....................................24
Owen Simpson (Keighley) 24

1990-91
Martin Offiah (Widnes) 49
Greg Austin (Halifax)......................................47
Martin Wood (Halifax) 31
Adrian Hadley (Salford)....................................31
Jonathan Davies (Widnes) 30
Ellery Hanley (Wigan)......................................29
Les Quirk (St. Helens) 26
Alan Hunte (St. Helens) 26
Garry Schofield (Leeds)....................................25
Graham Steadman (Castleford)...............................23
Andy Currier (Widnes)......................................23
John Devereux (Widnes).....................................23

1991-92
Shaun Edwards (Wigan) 40
John Devereux (Widnes).....................................35
Iva Ropati (Oldham) 33
Greg Austin (Halifax)......................................33
Vince Gribbin (Whitehaven) 31
Graham Steadman (Castleford)...............................31
Martin Offiah (Wigan)......................................30
David Myers (Wigan)..29
Paul Newlove (Featherstone R.) 28
Mark Preston (Halifax).....................................27

1992-93
Paul Newlove (Featherstone R.) 52
Shaun Edwards (Wigan) 46
Ellery Hanley (Leeds)......................................34
Owen Simpson (Featherstone R.) 34
Martin Offiah (Wigan)......................................32
Alan Hunte (St. Helens) 30
John Wasyliw (Keighley C.).................................29
Martin Pearson (Featherstone R.) 29
Greg Austin (Halifax)......................................27
Martin Wood (Keighley C.) 27

GOALS
(including drop goals)

1976-77
Geoff "Sammy" Lloyd (Castleford) 163
Steve Quinn (Featherstone R.)......................... 152
Geoff Pimblett (St. Helens)........................... 152
Steve Hesford (Warrington) 132
Iain MacCorquodale (Workington T.) 128
David Watkins (Salford) 125
Nigel Stephenson (Dewsbury) 106
George Fairbairn (Wigan) 105
Ray Dutton (Widnes) 97
John Woods (Leigh) 90

1977-78
Geoff Pimblett (St. Helens)................................. 178
Steve Hesford (Warrington) 158
John Woods (Leigh) 149
Iain MacCorquodale (Workington T.) 138
Paul Woods (Widnes)...................................... 122
David Watkins (Salford)................................... 110
Keith Mumby (Bradford N.)................................ 107
Geoff "Sammy" Lloyd (Castleford) 104
Neil Fox (Bradford N.) 95
Willie Oulton (Leeds)....................................... 80

1978-79
Geoff "Sammy" Lloyd (Hull) 172
Steve Hesford (Warrington) 170
Mick Burke (Widnes)....................................... 140
Iain MacCorquodale (Workington T.) 114
Geoff Pimblett (St. Helens)................................. 105
Graham Beale (Keighley) 96
John Woods (Leigh) 96
Jimmy Birts (Halifax)....................................... 86
George Fairbairn (Wigan)................................... 86
Paul Norton (Castleford) 82

1979-80
Steve Quinn (Featherstone R.)............................ 163
Steve Hubbard (Hull K.R.) 138
Steve Rule (Salford).. 134
Steve Hesford (Warrington) 128
Mick Burke (Widnes)....................................... 127
Ian Ball (Barrow) 119
Steve Diamond (Wakefield T.).............................. 116
Eric Fitzsimons (Oldham) 108
Mick Parrish (Hunslet) 98
Jimmy Birts (Halifax)....................................... 97

1980-81
Steve Hesford (Warrington) 147
Steve Quinn (Featherstone R.)............................ 123
Steve Diamond (Wakefield T.)............................. 112
Mick Burke (Widnes)....................................... 110
Steve Hubbard (Hull K.R.) 109
Ian Ball (Barrow) 104
Jimmy Birts (Halifax)....................................... 100
Graham Beale (Keighley) 97
Mick Parrish (Oldham)..................................... 95
George Fairbairn (Wigan)................................... 94

1981-82
Lyn Hopkins (Workington T.)............................. 190
George Fairbairn (Hull K.R.).............................. 168
Mick Parrish (Oldham)..................................... 164
John Woods (Leigh) 158
Steve Rule (Salford).. 130
Kevin Dick (Leeds)... 125
Steve Quinn (Featherstone R.) 120
Malcolm Agar (Halifax) 119
Lee Crooks (Hull)... 118
Steve Hesford (Warrington) 116

1982-83
Steve Diamond (Fulham) 136
Eric Fitzsimons (Hunslet).................................. 121
Lee Crooks (Hull) 120
Bob Beardmore (Castleford) 117
Steve Hesford (Warrington) 113
Steve Fenwick (Cardiff C.) 111
Ken Jones (Swinton).. 110
Colin Whitfield (Wigan)................................... 104
Shaun Kilner (Bramley).................................... 104
Steve Quinn (Featherstone R.)............................ 98

1983-84
Steve Hesford (Warrington) 142
Bob Beardmore (Castleford) 142
Lyn Hallett (Cardiff C.).................................... 140
Eric Fitzsimons (Hunslet).................................. 131
John Woods (Leigh) 124
Colin Whitfield (Wigan) 122
Ian Ball (Barrow) 104
Mick Parrish (Oldham) 101
Malcolm Agar (Halifax) 94
Steve Tickle (Barrow)....................................... 91

1984-85
Sean Day (St. Helens) 157
George Fairbairn (Hull K.R.) 141
Peter Wood (Runcorn H.) 126
Graham Steadman (York).................................. 122
Clive Griffiths (Salford).................................... 118
Mick Parrish (Oldham).................................... 117
Garry Schofield (Hull)..................................... 105
David Creasser (Leeds) 102
Malcolm Agar (Halifax) 87
Ken Jones (Swinton).. 87

1985-86
Chris Johnson (Leigh) 173
David Stephenson (Wigan) 128
David Noble (Doncaster) 118
Kevin Harcombe (Rochdale H.).......................... 115
Shaun Kilner (Bramley).................................... 110
John Dorahy (Hull K.R.)................................... 101
John Woods (Bradford N.) 98
David Creasser (Leeds) 84
Dean Carroll (Carlisle)..................................... 83
Gary Smith (Workington T.) 83

1986-87
Paul Loughlin (St. Helens) 190
Paul Bishop (Warrington) 117
David Noble (Doncaster) 114
Colin Whitfield (Halifax).................................. 109
Alan Platt (Hunslet) 102
Paul Topping (Swinton) 100
Chris Johnson (Leigh) 86
Martin Ketteridge (Castleford) 80
David Wood (Rochdale H.)................................ 80
Steve Quinn (Featherstone R.)............................ 77

1987-88

John Woods (Warrington)	152
Steve Quinn (Featherstone R.)	128
Kevin Harcombe (Wakefield T.)	116
Paul Loughlin (St. Helens)	114
Gary Pearce (Hull)	111
Mike Smith (Springfield B.)	98
David Stephenson (Leeds)	95
Mike Fletcher (Hull K.R.)	94
David Hobbs (Bradford N.)	83
Ken Jones (Salford)	79

1988-89

Mark Aston (Sheffield E.)	148
Martin Ketteridge (Castleford)	129
David Hobbs (Bradford N.)	118
Chris Johnson (Leigh)	117
Dean Marwood (Barrow)	115
Paul Loughlin (St. Helens)	113
David Noble (Doncaster)	110
John Woods (Warrington)	107
Andy Currier (Widnes)	107
Steve Turner (Rochdale H.)	104

1989-90

Mike Fletcher (Hull K.R.)	199
Paul Loughlin (St. Helens)	145
Duncan Platt (Oldham)	126
Colin Maskill (Leeds)	114
Mark Conway (Wakefield T.)	107
David Hobbs (Bradford N.)	104
Paul Eastwood (Hull)	101
Mark Aston (Sheffield E.)	99
Jonathan Davies (Widnes)	98
Steve Turner (Rochdale H.)	98

1990-91

Steve Kerry (Salford)	177
Frano Botica (Wigan)	126
Paul Eastwood (Hull)	119
Jonathan Davies (Widnes)	112
Simon Irving (Leeds)	99
Graham Sullivan (Ryedale-York)	94
Paul Loughlin (St. Helens)	94
Alan Platt (Halifax)	91
Barry Vickers (Carlisle)	88
Tim Lumb (Hunslet)	85

1991-92

Frano Botica (Wigan)	161
Steve Carroll (Bramley)	138
Deryck Fox (Featherstone R.)	115
Lee Crooks (Castleford)	113
David Hobbs (Bradford N.)	110
Chris Vasey (Dewsbury)	109
Paul Eastwood (Hull)	108
Steve Parrish (Batley)	106
Mark Aston (Sheffield E.)	104
Jonathan Davies (Widnes)	99

1992-93

John Wasyliw (Keighley C.)	187
Frano Botica (Wigan)	184
Dean Marwood (Workington T.)	179
Martin Pearson (Featherstone R.)	145
Paul Bishop (Halifax)	118
Lee Crooks (Castleford)	116
Jonathan Davies (Widnes)	116
Steve Gartland (Rochdale H.)	105
Steve Maguire (Whitehaven)	95
Andy Precious (Hunslet)	90

DROP GOALS

1976-77	Nigel Stephenson (Dewsbury)	16
1977-78	Jim Fiddler (Bramley, Leigh)	10
1978-79	Norman Turley (Blackpool B.)	18
1979-80	Tony Dean (Hunslet)	18
1980-81	Arnold Walker (Whitehaven)	22
1981-82	Malcolm Agar (Halifax)	17
	Steve Donlan (Leigh)	17
1982-83	Harry Pinner (St. Helens)	13
1983-84	Lyn Hallett (Cardiff C.)	29
1984-85	Peter Wood (Runcorn H.)	28
1985-86	Paul Bishop (Warrington)	13
1986-87	Billy Platt (Mansfield M.)	18
1987-88	Wayne Parker (Hull K.R.)	15
1988-89	Gary Pearce (Hull)	16
1989-90	Paul Harkin (Bradford N.)	12
1990-91	Ray Ashton (Workington T.)	13
	Dean Carroll (Doncaster)	13
1991-92	Andy Ruane (Leigh)	17
1992-93	Paul Shuttleworth (Dewsbury)	11

POINTS

1976-77	Geoff "Sammy" Lloyd (Castleford)	341
1977-78	Geoff Pimblett (St. Helens)	381
1978-79	Geoff "Sammy" Lloyd (Hull)	373
1979-80	Steve Quinn (Featherstone R.)	375
1980-81	Steve Hesford (Warrington)	310
1981-82	Lyn Hopkins (Workington T.)	446
1982-83	Steve Diamond (Fulham)	308
1983-84	John Woods (Leigh)	355
1984-85	Sean Day (St. Helens)	362
1985-86	Chris Johnson (Leigh)	400
1986-87	Paul Loughlin (St. Helens)	424
1987-88	John Woods (Warrington)	351
1988-89	Mark Aston (Sheffield E.)	307
1989-90	Mike Fletcher (Hull K.R.)	450
1990-91	Steve Kerry (Salford)	427
1991-92	Frano Botica (Wigan)	364
1992-93	John Wasyliw (Keighley C.)	490

ALL-TIME RECORDS

Most goals in a match:
22 by Jim Sullivan (Wigan) v. Flimby & Fothergill (Challenge Cup), 14 February 1925

Most goals in a season:
DAVID WATKINS holds the record for most goals in a season with 221 — all for Salford — in 1972-73. Watkins played and scored a goal in every match that season as follows:

1972

Aug.	19	Leeds .... (H)	5
	23	Featherstone R. ....(A)	3
	26	Whitehaven ....(A)	4
	28	Swinton .... (H)	1
Sep.	1	Oldham ....(LC) (H)	10
	9	Leeds .... (A)	2
	15	Rochdale H. .... (LC) (H)	11
	17	Leigh .... (A)	6
	24	Barrow ....(JP) (A)	4
	29	Huyton .... (H)	10
Oct.	3	Oldham .... (FT) (A)	4
	6	Wigan ....(LC) (A)	4
	8	Blackpool B. .... (A)	5
	13	Blackpool B. .... (H)	8
	21	Swinton .... (LCF)	5
Nov.	5	Huyton .... (A)	8
	10	Rochdale H. .... (H)	6
	17	Warrington ....(A)	4
	19	New Zealand .... (H)	10
	24	Dewsbury .... (JP) (H)	4
	26	Workington T. .... (H)	6
Dec.	1	Barrow .... (H)	9
	10	Bradford N. ....(JP) (H)	9
	13	Oldham .... (A)	4
	15	Leigh .... (H)	3
	24	Bradford N. .... (A)	5
	26	Workington T. ....(A)	3
	30	Hull K.R. .... (JP) (A)	5

1973

Jan.	3	Bradford N. .... (H)	6
	7	Rochdale H. ....(A)	2
	12	Featherstone R. .... (H)	4
	28	Featherstone R. .... (RL Cup) (A)	4
Feb.	2	Whitehaven .... (H)	4
	11	Barrow ....(A)	5
	23	St. Helens .... (H)	3
Mar.	7	Widnes ....(A)	3
	9	Dewsbury .... (H)	3
	16	St. Helens .... (A)	2
	24	Leeds ....(JP Final)	2
	30	Warrington .... (H)	1
Apr.	6	Widnes .... (H)	4
	13	Oldham .... (H)	3
	15	Dewsbury ....(A)	2
	17	Wigan ....(A)	3

20	Swinton .... (A)	7
23	Wigan .... (H)	3
29	Rochdale H. ....(top 16) (H)	2

	App	Goals
League	34	147
Lancs Cup	4	30
John Player	5	24
Tour match	1	10
RL Cup	1	4
Floodlit Cup	1	4
Top 16......................................	1	2
Totals	**47**	**221**

Fastest goals century:
Four players share the record of scoring the fastest 100 goals from the start of a season in terms of number of matches played. They are Bernard Ganley, David Watkins, Steve Quinn and John Wasyliw, who achieved the century in 18 matches.

Ganley reached 100 goals on 16 November 1957, after playing 17 matches for Oldham and one for Great Britain.

Watkins scored his 100th goal on 17 November 1972, all for Salford.

Quinn scored his 100th goal on 16 December 1979, all for Featherstone Rovers.

Wasyliw equalled the record with his 100th goal for Keighley Cougars on 31 January 1993.

Most goals in a career:
JIM SULLIVAN holds the record for most goals in a career with 2,867 between 1921-22 and 1945-46. He scored a century of goals in every season after leaving Welsh Rugby Union for Wigan until the war interrupted the 1939-40 campaign. The Test full back played all of his club rugby for Wigan apart from war-time appearances with Bradford Northern, Dewsbury and Keighley.

Sullivan's total includes 441 in representative matches, including three tours of Australasia. These figures are accepted by the Record Keepers' Club following research by James Carter and Malcolm Bentley.

Most one-point drop goals in a match:
5 by Danny Wilson (Swinton) v. Hunslet (John Player
    Special), 6 November 1983
    Peter Wood (Runcorn H.) v.Batley, 21 October 1984
    Paul Bishop (Warrington) at Wigan (Premiership
    semi-final), 11 May 1986

Most one-point drop goals in a season:
29 by Lyn Hallett (Cardiff C.) 1983-84

Most one-point drop goals in a career:
97 by Norman Turley (Warrington, Runcorn H.,
    Swinton, Blackpool B., Rochdale H., Barrow,
    Workington T., Trafford B.,
    Whitehaven) 1974-91

167

Most tries in a match:
11 by George West (Hull K.R.) v Brookland Rovers
(Challenge Cup), 4 March 1905

Most tries in a career:
BRIAN BEVAN holds the record for most tries in a career
with 796 between 1946 and 1964. His season-by-season
record is:

1946-47	48
1947-48	57
1948-49	56
1949-50	33
1950-51	68
1951-52	51
1952-53	72
1953-54	67
1954-55	63
1955-56	57
1956-57	17
1957-58	46
1958-59	54
1959-60	40
1960-61	35
1961-62	15
1962-63	10
1963-64	7

Totals

Warrington	740
Blackpool Borough	17
Other Nationalities	26
Other representative matches	13
Grand Total	**796**

The Australian winger played his first game for
Warrington on 17 November 1945 and his last on 23 April
1962 before having two seasons at Blackpool Borough. His
last match for Borough was on 22 February 1964.

Most tries in a season:
ALBERT ROSENFELD holds the record for most tries
in a season with 80 — all for Huddersfield — in 1913-14.

Rosenfeld's match-by-match record:
1913

Sep.	6	York	(A)	4
	8	Warrington	(H)	2
	13	Leeds	(H)	5
	20	Halifax	(A)	1
	27	Batley	(A)	0
Oct.	4	Oldham	(H)	2
	11	Rochdale H.	(A)	0
	18	Bramley	(YC) (H)	2
	25	Dewsbury	(A)	4
Nov.	1	Halifax	(YC) (A)	2
	8	Wigan	(A)	1
	15	Dewsbury	(YC) (H)	3

	19	Bradford N.	(H)	3
	22	Leeds	(A)	3
	29	Bradford N.	(Halifax, YCF)	1
Dec.	3	Halifax	(H)	3
	6	Hunslet	(A)	2
	13	Rochdale H.	(H)	3
	20	Hull K.R.	(A)	2
	25	Hull	(A)	1
	26	Wakefield T.	(H)	3
	27	Hunslet	(H)	0
1914				
Jan.	1	St. Helens	(A)	0
	3	Warrington	(A)	0
	10	York	(H)	3
	17	Keighley	(A)	2
	24	Dewsbury	(H)	1
	31	Batley	(H)	0
Feb.	7	Oldham	(A)	0
	14	Bramley	(H)	5
	21	Wigan	(H)	3
	28	Swinton Park R.	(RL Cup) (H)	7
Mar.	7	Wakefield T.	(A)	2
	14	Hull K.R.	(RL Cup) (A)	2
	18	Bramley	(A)	3
	21	Widnes	(RL Cup) (H)	0
	25	Keighley	(H)	3
	28	Hull K.R.	(H)	1
	30	Bradford N.	(A)	1
Apr.	4	Hull	(Leeds, RL Cup SF)	0
	11	Hull	(H) did not play	
	13	St. Helens	(H)	0
	20	Hull	(Play-off) (H) did not play	
	25	Salford	(Leeds, Championship final)	0

	App	Tries
League	33	63
Yorks Cup	4	8
RL Cup	4	9
Play-off	1	0
Totals	**42**	**80**

Most points in a season:
LEWIS JONES holds the record for most points in a
season with 496 from 194 goals and 36 tries for Leeds and
representative teams in 1956-57.

Jones's match-by-match record:

For Leeds

			G	T	Pts
1956					
Aug.	17	Halifax	(H) 3	0	6
	22	Bradford N.	(A) 11	3	31
	25	Wigan	(A) 4	0	8
	27	Featherstone R.	(H) 4	1	11
Sep.	1	Wakefield T.	(YC) (A) 3	1	9
	8	Dewsbury	(A) 6	0	12
	15	Warrington	(H) 7	0	14
	22	Huddersfield	(A) 3	0	6

	29	York .... (H)	6	0	12
Oct.	6	Batley ....(A)	4	2	14
	13	Australia .... (H)	Did not play		
	20	Hull K.R. .... (A)	Did not play		
	27	Wigan .... (H)	2	0	4
Nov.	3	Hunslet....................... (A)	1	0	2
	10	Barrow........................ (H)	3	2	12
	17	Halifax........................ (A)	4	0	8
	24	Keighley..................... (H)	3	3	15
Dec.	1	Barrow..........................(A)	4	0	8
	8	Bramley ....(A)	5	0	10
	15	Doncaster................... (H)	1	2	8
	22	Bradford N. ..(abandoned) (H)	1	1	5
	25	Batley .... (H)	8	1	19
	29	Keighley......................(A)	3	0	6
1957					
Jan.	5	Hull .... (H)	5	2	16
	12	Warrington...................(A)	0	3	9
	19	St. Helens .... (H)	5	1	13
	26	Doncaster................... (A)	Did not play		
Feb.	2	Huddersfield .... (H)	6	0	12
	9	Wigan .... (RL Cup) (H)	2	1	7
	16	York ....(A)	7	1	17
	23	Warrington..... (RL Cup) (H)	5	1	13
	27	Castleford .... (H)	4	1	11
Mar.	9	Halifax.......... (RL Cup) (A)	5	0	10
	16	Wakefield T. .... (H)	5	1	13
	20	Bradford N. .... (H)	5	1	13
	23	Hull .... (A)	2	0	4
	30	Whitehaven			
		..........(Odsal, RL Cup SF)	1	0	2
Apr.	3	Wakefield T. ....(A)	3	0	6
	6	St. Helens .... (A)	0	0	0
	12	Hull K.R. .... (H)	Did not play		
	13	Dewsbury .... (H)	6	2	18
	19	Hunslet....................... (H)	5	2	16
	20	Featherstone R. ....(A)	2	0	4
	22	Castleford .... (A)	2	0	4
	23	Bramley .... (H)	7	1	17
May	4	Oldham.......... (Play-off) (A)	3	0	6
	11	Barrow			
		.....(Wembley, RL Cup final)	0	0	0

Representative matches
For Great Britain:

Jan.	26	France .... (at Leeds)	9	1	21
Mar.	3	France .... (at Toulouse)	5	1	13
Apr.	10	France ....(at St. Helens)	7	1	17

For The Rest:

Oct.	3	Britain XIII .... (at Bradford)	4	0	8

For RL XIII:

Oct.	29	Australia .... (Leigh)	3	0	6

	App	G	T	Pts
League	36	147	30	384
RL Cup	5	13	2	32
Yorks Cup	1	3	1	9
Play-off..............................	1	3	0	6
Representative......................	5	28	3	65
Totals..............................	**48**	**194**	**36**	**496**

Most points in a match:

53 (11t,10g) by George West (Hull K.R.) v. Brookland Rovers (RL Cup), 4 March 1905

Most points in a career:

NEIL FOX holds the record for most points in a career with 6,220 between 1956 and 1979. This total does not include points scored during a spell of club rugby in New Zealand.

Fox was a month short of his 17th birthday when he made his debut for Wakefield Trinity on 10 April 1956. Apart from a brief time at Bradford Northern, Fox had 19 seasons at Wakefield before moving to a succession of clubs in later years.

After a long career as an international centre Fox moved into the forwards and played his last professional match for Bradford in their opening fixture of the 1979-80 season, on 19 August. That match enabled him to join the elite few who have played first team rugby at 40 years of age.

Fox's season-by-season tally is as follows:

	G	T	Pts
1955-56.............................	6	0	12
1956-57.............................	54	10	138
1957-58.............................	124	32	344
1958-59.............................	148	28	380
1959-60.............................	171	37	453
1960-61.............................	94	20	248
1961-62.............................	183	30	456
1962 Tour			
Australasia	85	19	227
South Africa	19	4	50
1962-63.............................	125	14	292
1963-64.............................	125	21	313
1964-65.............................	121	13	281
1965-66.............................	98	11	229
1966-67.............................	144	16	336
1967-68.............................	98	18	250
1968-69.............................	95	9	217
1969-70.............................	17	5	49
1970-71.............................	110	12	256
1971-72.............................	84	6	186
1972-73.............................	138	8	300
1973-74.............................	62	8	148
1974-75.............................	146(1)	14	333
1975-76.............................	102(1)	4	215
1976-77.............................	79(1)	6	175
1977-78.............................	95(1)	9	216
1978-79.............................	50	4	112
1979-80.............................	2	0	4

A breakdown of Fox's club and representative totals is as follows:

	App	G	T	Pts
Wakefield T.	574	1,836	272	4,488
Bradford N.	70	85(1)	12	205
Hull K.R.	59	212(2)	16	470
York	13	42	2	90
Bramley......................	23	73	6	164
Huddersfield..............	21	73(1)	5	160
Club Totals................	**760**	**2,321(4)**	**313**	**5,577**
Yorkshire	17	60	9	147
Britain v. Australia	8	26	3	61
New Zealand	4	11	1	25
France	17	56	10	142
Other representative games including tour	22	101	22	268
Representative Totals....	**68**	**254**	**45**	**643**
Grand Totals	**828**	**2,575(4)**	**358**	**6,220**

( ) Figures in brackets are one-point drop goals included in total.

Score-a-match:

The following players have appeared and scored in all of their club's matches in one season:

Jim Hoey (Widnes) 1932-33
Billy Langton (Hunslet) 1958-59
Stuart Ferguson (Leigh)............................... 1970-71
David Watkins (Salford).............................. 1972-73
David Watkins (Salford).............................. 1973-74
John Woods (Leigh) 1977-78
Steve Quinn (Featherstone R.)........................ 1979-80
Mick Parrish (Hunslet) 1979-80
John Gorton (Swinton) 1980-81
Mick Parrish (Oldham)............................... 1981-82
Peter Wood (Runcorn H.) 1984-85
David Noble (Doncaster) 1986-87
Mark Aston (Sheffield E.) 1988-89
Mike Fletcher (Hull K.R.) 1989-90
Steve Carroll (Bramley)............................... 1991-92
Paul Bishop (Halifax) 1992-93
John Wasyliw (Keighley C.)........................... 1992-93

Longest scoring run:

DAVID WATKINS holds the record for the longest scoring run, playing and scoring in 92 consecutive matches for Salford from 19 August 1972 to 25 April 1974. He totalled 403 goals, 41 tries and 929 points.

Longest run of appearances:

KEITH ELWELL holds the record for the longest run of appearances with one club with a total of 239 for Widnes. The consecutive run started at Wembley in the 1977 Challenge Cup final against Leeds on 7 May, and ended after he played in a Lancashire Cup tie at home to St. Helens on 5 September 1982. He was dropped for the match at Featherstone Rovers a week later. Although he went on as a substitute in the next match the record refers to full appearances only. Elwell played as a substitute in the next match and then made a full appearance before his run of all appearances ended at 242.

TEAM

Highest score:

Huddersfield 119 v. Swinton Park 2 (RL Cup)
.... 28 February 1914

Highest score away:

Nottingham C. 6 v. Hull K.R. 100 (Yorks Cup played at Doncaster) 19 Aug 1990

Most points in all matches in a season:

1,436 by Leigh from 43 matches in 1985-86 as follows:
34 Division Two matches 1,156
2 Lancashire Cup 54
4 John Player Special Trophy.......................... 161
3 RL Challenge Cup....................................... 65

Most League points in a season:

1,156 by Leigh from 34 Division Two matches in 1985-86.

Longest winning run:

29 by Wigan from February to October 1987, as follows: 20 Division One, 3 Premiership, 4 Lancashire Cup, 1 Charity Shield and 1 World Club Challenge.

Longest unbeaten run:

43 Cup and League matches, including two draws, by Huddersfield in 1914-19.

They were unbeaten in the last 38 matches of 1914-15 and after the interruption of the First World War won their next five competitive matches — four Yorkshire Cup ties in 1918-19 and the first League match of 1919-20.

Longest winning run in the League:

31 matches by Wigan. Last 8 matches of 1969-70 and first 23 of 1970-71.

● In 1978-79 Hull won all of their 26 Division Two matches, the only time a club has won all its League matches in one season.

Longest losing run:

61 Cup and League matches by Runcorn Highfield from January 1989 to February 1991. Made up of 55 Division Two, 2 Challenge Cup, 2 Regal Trophy and 2 Lancs Cup.

Longest run without a win:

75 Cup and League matches by Runcorn Highfield from October 1988 to March 1991. Made up of 67 Division Two, 3 Challenge Cup, 3 Regal Trophy and 2 Lancs Cup.

Longest League losing run and run without a win:

Included in the above.

● Only three teams have lost all their matches in a season: Liverpool City (1906-07)*, Runcorn Highfield (1989-90) and Nottingham City (1991-92).

*Liverpool drew a League match against Bramley but this was expunged from the records as the return fixture was cancelled.

Goals in a season record holder David Watkins, scorer of 1,342 goals and 3,117 points in a 15-year career with Salford, Swinton and Cardiff City.

CHARTS

Featured for the first time in *Rothmans Rugby League Yearbook*, this chapter gives extended charts of outstanding scoring and appearance records established by British-based players.

★Denotes amateur team

EIGHT OR MORE TRIES IN A MATCH
11 George West (Hull K.R.) v. Brookland R.★ .... 4 Mar. 1905
10 Lionel Cooper (Huddersfield) v. Keighley .... 17 Nov. 1951
   Martin Offiah (Wigan) v. Leeds .... 10 May 1992
   Shaun Edwards (Wigan) at Swinton .... 29 Sep. 1992
 9 Ray Markham (Huddersfield) v. Featherstone R. .... 21 Sep. 1935
 8 Dai Thomas (Dewsbury) v. Liverpool C. .... 13 Apr. 1907
   Albert Rosenfeld (Huddersfield) v. Wakefield T. .... 26 Dec. 1911
   Fred Webster (Leeds) v. Coventry .... 12 Apr. 1913
   Eric Harris (Leeds) v. Bradford N. .... 14 Sep. 1931
   Lionel Cooper (Huddersfield) v. Yorkshire Amateurs★ .... 11 Sep. 1948
   Keith Williams (Halifax) v. Dewsbury .... 9 Nov. 1957

14 OR MORE GOALS IN A MATCH
22 Jim Sullivan (Wigan) v. Flimby & Fothergill★ .... 14 Feb. 1925
18 Major Holland (Huddersfield) v. Swinton Park★ .... 28 Feb. 1914
17 Geoff "Sammy" Lloyd (Castleford) v. Millom★ .... 16 Sep. 1973
16 Paul Loughlin (St. Helens) v. Carlisle .... 14 Sep. 1986
15 Mick Stacey (Leigh) v. Doncaster .... 28 Mar. 1976
   John Wasyliw (Keighley C.) v. Nottingham C. .... 1 Nov. 1992
14 Alf Carmichael (Hull K.R.) v. Merthyr Tydfil .... 8 Oct. 1910
   Jim Kennedy (Hull) v. Rochdale H. .... 7 Apr. 1921
   Harold Palin (Warrington) v. Liverpool S. .... 13 Sep. 1950
   Joe Phillips (Bradford N.) v. Batley .... 6 Sep. 1952
   Bernard Ganley (Oldham) v. Liverpool C. .... 4 Apr. 1959
   Bruce Burton (Halifax) v. Hunslet .... 27 Aug. 1972
   Geoff "Sammy" Lloyd (Hull) v. Oldham .... 10 Sep. 1978
   Chris Johnson (Leigh) v. Keighley .... 30 Apr. 1986
   Steve Turner (Rochdale H.) v. Runcorn H. .... 5 Nov. 1989
   Mike Fletcher (Hull K.R.) v. Whitehaven .... 18 Mar. 1990
   Colin Armstrong (Hull K.R.) at Nottingham C. .... 19 Aug. 1990

On tour with Great Britain:
17 Ernest Ward v. Mackay (Australia) .... 2 Jul. 1946
15 Alf Wood v. South Australia .... 23 May 1914
   Jim Ledgard v. Wide Bay (Australia) .... 28 Jun. 1950
   Lewis Jones v. Southern New South Wales (Australia) .... 21 Aug. 1954
   Eric Fraser v. North Queensland (Australia) .... 29 Jun. 1958

35 POINTS OR MORE IN A MATCH

53 George West (Hull K.R.) v. Brookland R.★	4 Mar. 1905
44 Jim Sullivan (Wigan) v. Flimby & Fothergill★	14 Feb. 1925
43 Geoff "Sammy" Lloyd (Castleford) v. Millom★	16 Sep. 1973
42 Dean Marwood (Workington T.) v. Highfield	1 Nov. 1992
40 Paul Loughlin (St. Helens) v. Carlisle	14 Sep. 1986
Martin Offiah (Wigan) v. Leeds	10 May 1992
Shaun Edwards (Wigan) at Swinton	29 Sep. 1992
39 James Lomas (Salford) v. Liverpool C.	2 Feb. 1907
Major Holland (Huddersfield) v. Swinton Park★	28 Feb. 1914
38 John Woods (Leigh) v. Blackpool B.	11 Sep. 1977
Bob Beardmore (Castleford) v. Barrow	22 Mar. 1987
John Woods (Leigh) v. Ryedale-York	12 Jan. 1992
36 Jim Kennedy (Hull) v. Keighley	29 Jan. 1921
Mick Stacey (Leigh) v. Doncaster	28 Mar. 1976
John Woods (Bradford N.) v. Swinton	13 Oct. 1985
Graham Steadman (Castleford) v. Salford	1 Apr. 1990
John Wasyliw (Keighley C.) v. Nottingham C.★	31 Oct. 1993
35 Jim Bawden (Huddersfield) v. Swinton	20 Apr. 1946

Keighley Cougars winger John Wasyliw, match scorer of 15 goals in November 1992 and 36 points in October 1993.

Sammy Lloyd, third highest scorer of both goals and points in a match.

173

Great Britain winger Mick Sullivan, scorer of 50 tries in 1957-58 while serving both Huddersfield and Wigan.

South African wingman Tom Van Vollenhoven (right), who passed the half century of tries in a season landmark three times during an 11-year career with St. Helens.

50 TRIES OR MORE IN A SEASON

80	Albert Rosenfeld (Huddersfield)	1913-14
78	Albert Rosenfeld (Huddersfield)	1911-12
72	Brian Bevan (Warrington)	1952-53
71	Lionel Cooper (Huddersfield)	1951-52
68	Brian Bevan (Warrington)	1950-51
67	Brian Bevan (Warrington)	1953-54
66	Lionel Cooper (Huddersfield)	1954-55
63	Johnny Ring (Wigan)	1925-26
	Eric Harris (Leeds)	1935-36
	Jack McLean (Bradford N.)	1951-52
	Brian Bevan (Warrington)	1954-55
	Ellery Hanley (Wigan)	1986-87
62	Tom Van Vollenhoven (St. Helens)	1958-59
61	Jack McLean (Bradford N.)	1955-56
60	Lionel Cooper (Huddersfield)	1948-49
	Billy Boston (Wigan)	1956-57
	Martin Offiah (Widnes)	1988-89
59	Lionel Cooper (Huddersfield)	1950-51
	Jack McLean (Bradford N.)	1952-53
	Tom Van Vollenhoven (St. Helens)	1960-61
58	Eric Harris (Leeds)	1930-31
57	Eric Harris (Leeds)	1932-33
	Brian Bevan (Warrington)	1947-48
	Brian Nordgren (Wigan)	1949-50
	Brian Bevan (Warrington)	1955-56
56	Albert Rosenfeld (Huddersfield)	1912-13
	Albert Rosenfeld (Huddersfield)	1914-15
	Brian Bevan (Warrington)	1948-49
55	Alf Ellaby (St. Helens)	1926-27
	Ellery Hanley (Bradford N.)	1984-85
54	Stan Moorhouse (Huddersfield)	1911-12
	Johnny Ring (Wigan)	1924-25
	Brian Bevan (Warrington)	1958-59
	Billy Boston (Wigan)	1958-59
	Tom Van Vollenhoven (St. Helens)	1959-60
53	Ray Markham (Huddersfield)	1935-36
52	Jack Harrison (Hull)	1914-15
	Frank Castle (Barrow)	1951-52
	Jack McLean (Bradford N.)	1953-54
	Paul Newlove (Featherstone R.)	1992-93
51	Brian Bevan (Warrington)	1951-52
	Jim Lewthwaite (Barrow)	1956-57
	Billy Boston (Wigan)	1961-62
50	Ernest Mills (Huddersfield)	1931-32
	Lionel Cooper (Huddersfield)	1952-53
	Mick Sullivan (Huddersfield and Wigan)	1957-58

Nine half centuries for Brian Bevan.

A hat-trick of 50-plus landmarks for Billy Boston.

Twice topping the half century of touchdowns, Ellery Hanley.

170 GOALS OR MORE IN A SEASON
- Including drop goals

221 David Watkins (Salford)		1972-73
219 Bernard Ganley (Oldham)		1957-58
214 Kel Coslett (St. Helens)		1971-72
199 Mike Fletcher (Hull K.R.)		1989-90
194 Jim Sullivan (Wigan)		1933-34
Lewis Jones (Leeds)		1956-57
193 Kel Coslett (St. Helens)		1970-71
David Watkins (Salford)		1971-72
190 Bernard Ganley (Oldham)		1958-59
Lyn Hopkins (Workington T.)		1981-82
Paul Loughlin (St. Helens)		1986-87
189 Bernard Ganley (Oldham)		1956-57
188 Frano Botica (Wigan)		1993-94
187 John Wasyliw (Keighley C.)		1992-93
184 Frano Botica (Wigan)		1992-93
183 Fred Griffiths (Wigan)		1961-62
Neil Fox (Wakefield T.)		1961-62
David Watkins (Salford)		1973-74
181 Billy Langton (Hunslet)		1958-59
179 Dean Marwood (Workington T.)		1992-93
178 Jim Ledgard (Leigh)		1954-55
Geoff Pimblett (St. Helens)		1977-78
177 Steve Kerry (Salford)		1990-91
176 Fred Griffiths (Wigan)		1958-59
175 David Watkins (Salford)		1975-76
173 Eddie Tees (Bradford N.)		1971-72
Chris Johnson (Leigh)		1985-86
172 Geoff "Sammy" Lloyd (Hull)		1978-79
171 Austin Rhodes (St. Helens)		1959-60
Neil Fox (Wakefield T.)		1959-60
170 Harry Bath (Warrington)		1952-53
Steve Hesford (Warrington)		1978-79

Harry Bath.   *Neil Fox.*   *Jim Sullivan.*

370 OR MORE POINTS IN A SEASON

496	Lewis Jones (Leeds)	1956-57
493	David Watkins (Salford)	1972-73
490	John Wasyliw (Keighley C.)	1992-93
476	David Watkins (Salford)	1971-72
456	Neil Fox (Wakefield T.)	1961-62
453	Bernard Ganley (Oldham)	1957-58
	Neil Fox (Wakefield T.)	1959-60
452	Kel Coslett (St. Helens)	1971-72
450	Mike Fletcher (Hull K.R.)	1989-90
446	Lyn Hopkins (Workington T.)	1981-82
438	David Watkins (Salford)	1973-74
427	Steve Kerry (Salford)	1990-91
424	Paul Loughlin (St. Helens)	1986-87
423	Frano Botica (Wigan)	1992-93
422	Frano Botica (Wigan)	1993-94
418	Dean Marwood (Workington T.)	1992-93
406	Jim Sullivan (Wigan)	1933-34
405	Martin Pearson (Featherstone R.)	1992-93
400	Chris Johnson (Leigh)	1985-86
399	Austin Rhodes (St. Helens)	1959-60
395	Kel Coslett (St. Helens)	1970-71
394	Fred Griffiths (Wigan)	1958-59
390	Fred Griffiths (Wigan)	1961-62
385	Colin Tyrer (Wigan)	1969-70
	David Watkins (Salford)	1975-76
384	Bernard Ganley (Oldham)	1956-57
	John Gallagher (London C.)	1993-94
383	Bernard Ganley (Oldham)	1958-59
381	Geoff Pimblett (St. Helens)	1977-78
380	Neil Fox (Wakefield T.)	1958-59
	Billy Langton (Hunslet)	1958-59
379	Harry Bath (Warrington)	1952-53
	Mick Parrish (Oldham)	1981-82
376	Nigel Stephenson (Dewsbury)	1972-73
375	Steve Quinn (Featherstone R.)	1979-80
374	Jim Ledgard (Leigh)	1954-55
373	Geoff "Sammy" Lloyd (Hull)	1978-79
372	John Woods (Leigh)	1981-82

300 TRIES OR MORE IN A CAREER
796 Brian Bevan (Warrington, Blackpool B.).. 1945-1964
571 Billy Boston (Wigan, Blackpool B.) 1953-1970
446 Alf Ellaby (St. Helens, Wigan) 1926-1939
443 Eric Batten (Wakefield T., Hunslet, Bradford N., Featherstone R.)......... 1933-1954
441 Lionel Cooper (Huddersfield).. 1947-1955
415 Johnny Ring (Wigan, Rochdale H.).. 1922-1933
406 Clive Sullivan (Hull, Hull K.R., Oldham, Doncaster) 1961-1985
401 John Atkinson (Leeds, Carlisle) 1966-1983
399 Eric Harris (Leeds)... 1930-1939
395 Tom Van Vollenhoven (St. Helens)... 1957-1968
387 Ellery Hanley (Bradford N., Wigan, Leeds)....................................... 1978-
386 Albert Rosenfeld (Huddersfield, Wakefield T., Bradford N.)................. 1909-1924
383 Jim Lewthwaite (Barrow) 1943-1957
374 Ike Southward (Workington T., Oldham, Whitehaven)........................ 1952-1969
372 Barney Hudson (Salford).. 1928-1946
358 Neil Fox (Wakefield T., Bradford N., Hull K.R., York, Bramley,
    Huddersfield) 1956-1979
342 Mick Sullivan (Huddersfield, Wigan, St. Helens, York, Dewsbury)........ 1952-1966
325 Martin Offiah (Widnes, Wigan).. 1987-
321 Jim Lawrenson (Wigan, Workington T., Swinton)............................... 1939-1954
319 Eric Ashton (Wigan).. 1955-1969
314 Jim Leytham (Wigan) 1901-1912
312 Brian Nordgren (Wigan)... 1946-1955
311 Alan Smith (Leeds).. 1962-1983
310 Jim Lomas (Bramley, Salford, Oldham, York) 1902-1923
304 Alan Hardisty (Castleford, Leeds) 1958-1974
302 Maurice Richards (Salford) 1969-1983

Hull's Clive Sullivan, the seventh top try scorer of all time, also serving Hull K.R., Oldham and Doncaster, and capped by Great Britain and Wales.

1,000 OR MORE GOALS IN A CAREER

2,867	Jim Sullivan (Wigan)..	1921-1946
2,575	Neil Fox (Wakefield T., Bradford N., Hull K.R., York, Bramley, Huddersfield)...	1956-1979
1,768	Cyril Kellett (Hull K.R., Featherstone R.)..................................	1956-1974
1,698	Kel Coslett (St. Helens, Rochdale H.)......................................	1962-1979
1,677	Gus Risman (Salford, Workington T., Batley)	1929-1954
1,591	John Woods (Leigh, Bradford N., Warrington, Rochdale H.)	1976-1992
1,578	Steve Quinn (York, Featherstone R.)..	1970-1988
1,560	Jim Ledgard (Leeds, Dewsbury, Leigh)	1944-1961
1,478	Lewis Jones (Leeds)	1952-1964
1,398	Bernard Ganley (Oldham)...	1951-1961
1,376	Ray Dutton (Widnes, Whitehaven)	1966-1981
1,342	David Watkins (Salford, Swinton, Cardiff C.)	1967-1983
1,306	George Fairbairn (Wigan, Hull K.R.)...	1974-1990
1,272	Colin Tyrer (Leigh, Wigan, Barrow, Hull K.R.).............................	1962-1978
1,189	Frank Dyson (Huddersfield, Oldham)	1949-1965
1,179	Terry Clawson (Featherstone R., Bradford N., Hull K.R., Leeds, Oldham, York, Wakefield T., Huddersfield, Hull)	1957-1980
1,169	Steve Hesford (Warrington, Huddersfield B.)	1975-1986
1,154	Derek Whitehead (Swinton, Oldham, Warrington)..........................	1964-1979
1,127	Geoff "Sammy" Lloyd (Castleford, Hull)	1970-1983
1,092	John McKeown (Whitehaven)...	1948-1961
1,081	Vic Yorke (York)	1954-1967
1,075	Ken Gowers (Swinton)	1954-1973
1,044	Billy Langton (Hunslet)...	1955-1966
1,030	Ron James (Halifax)	1961-1971
1,016	Iain MacCorquodale (Salford, Workington T., Fulham, Blackpool B., Rochdale H.)	1970-1982

Lewis Jones, who tallied 1,478 goals in a 12-year career with Leeds.

Full back Cyril Kellett, third top goalkicker of all time, amassing 1,768 goals for Hull K.R. and Featherstone Rovers in an 18-year career span.

2,500 OR MORE POINTS IN A CAREER

6,220 Neil Fox (Wakefield T., Bradford N., Hull K.R., York, Bramley,
    Huddersfield) 1956-1979
6,022 Jim Sullivan (Wigan) 1921-1946
4,050 Gus Risman (Salford, Workington T., Batley) 1929-1954
3,985 John Woods (Leigh, Bradford N., Warrington, Rochdale H.) 1976-1992
3,686 Cyril Kellett (Hull K.R., Featherstone R.) 1956-1974
3,545 Kel Coslett (St. Helens, Rochdale H.) 1962-1979
3,445 Lewis Jones (Leeds) 1952-1964
3,438 Steve Quinn (York, Featherstone R.) 1970-1988
3,279 Jim Ledgard (Leeds, Dewsbury, Leigh) 1944-1961
3,117 David Watkins (Salford, Swinton, Cardiff C.) 1967-1982
2,902 Colin Tyrer (Leigh, Wigan, Barrow, Hull K.R.) 1962-1978
2,894 George Fairbairn (Wigan, Hull K.R.) 1974-1990
2,844 Bernard Ganley (Oldham) 1951-1961
2,786 Ray Dutton (Widnes, Whitehaven) 1966-1981
2,574 Terry Clawson (Featherstone R., Bradford N., Hull K.R., Leeds,
    Oldham, York, Wakefield T., Huddersfield, Hull) 1957-1980
2,561 Frank Dyson (Huddersfield, Oldham) 1949-1965

650 APPEARANCES OR MORE IN A CAREER

• Figures in brackets denote substitute appearances included in main total.

928   Jim Sullivan (Wigan) 1921-1946
873   Gus Risman (Salford, Workington T., Batley) 1929-1954
828 (28) Neil Fox (Wakefield T., Bradford N., Hull K.R., York, Bramley,
    Huddersfield) 1956-1979
760 (42) Jeff Grayshon (Dewsbury, Bradford N., Leeds, Featherstone R., Batley) 1969-
740 (46) Graham Idle (Bramley, Wakefield T., Bradford N., Hunslet, Rochdale H.,
    Sheffield E., Doncaster, Nottingham C., Highfield) 1969-1993
738 (25) Colin Dixon (Halifax, Salford, Hull K.R.) 1961-1981
727 (9) Paul Charlton (Workington T., Salford, Blackpool B.) 1961-1981
691 (1) Ernie Ashcroft (Wigan, Huddersfield, Warrington) 1942-1962
688   Brian Bevan (Warrington, Blackpool B.) 1945-1964
685 (20) Keith Mumby (Bradford N., Sheffield E., Keighley C.) 1973-
683 (24) John Wolford (Bramley, Bradford N., Dewsbury, Hunslet) 1962-1985
682   Joe Ferguson (Oldham) 1899-1923
679   Joe Oliver (Huddersfield, Batley, Hull, Hull K.R.) 1923-1945
669 (33) John Joyner (Castleford) 1973-1992
665   George Carmichael (Hull K.R., Bradford N.) 1929-1950
663 (25) John Holmes (Leeds) 1968-1989
662 (28) Mal Aspey (Widnes, Fulham, Wigan, Salford) 1964-1983
651   Jack Miller (Warrington, Leigh) 1926-1947

*World record Rugby Union signing Va'aiga Tuigamala holds
aloft the 1994 Silk Cut Challenge Cup.*

CUPS

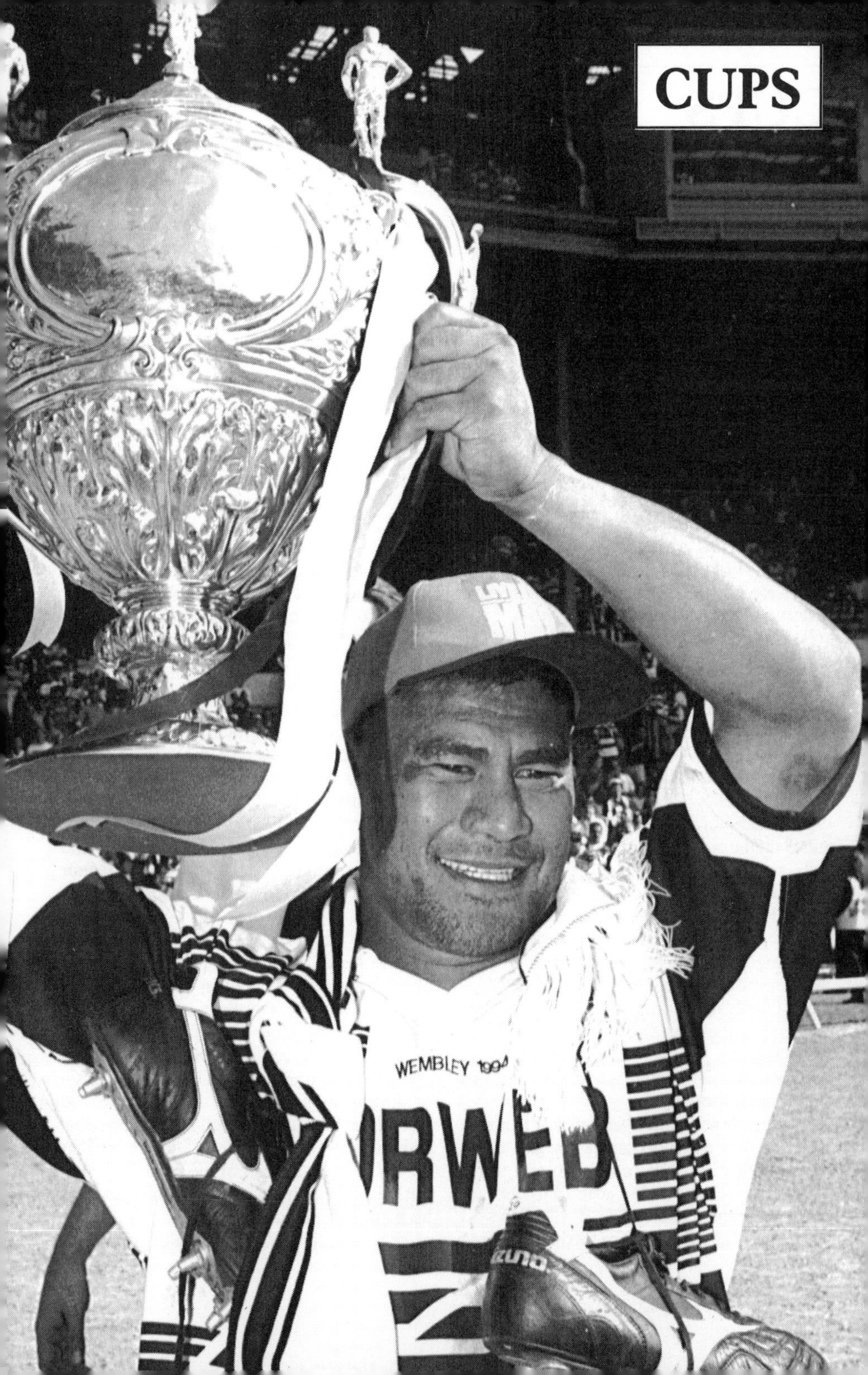

CUPS

RUGBY LEAGUE CHALLENGE CUP

1994 Final

Great Britain wingman Martin Offiah used Wembley as a world stage to confirm his return to top form, being awarded the Lance Todd Trophy as Man of the Match for the second time.

Wigan continued to rewrite the record books by beating Leeds 26-16 for a seventh consecutive Silk Cut Challenge Cup success, the fifth successive double with the Stones Bitter Championship Trophy. But it was the revitalised Offiah who grabbed the spotlight with two crucial tries which proved the difference between two sides meeting at Wembley for the first time.

Offiah's first touchdown in the 14th minute would rank as the best solo try in the 65-year history of Wembley finals.

Taking the ball five metres from his own line and just to the left of the posts, he shot past two defenders into the open. Then his carefully controlled running mesmerised the Leeds defence so that while he started to cruise nobody gained on him.

Leeds full back Alan Tait was equally transfixed. The fellow Test man tried to shepherd Offiah inside but lost him when the winger accelerated on the outside and finished off in glorious style near the right hand corner. The whole running distance covered well over 100 metres.

Leeds had matched Wigan in every department during that opening spell when the blistering pace matched the sweltering heat, the temperature topping 90°F inside the Wembley bowl. Offiah's spectacular try disheartened the Loiners on their return to Wembley after 16 years' absence, and they fell further behind to a try from second row man Andrew Farrell and two Frano Botica goals.

But the Yorkshiremen battled back from the 12-0 half-time deficit to narrow the gap to two points with tries from Jim Fallon and Garry Schofield and a penalty goal from teenage stand off Graham Holroyd.

A penalty goal from Botica further increased

Wigan's lead but just as Leeds were getting on top again Offiah struck a second time. Substitute Mick Cassidy created the opportunity with a strong burst deep inside his own half before handing on to Offiah, his thoroughbred style taking him over 60 metres to the line, a forlorn Fallon – Leeds's fastest man – giving chase in spirit only.

Botica's goal took the scoreline to 20-10 and the contest was virtually over on the hour. Every stride of that second try was a vote catcher for Offiah to become only the third player to win the Lance Todd Trophy twice, emulating Gerry Helme and Andy Gregory, both half backs.

While his attack was world class, Offiah was open to criticism on defence, being involved in the letting in of two of Leeds's three tries. Schofield, who had been invited by skipper Ellery Hanley to lead the team out before the match, brushed Offiah aside on his way to touch down in the 51st minute, while Francis Cummins sped 85 metres for the final try of a thrilling final after Offiah dropped the ball when he crossed over to the right wing in search of a third try that would have brought him Wembley's first Cup final hat-trick and a Silk Cut reward of £1,000.

Offiah's double strike was extra special and made him stand out on a day when all four wingers combined to produce a rare variety of wing play.

Former Bath RU star Fallon was an inspiration to Leeds during their post-interval rally, opening their try account in the 48th minute from James Lowes's throw-in style pass.

Over on the other flank, Cummins soon overcame any nerves from being the youngest-ever player by one day – at 17 years 200 days – to appear in a Wembley final. Within 90 seconds he fielded a high ball near his own line and broke away on a brilliant 65-metre run that set the pace for the rest of the game. The run was repeated in the last stages of the match for his memorable touchdown.

The 10th capacity crowd for a Cup final was

also enthralled by the Wembley debut of former New Zealand All Black winger Va'aiga Tuigamala, preferred to Great Britain's Jason Robinson. His rumbling charges created the occasional disturbance in the Leeds defence and his hefty tackle on Tait caused the Leeds full back to cough up the ball which led to substitute Sam Panapa scoring Wigan's last try.

Tait also failed to take the high ball which resulted in Andrew Farrell grabbing a soft 25th-minute touchdown, but he produced a first class attacking performance to match that of Wigan counterpart Gary Connolly.

Hanley battled until the 69th minute with the effects of a hamstring injury, while prop Neil Harmon played only a few days after having the plaster taken off a broken thumb. The main power base for the Loiners came from second row pairing Gary Mercer and Richard Eyres.

Leeds had been conscious of having no strength in depth and this was emphasised by Wigan's ability to bring on substitutes of the calibre of Panapa and Cassidy, both to play try-making roles.

Wigan captain Dean Bell marked his impending farewell to the club, to become skipper of Australian Premiership newcomers Auckland Warriors, by equalling the record of being a winning captain at Wembley in three successive seasons, so emulating his predecessor Hanley.

Botica's five goals took his Wembley total to a record 16 in four finals, passing the previous best of 15 by Neil Fox for Wakefield Trinity in three finals during the 1960s.

Leeds's substitute pairing also broke records of a contrasting nature. Mike O'Neill established a record for the longest playing span at Wembley, coming on for Harmon 15 years after first playing there, also as a substitute, for Widnes. Marcus Vassilakopoulos came on seven minutes later to become the youngest forward to play at Wembley, at 17 years and seven months.

Wigan scrum half Shaun Edwards picked up two Wembley records. He collected a record eighth Challenge Cup winners' medal after playing in his record-breaking ninth final, being the only ever-present in Wigan's run of 36 consecutive Challenge Cup wins.

But at the end of the day, despite the heat, the historic meeting of two of the greatest clubs, the records galore and the record receipts of over £2m, it would be the devastating skills of try merchant Offiah which will be recalled with most ease and pleasure.

Lance Todd Trophy winner Martin Offiah outstrips Leeds full back Alan Tait to score Wigan's opening try after a breathtaking 100-metre run.

SILK CUT CHALLENGE CUP FINAL
30 April   **Wembley**
WIGAN   26   ### LEEDS   16

Wigan	No.	Leeds
Gary Connolly	1.	Alan Tait
Va'aiga Tuigamala	2.	Jim Fallon
Dean Bell, Capt.	3.	Kevin Iro
Barrie-Jon Mather	4.	Craig Innes
Martin Offiah	5.	Francis Cummins
Frano Botica	6.	Graham Holroyd
Shaun Edwards	7.	Garry Schofield
Kelvin Skerrett	8.	Neil Harmon
Martin Dermott	9.	James Lowes
Andy Platt	10.	Harvey Howard
Denis Betts	11.	Gary Mercer
Andrew Farrell	12.	Richard Eyres
Philip Clarke	13.	Ellery Hanley, Capt.
Sam Panapa	14.	Marcus Vassilakopoulos
Mick Cassidy	15.	Mike O'Neill

T: Offiah (2), Farrell, Panapa
G: Botica (5)
Substitutions:
Cassidy for Farrell (52 min.)
Panapa for Platt (59 min.)
Half-time: 12-0
Referee: David Campbell (Widnes)

T: Fallon, Schofield, Cummins
G: Holroyd (2)
Substitutions:
O'Neill for Harmon (62 min.)
Vassilakopoulos for Hanley (69 min.)
Attendance: 78,348
Receipts: £2,032,839

Seventh heaven . . . Wigan celebrate their seventh successive Silk Cut Challenge Cup triumph, having defeated Leeds in their first meeting in the final.

1993-94 Round by Round

A major revamp of the early stages of the Silk Cut Challenge Cup saw the inclusion of 64 amateur teams, the scrapping of the much-criticised preliminary round, and the first-ever seeding of the First Division sides.

The amateur sides contested the first two rounds before Christmas, the 32 clubs in the National Conference League having home advantage in the first round, the second stage being drawn at random. Those 16 winners then played away to the professional Second Division clubs.

The 16-tie third round did not produce a giant killer, the nearest candidates being Saddleworth, who went down only 16-13 at bottom club Highfield. Keighley Cougars were the top scorers of the round with a 68-0 victory over Oulton, centre Nick Pinkney grabbing four tries. Darren Moxon and Steve Walker each collected a hat-trick of tries in Batley's 58-2 triumph over neighbouring amateurs Dewsbury Celtic. Hunslet's African winger Eric Kibe scored four tries in their 58-2 demolition of Barrow Island, while Dewsbury's Errol Johnson, Barrow's Bob Eccles and Doncaster's David Evans collected try hat-tricks.

The First Division sides entered the fourth round in a random draw. The televised encounter between Halifax and Warrington produced two memorable tries for Silk Cut Award winning Jonathan Davies and a 22-18 victory for the visitors. Bradford Northern registered a 58-30 success at Barrow in a 16-try extravaganza. Test centre Paul Newlove scored four of Northern's 11 touchdowns. Despite injuries before and during the tie, visitors Keighley Cougars were too powerful and imaginative for lacklustre hosts Batley, cruising to a 29-8 victory. Lowly Second Division side Bramley made Widnes, the previous year's Wembley finalists, struggle for a 20-11 victory,

Bramley holding a 5-4 lead after 37 minutes.

In a Cumbrian derby, Workington Town clinched a 13-12 victory at Carlisle with a 76th-minute drop goal from Wayne Kitchin. Castleford were virtually assured of victory over visitors Salford with an 18-0 lead after only 23 minutes, hat-trick hero Grant Anderson collecting the Silk Cut Award in a 36-4 triumph. Doncaster recorded an 18-6 home success over Dewsbury despite finishing with only 10 men after having two players sent off and one sin-binned. Bottom of the pile Highfield made visitors Whitehaven work for their 15-4 victory, the Cumbrians relying on the experience of their former New Zealand Test stars, player-coach Kurt Sorensen and half back Clayton Friend.

There was a standing ovation for Huddersfield and St. Helens at Leeds Road after the Second Division pacesetters led 12-6 at the break, before the Saints' extra pace and power took effect. Their 23-16 victory was sealed by Anthony Sullivan's try five minutes from time. Hull K.R.'s lowest crowd at their new ground of 1,878 witnessed a 16-6 success over Ryedale-York, Mike Bibby clinching victory with a last-minute try. Reshaped Second Division strugglers Hunslet were leading First Division Oldham 20-18, only for the visitors to score 12 points in a 10-minute spell to seal a 30-20 success. Featherstone Rovers gained revenge for their Regal Trophy exit at London Crusaders by registering a 28-14 victory, the visitors sealing success with three tries in 14 minutes late in the second half.

Rochdale Hornets centre Paul O'Keefe scored a hat-trick of tries but could not prevent Leeds strolling to a 40-18 away victory. New Leeds recruit Harvey Howard took the Silk Cut Award and centre Craig Innes made an impressive return after injury. Mark Aston was the scoring hero of Sheffield Eagles' 42-10 home defeat of First Division basement side Leigh, the half back tallying 22 points from a try and nine goals. Second Division strugglers Swinton belied their lowly position to dominate the first half against visitors Hull. But their 6-4 lead was not sufficient to prevent Hull fighting back for an 18-12 success. Holders Wigan entertained Wakefield Trinity who were level at 12-apiece before ex-Trinity star Nigel Wright came on as substitute to intercept a stray Matt Fuller pass and race the length of the field for a crucial touchdown which paved the way for a 24-16 Wigan triumph.

In the fifth round, Leeds entertained high-flying Warrington in the televised tie, producing their best performance under coach Doug Laughton. A devastating blend of youth and experience produced seven Leeds touchdowns, including two each from Jim Fallon and Innes in a 38-4 win. Doncaster's shock 20-0 win over First Division visitors Oldham put the future of Roughyeds' coach Peter Tunks in doubt. The Dons' third-ever quarter-final place was clinched by a second try from veteran second row man Audley Pennant, recipient of the Silk Cut Award. In the tie of the round, Hull squandered a 21-2 home lead over holders Wigan to lose 21-22. Hull winger Paul Eastwood missed a relatively easy 35-metre penalty goal attempt in the dying seconds. Despite lacking 11 regulars, Hull K.R. led 8-0 at home to Featherstone Rovers before Martin Pearson led a fightback with an 18-point haul in a 30-8 success.

The visit of Regal Trophy winners Castleford attracted a capacity crowd of 5,860 to Keighley, but Cougarmania lasted only six minutes as the visitors scored the first of their 10 tries in a 52-14 success. Great Britain forward Chris Joynt scored a hat-trick of tries as St. Helens ran up a 46-4 victory at Whitehaven, whose consolation try came from Billy Fisher on his 300th appearance for the club. Sheffield Eagles' hopes of reaching the quarter-finals for the first time were dashed by Widnes scrum half Bobby Goulding, who created two tries and kicked five goals from seven attempts to inspire a 22-6 home success. Workington Town were missing

three key forwards for the home tie with Bradford Northern, whose extra power told as they ran in three tries in the final 12 minutes to open a 32-0 winning margin.

In the quarter-finals, victory was secured by the four home teams. In-form Leeds disposed of arch-rivals Bradford Northern in an impressive 33-10 performance. In front of a crowd of over 22,000 Leeds scored six tries, all but one from long range, including the opening effort from 17-year-old Francis Cummins from 90 metres out. In the televised tie, Castleford beat Widnes 30-6 with top class performances from Silk Cut Award winner Mike Ford, scorer of two tries, five-goal Lee Crooks and second row man Tony Morrison. At Wigan, Featherstone Rovers conceded 10 points in the opening quarter before restricting their chances further through indiscipline. Steve Molloy of Rovers and Wigan's Andy Platt were sent off after a brawl involving nearly every player, including home forward Kelvin Skerrett who dived into the mêlée. Featherstone's Neil Roebuck was sin-binned in the same incident before being sent off in the last minute as Wigan finished 32-14 winners. Doncaster's hopes of a first-ever semi-final appearance were ended by a 40-9 defeat at St. Helens, but the Dons were gallant losers trailing only 18-9 midway through the second half as they bid to beat the Saints for the first time in their 42-year history.

In the semi-finals, Castleford could not repeat their Regal Trophy triumph at Headingley, crashing 20-6 to a Wigan side registering their 35th successive Challenge Cup victory and qualifying for a seventh successive Wembley appearance. Stand off Frano Botica took the Silk Cut Award with one try and four goals. In the second semi-final at Wigan, Leeds spent most of the afternoon on defence against a rampant St. Helens. But Leeds grabbed an 8-6 interval lead en route to a 20-8 triumph, scoring three tries to one. Man of the Match rating went to Leeds full back Alan Tait, although Tommy Martyn was outstanding for the Saints with a try and two goals.

1993-94 RESULTS

First Round

Askam	36	Orchard Park	20
Barrow Island	26	Moorends	13
Beverley	84	Cambridge E.	10
Blackpool G.	10	Park Amateurs	28
Chorley B.	30	Elland	2
Dewsbury C.	38	Fulham Travellers	15
Dudley Hill	8	Thatto Heath	22
East Leeds	25	Kells	12
Eastmoor	4	Irlam Hornets	12
Egremont	28	Ace	6
Greetland A.R.	0	Ellenborough	18
Hemel Hempstead	18	Hensingham	22
Heworth	24	Wigan St. Judes	8
Leigh East	14	Farnworth	10
Leigh M.W.	34	Eureka	14
Lock Lane	13	Mysons	16
Mayfield	24	Hull Dockers	12
Milford	18	Cardiff Institute	8
Millom	18	Westgate Redoubt	10
Moldgreen	23	Skirlaugh	5
Nottingham C.	8	Clayton	24
Oldham St. Annes	32	Bison	8
Oulton	27	Queens	6
Redhill	16	Littleborough	12
Saddleworth R.	13	Seaton	2
Shaw Cross	12	Fryston	6
Walney Central	11	Halton Simms C.	0
West Hull	36	Ovenden	9
Wigan St. Patricks	13	Wath Brow H.	6
Woolston R.	54	Upton/Frickley	12
York Acorn	32	Orrell St. James	32

Replay

Orrell St. James	24	York Acorn	5

Second Round

Askam	8	Chorley B.	3
Blackbrook	8	Beverley	17
Clayton	6	Oulton	23
Dewsbury C.	18	Heworth	10
East Leeds	14	Egremont	10
Ellenborough	4	Woolston R.	9
Hensingham	40	Mysons	0
Leigh East	14	Millom	26
Leigh M.W.	13	Moldgreen	11
Mayfield	14	Wigan St. Patricks	32
Milford	19	Irlam Hornets	20
Redhill	32	Orrell St. James	18
Saddleworth R.	12	Oldham St. Annes	4
Shaw Cross	11	Thatto Heath	4
Walney Central	4	Barrow Island	6
West Hull	47	Park Amateurs	14

Third Round

Barrow	34	East Leeds	10
Batley	58	Dewsbury C.	2
Bramley	46	Redhill	20
Carlisle	42	Askam	8
Dewsbury	64	Hensingham	6
Doncaster	36	Wigan St. Patricks	4
Highfield	16	Saddleworth R.	13
Huddersfield	42	Woolston R.	6
Hunslet	58	Barrow Island	2
Keighley C.	68	Oulton	0
London C.	40	Shaw Cross	14
Rochdale H.	32	Millom	0
Ryedale-York	52	Leigh M.W.	2
Swinton	30	Irlam Hornets	0
Whitehaven	44	West Hull	4
Workington T.	24	Beverley	10

Leeds second row man Gary Mercer subjected to a double Wigan tackle in the 1994 Silk Cut Challenge Cup final.

Fourth Round

Barrow	30	Bradford N.	58
Batley	8	Keighley C.	29
Bramley	11	Widnes	20
Carlisle	12	Workington T.	13
Castleford	36	Salford	4
Doncaster	18	Dewsbury	6
Halifax	18	Warrington	22
Highfield	4	Whitehaven	15
Huddersfield	16	St. Helens	23
Hull K.R.	16	Ryedale-York	6
Hunslet	20	Oldham	30
London C.	14	Featherstone R.	28
Rochdale H.	18	Leeds	40
Sheffield E.	42	Leigh	10
Swinton	12	Hull	18
Wigan	24	Wakefield T.	16

Fifth Round

Doncaster	20	Oldham	0
Hull	21	Wigan	22
Hull K.R.	8	Featherstone R.	30
Keighley C.	14	Castleford	52
Leeds	38	Warrington	4
Whitehaven	4	St. Helens	46
Widnes	22	Sheffield E.	6
Workington T.	0	Bradford N.	32

Sixth Round

Castleford	30	Widnes	6
Leeds	33	Bradford N.	10
St. Helens	40	Doncaster	9
Wigan	32	Featherstone R.	14

Semi-Finals

Castleford	6	Wigan	20
(at Leeds)			
Leeds	20	St. Helens	8
(at Wigan)			

Final

Wigan	26	Leeds	16
(at Wembley)			

1993-94 Prizes

Third Round..........	£2,675 to each Second Division club
Fourth Round..........	£2,675 to losers
Fifth Round............	£4,250 to losers
Quarter-Finals........	£6,725 to losers
Semi-Finals.............	£10,750 to losers
Runners-up.............	£20,000
Winners	£38,000
Total Prize Money	**£226,000**
Capital Development Fund	£134,000
Grand Total	**£360,000**

Leeds winger Francis Cummins, the youngest-ever player at Wembley, is halted by Wigan duo Dean Bell (upper) and Frano Botica.

CHALLENGE CUP ROLL OF HONOUR

Year	Winners		Runners-up		Venue	Attendance	Receipts
1897	Batley	10	St. Helens	3	Leeds	13,492	£624.17.7
1898	Batley	7	Bradford	0	Leeds	27,941	£1,586.3.0
1899	Oldham	19	Hunslet	9	Manchester	15,763	£946.16.0
1900	Swinton	16	Salford	8	Manchester	17,864	£1,100.0.0
1901	Batley	6	Warrington	0	Leeds	29,563	£1,644.16.0
1902	Broughton R.	25	Salford	0	Rochdale	15,006	£846.11.0
1903	Halifax	7	Salford	0	Leeds	32,507	£1,834.8.6
1904	Halifax	8	Warrington	3	Salford	17,041	£936.5.6
1905	Warrington	6	Hull K.R.	0	Leeds	19,638	£1,271.18.0
1906	Bradford	5	Salford	0	Leeds	15,834	£920.0.0
1907	Warrington	17	Oldham	3	Broughton	18,500	£1,010.0.0
1908	Hunslet	14	Hull	0	Huddersfield	18,000	£903.0.0
1909	Wakefield T.	17	Hull	0	Leeds	23,587	£1,490.0.0
1910	Leeds	7	Hull	7	Huddersfield	19,413	£1,102.0.0
Replay	Leeds	26	Hull	12	Huddersfield	11,608	£657.0.0
1911	Broughton R.	4	Wigan	0	Salford	8,000	£376.0.0
1912	Dewsbury	8	Oldham	5	Leeds	15,271	£853.0.0
1913	Huddersfield	9	Warrington	5	Leeds	22,754	£1,446.9.6
1914	Hull	6	Wakefield T.	0	Halifax	19,000	£1,035.5.0
1915	Huddersfield	37	St. Helens	3	Oldham	8,000	£472.0.0
1920	Huddersfield	21	Wigan	10	Leeds	14,000	£1,936.0.0
1921	Leigh	13	Halifax	0	Broughton	25,000	£2,700.0.0
1922	Rochdale H.	10	Hull	9	Leeds	32,596	£2,964.0.0
1923	Leeds	28	Hull	3	Wakefield	29,335	£2,390.0.0
1924	Wigan	21	Oldham	4	Rochdale	41,831	£3,712.0.0
1925	Oldham	16	Hull K.R.	3	Leeds	28,335	£2,879.0.0
1926	Swinton	9	Oldham	3	Rochdale	27,000	£2,551.0.0
1927	Oldham	26	Swinton	7	Wigan	33,448	£3,170.0.0
1928	Swinton	5	Warrington	3	Wigan	33,909	£3,158.1.11
1929	Wigan	13	Dewsbury	2	Wembley	41,500	£5,614.0.0
1930	Widnes	10	St. Helens	3	Wembley	36,544	£3,102.0.0
1931	Halifax	22	York	8	Wembley	40,368	£3,908.0.0
1932	Leeds	11	Swinton	8	Wigan	29,000	£2,479.0.0
1933	Huddersfield	21	Warrington	17	Wembley	41,874	£6,465.0.0
1934	Hunslet	11	Widnes	5	Wembley	41,280	£6,686.0.0
1935	Castleford	11	Huddersfield	8	Wembley	39,000	£5,533.0.0
1936	Leeds	18	Warrington	2	Wembley	51,250	£7,070.0.0
1937	Widnes	18	Keighley	5	Wembley	47,699	£6,704.0.0
1938	Salford	7	Barrow	4	Wembley	51,243	£7,174.0.0
1939	Halifax	20	Salford	3	Wembley	55,453	£7,681.0.0
1940	*No competition*						
1941	Leeds	19	Halifax	2	Bradford	28,500	£1,703.0.0
1942	Leeds	15	Halifax	10	Bradford	15,250	£1,276.0.0
1943	Dewsbury	16	Leeds	9	Dewsbury	10,470	£823.0.0
	Dewsbury	0	Leeds	6	Leeds	16,000	£1,521.0.0
	Dewsbury won on aggregate 16-15						
1944	Bradford N.	0	Wigan	3	Wigan	22,000	£1,640.0.0
	Bradford N.	8	Wigan	0	Bradford	30,000	£2,200.0.0
	Bradford won on aggregate 8-3						
1945	Huddersfield	7	Bradford N.	4	Huddersfield	9,041	£1,184.3.7
	Huddersfield	6	Bradford N.	5	Bradford	17,500	£2,050.0.0
	Huddersfield won on aggregate 13-9						

189

Year	Winners		Runners-up		Venue	Attendance	Receipts
1946	Wakefield T.	13	Wigan	12	Wembley	54,730	£12,013.13.6
1947	Bradford N.	8	Leeds	4	Wembley	77,605	£17,434.5.0
1948	Wigan	8	Bradford N.	3	Wembley	91,465	£21,121.9.9
1949	Bradford N.	12	Halifax	0	Wembley	*95,050	£21,930.5.0
1950	Warrington	19	Widnes	0	Wembley	94,249	£24,782.13.0
1951	Wigan	10	Barrow	0	Wembley	94,262	£24,797.19.0
1952	Workington T.	18	Featherstone R.	10	Wembley	72,093	£22,374.2.0
1953	Huddersfield	15	St. Helens	10	Wembley	89,588	£30,865.12.3
1954	Warrington	4	Halifax	4	Wembley	81,841	£29,706.7.3
Replay	Warrington	8	Halifax	4	Bradford	102,569	£18,623.7.0
1955	Barrow	21	Workington T.	12	Wembley	66,513	£27,453.16.0
1956	St. Helens	13	Halifax	2	Wembley	79,341	£29,424.7.6
1957	Leeds	9	Barrow	7	Wembley	76,318	£32,671.14.3
1958	Wigan	13	Workington T.	9	Wembley	66,109	£33,175.17.6
1959	Wigan	30	Hull	13	Wembley	79,811	£35,718.19.9
1960	Wakefield T.	38	Hull	5	Wembley	79,773	£35,754.16.0
1961	St. Helens	12	Wigan	6	Wembley	94,672	£38,479.11.9
1962	Wakefield T.	12	Huddersfield	6	Wembley	81,263	£33,390.18.4
1963	Wakefield T.	25	Wigan	10	Wembley	84,492	£44,521.17.0
1964	Widnes	13	Hull K.R.	5	Wembley	84,488	£44,840.19.0
1965	Wigan	20	Hunslet	16	Wembley	89,016	£48,080.4.0
1966	St. Helens	21	Wigan	2	Wembley	*98,536	£50,409.0.0
1967	Featherstone R.	17	Barrow	12	Wembley	76,290	£53,465.14.0
1968	Leeds	11	Wakefield T.	10	Wembley	87,100	£56,171.16.6
1969	Castleford	11	Salford	6	Wembley	*97,939	£58,848.1.0
1970	Castleford	7	Wigan	2	Wembley	95,255	£89,262.2.0
1971	Leigh	24	Leeds	7	Wembley	85,514	£84,452.15
1972	St. Helens	16	Leeds	13	Wembley	89,495	£86,414.30
1973	Featherstone R.	33	Bradford N.	14	Wembley	72,395	£125,826.40
1974	Warrington	24	Featherstone R.	9	Wembley	77,400	£132,021.05
1975	Widnes	14	Warrington	7	Wembley	85,098	£140,684.45
1976	St. Helens	20	Widnes	5	Wembley	89,982	£190,129.40
1977	Leeds	16	Widnes	7	Wembley	80,871	£241,488.00
1978	Leeds	14	St. Helens	12	Wembley	*96,000	£330,575.00
1979	Widnes	12	Wakefield T.	3	Wembley	94,218	£383,157.00
1980	Hull K.R.	10	Hull	5	Wembley	*95,000	£448,202.90
1981	Widnes	18	Hull K.R.	9	Wembley	92,496	£591,117.00
1982	Hull	14	Widnes	14	Wembley	92,147	£684,500.00
Replay	Hull	18	Widnes	9	Elland Rd, L'ds	41,171	£180,525.00
1983	Featherstone R.	14	Hull	12	Wembley	84,969	£655,510.00
1984	Widnes	19	Wigan	6	Wembley	80,116	£686,171.00
1985	Wigan	28	Hull	24	Wembley	*97,801	£760,322.00
1986	Castleford	15	Hull K.R.	14	Wembley	82,134	£806,676.00
1987	Halifax	19	St. Helens	18	Wembley	91,267	£1,009,206.00
1988	Wigan	32	Halifax	12	Wembley	*94,273	£1,102,247.00
1989	Wigan	27	St. Helens	0	Wembley	*78,000	£1,121,293.00
1990	Wigan	36	Warrington	14	Wembley	*77,729	£1,360,000.00
1991	Wigan	13	St. Helens	8	Wembley	75,532	£1,610,447.00
1992	Wigan	28	Castleford	12	Wembley	77,286	£1,877,564.00
1993	Wigan	20	Widnes	14	Wembley	*77,684	£1,981,591.00
1994	Wigan	26	Leeds	16	Wembley	*78,348	£2,032,839.00

*Indicates a capacity attendance, the limit being fixed annually taking into account variable factors.

RUGBY LEAGUE CHALLENGE CUP ....
A 20-YEAR REVIEW
Initials are included where more than one player shared a surname in a team in the same era.
1973-74
Warrington 24 Whitehead (7g); M. Philbin, Noonan, Whittle, Bevan; Murphy (2g) (Pickup), Gordon; D. Chisnall, Ashcroft (1t), Brady (Wanbon), Wright, Nicholas (1t), B. Philbin
Featherstone R. 9 Box (3g); Dyas, M. Smith, Hartley, Bray; Newlove (1t), Nash; Tonks, Bridges, Harris, Rhodes (Busfield), Thompson (Stone), Bell
Referee: S. Shepherd (Oldham)
1974-75
Widnes 14 Dutton (5g, 1dg); A. Prescott, George, Aspey, Anderson; Hughes, Bowden; Mills (1t), Elwell, Sheridan, Foran, Adams, Laughton
Warrington 7 Whitehead (2g); M. Philbin, Noonan, Reynolds (W. Briggs), Bevan (1t); Whittle, Gordon; D. Chisnall, Ashcroft, Wanbon, Conroy, Martyn (Nicholas), B. Philbin
Referee: P. Geraghty (York)
1975-76
St. Helens 20 G. Pimblett (3g, 2dg); L. Jones, Cunningham (1t), Noonan, Mathias; Benyon (Glynn 2t), Heaton (1t); Mantle (James), A. Karalius, Coslett, Nicholls, E. Chisnall, Hull
Widnes 5 Dutton (2g); A. Prescott (D. O'Neill), Hughes, George, Jenkins; Eckersley, Bowden; Nelson, Elwell (1dg), Wood, Foran (Sheridan), Adams, Laughton
Referee: R. Moore (Wakefield)
1976-77
Leeds 16 Murrell; Alan Smith (D. Smith), Hague, Dyl (1t), Atkinson (1t); Holmes, Dick (1t, 3g, 1dg); Harrison, Ward, Pitchford, Eccles, Cookson, Fearnley (Dickinson)
Widnes 7 Dutton (2g); S. Wright (George), Aspey (1t), Eckersley, D. O'Neill; Hughes, Bowden; Ramsey, Elwell, Mills, Dearden (Foran), Adams, Laughton
Referee: V. Moss (Manchester)
1977-78
Leeds 14 Oulton (1g); D. Smith (1t), Hague, Dyl, Atkinson (1t); Holmes (1dg), J. Sanderson (Dick); Harrison (Dickinson), Ward (2dg), Pitchford, Cookson (1t), Eccles, Crane
St. Helens 12 G. Pimblett (3g); L. Jones, Noonan, Glynn, Mathias; Francis (1t), K. Gwilliam; D. Chisnall, Liptrot (1t), James, Nicholls, Cunningham, Pinner
Referee: W.H. Thompson (Huddersfield)

1978-79
Widnes 12 Eckersley (1dg); S. Wright (1t), Aspey, George (Hull), Burke (2g); Hughes (1t), Bowden; Mills, Elwell (1dg), Shaw, Adams, Dearden (M. O'Neill), Laughton
Wakefield T. 3 Sheard; Fletcher (1t), K. Smith, Diamond, Juliff; Topliss, Lampkowski; Burke, McCurrie, Skerrett, Ashurst, Keith Rayne, Idle
Referee: J.E. Jackson (Pudsey)
1979-80
Hull K.R. 10 Hall; Hubbard (1t, 3g) (Hogan), M. Smith, Hartley, Sullivan; Millward (1dg), Agar; Holdstock, Watkinson, Lockwood, Lowe, Rose (Millington), Casey
Hull 5 Woods; Bray, Walters, Wilby (1t), Prendiville; Newlove (Hancock), Pickerill; Tindall, Wileman, Stone (Farrar), Birdsall, Lloyd (1g), Norton
Referee: G.F. Lindop (Wakefield)
1980-81
Widnes 18 Burke (1t, 4g); S. Wright, George (1t), Cunningham (J. Myler), Bentley; Hughes, Gregory (1t); M. O'Neill (Shaw), Elwell, Lockwood, L. Gorley, E. Prescott, Adams (1dg)
Hull K.R. 9 Hall; Hubbard (3g), M. Smith, Hogan, Muscroft; Hartley, Harkin; Holdstock (Millington), Watkinson, Crooks (Proctor), Lowe, Burton (1t), Casey
Referee: D.G. Kershaw (Easingwold)
1981-82
Hull 14 Kemble; O'Hara (1t), Day, S. Evans, Prendiville; Topliss, Harkin; Skerrett, Wileman, Stone, Crane (L. Crooks), Lloyd (4g), Norton (1t)
Widnes 14 Burke (1g) (A. Myler); S. Wright (1t), Keiron O'Loughlin, Cunningham (2t), Basnett; Hughes, Gregory (1g); M. O'Neill, Elwell (1dg), Lockwood (S. O'Neill), L. Gorley, E. Prescott, Adams
Referee: G.F. Lindop (Wakefield)
Replay
Hull 18 Kemble (1t); Sullivan, Leuluai, S. Evans, Prendiville; Topliss (2t), Dean; Tindall, Duke, Stone, Skerrett, L. Crooks (1t, 3g), Norton (Crane)
Widnes 9 Burke (3g); S. Wright (1t), Keiron O'Loughlin, Cunningham, Basnett; Hughes, Gregory; M. O'Neill, Elwell, Lockwood, L. Gorley, E. Prescott, Adams
Referee: G.F. Lindop (Wakefield)

1982-83
Featherstone R. 14 N. Barker; Marsden,
Quinn (4g), Gilbert (Lyman), K. Kellett;
A. Banks, Hudson; Gibbins, Handscombe,
Hankins, D. Hobbs (2t), Slatter (Siddall), P. Smith
Hull 12 Kemble; O'Hara, S. Evans, Leuluai (1t),
Prendiville; Topliss, Harkin (Day) (Crane);
Skerrett, Bridges, Stone, Rose, L. Crooks (1t, 3g),
Norton
Referee: R. Whitfield (Widnes)
1983-84
Widnes 19 Burke (3g); S. Wright, Hughes
(D. Hulme), Lydon (2t), Basnett;
Keiron O'Loughlin (1t), Gregory; S. O'Neill
(1dg), Elwell, K. Tamati, L. Gorley, M. O'Neill
(Whitfield), Adams
Wigan 6 Edwards; Ramsdale, Stephenson,
Whitfield (1g) (Elvin), Gill; Cannon, Stephens;
Hemsley (1t), H. Tamati, Case (Juliff), West,
Scott, Pendlebury
Referee: W.H. Thompson (Huddersfield)
1984-85
Wigan 28 Edwards (1t); Ferguson (2t),
Stephenson (1g), Donlan, Gill (1t, 3g);
Kenny (1t), M. Ford; Courtney, Kiss, Case
(Campbell), West, Dunn, Potter
Hull 24 Kemble; James (1t), S. Evans (1t),
Leuluai (2t), O'Hara (Schofield); Ah Kuoi,
Sterling; L. Crooks (2g), Patrick, Puckering
(Divorty 1t), Muggleton, Rose, Norton
Referee: R. Campbell (Widnes)
1985-86
Castleford 15 Lord (Roockley); Plange,
Marchant (1t), Hyde, Sandy (1t); Joyner,
R. Beardmore (1t, 1dg); Ward, K. Beardmore
(Horton), B. Johnson, England, Ketteridge (1g),
I. French
Hull K.R. 14 Fairbairn; Clark, M. Smith,
Prohm (2t), Laws; Dorahy (1g), Harkin; P.
Johnston, Watkinson, Ema, Kelly (G. Smith),
Des Harrison (Lydiat 1t), Miller
Referee: R. Whitfield (Widnes)
1986-87
Halifax 19 Eadie (1t); S. Wilson, Whitfield (3g),
Rix, George (1t); C. Anderson (Juliff), Stephens;
Beevers (James), McCallion (1t), Neller, Dixon,
Scott, Pendlebury (1dg)
St. Helens 18 Veivers; Ledger, Loughlin (1t, 3g),
Elia (1t), McCormack; Clark, Holding; Burke,
Liptrot, Fieldhouse, Platt, Haggerty (Round 1t),
Arkwright
Referee: J. Holdsworth (Kippax)
1987-88
Wigan 32 Lydon (1t, 1g); T. Iro (1t), K. Iro (2t),
Bell (1t), Gill (1t); Edwards (Byrne), Gregory
(1g); Case, Kiss, Shelford, Goodway, Potter
(Wane), Hanley (1t)

Halifax 12 Eadie; Meredith, T. Anderson (1t),
Wilkinson, Whitfield (2g); Grogan, S. Robinson
(Fairbank); James (1t), McCallion, Neller,
Holliday (Scott), Dixon, Pendlebury
Referee: G.F. Lindop (Wakefield)
1988-89
Wigan 27 Hampson (1t); T. Iro, K. Iro (2t),
Bell, Lydon (3g); Edwards, Gregory (1t, 1dg);
Lucas, Kiss (Betts), Shelford, Platt, Potter
(Goodway), Hanley (1t)
St. Helens 0 Connolly; O'Connor, Veivers,
Loughlin (Bloor), Quirk; Cooper, Holding;
Burke, Groves, Forber, Dwyer (Evans),
Haggerty, Vautin
Referee: R. Tennant (Castleford)
1989-90
Wigan 36 Hampson; Lydon (6g), K. Iro (2t),
Bell, Preston (2t) (Gildart); Edwards, Gregory;
Shelford, Dermott (Goulding), Platt, Betts (1t),
Goodway, Hanley (1t)
Warrington 14 Lyon (1t); Drummond, Mercer,
Darbyshire (1g), Forster; Crompton, Bishop (2g)
(McGinty); Burke, Mann, Harmon, Jackson
(Thomas), Sanderson, M. Gregory (1t)
Referee: J. Holdsworth (Kippax)
1990-91
Wigan 13 Hampson; Myers (1t), K. Iro, Bell,
Botica (1t, 2g); Edwards, Gregory (1dg); Lucas,
Dermott (Goulding), Platt, Betts, Clarke
(Goodway), Hanley
St. Helens 8 Veivers (Connolly); Hunte (1t),
Ropati, Loughlin, Quirk; Griffiths,
Bishop (2g); Neill (Groves), Dwyer, Ward,
Harrison, Mann, Cooper
Referee: J. Smith (Halifax)
1991-92
Wigan 28 Lydon (2dg); Botica (5g), Bell, Miles,
Offiah (2t); Edwards (1t), Gregory; Skerrett,
Dermott, Platt, Betts, McGinty (Hampson 1t)
(Cowie), Clarke
Castleford 12 Steadman; Wray, Ellis, Blackmore (1t),
Nelson; Anderson (T. Smith), Ford; Crooks
(Sampson), Southernwood, England (1t), Bradley,
Ketteridge (2g), Nikau
Referee: R. Whitfield (Widnes)
1992-93
Wigan 20 Hampson; Robinson, Lydon (Panapa 1t),
Farrar, Offiah; Botica (4g), Edwards; Skerrett (1t)
(Farrell), Dermott, Platt, Betts, Clarke, Bell (1t)
Widnes 14 Spruce; Devereux, Currier (McCurrie),
D. Wright, Myers; Davies (3g), Goulding;
Sorensen (1t), P. Hulme, Howard, R. Eyres (1t),
Faimalo (J. O'Neill), D. Hulme
Referee: R. Smith (Castleford)

RUGBY LEAGUE CHALLENGE CUP FINAL PLAYERS' REGISTER

The following is an index of players who have appeared in the Rugby League Challenge Cup final in the last 20 seasons. It also includes the pre-1975 record of any listed player. W — winners, L — losers, D — draw. Substitute appearances in lower case letters. The year denotes the second half of the season. * denotes replay.

ADAMS, Mick: Widnes 75W, 76L, 77L, 79W, 81W, 82DL*, 84W
AGAR, Allan: Hull K.R. 80W
AH KUOI, Fred: Hull 85L
ANDERSON, Chris: Widnes 75W; Halifax 87W
ANDERSON, Grant: Castleford 92L
ANDERSON, Tony: Halifax 88L
ARKWRIGHT, Chris: St. Helens 87L
ASHCROFT, Kevin: Leigh 71W; Warrington 74W, 75L
ASHURST, Bill: Wigan 70L; Wakefield T. 79L
ASPEY, Malcolm: Widnes 75W, 77L, 79W
ATKINSON, John: Leeds 68W, 71L, 72L, 77W, 78W

BANKS, Alan: Featherstone R. 83W
BARKER, Nigel: Featherstone R. 83W
BASNETT, John: Widnes 82DL*, 84W
BEARDMORE, Kevin: Castleford 86W
BEARDMORE, Bob: Castleford 86W
BEEVERS, Graham: Halifax 87W
BELL, Dean: Wigan 88W, 89W, 90W, 91W, 92W, 93W, 94W
BENTLEY, Keith: Widnes 81W
BENYON, Billy: St. Helens 66W, 72W, 76W
BETTS, Denis: Wigan 89w, 90W, 91W, 92W, 93W, 94W
BEVAN, John: Warrington 74W, 75L
BIRDSALL, Charlie: Hull 80L
BISHOP, Paul: Warrington 90L; St. Helens 91L
BLACKMORE, Richard: Castleford 92L
BLOOR, Darren: St. Helens 89l
BOTICA, Frano: Wigan 91W, 92W, 93W, 94W
BOWDEN, Reg: Widnes 75W, 76L, 77L, 79W
BRADLEY, Graeme: Castleford 92L
BRAY, Graham: Featherstone R. 74L; Hull 80L
BRIDGES, John "Keith": Featherstone R. 73W, 74L; Hull 83L
BRIGGS, Wilf: Warrington 75l
BURKE, John: Leeds 71L; Wakefield T. 79L
BURKE, Mick: Widnes 79W, 81W, 82DL*, 84W
BURKE, Tony: St. Helens 87L, 89L; Warrington 90L
BURTON, Chris: Hull K.R. 81L
BYRNE, Ged: Wigan 88w

CAMPBELL, Danny: Wigan 85w
CANNON, Mark: Wigan 84L
CASE, Brian: Wigan 84L, 85W, 88W
CASEY, Len: Hull K.R. 80W, 81L
CASSIDY, Mick: Wigan 94w
CHISNALL, Dave: Warrington 74W, 75L; St. Helens 78L
CHISNALL, Eric: St. Helens 72W, 76W
CLARK, Brett: St. Helens 87L
CLARK, Garry: Hull K.R. 86L
CLARKE, Phil: Wigan 91W, 92W, 93W, 94W
CONNOLLY, Gary: St. Helens 89L, 91l; Wigan 94W
CONROY, Tom: Warrington 75L
COOKSON, Phil: Leeds 72L, 77W, 78W
COOPER, Shane: St. Helens 89L, 91L
COSLETT, Kel: St. Helens 72W, 76W
COURTNEY, Neil: Wigan 85W
COWIE, Neil: Wigan 92w

CRANE, Mick: Leeds 78W; Hull 82Dw*, 83l
CROMPTON, Martin: Warrington 90L
CROOKS, Lee: Hull 82dW*, 83L, 85L; Castleford 92L
CROOKS, Steve: Hull K.R. 81L
CUMMINS, Francis: Leeds 94L
CUNNINGHAM, Eddie: St. Helens 76W, 78L; Widnes 81W, 82DL*
CURRIER, Andy: Widnes 93L

DARBYSHIRE, Paul: Warrington 90L
DAVIES, Jonathan: Widnes 93L
DAY, Terry: Hull 82D, 83l
DEAN, Tony: Hull 82W*
DEARDEN, Alan: Widnes 77L, 79W
DERMOTT, Martin: Wigan 90W, 91W, 92W, 93W, 94W
DEVEREUX, John: Widnes 93L
DIAMOND, Steve: Wakefield T. 79L
DICK, Kevin: Leeds 77W, 78w
DICKINSON, Roy: Leeds 77w, 78w
DIVORTY, Gary: Hull 85l
DIXON, Paul: Halifax 87W, 88L
DONLAN, Steve: Wigan 85W
DORAHY, John: Hull K.R. 86L
DRUMMOND, Des: Warrington 90L
DUKE, Tony: Hull 82W*
DUNN, Brian: Wigan 85W
DUTTON, Ray: Widnes 75W, 76L, 77L
DWYER, Bernard: St. Helens 89L, 91L
DYL, Les: Leeds 71l, 72L, 77W, 78W

EADIE, Graham: Halifax 87W, 88L
ECCLES, Graham: Leeds 77W, 78W
ECKERSLEY, David: Leigh 71W; Widnes 76L, 77L, 79W
EDWARDS, Shaun: Wigan 84L, 85W, 88W, 89W, 90W, 91W, 92W, 93W, 94W
ELIA, Mark: St. Helens 87L
ELLIS, St. John: Castleford 92L
ELVIN, Wayne: Wigan 84l
ELWELL, Keith: Widnes 75W, 76L, 77L, 79W, 81W, 82DL*, 84W
EMA, Asuquo: Hull K.R. 86L
ENGLAND, Keith: Castleford 86W, 92L
EVANS, Steve: Hull 82DW*, 83L, 85L
EVANS, Stuart: St. Helens 89l
EYRES, Richard: Widnes 93L; Leeds 94L

FAIMALO, Esene: Widnes 93L
FAIRBAIRN, George: Hull K.R. 86L
FAIRBANK, Dick: Halifax 88l
FALLON, Jim: Leeds 94L
FARRAR, Andrew: Wigan 93W
FARRAR, Vince: Featherstone R. 73W; Hull 80l
FARRELL, Andrew: Wigan 93w, 94W
FEARNLEY, Stan: Bradford N. 73L; Leeds 77W
FERGUSON, John: Wigan 85W
FIELDHOUSE, John: St. Helens 87L
FLETCHER, Andrew: Wakefield T. 79L
FORAN, John: Widnes 75W, 76L, 77l
FORBER, Paul: St. Helens 89L
FORD, Mike: Wigan 85W; Castleford 92L

193

FORSTER, Mark: Warrington 90L
FRANCIS, Bill: Wigan 70L; St. Helens 78L
FRENCH, Ian: Castleford 86W

GEORGE, Derek "Mick": Widnes 75W, 76L, 77l, 79W, 81W
GEORGE, Wilf: Halifax 87W
GIBBINS, Mick: Featherstone R. 83W
GILBERT, John: Featherstone R. 83W
GILDART, Ian: Wigan 90w
GILL, Henderson: Wigan 84L, 85W, 88W
GLYNN, Peter: St. Helens 76w, 78L
GOODWAY, Andy: Wigan 88W, 89w, 90W, 91w
GORDON, Parry: Warrington 74W, 75L
GORLEY, Les: Widnes 81W, 82DL*, 84W
GOULDING, Bobby: Wigan 90w, 91w; Widnes 93L
GREGORY, Andy: Widnes 81W, 82DL*, 84W; Wigan 88W, 89W, 90W, 91W, 92W
GREGORY, Mike: Warrington 90L
GRIFFITHS, Jonathan: St. Helens 91L
GROGAN, Bob: Halifax 88L
GROVES, Paul: St. Helens 89L, 91l
GWILLIAM, Ken: Salford 69L; St. Helens 78L

HAGGERTY, Roy: St. Helens 87L, 89L
HAGUE, Neil: Leeds 77W, 78W
HALL, David: Hull K.R. 80W, 81L
HAMPSON, Steve: Wigan 89W, 90W, 91W, 92w, 93W
HANCOCK, Brian: Hull 80l
HANDSCOMBE, Ray: Featherstone R. 83W
HANKINS, Steve: Featherstone R. 83W
HANLEY, Ellery: Wigan 88W, 89W, 90W, 91W; Leeds 94L
HARKIN, Kevin: Hull 82D, 83L
HARKIN, Paul: Hull K.R. 81L, 86L
HARMON, Neil: Warrington 90L; Leeds 94L
HARRISON, Des: Hull K.R. 86L
HARRISON, John: St. Helens 91L
HARRISON, Mick: Leeds 77W, 78W
HARTLEY, Steve: Hull K.R. 80W, 81L
HEATON, Jeff: St. Helens 72W, 76W
HEMSLEY, Kerry: Wigan 84L
HOBBS, David: Featherstone R. 83W
HOGAN, Phil: Hull K.R. 80w, 81L
HOLDING, Neil: St. Helens 87L, 89L
HOLDSTOCK, Roy: Hull K.R. 80W, 81L
HOLLIDAY, Les: Halifax 88L
HOLMES, John: Leeds 71L, 72L, 77W, 78W
HOLROYD, Graham: Leeds 94L
HORTON, Stuart: Castleford 86w
HOWARD, Harvey: Widnes 93L; Leeds 94L
HUBBARD, Steve: Hull K.R. 80W, 81L
HUDSON, Terry: Featherstone R. 83W
HUGHES, Eric: Widnes 75W, 76L, 77L, 79W, 81W, 82DL*, 84W
HULL, David: St. Helens 76W; Widnes 79w
HULME, David: Widnes 84w, 93L
HULME, Paul: Widnes 93L
HUNTE, Alan: St. Helens 91L
HYDE, Gary: Castleford 86W

IDLE, Graham: Wakefield T. 79L
INNES, Craig: Leeds 94L
IRO, Kevin: Wigan 88W, 89W, 90W, 91W; Leeds 94L
IRO, Tony: Wigan 88W, 89W

JACKSON, Bob: Warrington 90L
JAMES, Kevin: Hull 85L
JAMES, Mel: St. Helens 76w, 78L
JAMES, Neil: Halifax 87w, 88L
JENKINS, David: Widnes 76L
JOHNSON, Barry: Castleford 86W
JOHNSTON, Peter: Hull K.R. 86L
JONES, Les: St. Helens 72W, 76W, 78L
JOYNER, John: Castleford 86W
JULIFF, Brian: Wakefield T. 79L; Wigan 84l; Halifax 87w

KARALIUS, Tony: St. Helens 76W
KELLETT, Ken: Featherstone R. 73W, 83W
KELLY, Andy: Hull K.R. 86L
KEMBLE, Gary: Hull 82DW*, 83L, 85L
KENNY, Brett: Wigan 85W
KETTERIDGE, Martin: Castleford 86W, 92L
KISS, Nicky: Wigan 85W, 88W, 89W

LAMPKOWSKI, Mike: Wakefield T. 79L
LAUGHTON, Doug: Wigan 70L; Widnes 75W, 76L, 77L, 79W
LAWS, David: Hull K.R. 86L
LEDGER, Barry: St. Helens 87L
LEULUAI, James: Hull 82W*, 83L, 85L
LIPTROT, Graham: St. Helens 78L, 87L
LLOYD, Geoff "Sammy": Hull 80L, 82D
LOCKWOOD, Brian: Castleford 69W, 70W; Hull K.R. 80W; Widnes 81W, 82DL*
LORD, Gary: Castleford 86W
LOUGHLIN, Paul: St. Helens 87L, 89L, 91L
LOWE, Phil: Hull K.R. 80W, 81L
LOWES, James: Leeds 94L
LUCAS, Ian: Wigan 89W, 91W
LYDIAT, John: Hull K.R. 86l
LYDON, Joe: Widnes 84W; Wigan 88W, 89W, 90W, 92W, 93W
LYMAN, Paul: Featherstone R. 83w
LYON, David: Warrington 90L

McCALLION, Seamus: Halifax 87W, 88L
McCORMACK, Kevin: St. Helens 87L
McCURRIE, Alan: Wakefield T. 79L
McCURRIE, Steve: Widnes 93l
McGINTY, Billy: Warrington 90l; Wigan 92W
MANN, Duane: Warrington 90L
MANN, George: St. Helens 91L
MANTLE, John: St. Helens 66W, 72W, 76W
MARCHANT, Tony: Castleford 86W
MARSDEN, John: Featherstone R. 83W
MARTYN, Tommy: Warrington 75L
MATHER, Barrie-Jon: Wigan 94W
MATHIAS, Roy: St. Helens 76W, 78L
MERCER, Gary: Warrington 90L; Leeds 94L
MEREDITH, Martin: Halifax 88L
MILES, Gene: Wigan 92W
MILLER, Gavin: Hull K.R. 86L
MILLINGTON, John: Hull K.R. 80w, 81l
MILLS, Jim: Widnes 75W, 77L, 79W
MILLWARD, Roger: Hull K.R. 80W
MUGGLETON, John: Hull 85L
MURRELL, Brian: Leeds 77W
MUSCROFT, Peter: Hull K.R. 81L
MYERS, David: Wigan 91W; Widnes 93L

MYLER, John: Widnes 81w
MYLER, Tony: Widnes 82d

NEILL, Jonathan: St. Helens 91L
NELLER, Keith: Halifax 87W, 88L
NELSON, David: Castleford 92L
NELSON, Nick: Widnes 76L
NEWLOVE, John: Featherstone R. 73W, 74L; Hull 80L
NICHOLAS, Mike: Warrington 74W, 75l
NICHOLLS, George: St. Helens 76W, 78L
NIKAU, Tawera: Castleford 92L
NOONAN, Derek: Warrington 74W, 75L; St. Helens 76W, 78L
NORTON, Steve: Hull 80L, 82DW★, 83L, 85L

O'CONNOR, Michael: St. Helens 89L
OFFIAH, Martin: Wigan 92W, 93W, 94W
O'HARA, Dane: Hull 82D, 83L, 85L
O'LOUGHLIN, Keiron: Widnes 82DL★, 84W
O'NEILL, Dennis: Widnes 76l, 77L
O'NEILL, Julian: Widnes 93l
O'NEILL, Mike: Widnes 79w, 81W, 82DL★, 84W; Leeds 94l
O'NEILL, Steve: Widnes 82d, 84W
OULTON, Willie: Leeds 78W

PANAPA, Sam: Wigan 93w, 94w
PATRICK, Shaun: Hull 85L
PENDLEBURY, John: Wigan 84L; Halifax 87W, 88L
PHILBIN, Barry: Warrington 74W, 75L
PHILBIN, Mike: Warrington 74W, 75L
PICKERILL, Clive: Hull 80L
PIMBLETT, Geoff: St. Helens 72W, 76W, 78L
PINNER, Harry: St. Helens 78L
PITCHFORD, Steve: Leeds 77W, 78W
PLANGE, David: Castleford 86W
PLATT, Andy: St. Helens 87L; Wigan 89W, 90W, 91W, 92W, 93W, 94W
POTTER, Ian: Wigan 85W, 88W, 89W
PRENDIVILLE, Paul: Hull 80L, 82DW★, 83L
PRESCOTT, Alan: Widnes 75W, 76L
PRESCOTT, Eric: Widnes 81W, 82DL★
PRESTON, Mark: Wigan 90W
PROCTOR, Paul: Hull K.R. 81l
PROHM, Gary: Hull K.R. 86L
PUCKERING, Neil: Hull 85L

QUINN, Steve: Featherstone R. 83W
QUIRK, Les: St. Helens 89L, 91L

RAMSDALE, Denis: Wigan 84L
RAMSEY, Bill: Hunslet 65L; Leeds 68W, 71L, 72L; Widnes 77L
RAYNE, Keith: Wakefield T. 79L
REYNOLDS, Frank: Warrington 75L
RIX, Grant: Halifax 87W
ROBINSON, Jason: Wigan 93W
ROBINSON, Steve: Halifax 88L
ROOCKLEY, David: Castleford 86w
ROPATI, Tea: St. Helens 91L
ROSE, Paul: Hull K.R. 80W; Hull 83L, 85L
ROUND, Paul: St. Helens 87l

SAMPSON, Dean: Castleford 92l
SANDERSON, Gary: Warrington 90L

SANDERSON, John "Sammy": Leeds 78W
SANDY, Jamie: Castleford 86W
SCHOFIELD, Garry: Hull 85l; Leeds 94L
SCOTT, Mick: Wigan 84L; Halifax 87W, 88l
SHAW, Glyn: Widnes 79W, 81w
SHEARD, Les: Wakefield T. 79L
SHELFORD, Adrian: Wigan 88W, 89W, 90W
SHERIDAN, Barry: Widnes 75W, 76l
SIDDALL, Gary: Featherstone R. 83w
SKERRETT, Kelvin: Wigan 92W, 93W, 94W
SKERRETT, Trevor: Wakefield T. 79L; Hull 82DW★, 83L
SLATTER, Tim: Featherstone R. 83W
SMITH, Alan: Leeds 68W, 72L, 77W
SMITH, David: Leeds 77w, 78W
SMITH, Gordon: Hull K.R. 86l
SMITH, Keith: Wakefield T. 79L
SMITH, Mike: Hull K.R. 80W, 81L, 86L
SMITH, Peter: Featherstone R. 83W
SMITH, Tony: Castleford 92l
SORENSEN, Kurt: Widnes 93L
SOUTHERNWOOD, Graham: Castleford 92L
SPRUCE, Stuart: Widnes 93L
STEADMAN, Graham: Castleford 92L
STEPHENS, Gary: Wigan 84L; Halifax 87W
STEPHENSON, David: Wigan 84L, 85W
STERLING, Peter: Hull 85L
STONE, Richard "Charlie": Featherstone R. 73W, 74l; Hull 80L, 82DW★, 83L
SULLIVAN, Clive: Hull K.R. 80W; Hull 82W★

TAIT, Alan: Leeds 94L
TAMATI, Howie: Wigan 84L
TAMATI, Kevin: Widnes 84W
THOMAS, Mark: Warrington 90l
TINDALL, Keith: Hull 80L, 82W★
TOPLISS, David: Wakefield T. 79L; Hull 82DW★, 83L
TUIGAMALA, Va'aiga: Wigan 94W

VASSILAKOPOULOS, Marcus: Leeds 94l
VAUTIN, Paul: St. Helens 89L
VEIVERS, Phil: St. Helens 87L, 89L, 91L

WALTERS, Graham: Hull 80L
WANBON, Bobby: Warrington 74w, 75L
WANE, Shaun: Wigan 88w
WARD, David: Leeds 77W, 78W
WARD, Kevin: Castleford 86W; St. Helens 91L
WATKINSON, David: Hull K.R. 80W, 81L, 86L
WEST, Graeme: Wigan 84L, 85W
WHITEHEAD, Derek: Warrington 74W, 75L
WHITFIELD, Colin: Wigan 84L; Halifax 87W, 88L
WHITFIELD, Fred: Widnes 84w
WHITTLE, Alan: Warrington 74W, 75L
WILBY, Tim: Hull 80L
WILEMAN, Ron: Hull 80L, 82D
WILKINSON, Ian: Halifax 88L
WILSON, Scott: Halifax 87W
WOOD, John: Widnes 76L
WOODS, Paul: Hull 80L
WRAY, Jon: Castleford 92L
WRIGHT, Darren: Widnes 93L
WRIGHT, Stuart: Widnes 77L, 79W, 81W, 82DL★, 84W

THE LANCE TODD TROPHY

The Lance Todd Trophy is presented to the Man of the Match in the Rugby League Challenge Cup final, the decision being reached by a ballot of members of the Rugby League Writers' Association present at the game.

Lance Todd made his name in Britain as a player with Wigan and as manager of Salford. His untimely death in a road accident on the return journey from a game at Oldham was commemorated by the introduction of the Lance Todd Trophy.

The award was instituted by Australian-born Harry Sunderland, Warrington director Bob Anderton and Yorkshire journalist John Bapty.

Around 1950, the Red Devils' Association at Salford, comprising players and officials who had worked with Todd, raised sufficient funds to provide a trophy and replica for each winner.

Hull's Tommy Harris is the only hooker to earn the title; and Ray Ashby and Brian Gabbitas the only players to share the honour.

Following the 1954 replay, it was decided by the Red Devils that in the future the trophy would be awarded for the Wembley game. In 1954, Gerry Helme had received the trophy for his performance in the Odsal replay. In the 1982 replay at Elland Road, Leeds, the Man of the Match award went to Hull skipper David Topliss, the Lance Todd Trophy having been awarded to Eddie Cunningham, of Widnes, in the drawn Wembley tie.

In 1990 Andy Gregory, of Wigan, became the first player to win the trophy twice at Wembley, having also won it two years earlier, a feat emulated by Martin Offiah in 1992 and 1994.

The Lance Todd Trophy Roll of Honour

Year	Winner	Team	Position
1946	Billy Stott	Wakefield Trinity (v Wigan)	Centre
1947	Willie Davies	Bradford Northern (v Leeds)	Stand off
1948	Frank Whitcombe	Bradford Northern (v Wigan)	Prop
1949	Ernest Ward	Bradford Northern (v Halifax)	Centre
1950	Gerry Helme	Warrington (v Widnes)	Scrum half
1951	Cec Mountford	Wigan (v Barrow)	Stand off
1952	Billy Ivison	Workington T. (v Featherstone R.)	Loose forward
1953	Peter Ramsden	Huddersfield (v St. Helens)	Stand off
1954	Gerry Helme	Warrington (v Halifax)	Scrum half
1955	Jack Grundy	Barrow (v Workington Town)	Second row
1956	Alan Prescott	St. Helens (v Halifax)	Prop
1957	Jeff Stevenson	Leeds (v Barrow)	Scrum half
1958	Rees Thomas	Wigan (v Workington Town)	Scrum half
1959	Brian McTigue	Wigan (v Hull)	Second row
1960	Tommy Harris	Hull (v Wakefield Trinity)	Hooker
1961	Dick Huddart	St. Helens (v Wigan)	Second row
1962	Neil Fox	Wakefield Trinity (v Huddersfield)	Centre
1963	Harold Poynton	Wakefield Trinity (v Wigan)	Stand off
1964	Frank Collier	Widnes (v Hull K.R.)	Prop

1965	Ray Ashby	Wigan	Full back
	Brian Gabbitas	Hunslet	Stand off
1966	Len Killeen	St. Helens (v Wigan)	Winger
1967	Carl Dooler	Featherstone Rovers (v Barrow)	Scrum half
1968	Don Fox	Wakefield Trinity (v Leeds)	Prop
1969	Malcolm Reilly	Castleford (v Salford)	Loose forward
1970	Bill Kirkbride	Castleford (v Wigan)	Second row
1971	Alex Murphy	Leigh (v Leeds)	Scrum half
1972	Kel Coslett	St. Helens (v Leeds)	Loose forward
1973	Steve Nash	Featherstone R. (v Bradford N.)	Scrum half
1974	Derek Whitehead	Warrington (v Featherstone Rovers)	Full back
1975	Ray Dutton	Widnes (v Warrington)	Full back
1976	Geoff Pimblett	St. Helens (v Widnes)	Full back
1977	Steve Pitchford	Leeds (v Widnes)	Prop
1978	George Nicholls	St. Helens (v Leeds)	Second row
1979	David Topliss	Wakefield Trinity (v Widnes)	Stand off
1980	Brian Lockwood	Hull K.R. (v Hull)	Prop
1981	Mick Burke	Widnes (v Hull K.R.)	Full back
1982	Eddie Cunningham	Widnes (v Hull)	Centre
1983	David Hobbs	Featherstone Rovers (v Hull)	Second row
1984	Joe Lydon	Widnes (v Wigan)	Centre
1985	Brett Kenny	Wigan (v Hull)	Stand off
1986	Bob Beardmore	Castleford (v Hull K.R.)	Scrum half
1987	Graham Eadie	Halifax (v St. Helens)	Full back
1988	Andy Gregory	Wigan (v Halifax)	Scrum half
1989	Ellery Hanley	Wigan (v St. Helens)	Loose forward
1990	Andy Gregory	Wigan (v Warrington)	Scrum half
1991	Denis Betts	Wigan (v St. Helens)	Second row
1992	Martin Offiah	Wigan (v Castleford)	Winger
1993	Dean Bell	Wigan (v Widnes)	Loose forward
1994	Martin Offiah	Wigan (v Leeds)	Winger

1977 . . . Leeds prop Steve Pitchford.

1979 . . . Wakefield Trinity stand off David Topliss.

CHALLENGE CUP RECORDS

ALL ROUNDS

TEAM
Highest score:
Huddersfield 119 v. *Swinton Park 2 1914

INDIVIDUAL

Most goals in a match:
22 by Jim Sullivan (Wigan) v. *Flimby and Fothergill
. . . . 1925

Most tries in a match:
11 by George West (Hull K.R.) v. *Brookland Rovers
. . . . 1905

Most points in a match:
53 (11t,10g) by George West (Hull K.R.) as above.

*Amateur teams

FINAL RECORDS

TEAM

Most wins: 15 by Wigan

Most finals: 24 by Wigan

Highest score:
Wakefield T. 38 v. Hull 5 1960

Widest margin:
Huddersfield 37 v. St. Helens 3 1915

Biggest attendance:
102,569 Warrington v. Halifax (Replay) at Bradford
. . . . 1954

INDIVIDUAL

Most goals:
8 by Cyril Kellett (Featherstone R.) v. Bradford N.
. . . . 1973

Most tries:
3 by Bob Wilson (Broughton R.) v. Salford 1902
Stan Moorhouse (Huddersfield) v. Warrington . 1913
Tom Holliday (Oldham) v. Swinton 1927

Most points:
20 (2t,7g) by Neil Fox (Wakefield T.) v. Hull . . . 1960

WEMBLEY FACTS
WIGAN have made a record 20 appearances at Wembley and won there a record 14 times, including a record seven successive appearances from 1988.

A RECORD 10 overseas players trod the Wembley turf in 1985. Hull fielded six — a record for one club. The Airlie Birds sextet were Australians Peter Sterling and John Muggleton, plus New Zealanders Gary Kemble, James Leuluai, Dane O'Hara and Fred Ah Kuoi. Wigan added Australians John Ferguson and Brett Kenny together with New Zealanders Graeme West and Danny Campbell, who went on as substitute. South African Nick Du Toit was substitute back but did not play.

THE 1985 aggregates of 10 tries and 52 points were both record totals for a Challenge Cup final with Hull's 24 points the most by a losing side. There were also 10 tries in the 1915 final when Huddersfield beat St. Helens 37-3, which is the widest margin. Wakefield Trinity ran up the highest Cup final score when they beat Hull 38-5 in 1960.

WORLD RECORD receipts of £2,032,839 were taken at the 1994 final between Wigan and Leeds from a capacity crowd of 78,348.

SHAUN EDWARDS holds the record for most Cup-winning appearances at Wembley with eight from a record nine appearances.
Edwards made his debut in Wigan's losing side of 1984, earning winners' medals in 1985 and from 1988-94 inclusive.

ERIC ASHTON captained a record six teams at Wembley — Wigan in 1958, 1959, 1961, 1963, 1965 and 1966. His record of three wins (in 1958, 1959, 1965) is shared with Derek Turner (Wakefield Trinity 1960, 1962, 1963), Alex Murphy (St. Helens 1966, Leigh 1971 and Warrington 1974), Ellery Hanley (Wigan 1989, 1990, 1991) and Dean Bell (Wigan 1992, 1993 and 1994), Hanley's and Bell's being the only three successive wins.

THE YOUNGEST player to appear in a Wembley Cup final was Francis Cummins who was 17 years and 200 days when he played on the wing for Leeds against Wigan in 1994. Shaun Edwards was the youngest captain at Wembley, leading Wigan to success in the 1988 final against Halifax at the age of 21 years, 6 months and 14 days. The youngest winner at Wembley was Wigan's Andrew Farrell, a substitute in the 1993 final against Widnes at 17 years, 11 months. The youngest forward to play at Wembley is Marcus Vassilakopoulos of Leeds who went on as a substitute against Wigan in 1994 at 17 years and seven months.

ALEX MURPHY has been a record six times to Wembley as a coach. He was a winner as player-coach with Leigh (1971) and Warrington (1974), but losing each time when confined to the bench with Warrington (1975), Wigan (1984) and St. Helens (1987 and 1989). Murphy also went twice solely as a player, with St. Helens in 1961 and 1966.

MOST WINS as a coach at Wembley is four, by John Monie (Wigan 1990, 1991, 1992 and 1993).

THE OLDEST player at Wembley was Gus Risman, who at 41 years, 29 days led Workington Town to victory over Featherstone Rovers in 1952. He played full back.

THE TALLEST players at Wembley were St. Helens second row man John Harrison who appeared in the 1991 final, and Barrie-Jon Mather who was at centre for Wigan in 1994. Both were 6ft 7in.

SCHOOLBOYS who have appeared in an Under-11 curtain-raiser at Wembley and gone on to play in the major final at the stadium are Joe Lydon, David Hulme, Mike Ford, Neil Puckering, David Plange, Denis Betts, Bobby Goulding and Phil Clarke. Lydon became the first to achieve the feat with Widnes in the 1984 final against Wigan, followed by teammate Hulme who went on as a 72nd-minute substitute. Both had played in the first schoolboys' curtain-raiser in 1975 — Lydon for Wigan, and Hulme for Widnes.

CYRIL KELLETT holds the record for most goals in a Challenge Cup final with his eight for Featherstone Rovers in 1973.

In the most remarkable exhibition of kicking seen at Wembley, the veteran full back was successful with every one of his attempts as Bradford Northern crashed 33-14.

Nine years earlier he scored only one for Hull Kingston Rovers in the 13-5 defeat by Widnes.

NEIL FOX — the record aggregate points scorer of all time — piled up the most points in a Challenge Cup final in 1960. His 20 points helped Wakefield Trinity to a 38-5 defeat of Hull. Fox's points came from two tries and seven goals.

His three drop goals for Trinity in the 12-6 victory over Huddersfield two years later was another extraordinary feat in the days when the drop goal was a rarity.

NO player has scored a hat-trick of tries at Wembley, the feat being achieved only three times in the preceding era.

The last to do it was Oldham winger Tom Holliday in the 26-7 defeat of Swinton in 1927.

Bob Wilson, the Broughton Rangers centre and captain, was the first to score three tries, in the 25-0 victory over Salford in 1902.

In between, Stan Moorhouse's three-try feat accounted for all of Huddersfield's points when they beat Warrington 9-5 in 1913.

MANY great players have gone through an entire career without achieving their ambition of playing at Wembley. Hull's Mike Smith achieved it in his first senior game.

Smith made one of the most remarkable debuts in sporting history when he played in the second row of an injury-hit Boulevard side against Wakefield Trinity in 1960.

In contrast, Freddie Miller signed for Hull in 1932 and did not play at Wembley until 1952...two years after joining Featherstone Rovers.

Top Wembley coach, John Monie.

A NOTABLE Wembley captain was Gus Risman who led two clubs to victory...14 years apart. He was captain of Salford when they beat Barrow in 1938. At 41, he led Workington Town to their triumph over Featherstone Rovers in 1952.

Mike O'Neill holds the record for the longest playing span at Wembley of 15 years. He was a playing substitute for Widnes in 1979 and had the same role with Leeds in 1994. He played in five finals.

PROBABLY the unluckiest Challenge Cup finalist was Dai Davies who appeared in four finals and was on the losing side each time. Three of those occasions were at Wembley with different clubs. He was a loser with Warrington (1933), Huddersfield (1935) and Keighley (1937). Before the Wembley era he was also in Warrington's beaten team of 1928.

Steve Norton and Lee Crooks played at Wembley four times and were never on the winning side. Norton was in the beaten Hull teams of 1980, 1983 and 1985 in addition to playing in the 1982 drawn final. In 1970 he was a non-playing substitute for Castleford, who won the Cup.

Crooks was in the beaten Hull sides of 1983 and 1985 plus the drawn final of 1982. He was then in Castleford's beaten 1992 team.

Norton and Crooks both won winners' medals in the 1982 replay.

Bill Ramsey was on the losing side in four Wembley finals but gained a winners' medal with Leeds in 1968. He picked up losers' medals with Hunslet (1965), Leeds (1971 and 1972) and Widnes (1977).

ELEVEN of last season's clubs have never appeared at Wembley. They are: Batley, Bramley, Carlisle, Doncaster, Highfield, London Crusaders, Oldham, Rochdale Hornets, Sheffield Eagles, Swinton and Whitehaven.

Fate seems to be against Swinton and Oldham. In the five years preceding the move to Wembley, one or the other appeared in the final, twice meeting each other. Oldham played in four successive finals in that period. Swinton's run of three finals ended when the first Wembley took place in 1929. They got through to the final three years later ...only for it to be played at Wigan!

WEMBLEY ERA SEMI-FINALS

It is generally felt that it is better to have played at Wembley and lost than never to have played there at all. This makes the semi-final stage of the RL Challenge Cup almost as important as the final, with no consolation for the losers.

Of the 14 current clubs who have never appeared at Wembley, four have been beaten semi-finalists. They are Oldham (six times), Rochdale Hornets (twice), Swinton and Whitehaven.

Probably the unluckiest are Oldham. They have reached the penultimate stage six times without being able to realise their ambition. Oldham almost made it in 1964. After drawing 5-5 with Hull K.R., they were winning 17-14 in extra time of the replay when bad light stopped play and they were beaten in the third game.

Swinton did win a semi-final in 1932 but the final that year was switched from Wembley to Wigan!

There have been three occasions when Yorkshire has provided all four semi-finalists in one year — in 1962, 1973 and 1983. Four times have all four semi-finalists come from west of the Pennines — in 1930, 1989, 1990 and 1991.

Until 1962 the two semi-finals were always played on the same Saturday, but with four Yorkshire clubs competing for the first time it was decided to play one midweek. Both matches were played at Odsal Stadium, Bradford. The first was on a Wednesday evening — without floodlights — when 43,625 saw Wakefield Trinity beat Featherstone Rovers and on the following Saturday there were 31,423 to see Huddersfield beat Hull K.R.

The following year both semi-finals were again played on the same Saturday, but since then they have been staged on different Saturdays.

Some semi-final facts during the Wembley era are:

Biggest attendance: 69,898 Warrington v. Leeds at Bradford in 1950

Biggest aggregate: 104,453 in 1939 (Only other six-figure aggregate was 102,080 in 1951)

Record receipts: £177,161 St. Helens v. Wigan at Old Trafford, Manchester in 1990

Lowest attendance: 7,971 Featherstone R. v. Leigh at Leeds in 1974

Highest score and widest margin: Wigan 71 v. Bradford N. 10 in 1992

CHALLENGE CUP SEMI-FINALS

Year	Winners		Runners-up		Venue	Attendance	Receipts
1929	Dewsbury	9	Castleford	3	Huddersfield	25,000	£1,562
	Wigan	7	St. Helens Recs.	7	Swinton	31,000	£2,209
Replay	Wigan	13	St. Helens Recs.	12	Leigh	21,940	£1,437
1930	Widnes	10	Barrow	3	Warrington	25,500	£1,630
	St. Helens	5	Wigan	5	Swinton	37,169	£2,666
Replay	St. Helens	22	Wigan	10	Leigh	24,000	£1,657
1931	Halifax	11	St. Helens	2	Rochdale	21,674	£1,498
	York	15	Warrington	5	Leeds	32,419	£2,329
1932*	Leeds	2	Halifax	2	Huddersfield	31,818	£2,456
Replay	Leeds	9	Halifax	2	Wakefield	21,000	£1,417
	Swinton	7	Wakefield T.	4	Rochdale	21,273	£1,369
* Final was played at Wigan, not Wembley							
1933	Huddersfield	30	Leeds	8	Wakefield	36,359	£2,299
	Warrington	11	St. Helens	5	Swinton	30,373	£2,055
1934	Hunslet	12	Huddersfield	7	Wakefield	27,450	£1,797
	Widnes	7	Oldham	4	Swinton	17,577	£1,050

Year	Winners		Runners-up		Venue	Attendance	Receipts
1935	Castleford	11	Barrow	5	Swinton	24,469	£1,534
	Huddersfield	21	Hull	5	Leeds	37,111	£2,753
1936	Leeds	10	Huddersfield	5	Wakefield	37,906	£2,456
	Warrington	7	Salford	2	Wigan	41,538	£2,796
1937	Keighley	0	Wakefield T.	0	Leeds	39,998	£2,793
Replay	Keighley	5	Wakefield T.	3	Huddersfield	14,400	£1,052
	Widnes	13	Wigan	9	Warrington	29,260	£1,972
1938	Barrow	4	Halifax	2	Huddersfield	31,384	£2,431
	Salford	6	Swinton	0	Belle Vue, Manchester	31,664	£2,396
1939	Halifax	10	Leeds	4	Bradford	64,453	£3,645
	Salford	11	Wigan	2	Rochdale	40,000	£2,154

● *During the war the semi-finals were two-legged and the finals were not played at Wembley*

Year	Winners		Runners-up		Venue	Attendance	Receipts
1946	Wakefield T.	7	Hunslet	3	Leeds	33,000	£4,991
	Wigan	12	Widnes	5	Swinton	36,976	£4,746
1947	Bradford N.	11	Warrington	7	Swinton	33,474	£4,946
	Leeds	21	Wakefield T.	0	Huddersfield	35,136	£6,339
1948	Bradford N.	14	Hunslet	7	Leeds	38,125	£7,437
	Wigan	11	Rochdale H.	0	Swinton	26,004	£4,206
1949	Bradford N.	10	Barrow	0	Swinton	26,572	£4,646
	Halifax	11	Huddersfield	10	Bradford	61,875	£8,638
1950	Warrington	16	Leeds	4	Bradford	69,898	£9,861
	Widnes	8	Bradford N.	0	Wigan	25,390	£3,936
1951	Barrow	14	Leeds	14	Bradford	57,459	£8,248
Replay	Barrow	28	Leeds	13	Huddersfield	31,078	£5,098
	Wigan	3	Warrington	2	Swinton	44,621	£7,358
1952	Featherstone R.	6	Leigh	2	Leeds	35,621	£6,494
	Workington T.	5	Barrow	2	Wigan	31,206	£4,782
1953	Huddersfield	7	Wigan	0	Bradford	58,722	£10,519
	St. Helens	9	Warrington	3	Swinton	38,059	£7,768
1954	Halifax	18	Hunslet	3	Bradford	46,961	£8,243
	Warrington	8	Leeds	4	Swinton	36,993	£7,596
1955	Barrow	9	Hunslet	6	Wigan	25,493	£4,671
	Workington T.	13	Featherstone R.	2	Leeds	33,499	£7,305
1956	Halifax	11	Wigan	10	Bradford	51,889	£9,054
	St. Helens	5	Barrow	5	Swinton	38,897	£7,793
Replay	St. Helens	10	Barrow	5	Wigan	44,731	£7,750
1957	Barrow	2	Leigh	2	Wigan	34,628	£6,340
Replay	Barrow	15	Leigh	10	Swinton	28,081	£5,695
	Leeds	10	Whitehaven	9	Bradford	49,094	£8,987
1958	Wigan	5	Rochdale H.	3	Swinton	28,597	£6,354
	Workington T.	8	Featherstone R.	2	Bradford	31,517	£6,325
1959	Wigan	5	Leigh	0	Swinton	27,906	£6,068
	Hull	15	Featherstone R.	5	Bradford	52,131	£9,776
1960	Wakefield T.	11	Featherstone R.	2	Bradford	55,935	£10,390
	Hull	12	Oldham	9	Swinton	27,545	£6,093
1961	St. Helens	26	Hull	9	Bradford	42,935	£9,231
	Wigan	19	Halifax	10	Swinton	35,118	£7,557
1962	Wakefield T.	9	Featherstone R.	0	Bradford	43,625	£8,496
	Huddersfield	6	Hull K.R.	0	Bradford	31,423	£6,685

Year	Winners		Runners-up		Venue	Attendance	Receipts
1963	Wakefield T.	5	Warrington	2	Swinton	15,565	£3,530
	Wigan	18	Hull K.R.	4	Leeds	21,420	£6,029
1964	Widnes	7	Castleford	7	Swinton	25,603	£5,541
Replay	Widnes	7	Castleford	5	Wakefield	28,739	£5,313
	Hull K.R.	5	Oldham	5	Leeds	28,823	£7,411
Replay	Hull K.R.	14	Oldham	17	Swinton	27,209	£5,929

● *Score after 80 minutes was 14-14, then bad light caused match to be abandoned after 12 minutes of extra time with Oldham winning 17-14*

Year	Winners		Runners-up		Venue	Attendance	Receipts
Second Replay	Hull K.R.	12	Oldham	2	Huddersfield	28,732	£6,183
1965	Wigan	25	Swinton	10	St. Helens	26,658	£6,384
	Hunslet	8	Wakefield T.	0	Leeds	21,262	£6,090
1966	St. Helens	12	Dewsbury	5	Swinton	13,046	£3,102
	Wigan	7	Leeds	2	Huddersfield	22,758	£5,971
1967	Featherstone R.	16	Leeds	8	Huddersfield	20,052	£6,276
	Barrow	14	Dewsbury	9	Swinton	13,744	£4,560
1968	Leeds	25	Wigan	4	Swinton	30,058	£9,845
	Wakefield T.	0	Huddersfield	0	Bradford	21,569	£6,196
Replay	Wakefield T.	15	Huddersfield	10	Leeds	20,983	£6,425
1969	Castleford	16	Wakefield T.	10	Leeds	21,497	£8,477
	Salford	15	Warrington	8	Wigan	20,600	£7,738
1970	Castleford	6	St. Helens	3	Swinton	18,913	£7,171
	Wigan	19	Hull K.R.	8	Leeds	18,495	£7,862
1971	Leeds	19	Castleford	8	Bradford	24,464	£9,120
	Leigh	10	Huddersfield	4	Wigan	14,875	£5,670
1972	St. Helens	10	Warrington	10	Wigan	19,300	£8,250
Replay	St. Helens	10	Warrington	6	Wigan	32,380	£12,604
	Leeds	16	Halifax	3	Bradford	16,680	£6,851
1973	Featherstone R.	17	Castleford	3	Leeds	15,369	£9,454
	Bradford N.	23	Dewsbury	7	Leeds	14,028	£9,221
1974	Warrington	17	Dewsbury	7	Wigan	11,789	£6,821
	Featherstone R.	21	Leigh	14	Leeds	7,971	£4,461
1975	Widnes	13	Wakefield T.	7	Bradford	9,155	£5,856
	Warrington	11	Leeds	4	Wigan	13,168	£9,581
1976	Widnes	15	Featherstone R.	9	Swinton	13,019	£9,078
	St. Helens	5	Keighley	4	Huddersfield	9,829	£6,113
1977	Leeds	7	St. Helens	2	Wigan	12,974	£11,379
	Widnes	14	Hull K.R.	5	Leeds	17,053	£16,068
1978	Leeds	14	Featherstone R.	9	Bradford	12,824	£11,322
	St. Helens	12	Warrington	8	Wigan	16,167	£13,960
1979	Widnes	14	Bradford N.	11	Swinton	14,324	£16,363
	Wakefield T.	9	St. Helens	7	Leeds	12,393	£14,195
1980	Hull K.R.	20	Halifax	7	Leeds	17,910	£31,650
	Hull	10	Widnes	5	Swinton	18,347	£29,415
1981	Widnes	17	Warrington	9	Wigan	12,624	£20,673
	Hull K.R.	22	St. Helens	5	Leeds	17,073	£30,616
1982	Hull	15	Castleford	11	Leeds	21,207	£41,867
	Widnes	11	Leeds	8	Swinton	13,075	£25,796
1983	Featherstone R.	11	Bradford N.	6	Leeds	10,784	£22,579
	Hull	14	Castleford	7	Elland Rd, L'ds	26,031	£65,498
1984	Wigan	14	York	8	Elland Rd, L'ds	17,156	£52,888
	Widnes	15	Leeds	4	Swinton	14,046	£37,183

Year	Winners		Runners-up		Venue	Attendance	Receipts
1985	Wigan	18	Hull K.R.	11	Elland Rd, L'ds	19,275	£70,192
	Hull	10	Castleford	10	Leeds	20,982	£64,163
Replay	Hull	22	Castleford	16	Leeds	20,968	£65,005
1986	Castleford	18	Oldham	7	Wigan	12,430	£38,296
	Hull K.R.	24	Leeds	24	Elland Rd, L'ds	23,866	£83,757
Replay	Hull K.R.	17	Leeds	0	Elland Rd, L'ds	32,485	£113,345
1987	St. Helens	14	Leigh	8	Wigan	13,105	£48,627
	Halifax	12	Widnes	8	Leeds	16,064	£61,260
1988	Wigan	34	Salford	4	Bolton W. FC	20,783	£95,876
	Halifax	0	Hull	0	Leeds	20,534	£82,026
Replay	Halifax	4	Hull	3	Elland Rd, L'ds	25,117	£113,679
1989	St. Helens	16	Widnes	14	Wigan	17,119	£70,411
	Wigan	13	Warrington	6	Man. C. FC	26,529	£144,056
1990	Wigan	20	St. Helens	14	Man. U. FC	26,489	£177,161
	Warrington	10	Oldham	6	Wigan	15,631	£80,500
1991	Wigan	30	Oldham	16	Bolton W. FC	19,057	£116,937
	St. Helens	19	Widnes	2	Wigan	16,109	£81,342
1992	Castleford	8	Hull	4	Leeds	14,636	£91,225
	Wigan	71	Bradford N.	10	Bolton W. FC	18,027	£131,124
1993	Widnes	39	Leeds	4	Wigan	13,823	£83,914
	Wigan	15	Bradford N.	6	Elland Rd, L'ds	20,085	£150,167
1994	Wigan	20	Castleford	6	Leeds	17,049	£115,842
	Leeds	20	St. Helens	8	Wigan	20,771	£135,722

NON-LEAGUE CLUBS IN THE CHALLENGE CUP

AMATEUR clubs were invited to compete in the 1986 Rugby League Challenge Cup after a five-year break. The League asked for two of the three county cup competition winners to enter the preliminary round.

The League later decided that from 1987 the Silk Cut Challenge Cup campaign would feature 38 teams, amateur clubs joining the professionals for a preliminary round of six ties. But amateur clubs were not invited to enter the 1993 tournament due to a prolonged dispute between the League and BARLA.

In 1993-94 the competition was expanded with the first round consisting of 64 amateur clubs, half of them from the National Conference League who had home advantage against the rest. The second round was also restricted to amateur clubs but with a random draw. Those 16 winners played away to Division Two professional opposition in the third round, before the Division One clubs entered in the fourth round.

In the early years of the Northern Union Challenge Cup — as it was then called — the line between professional and amateur was less clearly defined.

A variety of Leagues also make it difficult to set non-League clubs apart. Fifty-six clubs appeared in the inaugurating first round of 1897 and four others received byes. The complications continued until 1904 when the League format settled down and non-League clubs had to qualify for the first round.

Not since 1909 when BEVERLEY beat Ebbw Vale 7-2 has a senior team been knocked out by a non-League club although amateur teams twice had victories in the two-leg era of 1946-54.

NON-LEAGUE CLUB VICTORIES OVER SENIOR CLUBS SINCE 1904

(Excluding preliminary rounds before 1908)
Non-League Clubs in Capitals

1905-06
*FEATHERSTONE ROVERS 23 v. Widnes 2
(second round)

1907-08
WHITEHAVEN RECREATION 13 v. St. Helens 8
(Lost 33-5 at Merthyr Tydfil in second round)

1908-09
BEVERLEY 7 v. Ebbw Vale 2
(Lost 53-2 at Halifax in second round)

1945-46
SHARLSTON 12 v. Workington Town 7
(1st leg) (Workington Town won 2nd leg 16-2)

1947-48
RISEHOW AND GILLHEAD 10 v. Keighley 2 (2nd leg)
(Keighley won 1st leg 11-0)

*FEATHERSTONE ROVERS are the only non-League club to appear in the old third round when they lost 3-0 at Keighley. In the first round they beat BROOKLAND ROVERS 16-5.

There have been seven drawn clashes, with the professional club winning through each time. The last draw was in 1986-87 when KELLS drew 4-4 with Fulham at Whitehaven. Fulham won the replay 22-14 at Chiswick.

CHALLENGE CUP PROGRESS CHART

A 20-year review . . . .

Key: W — Winners. F — Beaten finalists. SF — Semi-final. P — Preliminary round.

	1993-94*	1992-93	1991-92	1990-91	1989-90	1988-89	1987-88	1986-87	1985-86	1984-85	1983-84	1982-83	1981-82	1980-81	1979-80	1978-79	1977-78	1976-77	1975-76	1974-75
BARROW	4	1	2	2	1	2	1	2	2	P	1	2	2	1	2	3	1	2	1	1
BATLEY	4	2	1	1	1	1	1	1	1	1	1	1	2	1	1	1	1	1	1	1
BLACKPOOL G.	1	P	1	1	2	2	2	1	2	1	1	1	1	1	1	1	1	1	1	1
BRADFORD N.	6	SF	SF	3	3	2	1	2	3	3	3	SF	3	1	3	SF	3	3	2	3
BRAMLEY	4	1	P	1	1	P	P	1	2	3	1	1	1	1	1	2	1	1	1	1
CARLISLE	4	1	P	P	1	2	1	2	1	1	P	1	1							
CASTLEFORD	SF	3	F	1	P	2	1	1	W	SF	3	SF	SF	2	2	3	3	3	1	1
CHORLEY B.	2	1	P	1	1															
DEWSBURY	4	1	2	1	2	1	1	1	1	1	1	1	2	1	2	1	3	1	1	
DONCASTER	6	1	2	1	P	1	3	1	2	P	2	1	1	1	1	1	1	1	2	1
FEATHERSTONE R.	6	1	3	1	1	3	2	1	1	P	1	W	P	3	1	1	SF	2	SF	1
HALIFAX	4	3	3	3	1	1	F	W	1	2	1	2	3	2	SF	1	1	1	1	1
HIGHFIELD	4	1	1	1	1	1	1	1	1	2	1	2	1	1	1	1	1	1	1	
HUDDERSFIELD	4	2	P	P	P	1	P	1	1	1	2	1	2	3	3	1	1	1		
HULL	5	P	SF	P	2	1	SF	3	1	F	2	F	W	2	F	3	2	2	1	2
HULL K.R.	5	3	1	1	1	3	3	3	F	SF	3	1	2	F	W	2	1	SF	2	3
HUNSLET	4	2	2	1	1	P	1	2	1	3	2	3	1	1	1	1	2	1	2	3
KEIGHLEY C.	5	2	1	2	2	2	2	2	1	1	1	1	2	1	2	1	1	1	SF	1
LEEDS	F	SF	2	2	P	3	2	3	SF	1	SF	2	SF	1	2	1	W	W	3	SF
LEIGH	4	1	1	1	1	1	1	SF	3	2	1	1	3	2	1	2	1	1	3	2
LONDON C.	4	1	2	1	2	1	1	1	1	1	2	2	2	1						
NOTTINGHAM C.	1	1	P	1	1	1	2	2	P	1										
OLDHAM	5	3	1	SF	SF	3	1	2	SF	1	2	1	2	3	2	2	2	1	3	3
ROCHDALE H.	4	2	1	2	2	1	2	1	2	2	1	1	2	1	2	2	1	2	1	2
RYEDALE-YORK	4	1	1	1	1	1	1	P	2	1	SF	1	1	2	2	1	1	1	2	2
ST. HELENS	SF	2	3	F	SF	F	3	F	2	1	3	3	1	SF	2	SF	F	SF	W	2
SALFORD	4	1	1	3	2	1	SF	1	1	2	1	2	1	3	3	1	2	2	2	2
SHEFFIELD E.	5	2	2	2	2	2	2	1	1											
SWINTON	4	P	1	1	1	1	1	P	P	1	P	2	1	1	1	1	2	2	1	1
WAKEFIELD T.	4	2	1	2	3	2	1	2	1	2	2	2	3	3	3	F	2	2	1	SF
WARRINGTON	5	1	2	3	F	SF	2	1	2	2	2	3	1	SF	3	1	SF	1	3	F
WHITEHAVEN	5	1	1	2	3	1	P	3	1	1	1	1	1	1	1	1	1	1	1	1
WIDNES	6	F	1	SF	3	SF	3	SF	3	3	W	1	F	W	SF	W	3	F	F	W
WIGAN	W	W	W	W	W	W	W	1	3	W	F	1	2	1	1	2	2	2	2	2
WORKINGTON T.	5	1	3	2	1	P	1	P	1	2	2	3	2	2	1	1	2	3	2	2

* Second Division clubs entered the new-style tournament in the third round, First Division clubs being exempt until the fourth round, there being six rounds before the semi-finals.

REGAL TROPHY

1993-94 Final

Underdogs Castleford — given an eight-point start on the bookmakers' handicap coupons — turned the tables to give mighty Wigan their biggest thrashing in 87 major finals.

The Tigers roared to a 33-2 Regal Trophy success, their second in two finals in the 23-year history of the competition, rewriting the record books for the Imperial Tobacco-sponsored final:

★ Highest score and widest margin
★ Record points haul by skipper Lee Crooks with 16 from a try and six goals
★ Equalling of the goals record by Crooks

Never were such hot favourites been beaten so comprehensively in a big match as the champions drowned under wave after wave of Castleford attacks in a vastly entertaining Headingley final.

But just as impressive was Castleford's defence, which prevented Wigan's much-vaunted attack from scoring even one try. That gave Castleford coach John Joyner, in his debut campaign, as much satisfaction as the record score, stressing the point that all-out attacking rugby can be balanced by a tight defence.

Joyner asked each player to write his objectives on a card above his dressing room peg in a bid to focus aims and intentions. That single-minded approach produced a fervour bordering on fanaticism.

Such was Castleford's dominance by combining individual brilliance with balanced teamwork that the selection of the Regal Man of the Match award was always going to be finely judged. As the game entered the final 10 minutes there were two outstanding candidates, the pair of Castleford props, Crooks and Martin Ketteridge.

The latter was announced as the winner just as he sat on the substitutes' bench to a great ovation after perhaps the best 74 minutes of his 11-year career. It included two tries, a big

tackle count and a succession of forward charges as he dominated Wigan skipper Andy Platt, generally reckoned to be the world's best prop.

But Crooks then scored the fifth and final try of an absorbing afternoon, adding the goal to establish a new points record and equalling the goals record. The consensus in the press box was that a delay of the Man of the Match voting until the final whistle would have given the Castleford captain the individual honour.

Crooks not only fulfilled the aims outlined on his dressing room card, but wrote his own testimonial for a return to the Great Britain ranks. He slipped out world-class passes to spark off numerous attacks, drove in hard and relentlessly, tackled non-stop, kicked six goals from six attempts and blasted through from 20 metres for his touchdown.

Crooks was one of many Castleford performers who outplayed his opposite number.

Mike Ford pushed himself into the spotlight for a full Test appearance, after two substitute roles, by overshadowing incumbent scrum half Shaun Edwards. The ex-Wiganer was involved in all the moves that brought his side's five tries, including the high kick that Ketteridge touched down and the astute pass which sent Crooks pounding through to the try line.

Simon Middleton beat Test winger Jason Robinson at his own game of coming inside for defence-relieving runs down the middle. Fellow winger St. John Ellis made up for not adding to his season's tally of 23 tries by blotting out Martin Offiah, who failed to score for the first time in 12 club and representative appearances during the current campaign.

Castleford hooker Richard Russell sneaked more yards than Martin Dermott; Grant Anderson edged Gary Connolly in the centre; while Ian Smales was more prominent than any of Wigan's international back row forwards.

Only full back Joe Lydon could claim any Wigan satisfaction from the afternoon, his keen anticipation and timing twice foiling Castleford breakaways and preventing an even greater destruction.

REGAL TROPHY FINAL

22 January   **Leeds**

CASTLEFORD 33   **WIGAN   2**

Castleford	No.	Wigan
Graham Steadman	1.	Joe Lydon
St. John Ellis	2.	Jason Robinson
Richard Blackmore	3.	Barrie-Jon Mather
Grant Anderson	4.	Gary Connolly
Simon Middleton	5.	Martin Offiah
Tony Kemp	6.	Frano Botica
Mike Ford	7.	Shaun Edwards
Lee Crooks, Capt.	8.	Kelvin Skerrett
Richard Russell	9.	Martin Dermott
Martin Ketteridge	10.	Andy Platt, Capt.
Tony Morrison	11.	Neil Cowie
Ian Smales	12.	Andrew Farrell
Tawera Nikau	13.	Phil Clarke
Andy Hay	14.	Sam Panapa
Dean Sampson	15.	Mick Cassidy

T: Ketteridge (2), Nikau,
Anderson, Crooks
G: Crooks (6), Kemp (dg)
Substitutions:
Hay for Anderson (63 min.)
Sampson for Ketteridge (74 min.)
Attendance: 15,626

G: Botica
Substitutions:
Cassidy for Cowie (30 min.)
Panapa for Edwards (51 min.)
Half-time: 20-2
Referee: David Campbell (Widnes)

Dressing-room celebrations for 1993-94 Regal Trophy victors Castleford.

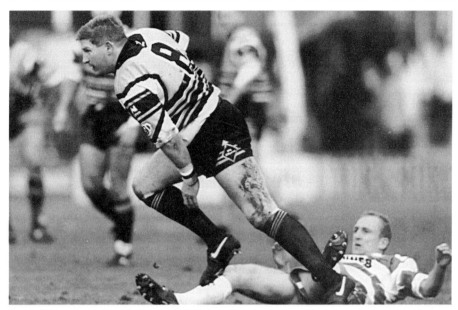

Castleford skipper Lee Crooks evades Wigan scrum half Shaun Edwards en route to a Regal Trophy final record-equalling 16-point tally.

Coach John Joyner shows off his first trophy in his debut season, Castleford having won the 1993-94 Regal Trophy by a record score.

1993-94 Round by Round

A new-look Regal Trophy format encompassed the first-ever seeding for First Division clubs, the second successive appearance of top French sides and the largest-ever presence of amateur teams in a new-style first round which rid the competition of the disliked preliminary round.

In the first round, the 16 Second Division clubs were given a guaranteed home draw against a variety of non-League sides. The two French qualifiers were Carcassonne and St. Esteve. The three clubs demoted from the previous season's now defunct Third Division — Blackpool Gladiators, Chorley Borough and Nottingham City — plus fellow National Conference League entrant Hemel Hempstead, formerly competing in the Younger's Alliance, all qualified for the cup. The remaining 10 first round competitors were submitted by BARLA in the shape of the five 1992-93 regional champions, Ellenborough (Cumbria), Mysons (Humberside), Irlam Hornets (North West Counties), West Bowling (Pennine) and Queens (Yorkshire), and the top five in last season's National League, Saddleworth, Egremont, Wigan St. Patricks, Woolston and Leigh Miners.

All the Second Division sides won through, though four were made to battle for victory. Bramley beat Woolston 17-8, Carlisle toppled Carcassonne 36-24, Highfield defeated Ellenborough 30-22 while Swinton disposed of Saddleworth 24-13. In contrast, eight professional sides topped the 50-mark, Rochdale Hornets running in 80 against Blackpool Gladiators and Workington Town 74 points past Wigan St. Patricks.

Second Division Batley, Carlisle and London were the giant-killers of the second round, the 16 Stones Bitter Championship clubs having entered the random draw. Batley's Australian scrum half Glen Tomlinson scored their two tries in an 8-6 victory over First Division Sheffield Eagles in the clinging mud at Mount Pleasant. Up in Cumbria, Wakefield Trinity had skipper David Woods sent off after only eight minutes, Carlisle leading 20-0 on the half hour en route to a commanding 28-12 success. First Division Featherstone Rovers travelled to London Crusaders to be knocked out by 26-12, two late tries by Mark Johnson in the 74th minute, and Abi Ekoku four minutes later, sealing their fate.

In the televised tie, Salford entertained Leeds, with two forgotten men being the heroes in a 21-12 victory. Recalled hooker Mark Lee scored two tries, with scrum half Shaun Brown celebrating his first appearance of the season with an outstanding performance. Championship title pacesetters Bradford Northern scored five tries to two in a 28-8 success at Barrow, while Dewsbury paid the price for two defensive errors in the first half to trail 18-2 at the break before going down 20-6 at home to St. Helens.

Having failed to postpone the tie because of an outbreak of flu, Second Division promotion favourites Keighley Cougars almost pulled off a shock victory at arch-rivals Halifax, losing 19-10 after running out of steam. Lowly Highfield stemmed the tide in the second half of their home tie with Oldham, who led 26-0 at half-time before the bottom club in the league pulled back to 26-8. Test full back Graham Steadman was Castleford's villain turned hero in their 16-12 victory at Hull K.R., making up for spilling a high kick which allowed Paul Fletcher to touch down by putting in a long kick three minutes from time with the scores level at 12-12, and sprinting through to claim the winning try. Leigh's first victory of the season, sealed with second-half tries from Paul Rowley and Gareth Pratt, was the first defeat inflicted on Second Division leaders Huddersfield, who went down 20-12 at Hilton Park.

A drop goal by Dean Blankley 15 minutes from time gave Bramley their first victory of the season with an 11-10 success at fellow Second Division Rochdale Hornets. In another one-point decider, Second Division promotion candidates Workington Town went out at

Ryedale-York, their 12-11 exit being sealed by a David Close drop goal with three minutes to go, the home side's only second-half score.

Hull's 36-14 victory at Swinton featured a try from ex-Swinton prop Tim Street, his first for the Airlie Birds since leaving Leigh a fortnight earlier. Teenagers Lee Penny and Iestyn Harris each scored a hat-trick of tries as Warrington disposed of Second Division Hunslet 58-16 at Wilderspool. Player-coach Kurt Sorensen inspired home-based Whitehaven to trail only 12-8 to the mighty Wigan early in the second half, having come back from a 12-0 interval deficit, Wigan's power opening up a 22-8 final scoreline. Doncaster failed to register a first-ever victory at Widnes, trailing 18-4 at the break but restricting the Chemics to only one further try in the second period to go down 24-4.

In the third round, Jonathan Davies dominated the televised tie as Warrington knocked out St. Helens by 16-8 at Knowsley Road. The Wales skipper scored four goals, made a vital try-saving tackle and set up Rob Myler's matchwinning try in a Man of the Match performance, Saints' half back Tommy Martyn being sent off for tripping, inevitably, Davies. In a West Yorkshire derby, Bradford Northern disposed of visitors Halifax, who trailed only 10-8 with three minutes left before Northern loose forward Karl Fairbank raced over for the clinching try. Second Division Batley were heading for a giant-killing triumph with an 8-0 lead over First Division Salford before the second-half entry of new signing Andy Gregory, who scored his first try for the club as the visitors mastered the Mount Pleasant quagmire to register a hard-earned 12-8 success. Hull beat Widnes 10-6 at a rainswept Boulevard, the foundation being laid by packmen Street and Daniel Divet although the scoring honours went to the Nolan brothers, Gary and Rob, who each touched down.

Holders Wigan overcame atrocious weather conditions and a robust Oldham side to record a 16-8 victory at the Watersheddings, Test winger Jason Robinson celebrating his return to the side after a seven-week injury absence with a try as Wigan ran up a 16-2 half-time lead. Multi-nation London Crusaders travelled to all-English Ryedale-York for a 42-10 success, Australian centre Scott Roskell scoring a hat-trick of tries and Man of the Match Steve Rosolen adding a try in the last minute. Castleford's 54-14 home hammering of lowly Leigh was highlighted by half their 10-try tally coming from the wingers, Simon Middleton registering a hat-trick and St. John Ellis contributing a brace. Carlisle reached the quarter-finals for the first time in their 12-year history with a 34-4 home defeat of Bramley, the Border Raiders' Scottish prop-cum-stand off George Graham scoring a hat-trick of tries, skipper Kevin Pape adding two more.

In the quarter-finals, ruthless Wigan served up a five-star display to dispose of heir apparents Warrington 27-10 at Wilderspool. Great Britain winger Robinson stole the limelight with two tries as Wigan allowed themselves the luxury of leaving Test duo Shaun Edwards and Martin Offiah on the substitutes' bench. Salford's meagre £10,000 investment in the recruitment of Leeds scrum half Gregory again paid rich dividends as he continued an unbeaten run in their colours, tormenting Hull in a fifth successive victory. Gregory scored two tries in a 26-6 demolition of the visitors. The two remaining Second Division sides were unable to pull off shock victories, Carlisle going down 44-4 at Castleford, who led only 14-0 at the interval before adding a further six tries as Carlisle wilted, while Bradford Northern won 22-10 at London Crusaders, ending the Second Division club's 10-match winning run, Northern's Test centre Paul Newlove contributing two tries.

In the semi-finals, Castleford and Wigan registered victories away from home to set up a final at Headingley, Leeds. Skipper Lee Crooks inspired Castleford to their first Regal Trophy final for 17 years, being a try creator as well as contributing three goals and a drop goal in a convincing 23-10 success, despite claims by Northern that he should have been sent off for a high challenge on Test centre Newlove. In the all-Lancashire clash, Wigan triumphed 18-12 at Salford to reach their fourth Trophy final in six years. But Salford came within millimetres of pulling off a shock victory with the scores level at 12-12 midway through the second half, a penalty attempt by Steve Blakeley and a drop goal effort by Gregory both hitting the woodwork, before Wigan centre Barrie-Jon Mather scored the clinching try in the final seconds.

1993-94 RESULTS

First Round

Barrow	54	Leigh M.W.	12
Batley	64	Queens	1
Bramley	17	Woolston R.	8
Carlisle	36	Carcassonne	24
Dewsbury	56	West Bowling	10
Doncaster	62	Mysons	4
Highfield	30	Ellenborough	22
Huddersfield	36	Irlam	8
Hunslet	30	Chorley B.	19
Keighley C.	72	Nottingham C.	12
London C.	48	St. Esteve	16
Rochdale H.	80	Blackpool G.	10
Ryedale-York	66	Hemel Hempstead	14
Swinton	24	Saddleworth R.	13
Whitehaven	46	Egremont	0
Workington T.	74	Wigan St. Patricks	6

Second Round

Barrow	8	Bradford N.	28
Batley	8	Sheffield E.	6
Carlisle	28	Wakefield T.	12
Dewsbury	6	St. Helens	20
Halifax	19	Keighley C.	10
Highfield	8	Oldham	26
Hull K.R.	12	Castleford	16
Leigh	20	Huddersfield	12
London C.	26	Featherstone R.	12
Rochdale H.	10	Bramley	11
Ryedale-York	12	Workington T.	11
Salford	21	Leeds	12
Swinton	14	Hull	36
Warrington	58	Hunslet	16
Whitehaven	8	Wigan	22
Widnes	24	Doncaster	4

Third Round

Batley	8	Salford	12
Bradford N.	16	Halifax	8
Carlisle	34	Bramley	4
Castleford	54	Leigh	14
Hull	10	Widnes	6
Oldham	8	Wigan	16
Ryedale-York	10	London C.	42
St. Helens	8	Warrington	16

Fourth Round

Castleford	44	Carlisle	4
London C.	10	Bradford N.	22
Salford	26	Hull	6
Warrington	10	Wigan	27

Semi-finals

Bradford N.	10	Castleford	23
Salford	12	Wigan	18

Final

Castleford	33	Wigan	2
(at Leeds)			

1993-94 PRIZES

First Round .... £2,650 to each RFL club and two French clubs
£1,000 to each amateur club
Second Round......................... £2,650 to losers
Third Round .... £4,000 to losers
Quarter-finals........................ £6,225 to losers
Semi-finals .... £9,750 to losers
Runners-up £18,500
Winners £35,000

Total Prize Money	£234,000
Capital Development Fund	£126,000
Grand Total	£360,000

REGAL TROPHY ROLL OF HONOUR

Season	Winners		Runners-up		Venue	Attendance	Receipts
1971-72	Halifax	22	Wakefield T.	11	Bradford	7,975	£2,545
1972-73	Leeds	12	Salford	7	Huddersfield	10,102	£4,563
1973-74	Warrington	27	Rochdale H.	16	Wigan	9,347	£4,380
1974-75	Bradford N.	3	Widnes	2	Warrington	5,935	£3,305
1975-76	Widnes	19	Hull	13	Leeds	9,035	£6,275
1976-77	Castleford	25	Blackpool B.	15	Salford	4,512	£2,919
1977-78	Warrington	9	Widnes	4	St. Helens	10,258	£8,429
1978-79	Widnes	16	Warrington	4	St. Helens	10,743	£11,709
1979-80	Bradford N.	6	Widnes	0	Leeds	9,909	£11,560
1980-81	Warrington	12	Barrow	5	Wigan	12,820	£21,020
1981-82	Hull	12	Hull K.R.	4	Leeds	25,245	£42,987
1982-83	Wigan	15	Leeds	4	Elland Rd, Leeds	19,553	£49,027
1983-84	Leeds	18	Widnes	10	Wigan	9,510	£19,824
1984-85	Hull K.R.	12	Hull	0	Hull City FC	25,326	£69,555
1985-86	Wigan	11	Hull K.R.	8	Elland Rd, Leeds	17,573	£66,714
1986-87	Wigan	18	Warrington	4	Bolton W. FC	21,144	£86,041
1987-88	St. Helens	15	Leeds	14	Wigan	16,669	£62,232
1988-89	Wigan	12	Widnes	6	Bolton W. FC	20,709	£94,874
1989-90	Wigan	24	Halifax	12	Leeds	17,810	£73,688
1990-91	Warrington	12	Bradford N.	2	Leeds	11,154	£57,652
1991-92	Widnes	24	Leeds	0	Wigan	15,070	£90,453
1992-93	Wigan	15	Bradford N.	8	Elland Rd, Leeds	13,221	£90,204
1993-94	Castleford	33	Wigan	2	Leeds	15,626	£99,804

REGAL TROPHY FINAL ....
A REVIEW
1971-72
Halifax 22 Hepworth; Rayner, Davies (1t),
Willicombe (1t), Kelly (1t); Burton (5g), Baker
(Sanderson); Dewhirst, Hawksley, Callon (1t)
(Reeves), Fogerty, Martin, Halmshaw
Wakefield T. 11 Wraith (Ward); Slater (1t),
Marston, Hegarty, Major; Topliss (1t), Harkin;
Jeanes, Morgan, Lyons, Harrison (Spencer),
Valentine (1t), N. Fox (1g)
Referee: S. Shepherd (Oldham)
1972-73
Leeds 12 Holmes (1g); Alan Smith, Hynes,
Dyl, Atkinson (2t); Hardisty, Hepworth;
Clawson (2g) (Ward), Fisher (Pickup), Jeanes,
Haigh, Cookson, Eccles
Salford 7 Charlton; Colloby, Watkins (2g),
Hesketh, Richards; Gill (P. Ward), Banner;
Ramshaw, J. Ward, Mackay, Grice (Davies),
Kirkbride, Dixon (1t)
Referee: W.H. Thompson (Huddersfield)

1973-74
Warrington 27 Whitehead (1t, 6g); M. Philbin,
Noonan (2t), Reynolds (Pickup), Bevan (1t);
Whittle, Gordon; D. Chisnall (Nicholas 1t),
Ashcroft, Brady, Wright, Wanbon, B. Philbin
Rochdale H. 16 Crellin; Brelsford (2t), Brophy
(1t), Taylor (1t), Aspinall; Butler (Wood),
Gartland; Holliday (2g), Harris, Whitehead,
Fogerty, Sheffield, Halmshaw
Referee: D.G. Kershaw (York)
1974-75
Bradford N. 3 Carlton (1t); Francis, Ward,
Gant, D. Redfearn; Blacker, Seabourne; Earl,
Jarvis, Jackson, Joyce, Trotter, Fearnley
Widnes 2 Dutton (1g); A. Prescott, D. O'Neill,
Aspey, Anderson; Hughes, Bowden; Mills,
Elwell, Sheridan, Adams, Blackwood,
Laughton
Referee: G.F. Lindop (Wakefield)

1975-76
Widnes 19 Dutton (3g); A. Prescott, George, Aspey, Jenkins (2t); Hughes, Bowden (1t, 1dg); Mills, Elwell, Wood, Foran, Sheridan, Adams (1t)
Hull 13 Stephenson; Macklin, Clark, Portz, Hunter (1t); Hancock, Foulkes (Davidson); Ramsey, Flanagan, Wardell, Boxall (2g), Walker, Crane (2t)
Referee: J.V. Moss (Manchester)
1976-77
Castleford 25 Wraith (1t); Fenton, Joyner (1t), P. Johnson (1t), Briggs; Burton (1t), Stephens (1t); Khan, Spurr, A. Dickinson, Reilly, Lloyd (5g), S. Norton
Blackpool B. 15 Reynolds; Robinson, Heritage, Machen (1t), Pitman (Lamb); Marsh, Newall; Hamilton, Allen (1t), Egan (1t, 3g), Gamble, Groves (Hurst), M. Pattinson
Referee: M.J. Naughton (Widnes)
1977-78
Warrington 9 Finnigan; Hesford (3g), Benyon, Wilson, Bevan (1t); K. Kelly, Gordon; Lester, Dalgreen, Nicholas, Martyn, B. Philbin, Potter
Widnes 4 Eckersley; S. Wright, Aspey, George, Woods (2g); Hughes, Bowden; Ramsey, Elwell, Shaw (Dearden), Adams, Hull, Laughton
Referee: W.H. Thompson (Huddersfield)
1978-79
Widnes 16 Eckersley; S. Wright (1t), Aspey, Hughes, Burke (3g); Moran, Bowden; Mills, Elwell (2dg), Shaw, Dearden, Hull (1t), Adams (2dg)
Warrington 4 Finnigan; M. Kelly, Hesford (2g), Benyon, Sutton; K. Kelly (Hunter), Gordon; Lester, Waller, Nicholas, Case, Martyn, A. Gwilliam
Referee: G.F. Lindop (Wakefield)
1979-80
Bradford N. 6 Mumby (1g); Barends, D. Redfearn, D. Parker (1t), Gant; Stephenson (1dg), A. Redfearn; Thompson, Bridges, Forsyth (I. Van Bellen), Grayshon, G. Van Bellen (Ferres), Casey
Widnes 0 Eckersley; S. Wright, Aspey, George, Burke; Hughes, Bowden; Hogan (Mills), Elwell, Shaw, L. Gorley, Hull, Adams
Referee: W.H. Thompson (Huddersfield)
1980-81
Warrington 12 Hesford (2g, 2dg); Thackray, I. Duane, Bevan (2t), M. Kelly; K. Kelly, A. Gwilliam; Courtney, Waller, Case, Martyn, Potter, Hunter (Eccles)
Barrow 5 Elliott; McConnell, French, Ball (1g), Wainwright; Mason (1t), Cairns; D. Chisnall, Allen (Szymala), Flynn, K. James, Kirkby, Hadley
Referee: W.H. Thompson (Huddersfield)

1981-82
Hull 12 Banks; O'Hara, Harrison, Leuluai, Prendiville; Day, Dean (1dg) (Harkin); Skerrett, Wileman (1t), Stone, Crane, L. Crooks (4g), Norton
Hull K.R. 4 Fairbairn (2g); Hubbard, M. Smith, Hogan, Muscroft; Hartley, Harkin (Burton); Holdstock (Millington), Watkinson, Crooks, Lowe, Casey, Hall
Referee: G.F. Lindop (Wakefield)
1982-83
Wigan 15 Williams; Ramsdale, Stephenson, Whitfield (4g, 1dg), Gill (Juliff 1t); Foy, Fairhurst; Shaw, Kiss, Campbell, West (Case), Scott, Pendlebury
Leeds 4 Hague; Campbell, Wilkinson, Dyl, Andy Smith; Holmes, Dick (2g); Dickinson, Ward, Burke, Sykes, W. Heron, D. Heron
Referee: R. Campbell (Widnes)
1983-84
Leeds 18 Wilkinson; Prendiville, Creasser (5g), Bell, Andy Smith; Holmes (1t), Dick (1t); Keith Rayne, Ward (Squire), Kevin Rayne, Moorby, Laurie, Webb
Widnes 10 Burke (1g); S. Wright, Keiron O'Loughlin, Lydon (1t), Linton (1t); Hughes, Gregory; S. O'Neill, Elwell, Tamati, L. Gorley, Whitfield, Adams
Referee: W.H. Thompson (Huddersfield)
1984-85
Hull K.R. 12 Fairbairn; Clark (1t), Robinson, Prohm (1t), Laws; M. Smith, Harkin; Broadhurst, Watkinson, Ema, Burton, Hogan (1t), Miller
Hull 0 Kemble (Schofield); S. Evans, Ah Kuoi, Leuluai, O'Hara; Topliss, Sterling; Edmonds (Dannatt), Patrick, Rose, L. Crooks, Proctor, Divorty
Referee: S. Wall (Leigh)
1985-86
Wigan 11 Hampson; Mordt, Stephenson (1g), Hanley, Gill (Edwards); Ella, M. Ford (1t); Dowling (1dg), Kiss, Wane (1t), West, Goodway, Potter (Du Toit)
Hull K.R. 8 Lydiat (1t); Clark, M. Smith, Dorahy, Laws (1t); G. Smith, Harkin; P. Johnston (Robinson), Watkinson, Ema, Burton, Kelly, Miller
Referee: J. Holdsworth (Kippax)
1986-87
Wigan 18 Hampson; Stephenson, Lydon, Bell (1t), Gill (2t, 1g); Hanley, Edwards; West, Dermott, Case, Roberts, Potter, Goodway (1t)
Warrington 4 Johnson; Meadows, Cullen, Ropati, Forster (1t); K. Kelly, Peters (R. Duane); Boyd, Tamati (Rathbone), Jackson, Sanderson, Roberts, M. Gregory
Referee: J. Holdsworth (Kippax)

1987-88
St. Helens 15 Veivers; Tanner, Loughlin
(2t, 3g), Elia, Quirk; Cooper, Holding (1dg);
Burke, Groves, Souto (Evans), Forber,
Haggerty, Platt
Leeds 14 Gurr; Morris, Schofield, Jackson (1t),
Basnett (Gibson); Creasser (1t, 3g), Ashton;
Tunks, Maskill, Kevin Rayne (Fairbank),
Powell, Medley, D. Heron
Referee: G.F. Lindop (Wakefield)
1988-89
Wigan 12 Hampson; Bell, K. Iro (1t), Lydon
(2g) (Gregory), T. Iro; Byrne, Edwards;
Shelford (Goodway), Dermott, Wane, Betts,
Potter, Hanley (1t)
Widnes 6 Tait; Thackray, Currier (1g), D. Wright
(1t), Offiah; A. Myler, D. Hulme; Sorensen,
McKenzie, Grima, M. O'Neill, Koloto
(P. Hulme), R. Eyres
Referee: J. Holdsworth (Kippax)
1989-90
Wigan 24 Lydon (2g); Marshall, K. Iro, Bell,
Preston; Edwards (1t), Gregory; Lucas (Wane),
Dermott, Platt, Betts, Gildart (Goodway 1t),
Hanley (3t)
Halifax 12 Whitfield (Smith) (Scott);
Riddlesden, T. Anderson, Hetherington, George;
Dorahy, Lyons; Hill (1t), McCallion, Johnston,
Bell, Milner, Holliday (4g)
Referee: D.G. Kershaw (Easingwold)

1990-91
Warrington 12 Lyon (4g); Drummond,
Bateman, Thorniley, Forster; O'Sullivan, Ellis;
Harmon (Phillips), Mann, Chambers
(Thomas 1t), Mercer, McGinty, Cullen
Bradford N. 2 Wilkinson; Cordle, Shelford,
Simpson, Marchant (Hellewell); Summers, Iti;
Hobbs (1g), Noble, Hamer, Medley, Croft,
Pendlebury
Referee: J. Smith (Halifax)
1991-92
Widnes 24 Tait (1t); Devereux, Currier,
D. Wright, Sarsfield (Atcheson); Davies (1t, 3g,
1dg), Dowd; Sorensen (1t), P. Hulme, D. Smith,
Howard, R. Eyres, Holliday (1t, 1dg) (Grima)
Leeds 0 Edwards; Ford, Creasser, Irving (Gibson),
Bentley; Schofield, Goulding; Wane (Molloy),
Gunn, O'Neill, Powell, Dixon, Divorty
Referee: B. Galtress (Bradford)
1992-93
Wigan 15 Hampson (1dg); Robinson (1t), Bell,
Farrar, Offiah (Lydon); Botica (3g), Edwards (1t);
Cowie, Dermott, Platt, Betts, McGinty,
Clarke (Panapa)
Bradford N. 8 Watson; Marchant, McGowan (1t),
Anderson (Mumby 1g), Simpson; Summers, Fox;
Hobbs (1g), Noble (Clark), R. Powell, Medley,
Fairbank, D. Heron
Referee: J. Holdsworth (Kippax)

REGAL TROPHY MAN OF THE MATCH

Season	Winner	Team	Position
1971-72	Bruce Burton	Halifax (v. Wakefield T.)	Stand off
1972-73	Keith Hepworth	Leeds (v. Salford)	Scrum half
1973-74	Kevin Ashcroft	Warrington (v. Rochdale H.)	Hooker
1974-75	Barry Seabourne	Bradford N. (v. Widnes)	Scrum half
1975-76	Reg Bowden	Widnes (v. Hull)	Scrum half
1976-77	Gary Stephens	Castleford	Scrum half
	Howard Allen	Blackpool B.	Hooker
1977-78	Steve Hesford	Warrington (v. Widnes)	Winger
1978-79	David Eckersley	Widnes (v. Warrington)	Full back
1979-80	Len Casey	Bradford N. (v. Widnes)	Loose forward
1980-81	Tommy Martyn	Warrington (v. Barrow)	Second row
1981-82	Trevor Skerrett	Hull (v. Hull K.R.)	Prop
1982-83	Martin Foy	Wigan (v. Leeds)	Stand off
1983-84	Mark Laurie	Leeds (v. Widnes)	Second row
1984-85	Paul Harkin	Hull K.R. (v. Hull)	Scrum half
1985-86	Paul Harkin	Hull K.R. (v. Wigan)	Scrum half
1986-87	Andy Goodway	Wigan (v. Warrington)	Loose forward
1987-88	Paul Loughlin	St. Helens (v. Leeds)	Centre
1988-89	Ellery Hanley	Wigan (v. Widnes)	Loose forward
1989-90	Ellery Hanley	Wigan (v. Halifax)	Loose forward

213

Season	Winner	Team	Position
1990-91	Billy McGinty	Warrington (v. Bradford N.)	Second row
1991-92	Les Holliday	Widnes (v. Leeds)	Loose forward
1992-93	Shaun Edwards	Wigan (v. Bradford N.)	Scrum half
1993-94	Martin Ketteridge	Castleford (v. Wigan)	Prop

REGAL TROPHY FINAL PLAYERS' REGISTER

The following is an index of players who have appeared in the Regal Trophy final since its inauguration as the Player's No. 6 Trophy in 1971-72.
W — winners, L — losers. Substitute appearances in lower case letters. The year denotes the second half of the season.

ADAMS, Mick: Widnes 75L, 76W, 78L, 79W, 80L, 84L
AH KUOI, Fred: Hull 85L
ALLEN, Howard: Blackpool B. 77L; Barrow 81L
ANDERSON, Chris: Widnes 75L
ANDERSON, Grant: Castleford 94W
ANDERSON, Tony: Halifax 90L; Bradford N. 93L
ASHCROFT, Kevin: Warrington 74W
ASHTON, Ray: Leeds 88L
ASPEY, Mal: Widnes 75L, 76W, 78L, 79W, 80L
ASPINALL, Willie: Rochdale H. 74L
ATCHESON, Paul: Widnes 92w
ATKINSON, John: Leeds 73W

BAKER, Gordon: Halifax 72W
BALL, Ian: Barrow 81L
BANKS, Barry: Hull 82W
BANNER, Peter: Salford 73L
BARENDS, David: Bradford N. 80W
BASNETT, John: Leeds 88L
BATEMAN, Allan: Warrington 91W
BELL, Dean: Leeds 84W; Wigan 87W, 89W, 90W, 93W
BELL, Peter: Halifax 90L
BENTLEY, John: Leeds 92L
BENYON, Billy: Warrington 78W, 79L
BETTS, Denis: Wigan 89W, 90W, 93W
BEVAN, John: Warrington 74W, 78W, 81W
BLACKER, Mick: Bradford N. 75W
BLACKMORE, Richard: Castleford 94W
BLACKWOOD, Bob: Widnes 75L
BOTICA, Frano: Wigan 93W, 94L
BOWDEN, Reg: Widnes 75L, 76W, 78L, 79W, 80L
BOXALL, Keith: Hull 76L
BOYD, Les: Warrington 87L
BRADY, Brian: Warrington 74W
BRELSFORD, Norman: Rochdale H. 74L
BRIDGES, John "Keith": Bradford N. 80W
BRIGGS, Trevor: Castleford 77W
BROADHURST, Mark: Hull K.R. 85W
BROPHY, Tom: Rochdale H. 74L
BURKE, Mick: Widnes 79W, 80L, 84L
BURKE, Tony: Leeds 83L; St. Helens 88W

BURTON, Bruce: Halifax 72W; Castleford 77W
BURTON, Chris: Hull K.R. 82l, 85W, 86L
BUTLER, John: Rochdale H. 74L
BYRNE, Ged: Wigan 89W

CAIRNS, David: Barrow 81L
CALLON, David: Halifax 72W
CAMPBELL, Danny: Wigan 83W
CAMPBELL, Mark: Leeds 83l
CARLTON, Stuart: Bradford N. 75W
CASE, Brian: Warrington 79L, 81W; Wigan 83w, 87W
CASEY, Len: Bradford N. 80W; Hull K.R. 82L
CASSIDY, Mick: Wigan 94l
CHAMBERS, Gary: Warrington 91W
CHARLTON, Paul: Salford 73L
CHISNALL, Dave: Warrington 74W; Barrow 81L
CLARK, Garry: Hull K.R. 85W, 86L
CLARK, George: Hull 76L
CLARK, Trevor: Bradford N. 93l
CLARKE, Phil: Wigan 93W, 94L
CLAWSON, Terry: Leeds 73W
COLLOBY, Tony: Salford 73L
CONNOLLY, Gary: Wigan 94L
COOKSON, Phil: Leeds 73W
COOPER, Shane: St. Helens 88W
CORDLE, Gerald: Bradford N. 91L
COURTNEY, Neil: Warrington 81W
COWIE, Neil: Wigan 93W, 94L
CRANE, Mick: Hull 76L, 82W
CREASSER, David: Leeds 84W, 88L, 92L
CRELLIN, Jim: Rochdale H. 74L
CROFT, David: Bradford N. 91L
CROOKS, Lee: Hull 82W, 85L; Castleford 94W
CROOKS, Steve: Hull K.R. 82L
CULLEN, Paul: Warrington 87L, 91W
CURRIER, Andy: Widnes 89L, 92W

DALGREEN, John: Warrington 78W
DANNATT, Andy: Hull 85l
DAVIDSON, Chris: Hull 76l
DAVIES, Doug: Salford 73l
DAVIES, Jonathan: Widnes 92W
DAVIES, Phil: Halifax 72W

DAY, Terry: Hull 82W
DEAN, Tony: Hull 82W
DEARDEN, Alan: Widnes 78l, 79W
DERMOTT, Martin: Wigan 87W, 89W, 90W, 93W, 94L
DEVEREUX, John: Widnes 92W
DEWHIRST, Terry: Halifax 72W
DICK, Kevin: Leeds 83L, 84W
DICKINSON, Alan: Castleford 77W
DICKINSON, Roy: Leeds 83L
DIVORTY, Gary: Hull 85L; Leeds 92L
DIXON, Colin: Salford 73L
DIXON, Paul: Leeds 92L
DORAHY, John: Hull K.R. 86L; Halifax 90L
DOWD, Barry: Widnes 92W
DOWLING, Greg: Wigan 86W
DRUMMOND, Des: Warrington 91W
DUANE, Ian: Warrington 81W
DUANE, Ronnie: Warrington 87L
DU TOIT, Nick: Wigan 86w
DUTTON, Ray: Widnes 75L, 76W
DYL, Les: Leeds 73W, 83L

EARL, Kelvin: Bradford N. 75W
ECCLES, Bob: Warrington 81w
ECCLES, Graham: Leeds 73W
ECKERSLEY, David: Widnes 78L 79W, 80L
EDMONDS, Phil: Hull 85L
EDWARDS, Morvin: Leeds 92L
EDWARDS, Shaun: Wigan 86W, 87W, 89W, 90W, 93W, 94L
EGAN, Joe: Blackpool B. 77L
ELIA, Mark: St. Helens 88W
ELLA, Steve: Wigan 86W
ELLIOTT, David: Barrow 81L
ELLIS, Kevin: Warrington 91W
ELLIS, St. John; Castleford 94W
ELWELL, Keith: Widnes 75L, 76W, 78L, 79W, 80L, 84L
EMA, Asuquo: Hull K.R. 85W, 86L
EVANS, Steve: Hull 85L
EVANS, Stuart: St. Helens 88w
EYRES, Richard: Widnes 89L, 92W

FAIRBAIRN, George: Hull K.R. 82L, 85W
FAIRBANK, John: Leeds 88l
FAIRBANK, Karl: Bradford N. 93L
FAIRHURST, Jimmy: Wigan 83W
FARRAR, Andrew: Wigan 93W
FARRELL, Andrew: Wigan 94L
FEARNLEY, Stan: Bradford N. 75W
FENTON, Steve: Castleford 77W
FERRES, Steve: Bradford N. 80w
FINNIGAN, Derek: Warrington 78W, 79L
FISHER, Tony: Leeds 73W
FLANAGAN, Peter: Hull 76L
FLYNN, Malcolm: Barrow 81L

FOGERTY, Terry: Halifax 72W; Rochdale H. 74L
FORAN, John: Widnes 76W
FORBER, Paul: St. Helens 88W
FORD, Mike: Wigan 86W; Castleford 94W
FORD, Phil: Leeds 92L
FORSTER, Mark: Warrington 87L, 91W
FORSYTH, Colin: Bradford N. 80W
FOULKES, Kenny: Hull 76L
FOX, Deryck: Bradford N. 93L
FOX, Neil: Wakefield T. 72L
FOY, Martin: Wigan 83W
FRANCIS, Rudi: Bradford N. 75W
FRENCH, Nigel: Barrow 81L

GAMBLE, Paul: Blackpool B. 77L
GANT, Les: Bradford N. 75W, 80W
GARTLAND, Peter: Rochdale H. 74L
GEORGE, Derek "Mick": Widnes 76W, 78L, 80L
GEORGE, Wilf: Halifax 90L
GIBSON, Carl: Leeds 88L, 92l
GILDART, Ian: Wigan 90W
GILL, Henderson: Wigan 83W, 86W, 87W
GILL, Ken: Salford 73L
GOODWAY, Andy: Wigan 86W, 87W, 89w, 90w
GORDON, Parry: Warrington 74W, 78W, 79L
GORLEY, Les: Widnes 80L, 84L
GOULDING, Bobby: Leeds 92L
GRAYSHON, Jeff: Bradford N. 80W
GREGORY, Andy: Widnes 84L; Wigan 89w, 90W
GREGORY, Mike: Warrington 87L
GRICE, Alan: Salford 73L
GRIMA, Joe: Widnes 89L, 92w
GROVES, Ken: Blackpool B. 77L
GROVES, Paul: St. Helens 88W
GUNN, Richard: Leeds 92L
GURR, Marty: Leeds 88L
GWILLIAM, Alan: Warrington 79L, 81W

HADLEY, Derek: Barrow 81L
HAGGERTY, Roy: St. Helens 88W
HAGUE, Neil: Leeds 83l
HAIGH, Bob: Leeds 73W
HALL, David: Hull K.R. 82L
HALMSHAW, Tony: Halifax 72W; Rochdale H. 74L
HAMER, Jon: Bradford N. 91L
HAMILTON, Jim: Blackpool B. 77L
HAMPSON, Steve: Wigan 86W, 87W, 89W, 93W
HANCOCK, Brian: Hull 76L
HANLEY, Ellery: Wigan 86W, 87W, 89W, 90W
HARDISTY, Alan: Leeds 73W
HARKIN, Kevin: Wakefield T. 72L; Hull 82w
HARKIN, Paul: Hull K.R. 82L, 85W, 86L
HARMON, Neil: Warrington 91W
HARRIS, Ray: Rochdale H. 74L
HARRISON, Chris: Hull 82W
HARRISON, Peter: Wakefield T. 72L

HARTLEY, Steve: Hull K.R. 82L
HAWKSLEY, Roy: Halifax 72W
HAY, Andy: Castleford 94w
HEGARTY, John: Wakefield T. 72L
HELLEWELL, Phil: Bradford N. 911
HEPWORTH, Keith: Leeds 73W
HEPWORTH, Tony: Halifax 72W
HERITAGE, John: Blackpool B. 77L
HERON, David: Leeds 83L, 88L; Bradford N. 93L
HERON, Wayne: Leeds 83L
HESFORD, Steve: Warrington 78W, 79L, 81W
HESKETH, Chris: Salford 73L
HETHERINGTON, Brian: Halifax 90L
HILL, Brendan: Halifax 90L
HOBBS, David: Bradford N. 91L, 93L
HOGAN, Brian: Widnes 80L
HOGAN, Phil: Hull K.R. 82L, 85W
HOLDING, Neil: St. Helens 88W
HOLDSTOCK, Roy: Hull K.R. 82L
HOLLIDAY, Bill: Rochdale H. 74L
HOLLIDAY, Les: Halifax 90L; Widnes 92W
HOLMES, John: Leeds 73W, 83L, 84W
HOWARD, Harvey: Widnes 92W
HUBBARD, Steve: Hull K.R. 82L
HUGHES, Eric: Widnes 75L, 76W, 78L, 79W,
    80L, 84L
HULL, David: Widnes 78L, 79W, 80L
HULME, David: Widnes 89L
HULME, Paul: Widnes 89l, 92W
HUNTER, Eddie: Warrington 79l, 81W
HUNTER, Paul: Hull 76L
HURST, Phil: Blackpool B. 77l
HYNES, Syd: Leeds 73W

IRO, Kevin: Wigan 89W, 90W
IRO, Tony: Wigan 89W
IRVING, Simon: Leeds 92L
ITI, Brett: Bradford N. 91L

JACKSON, Bob: Warrington 87L
JACKSON, Peter: Leeds 88L
JACKSON, Phil: Bradford N. 75W
JAMES, Kevin: Barrow 81L
JARVIS, Francis: Bradford N. 75W
JEANES, David: Wakefield T. 72L; Leeds 73W
JENKINS, David: Widnes 76W
JOHNSON, Brian: Warrington 87L
JOHNSON, Phil: Castleford 77W
JOHNSTON, Lindsay: Halifax 90L
JOHNSTON, Peter: Hull K.R. 86L
JOYCE, Graham: Bradford N. 75W
JOYNER, John: Castleford 77W
JULIFF, Brian: Wigan 83w

KAHN, Paul: Castleford 77W
KELLY, Andy: Hull K.R. 86L
KELLY, Ken: Warrington 78W, 79L, 81W, 87L

KELLY, Mike: Halifax 72W
KELLY, Mike: Warrington 79L, 81W
KEMBLE, Gary: Hull 85L
KEMP, Tony: Castleford 94W
KETTERIDGE, Martin: Castleford 94W
KIRKBRIDE, Bill: Salford 73L
KIRKBY, Steve: Barrow 81L
KISS, Nicky: Wigan 83W, 86W
KOLOTO, Emosi: Widnes 89L

LAMB, Cliff: Blackpool B. 77l
LAUGHTON, Doug: Widnes 75L, 78L
LAURIE, Mark: Leeds 84W
LAWS, David: Hull K.R. 85W, 86L
LESTER, Roy: Warrington 78W, 79L
LEULUAI, James: Hull 82W, 85L
LINTON, Ralph: Widnes 84L
LLOYD, Geoff "Sammy": Castleford 77W
LOUGHLIN, Paul: St. Helens 88W
LOWE, Phil: Hull K.R. 82L
LUCAS, Ian: Wigan 90W
LYDIAT, John: Hull K.R. 86L
LYDON, Joe: Widnes 84L; Wigan 87W, 89W,
    90W, 93w, 94L
LYON, David: Warrington 91W
LYONS, John: Halifax 90L
LYONS, Steve: Wakefield T. 72L

McCALLION, Seamus: Halifax 90L
McCONNELL, Ralph: Barrow 81L
McGINTY, Billy: Warrington 91W; Wigan 93W
McGOWAN, Steve: Bradford N. 93L
MACKAY, Graham: Salford 73L
McKENZIE, Phil: Widnes 89L
MACHEN, Paul: Blackpool B. 77L
MACKLIN, Alf: Hull 76L
MAJOR, Mick: Wakefield T. 72L
MANN, Duane: Warrington 91W
MARCHANT, Tony: Bradford N. 91L, 93L
MARSH, Ged: Blackpool B. 77L
MARSHALL, David: Wigan 90W
MARSTON, Jack: Wakefield T. 72L
MARTIN, John: Halifax 72W
MARTYN, Tommy: Warrington 78W, 79L, 81W
MASKILL, Colin: Leeds 88L
MASON, Mel: Barrow 81L
MATHER, Barrie-Jon: Wigan 94L
MEADOWS, Kevin: Warrington 87L
MEDLEY, Paul: Leeds 88L; Bradford N. 91L, 93L
MERCER, Gary: Warrington 91W
MIDDLETON, Simon: Castleford 94W
MILLER, Gavin: Hull K.R. 85W, 86L
MILLINGTON, John: Hull K.R. 821
MILLS, Jim: Widnes 75L, 76W, 79W, 80l
MILNER, Richard: Halifax 90L
MOLLOY, Steve: Leeds 92l
MOORBY, Gary: Leeds 84W

MORAN, Dave: Widnes 79W
MORDT, Ray: Wigan 86W
MORGAN, Mick: Wakefield T. 72L
MORRIS, Steve: Leeds 88L
MORRISON, Tony: Castleford 94W
MUMBY, Keith: Bradford N. 80W, 93l
MUSCROFT, Peter: Hull K.R. 82L
MYLER, Tony: Widnes 89L

NEWALL, Jackie: Blackpool B. 77L
NICHOLAS, Mike: Warrington 74w, 78W, 79L
NIKAU, Tawera: Castleford 94W
NOBLE, Brian: Bradford N. 91L, 93L
NOONAN, Derek: Warrington 74W
NORTON, Steve: Castleford 77W; Hull 82W

OFFIAH, Martin: Widnes 89L; Wigan 93W, 94L
O'HARA, Dane: Hull 82W, 85L
O'LOUGHLIN, Keiron: Widnes 84L
O'NEILL, Dennis: Widnes 75L
O'NEILL, Mike: Widnes 89L; Leeds 92L
O'NEILL, Steve: Widnes 84L
O'SULLIVAN, Chris: Warrington 91W

PANAPA, Sam: Wigan 93w, 94l
PARKER, Derek: Bradford N. 80W
PATRICK, Shaun: Hull 85L
PATTINSON, Malcolm: Blackpool B. 77L
PENDLEBURY, John: Wigan 83W;
    Bradford N. 91L
PETERS, Steve: Warrington 87L
PHILBIN, Barry: Warrington 74W, 78W
PHILBIN, Mike: Warrington 74W
PHILLIPS, Rowland: Warrington 91w
PICKUP, Bill: Warrington 74w
PICKUP, Fred: Leeds 73w
PITMAN, Phil: Blackpool B. 77L
PLATT, Andy: St. Helens 88W; Wigan 90W,
    93W, 94L
PORTZ, Steve: Hull 76L
POTTER, Ian: Warrington 78W, 81W;
    Wigan 86W, 87W, 89W
POWELL, Roy: Leeds 88L, 92L; Bradford N.
    93L
PRENDIVILLE, Paul: Hull 82W; Leeds 84W
PRESCOTT, Alan: Widnes 75L, 76W
PRESTON, Mark: Wigan 90W
PROCTOR, Wayne: Hull 85L
PROHM, Gary: Hull K.R. 85W

QUIRK, Les: St. Helens 88W

RAMSDALE, Denis: Wigan 83W
RAMSEY, Bill: Hull 76L; Widnes 78L
RAMSHAW, Terry: Salford 73L
RATHBONE, Alan: Warrington 87l
RAYNE, Keith: Leeds 84W

RAYNE, Kevin: Leeds 84W, 88L
RAYNER, David: Halifax 72W
REDFEARN, Alan: Bradford N. 80W
REDFEARN, David: Bradford N. 75W, 80W
REEVES, Derek: Halifax 72w
REILLY, Malcolm: Castleford 77W
REYNOLDS, Doug: Blackpool B. 77L
REYNOLDS, Frank: Warrington 74W
RICHARDS, Maurice: Salford 73L
RIDDLESDEN, Eddie: Halifax 90L
ROBERTS, Ian: Wigan 87W
ROBERTS, Mark: Warrington 87L
ROBINSON, Doug: Blackpool B. 77L
ROBINSON, Ian: Hull K.R. 85W, 86l
ROBINSON, Jason: Wigan 93W, 94L
ROPATI, Joe: Warrington 87L
ROSE, Paul: Hull 85L
RUSSELL, Richard: Castleford 94W

SAMPSON, Dean: Castleford 94w
SANDERSON, Gary: Warrington 87L
SANDERSON, John "Sammy": Halifax 72w
SARSFIELD, Mark: Widnes 92W
SCHOFIELD, Garry: Hull 85l; Leeds 88L, 92L
SCOTT, Mick: Wigan 83W; Halifax 90l
SEABOURNE, Barry: Bradford N. 75W
SHAW, Glyn: Widnes 78L, 79W, 80L; Wigan 83W
SHEFFIELD, Bill: Rochdale H. 74L
SHELFORD, Adrian: Wigan 89W
SHELFORD, Darrall: Bradford N. 91L
SHERIDAN, Barry: Widnes 75L, 76W
SIMPSON, Roger: Bradford N. 91L, 93L
SKERRETT, Kelvin: Wigan 94L
SKERRETT, Trevor: Hull 82W
SLATER, Keith: Wakefield T. 72L
SMALES, Ian: Castleford 94W
SMITH, Alan: Leeds 73W
SMITH, Andy: Leeds 83L, 84W
SMITH, David: Widnes 92W
SMITH, Gordon: Hull K.R. 86L
SMITH, Mike: Hull K.R. 82L, 85W, 86L
SMITH, Steve: Halifax 90l
SORENSEN, Kurt: Widnes 89L, 92W
SOUTO, Peter: St. Helens 88W
SPENCER, Ray: Wakefield T. 72l
SPURR, Bob: Castleford 77W
SQUIRE, Kevin: Leeds 84w
STEADMAN, Graham: Castleford 94W
STEPHENS, Gary: Castleford 77W
STEPHENSON, David: Wigan 83W, 86W, 87W
STEPHENSON, Mike: Hull 76L
STEPHENSON, Nigel: Bradford N. 80W
STERLING, Peter: Hull 85L
STONE, Richard "Charlie": Hull 82W
SUMMERS, Neil: Bradford N. 91L, 93L
SUTTON, Dave: Warrington 79L
SYKES, Andy: Leeds 83L
SZYMALA, Eddie: Barrow 81l

217

TAIT, Alan: Widnes 89L, 92W
TAMATI, Kevin: Widnes 84L; Warrington 87L
TANNER, David: St. Helens 88W
TAYLOR, David: Rochdale H. 74L
THACKRAY, Rick: Warrington 81W; Widnes 89L
THOMAS, Mark: Warrington 91w
THOMPSON, Jimmy: Bradford N. 80W
THORNILEY, Tony: Warrington 91W
TOPLISS, David: Wakefield T. 72L; Hull 85L
TROTTER, Dennis: Bradford N. 75W
TUNKS, Peter: Leeds 88L

VALENTINE, Rob: Wakefield T. 72L
VAN BELLEN, Gary: Bradford N. 80W
VAN BELLEN, Ian: Bradford N. 80w
VEIVERS, Phil: St. Helens 88W

WAINWRIGHT, Tony: Barrow 81L
WALKER, Malcolm: Hull 76L
WALLER, Tony: Warrington 79L, 81W
WANBON, Bobby: Warrington 74W
WANE, Shaun: Wigan 86W, 89W, 90w; Leeds 92L
WARD, Bernard: Wakefield T. 72l
WARD, David: Leeds 73w, 83L, 84W
WARD, Johnny: Salford 73L
WARD, Phil: Salford 73l; Bradford N. 75W
WARDELL, Alan: Hull 76L
WATKINS, David: Salford 73L
WATKINSON, David: Hull K.R. 82L, 85W, 86L
WATSON, David: Bradford N. 93L
WEBB, Terry: Leeds 84W
WEST, Graeme: Wigan 83W, 86W, 87W
WHITEHEAD, Derek: Warrington 74W
WHITEHEAD, Stuart: Rochdale H. 74L
WHITFIELD, Colin: Wigan 83W; Halifax 90L
WHITFIELD, Fred: Widnes 84L
WHITTLE, Alan: Warrington 74W
WILEMAN, Ron: Hull 82W
WILKINSON, Ian: Leeds 83L, 84W;
    Bradford N. 91L
WILLIAMS, Barry: Wigan 83W
WILLICOMBE, David: Halifax 72W
WILSON, Frank: Warrington 78W
WOOD, Harry: Rochdale H. 74l
WOOD, John: Widnes 76W
WOODS, Paul: Widnes 78L
WRAITH, Geoff: Wakefield T. 72L;
    Castleford 77W
WRIGHT, Darren: Widnes 89L, 92W
WRIGHT, Dave: Warrington 74W
WRIGHT, Stuart: Widnes 78L, 79W, 80L, 84L

REGAL TROPHY RECORDS

ALL ROUNDS

TEAM
Highest score: Wigan 92 v. Runcorn H. 2 (1988-89)
Biggest attendance: 25,326 Hull v. Hull K.R.
                (at Hull C. FC) ....Final 1984-85

INDIVIDUAL
Most tries: 6 by Vince Gribbin (Whitehaven) v. Doncaster
                1984-85
            6 by Steve McGowan (Bradford N.) v. Barrow
                1992-93
*Most goals: 17 by Sammy Lloyd (Castleford)
*Most points: 43 (3t,17g) by Sammy Lloyd (Castleford)
*The above records were achieved in the Castleford v.
Millom first round tie in 1973-74.

REGAL TROPHY FINAL RECORDS

Most final appearances: 8 by Widnes
Most wins: 6 by Wigan
Most tries: 3 by Ellery Hanley (Wigan) v. Halifax
           1989-90
Most goals: 6 by Derek Whitehead (Warrington) v.
            Rochdale H...............................1973-74
            6 by Lee Crooks (Castleford) v. Wigan
           1993-94
Most points: 16 (1t,6g) by Lee Crooks (Castleford)
            v. Wigan 1993-94
Highest score and widest margin win: Castleford
            33 v. Wigan 2..........................1993-94
Biggest attendance: 25,326 Hull v. Hull K.R.
            (at Hull C. FC) 1984-85
Biggest receipts: £94,874 Widnes v. Wigan
            (at Bolton W. FC)..................1988-89

● *BEFORE 1977-78 the competition was known as the Player's No.6 Trophy, then the John Player Trophy. In 1983-84 it became the John Player Special Trophy, renamed the Regal Trophy in 1989-90. It was not until 1979-80 that semi-finals were played at neutral venues, reverting to home advantage in 1992-93.*

FRENCH CLUBS IN REGAL TROPHY
French clubs were admitted into the Regal tournament for the first time in 1992-93. The inaugural entrants were champions Carcassonne and XIII Catalan who qualified through a play-off.

NON-LEAGUE CLUBS IN THE REGAL TROPHY

Amateur clubs have entered the Regal tournament in every season apart from a period between 1981 and 1984, plus 1992-93 when the League and BARLA were in dispute. Two figured in the first round up to 1979-80 and one the following season. They were then left out from 1981-82 because the number of professional clubs had grown beyond the number mathematically suitable 32.

But the amateurs returned in 1984-85 with two clubs joining the professionals in a small preliminary round, the number being increased to three in 1989-90. A new-style

format in 1993-94 saw the preliminary round scrapped, replaced by a full first round of 16 Second Division clubs, two French sides, the three professional clubs demoted in 1992-93 plus Hemel Hempstead and 10 selected amateur sides.

The fate of the amateurs has varied from the record 88-5 hammering Millom received at Castleford to victories by Cawoods over Halifax, Myson over Batley and Leigh East over Chorley.

The full list of amateur clubs' results up to 1991-92 — all first round matches except where stated (P) Preliminary (2) Second Round — is:

Season							Attendance
1971-72		Wigan	33	v	Ace Amateurs (Hull)	9	2,678
		Thames Board Mill (Warr.)	7	v	Huddersfield	27	1,175
1972-73		Bramley	26	v	Pilkington Recs. (St. Helens)	5	616
		Dewsbury	22	v	Dewsbury Celtic	4	1,897
1973-74		Whitehaven	26	v	Dewsbury Celtic	3	1,276
		Castleford	88	v	Millom (Cumbria)	5	1,031
1974-75		Whitehaven	32	v	Lock Lane (Castleford)	6	537
		Doncaster	15	v	Kippax White Swan	6	453
1975-76		Salford	57	v	Mayfield (Rochdale)	3	3,449
		Barrow	16	v	Pilkington Recs. (St. Helens)	9	612
1976-77		Halifax	24	v	Ovenden (Halifax)	4	3,680
		Salford	39	v	Ace Amateurs (Hull)	15	3,037
1977-78		N.D.L.B. (Hull)	4	v	New Hunslet	18	3,845
		Halifax	8	v	Cawoods (Hull)	9	1,168
	(2)	Wakefield T.	31	v	Cawoods (Hull)	7	3,380
1978-79		Leigh Miners Welfare	9	v	Halifax	21	1,621
		Milford (Leeds)	5	v	Dewsbury	38	3,129
1979-80		Pilkington Recs. (St. Helens)	9	v	Wigan	18	6,707
		Blackpool B.	6	v	West Hull	3	555
1980-81		Castleford	30	v	Pilkington Recs. (St. Helens)	17	2,823
1984-85	(P)	Myson (Hull)	2	v	Dewsbury	8	1,572
	(P)	Keighley	24	v	Dudley Hill (Bradford)	10	1,570
1985-86	(P)	Keighley	24	v	Jubilee (Featherstone)	6	1,007
	(P)	West Hull	10	v	Castleford	24	2,500
1986-87	(P)	Batley	2	v	Myson (Hull)	8	687
	(P)	Millom (Cumbria)	4	v	Wakefield T.	18	2,000
		Myson (Hull)	11	v	Swinton	18	1,648
1987-88	(P)	Featherstone R.	34	v	Thatto Heath (St. Helens)	16	1,045
	(P)	Heworth (York)	5	v	Swinton	32	1,063
1988-89	(P)	Wigan St. Patricks	36	v	Elland (Halifax)	2	2,510
		Sheffield E.	80	v	Wigan St. Patricks	8	621
1989-90	(P)	Batley	28	v	West Hull	14	844
	(P)	Crosfields (Warrington)	14	v	Workington T.	19	942
	(P)	Kells (Whitehaven)	2	v	Doncaster	28	2,127
1990-91	(P)	Dudley Hill (Bradford)	18	v	Dewsbury	24	970
	(P)	Saddleworth R. (Oldham)	35	v	Egremont (Cumbria)	18	900
		Rochdale H.	30	v	Saddleworth R. (Oldham)	10	2,434
1991-92	(P)	Saddleworth R. (Oldham)	0	v	Workington T.	30	1,650
	(P)	Leigh East	20	v	Chorley	10	1,393
		Bradford N.	76	v	Leigh East	0	1,613

219

REGAL TROPHY PROGRESS CHART

Key: W — Winners. F — Beaten finalists. SF — Semi-final. P — Preliminary round.

	1993-94	1992-93	1991-92	1990-91	1989-90	1988-89	1987-88	1986-87	1985-86	1984-85	1983-84	1982-83	1981-82	1980-81	1979-80	1978-79	1977-78	1976-77	1975-76	1974-75	1973-74	1972-73	1971-72
BARROW	2	1	1	1	1	1	1	3	2	1	2	3	3	F	1	1	1	1	2	1	1	1	3
BATLEY	3	1	1	3	1	1	2	P	1	1	P	1	1	1	1	1	1	1	2	1	1	2	1
BLACKPOOL G.	(1)	P	1	1	1	2	3	2	1	1	1	2	P	2	2	1	1	F	1	1	1	1	3
BRADFORD N.	SF	F	3	F	2	SF	1	3	2	2	1	3	2	1	W	SF	SF	2	1	W	1	3	1
BRAMLEY	3	1	1	2	1	2	P	1	1	3	*	1	1	1	2	1	1	2	1	2	SF	2	2
CARLISLE	4	2	2	P	1	1	2	P	P	2	2	2											
CASTLEFORD	W	SF	3	3	SF	2	2	2	1	2	1	1	2	SF	3	3	2	W	SF	1	2	1	2
CHORLEY B.	(1)	P	P	1	1																		
DEWSBURY	2	1	P	1	2	1	2	1	1	3	1	1	1	1	1	2	1	1	1	1	3	2	1
DONCASTER	2	1	2	2	1	2	1	2	2	1	1	1	1	1	1	1	1	1	2	1	1	1	
FEATHERSTONE R.	2	2	3	2	3	1	1	2	P	2	3	1	2	2	2	2	3	2	1	1	1	2	1
HALIFAX	3	2	2	P	F	2	2	2	1	SF	1	1	1	3	1	2	1	2	1	1	2	1	W
HIGHFIELD	2	P	1	1	1	1	1	1	1	2	2	P	1	1	1	1	1	1	1	2	1	1	1
HUDDERSFIELD	2	P	1	1	2	1	1	P	1	1	1	2	2	2	1	1	3	1	3	1	1	2	2
HULL	4	SF	2	1	1	2	3	SF	3	F	2	2	W	SF	1	2	1	3	F	1	1	3	3
HULL K.R.	2	2	1	1	3	2	1	F	W	2	3	F	2	1	SF	1	1	3	SF	1	SF	2	
HUNSLET	2	2	1	1	2	P	1	1	2	P	1	1	1	2	1	1	2	1	2	1	1	1	1
KEIGHLEY C.	2	1	2	2	1	1	1	1	2	1	2	1	2	1	2	3	2	1	1	2	3	1	2
LEEDS	2	1	F	2	3	1	F	1	1	SF	W	F	3	1	2	1	1	3	2	3	3	W	SF
LEIGH	3	3	P	2	1	3	2	3	SF	1	SF	2	1	3	3	3	3	SF	2	1	2	2	1
LONDON C.	4	2	1	1	1	P	P	1	1	1	1	1	1	2									
NOTTINGHAM C.	(1)	1	1	1	1	1	2	1	1	1													
OLDHAM	3	1	2	2	3	1	SF	1	2	2	1	1	SF	1	1	1	2	2	2	2	1	1	1
ROCHDALE H.	2	2	P	SF	1	2	1	1	1	2	1	2	1	1	1	1	1	1	1	1	F	1	2
RYEDALE-YORK	3	1	1	P	P	1	1	P	3	1	1	2	1	2	2	1	3	1	2	2	2	2	
ST. HELENS	3	3	SF	3	SF	SF	W	3	SF	3	SF	2	1	1	2	2	2	2	3	1	SF	SF	SF
SALFORD	SF	1	SF	1	2	1	3	1	2	1	2	3	3	2	SF	2	2	2	SF	3	2	F	1
SCARBOROUGH P.		P																					
SHEFFIELD E.	2	1	2	P	3	2	1	2	1	1													
SWINTON	2	P	1	1	2	1	1	2	1	1	3	1	SF	1	1	1	1	1	1	3	1	3	1
WAKEFIELD T.	2	1	2	2	P	3	2	2	2	P	1	1	1	SF	3	SF	1	2	2	3	2	F	
WARRINGTON	4	2	1	W	P	3	3	F	3	1	2	SF	2	W	3	F	W	1	1	3	W	1	1
WHITEHAVEN	2	1	1	1	2	1	1	1	1	2	P	1	1	3	1	1	1	1	SF	2	1	2	
WIDNES	3	3	W	SF	2	F	1	SF	3	3	F	SF	3	3	F	W	F	SF	W	F	1	3	1
WIGAN	F	W	3	3	W	W	SF	W	W	2	3	W	1	1	2	2	3	2	2	2	2	1	3
WORKINGTON T.	2	3	1	1	1	P	1	1	1	1	1	1	2	1	3	2	2	3	3	1	2	1	1

*Bramley withdrew from the Trophy while in liquidation, opponents Hull K.R. receiving a bye.
( ) Entrant as non-League side

PREMIERSHIP TROPHY

1994 Final

Wigan completed a second end-of-season triple haul of Cup, League and Premiership trophies with a 24-20 success over Castleford which was achieved with more ease than the final scoreline suggested.

The Riversiders finished off the treble, repeating their historic feat of 1992, despite a change of coach as caretaker Graeme West made a bid for the permanent position after the post-Wembley dismissal of Australian John Dorahy.

The Old Trafford triumph was soured only by a 56th-minute injury to Test prop Kelvin Skerrett, who suffered a double fracture of the jaw in a clash with Castleford counterpart Dean Sampson. The injury ruled Skerrett out of the World Club Challenge in Brisbane 10 days later, while Sampson was subsequently suspended for four matches after a "trial by video", having been cited by Wigan.

Otherwise the Stones Bitter Premiership provided ideal preparation for Wigan's world title encounter with Australian Grand Final winners Brisbane Broncos, while rounding off a dramatic and controversial 1993-94 campaign with three trophies and a set of runners-up medals from the four competitions.

The crowd of 35,644, paying Premiership record receipts of more than £475,000, saw Wigan perform ruthlessly in a first half which opened with Castleford in dominating form. The champions were not as authoritative in the second period but their extra pace helped them win convincingly enough despite two late Castleford tries.

Castleford, making their second appearance in the Premiership final having been beaten by Hull K.R. in 1984, opened in promising style with a try from Sampson, created by stand off

Graham Steadman. Two goals by skipper Lee Crooks extended their lead to 8-0 after 19 minutes.

Wigan then took control with teenage second row man Andrew Farrell forcing his way over from a pass by Kiwi stand off Frano Botica. Castleford's mediocre kicking game failed to relieve the increasing pressure while, in contrast, Wigan skipper Shaun Edwards gave a faultless display of tactical prowess with the boot.

With second row pairing Farrell and the revitalised Denis Betts combining well, the Yorkshiremen's defence became stretched and inevitably cracked.

But it still needed a bad error by St. John Ellis to give Wigan the initiative, the Castleford full back losing the ball in a tackle by Martin Offiah three minutes after Farrell's touchdown.

The champions took a couple of tackles to find the gap but the crucial score fell fittingly to centre Sam Panapa, who went over from Edwards's pass en route to becoming the first New Zealander to be awarded the Harry Sunderland Trophy as Man of the Match.

Botica, who finished with four goals from five attempts to extend his lead at the top of the season's goals chart, sprinted over for the third try in the 35th minute. Though the second half never lived up to the standards of the first, Castleford rarely looked like breaking through a solid Wigan defence until it was too late.

Substitute Mick Cassidy set up Wigan's fourth try for Betts in the 70th minute and though the Tigers scored 12 points in a late flurry, the burst could not mask Wigan's superiority as they claimed a third Premiership success.

An unusual try by teenage substitute Nathan Sykes, who touched down from Sampson's pass after the ball had rebounded from his head, and an injury time try from the impressive Steadman gave Castleford some reward.

STONES BITTER PREMIERSHIP FINAL

22 May   Old Trafford, Manchester

WIGAN   24   **CASTLEFORD   20**

Wigan	No.	Castleford
Paul Atcheson	1.	St. John Ellis
Jason Robinson	2.	Chris Smith
Sam Panapa	3.	Richard Blackmore
Gary Connolly	4.	Tony Smith
Martin Offiah	5.	Simon Middleton
Frano Botica	6.	Graham Steadman
Shaun Edwards, Capt.	7.	Mike Ford
Kelvin Skerrett	8.	Lee Crooks, Capt.
Martin Hall	9.	Richard Russell
Neil Cowie	10.	Dean Sampson
Denis Betts	11.	Martin Ketteridge
Andrew Farrell	12.	Andy Hay
Phil Clarke	13.	Tawera Nikau
Joe Lydon	14.	Ian Smales
Mick Cassidy	15.	Nathan Sykes

T: Farrell, Panapa, Botica, Betts   T: Sampson, Sykes, Steadman
G: Botica (4)   G: Crooks (2), Steadman (2)
Substitutions: Substitutions:
Cassidy for Cowie (54 min.)   Smales for Ketteridge (49 min.)
Lydon for Panapa (72 min.)   Sykes for Crooks (72 min.)
Half-time: 16-8   Referee: Stuart Cummings (Widnes)
Attendance: 35,644   Receipts: £475,000

1994 Round by Round

In the four-tie first round, only sixth-placed Sheffield Eagles registered an away victory, beating third-placed Warrington 32-16. The Eagles led 18-0 at half-time, putting the issue beyond doubt at 28-6 before the Wire came to life in the last quarter with tries from Kelly Shelford and Jonathan Davies. Champions Wigan allowed arch-rivals St. Helens to open a 12-0 lead before clicking into gear either side of the interval, clinching a 34-16 success with a scoring burst of 16 points in 12 minutes midway through the second half.

In another derby match, title runners-up Bradford Northern saw off Wembley finalists Leeds 42-16 at Odsal. Test centre Paul Newlove registered his third hat-trick of tries of the season in a seven-try romp, Northern skipper Deryck Fox adding seven goals. Halifax coach Malcolm Reilly returned to his old stamping ground of Castleford to suffer a 28-23 defeat, brilliant solo tries by Graham Steadman and Richard Blackmore inside the space of three minutes clinching the success.

In the semi-finals, Sheffield Eagles' dreams of adding a First Division Premiership final appearance to their twin Second Division triumphs of 1989 and 1992 were shattered by a rampant Wigan who soaked up early pressure to romp home 52-18. Martin Offiah took the scoring honours with three tries. Castleford winger Simon Middleton shot in for a quickfire hat-trick of tries in a 14-minute spell to derail Bradford Northern 24-16 at a rain-sodden Odsal, a repeat of the Tigers' mid-season success in the Regal Trophy semi-final.

1994 Results
First Round

Bradford N.	42	Leeds	16
Castleford	28	Halifax	23
Warrington	16	Sheffield E.	32
Wigan	34	St. Helens	16

Semi-Finals

Bradford N.	16	Castleford	24
Wigan	52	Sheffield E.	18

Final

Wigan	24	Castleford	20

(at Old Trafford, Manchester)

1994 Prizes

Winners: £22,000
Runners-up: £10,000

History

With the reintroduction of two divisions in 1973-74 there was no longer a need for a play-off to decide the championship.

However, it was decided to continue the tradition of an end-of-season play-off, the winners to receive the newly instituted Premiership Trophy.

In the first season of the Premiership, 1974-75, the top 12 Division One clubs and the top four from Division Two went into a first round draw, the luck of the draw operating through to the final, played at a neutral venue.

The following season the play-off was reduced to the top eight clubs in the First Division, the ties being decided on a merit basis, i.e., 1st v. 8th, 2nd v. 7th, etc. At the semi-final stage the highest placed clubs had the option of when to play at home in the two-legged tie.

In 1978-79 the two-leg system was suspended because of fixture congestion, and the higher-placed clubs had home advantage right through to the neutrally staged final.

Two legs returned the following season, but were finally abolished from 1980-81.

1994 Harry Sunderland Trophy winner, Wigan's Sam Panapa.

PREMIERSHIP ROLL OF HONOUR

Year	Winners	Runners-up	Venue	Attendance	Receipts
1975	Leeds (3)............26	St. Helens (1) 11	Wigan 14,531		£7,795
1976	St. Helens (4) 15	Salford (1) 2	Swinton 18,082		£13,138
1977	St. Helens (2) 32	Warrington (5).....20	Swinton 11,178		£11,626
1978	Bradford N. (2)....17	Widnes (1)........... 8	Swinton 16,813		£18,677
1979	Leeds (4)............24	Bradford N. (8).... 2	Huddersfield 19,486		£21,291
1980	Widnes (2)..........19	Bradford N. (1).... 5	Swinton 10,215		£13,665
1981	Hull K.R. (3) 11	Hull (7)............. 7	Leeds 29,448		£47,529
1982	Widnes (3)..........23	Hull (2)............. 8	Leeds 12,100		£23,749
1983	Widnes (5)..........22	Hull (1).............10	Leeds 17,813		£34,145
1984	Hull K.R. (1) 18	Castleford (4).......10	Leeds 12,515		£31,769
1985	St. Helens (2) 36	Hull K.R. (1) 16	Elland Rd, Leeds 15,518		£46,950
1986	Warrington (4).....38	Halifax (1) 10	Elland Rd, Leeds 13,683		£50,879
1987	Wigan (1) 8	Warrington (3)..... 0	Old Trafford, Man'r 38,756		£165,166
1988	Widnes (1)..........38	St. Helens (2) 14	Old Trafford, Man'r 35,252		£202,616
1989	Widnes (1)..........18	Hull (4).............10	Old Trafford, Man'r 40,194		£264,242
1990	Widnes (3)..........28	Bradford N. (4).... 6	Old Trafford, Man'r 40,796		£273,877
1991	Hull (3).............14	Widnes (2).......... 4	Old Trafford, Man'r 42,043		£384,300
1992	Wigan (1) 48	St. Helens (2) 16	Old Trafford, Man'r 33,157		£389,988
1993	St. Helens (2) 10	Wigan (1) 4	Old Trafford, Man'r 36,598		£454,013
1994	Wigan (1) 24	Castleford (4).......20	Old Trafford, Man'r 35,644		£475,000

() denotes final League position

PREMIERSHIP FINAL . . . . A REVIEW

Initials are included where more than one player shared a surname in the club in the same era.

1974-75
Leeds 26 Holmes (2g) (Marshall 3g); Alan Smith (1t), Hynes (1t, 1dg) (Eccles), Dyl, Atkinson (2t); Mason (1t), Hepworth; Dickinson, Ward, Pitchford, Cookson, Batten, Haigh
St. Helens 11 G. Pimblett; L. Jones (1t), Wilson, Hull, Mathias (1t); Walsh, Heaton (1t); Warlow (Cunningham), A. Karalius, Mantle (K. Gwilliam), E. Chisnall, Nicholls, Coslett (1g)
Referee: W.H. Thompson (Huddersfield)

1975-76
St. Helens 15 G. Pimblett (3g); L. Jones, Glynn (1t), Noonan, Mathias; Benyon, Heaton (K. Gwilliam); Mantle, A. Karalius (1t), James, Nicholls, E. Chisnall (1t), Coslett
Salford 2 Watkins (2dg); Fielding, Richards, Hesketh, Graham; Butler, Nash; Coulman, Raistrick, Sheffield, Knighton (Turnbull), Dixon, E. Prescott
Referee: M.J. Naughton (Widnes)

1976-77
St. Helens 32 G. Pimblett (1t, 7g); L. Jones, Benyon (1t), Cunningham (1t), Mathias (1t); Glynn (Ashton), K. Gwilliam (1t); D. Chisnall, Liptrot, James (1t), Nicholls (A. Karalius), E. Chisnall, Pinner
Warrington 20 Finnegan; Curling, Bevan (Cunliffe), Hesford (4g), M. Kelly; A. Gwilliam (1t), Gordon (1t); Weavill (1t), Price, Case, Martyn (Peers), Lester, B. Philbin (1t)
Referee: G.F. Lindop (Wakefield)

1977-78
Bradford N. 17 Mumby (2g); Barends (1t), Roe (1t), Austin, D. Redfearn (1t); Wolford (1dg), A. Redfearn; I. Van Bellen (N. Fox), Raistrick, Thompson, Joyce (Forsyth), Trotter, Haigh (1t)
Widnes 8 Eckersley; S. Wright, Hughes, Aspey (2t), Woods (1g); Gill, Bowden; Mills, Elwell, Shaw (Ramsey) (George), Adams, Hull, Laughton
Referee: J.E. Jackson (Pudsey)

1978-79
Leeds 24 Hague; Alan Smith (1t), D. Smith (1t), Dyl (Fletcher), Atkinson; Dick (7g, 1dg), J. Sanderson; Harrison, Ward (1t), Pitchford, Joyce, Eccles (Adams), Cookson
Bradford N. 2 Mumby; D. Parker, Okulicz, Gant, Spencer; Ferres (1g), A. Redfearn; Thompson, Bridges, Forsyth (I. Van Bellen), Trotter (Mordue), J. Grayshon, Casey
Referee: W.H. Thompson (Huddersfield)

1979-80
Widnes 19 Burke (1g); S. Wright (1t), George, Aspey (1t), Bentley (1t); Eckersley (1dg), Bowden; Shaw, Elwell (1t, 1dg), M. O'Neill, L. Gorley (1t), Hull (Hogan), Adams
Bradford N. 5 Mumby (1g); MacLean (Ferres), D. Redfearn (1t), D. Parker, Gant; Stephenson, A. Redfearn; Thompson, Bridges, Forsyth, Clarkson (G. Van Bellen), J. Grayshon, Hale
Referee: W.H. Thompson (Huddersfield)

1980-81
Hull K.R. 11 Proctor; Hubbard (1g), M. Smith (1t), Hogan (1t), Muscroft; Hartley (1t), Harkin; Holdstock, Watkinson, Millington, Lowe, Casey, Hall (Burton)
Hull 7 Woods (2g); Peacham, Elliott, Wilby, Prendiville; Banks, Dean; Tindall, Wileman, Stone, Skerrett (Madley), Crane (1t), Norton
Referee: J. Holdsworth (Kippax)

1981-82
Widnes 23 Burke (1t, 4g); S. Wright (1t), Kieron O'Loughlin, Cunningham (A. Myler), Basnett (1t); Hughes (1t), Gregory; M. O'Neill, Elwell, Lockwood (Whitfield), L. Gorley, Prescott, Adams (1t)
Hull 8 Kemble; O'Hara (Day), Leuluai, S. Evans, Prendiville; Topliss, Harkin; Tindall, Wileman (Lloyd), Stone, Skerrett, L. Crooks (1t, 2g, 1dg), Norton
Referee: S. Wall (Leigh)

1982-83
Widnes 22 Burke; Linton, Hughes, Lydon (5g), Basnett (2t); A. Myler (1t), Gregory (1t) (D. Hulme); M. O'Neill, Elwell, L. Gorley, Whitfield (S. O'Neill), Prescott, Adams
Hull 10 Kemble; O'Hara (1t), Day (Solal), Leuluai, S. Evans; Topliss (1t), Dean; Skerrett, Bridges, Stone, Rose, L. Crooks (2g), Norton (Crane)
Referee: G.F. Lindop (Wakefield)

1983-84
Hull K.R. 18 Fairbairn; G. Clark, M. Smith (1t), Prohm (1t), Laws (1t); Dorahy (1t, 1g), Harkin; Holdstock, Rudd, Millington (Robinson), Burton (Lydiat), Broadhurst, Hall
Castleford 10 Roockley; Coen, Marchant, Hyde, Kear (1t); Robinson, R. Beardmore (3g); Ward, Horton, Connell, Crampton, B. Atkins, Joyner
Referee: R. Campbell (Widnes)

1984-85
St. Helens 36 Veivers (1t); Ledger (2t), Peters, Meninga (2t) (Allen), Day (4g); Arkwright, Holding; Burke (Forber), Ainsworth (1t), P. Gorley, Platt, Haggerty, Pinner (1t)

Hull K.R. 16 Fairbairn (1t, 2g); G. Clark,
Robinson (1t), Prohm, Laws (1t); M. Smith,
G. Smith (Harkin); Broadhurst, Watkinson,
Ema (Lydiat), Kelly, Hogan, Hall
Referee: S. Wall (Leigh)
1985-86
Warrington 38 Paul Ford (Johnson 1t);
Forster (1t), Cullen, R. Duane, Carbert;
Bishop (1t, 5g), A. Gregory; Boyd (2t),
Tamati (1t), Jackson (1t), Sanderson (McGinty),
Roberts, M. Gregory
Halifax 10 Whitfield (3g) (Smith); Riddlesden,
T. Anderson, C. Anderson (1t), S. Wilson;
Crossley, Stephens; Scott, McCallion, G. Robinson,
Juliff, James (Bond), Dixon
Referee: G.F. Lindop (Wakefield)

1986-87
Wigan 8 Hampson; Gill (1g), Stephenson (1g),
Bell, Lydon (1t) (Russell); Edwards, Gregory;
Case, Kiss, Wane (West), Goodway, Potter,
Hanley
Warrington 0 Johnson; Drummond, Ropati, B.
Peters, Forster; Cullen, Bishop; Tamati, Roberts
(Eccles), Jackson, Humphries (M. Gregory),
Sanderson, R. Duane
Referee: K. Allatt (Southport)

1987-88
Widnes 38 Platt (1g); Thackray (Tait 1t), Currier
(4g), D. Wright (2t), Offiah; Dowd, D. Hulme
(2t); Sorensen (1t), McKenzie (1t), Grima
(S. O'Neill), M. O'Neill, P. Hulme, R. Eyres
St. Helens 14 Loughlin (3g); Ledger (1t),
Tanner, Elia, Quirk; Bailey, Holding; Burke,
Groves, Evans (Dwyer), Forber, Fieldhouse
(Allen), Haggerty (1t)
Referee: J. Holdsworth (Kippax)

1988-89
Widnes 18 Tait; Davies (3g), Currier (1t) (Pyke),
D. Wright (1t), Offiah (1t); D. Hulme (A. Myler),
P. Hulme; Sorensen, McKenzie, Grima,
M. O'Neill, Koloto, R. Eyres
Hull 10 Fletcher; Eastwood, Blacker, Price
(Wilby), O'Hara; Pearce (3g), Windley (R. Nolan);
Dannatt, L. Jackson, S. Crooks, Welham (1t),
Sharp, Divorty
Referee: J. Holdsworth (Kippax)

1989-90
Widnes 28 Tait (2t); Davies (4g), Currier (2t),
D. Wright, Offiah; D. Hulme, P. Hulme;
Sorensen (A. Myler), McKenzie, M. O'Neill,
Koloto (Grima), R. Eyres, Holliday (1t)
Bradford N. 6 Wilkinson; Cordle, McGowan
(Cooper), Marchant (1t), Francis; Simpson,
Harkin; Skerrett, Noble (Richards), Hobbs,
Medley, Fairbank, Mumby (1g)
Referee: C. Morris (Huddersfield)

1990-91
Hull 14 Gay (1t); Eastwood (1g), McGarry
(G. Nolan 1t), Webb, Turner; Mackey, Entat;
Harrison, L. Jackson, Dannatt, Marlow
(Busby), Walker (1t), Sharp
Widnes 4 Tait; Devereux, Currier, Davies,
Offiah (1t); Dowd, D. Hulme; Sorensen,
McKenzie (D. Wright), Grima, P. Hulme, Koloto
(Howard), McCurrie
Referee: J. Holdsworth (Kippax)
1991-92
Wigan 48 Hampson (Myers 1t); Lydon, Bell, Miles
(1t), Offiah (2t); Botica (10g), Edwards; Cowie,
Dermott, Platt (1t), Betts (2t), McGinty (Panapa),
Clarke
St. Helens 16 Veivers; Hunte, Connolly
(Griffiths), Loughlin (1t, 2g), Sullivan (2t); Ropati,
Bishop; Neill (Groves), Dwyer, Ward, Nickle,
Mann, Cooper
Referee: J. Holdsworth (Kippax)
1992-93
St. Helens 10 Lyon; Riley, Connolly (1t), Loughlin
(1t), Hunte; Ropati, O'Donnell (2dg); Neill,
Dwyer, Mann (Griffiths), Joynt, Nickle, Cooper
Wigan 4 Atcheson; Robinson, Panapa, Farrar,
Offiah; Botica, Edwards; Cowie, Dermott,
Skerrett (Gildart), Cassidy (Forshaw 1t), Farrell,
Clarke
Referee: J. Holdsworth (Kippax)

PREMIERSHIP TROPHY FINAL PLAYERS' REGISTER

The following is an index of players who have
appeared in the Premiership final since the first in
1975. W — winners, L — losers. Substitute
appearances in lower case letters. The year denotes
the second half of the season.

ADAMS, Bryan: Leeds 79w
ADAMS, Mick: Widnes 78L, 80W, 82W, 83W
AINSWORTH, Gary: St. Helens 85W
ALLEN, Shaun: St. Helens 85w, 88l
ANDERSON, Chris: Halifax 86L
ANDERSON, Tony: Halifax 86L
ARKWRIGHT, Chris: St. Helens 85W
ASHTON, Alan: St. Helens 77l
ASPEY, Malcolm: Widnes 78L, 80W
ATCHESON, Paul: Wigan 93L, 94W
ATKINS, Brett: Castleford 84L
ATKINSON, John: Leeds 75W, 79W
AUSTIN, Jack: Bradford N. 78W

BAILEY, Mark: St. Helens 88L
BANKS, Barry: Hull 81L
BARENDS, David: Bradford N. 78W
BASNETT, John: Widnes 82W, 83W
BATTEN, Ray: Leeds 75W
BEARDMORE, Bob: Castleford 84L
BELL, Dean: Wigan 87W, 92W
BENTLEY, Keith: Widnes 80W
BENYON, Billy: St. Helens 76W, 77W

BETTS, Denis: Wigan 92W, 94W
BEVAN, John: Warrington 77L
BISHOP, Paul: Warrington 86W, 87L; St. Helens 92L
BLACKER, Brian: Hull 89L
BLACKMORE, Richard: Castleford 94L
BOND, Steve: Halifax 86l
BOTICA, Frano: Wigan 92W, 93L, 94W
BOWDEN, Reg: Widnes 78L, 80W
BOYD, Les: Warrington 86W
BRIDGES, John "Keith": Bradford N. 79L, 80L;
   Hull 83L
BROADHURST, Mark: Hull K.R. 84W, 85L
BURKE, Mick: Widnes 80W, 82W, 83W
BURKE, Tony: St. Helens 85W, 88L
BURTON, Chris: Hull K.R. 81w, 84W
BUSBY, Dean: Hull 91w
BUTLER, John: Salford 76L

CARBERT, Brian: Warrington 86W
CASE, Brian: Warrington 77L; Wigan 87W
CASEY, Len: Bradford N. 79L; Hull K.R. 81W
CASSIDY, Mick: Wigan 93L, 94w
CHISNALL, Dave: St. Helens 77W
CHISNALL, Eric: St. Helens 75L, 76W, 77W
CLARK, Garry: Hull K.R. 84W, 85L
CLARKE, Phil: Wigan 92W, 93L, 94W
CLARKSON, Geoff: Bradford N. 80L
COEN, Darren: Castleford 84L
CONNELL, Gary: Castleford 84L
CONNOLLY, Gary: St. Helens 92L, 93W;
   Wigan 94W
COOKSON, Phil: Leeds 75W, 79W
COOPER, David: Bradford N. 90l
COOPER, Shane: St. Helens 92L, 93W
CORDLE, Gerald: Bradford N. 90L
COSLETT, Kel: St. Helens 75L, 76W
COULMAN, Mike: Salford 76L
COWIE, Neil: Wigan 92W, 93L, 94W
CRAMPTON, Jimmy: Castleford 84L
CRANE, Mick: Hull 81L, 83l
CROOKS, Lee: Hull 82L, 83L; Castleford 94L
CROOKS, Steve: Hull 89L
CROSSLEY, John: Halifax 86L
CULLEN, Paul: Warrington 86W, 87L
CUNLIFFE, Dave: Warrington 77l
CUNNINGHAM, Eddie: St. Helens 75l, 77W;
   Widnes 82W
CURLING, Denis: Warrington 77L
CURRIER, Andy: Widnes 88W, 89W, 90W, 91L

DANNATT, Andy: Hull 89L, 91W
DAVIES, Jonathan: Widnes 89W, 90W, 91L
DAY, Sean: St. Helens 85W
DAY, Terry: Hull 82l, 83L
DEAN, Tony: Hull 81L, 83L
DERMOTT, Martin: Wigan 92W, 93L
DEVEREUX, John: Widnes 91L
DICK, Kevin: Leeds 79W
DICKINSON, Roy: Leeds 75W
DIVORTY, Gary: Hull 89L
DIXON, Colin: Salford 76L
DIXON, Paul: Halifax 86L

DORAHY, John: Hull K.R. 84W
DOWD, Barry: Widnes 88W, 91L
DRUMMOND, Des: Warrington 87L
DUANE, Ronnie: Warrington 86W, 87L
DWYER, Bernard: St. Helens 88l, 92L, 93W
DYL, Les: Leeds 75W, 79W

EASTWOOD, Paul: Hull 89L, 91W
ECCLES, Bob: Warrington 87l
ECCLES, Graham: Leeds 75w, 79W
ECKERSLEY, David: Widnes 78L, 80W
EDWARDS, Shaun: Wigan 87W, 92W, 93L, 94W
ELIA, Mark: St. Helens 88L
ELLIOTT, David: Hull 81L
ELLIS, St. John: Castleford 94L
ELWELL, Keith: Widnes 78L, 80W, 82W, 83W
EMA, Asuquo: Hull K.R. 85L
ENTAT, Patrick: Hull 91W
EVANS, Steve: Hull 82L, 83L
EVANS, Stuart: St. Helens 88L
EYRES, Richard: Widnes 88W, 89W, 90W

FAIRBAIRN, George: Hull K.R. 84W, 85L
FAIRBANK, Karl: Bradford N. 90L
FARRAR, Andrew: Wigan 93L
FARRELL, Andrew: Wigan 93L, 94W
FERRES, Steve: Bradford N. 79L, 80l
FIELDHOUSE, John: St. Helens 88L
FIELDING, Keith: Salford 76L
FINNEGAN, Derek: Warrington 77L
FLETCHER, Paul: Hull 89L
FLETCHER, Paul: Leeds 79w
FORBER, Paul: St. Helens 85w, 88L
FORD, Mike: Castleford 94L
FORD, Paul: Warrington 86W
FORSHAW, Mike: Wigan 93l
FORSTER, Mark: Warrington 86W, 87L
FORSYTH, Colin: Bradford N. 78w, 79L, 80L
FOX, Neil: Bradford N. 78w
FRANCIS, Richard: Bradford N. 90L

GANT, Les: Bradford N. 79L, 80L
GAY, Richard: Hull 91W
GEORGE, Derek "Mick": Widnes 78l, 80W
GILDART, Ian: Wigan 93l
GILL, Henderson: Wigan 87W
GILL, Ken: Widnes 78L
GLYNN, Peter: St. Helens 76W, 77W
GOODWAY, Andy: Wigan 87W
GORDON, Parry: Warrington 77L
GORLEY, Les: Widnes 80W, 82W, 83W
GORLEY, Peter: St. Helens 85W
GRAHAM, Gordon: Salford 76L
GRAYSHON, Jeff: Bradford N. 79L, 80L
GREGORY, Andy: Widnes 82W, 83W;
   Warrington 86W; Wigan 87W
GREGORY, Mike: Warrington 86W, 87l
GRIFFITHS, Jonathan: St. Helens 92l, 93w
GRIMA, Joe: Widnes 88W, 89W, 90w, 91L
GROVES, Paul: St. Helens 88L, 92l
GWILLIAM, Alan: Warrington 77L
GWILLIAM, Ken: St. Helens 75l, 76w, 77W

HAGGERTY, Roy: St. Helens 85W, 88L
HAGUE, Neil: Leeds 79W
HAIGH, Bob: Leeds 75W; Bradford N. 78W
HALE, Gary: Bradford N. 80L
HALL, David: Hull K.R. 81W, 84W, 85L
HALL, Martin: Wigan 94W
HAMPSON, Steve: Wigan 87W, 92W
HANLEY, Ellery: Wigan 87W
HARKIN, Kevin: Hull 82L
HARKIN, Paul: Hull K.R. 81W, 84W, 85l;
    Bradford N. 90L
HARRISON, Karl: Hull 91W
HARRISON, Mick: Leeds 79W
HARTLEY, Steve: Hull K.R. 81W
HAY, Andy: Castleford 94L
HEATON, Jeff: St. Helens 75L, 76W
HEPWORTH, Keith: Leeds 75W
HESFORD, Steve: Warrington 77L
HESKETH, Chris: Salford 76L
HOBBS, David: Bradford N. 90L
HOGAN, Brian: Widnes 80w
HOGAN, Phil: Hull K.R. 81W, 85L
HOLDING, Neil: St. Helens 85W, 88L
HOLDSTOCK, Roy: Hull K.R. 81W, 84W
HOLLIDAY, Les: Widnes 90W
HOLMES, John: Leeds 75W
HORTON, Stuart: Castleford 84L
HOWARD, Harvey: Widnes 911
HUBBARD, Steve: Hull K.R. 81W
HUGHES, Eric: Widnes 78L, 82W, 83W
HULL, David: St. Helens 75L; Widnes 78L, 80W
HULME, David: Widnes 83w, 88W, 89W, 90W, 91L
HULME, Paul: Widnes 88W, 89W, 90W, 91L
HUMPHRIES, Tony: Warrington 87L
HUNTE, Alan: St. Helens 92L, 93W
HYDE, Gary: Castleford 84L
HYNES, Syd: Leeds 75W

JACKSON, Bob: Warrington 86W, 87L
JACKSON, Lee: Hull 89L, 91W
JAMES, Mel: St. Helens 76W, 77W
JAMES, Neil: Halifax 86L
JOHNSON, Brian: Warrington 86w, 87L
JONES, Les: St. Helens 75L, 76W, 77W
JOYCE, Graham: Bradford N. 78W; Leeds 79W
JOYNER, John: Castleford 84L
JOYNT, Chris: St. Helens 93W
JULIFF, Brian: Halifax 86L

KARALIUS, Tony: St. Helens 75L, 76W, 77w
KEAR, John: Castleford 84L
KELLY, Andy: Hull K.R. 85L
KELLY, Mike: Warrington 77L
KEMBLE, Gary: Hull 82L, 83L
KETTERIDGE, Martin: Castleford 94L
KISS, Nicky: Wigan 87W
KNIGHTON, John: Salford 76L
KOLOTO, Emosi: Widnes 89W, 90W, 91L

LAUGHTON, Doug: Widnes 78L
LAWS, David: Hull K.R. 84W, 85L
LEDGER, Barry: St. Helens 85W, 88L
LESTER, Roy: Warrington 77L

LEULUAI, James: Hull 82L, 83L
LINTON, Ralph: Widnes 83W
LIPTROT, Graham: St. Helens 77W
LLOYD, Geoff "Sammy": Hull 821
LOCKWOOD, Brian: Widnes 82W
LOUGHLIN, Paul: St. Helens 88L, 92L, 93W
LOWE, Phil: Hull K.R. 81W
LYDIAT, John: Hull K.R. 84w, 851
LYDON, Joe: Widnes 83W; Wigan 87W, 92W, 94w
LYON, David: St. Helens 93W

McCALLION, Seamus: Halifax 86L
McCURRIE, Steve: Widnes 91L
McGARRY, Damien: Hull 91W
McGINTY, Billy: Warrington 86w; Wigan 92W
McGOWAN, Steve: Bradford N. 90L
McKENZIE, Phil: Widnes 88W, 89W, 90W, 91L
MACKEY, Greg: Hull 91W
MacLEAN, Ian: Bradford N. 80L
MADLEY, Ian: Hull 811
MANN, George: St. Helens 92L, 93W
MANTLE, John: St. Helens 75L, 76W
MARCHANT, Tony: Castleford 84L;
    Bradford N. 90L
MARLOW, Ian: Hull 91W
MARSHALL, David: Leeds 75w
MARTYN, Tommy: Warrington 77L
MASON, Mel: Leeds 75W
MATHIAS, Roy: St. Helens 75L, 76W, 77W
MEDLEY, Paul: Bradford N. 90L
MENINGA, Mal: St. Helens 85W
MIDDLETON, Simon: Castleford 94L
MILES, Gene: Wigan 92W
MILLINGTON, John: Hull K.R. 81W, 84W
MILLS, Jim: Widnes 78L
MORDUE, David: Bradford N. 79l
MUMBY, Keith: Bradford N. 78W, 79L, 80L, 90L
MUSCROFT, Peter: Hull K.R. 81W
MYERS, David: Wigan 92w
MYLER, Tony: Widnes 82w, 83W, 89w, 90w

NASH, Steve: Salford 76L
NEILL, Jonathan: St. Helens 92L, 93W
NICHOLLS, George: St. Helens 75L, 76W, 77W
NICKLE, Sonny: St. Helens 92L, 93W
NIKAU, Tawera: Castleford 94L
NOBLE, Brian: Bradford N. 90L
NOLAN, Gary: Hull 91w
NOLAN, Rob: Hull 891
NOONAN, Derek: St. Helens 76W
NORTON, Steve: Hull 81L, 82L, 83L

O'DONNELL, Gus: St. Helens 93W
OFFIAH, Martin: Widnes 88W, 89W, 90W, 91L;
    Wigan 92W, 93L, 94W
O'HARA, Dane: Hull 82L, 83L, 89L
OKULICZ, Eddie: Bradford N. 79L
O'LOUGHLIN, Kieron: Widnes 82W
O'NEILL, Mike: Widnes 80W, 82W, 83W,
    88W, 89W, 90W
O'NEILL, Steve: Widnes 83w, 88w

PANAPA, Sam: Wigan 92w, 93L, 94W
PARKER, Derek: Bradford N. 79L, 80L

227

PEACHAM, Gary: Hull 81L
PEARCE, Gary: Hull 89L
PEERS, Mike: Warrington 77l
PETERS, Barry: Warrington 87L
PETERS, Steve: St. Helens 85W
PHILBIN, Barry: Warrington 77L
PIMBLETT, Geoff: St. Helens 75L, 76W, 77W
PINNER, Harry: St. Helens 77W, 85W
PITCHFORD, Steve: Leeds 75W, 79W
PLATT, Andy: St. Helens 85W; Wigan 92W
PLATT, Duncan: Widnes 88W
POTTER, Ian: Wigan 87W
PRENDIVILLE, Paul: Hull 81L, 82L
PRESCOTT, Eric: Salford 76L; Widnes 82W, 83W
PRICE, Joe: Warrington 77L
PRICE, Richard; Hull 89L
PROCTOR, Paul: Hull K.R. 81W
PROHM, Gary: Hull K.R. 84W, 85L
PYKE, Derek: Widnes 89w

QUIRK, Les: St. Helens 88L

RAISTRICK, Dean: Salford 76L; Bradford N. 78W
RAMSEY, Bill: Widnes 78l
REDFEARN, Alan: Bradford N. 78W, 79L, 80L
REDFEARN, David: Bradford N. 78W, 80L
RICHARDS, Craig: Bradford N. 90l
RICHARDS, Maurice: Salford 76L
RIDDLESDEN, Eddie: Halifax 86L
RILEY, Mike: St. Helens 93W
ROBERTS, Mark: Warrington 86W, 87L
ROBINSON, Geoff: Halifax 86L
ROBINSON, Ian: Hull K.R. 84w, 85L
ROBINSON, Jason: Wigan 93L, 94W
ROBINSON, Steve: Castleford 84L
ROE, Peter: Bradford N. 78W
ROOCKLEY, David: Castleford 84L
ROPATI, Joe: Warrington 87L
ROPATI, Tea: St. Helens 92L, 93W
ROSE, Paul: Hull 83L
RUDD, Chris: Hull K.R. 84W
RUSSELL, Richard: Wigan 87w; Castleford 94L

SAMPSON, Dean: Castleford 94L
SANDERSON, Gary: Warrington 86W, 87L
SANDERSON, John "Sammy": Leeds 79W
SCOTT, Mick: Halifax 86L
SHARP, Jon: Hull 89L, 91W
SHAW, Glyn: Widnes 78L, 80W
SHEFFIELD, Bill: Salford 76L
SIMPSON, Roger: Bradford N. 90L
SKERRETT, Kelvin: Bradford N. 90L; Wigan 93L, 94W
SKERRETT, Trevor: Hull 81L, 82L, 83L
SMALES, Ian: Castleford 94l
SMITH, Alan: Leeds 75W, 79W
SMITH, Chris: Castleford 94L
SMITH, David: Leeds 79W
SMITH, Gordon: Hull K.R. 85L
SMITH, Mike: Hull K.R. 81W, 84W, 85L
SMITH, Steve: Halifax 86l
SMITH, Tony: Castleford 94L
SOLAL, Patrick: Hull 83l

SORENSEN, Kurt: Widnes 88W, 89W, 90W, 91L
SPENCER, Alan: Bradford N. 79L
STEADMAN, Graham: Castleford 94L
STEPHENS, Gary: Halifax 86L
STEPHENSON, David: Wigan 87W
STEPHENSON, Nigel: Bradford N. 80L
STONE, Richard "Charlie": Hull 81L, 82L, 83L
SULLIVAN, Anthony: St. Helens 92L
SYKES, Nathan: Castleford 94l

TAIT, Alan: Widnes 88w, 89W, 90W, 91L
TAMATI, Kevin: Warrington 86W, 87L
TANNER, David: St. Helens 88L
THACKRAY, Rick: Widnes 88W
THOMPSON, Jimmy: Bradford N. 78W, 79L, 80L
TINDALL, Keith: Hull 81L, 82L
TOPLISS, David: Hull 82L, 83L
TROTTER, Dennis: Bradford N. 78W, 79L
TURNBULL, Sam: Salford 76l
TURNER, Neil: Hull 91W

VAN BELLEN, Gary: Bradford N. 80l
VAN BELLEN, Ian: Bradford N. 78W, 79l
VEIVERS, Phil: St. Helens 85W, 92L

WALKER, Russ: Hull 91W
WALSH, John: St. Helens 75L
WANE, Shaun: Wigan 87W
WARD, David: Leeds 75W, 79W
WARD, Kevin: Castleford 84L; St. Helens 92L
WARLOW, John: St. Helens 75L
WATKINS, David: Salford 76L
WATKINSON, David: Hull K.R. 81W, 85L
WEAVILL, Dave: Warrington 77L
WEBB, Brad: Hull 91W
WELHAM, Paul: Hull 89L
WEST, Graeme: Wigan 87w
WHITFIELD, Colin: Halifax 86L
WHITFIELD, Fred: Widnes 82w, 83W
WILBY, Tim: Hull 81L, 89l
WILEMAN, Ronnie: Hull 81L, 82L
WILKINSON, Ian: Bradford N. 90L
WILSON, Frank: St. Helens 75L
WILSON, Scott: Halifax 86L
WINDLEY, Phil: Hull 89L
WOLFORD, John: Bradford N. 78W
WOODS, Paul: Widnes 78L; Hull 81L
WRIGHT, Darren: Widnes 88W, 89W, 90W, 91l
WRIGHT, Stuart: Widnes 78L, 80W, 82W

THE HARRY SUNDERLAND TROPHY

The trophy, in memory of the famous Queenslander, a former Australian tour manager, broadcaster and journalist, is presented to the Man of the Match in the end-of-season Championship or Premiership final.

The award is donated and judged by the Rugby League Writers' Association and is sponsored by Stones Bitter.

The Harry Sunderland Trophy Roll of Honour

Year	Winner	Team	Position
1965	Terry Fogerty	Halifax (v. St. Helens)	Second row
1966	Albert Halsall	St. Helens (v. Halifax)	Prop
1967	Ray Owen	Wakefield T. (v. St. Helens)	Scrum half
1968	Gary Cooper	Wakefield T. (v. Hull K.R.)	Full back
1969	Bev Risman	Leeds (v. Castleford)	Full back
1970	Frank Myler	St. Helens (v. Leeds)	Stand off
1971	Bill Ashurst	Wigan (v. St. Helens)	Second row
1972	Terry Clawson	Leeds (v. St. Helens)	Prop
1973	Mick Stephenson	Dewsbury (v. Leeds)	Hooker
1974	Barry Philbin	Warrington (v. St. Helens)	Loose forward
1975	Mel Mason	Leeds (v. St. Helens)	Stand off
1976	George Nicholls	St. Helens (v. Salford)	Second row
1977	Geoff Pimblett	St. Helens (v. Warrington)	Full back
1978	Bob Haigh	Bradford N. (v. Widnes)	Loose forward
1979	Kevin Dick	Leeds (v. Bradford N.)	Stand off
1980	Mal Aspey	Widnes (v. Bradford N.)	Centre
1981	Len Casey	Hull K.R. (v. Hull)	Second row
1982	Mick Burke	Widnes (v. Hull)	Full back
1983	Tony Myler	Widnes (v. Hull)	Stand off
1984	John Dorahy	Hull K.R. (v. Castleford)	Stand off
1985	Harry Pinner	St. Helens (v. Hull K.R.)	Loose forward
1986	Les Boyd	Warrington (v. Halifax)	Prop
1987	Joe Lydon	Wigan (v. Warrington)	Winger
1988	David Hulme	Widnes (v. St. Helens)	Scrum half
1989	Alan Tait	Widnes (v. Hull)	Full back
1990	Alan Tait	Widnes (v. Bradford N.)	Full back
1991	Greg Mackey	Hull (v. Widnes)	Stand off
1992	Andy Platt	Wigan (v. St. Helens)	Prop
1993	Chris Joynt	St. Helens (v. Wigan)	Second row
1994	Sam Panapa	Wigan (v. Castleford)	Centre

PREMIERSHIP RECORDS   First staged 1975
ALL ROUNDS
TEAM
Highest score: Wigan 74 v. Leeds 6 1992
(Also widest margin)
Biggest attendance: 42,043 Hull v. Widnes
.... Final at Old Trafford 1991

INDIVIDUAL
Most goals:
10 by Frano Botica (Wigan) v. St. Helens ...... Final 1992
Most tries:
10 by Martin Offiah (Wigan) v. Leeds
.... Semi-final 1992
Most points:
40 (10t) by Martin Offiah (Wigan) v. Leeds
.... Semi-final 1992

PREMIERSHIP FINAL
TEAM
Most appearances: 8 by Widnes
Most wins: 6 by Widnes
Highest score:
Wigan 48 v. St. Helens 16 (also widest margin) 1992
Biggest attendance:
42,043 Hull v. Widnes
(at Old Trafford, Man'r) 1991

INDIVIDUAL
Most tries:
No player has scored 3 or more
Most goals:
10 by Frano Botica (Wigan) v. St. Helens 1992
Most points:
20 (10g) by Frano Botica (Wigan) v. St. Helens 1992

SECOND DIVISION PREMIERSHIP TROPHY

1994 Final

Workington Town completed the double by adding the Stones Bitter Second Division Premiership Trophy to the Second Division Championship title, outclassing London Crusaders who were in the first final of their 14-season history.

After two close League encounters between the sides, the Cumbrians opened at a blistering pace and demolished the Southerners with a devastating five-try haul in the first half.

While Workington helped Australian coach Peter Walsh celebrate his new two-year contract, London said farewell to Kiwi coach Tony Gordon with a below-par performance influenced by the loss through injury of key men in hooker Scott Carter and playmaker Mark Riley within the first quarter.

Inadequate reserve cover had hampered the Crusaders' bid for promotion, finishing in third spot, and their shallowness of strength was apparent when scrum half Riley, the mainspring of their attack in a record-breaking season, was replaced by second row man Geoff Luxon.

The dual loss completely disrupted the Londoners, with loose forward Neville Ramsey taking over the scrum pivot role. Even so, Town's quality of attacking play could not be overshadowed by London's ill luck.

Workington became the fifth side to complete the League-Premiership double in the eight years of Second Division Premiership history, following in the footsteps of Oldham, Salford, Sheffield Eagles and Featherstone Rovers. Featherstone had beaten Town 12 months earlier when the Cumbrians qualified for the Old Trafford showpiece as runners-up in the now-defunct Third Division.

London's showing in the second quarter was marred by repeated handling errors in the greasy conditions, which never allowed them to stabilise after the double injury blow. They could not contain a Workington pack in which props James Pickering and Colin Armstrong figured prominently.

The Cumbrians looked assured as they opened at breakneck speed to continue the tradition of Second Division finals providing fast, open football. They trailed only once in a contest effectively decided in the first 35 minutes, the first of John Gallagher's three goals after winger Mark Johnson's initial try giving the Londoners the lead after eight minutes.

South African Johnson claimed the mantle of top try scorer with a final record-equalling hat-trick of touchdowns taking his season's tally to 43 – three ahead of Castleford's St. John Ellis, who failed to add to his total in the subsequent Stones Bitter Premiership final.

Having cancelled out Ged Byrne's opening score, London's joy was shortlived as loose forward Byrne, poised for retirement, sent centre Tony Kay over in the 24th minute.

Then wingers Stuart Cocker and Des Drummond, plus full back Mark Mulligan, added tries to give Town a 24-6 interval lead.

Without Riley, the Crusaders were rudderless and floundered under the waves of Workington attack. But the never-say-die spirit of the underdogs paid dividends with a late rally inspired by New Zealand centre Logan Campbell, who was involved in the move which sent Johnson over for his second try in the 66th minute before scoring himself four minutes from time.

In between, Byrne sent Cocker away for his second try and Man of the Match Dean Marwood landed his third goal. London, however, had the last word when Johnson claimed his hat-trick of tries in injury time.

STONES BITTER SECOND DIVISION PREMIERSHIP FINAL

22 May   Old Trafford, Manchester

WORKINGTON TOWN   30   **LONDON CRUSADERS   22**

Workington Town	No.	London Crusaders
Mark Mulligan	1.	Andre Stoop
Des Drummond	2.	John Gallagher
Tony Kay	3.	Scott Roskell
Paul Burns	4.	Logan Campbell
Stuart Cocker	5.	Mark Johnson
Wayne Kitchin	6.	Dixon McIvor
Dean Marwood	7.	Mark Riley
James Pickering	8.	Chris Whiteley
Phil McKenzie	9.	Scott Carter
Colin Armstrong, Capt.	10.	Dave Rotheram
Brad Hepi	11.	Steve Rosolen
Martin Oglanby	12.	Sam Stewart, Capt.
Ged Byrne	13.	Neville Ramsey
Peter Riley	14.	Kris Smith
Paul Penrice	15.	Geoff Luxon

T: Cocker (2), Byrne, Kay,
   Drummond, Mulligan
G: Marwood (3)
Substitutions:
Riley for Pickering (46 min.)
Penrice for Byrne (50 min.)
Half-time: 24-6

T: Johnson (3), Campbell
G: Gallagher (3)
Substitutions:
Smith for Carter (6 min.)
Luxon for Riley (13 min.)
Referee: John Connolly (Wigan)

1994 Round by Round

The four-tie first round went according to form with the home sides recording comfortable victories. The closest contest was at Batley, who registered a 28-17 success over Huddersfield after the visitors had led 13-6 at the break before home skipper Michael Booth scored two tries to spark a second half revival. Promoted Doncaster clinched an unexpectedly easy 48-18 victory over visitors Dewsbury to reach the semi-final stage for the first time, two-try Man of the Match Audley Pennant opening the scoring after 12 minutes.

London Crusaders rattled up a club record score with a 66-12 hammering of disappointing Keighley Cougars at Barnet Copthall Stadium, South African winger Mark Johnson leading the 12-try romp with a hat-trick. Champions Workington Town disposed of Rochdale

Hornets 50-6 at Derwent Park, Australian full back Mark Mulligan scoring twice in a nine-try performance.

In the semi-finals, London Crusaders pulled off a surprise 16-6 victory at Doncaster with a late comeback. Doncaster's hard earned 6-4 second half lead was wiped out when South African full back Andre Stoop sprinted through the heavy mud to kick ahead for fellow countryman Johnson to register his 40th try of the season. Australian centre Scott Roskell added a final touchdown four minutes from time to seal the success. Batley travelled to Workington for a virtual repeat of their League defeat four months earlier, Glen Tomlinson's sin-bin punishment again sealing their fate. While the Australian scrum half was off the field, Town extended their lead to 12-0 en route to a 19-4 passage to Old Trafford for a second successive season.

1994 Results

First Round

Batley	28	Huddersfield	17
Doncaster	48	Dewsbury	18
London C.	66	Keighley C.	12
Workington T.	50	Rochdale H.	6

Semi-Finals

Doncaster	6	London C.	16
Workington T.	19	Batley	4

Final

Workington T.	30	London C.	22

(at Old Trafford, Manchester)

1994 Prizes

Winners:	£12,500
Runners-up:	£5,250

History

A Second Division Premiership tournament was introduced for the first time in 1986-87, Manchester United's Old Trafford being selected as a new fixed venue for a double-header final. With the introduction of a Third Division in 1991-92, the top eight Division Three clubs played off to visit the top four Second Division clubs, the second tier event being renamed the Divisional Premiership. But three divisions lasted only two seasons and the Second Division Premiership returned in 1994.

ROLL OF HONOUR
SECOND DIVISION PREMIERSHIP

Year	Winners		Runners-up		Venue
1987	Swinton (2)	27	Hunslet (1)	10	Old Trafford, Manchester
1988	Oldham (1)	28	Featherstone R. (2)	26	Old Trafford, Manchester
1989	Sheffield E. (3)	43	Swinton (5)	18	Old Trafford, Manchester
1990	Oldham (3)	30	Hull K.R. (1)	29	Old Trafford, Manchester
1991	Salford (1)	27	Halifax (2)	20	Old Trafford, Manchester
†1992	Sheffield E. (1)	34	Oldham (3)	20	Old Trafford, Manchester
†1993	Featherstone R. (1)	20	Workington T. (*2)	16	Old Trafford, Manchester
1994	Workington T. (1)	30	London C. (3)	22	Old Trafford, Manchester

( )Denotes Second Division position
(*)Denotes Third Division position
† Divisional Premiership, three-division era

THE TOM BERGIN TROPHY

The trophy, in honour of the president of the Rugby League Writers' Association and former editor of the *Salford City Reporter*, is presented to the Man of the Match in the end-of-season Second Division, later Divisional, Premiership final. The award is donated and judged by the Association and sponsored by Stones Bitter.

Year	Winner	Team	Position
1987	Gary Ainsworth	Swinton (v. Hunslet)	Hooker
1988	Des Foy	Oldham (v. Featherstone R.)	Centre
1989	Mark Aston	Sheffield E. (v. Swinton)	Stand off
1990	Mike Ford	Oldham (v. Hull K.R.)	Scrum half
1991	Steve Kerry	Salford (v. Halifax)	Scrum half
1992	Daryl Powell	Sheffield (v. Oldham)	Centre
1993	Paul Newlove	Featherstone R. (v. Workington T.)	Centre
1994	Dean Marwood	Workington T. (v. London C.)	Scrum half

SECOND DIVISION/DIVISIONAL PREMIERSHIP. . . . A REVIEW

1986-87
Swinton 27 Viller; Bate (1t), Topping (Ratcliffe), Brown, Rippon (3g); Snape, Lee (1t); Grima (1t), Ainsworth (1t), Muller, Derbyshire (1t), M. Holliday (Allen), L. Holliday (1dg)
Hunslet 10 Kay; Tate, Penola, Irvine, Wilson; Coates, King; Sykes, Gibson (Senior), Bateman (2t), Platt (1g) (Mason), Bowden, Jennings
Referee: J. McDonald (Wigan)

1987-88
Oldham 28 Burke (Irving); Round, D. Foy (2t), McAlister (4g), Meadows (1t); Walsh (1t), Ford; Sherratt (Warnecke), Sanderson, Waddell, Hawkyard, Graham, Flanagan (1t)
Featherstone R. 26 Quinn (5g); Bannister (1t), Sykes (1t), Banks, Marsh (Crossley); Steadman (2t), Fox; Siddall (Bastian), K. Bell, Harrison, Hughes, Smith, Lyman
Referee: R. Whitfield (Widnes)

1988-89
Sheffield E. 43 Gamson; Cartwright, Dickinson, Powell (3t), Young; Aston (1t, 7g, 1dg), Close (Evans); Broadbent (1t), Cook (1t), Van Bellen, Nickle, Fleming (McDermott 1t), Smiles
Swinton 18 Topping; Ranson (1t), Viller (Maloney), Snape, Bate; Frodsham (1t), Hewitt; Mooney, Melling (1t), S. O'Neill, Ainsworth, Allen (Horrocks), J. Myler (3g)
Referee: R. Whitfield (Widnes)

1989-90
Oldham 30 Platt (1g) (Martyn 1t); Irving (1t), Hyde (2g), Henderson (1t), Lord (1t); Brett Clark, Ford (1t); Casey (Newton), Ruane (1t), Fieldhouse, Round, McAlister, Russell
Hull K.R. 29 Lightfoot; G. Clark (1t), M. Fletcher (4g), Austin, Sullivan; Parker (2t, 1dg), Bishop (Irvine); Niebling, Rudd, Ema, Des Harrison (1t) (Armstrong), Thompson, Lyman (1t)
Referee: R. Whitfield (Widnes)

1990-91
Salford 27 Gibson; Evans (1t), Gilfillan (1t), Birkett, Hadley (Dean); Cassidy (1dg), Kerry (2t, 4g, 1dg); Worrall, Lee (1dg), Hansen, Bradshaw (Sherratt), Blease, Burgess
Halifax 20 Smith; Wood (1t), W. Wilson (1t), Austin, Silva (Platt 2g); Lyons, R. Southernwood (1t); Hill (1t), Ramshaw, Bell (Scott), Brown, Milner, Keebles
Referee: B. Galtress (Bradford)

1991-92
Sheffield E. 34 Mycoe (1t); Gamson, McAlister, Powell (3t), Plange; Price, Aston (5g); Broadbent, Cook, Waddell, Laughton (Lumb 1t), Hughes (Mumby 1t), Farrell

Oldham 20 Platt (1t); Ranson (1t), Nicklin, Ropati, Tyrer; Russell (Warburton), Martyn (2g); Sherratt, Pachniuk, Newton (1t), Joynt, Tupaea (Street), Byrne (1t)
Referee: S. Cummings (Widnes)

1992-93
Featherstone R. 20 Pearson (4g); Butt, Manning, Newlove (2t), Simpson (Roebuck); Maloney (1t), Daunt; Casey (Gunn), Wilson, Taekata, G.S. Price, Smales, Tuuta
Workington T. 16 Mulligan; Drummond, Kay, Hepi, Smith; Byrne, Marwood (4g); Pickering, McKenzie (1t), Riley (Schubert), Scott, Armstrong, Kitchin (Oglanby 1t)
Referee: J. Connolly (Wigan)

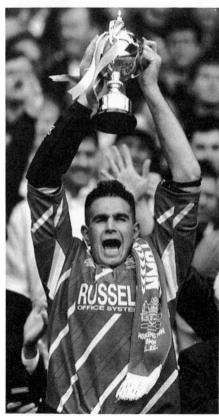

Triumphant Workington Town skipper Colin Armstrong holds aloft the 1994 Stones Bitter Second Division Premiership Trophy.

233

London Crusaders centre Scott Roskell in 1994 Old Trafford action.

Workington Town second row man Brad Hepi offloads despite a double London Crusaders tackle in the 1994 showpiece.

SECOND DIVISION/DIVISIONAL PREMIERSHIP TROPHY FINAL PLAYERS' REGISTER

The following is an index of players who have appeared in the Second Division Premiership final since the first in 1987. It also includes the Divisional finals of 1992 and 1993 when Third Division clubs were included in the competition. W – winners, L – losers. Substitute appearances in lower case letters. The year denotes the second half of the season.

AINSWORTH, Gary: Swinton 87W, 89L
ALLEN, John: Swinton 87w, 89L
ARMSTRONG, Colin: Hull K.R. 90l; Workington T. 93L, 94W
ASTON, Mark: Sheffield E. 89W, 92W
AUSTIN, Greg: Hull K.R. 90L; Halifax 91L

BANKS, Alan: Featherstone R. 88L
BANNISTER, Andy: Featherstone R. 88L
BASTIAN, John: Featherstone R. 88l
BATE, Derek: Swinton 87W, 89L
BATEMAN, Andy: Hunslet 87L
BELL, Keith: Featherstone R. 88L
BELL, Peter: Halifax 91L
BIRKETT, Martin: Salford 91W
BISHOP, David: Hull K.R. 90L
BLEASE, Ian: Salford 91W
BOWDEN, Chris: Hunslet 87L
BRADSHAW, Arthur: Salford 91W

BROADBENT, Paul: Sheffield E. 89W, 92W
BROWN, Jeff: Swinton 87W
BROWN, Peter: Halifax 91L
BURGESS, Andy: Salford 91W
BURKE, Mick: Oldham 88W
BURNS, Paul: Workington T. 94W
BUTT, Ikram: Featherstone R. 93W
BYRNE, Ged: Oldham 92L; Workington T. 93L, 94W

CAMPBELL, Logan: London C. 94L
CARTER, Scott: London C. 94L
CARTWRIGHT, Phil: Sheffield E. 89W
CASEY, Leo: Oldham 90W; Featherstone R. 93W
CASSIDY, Frank: Salford 91W
CLARK, Brett: Oldham 90W
CLARK, Garry: Hull K.R. 90L
CLOSE, David: Sheffield E. 89W
COATES, Ged: Hunslet 87L
COCKER, Stuart: Workington T. 94W
COOK, Mick: Sheffield E. 89W, 92W
CROSSLEY, John: Featherstone R. 88l

DAUNT, Brett: Featherstone R. 93W
DEAN, Mick: Salford 91w
DERBYSHIRE, Alan: Swinton 87W
DICKINSON, Andy: Sheffield E. 89W
DRUMMOND, Des: Workington T. 93L, 94W

EMA, Asuquo: Hull K.R. 90L
EVANS, Steve: Sheffield E. 89w
EVANS, Tex: Salford 91W

FARRELL, Anthony: Sheffield E. 92W
FIELDHOUSE, John: Oldham 90W
FLANAGAN, Terry: Oldham 88W
FLEMING, Mark: Sheffield E. 89W
FLETCHER, Mike: Hull K.R. 90L
FORD, Mike: Oldham 88W, 90W
FOX, Deryck: Featherstone R. 88L
FOY, Des: Oldham 88W
FRODSHAM, Tommy: Swinton 89L

GALLAGHER, John: London C. 94L
GAMSON, Mark: Sheffield E. 89W, 92W
GIBSON, Phil: Hunslet 87L
GIBSON, Steve: Salford 91W
GILFILLAN, John: Salford 91W
GRAHAM, Mal: Oldham 88W
GRIMA, Joe: Swinton 87W
GUNN, Richard: Featherstone R. 93w

HADLEY, Adrian: Salford 91W
HANSEN, Shane: Salford 91W
HARRISON, Des: Hull K.R. 90L
HARRISON, Karl: Featherstone R. 88L
HAWKYARD, Colin: Oldham 88W
HENDERSON, John: Oldham 90W
HEPI, Brad: Workington T. 93L, 94W
HEWITT, Tony: Swinton 89L
HILL, Brendan: Halifax 91L
HOLLIDAY, Les: Swinton 87W
HOLLIDAY, Mike: Swinton 87W
HORROCKS, John: Swinton 89l
HUGHES, Ian: Sheffield E. 92W
HUGHES, Paul: Featherstone R. 88L
HYDE, Gary: Oldham 90W

IRVINE, Jimmy: Hunslet 87L; Hull K.R. 90l
IRVING, Richard: Oldham 88w, 90W

JENNINGS, Graeme: Hunslet 87L
JOHNSON, Mark: London C. 94L
JOYNT, Chris: Oldham 92L

KAY, Andy: Hunslet 87L
KAY, Tony: Workington T. 93L, 94W
KING, Graham: Hunslet 87L
KEEBLES, Mick: Halifax 91L
KERRY, Steve: Salford 91W
KITCHIN, Wayne: Workington T. 93L, 94W

LAUGHTON, Dale: Sheffield E. 92W
LEE, Mark: Salford 91W
LEE, Martin: Swinton 87W
LORD, Paul: Oldham 90W
LIGHTFOOT, David: Hull K.R. 90L
LUMB, Tim: Sheffield E. 92w
LUXON, Geoff: London C. 94l
LYMAN, Paul: Featherstone R. 88L;
 Hull K.R. 90L
LYONS, John: Halifax 91L

McALISTER, Charlie: Oldham 88W, 90W;
 Sheffield E. 92W
McDERMOTT, Paul: Sheffield E. 89w
McIVOR, Dixon: London C. 94L
McKENZIE, Phil: Workington T. 93L, 94W
MALONEY, Dave: Swinton 89l
MALONEY, Francis: Featherstone R. 93W
MANNING, Terry: Featherstone R. 93W
MARSH, Richard: Featherstone R. 88L
MARTYN, Tommy: Oldham 90w, 92L
MARWOOD, Dean: Workington T. 93L, 94W
MASON, Keith: Hunslet 87l
MEADOWS, Kevin: Oldham 88W
MELLING, Alex: Swinton 89L
MILNER, Richard: Halifax 91L
MOONEY, Frank: Swinton 89L
MULLER, Roby: Swinton 87W
MULLIGAN, Mark: Workington T. 93L, 94W
MUMBY, Keith: Sheffield E. 92w
MYCOE, David: Sheffield E. 92W
MYLER, John: Swinton 89L

NEWLOVE, Paul: Featherstone R. 93W
NEWTON, Keith: Oldham 90w, 92L
NICKLE, Sonny: Sheffield E. 89W
NICKLIN, Vince: Oldham 92L
NIEBLING, Bryan: Hull K.R. 90L

OGLANBY, Martin: Workington T. 93l, 94W
O'NEILL, Steve: Swinton 89L

PACHNIUK, Richard: Oldham 92L
PARKER, Wayne: Hull K.R. 90L
PEARSON, Martin: Featherstone R. 93W
PENOLA, Colin: Hunslet 87L
PENRICE, Paul: Workington T. 94w
PICKERING, James: Workington T. 93L, 94W
PLANGE, David: Sheffield E. 92W
PLATT, Alan: Hunslet 87L; Halifax 91l
PLATT, Duncan: Oldham 90W, 92L
POWELL, Daryl: Sheffield E. 89W, 92W
PRICE, Gary S.: Featherstone R. 93W
PRICE, Richard: Sheffield E. 92W

QUINN, Steve: Featherstone R. 88L

RAMSEY, Neville: London C. 94L
RAMSHAW, Jason: Halifax 91L
RANSON, Scott: Swinton 89L; Oldham 92L
RATCLIFFE, Alan: Swinton 87w
RILEY, Mark: London C. 94L
RILEY, Peter: Workington T. 93L, 94w
RIPPON, Andy: Swinton 87W
ROEBUCK, Neil: Featherstone R. 93w
ROPATI, Iva: Oldham 92L
ROSKELL, Scott: London C. 94L
ROSOLEN, Steve: London C. 94L
ROTHERAM, Dave: London C. 94L
ROUND, Paul: Oldham 88W, 90W
RUANE, Andy: Oldham 90W
RUDD, Chris: Hull K.R. 90L

RUSSELL, Richard: Oldham 90W, 92L
SANDERSON, Ian: Oldham 88W
SCHUBERT, Gary: Workington T. 93l
SCOTT, Ian: Workington T. 93L
SCOTT, Mick: Halifax 91l
SENIOR, Gary: Hunslet 87l
SHERRATT, Ian: Oldham 88W, 92L; Salford 91w
SIDDALL, Gary: Featherstone R. 88L
SILVA, Matthew: Halifax 91L
SIMPSON, Owen: Featherstone R. 93W
SMALES, Ian: Featherstone R. 93W
SMILES, Warren: Sheffield E. 89W
SMITH, Kris: London C. 94l
SMITH, Gary: Workington T. 93L
SMITH, Peter: Featherstone R. 88L
SMITH, Steve: Halifax 91L
SNAPE, Steve: Swinton 87W, 89L
SOUTHERNWOOD, Roy: Halifax 91L
STEADMAN, Graham: Featherstone R. 88L
STEWART, Sam: London C. 94L
STOOP, Andre: London C. 94L
STREET, Tim: Oldham 92l
SULLIVAN, Anthony: Hull K.R. 90L
SYKES, Andy: Hunslet 87L
SYKES, David: Featherstone R. 88L

TAEKATA, Wayne: Featherstone R. 93W
TATE, Phil: Hunslet 87L
THOMPSON, Andy: Hull K.R. 90L
TOPPING, Paul: Swinton 87W, 89L
TUPAEA, Shane: Oldham 92L
TUUTA, Brendon: Featherstone R. 93W
TYRER, Sean: Oldham 92L

VAN BELLEN, Gary: Sheffield E. 89W
VILLER, Mark: Swinton 87W, 89L

WADDELL, Hugh: Oldham 88W;
    Sheffield E. 92W
WALSH, Peter: Oldham 88W
WARBURTON, Steve: Oldham 92l
WARNECKE, Gary: Oldham 88w
WHITELEY, Chris: London C. 94L
WILSON, Mark: Featherstone R. 93W
WILSON, Warren: Hunslet 87L; Halifax 91L
WOOD, Martin: Halifax 91L
WORRALL, Mick: Salford 91W

YOUNG, Andy: Sheffield E. 89W

SECOND DIVISION/DIVISIONAL PREMIERSHIP RECORDS
First staged 1987
ALL ROUNDS
TEAM
Highest score: Sheffield E. 72 v. Keighley C. 14......1992
(Also widest margin)
Biggest attendance: 5,885 Halifax v. Leigh.............1991
(Not including final)
INDIVIDUAL
Most goals:
12 by Mark Aston (Sheffield E.) v. Keighley C. 1992
Most tries:
4 by Martin Wood (Halifax) v. Fulham 1991
Most points:
26 (3t, 7g) by Martin Pearson (Featherstone R.) v.
Ryedale-York 1993

FINAL ONLY
TEAM
Most appearances: 3 by Oldham
Most wins: 2 by Oldham, Sheffield E.
Highest score:
Sheffield E. 43 v. Swinton 18 1989
(Also widest margin)

INDIVIDUAL
Most goals:
8 by Mark Aston (Sheffield E.) v. Swinton.............1989
Most tries:
3 by Daryl Powell (Sheffield E.) v. Swinton...........1989
    Daryl Powell (Sheffield E.) v. Oldham...........1992
    Mark Johnson (London C.) v. Workington T ...1994
Most points:
19 (1t,7g,1dg) by Mark Aston (Sheffield E. v. Swinton)
.............1989

LANCASHIRE CUP

ROLL OF HONOUR

Season	Winners		Runners-up		Venue	Attendance	Receipts
1905-06	Wigan	0	Leigh	0	Broughton	16,000	£400
(replay)	Wigan	8	Leigh	0	Broughton	10,000	£200
1906-07	Broughton R.	15	Warrington	6	Wigan	14,048	£392
1907-08	Oldham	16	Broughton R.	9	Rochdale	14,000	£340
1908-09	Wigan	10	Oldham	9	Broughton	20,000	£600
1909-10	Wigan	22	Leigh	5	Broughton	14,000	£296
1910-11	Oldham	4	Swinton	3	Broughton	14,000	£418
1911-12	Rochdale H.	12	Oldham	5	Broughton	20,000	£630
1912-13	Wigan	21	Rochdale H.	5	Salford	6,000	£200
1913-14	Oldham	5	Wigan	0	Broughton	18,000	£610
1914-15	Rochdale H.	3	Wigan	2	Salford	4,000	£475
1915-16 to 1917-18 *Competition suspended during war-time*							
1918-19	Rochdale H.	22	Oldham	0	Salford	18,617	£1,365
1919-20	Oldham	7	Rochdale H.	0	Salford	19,000	£1,615
1920-21	Broughton R.	6	Leigh	3	Salford	25,000	£1,800
1921-22	Warrington	7	Oldham	5	Broughton	18,000	£1,200
1922-23	Wigan	20	Leigh	2	Salford	15,000	£1,200
1923-24	St. Helens Recs.	17	Swinton	0	Wigan	25,656	£1,450
1924-25	Oldham	10	St. Helens Recs.	0	Salford	15,000	£1,116
1925-26	Swinton	15	Wigan	11	Broughton	17,000	£1,115
1926-27	St. Helens	10	St. Helens Recs.	2	Warrington	19,439	£1,192
1927-28	Swinton	5	Wigan	2	Oldham	22,000	£1,275
1928-29	Wigan	5	Widnes	4	Warrington	19,000	£1,150
1929-30	Warrington	15	Salford	2	Wigan	21,012	£1,250
1930-31	St. Helens Recs.	18	Wigan	3	Swinton	16,710	£1,030
1931-32	Salford	10	Swinton	8	Broughton	26,471	£1,654
1932-33	Warrington	10	St. Helens	9	Wigan	28,500	£1,675
1933-34	Oldham	12	St. Helens Recs.	0	Swinton	9,085	£516
1934-35	Salford	21	Wigan	12	Swinton	33,544	£2,191
1935-36	Salford	15	Wigan	7	Warrington	16,500	£950
1936-37	Salford	5	Wigan	2	Warrington	17,500	£1,160
1937-38	Warrington	8	Barrow	4	Wigan	14,000	£800
1938-39	Wigan	10	Salford	7	Swinton	27,940	£1,708
1939-40★	Swinton	5	Widnes	4	Widnes	5,500	£269
	Swinton	16	Widnes	11	Swinton	9,000	£446
	Swinton won on aggregate 21-15						
1940-41 to 1944-45 *Competition suspended during war-time*							
1945-46	Widnes	7	Wigan	3	Warrington	28,184	£2,600
1946-47	Wigan	9	Belle Vue R.	3	Swinton	21,618	£2,658
1947-48	Wigan	10	Belle Vue R.	7	Warrington	23,110	£3,043
1948-49	Wigan	14	Warrington	8	Swinton	39,015	£5,518
1949-50	Wigan	20	Leigh	7	Warrington	33,701	£4,751
1950-51	Wigan	28	Warrington	5	Swinton	42,541	£6,222
1951-52	Wigan	14	Leigh	6	Swinton	33,230	£5,432
1952-53	Leigh	22	St. Helens	5	Swinton	34,785	£5,793
1953-54	St. Helens	16	Wigan	8	Swinton	42,793	£6,918
1954-55	Barrow	12	Oldham	2	Swinton	25,204	£4,603
1955-56	Leigh	26	Widnes	9	Wigan	26,507	£4,090
1956-57	Oldham	10	St. Helens	3	Wigan	39,544	£6,274
1957-58	Oldham	13	Wigan	8	Swinton	42,747	£6,918
1958-59	Oldham	12	St. Helens	2	Swinton	38,780	£6,933
1959-60	Warrington	5	St. Helens	4	Wigan	39,237	£6,424

Season	Winners		Runners-up		Venue	Attendance	Receipts
1960-61	St. Helens	15	Swinton	9	Wigan	31,755	£5,337
1961-62	St. Helens	25	Swinton	9	Wigan	30,000	£4,850
1962-63	St. Helens	7	Swinton	4	Wigan	23,523	£4,122
1963-64	St. Helens	15	Leigh	4	Swinton	21,231	£3,857
1964-65	St. Helens	12	Swinton	4	Wigan	17,383	£3,393
1965-66	Warrington	16	Rochdale H.	5	St. Helens	21,360	£3,800
1966-67	Wigan	16	on	5	Swinton	42,541	£6,222
1967-68	St. Helens	2	Warrington	2	Wigan	16,897	£3,886
Replay	St. Helens	13	Warrington	10	Swinton	7,577	£2,485
1968-69	St. Helens	30	Oldham	2	Wigan	17,008	£4,644
1969-70	Swinton	11	Leigh	2	Wigan	13,532	£3,651
1970-71	Leigh	7	St. Helens	4	Swinton	10,776	£3,136
1971-72	Wigan	15	Widnes	8	St. Helens	6,970	£2,204
1972-73	Salford	25	Swinton	11	Warrington	6,865	£3,321
1973-74	Wigan	19	Salford	9	Warrington	8,012	£2,750
1974-75	Widnes	6	Salford	2	Wigan	7,403	£2,833
1975-76	Widnes	16	Salford	7	Wigan	7,566	£3,880
1976-77	Widnes	16	Workington T.	11	Wigan	8,498	£6,414
1977-78	Workington T.	16	Wigan	13	Warrington	9,548	£5,038
1978-79	Widnes	15	Workington T.	13	Wigan	10,020	£6,261
1979-80	Widnes	11	Workington T.	0	Salford	6,887	£7,100
1980-81	Warrington	26	Wigan	10	St. Helens	6,442	£8,629
1981-82	Leigh	8	Widnes	3	Wigan	9,011	£14,029
1982-83	Warrington	16	St. Helens	0	Wigan	6,462	£11,732
1983-84	Barrow	12	Widnes	8	Wigan	7,007	£13,160
1984-85	St. Helens	26	Wigan	18	Wigan	26,074	£62,139
1985-86	Wigan	34	Warrington	8	St. Helens	19,202	£56,030
1986-87	Wigan	27	Oldham	6	St. Helens	20,180	£60,329
1987-88	Wigan	28	Warrington	16	St. Helens	20,237	£67,339
1988-89	Wigan	22	Salford	17	St. Helens	19,154	£71,879
1989-90	Warrington	24	Oldham	16	St. Helens	9,990	£41,804
1990-91	Widnes	24	Salford	18	Wigan	7,485	£36,867
1991-92	St. Helens	24	Rochdale H.	14	Warrington	9,269	£44,278
1992-93	Wigan	5	St. Helens	4	St. Helens	20,534	£122,327

*Emergency war-time competition

LANCASHIRE CUP FINAL ....
A 20-YEAR REVIEW
1973-74
Wigan 19 Francis; Vigo, D. Hill, Keiron O'Loughlin (2t), Wright (1t); Cassidy, Ayres (1g); Smethurst, Clarke, Gray (4g), Irving, D. Robinson, Cunningham
Salford 9 Charlton; Fielding, Watkins (1t, 3g), Hesketh, Holland; Gill, Banner; Mackay, Walker, Davies (Grice), Dixon, Kear (Knighton), E. Prescott
Referee: W.H. Thompson (Huddersfield)
1974-75
Widnes 6 Dutton (1g); George (1t), D. O'Neill, Aspey, A. Prescott; Hughes (1dg), Bowden; Mills, Elwell, J. Stephens, Adams, Blackwood, Laughton
Salford 2 Charlton; Fielding (1g), Dixon, Graham, Richards; Taylor, Banner; Mackay, Devlin, Grice, Knighton, Coulman, E. Prescott
Referee: G.F. Lindop (Wakefield)

1975-76
Widnes 16 Dutton (3g, 1dg); A. Prescott (1t), George (1t), Aspey (1t), Jenkins; Hughes, Bowden; Mills, Elwell, Nelson, Foran, Fitzpatrick (Sheridan), Adams
Salford 7 Watkins (2g); Fielding, Butler, Hesketh, Richards (1t); Gill, Nash; Fiddler, Hawksley, Dixon (Mackay), Turnbull, Knighton, E. Prescott
Referee: W.H. Thompson (Huddersfield)
1976-77
Widnes 16 Dutton (4g, 1dg); S. Wright (1t), Aspey, George (1t), A. Prescott; Eckersley, Bowden (1dg); Ramsey, Elwell, Nelson, Dearden, Adams, Laughton
Workington T. 11 Charlton; Collister, Wilkins (1t), Wright, MacCorquodale (4g); Lauder, Walker; Mills, Banks, Calvin, Bowman, L. Gorley, W. Pattinson (P. Gorley)
Referee: W.H. Thompson (Huddersfield)

1977-78
Workington T. 16 Charlton (Atkinson);
Collister, Risman, Wright (1t), MacCorquodale
(4g); Wilkins (1t), Walker (2dg); Watts, Banks,
Bowman, L. Gorley, W. Pattinson, P. Gorley
Wigan 13 Swann; Vigo, Davies (Burke 1g),
Willicombe (1t), Hornby; Taylor, Nulty (1t, 1g);
Hogan, Aspinall, Irving, Ashurst (1t),
Blackwood, Melling (Regan)
Referee: W.H. Thompson (Huddersfield)
1978-79
Widnes 15 Eckersley; S. Wright (1t), Aspey,
George, Burke (3g); Hughes, Bowden; Mills,
Elwell, Shaw, Adams, Dearden (Hull),
Laughton (2t)
Workington T. 13 Charlton; Collister, Risman,
Wilkins (1t), MacCorquodale (1t, 2g); McMillan,
Walker; Beverley, Banks, Bowman, Blackwood,
P. Gorley, W. Pattinson (L. Gorley 1t)
Referee: W.H. Thompson (Huddersfield)
1979-80
Widnes 11 Eckersley; S. Wright, Aspey, Hughes
(George), Burke (2g); Moran (1t), Bowden;
Hogan, Elwell (1dg), Shaw, L. Gorley, Dearden,
Adams (1t)
Workington T. 0 Charlton; MacCorquodale,
Maughan, Thompson, Beck; Rudd, Walker
(Roper); Beverley, Banks, Wallbanks (Varty),
W. Pattinson, Lewis, Dobie
Referee: W.H. Thompson (Huddersfield)
1980-81
Warrington 26 Finnegan; Thackray (1t),
I. Duane, Bevan (1t), Hesford (1t, 7g);
K. Kelly, A. Gwilliam; Courtney, Waller, Case,
Martyn (1t), Eccles (Potter), Hunter
Wigan 10 Fairbairn (1t, 2g); Ramsdale (1t),
Willicombe, Davies, Hornby; Foy, Bolton (Coyle);
Breheny, Pendlebury (M. Smith), S. O'Neill,
Melling, Clough, Hollingsworth
Referee: D.G. Kershaw (Easingwold)
1981-82
Leigh 8 Hogan; Drummond, Bilsbury (1t),
Donlan (1dg), Worgan; Woods (2g), Green;
Wilkinson, Tabern, Cooke, Martyn (B. Platt),
Clarkson, McTigue
Widnes 3 Burke; George, Hughes,
Cunningham, Bentley (1t); Moran, Gregory;
M. O'Neill, Elwell, Lockwood, L. Gorley,
E. Prescott, Adams
Referee: W.H. Thompson (Huddersfield)
1982-83
Warrington 16 Hesford (2g); Fellows (1t),
R. Duane, Bevan, M. Kelly (1t); Cullen,
K. Kelly (1t); Courtney, Webb, Cooke
(D. Chisnall), Eccles (1t), Fieldhouse, M. Gregory

St. Helens 0 Parkes (Smith); Ledger,
Arkwright, Haggerty, Litherland; Peters,
Holding; James, Liptrot, Bottell (Mathias),
Moorby, P. Gorley, Pinner
Referee: J. Holdsworth (Leeds)
1983-84
Barrow 12 Tickle (1dg); Moore, Whittle,
Ball (3g, 1dg), Milby; McConnell (1t), Cairns;
Hodkinson, Wall, McJennett, Herbert, Szymala,
Mossop
Widnes 8 Burke; Lydon (1t, 2g), Hughes,
Keiron O'Loughlin, Basnett; A. Myler,
Gregory; S. O'Neill, Elwell, Tamati, Whitfield,
E. Prescott, Adams
Referee: K. Allatt (Southport)
1984-85
St. Helens 26 Veivers (Haggerty 1t); Ledger,
Allen, Meninga (2t), Day (1t, 5g); Arkwright,
Holding; Burke, Liptrot, P. Gorley, Platt,
Round, Pinner
Wigan 18 Edwards; Ferguson, Stephenson,
Whitfield (3g), Gill (1t) (Pendlebury); Cannon,
Fairhurst; Courtney, Kiss (1t), Case, West (1t),
Wane, Potter
Referee: R. Campbell (Widnes)
1985-86
Wigan 34 Edwards (1t); Henley-Smith
(Hampson), Stephenson (7g), Hanley (1t),
Whitfield; Ella (2t), M. Ford; Dowling, Kiss
(1t), Wane (Case), Du Toit, Goodway, Potter
Warrington 8 Johnson (1t); Carbert (2g), Cullen,
Blake (Forster), Thackray; K. Kelly, A. Gregory;
Eccles, Webb, Jackson, Boyd (Tamati),
M. Gregory, Rathbone
Referee: J. Holdsworth (Kippax)
1986-87
Wigan 27 Edwards (2t); Lydon (1t, 1dg),
Stephenson, Bell, Gill (5g); Hanley, M. Ford
(1t); West, Dermott, Case, Roberts (Louw),
Potter, Goodway
Oldham 6 M'Barki; Sherman, Bridge (1t),
Warnecke, Taylor; Topliss, Kirwan; Bruce Clark,
Flanagan, Hobbs (1g), Nadiole, M. Worrall,
Raper (Hawkyard)
Referee: J.E. Smith (Halifax)
1987-88
Wigan 28 Hampson; Russell, Stephenson (1g)
(Bell), Lydon (5g), Gill (1t); Edwards,
Gregory; Case, Kiss, Wane (West 1t),
Goodway, Potter, Hanley (2t)
Warrington 16 Johnson; Drummond, Forster
(2t), Peters, Carbert; Woods (2g), Holden;
Tamati, Webb (Harmon), Humphries,
Sanderson, Roberts, M. Gregory (1t)
Referee: G.F. Lindop (Wakefield)

239

1988-89
Wigan 22 Hampson; T. Iro, K. Iro (2t, 3g), Bell (1t), Lydon (Byrne); Edwards, Gregory; Lucas (Betts), Dermott, Shelford (1t), Platt, Goodway, Hanley
Salford 17 Williams (Blease); Evans (1t), Bentley (1t), Jones, Hadley; Shaw, Cairns; Herbert (1t), Moran, P. Brown (2g), Gormley, M. Worrall (1dg), Horo (McTigue)
Referee: K. Allatt (Southport)
1989-90
Warrington 24 Lyon (Darbyshire); Drummond, Ropati (1t), Thorniley, Forster (1t); Turner (4g), Mackey; Burke, Roskell, Molloy, Jackson (2t), Sanderson (R. Duane), M. Gregory
Oldham 16 Platt (1g) (Russell); Robinson (1t), Hyde (1g), Irving (1t), Lord (1t); Brett Clark, Ford; Casey (Fairbank), A. Ruane, Fieldhouse, Allen, Newton, Cogger
Referee: R. Tennant (Castleford)
1990-91
Widnes 24 Tait; D. Wright, Currier (1t), Davies (4g), Offiah (1t); A. Myler (1t), D. Hulme; Sorensen, McKenzie, Ashurst (D. Smith 1t), R. Eyres, Koloto, Holliday

Salford 18 Gibson; Evans, Birkett, Williams (1t), Hadley; Fell (1t), Kerry (3g) (Cassidy); Sherratt, Lee, Whiteley (Hansen), Bradshaw, Blease (1t), Burgess
Referee: A. Burke (Oldham)
1991-92
St Helens 24 Tanner; Riley, Connolly (Bailey), Ropati, Sullivan; Veivers (2t), Bishop (1t, 2g); Neill (Forber), Groves, Ward, Harrison, Mann (2t), Cooper
Rochdale H. 14 Whitfield (1g); Fox (Calland), Abram (1t), Duane (1t), Garritty; Clark, Gartland; Humphries, M. Hall, Marsden, C. Eccles (Bamber), Okesene, Kuiti (1t)
Referee: D. Campbell (Widnes)
1992-93
Wigan 5 Hampson (Cowie); Robinson, Lydon, Farrar, Offiah (Crompton); Botica (2g, 1dg), Edwards; Skerrett, Dermott, Platt, Betts, McGinty, Bell
St. Helens 4 Veivers (O'Donnell); Hunte, Connolly, McCracken, Sullivan; Ropati, Griffiths; Harrison (Forber), Dwyer (2g), Ward, Joynt, Nickle, Cooper
Referee: S. Cummings (Widnes)

MAN OF THE MATCH AWARDS

Season	Winner	Team	Position
1974-75	Mike Coulman	Salford (v. Widnes)	Second row
1975-76	Mick George	Widnes (v. Salford)	Centre
1976-77	David Eckersley	Widnes (v. Workington T.)	Stand off
1977-78	Arnold Walker	Workington T. (v. Wigan)	Scrum half
1978-79	Arnold Walker	Workington T. (v. Widnes)	Scrum half
1979-80	Mick Adams	Widnes (v. Workington T.)	Loose forward
1980-81	Tony Waller	Warrington (v. Wigan)	Hooker
1981-82	Ray Tabern	Leigh (v. Widnes)	Hooker
1982-83	Steve Hesford	Warrington (v. St. Helens)	Full back
1983-84	David Cairns	Barrow (v. Widnes)	Scrum half
1984-85	Mal Meninga	St. Helens (v. Wigan)	Centre
1985-86	Steve Ella	Wigan (v. Warrington)	Stand off
1986-87	Mike Ford	Wigan (v. Oldham)	Scrum half
1987-88	Shaun Edwards	Wigan (v. Warrington)	Stand off
1988-89	Paul Shaw	Salford (v. Wigan)	Stand off
1989-90	Bob Jackson	Warrington (v. Oldham)	Second row
1990-91	David Fell	Salford (v. Widnes)	Stand off
1991-92	Bob Marsden	Rochdale H. (v. St. Helens)	Prop
1992-93	Denis Betts	Wigan (v. St. Helens)	Second row

LANCASHIRE CUP FINAL RECORDS
TEAM
Most appearances: 35 by Wigan
Most wins: 21 by Wigan
Highest score: Wigan 34 v. Warrington 8 1985
Widest margin: St. Helens 30 v. Oldham 2 1968
Biggest attendance:
42,793 St. Helens v. Wigan (at Swinton) 1953

INDIVIDUAL
Most tries:
4 by Brian Nordgren (Wigan) v. Leigh 1949
Most goals:
7 by Jim Ledgard (Leigh) v. Widnes 1955
    Steve Hesford (Warrington) v. Wigan 1980
    David Stephenson (Wigan) v. Warrington 1985
Most points:
17 (1t, 7g) by Steve Hesford (Warrington) v. Wigan
    1980

YORKSHIRE CUP
ROLL OF HONOUR

Year	Winners		Runners-up		Venue	Attendance	Receipts
1905-06	Hunslet	13	Halifax	3	Bradford P.A.	18,500	£465
1906-07	Bradford	8	Hull K.R.	5	Wakefield	10,500	£286
1907-08	Hunslet	17	Halifax	0	Leeds	15,000	£397
1908-09	Halifax	9	Hunslet	5	Wakefield	13,000	£356
1909-10	Huddersfield	21	Batley	0	Leeds	22,000	£778
1910-11	Wakefield T.	8	Huddersfield	2	Leeds	19,000	£696
1911-12	Huddersfield	22	Hull K.R.	10	Wakefield	20,000	£700
1912-13	Batley	17	Hull	3	Leeds	16,000	£523
1913-14	Huddersfield	19	Bradford N.	3	Halifax	12,000	£430
1914-15	Huddersfield	31	Hull	0	Leeds	12,000	£422
1918-19	Huddersfield	14	Dewsbury	8	Leeds	21,500	£1,309
1919-20	Huddersfield	24	Leeds	5	Halifax	24,935	£2,096
1920-21	Hull K.R.	2	Hull	0	Leeds	20,000	£1,926
1921-22	Leeds	11	Dewsbury	3	Halifax	20,000	£1,650
1922-23	York	5	Batley	0	Leeds	33,719	£2,414
1923-24	Hull	10	Huddersfield	4	Leeds	23,300	£1,728
1924-25	Wakefield T.	9	Batley	8	Leeds	25,546	£1,912
1925-26	Dewsbury	2	Huddersfield	0	Wakefield	12,616	£718
1926-27	Huddersfield	10	Wakefield T.	3	Leeds	11,300	£853
1927-28	Dewsbury	8	Hull	2	Leeds	21,700	£1,466
1928-29	Leeds	5	Featherstone R.	0	Wakefield	13,000	£838
1929-30	Hull K.R.	13	Hunslet	7	Leeds	11,000	£687
1930-31	Leeds	10	Huddersfield	2	Halifax	17,812	£1,405
1931-32	Huddersfield	4	Hunslet	2	Leeds	27,000	£1,764
1932-33	Leeds	8	Wakefield T.	0	Huddersfield	17,685	£1,183
1933-34	York	10	Hull K.R.	4	Leeds	22,000	£1,480
1934-35	Leeds	5	Wakefield T.	5	Dewsbury	22,598	£1,529
Replay	Leeds	2	Wakefield T.	2	Huddersfield	10,300	£745
Replay	Leeds	13	Wakefield T.	0	Hunslet	19,304	£1,327
1935-36	Leeds	3	York	0	Halifax	14,616	£1,113
1936-37	York	9	Wakefield T.	2	Leeds	19,000	£1,294
1937-38	Leeds	14	Huddersfield	8	Wakefield	22,000	£1,508
1938-39	Huddersfield	18	Hull	10	Bradford	28,714	£1,534
1939-40	Featherstone R.	12	Wakefield T.	9	Bradford	7,077	£403
1940-41	Bradford N.	15	Dewsbury	5	Huddersfield	13,316	£939
1941-42	Bradford N.	24	Halifax	0	Huddersfield	5,989	£635
1942-43	Dewsbury	7	Huddersfield	0	Dewsbury	11,000	£680
	Huddersfield	2	Dewsbury	0	Huddersfield	6,252	£618
	Dewsbury won on aggregate 7-2						
1943-44	Bradford N.	5	Keighley	2	Bradford	10,251	£757
	Keighley	5	Bradford N.	5	Keighley	8,993	£694
	Bradford N. won on aggregate 10-7						
1944-45	Hunslet	3	Halifax	12	Hunslet	11,213	£744
	Halifax	2	Hunslet	0	Halifax	9,800	£745
	Halifax won on aggregate 14-3						

Year	Winners		Runners-up		Venue	Attendance	Receipts
1945-46	Bradford N.	5	Wakefield T.	2	Halifax	24,292	£1,934
1946-47	Wakefield T.	10	Hull	0	Leeds	34,300	£3,718
1947-48	Wakefield T.	7	Leeds	7	Huddersfield	24,344	£3,461
Replay	Wakefield T.	8	Leeds	7	Bradford	32,000	£3,251
1948-49	Bradford N.	18	Castleford	9	Leeds	31,393	£5,053
1949-50	Bradford N.	11	Huddersfield	4	Leeds	36,000	£6,365
1950-51	Huddersfield	16	Castleford	3	Leeds	28,906	£5,152
1951-52	Wakefield T.	17	Keighley	3	Huddersfield	25,495	£3,347
1952-53	Huddersfield	18	Batley	8	Leeds	14,705	£2,471
1953-54	Bradford N.	7	Hull	2	Leeds	22,147	£3,833
1954-55	Halifax	22	Hull	14	Leeds	25,949	£4,638
1955-56	Halifax	10	Hull	10	Leeds	23,520	£4,385
Replay	Halifax	7	Hull	0	Bradford	14,000	£2,439
1956-57	Wakefield T.	23	Hunslet	5	Leeds	30,942	£5,609
1957-58	Huddersfield	15	York	8	Leeds	22,531	£4,123
1958-59	Leeds	24	Wakefield T.	20	Bradford	26,927	£3,833
1959-60	Featherstone R.	15	Hull	14	Leeds	23,983	£4,156
1960-61	Wakefield T.	16	Huddersfield	10	Leeds	17,456	£2,937
1961-62	Wakefield T.	19	Leeds	9	Bradford	16,329	£2,864
1962-63	Hunslet	12	Hull K.R.	2	Leeds	22,742	£4,514
1963-64	Halifax	10	Featherstone R.	0	Wakefield	13,238	£2,471
1964-65	Wakefield T.	18	Leeds	2	Huddersfield	13,527	£2,707
1965-66	Bradford N.	17	Hunslet	8	Leeds	17,522	£4,359
1966-67	Hull K.R.	25	Featherstone R.	12	Leeds	13,241	£3,482
1967-68	Hull K.R.	8	Hull	7	Leeds	16,729	£5,515
1968-69	Leeds	22	Castleford	11	Wakefield	12,573	£3,746
1969-70	Hull	12	Featherstone R.	9	Leeds	11,089	£3,419
1970-71	Leeds	23	Featherstone R.	7	Bradford	6,753	£1,879
1971-72	Hull K.R.	11	Castleford	7	Wakefield	5,536	£1,589
1972-73	Leeds	36	Dewsbury	9	Bradford	7,806	£2,659
1973-74	Leeds	7	Wakefield T.	2	Leeds	7,621	£3,728
1974-75	Hull K.R.	16	Wakefield T.	13	Leeds	5,823	£3,090
1975-76	Leeds	15	Hull K.R.	11	Leeds	5,743	£3,617
1976-77	Leeds	16	Featherstone R.	12	Leeds	7,645	£5,198
1977-78	Castleford	17	Featherstone R.	7	Leeds	6,318	£4,528
1978-79	Bradford N.	18	York	8	Leeds	10,429	£9,188
1979-80	Leeds	15	Halifax	6	Leeds	9,137	£9,999
1980-81	Leeds	8	Hull K.R.	7	Huddersfield	9,751	£15,578
1981-82	Castleford	10	Bradford N.	5	Leeds	5,852	£10,359
1982-83	Hull	18	Bradford N.	7	Leeds	11,755	£21,950
1983-84	Hull	13	Castleford	2	Elland Rd, Leeds	14,049	£33,572
1984-85	Hull	29	Hull K.R.	12	Hull C. FC	25,237	£68,639
1985-86	Hull K.R.	22	Castleford	18	Leeds	12,686	£36,327
1986-87	Castleford	31	Hull	24	Leeds	11,132	£31,888
1987-88	Bradford N.	12	Castleford	12	Leeds	10,947	£40,283
Replay	Bradford N.	11	Castleford	2	Elland Rd, Leeds	8,175	£30,732
1988-89	Leeds	33	Castleford	12	Elland Rd, Leeds	22,968	£76,658
1989-90	Bradford N.	20	Featherstone R.	14	Leeds	12,607	£50,775
1990-91	Castleford	11	Wakefield T.	8	Elland Rd, Leeds	12,420	£61,432
1991-92	Castleford	28	Bradford N.	6	Elland Rd, Leeds	8,916	£54,183
1992-93	Wakefield T.	29	Sheffield E.	16	Elland Rd, Leeds	7,918	£49,845

YORKSHIRE CUP FINAL ....
A 20-YEAR REVIEW
1973-74
Leeds 7 Holmes; Langley (1t) (Marshall 1g),
Hynes (1g), Dyl, Atkinson; Hardisty,
Hepworth; Jeanes (Ramsey), Ward, Clarkson,
Eccles, Cookson, Batten
Wakefield T. 2 Wraith (Sheard); D. Smith,
Crook (1g), Hegarty, B. Parker; Topliss,
Bonnar; Valentine, Morgan, Bratt, Knowles
(Ballantyne), Endersby, Holmes
Referee: M.J. Naughton (Widnes)
1974-75
Hull K.R. 16 Smithies; Sullivan (Dunn 1t),
Watson (2t), Coupland, Kirkpatrick (1t);
Millward, Stephenson; Millington, Heslop,
Rose, Wallis, Fox (2g) (Madley), Brown
Wakefield T. 13 Sheard; D. Smith (1t), Crook
(2g), Hegarty (1t), Archer; Topliss, Bonnar;
Ballantyne, Handscombe, Bratt (1t), Skerrett,
A. Tonks (Goodwin) (Holmes), Morgan
Referee: M.J. Naughton (Widnes)
1975-76
Leeds 15 Marshall; Alan Smith, Hague, Dyl
(1t), Atkinson; Holmes (4g, 1dg), Hynes;
Harrison, Payne, Pitchford (Dickinson),
Eccles, Batten, Cookson (1t)
Hull K.R. 11 Wallace; Dunn, A. Burwell,
Watson, Sullivan (1t); Turner, Millward (1dg);
Millington, Dickinson, Lyons, Rose, Fox (1t, 2g),
Hughes (Holdstock)
Referee: J.V. Moss (Manchester)
1976-77
Leeds 16 Marshall (2g); Hague, Hynes, Dyl
(2t), D. Smith; Holmes, Banner; Dickinson,
Ward, Pitchford, Eccles (1t), Burton, Cookson
(1t)
Featherstone R. 12 Box; Bray (1t), Coventry,
Quinn (3g), K. Kellett; Newlove, Fennell;
Gibbins, Bridges, Farrar, Stone, P. Smith (1t),
Bell (Spells)
Referee: M.J. Naughton (Widnes)
1977-78
Castleford 17 Wraith; Richardson, Joyner,
P. Johnson, Fenton; Burton (2t, 1dg), Pickerill
(Stephens); Fisher (Woodall), Spurr, Weston,
Huddlestone, Reilly, Lloyd (5g)
Featherstone R. 7 Marsden; Evans, Gilbert,
Quinn (1g) (N. Tuffs), K. Kellett; Newlove,
Butler; Townend (1g), Bridges, Farrar,
Gibbins, Stone (P. Smith 1t), Bell
Referee: M.J. Naughton (Widr .
1978-79
Bradford N. 18 Mumby; Barends, Gant (1t),
D. Parker (1t), D. Redfearn; Slater (Wolford),
A. Redfearn (1t); Thompson, Fisher, Forsyth
(Joyce), Fox (3g), Trotter, Haigh (1t)

York 8 G. Smith (1t); T. Morgan, Day
(Crossley), Foster, Nicholson; Banks (2g),
Harkin; Dunkerley, Wileman, Harris, Rhodes,
Hollis (1dg) (Ramshaw), Cooper
Referee: M.J. Naughton (Widnes)
1979-80
Leeds 15 Hague; Alan Smith (2t), D. Smith
(1t), Dyl, Atkinson; Holmes (J. Sanderson),
Dick (3g); Dickinson, Ward, Pitchford, Eccles,
D. Heron (Adams), Cookson
Halifax 6 Birts (3g); Howard (Snee), Garrod,
Cholmondeley, Waites; Blacker, Langton;
Jarvis (Callon), Raistrick, Wood, Scott, Sharp,
Busfield
Referee: M.J. Naughton (Widnes)
1980-81
Leeds 8 Hague; Alan Smith (1t), D. Smith,
Atkinson, Oulton; Holmes, Dick (2g, 1dg);
Harrison, Ward, Pitchford, Eccles, Cookson
(Carroll), D. Heron
Hull K.R. 7 Robinson; McHugh (1t),
M. Smith, Hogan (2g), Youngman; Hall,
Harkin; Holdstock, Price, Crooks (Rose),
Lowe, Casey, Crane
Referee: R. Campbell (Widnes)
1981-82
Castleford 10 Claughton; Richardson, Fenton,
Hyde (1t), Morris; Joyner (1t), R. Beardmore;
Hardy (P. Norton), Spurr, B. Johnson, Finch
(2g), Ward, Timson
Bradford N. 5 Mumby; Barends, Hale,
A. Parker (1t), Gant; Hanley (1g), A. Redfearn;
Grayshon, Noble, Sanderson (D. Redfearn),
G. Van Bellen (Jasiewicz), Idle, Rathbone
Referee: R. Whitfield (Widnes)
1982-83
Hull 18 Kemble; S. Evans (1t), Day, Leuluai,
Prendiville (1t); Topliss, Harkin; Skerrett,
Bridges, Stone, Rose (2t), L. Crooks (2g, 2dg),
Crane (Norton)
Bradford N. 7 Mumby; Barends, Gant,
A. Parker, Pullen (Smith); Whiteman (1t),
Carroll (1g, 2dg); Grayshon, Noble, G. Van
Bellen (Sanderson), Idle, Jasiewicz, Hale
Referee: S. Wall (Leigh)
1983-84
Hull 13 Kemble; Solal, Schofield, Leuluai,
O'Hara (1t); Topliss, Dean; Edmonds,
Wileman, Skerrett, Proctor (1t), L. Crooks,
Crane (1t, 1dg)
Castleford 2 Coen; Fenton, Marchant, Hyde
(Orum), Kear; Joyner, R. Beardmore (1g);
Connell, Horton, Reilly, Timson, James,
England
Referee: W.H. Thompson (Huddersfield)

243

1984-85
Hull 29 Kemble (2t); Leuluai, Schofield (4g, 1dg), S. Evans (1t), O'Hara; Ah Kuoi, Sterling; Edmonds, Patrick, L. Crooks (1t), Norton (1t), Proctor, Divorty (Rose)
Hull K.R. 12 Fairbairn (1t); Clark, Robinson (1t), Prohm, Laws; M. Smith, Harkin (Rudd); Broadhurst, Watkinson, Ema (Hartley), Burton, Kelly, Hall (1t)
Referee: G.F. Lindop (Wakefield)
1985-86
Hull K.R. 22 Fairbairn (Lydiat); Clark (1t), Dorahy (5g), Prohm, Laws; G. Smith, Harkin; Des Harrison, Watkinson, Ema, Burton, Hogan (Kelly), Miller (2t)
Castleford 18 Lord; Plange, Marchant (2t), Hyde, Spears; Diamond (1g), R. Beardmore (1t, 2g); Ward, K. Beardmore, B. Johnson, England, Ketteridge, Joyner
Referee: R. Campbell (Widnes)
1986-87
Castleford 31 Scott; Plange, Marchant, Johns, Hyde (Lord); Joyner, R. Beardmore (1dg); Ward (1t), K. Beardmore (2t), B. Johnson, Ketteridge (1t, 5g), B. Atkins (1t) (Shillito), England
Hull 24 Kemble; Brand (2t), Schofield, O'Hara (2t), Eastwood; Ah Kuoi, Windley; Brown (Puckering), Patrick, Dannatt, Norton (Divorty), L. Crooks (4g), Sharp
Referee: J. McDonald (Wigan)
1987-88
Bradford N. 12 Mercer; Ford, McGowan, Simpson, Francis; Mumby (2g), Harkin; Grayshon (Hobbs 2g), Noble, Hill, Skerrett, Fairbank (1t), Holmes (Roebuck)
Castleford 12 Roockley; Plange (1t), Marchant, Beattie, Hyde; Joyner, R. Southernwood; Shillito (R. Beardmore), K. Beardmore (Sampson), Ward, Ketteridge (2g), Fifita, Lindner (1t)
Referee: K. Allatt (Southport)
Replay
Bradford N. 11 Mumby; Ford, McGowan, Mercer, Simpson; Stewart, Harkin; Hobbs (1g, 1dg), Noble, Hill (1t), Skerrett, Fairbank, W. Heron (1t)
Castleford 2 Roockley; Plange, Marchant, Beattie, Hyde; R. Southernwood, R. Beardmore; Ward, Hill, Fifita (Sampson), Ketteridge (1g), England (Boothroyd), Joyner
Referee: K. Allatt (Southport)

1988-89
Leeds 33 Spencer; Ettingshausen, Schofield (2t, 1dg), Stephenson (6g), Gibson (2t); C. Lyons, Ashton; Crooks, Maskill, Waddell (Backo), Powell, Brooke-Cowden (Medley 1t), D. Heron
Castleford 12 Belcher; Plange, Marchant, Boothroyd (1t), Chapman (Roockley) (Sampson); Anderson, R. Beardmore; Ward, K. Beardmore, England, Ketteridge (2g), Gibbs, Joyner (1t)
Referee: R. Whitfield (Widnes)
1989-90
Bradford N. 20 Wilkinson; Cordle (2t), McGowan, Simpson, Francis; Henjak (Mumby), Harkin (2t); Skerrett, Barraclough, Hamer (Medley), Hobbs (2g), Fairbank, Pendlebury
Featherstone R. 14 Bibb; Drummond, I. Ropati (1t), Newlove, A. Banks; Smales, Fox (3g); Grayshon, Clark, G. Bell (Dakin), G.S. Price, Booth (Fisher), P. Smith (1t)
Referee: R. Whitfield (Widnes)
1990-91
Castleford 11 Larder; Ellis, Irwin, Anderson, Plange (1t); Steadman, G. Atkins (1t) (England); Crooks (1g), G. Southernwood, Sampson, Battye (Ketteridge), Hardy, Roebuck (1dg)
Wakefield T. 8 Harcombe (2g); Jones, Mason (1t), Eden, Wilson; Lazenby, M. Conway; Shelford, B. Conway (Slater), Thompson, Kelly (Perry), G.H. Price, Bell
Referee: J. Smith (Halifax)
1991-92
Castleford 28 Steadman (2t, 4g); Ellis, Bradley, Blackmore, Nelson; T. Smith (1t), Ford (1t); Sampson (Ketteridge), G. Southernwood, England, Battye (1t), Irwin, Nikau
Bradford N. 6 Simpson; D. Powell (1t), Shelford, McGowan, Marchant; Anderson, Iti (Croft); Hobbs (1g), Noble, Hamer, Medley (Richards), Fairbank, Barnett
Referee: J. Holdsworth (Kippax)
1992-93
Wakefield T. 29 Spencer (1t); Jones, Mason (1t), Benson (3g), Wilson (Goddard); Wright (1g, 1dg), Bagnall (1t); Webster (B. Conway), Bell, Glancy, G.H. Price (1t), Fritz, Slater (1t)
Sheffield E. 16 Jack; Gamson (1t), R. Price, Mycoe (2g), Plange; Aston, Lumb; Broadbent, Cook, Laughton (Waddell), McGuire (2t), Carr (Young), Farrell
Referee: R. Smith (Castleford)

THE WHITE ROSE TROPHY

First awarded in 1966, the trophy is presented to the adjudged Man of the Match in the Yorkshire Cup final.

Donated by the late T.E. Smith, of York, the award is organised by the Yorkshire

Federation of Rugby League Supporters' Clubs and judged by a panel of the Press.

The trophy is not awarded in replays, although Bradford Northern's Brendan Hill was named Man of the Match in the second game against Castleford in 1987.

Season	Winner	Team	Position
1966-67	Cyril Kellett	Hull K.R. (v. Featherstone R.)	Full back
1967-68	Chris Davidson	Hull (v. Hull K.R.)	Scrum half
1968-69	Barry Seabourne	Leeds (v. Castleford)	Scrum half
1969-70	Joe Brown	Hull (v. Featherstone R.)	Loose forward
1970-71	Syd Hynes	Leeds (v. Featherstone R.)	Centre
1971-72	Ian Markham	Hull K.R. (v. Castleford)	Full back
1972-73	John Holmes	Leeds (v. Dewsbury)	Full back
1973-74	Keith Hepworth	Leeds (v. Wakefield T.)	Scrum half
1974-75	Roger Millward	Hull K.R. (v. Wakefield T.)	Stand off
1975-76	Neil Fox	Hull K.R. (v. Leeds)	Second row
1976-77	Les Dyl	Leeds (v. Featherstone R.)	Centre
1977-78	Bruce Burton	Castleford (v. Featherstone R.)	Stand off
1978-79	Bob Haigh	Bradford N. (v. York)	Loose forward
1979-80	Alan Smith	Leeds (v. Halifax)	Winger
1980-81	Kevin Dick	Leeds (v. Hull K.R.)	Scrum half
1981-82	Barry Johnson	Castleford (v. Bradford N.)	Prop
1982-83	Keith Mumby	Bradford N. (v. Hull)	Full back
1983-84	Mick Crane	Hull (v. Castleford)	Loose forward
1984-85	Peter Sterling	Hull (v. Hull K.R.)	Scrum half
1985-86	Gavin Miller	Hull K.R. (v. Castleford)	Loose forward
1986-87	Kevin Beardmore	Castleford (v. Hull)	Hooker
1987-88	Paul Harkin	Bradford N. (v. Castleford)	Scrum half
1988-89	Cliff Lyons	Leeds (v. Castleford)	Stand off
1989-90	Paul Harkin	Bradford N. (v. Featherstone R.)	Scrum half
1990-91	Tracy Lazenby	Wakefield T. (v. Castleford)	Stand off
1991-92	Graham Steadman	Castleford (v. Bradford N.)	Full back
1992-93	Nigel Wright	Wakefield T. (v. Sheffield E.)	Stand off

YORKSHIRE CUP FINAL RECORDS

TEAM
Most appearances: 21 Leeds
Most wins: 17 Leeds
Highest score: Leeds 36 v. Dewsbury 9............... 1972
Widest margin win: Huddersfield 31 v. Hull 0 1914
Biggest attendance:
36,000 Bradford N. v. Huddersfield (at Leeds)...... 1949

INDIVIDUAL
Most tries:
4 by Stan Moorhouse (Huddersfield) v. Leeds....... 1919
Most goals:
6 by David Stephenson (Leeds) v. Castleford 1988
Most points:
16 (2t, 4g) by Graham Steadman (Castleford)
v. Bradford N. 1991

CHARITY SHIELD
● From 1985-86 to 1992-93, the Charity Shield was contested between the previous season's Challenge Cup winners and Division One Champions. When Wigan won both trophies in 1990 and 1991 they met the previous season's Premiership final winners. When Wigan won the Championship, Challenge Cup and Premiership in 1992, they met the previous season's Division One title runners-up.

CHARITY SHIELD ROLL OF HONOUR

Year	Winners		Runners-up		Venue	Attendance
1985-86	Wigan	34	*Hull K.R.	6	Isle of Man	4,066
1986-87	*Halifax	9	Castleford	8	Isle of Man	3,276
1987-88	*Wigan	44	Halifax	12	Isle of Man	4,804
1988-89	*Widnes	20	Wigan	14	Isle of Man	5,044
1989-90	*Widnes	27	Wigan	22	Liverpool FC	17,263
1990-91	†Widnes	24	*Wigan	8	Swansea C. FC	11,178
1991-92	*Wigan	22	†Hull	8	Gateshead	10,248
1992-93	#St. Helens	17	*Wigan	0	Gateshead	7,364

*Denotes previous season's Champions; † Premiership winners; unmarked, Challenge Cup winners;
Championship runners-up

CHARITY SHIELD .... A REVIEW

1985-86
Wigan 34 Hampson; P. Ford, Stephenson (7g), Donlan (2t), Gill (2t); Edwards, M. Ford (1t); Courtney (Mayo), Kiss, Campbell, West (Lucas), Du Toit, Wane
Hull K.R. 6 Fairbairn (Lydiat 1g); Clark (1t), Robinson, Prohm, Laws; M. Smith, G. Smith; Des Harrison, Watkinson, Ema, Kelly (Rudd), Burton, Hogan
Referee: R. Campbell (Widnes)

1986-87
Halifax 9 Smith (Wilson); Riddlesden, Whitfield (1t), Hague (1dg), George (1t); C. Anderson, Stephens; Dickinson, McCallion, Juliff, Scott (James), Bell, Dixon
Castleford 8 Roockley; Plange, Lord (1t), Irwin (R. Southernwood), Spears; Joyner (Fletcher), R. Beardmore; Ward, K. Beardmore, Johnson, Ketteridge (2g), Mountain, England
Referee: G.F. Lindop (Wakefield)

Halifax celebrate their 1986-87 Charity Shield success over Castleford on the Isle of Man.

1987-88
Wigan 44 Hampson (2t); Stephenson (8g),
Byrne (Russell), Bell (2t), Gill (1t); Edwards
(2t), Gregory; West, Kiss, Case, Gildart
(Wane), Potter, Goodway
Halifax 12 Eadie (2g); Taylor, Wilson,
T. Anderson, George; Simpson (Juliff 1t),
Stephens; Dickinson, Pendlebury, Beevers,
James, Scott (Bell), Dixon (1t)
Referee: J. Holdsworth (Kippax)
1988-89
Widnes 20 Tait; Thackray, Currier (4g),
D. Wright (1t), Offiah (1t); Dowd, D. Hulme;
Sorensen, McKenzie (1t), Grima (Pyke),
M. O'Neill, P. Hulme, R. Eyres
Wigan 14 Hampson; Gill, Lydon (1t, 1g), Bell,
Preston (Lucas); Byrne, Gregory; Shelford
(Betts), Kiss, Case, T. Iro (2t), Wane,
Goodway
Referee: R. Tennant (Castleford)
1989-90
Widnes 27 Tait (1dg); Kebbie (1t), Davies
(1t, 5g), D. Wright, Offiah (1t); A. Myler,
D. Hulme (1t); Sorensen, P. Hulme, Grima
(Pyke), M. O'Neill, Koloto, R. Eyres
Wigan 22 Hampson; Bell (Gilfillan), K. Iro
(1t), Lydon (1t, 5g), Preston; Byrne, Gregory;
Lucas, Kiss, Platt (1t) (Stazicker), Betts,
Gildart, Goodway
Referee: J. Holdsworth (Kippax)
1990-91
Widnes 24 Tait; Devereux (1t), Currier, Davies
(3t, 2g), Offiah (1t); A. Myler, D. Hulme;
Ashurst (D. Wright), McKenzie, Grima, P. Hulme
(Sorensen), Koloto, Holliday
Wigan 8 Gilfillan; Myers, Bell, Byrne, Preston;
Botica (1t, 2g) (Edwards), Goulding; Skerrett,
Bridge, Wane, Gildart (Forshaw), Platt, Betts
Referee: C. Morris (Huddersfield)

1991-92
Wigan 22 Hampson; Myers (1t), Bell (2t), Lydon,
Botica (3g); Edwards (1t), Gregory; Lucas
(Gildart), Dermott, Skerrett, Betts, Platt
(Forshaw), Goodway
Hull 8 Feather; Eastwood (2g), Blacker, G. Nolan
(1t), Turner; Hanlan, Mackey; Durham (Dixon),
L. Jackson, Marlow, McNamara (Jones), Walker,
Busby
Referee: R. Whitfield (Widnes)
1992-93
St. Helens 17 Hunte; Riley, Connolly, Ropati (1t,
2g), Sullivan (1t); Griffiths, O'Donnell (1dg)
(Quirk); Neill, Dwyer, Ward, Harrison, Mann
(Forber), Cooper (1t)
Wigan 0 Hampson; Panapa, Bell, Lydon (Myers),
Offiah; Botica, Crompton; Lucas, Cassidy, Skerrett
(Goodway), Betts, McGinty, Clarke
Referee: S. Cummings (Widnes)

CHARITY SHIELD RECORDS

TEAM
Most appearances: 7 Wigan
Most wins: 3 Widnes, Wigan
Highest score: Wigan 44 v. Halifax 12 1987
(Also widest margin)
Biggest attendance:
17,263 Widnes v. Wigan (at Liverpool FC) 1989

INDIVIDUAL
Most tries:
3 by Jonathan Davies (Widnes) v. Wigan 1990
Most goals:
8 by David Stephenson (Wigan) v. Halifax 1987
Most points:
16 (8g) by David Stephenson (Wigan) v. Halifax ... 1987
   (3t,2g) Jonathan Davies (Widnes) v. Wigan 1990

MAN OF THE MATCH AWARDS

Season	Winner	Team	Position
1985-86	Shaun Edwards	Wigan (v. Hull K.R.)	Stand off
1986-87	Chris Anderson	Halifax (v. Castleford)	Stand off
1987-88	Shaun Edwards	Wigan (v. Halifax)	Stand off
1988-89	Phil McKenzie	Widnes (v. Wigan)	Hooker
1989-90	Denis Betts	Wigan (v. Widnes)	Second row
1990-91	Jonathan Davies	Widnes (v. Wigan)	Centre
1991-92	Dean Bell	Wigan (v. Hull)	Centre
1992-93	Alan Hunte	St. Helens (v. Wigan)	Full back

● From 1987 it became the Jack Bentley Trophy in memory of the former *Daily Express* Rugby
League journalist.

WORLD CLUB CHALLENGE 1994

Wigan produced one of their most impressive displays of physical and mental strength to beat Australian champions Brisbane Broncos 20-14 in the first official World Club Challenge encounter to be staged Down Under.

The Riversiders took their tryscoring chances superbly and were magnificent on defence, especially taking into account their recent completion of a 45-match domestic programme and a round-the-world journey for the Brisbane showdown.

And the narrow, but thoroughly deserved, victory was executed in front of a home crowd of more than 54,000 partisan fans in the Broncos' ANZ Stadium.

The hard-earned success boosted Wigan caretaker coach Graeme West's chances of landing the job permanently as the Britons collected a winner-takes-all £200,000 cash prize, achieved without first choice Test props Kelvin Skerrett and Andy Platt.

Having opened a 12-0 lead inside the first 16 minutes, Wigan sustained a 25-minute spell of intense pressure from the double Sydney Grand Final victors, who entered the last quarter only four points adrift.

Wigan's heroic stubborn defence held out for a memorable victory which gained revenge for the 22-8 defeat by Brisbane 17 months earlier at Central Park. Wigan's two previous World Club Challenge triumphs had been gained on British soil amid Australian claims of British advantage of venue and timing.

It was vital that Wigan scored first and when full back Willie Carne found himself badly positioned to field a bomb from Wigan skipper Shaun Edwards, second row man Denis Betts manoeuvred the bouncing ball with one hand to touch down for the opening score after seven minutes, Frano Botica adding the goal.

Nine minutes later, Wigan struck again with loose forward Phil Clarke sending Barrie-Jon Mather away, the tall centre easily evading opposite number Steve Renouf and using wing partner Martin Offiah as a decoy to drift past Wendell Sailor for the second try, Botica again obliging with the goal.

Jason Robinson, Sam Panapa, Offiah and Gary Connolly all made try saving tackles before the outstanding Sailor replied for Brisbane in the 27th minute, going outside Offiah to score in the corner to give a half-time scoreline of 12-4 to the visitors.

Robinson opened the second half with an opportunist try after Kangaroo Test winger Michael Hancock spilled the ball and, with Botica again adding the goal, Wigan looked set for a comfortable run-in to victory at 18-4.

But the battling Broncos, whose recent League form had been below par, staged an attacking onslaught, which even two years ago would have seen an English club defence wilt. Despite Wigan's Herculean efforts, their defence gave way twice, conceding tries to Hancock in the 46th minute and former Widnes utility man Julian O'Neill 13 minutes later, the loose forward adding the goal to his own try to close the gap to 18-14.

But Wigan's renowned mental strength prevented a collapse and, when Carne fouled Betts 14 minutes from time, Botica's successful penalty kick provided valuable breathing space after which Wigan unsuccessfully tried a series of drop goal attempts to put the result beyond doubt.

Edwards took the official Man of the Match award but there were also outstanding contributions from the devastating Robinson and full back Connolly, plus the excellent back three of Betts, Andrew Farrell and Clarke.

MAN OF THE MATCH AWARDS
1987: Shaun Wane (Wigan)
1989: David Hulme (Widnes)
1991: Frano Botica (Wigan)
1992: Terry Matterson (Brisbane B.)
1994: Shaun Edwards (Wigan)

WORLD CLUB CHALLENGE

1 June 1994 ANZ Stadium, Brisbane

WIGAN 20		BRISBANE BRONCOS 14
Gary Connolly	1.	Willie Carne
Jason Robinson	2.	Wendell Sailor
Sam Panapa	3.	Steve Renouf
Barrie-Jon Mather	4.	Chris Johns
Martin Offiah	5.	Michael Hancock
Frano Botica	6.	Kevin Walters
Shaun Edwards, Capt.	7.	Allan Langer, Capt.
Neil Cowie	8.	Glenn Lazarus
Martin Dermott	9.	Kerrod Walters
Billy McGinty	10.	Andrew Gee
Denis Betts	11.	Mark Hohn
Andrew Farrell	12.	Alan Cann
Philip Clarke	13.	Julian O'Neill
Va'aiga Tuigamala	14.	John Plath
Martin Hall	15.	Peter Ryan
Paul Atcheson	16.	Brett Galea
Mick Cassidy	17.	Chris McKenna

T: Betts, Mather, Robinson
G: Botica (4)
Substitutions:
Hall for Dermott (23 min.)
Cassidy for McGinty (26 min.)
Atcheson for Mather (50 min.)
Half-time: 12-4
Referee: Greg McCallum (Australia)

T: Sailor, Hancock, O'Neill
G: O'Neill
Substitutions:
Plath for Kevin Walters (6 min.)
Ryan for Renouf (23 min.)
Galea for Gee (65 min.)
McKenna for Plath (74 min.)
Attendance: 54,220

Year	Winners		Runners-up		Venue	Attendance	Receipts
1987	Wigan	8	Manly-Warringah	2	Wigan	36,895	£131,000
1989	Widnes	30	Canberra	18	Old Trafford, Man'r	30,786	£207,764
1991	Wigan	21	Penrith	4	Anfield, Liverpool	20,152	£179,797
1992	Brisbane B.	22	Wigan	8	Wigan	17,746	£170,911
1994	Wigan	20	Brisbane B.	14	Brisbane	54,220	$448,041

1987-88
Wigan 8 Hampson; Russell, Stephenson (4g), Lydon, Gill; Edwards, Gregory; Case (Lucas), Kiss, Wane, Goodway, Potter, Hanley
Manly 2 Shearer; Ronson, Williams (Ticehurst), O'Connor (1g), Davis; Lyons, Hasler; Daley, Cochrane, Gately (Brokenshire), Gibbs, Cunningham (Shaw), Vautin
Referee: J. Holdsworth (Kippax)
1989-90
Widnes 30 Tait; Currier, Davies (1t, 3g), D. Wright (1t), Offiah (2t); A. Myler (Dowd), D. Hulme; Grima (Moriarty), McKenzie, Pyke, Sorensen, P. Hulme (1t), R. Eyres (1t)
Canberra 18 Belcher; Wood (2g), Meninga (1t) (Martin), Daley, Ferguson; O'Sullivan (1t, 1g), Stuart; Jackson (Lowry), Walters (1t), Lazarus, Lance, Coyne, Clyde
Referee: F. Desplas (France)

1991-92
Wigan 21 Hampson; Myers (1t), Panapa (1t), Lydon (1dg), Botica (6g); Edwards, Gregory; Skerrett (Cowie) (Lucas), Dermott, Platt, Betts, McGinty (Gildart), Clarke (Forshaw)
Penrith 4 Barwick (B. Alexander); Willis (1t) (Smith), Bradley, B. Izzard, Mackay; Carter, G. Alexander; Lee (G. Izzard), Simmons, Dunn, Clarke, Cartwright, Van Der Voort (Xuereb)
Referee: A. Sablayrolles (France)
1992-93
Brisbane B. 22 O'Neill (1t) (Plowman); Carne, Renouf, Johns (Currie), Hancock (2t); Kevin Walters, Langer (Plath); Lazarus, Kerrod Walters (1t), Gee (Ryan), Gillmeister, Hohn, Matterson (3g)
Wigan 8 Stoop (Crompton); Robinson, Bell, Farrar, Offiah; Botica (2g), Edwards (1t); Skerrett (Lucas), Dermott, Platt (Cowie), Betts, McGinty (Panapa), Clarke
Referee: D. Hale (New Zealand)

249

BBC-2 FLOODLIT TROPHY

The BBC-2 Floodlit Trophy competition was launched in 1965. Eight clubs competed in the first year and the total had grown to 22 by 1980 when the competition was abolished as part of the BBC's financial cut-backs.

For 15 years the matches were a regular television feature on Tuesday evenings throughout the early winter months.

Although the format changed slightly over the years, it was basically a knockout competition on the lines of the Challenge Cup.

In 1966 the Floodlit Competition was used to introduce the limited tackle rule, then four tackles, which proved such a great success it was adopted in all other matches before the end of the year.

BBC-2 FLOODLIT TROPHY FINALS
(Only the 1967, at Leeds, and 1972, at Wigan, finals were played on neutral grounds)

Season	Winners		Runners-up		Venue	Attendance	Receipts
1965-66	Castleford	4	St. Helens	0	St. Helens	11,510	£1,548
1966-67	Castleford	7	Swinton	2	Castleford	8,986	£1,692
1967-68	Castleford	8	Leigh	5	Leeds	9,716	£2,099
1968-69	Wigan	7	St. Helens	4	Wigan	13,479	£3,291
1969-70	Leigh	11	Wigan	6	Wigan	12,312	£2,854
1970-71	Leeds	9	St. Helens	5	Leeds	7,612	£2,189
1971-72	St. Helens	8	Rochdale H.	2	St. Helens	9,300	£2,493
1972-73	Leigh	5	Widnes	0	Wigan	4,691	£1,391
1973-74	Bramley	15	Widnes	7	Widnes	4,422	£1,538
1974-75	Salford	0	Warrington	0	Salford	4,473	£1,913
Replay	Salford	10	Warrington	5	Warrington	5,778	£2,434
1975-76	St. Helens	22	Dewsbury	2	St. Helens	3,858	£1,747
1976-77	Castleford	12	Leigh	4	Leigh	5,402	£2,793
1977-78	Hull K.R.	26	St. Helens	11	Hull K.R.	10,099	£6,586
1978-79	Widnes	13	St. Helens	7	St. Helens	10,250	£7,017
1979-80	Hull	13	Hull K.R.	3	Hull	18,500	£16,605

BBC-2 FLOODLIT TROPHY . . . A REVIEW
1965-66
Castleford 4 Edwards; C. Battye, M. Battye, Willett (2g), Briggs; Hardisty, Millward; Terry, J. Ward, C. Dickinson, Bryant, Taylor, Small
St. Helens 0 F. Barrow; Vollenhoven, Wood, Benyon, Killeen; Murphy, Prosser; French, Dagnall, Watson, Hicks, Mantle, Laughton
Referee: L. Gant (Wakefield)
1966-67
Castleford 7 Edwards; Howe, Stenton, Willett (1g), Austin (1t); Hardisty, Hepworth (1g); Hartley, C. Dickinson, McCartney, Bryant, Small, Walker
Swinton 2 Gowers; Whitehead (1g), Gomersall, Buckley, Davies; Fleet, G. Williams; Halliwell, D. Clarke, Scott (Cummings), Rees, Simpson, Robinson
Referee: J. Manley (Warrington)
1967-68
Castleford 8 Edwards; Harris, Thomas, Stenton, Willett (4g); Hardisty, Hepworth; Hartley, J. Ward, Walton, Bryant (C. Dickinson), Redfearn, Reilly

Leigh 5 Grainey; Tickle (1t), Lewis, Collins, Walsh; Entwistle, A. Murphy; Whitworth, Ashcroft, Major, Welding, M. Murphy, Gilfedder (1g)
Referee: G.F. Lindop (Wakefield)
1968-69
Wigan 7 Tyrer (2g); Francis, Ashton, Ashurst, Rowe; C. Hill (1t), Jackson; J. Stephens, Clarke, Mills, Fogerty (Lyon), Kevin O'Loughlin, Laughton
St. Helens 4 Williams; Wilson, Benyon, Myler, Wills; Whittle, Bishop; Warlow, Sayer, Watson, Mantle, Hogan, Coslett (2g)
Referee: E. Clay (Leeds)
1969-70
Leigh 11 Ferguson (3g) (Lewis); Tickle (1t), Dorrington, Collins, Walsh; Eckersley, Murphy (1g); D. Chisnall, Ashcroft, Watts, Welding, Grimes, Lyon
Wigan 6 C. Hill; Wright, Francis (2g), Rowe, Kevin O'Loughlin; D. Hill (1g), Jackson; J. Stephens, Clarke, Ashcroft, Ashurst, Mills, Laughton
Referee: W.H. Thompson (Huddersfield)

1970-71
Leeds 9 Holmes (2g); Alan Smith, Hynes
(1t, 1g), Cowan, Atkinson; Wainwright,
Shoebottom; J. Burke, Fisher, Barnard, Haigh,
Ramsey, Batten
St. Helens 5 F. Barrow; L. Jones (1t), Benyon,
Walsh, Wilson; Whittle, Heaton; Rees,
A. Karalius, E. Chisnall, Mantle, E. Prescott,
Coslett (1g)
Referee: E. Lawrinson (Warrington)
1971-72
St. Helens 8 G. Pimblett; L. Jones, Benyon,
Walsh, Wilson; Kelly, Heaton; Rees,
A. Karalius, E. Chisnall, E. Prescott, Mantle,
Coslett (4g)
Rochdale H. 2 Chamberlain (1g); Brelsford,
Crellin, Taylor, Glover; Myler, Gartland;
Birchall, P. Clarke, Brown, Welding, Sheffield
(Hodkinson), Delooze
Referee: E. Clay (Leeds)
1972-73
Leigh 5 Hogan; Lawson (1t) (Lester), Atkin,
Collins, Stacey; A. Barrow, Sayer (Ryding);
Grimes, D. Clarke, Fletcher, Fiddler (1g),
F. Barrow, Martyn
Widnes 0 Dutton; A. Prescott, Aspey,
Blackwood, McDonnell; Lowe, Ashton;
Mills, Elwell, Warlow, Foran, Sheridan,
Nicholls
Referee: G.F. Lindop (Wakefield)
1973-74
Bramley 15 Keegan; Goodchild (1t), Bollon,
Hughes, Austin (1t); T. Briggs, Ward (1g)
(Ashman); D. Briggs, Firth, Cheshire,
D. Sampson (1t), Idle, Wolford (2g)
Widnes 7 Dutton (2g); D. O'Neill, Hughes,
Aspey, Macko (1t); Warburton, Bowden;
Hogan, Elwell, Nelson, Sheridan, Blackwood
(Foran), Laughton
Referee: D.G. Kershaw (York)
1974-75
Salford 0 Charlton; Fielding, Hesketh,
Graham, Richards; Brophy (Taylor), Banner;
Coulman, Devlin, Grice, Knighton, Dixon,
E. Prescott
Warrington 0 Whitehead; Sutton, Cunliffe
(Lowe), Whittle, Bevan; Briggs, Gordon;
D. Chisnall, Ashcroft, Wright, Gaskell, Conroy,
B. Philbin (Jewitt)
Referee: W.H. Thompson (Huddersfield)
Replay
Salford 10 Stead; Fielding (1t), Watkins (2g),
Hesketh, Richards (1t); Gill, Banner; Grice,
Walker, Mackay, Dixon, Knighton, E. Prescott

Warrington 5 Cunliffe; Whitehead (1g), Pickup,
Whittle, Bevan (1t); Noonan (Briggs), Gordon;
D. Chisnall, Ashcroft, Wanbon, Conroy,
Nicholas (Brady), B. Philbin
Referee: W.H. Thompson (Huddersfield)
1975-76
St. Helens 22 G. Pimblett (2g); L. Jones,
Benyon (1t), Hull (1t), Mathias (2t); Wilson
(1t), Heaton (1dg); Mantle, A. Karalius, James,
Nicholls, E. Chisnall, Coslett (1g)
Dewsbury 2 Langley; Hegarty, Chalkley,
Simpson, Mitchell; N. Stephenson (1g) (Lee),
A. Bates; Beverley, Price, Hankins, Halloran
(Artis), Bell, Grayshon
Referee: W.H. Thompson (Huddersfield)
1976-77
Castleford 12 Wraith; Fenton, Joyner, P.
Johnson, Walsh (1t); Burton (1t), Stephens;
Khan, Spurr, A. Dickinson, Reilly, Lloyd (3g),
S. Norton
Leigh 4 Hogan; A. Prescott, Stacey, Woods,
Walsh (1t); Taylor, Sayer; D. Chisnall, Ashcroft
(1dg), Fletcher, Macko, Grimes, Boyd
Referee: J.E. Jackson (Pudsey)
1977-78
Hull K.R. 26 Hall (4g); Dunn (2t), M. Smith
(1t), Watson, Sullivan (1t); Hartley (1t),
Millward; Millington, Watkinson, Cunningham
(Hughes), Lowe, Rose (1t), Casey
St. Helens 11 G. Pimblett (Platt); L. Jones
(Courtney), Noonan, Cunningham (1t), Glynn
(2t, 1g); Francis, K. Gwilliam; D. Chisnall,
Liptrot, James, Hope, A. Karalius, Pinner
Referee: M.J. Naughton (Widnes)
1978-79
Widnes 13 Eckersley; Wright (2t), Hughes,
Aspey, P. Shaw; Burke (1t, 2g), Bowden;
Hogan, Elwell, Mills, Adams, Dearden,
Laughton
St. Helens 7 G. Pimblett (2g); L. Jones,
Glynn, Cunningham, Mathias; Francis,
Holding; D. Chisnall (1t), Liptrot, James,
Nicholls, Knighton (E. Chisnall), Pinner
Referee: J. McDonald (Wigan)
1979-80
Hull 13 Woods; Bray, G. Evans (1t), Coupland,
Dennison (1t, 2g); Newlove, Hepworth;
Tindall, Wileman, Farrar, Stone, Boxall
(Birdsall 1t), Norton
Hull K.R. 3 Robinson; Hubbard (1t),
M. Smith, Watson, Sullivan; Hall, Agar;
Holdstock, Tyreman, Lockwood, Clarkson
(Hartley), Lowe, Hogan (Millington)
Referee: W.H. Thompson (Huddersfield)

CAPTAIN MORGAN TROPHY

This sponsored competition, with a winners' prize of £3,000, lasted only one season. Entry was restricted to the 16 clubs who won their Yorkshire and Lancashire Cup first round ties. The Lancashire contingent was made up to eight by including the side which lost their first round county cup tie by the narrowest margin. The first round of the Captain Morgan Trophy was zoned with clubs being drawn against those in their own county. The remainder of the competition was integrated. The final was on a neutral ground as follows:

1973-74	Warrington 4	Featherstone R. 0	Salford	5,259	£2,265

1973-74

Warrington 4 Whitehead (2g); M. Philbin, Noonan, Reynolds (Pickup), Bevan; Whittle, Gordon; D. Chisnall, Ashcroft, Brady, Wanbon (Price), Wright, Mather

Featherstone R. 0 Box; Coventry, M. Smith, Hartley, Bray; Mason, Wood; Tonks, Bridges, Harris, Gibbins (Stone), Rhodes, Bell
Referee: G.F. Lindop (Wakefield)

Workington Town won the Second Division title for the first time in 1993-94, skipper Colin Armstrong holding aloft the bowl.

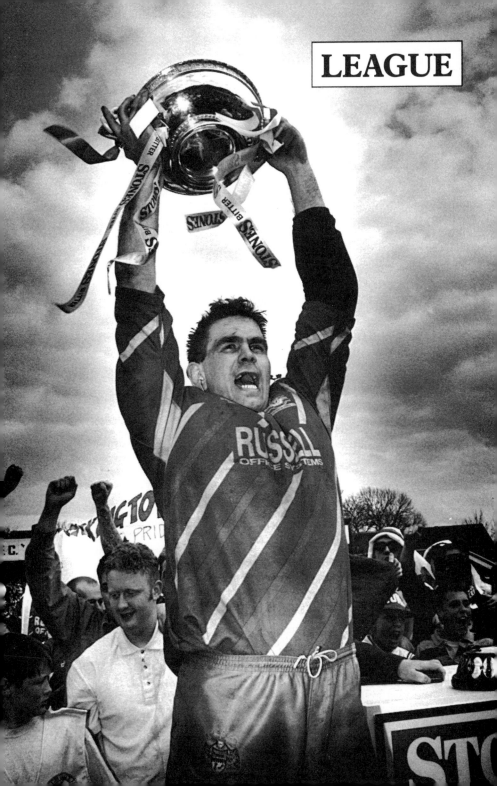

LEAGUE

1993-94 CHAMPIONSHIP

Bradford Northern, Warrington and Wigan formed a three-horse race for the 1993-94 Stones Bitter Championship, finishing neck and neck with 46 points. Each lost seven matches, but Wigan won the photo finish with a vastly superior points difference to claim a record-extending fifth successive title.

The First Division reverted to 16 clubs after six seasons of 14, following the scrapping of three divisions after only two seasons.

The chase for the £56,000 Stones Bitter prize cheque went the whole distance of the eight-month campaign with the leading trio entering the final weekend level on points with one round of matches left.

Controversy entered the last lap of the title race when the League agreed to a request from BSkyB Television to stage the three deciding fixtures over three separate days.

Warrington had already been allocated the Friday night live BSkyB game at the start of the season and were happy to fulfil the obligation. Wigan, the title favourites, did not object to moving their Sunday afternoon game at Oldham to a live evening kick-off.

However, Bradford Northern were angry at having to move their scheduled Sunday afternoon match at Leeds forward 24 hours, claiming that all the title contenders should kick off at the same time on the same day. When Northern's protests went unheeded, club chairman Chris Caisley resigned from the League's Board of Directors pointing out that, not for the first time that season, there had been a clash of interests between his services to club and League.

Thus the three title contenders approached the final hurdle level on 44 points apiece. Warrington disposed of a weakened Sheffield Eagles at Wilderspool by 36-18 to top the table. Bradford Northern then faced Wembley-bound Leeds at Headingley and, against a side starting with only four of their Cup final team, recorded a 52-10 rout, scoring nine tries to two.

Northern went to the top for the next 24 hours until Wigan soaked up a spirited opening quarter from Oldham, fourth from bottom, before showing Championship style in a 50-6 victory, running in nine tries.

The triple success meant that, for the first time in Rugby League history, the title was decided from three clubs tied on equal points. Wigan retained their premier rating with a scoring difference of 377 points, well clear of Bradford Northern's 229 and Warrington's 198.

Warrington's progress from the previous season's ranking of eighth to joint top after starting as 50-1 outsiders for the title was outstanding. The close season signing of Jonathan Davies proved to be a masterstroke as the Welsh scoring machine was inspirational in his appointed centre role, encouraging the Wire to adopt a more flamboyant gameplan. Skipper Greg Mackey and loose forward Kelly Shelford were the creative engine room of the revitalised Wilderspool outfit.

Ironically, Warrington did not take any points off their fellow title chasers, whereas Bradford Northern and Wigan shared the spoils in their two encounters four days apart in April. It was the home defeat by Wigan which was to cause Warrington to reflect on what might have been.

Their first game of 1994 was heading for a draw at 6-6 when referee Russell Smith penalised Warrington, first for foul play and then Davies talking back, to give Frano Botica an easy chance to boot Wigan to a last second 8-6 victory. That point would have ultimately given Warrington the title.

But it was a season of what might have beens, with each of the trio of contenders losing unexpected matches which continually affected the make-up of the top of the table.

Northern were in contention throughout the season, leading the table after five matches at the end of September. They were still there after 10 rounds at the start of November, level on points with Warrington and Castleford.

As the new year opened, the top three spots had taken on a familiar look with Wigan on top. They were followed by Warrington, who had played two more matches, and Northern.

Wigan dropped to third place during February as they started to lag behind in fixture fulfilment due to their cup and international commitments, bringing their now traditional end of season fixture pile-up.

As the Stones Bitter Championship race entered the last two months, title nerves emerged. Warrington were to pay the price for lack of success against their fellow title contenders, their other defeats being at Halifax, Leeds and Wakefield Trinity.

But both Bradford and Wigan started dropping points against the form guide. Northern's jitters came in mid-March at home to relegation-bound Leigh. With the pundits having merrily pinpointed the need for a big win to improve their points difference margin compared with rivals Wigan, Northern lost 24-14 to the bottom club.

Wigan then lost twice in five days, both away, 18-4 at Hull and 10-5 at in-form Sheffield.

The nerves became even more frayed as April opened. Northern suffered two bad defeats over Easter, 27-18 at Halifax and then 32-30 at home to Hull. Wigan had regained their composure with victories over St. Helens, Halifax and Warrington, before travelling to relegation-bound Hull Kingston Rovers the weekend after Easter, only to go down 21-10. The title was wide open again, setting up the most exciting gallop in the 98-year history of the Championship.

At the bottom end of the table, Leigh propped up the other 15 clubs for the whole of the season to make relegation a formality, going down for the third time in 10 years and the fifth since two divisions were reintroduced in 1973-74.

They were joined by Hull K.R. who had finished bottom the previous season and escaped the drop because of the restructuring of the League system from three divisions to two. The Robins were doomed to a third season in the Second Division during the current divisional period despite late form which claimed the scalps of Wigan and Widnes in the final weeks.

The Second Division title race was also a thriller. After a promising start, Huddersfield and joint-title favourites Keighley Cougars both faded in the run-in to finish outside the top four. Joint 9-4 favourites Workington Town clinched the Stones Bitter prize cheque for £28,000 with a 52-8 win at Bramley on the final day of the campaign, but it was the runners-up spot which caused the most interest.

The last afternoon of the League season saw Batley entertain Doncaster, victory either way clinching promotion. A draw, however, would allow London Crusaders, if victorious at Carlisle, to leapfrog over them both to be upgraded.

In a tense encounter at a packed Mount Pleasant, the first half remained scoreless, Batley breaking the deadlock to lead 5-0 at threequarter-time. The dismissal of veteran prop Jeff Grayshon sparked a comeback by Doncaster who ran in two late tries to steal the honours, the Dons' first promotion since formation in 1951.

At the other end of the table, Highfield won one game and drew one to become the first side to face relegation to the National Conference League, but were reprieved. Leeds-based duo Bramley and Hunslet also failed to reach double figures in the points column.

Dean Bell, 1993-94 Championship winning skipper of Wigan before his departure for Auckland Warriors.

FINAL TABLES 1993-94

STONES BITTER CHAMPIONSHIP

	P.	W.	D.	L.	Dg.	Gls.	Trs.	Pts.	Dg.	Gls.	Trs.	Pts.	Pts.
						FOR				**AGAINST**			
Wigan	30	23	0	7	8	124	131	780	3	68	66	403	46
Bradford N.	30	23	0	7	10	107	140	784	3	80	98	555	46
Warrington	30	23	0	7	16	98	104	628	10	72	69	430	46
Castleford	30	19	1	10	3	112	140	787	10	74	77	466	39
Halifax	30	17	2	11	4	97	121	682	5	86	101	581	36
Sheffield E.	30	16	2	12	8	102	123	704	11	102	114	671	34
Leeds	30	15	2	13	5	102	116	673	6	107	115	680	32
St. Helens	30	15	1	14	18	109	117	704	9	86	89	537	31
Hull	30	14	2	14	4	82	92	536	8	79	91	530	30
Widnes	30	14	0	16	3	84	88	523	10	94	111	642	28
Featherstone R.	30	13	1	16	3	98	113	651	7	105	116	681	27
Salford	30	11	0	19	6	80	97	554	4	105	109	650	22
Oldham	30	10	1	19	8	80	96	552	5	97	113	651	21
Wakefield T.	30	9	1	20	2	68	80	458	6	99	126	708	19
Hull K.R.	30	9	0	21	5	88	78	493	4	107	141	782	18
Leigh	30	2	1	27	4	57	63	370	6	127	163	912	5

SECOND DIVISION

	P.	W.	D.	L.	Dg.	Gls.	Trs.	Pts.	Dg.	Gls.	Trs.	Pts.	Pts.
						FOR				**AGAINST**			
Workington T.	30	22	2	6	4	114	132	760	7	54	54	331	46
Doncaster	30	22	1	7	11	99	130	729	8	67	86	486	45
London C.	30	21	2	7	4	119	150	842	4	81	89	522	44
Batley	30	21	1	8	3	96	128	707	4	63	74	426	43
Huddersfield	30	20	0	10	3	107	111	661	10	76	89	518	40
Keighley C.	30	19	1	10	4	104	161	856	8	66	83	472	39
Dewsbury	30	18	1	11	2	120	131	766	4	68	77	448	37
Rochdale H.	30	18	0	12	10	101	123	704	4	72	96	532	36
Ryedale-York	30	17	1	12	12	89	118	662	6	73	91	516	35
Whitehaven	30	14	4	12	5	75	104	571	3	69	74	437	32
Barrow	30	13	1	16	13	82	101	581	7	104	132	743	27
Swinton	30	11	0	19	6	77	92	528	7	91	123	681	22
Carlisle	30	9	0	21	6	79	94	540	6	132	152	878	18
Hunslet	30	3	1	26	1	62	80	445	12	109	146	814	7
Bramley	30	3	0	27	4	40	73	376	1	132	173	957	6
Highfield	30	1	1	28	5	47	42	267	2	154	231	1,234	3

1993-94 PRE-SEASON BETTING FOR THE CHAMPIONSHIPS
Coral's pre-season betting:
For the Stones Bitter Championship: 4-6 Wigan; 7-2 St. Helens; 5-1 Bradford N.; 8-1 Halifax; 10-1 Leeds; 14-1 Castleford; 25-1 Widnes; 50-1 Warrington; 150-1 Hull; 200-1 Featherstone R., Oldham; 300-1 Sheffield E., Salford; 500-1 Hull K.R., Leigh, Wakefield T.
For the Second Division Championship: 9-4 Keighley C., Workington T.; 100-30 London C.; 9-1 Huddersfield; 12-1 Dewsbury, Rochdale H.; 16-1 Swinton; 20-1 Whitehaven; 28-1 Ryedale-York; 33-1 Batley; 40-1 Carlisle; 66-1 Bramley, Doncaster, Hunslet; 250-1 Barrow; 1,000-1 Highfield.

TWO DIVISION CHAMPIONSHIP ROLL OF HONOUR

	FIRST DIVISION	SECOND DIVISION
1902-03	Halifax	Keighley
1903-04	Bradford	Wakefield Trinity
1904-05	Oldham	Dewsbury
1962-63	Swinton	Hunslet
1963-64	Swinton	Oldham
1973-74	Salford	Bradford Northern
1974-75	St. Helens	Huddersfield
1975-76	Salford	Barrow
1976-77	Featherstone Rovers	Hull
1977-78	Widnes	Leigh
1978-79	Hull Kingston Rovers	Hull
1979-80	Bradford Northern	Featherstone Rovers
1980-81	Bradford Northern	York
1981-82	Leigh	Oldham
1982-83	Hull	Fulham
1983-84	Hull Kingston Rovers	Barrow
1984-85	Hull Kingston Rovers	Swinton
1985-86	Halifax	Leigh
1986-87	Wigan	Hunslet
1987-88	Widnes	Oldham
1988-89	Widnes	Leigh
1989-90	Wigan	Hull Kingston Rovers
1990-91	Wigan	Salford
1991-92	Wigan	Sheffield Eagles
1992-93	Wigan	Featherstone Rovers
1993-94	Wigan	Workington Town

THIRD DIVISION CHAMPIONS

1991-92	Huddersfield
1992-93	Keighley Cougars

RELEGATION AND PROMOTION
Since reintroduction of two divisions in 1973-74.

●Figure in brackets indicates position in division.

	RELEGATED	PROMOTED
1973-74	Oldham (13) Hull K.R. (14) Leigh (15) Whitehaven (16)	Bradford Northern (1) York (2) Keighley (3) Halifax (4)
1974-75	York (13) Bramley (14) Rochdale Hornets (15) Halifax (16)	Huddersfield (1) Hull K.R. (2) Oldham (3) Swinton (4)
1975-76	Dewsbury (13) Keighley (14) Huddersfield (15) Swinton (16)	Barrow (1) Rochdale Hornets (2) Workington Town (3) Leigh (4)
1976-77	Rochdale Hornets (13) Leigh (14) Barrow (15) Oldham (16)	Hull (1) Dewsbury (2) Bramley (3) New Hunslet (4)
1977-78	Hull (13) New Hunslet (14) Bramley (15) Dewsbury (16)	Leigh (1) Barrow (2) Rochdale Hornets (3) Huddersfield (4)
1978-79	Barrow (13) Featherstone Rovers (14) Rochdale Hornets (15) Huddersfield (16)	Hull (1) New Hunslet (2) York (3) Blackpool Borough (4)
1979-80	Wigan (13) Hunslet (14) York (15) Blackpool Borough (16)	Featherstone Rovers (1) Halifax (2) Oldham (3) Barrow (4)
1980-81	Halifax (13) Salford (14) Workington Town (15) Oldham (16)	York (1) Wigan (2) Fulham (3) Whitehaven (4)
1981-82	Fulham (13) Wakefield Trinity (14) York (15) Whitehaven (16)	Oldham (1) Carlisle (2) Workington Town (3) Halifax (4)
1982-83	Barrow (13) Workington Town (14) Halifax (15) Carlisle (16)	Fulham (1) Wakefield Trinity (2) Salford (3) Whitehaven (4)
1983-84	Fulham (13) Wakefield Trinity (14) Salford (15) Whitehaven (16)	Barrow (1) Workington Town (2) Hunslet (3) Halifax (4)

1984-85	Barrow (13) Leigh (14) Hunslet (15) Workington Town (16)	Swinton (1) Salford (2) York (3) Dewsbury (4)
1985-86	York (14) Swinton (15) Dewsbury (16)	Leigh (1) Barrow (2) Wakefield Trinity (3)
1986-87	Oldham (13) Featherstone Rovers (14) Barrow (15) Wakefield Trinity (16)	Hunslet (1) Swinton (2)
1987-88	Leigh (12) Swinton (13) Hunslet (14)	Oldham (1) Featherstone Rovers (2) Wakefield Trinity (3)
1988-89	Oldham (12) Halifax (13) Hull K.R. (14)	Leigh (1) Barrow (2) Sheffield Eagles (3)
1989-90	Leigh (12) Salford (13) Barrow (14)	Hull K.R. (1) Rochdale Hornets (2) Oldham (3)
1990-91	Oldham (12) Sheffield Eagles (13) Rochdale Hornets (14)	Salford (1) Halifax (2) Swinton (3)

	FIRST DIVISION	SECOND DIVISION	THIRD DIVISION
1991-92	Down: Featherstone R. (13) Swinton (14)	Up: Sheffield E. (1) Leigh (2) Down: Ryedale-York (7) Workington Town (8)	Up: Huddersfield (1) Bramley (2)
1992-93	—	Up: Featherstone R. (1) Oldham (2)	—
1993-94	RELEGATED Hull K.R. (15) Leigh (16)	PROMOTED Workington Town (1) Doncaster (2)	

Workington Town winger Stuart Cocker, a prolific try scorer for the 1993-94 Second Division champions.

FIRST DIVISION RECORDS
Since reintroduction in 1973

INDIVIDUAL
Match records

Most tries:
6 Shane Cooper (St. Helens) v. Hull, 17 February 1988

Most goals: 13 Geoff Pimblett (St. Helens) v. Bramley, 5 March 1978

Most points: 38 (4t,11g) Bob Beardmore (Castleford) v. Barrow, 22 March 1987

Season records

Most tries: 44 Ellery Hanley (Wigan) 1986-87
Most goals: 130 Steve Hesford (Warrington) 1978-79
Most points: 295 (23t,101g,1dg) John Woods (Leigh) 1983-84

TEAM

Highest score and widest margin: Leeds 90 v. Barrow 0, 11 February 1990

Highest away score: Rochdale H. 12 v. Castleford 76, 3 March 1991

Widest away margin: Wakefield T. 6 v. Wigan 72, 29 March 1987; Barrow 0 v. Wigan 66, 1 October 1989

Most points by losing team: Hunslet 40 v. Barrow 41, 9 September 1984

Scoreless draw: Wigan 0 v. Castleford 0, 26 January 1974

Highest score draw: Leeds 46 v. Sheffield E. 46, 10 April 1994

Best opening sequence: 13 wins then a draw by Widnes 1981-82

Longest winning run: 25 by St. Helens. Won last 13 of 1985-86 and first 12 of 1986-87 (Also longest unbeaten run)

Longest losing run: 20 by Whitehaven 1983-84; Rochdale H. 1990-91

Longest run without a win: 23, including 3 draws, by Whitehaven 1981-82 (Also worst opening sequence)

Biggest attendance: 29,839 Wigan v. St. Helens, 9 April 1993

Top ten Division One career tries
250 Ellery Hanley (Bradford N., Wigan, Leeds)
174 Martin Offiah (Widnes, Wigan)
165 Keith Fielding (Salford)
165 Phil Ford (Warrington, Wigan, Bradford N., Leeds, Salford)
154 Garry Schofield (Hull, Leeds)
144 David Smith (Wakefield T., Leeds, Bradford N.)
144 Shaun Edwards (Wigan)
139 Stuart Wright (Wigan, Widnes)
136 Roy Mathias (St. Helens)
133 John Joyner (Castleford)

Most Division One career goals
862 John Woods (Leigh, Bradford N., Warrington)

Most Division One career points
2,150 John Woods (Leigh, Bradford N., Warrington)

20 Division One tries in a season

Season		
1973-74	36	Keith Fielding (Salford)
	29	Roy Mathias (St. Helens)
	21	David Smith (Wakefield T.)
1974-75	21	Maurice Richards (Salford)
	21	Roy Mathias (St. Helens)
1975-76	26	Maurice Richards (Salford)
	20	David Smith (Wakefield T.)
1976-77	22	David Topliss (Wakefield T.)
	21	Keith Fielding (Salford)
	21	Ged Dunn (Hull K.R.)
	20	David Smith (Leeds)
	20	Stuart Wright (Widnes)
1977-78	26	Keith Fielding (Salford)
	25	Steve Fenton (Castleford)
	24	Stuart Wright (Widnes)
	20	David Smith (Leeds)
	20	Bruce Burton (Castleford)
	20	John Bevan (Warrington)
1978-79	28	Steve Hartley (Hull K.R.)
1979-80	24	Keith Fielding (Salford)
	21	Roy Mathias (St. Helens)
	21	Steve Hubbard (Hull K.R.)
	20	David Smith (Leeds)
1980-81	20	Steve Hubbard (Hull K.R.)
1981-82		David Hobbs (Featherstone R.) was top scorer with 19 tries.
1982-83	22	Bob Eccles (Warrington)
	20	Steve Evans (Hull)
1983-84	28	Garry Schofield (Hull)
	23	John Woods (Leigh)
	20	James Leuluai (Hull)
1984-85	40	Ellery Hanley (Bradford N.)
	34	Gary Prohm (Hull K.R.)
	23	Henderson Gill (Wigan)
	22	Barry Ledger (St. Helens)
	22	Mal Meninga (St. Helens)
1985-86	22	Ellery Hanley (Wigan)
1986-87	44	Ellery Hanley (Wigan)
	24	Phil Ford (Bradford N.)
	24	Henderson Gill (Wigan)
	23	Garry Schofield (Hull)
	21	John Henderson (Leigh)
1987-88	33	Martin Offiah (Widnes)
	22	Ellery Hanley (Wigan)
1988-89	37	Martin Offiah (Widnes)
	20	Grant Anderson (Castleford)
1989-90	28	Martin Offiah (Widnes)
	25	Mark Preston (Wigan)
	20	Steve Larder (Castleford)
1990-91	22	Martin Offiah (Widnes)
	22	Les Quirk (St. Helens)
	20	Ellery Hanley (Wigan)
1991-92	31	John Devereux (Widnes)
	27	Greg Austin (Halifax)
	25	Shaun Edwards (Wigan)
	23	Mark Preston (Halifax)
1992-93	24	Shaun Edwards (Wigan)
	23	Ellery Hanley (Leeds)
	20	Martin Offiah (Wigan)
	20	Alan Hunte (St. Helens)
1993-94	30	St. John Ellis (Castleford)
	26	Martin Offiah (Wigan)
	24	Jason Critchley (Salford)
	23	Paul Newlove (Bradford N.)
	21	John Bentley (Halifax)
	20	Anthony Sullivan (St. Helens)

Top Division One goalscorers

1973-74	126	David Watkins (Salford)
1974-75	96	Sammy Lloyd (Castleford)
1975-76	118	Sammy Lloyd (Castleford)
1976-77	113	Steve Quinn (Featherstone R.)
1977-78	116	Steve Hesford (Warrington)
1978-79	130	Steve Hesford (Warrington)
1979-80	104	Steve Hubbard (Hull K.R.)
1980-81	96	Steve Diamond (Wakefield T.)
1981-82	110	Steve Quinn (Featherstone R.)
		John Woods (Leigh)
1982-83	105	Bob Beardmore (Castleford)
1983-84	106	Steve Hesford (Warrington)
1984-85	114	Sean Day (St. Helens)
1985-86	85	David Stephenson (Wigan)
1986-87	120	Paul Loughlin (St. Helens)
1987-88	95	John Woods (Warrington)
1988-89	95	David Hobbs (Bradford N.)
1989-90	96	Paul Loughlin (St. Helens)
1990-91	85	Paul Eastwood (Hull)
1991-92	86	Frano Botica (Wigan)
1992-93	107	Frano Botica (Wigan)
1993-94	123	Frano Botica (Wigan)

Top Division One points-scorer 1993-94
273 (8t,118g,5dg) Frano Botica (Wigan)

SECOND DIVISION RECORDS
Since reintroduction in 1973

INDIVIDUAL
Match records
Most tries: 6 Ged Dunn (Hull K.R.) v. New Hunslet, 2 February 1975; David Kettlestring (Ryedale-York) at Keighley, 11 March 1990; Greg Austin (Halifax) v. Trafford B., 7 April 1991

Most goals: 15 Mick Stacey (Leigh) v. Doncaster, 28 March 1976

Most points: 38 (4t,13g) John Woods (Leigh) v. Blackpool B., 11 September 1977; 38 (4t,11g) John Woods (Leigh) v. Ryedale-York, 12 January 1992

Season records
Most tries: 48 Steve Halliwell (Leigh) 1985-86

Most goals: 167 Mike Fletcher (Hull K.R.) 1989-90

Most points: 395 (22t,163g,3dg) Lyn Hopkins (Workington T.) 1981-82

TEAM
Highest score: Doncaster 96 v. Highfield 0, 20 March 1994

Highest away: Runcorn H. 2 v. Leigh 88, 15 January 1989 (Also widest margin)

Most points by losing team:
Dewsbury 36 v. Rochdale H. 34, 9 October 1988; Oldham 50 v. Keighley 34, 12 November 1989 Swinton 40 v. Hunslet 34, 24 April 1994

Highest score draw: Huddersfield B. 32 v. Keighley 32, 17 April 1986

Scoreless draw: Dewsbury 0 v. Rochdale H. 0, 30 January 1983; Whitehaven 0 v. Workington T. 0, 28 December 1993

Longest winning run: 30 by Leigh in 1985-86. Hull won all 26 matches in 1978-79

Longest losing run: 55 by Runcorn H. (9 in 1988-89, all 28 in 1989-90 and 18 in 1990-91)

Longest run without a win: 67, inc 2 draws, by Runcorn H. (19 in 1988-89, all 28 in 1989-90 and 20 in 1990-91)

Biggest attendance: 12,424 Hull v. New Hunslet, 18 May 1979

1993-94 Top Division Two scorers
Most tries: 32 Mark Johnson (London C.)

Most goals: 121 John Gallagher (London C.)

Most points: 300 (15t,119g,2dg) John Gallagher (London C.)

THIRD DIVISION RECORDS
Two seasons only, 1991-92 and 1992-93

INDIVIDUAL
Match records
Most tries: 6 Steve Rowan (Barrow) at Nottingham C., 15 November 1992

Most goals: 15 John Wasyliw (Keighley C.) v. Nottingham C., 1 November 1992

Most points: 42 (4t,13g) Dean Marwood (Workington T.) v. Highfield, 1 November 1992

Season records
Most tries: 31 Vince Gribbin (Whitehaven) 1991-92

Most goals: 146 John Wasyliw (Keighley C.) 1992-93

Most points: 380 (22t,146g) John Wasyliw (Keighley C.) 1992-93

TEAM
Highest score: Blackpool G. 5 v. Dewsbury 90, 14 April 1993 (Also highest away score)

Widest margin: Keighley C. 86 v. Nottingham C. 0, 1 November 1992

Most points by losing team: Hunslet 33 v. Doncaster 32, 16 February 1992

Highest score draw: None of 20-20 or more

Scoreless draw: None

Longest winning run: 14 by Keighley C. 1992-93 (Also longest unbeaten)

Longest losing run: 27 by Nottingham C. All 26 in 1991-92 and first of 1992-93 (Also longest without win)

Biggest attendance: 5,226 Keighley C. v. Batley, 9 April 1993

● League match records do not include scores in abandoned matches that were replayed.

THE 21-SEASON TABLE

St. Helens have been the most consistently successful club over 21 seasons of Division One rugby in terms of total points gained. Although St. Helens have won the title only once since the reintroduction of two divisions in 1973 they head a 21-season table with 790 points from 606 matches.

The Saints are also the only club to finish in the top eight throughout the 21 seasons. The only other clubs to have remained in Division One are Widnes, Leeds, Warrington and Castleford.

Bradford Northern, Hull and Leigh were all Division Two champions who went on to win the Division One title a few years after being promoted, while Hull Kingston Rovers, Halifax and Wigan are other former lower grade clubs who later won the major championship.

The highest place gained by a newly-promoted club is third by Hull in 1979-80 after winning the Division Two title with a 100 per cent record the previous season.

Division One champions who were relegated a few seasons after winning the Division One title were Salford, Featherstone Rovers, Leigh, Halifax and Hull K.R.

The records of the five clubs who have appeared in Division One throughout the 21 seasons are as follows:

FIRST DIVISION SCORING

The following table shows the scoring totals for each season since the inauguration of two divisions in 1973-74:

DIVISION ONE

Season	Matches each club played	Goals	1-Point drop goals	Tries	Pts
1973-74	30	1,508	—	1,295	6,901
1974-75	30	1,334	48	1,261	6,499
1975-76	30	1,498	53	1,331	7,042
1976-77	30[1]	1,435	91	1,423	7,230
1977-78	30[2]	1,402	99	1,443	7,232
1978-79	30	1,367	119	1,448	7,197
1979-80	30	1,389	131	1,349	6,956
1980-81	30	1,439	147	1,342	7,051
1981-82	30	1,486	132	1,354	7,166
1982-83	30	1,369	64	1,386	6,960
1983-84	30	1,472	108	1,479	8,968
1984-85	30	1,464	84	1,595	9,392
1985-86	30	1,296	80	1,435	8,412
1986-87	30	1,412	90	1,607	9,342
1987-88	26	1,070	75	1,170	6,895
1988-89	26	1,107	80	1,154	6,910
1989-90	26	1,198	80	1,295	7,656
1990-91	26	1,115	58	1,189	7,044
1991-92	26	1,026	46	1,178	6,810
1992-93	26	1,082	57	1,215	7,081
1993-94	30	1,488	107	1,699	9,879

[1] Salford & Leeds played 29 matches — their final match was abandoned and not replayed. This match was expunged from league records.
[2] Featherstone R. & Bradford N. played 29 matches — their final match was cancelled following Featherstone's strike.

	P.	W.	D.	L.	F.	A.	Pts
1. St. Helens	606	383	24	199	12,876	8,701	790
2. Widnes	606	379	20	207	11,414	8,307	778
3. Leeds	605	347	26	232	11,730	9,367	720
4. Warrington	606	333	21	252	10,472	8,932	687
5. Castleford	606	320	29	257	11,824	9,666	669

●Although Wigan have had only 20 seasons in Division One they have totalled 757 points from 576 matches.

CHAMPIONSHIP PLAY-OFFS

Following the breakaway from the English Rugby Union, 22 clubs formed the Northern Rugby Football League. Each club played 42 matches and Manningham won the first Championship as league leaders in 1895-96.

This format was then abandoned and replaced by the Yorkshire Senior and Lancashire Senior Combination leagues until 1901-02 when 14 clubs broke away to form the Northern Rugby League with Broughton Rangers winning the first Championship.

The following season two divisions were formed with the Division One title going to Halifax (1902-03), Bradford (1903-04), who won a play-off against Salford 5-0 at Halifax after both teams tied with 52 points, and Oldham (1904-05).

In 1905-06 the two divisions were merged with Leigh taking the Championship as league leaders. They won the title on a percentage basis as the 31 clubs did not play the same number of matches. The following season the top four play-off was introduced as a fairer means of deciding the title.

The top club played the fourth-placed, the second meeting the third, with the higher club having home advantage. The final was staged at a neutral venue.

It was not until 1930-31 that all clubs played the same number of league matches, but not all against each other, the top four play-off being a necessity until the reintroduction of two divisions in 1962-63.

This spell of two division football lasted only two seasons and the restoration of the one-league Championship table brought about the introduction of a top-16 play-off, this format continuing until the reappearance of two divisions in 1973-74.

Since then the Championship Trophy has been awarded to the leaders of the First Division, with the Second Division champions receiving a silver bowl. A Third Division was introduced for two years from 1991-92.

Slalom Lager launched a three-year sponsorship deal of the Championship and the Premiership in 1980-81 in a £215,000 package, extending the deal for another three years from 1983-84 for £270,000. From 1986-87, the sponsorship was taken over by brewers Bass, under the Stones Bitter banner, in a new £400,000 three-year deal, twice renewed through until 1996.

CHAMPIONSHIP PLAY-OFF FINALS

Season	Winners		Runners-up		Venue	Attendance	Receipts
Top Four Play-Offs							
1906-07	Halifax	18	Oldham	3	Huddersfield	13,200	£722
1907-08	Hunslet	7	Oldham	7	Salford	14,000	£690
Replay	Hunslet	12	Oldham	2	Wakefield	14,054	£800
1908-09	Wigan	7	Oldham	3	Salford	12,000	£630
1909-10	Oldham	13	Wigan	7	Broughton	10,850	£520
1910-11	Oldham	20	Wigan	7	Broughton	15,543	£717
1911-12	Huddersfield	13	Wigan	5	Halifax	15,000	£591
1912-13	Huddersfield	29	Wigan	2	Wakefield	17,000	£914
1913-14	Salford	5	Huddersfield	3	Leeds	8,091	£474
1914-15	Huddersfield	35	Leeds	2	Wakefield	14,000	£750
COMPETITION SUSPENDED DURING WAR-TIME							
1919-20	Hull	3	Huddersfield	2	Leeds	12,900	£1,615
1920-21	Hull	16	Hull K.R.	14	Leeds	10,000	£1,320
1921-22	Wigan	13	Oldham	2	Broughton	26,000	£1,825
1922-23	Hull K.R.	15	Huddersfield	5	Leeds	14,000	£1,370
1923-24	Batley	13	Wigan	7	Broughton	13,729	£968
1924-25	Hull K.R.	9	Swinton	5	Rochdale	21,580	£1,504
1925-26	Wigan	22	Warrington	10	St. Helens	20,000	£1,100
1926-27	Swinton	13	St. Helens Recs.	8	Warrington	24,432	£1,803
1927-28	Swinton	11	Featherstone R.	0	Oldham	15,451	£1,136
1928-29	Huddersfield	2	Leeds	0	Halifax	25,604	£2,028
1929-30	Huddersfield	2	Leeds	2	Wakefield	32,095	£2,111
Replay	Huddersfield	10	Leeds	0	Halifax	18,563	£1,319
1930-31	Swinton	14	Leeds	7	Wigan	31,000	£2,100
1931-32	St. Helens	9	Huddersfield	5	Wakefield	19,386	£943
1932-33	Salford	15	Swinton	5	Wigan	18,000	£1,053
1933-34	Wigan	15	Salford	3	Warrington	31,564	£2,114
1934-35	Swinton	14	Warrington	3	Wigan	27,700	£1,710
1935-36	Hull	21	Widnes	2	Huddersfield	17,276	£1,208

Season	Winners		Runners-up		Venue	Attendance	Receipts
1936-37	Salford	13	Warrington	11	Wigan	31,500	£2,000
1937-38	Hunslet	8	Leeds	2	Elland Rd., Leeds	54,112	£3,572
1938-39	Salford	8	Castleford	6	Man. C. FC	69,504	£4,301

WAR-TIME EMERGENCY PLAY-OFFS
For the first two seasons the Yorkshire League and Lancashire League champions met in a two-leg final as follows:

1939-40	*Swinton*	*13*	*Bradford N.*	*21*	*Swinton*	*4,800*	*£237*
	Bradford N.	*16*	*Swinton*	*9*	*Bradford*	*11,721*	*£570*
	Bradford N. won 37-22 on aggregate						
1940-41	*Wigan*	*6*	*Bradford N.*	*17*	*Wigan*	*11,245*	*£640*
	Bradford N.	*28*	*Wigan*	*9*	*Bradford*	*20,205*	*£1,148*
	Bradford N. won 45-15 on aggregate						

For the remainder of the war the top four in the War League played-off as follows:

1941-42	*Dewsbury*	*13*	*Bradford N.*	*0*	*Leeds*	*18,000*	*£1,121*
1942-43	*Dewsbury*	*11*	*Halifax*	*3*	*Dewsbury*	*7,000*	*£400*
	Halifax	*13*	*Dewsbury*	*22*	*Halifax*	*9,700*	*£683*

Dewsbury won 33-16 on aggregate but the Championship was declared null and void because they had played an ineligible player

1943-44	*Wigan*	*13*	*Dewsbury*	*9*	*Wigan*	*14,000*	*£915*
	Dewsbury	*5*	*Wigan*	*12*	*Dewsbury*	*9,000*	*£700*
	Wigan won 25-14 on aggregate						
1944-45	*Halifax*	*9*	*Bradford N.*	*2*	*Halifax*	*9,426*	*£955*
	Bradford N.	*24*	*Halifax*	*11*	*Bradford*	*16,000*	*£1,850*
	Bradford N. won 26-20 on aggregate						
1945-46	Wigan	13	Huddersfield	4	Man. C. FC	67,136	£8,387
1946-47	Wigan	13	Dewsbury	4	Man. C. FC	40,599	£5,895
1947-48	Warrington	15	Bradford N.	5	Man. C. FC	69,143	£9,792
1948-49	Huddersfield	13	Warrington	12	Man. C. FC	75,194	£11,073
1949-50	Wigan	20	Huddersfield	2	Man. C. FC	65,065	£11,500
1950-51	Workington T.	26	Warrington	11	Man. C. FC	61,618	£10,993
1951-52	Wigan	13	Bradford N.	6	Huddersfield Town FC	48,684	£8,215
1952-53	St. Helens	24	Halifax	14	Man. C. FC	51,083	£11,503
1953-54	Warrington	8	Halifax	7	Man. C. FC	36,519	£9,076
1954-55	Warrington	7	Oldham	3	Man. C. FC	49,434	£11,516
1955-56	Hull	10	Halifax	9	Man. C. FC	36,675	£9,179
1956-57	Oldham	15	Hull	14	Bradford	62,199	£12,054
1957-58	Hull	20	Workington T.	3	Bradford	57,699	£11,149
1958-59	St. Helens	44	Hunslet	22	Bradford	52,560	£10,146
1959-60	Wigan	27	Wakefield T.	3	Bradford	83,190	£14,482
1960-61	Leeds	25	Warrington	10	Bradford	52,177	£10,475
1961-62	Huddersfield	14	Wakefield T.	5	Bradford	37,451	£7,979

TWO DIVISIONS 1962-63 and 1963-64

Top Sixteen Play-Offs

1964-65	Halifax	15	St. Helens	7	Swinton	20,786	£6,141
1965-66	St. Helens	35	Halifax	12	Swinton	30,634	£8,750
1966-67	Wakefield T.	7	St. Helens	7	Leeds	20,161	£6,702
Replay	Wakefield T.	21	St. Helens	9	Swinton	33,537	£9,800
1967-68	Wakefield T.	17	Hull K.R.	10	Leeds	22,586	£7,697
1968-69	Leeds	16	Castleford	14	Bradford	28,442	£10,130
1969-70	St. Helens	24	Leeds	12	Bradford	26,358	£9,791
1970-71	St. Helens	16	Wigan	12	Swinton	21,745	£10,200
1971-72	Leeds	9	St. Helens	5	Swinton	24,055	£9,513
1972-73	Dewsbury	22	Leeds	13	Bradford	18,889	£9,479

A pensive Malcolm Reilly, current coach of Great Britain and Halifax.

COACHES

COACHES

INDEX OF COACHES

The following is an index of the 268 coaches who have held first team coaching posts since the start of the 1974-75 season to 1 June 1994.

It includes the alphabetical listing of British clubs they coached in the period.

Ten new coaches were added to the list during the past 12 months when 14 clubs made at least one change.

Although some clubs appoint team managers with a coach as his assistant, the list refers only to the man generally recognised as being in overall charge of team affairs.

A caretaker coach, who stands in while the club is seeking a permanent appointment, is only listed if he takes charge for more than a few matches.

For a list of each club's appointments since 1974 see CLUBS section.

Ray Abbey (Dewsbury)
Jack Addy (Dewsbury, Huddersfield B.)
Allan Agar (Bramley, Carlisle, Featherstone R., Rochdale H.)
Gary Ainsworth (Trafford B.)
Dave Alred (Bridgend)
Chris Anderson (Halifax)
Harry Archer (Workington T.)
Chris Arkwright (Highfield)
Kevin Ashcroft (Leigh, Salford, Warrington)
Eric Ashton (St. Helens)
Ray Ashton (Bramley, Workington T.)
Bill Ashurst (Runcorn H., Wakefield T.)
Mal Aspey (Salford)
John Atkinson (Carlisle)
Jack Austin (Hunslet)

Trevor Bailey (Scarborough P., Wakefield T.)
Maurice Bamford (Bramley, Dewsbury, Halifax, Huddersfield, Leeds, Wigan, Workington T.)
Frank Barrow (Oldham, Swinton)
Tony Barrow (Oldham, Swinton, Warrington)
Ray Batten (Wakefield T.)
Jeff Bawden (Whitehaven)
Mel Bedford (Huddersfield)
Cameron Bell (Carlisle)
Billy Benyon (Leigh, St. Helens, Warrington)
Les Bettinson (Salford)
Charlie Birdsall (Rochdale H.)
Alan Bishop (Runcorn H.)

Tommy Bishop (Barrow, Leigh, Workington T.)
Mick Blacker (Halifax, Huddersfield, Mansfield M.)
Tommy Blakeley (Blackpool B.)
Dick Bonser (Rochdale H.)
Reg Bowden (Fulham, Warrington)
Carl Briscoe (Chorley B.)
Drew Broatch (Hunslet)
Ian Brooke (Bradford N., Huddersfield, Wakefield T.)
Arthur Bunting (Hull, Hull K.R.)
Mark Burgess (Nottingham C.)
Dave Busfield (Dewsbury)

Len Casey (Hull, Scarborough P., Wakefield T.)
Jim Challinor (Oldham)
Paul Charlton (Workington T.)
Eddie Cheetham (Leigh)
Dave Chisnall (Runcorn H.)
Colin Clarke (Leigh, Wigan)
Terry Clawson (Featherstone R.)
Noel Cleal (Hull)
Malcolm Clift (Leeds)
Joe Coan (Wigan)
John Cogger (Runcorn H.)
Gary Cooper (York)
Kel Coslett (Rochdale H., St. Helens, Wigan)
Gordon Cottier (Whitehaven)
Keith Cotton (Featherstone R.)
Mike Coulman (Salford)
Les Coulter (Keighley)
Dave Cox (Batley, Castleford, Dewsbury, Huyton, Oldham, Workington T.)
Jim Crellin (Blackpool B., Halifax, Leigh, Mansfield M., Rochdale H., Swinton)
Terry Crook (Batley, Dewsbury)
Steve Crooks (Hull K.R., Ryedale-York)

Arthur Daley (Runcorn H.)
Paul Daley (Batley, Featherstone R., Hunslet, York)
Jackie Davidson (Whitehaven, Workington T.)
Keith Davies (Workington T.)
Tommy Dawes (Barrow, Carlisle, Whitehaven)
Harry Dawson (Widnes)
Tony Dean (Hull, Wakefield T.)
Henry Delooze (Rochdale H.)
Steve Dennison (Mansfield M.)
Robin Dewhurst (Leeds)
Bakary Diabira (Blackpool B., Keighley)
Tommy Dickens (Blackpool B., Leigh)
Roy Dickinson (Bramley)
Colin Dixon (Halifax, Keighley, Salford)

Mal Dixon (York)
John Dorahy (Halifax, Wigan)
David Doyle-Davidson (Hull, York)
Ray Dutton (Whitehaven)

Graham Eadie (Halifax)
Bob Eccles (Blackpool G., Chorley)
Derek Edwards (Doncaster)
Joe Egan Jnr. (Blackpool B.)

George Fairbairn (Hull K.R., Wigan)
Vince Farrar (Featherstone R.)
Albert Fearnley (Batley, Blackpool B., Keighley)
Steve Ferres (Hunslet)
John Fieldhouse (Oldham)
Tony Fisher (Bramley, Doncaster, Keighley)
Eric Fitzsimons (Oldham, Rochdale H.,
    Whitehaven)
Bob Fleet (Swinton)
Geoff Fletcher (Huyton, Runcorn H.)
Terry Fogerty (Rochdale H.)
Chris Forster (Bramley, Huddersfield B.)
Derek Foster (Ryedale-York)

Wigan coach John Dorahy shows off the Silk Cut Challenge Cup days before being sacked.

Frank Foster (Barrow, Whitehaven)
Kenny Foulkes (Hull)
Don Fox (Batley)
Harry Fox (Halifax)
Neil Fox (Huddersfield)
Peter Fox (Bradford N., Bramley, Featherstone R.,
    Leeds, Wakefield T.)
Bill Francis (Oldham)
Roy Francis (Bradford N., Leeds)

Paul Gamble (Blackpool G.)
Bill Gardner (Sheffield E.)
Brian Gartland (Oldham)
Steve Gibson (Rochdale H.)
Stan Gittins (Blackpool B., Chorley, Rochdale H.,
    Springfield B.)
Andy Goodway (Oldham)
Bill Goodwin (Fulham, Kent Invicta)
Tony Gordon (Hull, London C.)
Terry Gorman (Huyton, Swinton)
Keith Goulding (Featherstone R., Huddersfield,
    York)
Mal Graham (Oldham)
Tom Grainey (Leigh, Swinton)
Jeff Grayshon (Dewsbury)
Lee Greenwood (Keighley, Mansfield M./
    Nottingham C.)
Gary Grienke (London B.)
Geoff Gunney (Wakefield T.)

Bob Haigh (Wakefield T.)
Derek Hallas (Halifax)
Ken Halliwell (Swinton)
Alan Hardisty (Dewsbury, Halifax, York)
Arnold Hema (Nottingham C.)
Graham Heptinstall (Doncaster)
Alan Hepworth (Batley)
Keith Hepworth (Bramley, Hull)
Gary Hetherington (Sheffield E.)
Ron Hill (Dewsbury)
David Hobbs (Bradford N., Wakefield T.)
Neil Holding (Rochdale H.)
Bill Holliday (Swinton)
Eric Hughes (Rochdale H., St. Helens, Widnes)
Syd Hynes (Leeds)

Bob Irving (Blackpool B.)
Keith Irving (Workington T.)

Garry Jack (Salford)
Dennis Jackson (Barrow)
Francis Jarvis (Huddersfield)
Peter Jarvis (Bramley, Hunslet)
Graeme Jennings (Hunslet)
Barry Johnson (Bramley)
Brian Johnson (Warrington)
Willie Johnson (Highfield)
Allen Jones (Huddersfield B.)
Lewis Jones (Dewsbury)
John Joyner (Castleford)

Vince Karalius (Widnes, Wigan)
Paul Kavanagh (Barrow)
John Kear (Bramley)
Arthur Keegan (Bramley)
Ivor Kelland (Barrow)
Alan Kellett (Carlisle, Halifax, Keighley)
Bill Kenny (Doncaster)
Bill Kindon (Leigh)
Bill Kirkbride (Mansfield M., Rochdale H.,
    Wakefield T., York)
Phil Kitchin (Whitehaven, Workington T.)

Dave Lamming (Wakefield T.)
Steve Lane (Kent Invicta)
Phil Larder (Keighley C., Widnes)
Doug Laughton (Leeds, Widnes)
Roy Lester (Carlisle, Fulham)
Bob Lindner (Oldham)
Alan Lockwood (Dewsbury)
Brian Lockwood (Batley, Huddersfield,
    Wakefield T.)
Paul Longstaff (Rochdale H.)
Graham Lowe (Wigan)
Phil Lowe (York)
Trevor Lowe (Batley, Doncaster)
Ken Loxton (Bramley)
Geoff Lyon (Blackpool B.)

Mike McClennan (St. Helens)
Stan McCormick (Salford)

John McFarlane (Whitehaven)
Alan McInnes (Salford, Wigan)
John Mantle (Blackpool B., Cardiff C., Leigh)
Steve Martin (Featherstone R.)
Jack Melling (Blackpool G.)
Roger Millward (Halifax, Hull K.R.)
John Monie (Wigan)
Mick Morgan (Carlisle)
Geoff Morris (Doncaster)
David Mortimer (Huddersfield)
Alex Murphy (Huddersfield, Leigh, St. Helens,
    Salford, Warrington, Wigan)
Frank Myler (Oldham, Rochdale H., Swinton,
    Widnes)
Tony Myler (Widnes)

Steve Nash (Mansfield M.)
Steve Norton (Barrow)

Chris O'Sullivan (Swinton)

Les Pearce (Bramley, Halifax)
Mike Peers (Blackpool G., Chorley B./Trafford B.,
    Highfield, Swinton)
Geoff Peggs (Keighley)
George Pieniazek (Batley, Featherstone R.)
Billy Platt (Mansfield M.)
Harry Poole (Hull K.R.)

Denis Ramsdale (Barrow)
Bill Ramsey (Hunslet)
Terry Ramshaw (Oldham)
Keith Rayne (Batley)
Rod Reddy (Barrow)
Graham Rees (Blackpool B.)
Peter Regan (Rochdale H.)
Malcolm Reilly (Castleford, Halifax, Leeds)
Alan Rhodes (Doncaster, Sheffield E.)
Austin Rhodes (Swinton)
Bev Risman (Fulham)
Ken Roberts (Halifax)
Don Robinson (Bramley)
Don Robson (Doncaster)
Peter Roe (Halifax, Keighley)
Sol Roper (Workington T.)

Roy Sabine (Keighley)
Dave Sampson (Castleford, Doncaster,
    Nottingham C.)
Barry Seabourne (Bradford N., Huddersfield,
    Keighley)

*Peter Roe, who ended a second spell as coach of
Keighley Cougars by resigning as the season approached
its close in April 1994.*

Norman Smith, promoted to coach of Dewsbury in August 1993.

Australian Peter Walsh, coach of Workington Town who lifted the 1993-94 Second Division Championship and Premiership double.

Les Sheard (Huddersfield)
Danny Sheehan (York)
John Sheridan (Doncaster)
Royce Simmons (Hull)
Steve Simms (Leigh)
Tommy Smales [*Scrum half*] (Featherstone R.)
Tommy Smales [*Forward*] (Batley, Bramley, Dewsbury, Doncaster, Featherstone R.)
Peter Smethurst (Leigh, Oldham)
Barry Smith (Whitehaven)
Bill Smith (Whitehaven, Workington T.)
Brian Smith (Huddersfield)
Brian Smith [*Australian*] (Hull)
Norman Smith (Dewsbury)
Kurt Sorensen (Whitehaven)
Ike Southward (Whitehaven, Workington T.)
Graham Starkey (Oldham, Rochdale H.)
Gary Stephens (York)
Nigel Stephenson (Huddersfield, Hunslet)
Dave Stockwell (Batley, Bramley)
John Stopford (Swinton)
Ted Strawbridge (Doncaster)
Ross Strudwick (Fulham/London C., Halifax)
Clive Sullivan (Doncaster, Hull)
Phil Sullivan (Fulham)

Kevin Tamati (Salford)
John Taylor (Chorley B.)
Bob Tomlinson (Huddersfield)
Ted Toohey (Wigan)
David Topliss (Wakefield T.)

Peter Tunks (Oldham)
Norman Turley (Trafford B., Whitehaven, Workington T.)
Derek Turner (Wakefield T.)
Colin Tyrer (Widnes)

Darryl Van de Velde (Castleford)
Don Vines (Doncaster)

Hugh Waddell (Carlisle)
Arnold Walker (Whitehaven)
Trevor Walker (Batley)
Peter Walsh (Workington T.)
David Ward (Batley, Hunslet, Leeds)
John Warlow (Bridgend)
David Watkins (Cardiff C.)
Bernard Watson (Dewsbury)
Graeme West (Wigan)
Neil Whittaker (Huddersfield B.)
Mel Wibberley (Nottingham C.)
Ron Willey (Bradford N.)
Dean Williams (Workington T.)
Frank Wilson (Runcorn H.)
John Wolford (Hunslet)
Jeff Woods (Bridgend)
John Woods (Leigh)
Paul Woods (Runcorn H.)
Geoff Worrall (Barrow)
Geoff Wraith (Wakefield T.)

Billy Yates (Doncaster)

269

DOSSIER OF 1993-94 COACHES

The following is a dossier of the British coaching and playing careers of coaches holding first team posts from June 1993 to 1 June 1994. Overseas details are not included.

● BF — beaten finalist.

JACK ADDY

Dewsbury:	Feb. 84 - Jan. 87 (Promotion)
Huddersfield B.:	Jan. 87 - Mar. 88
Dewsbury:	Dec. 90 - Aug. 93

Played for: Dewsbury

MAURICE BAMFORD

Dewsbury:	Aug. 74 - Oct. 74
Halifax:	Feb. 78 - May 80
	(Yorks. Cup BF, Promotion)
Huddersfield:	May 80 - May 81
Wigan:	May 81 - May 82
Bramley:	May 82 - Oct. 83
Leeds:	Nov. 83 - Feb. 85
	(John Player winners)
Leeds:	Dec. 86 - Apr. 88
	(John Player BF)
Workington T.:	July 88 - Dec. 88
Dewsbury:	Dec. 88 - Dec. 90
Bramley:	Apr. 92 - Sep. 93 (Promotion)
Great Britain &	
Under-21s:	Oct. 84 - Dec. 86

Played for: Dewsbury, Batley

TONY BARROW

Warrington:	Mar. 86 - Nov. 88 (Premier winners & BF, John Player BF, Lancs. Cup BF)
Oldham:	Nov. 88 - Jan. 91 (Promotion, Lancs. Cup BF, Div. 2 Premier winners)
Swinton:	Jan. 92 -

Played for: St. Helens, Leigh

CAMERON BELL (New Zealander)

Carlisle:	Feb. 90 - Apr. 94

STEVE CROOKS

Ryedale-York	Nov. 92 - May 94
Hull K.R.	May 94 -

Played for: Hull K.R., Hull, York

PAUL DALEY

New Hunslet:	Apr. 74 - Aug. 78 (Promotion)
York:	Jan. 79 - May 79 (Promotion)

Featherstone R.:	May 79 - Jan. 81 (Div. 2 champs)
Hunslet:	Apr. 81 - Nov. 85 (Promotion)
Featherstone R.:	Nov. 86 - Apr. 87
Batley:	July 87 - Apr. 90
Hunslet:	May 90 - Dec. 93

Played for: Halifax, Bradford N., Hull K.R., Hunslet

JOHN DORAHY (Australian)

Halifax:	June 89 - Aug. 90
	(Regal Trophy BF)
Wigan:	June 93 - May 94
	(Div. 1 champs, RL Cup winners, Regal Trophy BF)

Played for: Leigh, Hull K.R., Halifax

GEORGE FAIRBAIRN

Wigan:	Apr. 80 - May 81 (Promotion)
Hull K.R.:	May 91 - May 94

Played for: Wigan, Hull K.R.

STEVE FERRES

Hunslet:	Jan. 94 -

Played for: Bramley, York, Dewsbury, Bradford N., Carlisle, Kent I., Keighley, Batley, Sheffield E.

TONY FISHER

Bramley:	Nov. 87 - Feb. 89
Keighley:	June 90 - Sep. 91
Doncaster:	Nov. 92 - (Promotion)

Played for: Bradford N., Leeds, Castleford

PETER FOX

Featherstone R.:	Jan. 71 - May 74
	(RL Cup winners & BF)
Wakefield T.:	June 74 - May 76
	(Yorks. Cup BF)
Bramley:	Sep. 76 - Apr. 77 (Promotion)
Bradford N.:	Apr. 77 - May 85 (Div. 1 champs (2), Yorks. Cup winners & BF (2), Premier winners & BF (2), John Player winners)
Leeds:	May 85 - Dec. 86
Featherstone R.:	May 87 - Oct. 91 (Promotion, Div. 2 Premier BF, Yorks. Cup BF)
Bradford N.:	Oct. 91 - (Regal Trophy BF)
England:	1977 (2 matches)
Great Britain:	1978 (3 Tests v. Australia)
Yorkshire:	1985-86 to 1991-92

Played for: Featherstone R., Batley, Hull K.R., Wakefield T.

BILL GARDNER (Australian)
Sheffield E.: May 93 - Dec. 93

STEVE GIBSON (Australian)
Rochdale H.: Oct. 93-
Played for: Salford, Rochdale H.

ANDY GOODWAY
Oldham: May 94 -
Played for: Oldham, Wigan, Leeds

TONY GORDON (New Zealander)
London C.: Feb. 93 - May 94
(Div. 2 Premier BF)
Hull: May 94 -

GARY GRIENKE (Australian)
London B.: May 94 -
Played for: St. Helens

GARY HETHERINGTON
Sheffield E.: July 86 - May 93 (Div. 2 champs,
Promotion (2),
Div. 2 Premier winners,
Divisional Premier winners,
Yorks. Cup BF)
Sheffield E.: Dec. 93 -
Played for: York, Leeds, Kent I., Sheffield E.

DAVID HOBBS
Bradford N.: Mar. 90 - Oct. 91 (Premier BF,
Regal BF, Yorks. Cup BF)
Wakefield T.: May 94 -
Played for: Featherstone R., Oldham, Bradford N.,
Wakefield T.

ERIC HUGHES
Widnes: June 84 - Jan. 86
Rochdale H. June 87 - June 88
St. Helens: Jan. 94 -
Played for: Widnes, St. Helens, Rochdale H.

GARRY JACK (Australian)
Salford: July 93 -
Played for: Sheffield E., Salford

BRIAN JOHNSON (Australian)
Warrington: Nov. 88 - (Lancs. Cup winners,
RL Cup BF, Regal winners)
Played for: Warrington

JOHN JOYNER
Castleford: May 93 - (Regal Trophy winners,
Premier BF)
Played for: Castleford

*New St. Helens coach Eric Hughes, appointed in succession
to Mike McClennan in January 1994.*

PHIL LARDER
Widnes: May 92 - May 94 (RL Cup BF)
Keighley C.: May 94 -
Great Britain
Under-21s: 1990-91, 1991-92
Played for: Oldham, Whitehaven

DOUG LAUGHTON
Widnes: May 78 - Mar. 83
(RL Cup winners (2) & BF,
Lancs. Cup winners (2) & BF,
John Player winners & BF,
Premier winners (2), Floodlit
Trophy winners)
Widnes: Jan. 86 - May 91 (Div. 1
champs (2), Premier winners
(3) & BF, Charity Shield
winners (3), John Player BF,
Lancs. Cup winners, World
Club Challenge winners)
Leeds: May 91 - (Regal Trophy BF,
RL Cup BF)
Lancashire: 1982-83, 1988-89, 1989-90
Played for: Wigan, St. Helens, Widnes

271

Australian Test forward Bob Lindner who helped secure 1993-94 Stones Bitter Championship survival for Oldham during a three-month spell as player-coach.

BOB LINDNER (Australian)
Oldham: Feb. 94 - Apr. 94
Played for: Castleford, Oldham

MIKE McCLENNAN (New Zealander)
St. Helens: Feb. 90 - Dec. 93 (RL Cup BF, Premier winners & BF, Lancs. Cup winners & BF, Charity Shield winners)

STEVE MARTIN (Australian)
Featherstone R.:   Sep. 92 - (Div. 2 champs, Divisional Premier winners)
Played for: Barrow, Leeds

ALEX MURPHY
Leigh: Nov. 66 - May 71 (RL Cup winners, Lancs. Cup winners & BF, Floodlit Trophy winners & BF)

Warrington: May 71 - May 78 (League Leaders, Club Merit winners, RL Cup winners & BF, John Player winners (2), Floodlit Trophy BF, Capt. Morgan winners, Premier BF)

Salford: May 78 - Nov. 80
Leigh: Nov. 80 - June 82 (Div. 1 champs, Lancs. Cup winners)
Wigan: June 82 - Aug. 84 (John Player winners, RL Cup BF)
Leigh: Feb. 85 - Nov. 85
St. Helens: Nov. 85 - Jan. 90 (RL Cup BF (2), John Player winners, Premier BF)
Leigh: Mar. 90 - Aug. 91
Huddersfield: Sep. 91 - May 94 (Div. 3 champs)
Lancashire: 1973-74 to 1977-78 (Champions (2)); 1985-86 to 1987-88
England: 1975 (including World Championship (European Champions))
Played for: St. Helens, Leigh, Warrington

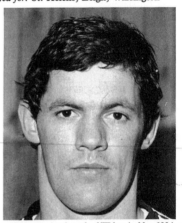

Tony Myler, appointed coach of Widnes in May 1994, only weeks after announcing his retirement as a player.

TONY MYLER
Widnes: May 94 -
Played for: Widnes

MIKE PEERS
Swinton: June 86 - Oct. 87 (Promotion, Div. 2 Premier winners)
Springfield B./
Chorley B./
Trafford B.: Aug. 87 - May 91
Blackpool G.: Jan. 93 - Feb. 93
Highfield: Apr. 93 -
Played for: Warrington, Swinton

DENIS RAMSDALE
Barrow: May 93 -
Played for: Wigan

PETER REGAN (Australian)
Rochdale H.:   Jan. 93 - Oct. 93

MALCOLM REILLY
Castleford: Dec. 74 - May 87
                 (RL Cup winners, John Player
                 winners, Premier BF, Yorks. Cup
                 winners (3) & BF (2), Charity
                 Shield BF, Floodlit Trophy
                 winners)
Leeds: Aug. 88 - Sep. 89
                 (Yorks. Cup winners)
Halifax: Jan. 93 -
Great Britain: Jan. 87 -
Under-21s: 1986-87, 1987-88, 1989-90,
                 1991-92, 1992-93
Played for: Castleford

PETER ROE
Keighley: Sep. 85 - July 86
Halifax: Aug. 90 - May 91 (Promotion,
                 Div. 2 Premier BF)
Keighley C.:   Sep. 91 - Apr. 94 (Div. 3 champs)
Played for: Keighley, Bradford N., York, Hunslet

ROYCE SIMMONS (Australian)
Hull: May 92 - Apr. 94

STEVE SIMMS (Australian)
Leigh: Nov. 92 -

NORMAN SMITH
Dewsbury: Aug. 93 -
Played for: Bramley, Dewsbury

KURT SORENSEN (New Zealander)
Whitehaven: May 93 -
Played for: Widnes, Wigan, Whitehaven

KEVIN TAMATI (New Zealander)
Salford: Oct. 89 - June 93 (Lancs. Cup
                 BF, Div. 2 champs, Div. 2
                 Premier winners)
Played for: Widnes, Warrington, Salford

DAVID TOPLISS
Wakefield T.:   May 87 - Apr. 94 (Promotion,
                 Yorks. Cup winners & BF)
GB Under-21s: 1988-89
Played for: Wakefield T., Hull, Oldham

New Zealander Graeme West, put in charge of Wigan in May 1994, steering the Riversiders to the Stones Bitter Premiership and the World Club Challenge.

PETER TUNKS (Australian)
Oldham: Apr. 91 - Feb. 94 (Promotion,
                 Div. 2 Premier BF)
Played for: Leeds, Salford, Sheffield E.

HUGH WADDELL
Carlisle: Apr. 94 -
Played for: Blackpool B., Oldham, Leeds,
Sheffield E., Swinton, Wakefield T., Carlisle

PETER WALSH (Australian)
Workington T.:   Apr. 92 - (Div. 2 champs, Div. 2
                 Premier winners, Divisional
                 Premier BF)
Played for: Oldham

DAVID WARD
Hunslet: July 86 - Apr. 88 (Div. 2
                 champs, Div. 2 Premier BF)
Hunslet: Jan. 89 - May 89
Leeds: Sep. 89 - May 91
Batley: May 91 -
Played for: Leeds, Workington T.

GRAEME WEST (New Zealander)
Wigan: May 94 - (Premier winners,
                 World Club Challenge winners)
Played for: Wigan

273

REPRESENTATIVE REGISTER

The following is a list of international and county coaches since 1974-75.

GREAT BRITAIN
Jim Challinor	Dec. 71 - Aug. 74 (Inc. tours)
David Watkins	1977 World Championship
Peter Fox	1978
Eric Ashton	1979 tour
Johnny Whiteley	Aug. 80 - Nov. 82
Frank Myler	Dec. 82 - Aug. 84 (Inc. tour)
Maurice Bamford	Oct. 84 - Dec. 86
Malcolm Reilly	Jan. 87 - (Inc. tours)

ENGLAND
Alex Murphy	Jan. 75 - Nov. 75 (Inc. World Championship tour)
Peter Fox	1976-77
Frank Myler	1977-78
Eric Ashton	1978-79, 1979-80
Johnny Whiteley	1980-81, 1981-82
Reg Parker (Mgr)	1984-85
Malcolm Reilly	1992-93

WALES
Les Pearce	Jan. 75 - Nov. 75 (Inc. World Championship tour)
David Watkins / Bill Francis	1976-77
Kel Coslett / Bill Francis	1977-78
Kel Coslett	1978-79 to 1981-82
David Watkins	1982-83, 1984-85
Clive Griffiths	1991-92, 1992-93, 1993-94

GREAT BRITAIN UNDER-24s
Johnny Whiteley	1976-82
Frank Myler	1983-84

GREAT BRITAIN UNDER-21s
Maurice Bamford	Oct. 84 - Dec. 86
Malcolm Reilly	1986-87, 1987-88, 1989-90, 1991-92, 1992-93, 1993-94
David Topliss	1988-89
Phil Larder	1990-91, 1991-92

CUMBRIA
Ike Southward	1975-76
Frank Foster	1976-77 to 1977-78
Sol Roper	1978-79
Frank Foster	1979-80
Phil Kitchin	1980-81 to 1981-82
Frank Foster	1982-83
Jackie Davidson	1985-86
Phil Kitchin	1986-87 to 1991-92
Gordon Cottier	1992-93

LANCASHIRE
Alex Murphy	1973-74 to 1977-78
Eric Ashton	1978-79 to 1979-80
Tom Grainey	1980-81 to 1981-82
Doug Laughton	1982-83
Alex Murphy	1985-86 to 1987-88
Doug Laughton	1988-89 to 1989-90
Ray Ashton	1991-92

YORKSHIRE
Johnny Whiteley	1970-71 to 1979-80
Arthur Keegan	1980-81
Johnny Whiteley	1981-82 to 1982-83
Peter Fox	1985-86 to 1991-92

OTHER NATIONALITIES
Dave Cox	1974-75 to 1975-76

Legendary Australian captain Reg Gasnier, a triple Kangaroo in 1959, 1963 and 1967 and regarded as the greatest Australian centre of all time.

AUSTRALIA

AUSTRALIA

The following is a list of international matches involving Australia. For Tests versus Great Britain see the GREAT BRITAIN section.

Australia v. France Tests

Date		Score	Venue
2 Jan. 1938	W	35-6	Paris
16 Jan. 1938	W	16-11	Marseilles
9 Jan. 1949	W	29-10	Marseilles
23 Jan. 1949	W	10-0	Bordeaux
11 Jun. 1951	L	15-26	Sydney
30 Jun. 1951	W	23-11	Brisbane
21 Jul. 1951	L	14-35	Sydney
27 Dec. 1952	W	16-12	Paris
11 Jan. 1953	L	0-5	Bordeaux
25 Jan. 1953	L	5-13	Lyons
11 Jun. 1955	W	20-8	Sydney
2 Jul. 1955	L	28-29	Brisbane
27 Jul. 1955	L	5-8	Sydney
1 Nov. 1956	W	15-8	Paris
23 Dec. 1956	W	10-6	Bordeaux
13 Jan. 1957	W	25-21	Lyons
31 Oct. 1959	W	20-19	Paris
20 Dec. 1959	W	17-2	Bordeaux
20 Jan. 1960	W	16-8	Roanne
11 Jun. 1960	D	8-8	Sydney
2 Jul. 1960	W	56-6	Brisbane
16 Jul. 1960	L	5-7	Sydney
8 Dec. 1963	L	5-8	Bordeaux
22 Dec. 1963	W	21-9	Toulouse
18 Jan. 1964	W	16-8	Paris
13 Jun. 1964	W	20-6	Sydney
4 Jul. 1964	W	27-2	Brisbane
18 Jul. 1964	W	35-9	Sydney
17 Dec. 1967	D	7-7	Marseilles
24 Dec. 1967	L	3-10	Carcassonne
7 Jan. 1968	L	13-16	Toulouse
9 Dec. 1973	W	21-9	Perpignan
16 Dec. 1973	W	14-3	Toulouse
26 Nov. 1978	L	10-13	Carcassonne
10 Dec. 1978	L	10-11	Toulouse
4 Jul. 1981	W	43-3	Sydney
18 Jul. 1981	W	17-2	Brisbane
5 Dec. 1982	W	15-4	Avignon
18 Dec. 1982	W	23-9	Narbonne
30 Nov. 1986	W	44-2	Perpignan
*13 Dec. 1986	W	52-0	Carcassonne
*27 Jun. 1990	W	34-2	Parkes
2 Dec. 1990	W	60-4	Avignon
*9 Dec. 1990	W	34-10	Perpignan

*Also World Cup

	P	W	D	L	F	A
TOTALS	44	30	2	12	912	406

Australia v. France World Cup

Date		Score	Venue
11 Nov. 1954	L	5-15	Nantes
22 Jun. 1957	W	26-9	Sydney
24 Sep. 1960	W	13-12	Wigan
8 Jun. 1968	W	37-4	Brisbane
10 Jun. 1968	W	20-2	Sydney
1 Nov. 1970	L	15-17	Bradford
5 Nov. 1972	W	31-9	Toulouse
22 Jun. 1975	W	26-6	Brisbane
26 Oct. 1975	W	41-2	Perpignan
11 Jun. 1977	W	21-9	Sydney

Australia v. France other matches

Date		Score	Venue
16 Oct. 1960	W	37-12	Toulouse
11 Nov. 1970	W	7-4	Perpignan

Australia v. Great Britain Tests
see GREAT BRITAIN section.

Australia v. Great Britain World Cup

Date		Score	Venue
31 Oct. 1954	L	13-28	Lyons
17 Jun. 1957	W	31-6	Sydney
8 Oct. 1960	L	3-10	Bradford
25 May 1968	W	25-10	Sydney
24 Oct. 1970	L	4-11	Leeds
7 Nov. 1970	W	12-7	Leeds
29 Oct. 1972	L	21-27	Perpignan
11 Nov. 1972	D	10-10	Lyons
18 Jun. 1977	W	19-5	Brisbane
25 Jun. 1977	W	13-12	Sydney
24 Oct. 1992	W	10-6	Wembley

1975 France (WC)
Perpignan: 26 Oct.
Won 41-2
Eadie 1t, 7g
Rhodes 1t
Rogers 2t
Brass
Porter
Peard 1t
Raudonikis 1t
*Beetson
Lang
Randall 1t
Platz, L. 1t
Higgs 1t
Pierce
Sub: Schubert

1975 England (WC)
Wigan: 1 Nov.
Lost 13-16
Eadie
Schubert 3t
Brass
Cronin 2g
Rhodes
Peard
Mayes
*Beetson
Piggins
Mackay, I.
Higgs
Randall
Pierce
Sub: Rogers

1977 New Zealand (WC)
Auckland: 29 May
Won 27-12
Eadie
Harris 1t
Cronin 6g
Thomas 1t
McMahon 2t
Peard 1t
Raudonikis
*Veivers
Geiger
Fitzgerald
Randall
Higgs
Pierce

1977 France (WC)
Sydney: 11 June
Won 21-9
Eadie 2t
McMahon 1t
Cronin 3g
Thomas
Fahey
Peard
Raudonikis
Veivers 1t
Geiger
Fitzgerald 1t
Randall
*Beetson
Reddy
Subs: Gartner
     Higgs

1977 Great Britain (WC)
Brisbane: 18 June
Won 19-5
Eadie 2t
McMahon
Cronin 5g
Thomas
Fahey
Peard
Raudonikis
Fitzgerald
Geiger
Veivers
*Beetson
Randall 1t
Pierce
Sub: Higgs

1977 Great Britain (WC)
Sydney: 25 June
Won 13-12
Eadie
McMahon 1t
Cronin 2g
Gartner 1t
Harris
Peard
Kolc 1t
Veivers
Geiger
Randall
*Beetson
Higgs
Pierce
Sub: Fitzgerald

1978 New Zealand
Sydney: 24 June
Won 24-2
Eadie
Fahey 1t
Cronin 6g
Rogers 1t
Boustead 1t
*Fulton
Morris, S.
Olling
Peponis 1t
Thomson
Pierce
Reddy
Price
Sub: Oliphant

1978 New Zealand
Brisbane: 15 July
Won 38-7
Dorahy
Boustead 2t
Cronin 7g
Rogers 1t
Glover 2t
*Fulton
Oliphant
Donnelly
Lang
Olling
Platz, G.
Reddy 1t
Price 2t
Sub: Morris, R.

1978 New Zealand
Sydney: 22 July
Won 33-16
Dorahy 1t
Glover
Cronin 9g
Rogers
Boustead 1t
*Fulton 2t
Raudonikis
Morris, R.
Krilich
Young
Pierce 1t
Reddy
Price

1978 Great Britain
Wigan: 21 Oct.
Won 15-9
Eadie
Boustead 1t
Rogers
Cronin 4g
Anderson
*Fulton 1t, 1dg
Raudonikis
Young
Krilich
Olling
Gerard
Reddy
Price

1978 France
Carcassonne: 26 Nov.
Lost 10-13
Eadie 1t
Boustead
Cronin 1t, 2g
Martin
Anderson
*Fulton
Raudonikis
Morris, R.
Peponis
Young
Gerard
Boyd
Price

1979 Great Britain
Sydney: 30 June
Won 24-16
Eadie
Corowa
Rogers 1t
Cronin 2t, 6g
Boustead
Thompson
Raudonikis
Young
*Peponis
Morris, R.
Reddy 1t
Boyd
Price

1978 Great Britain
Bradford: 5 Nov.
Lost 14-18
Eadie
Boustead
Rogers 1t, 2g
Cronin 2g
Anderson
*Fulton
Raudonikis
Olling
Krilich
Young
Gerard
Reddy
Price 1t
Subs: Thompson
Boyd

1978 France
Toulouse: 10 Dec.
Lost 10-11
Eadie
Boustead 1t
Rogers 1t
Cronin 2g
Anderson
*Fulton
Raudonikis
Thomson
Hilditch
Young
Gerard
Reddy
Price

1979 Great Britain
Sydney: 14 July
Won 28-2
Eadie 1t
Anderson
Cronin 8g
Rogers
Fahey
Thompson
Raudonikis
Young
*Peponis
Morris, R.
Reddy 1t
Boyd 1t
Price 1t

1978 Great Britain
Leeds: 18 Nov.
Won 23-6
Eadie
Boustead
Rogers
Cronin 5g
Anderson
*Fulton 1dg
Raudonikis 1t
Young
Peponis 1t
Morris, R.
Gerard 1t
Boyd 1t
Price
Subs: Thompson
Thomson

1979 Great Britain
Brisbane: 16 June
Won 35-0
Eadie
Corowa 1t
Rogers
Cronin 10g
Boustead 2t
Thompson
Raudonikis
Young
*Peponis
Morris, R.
Reddy
Boyd
Price 2t

1980 New Zealand
Auckland: 1 June
Won 27-6
Dowling, Gary
Boustead 1t
Cronin 6g
Brentnall
Anderson
Thompson 2t
Raudonikis
Morris, R.
*Peponis
Young 1t
Reddy 1t
Boyd
Price

1980 New Zealand
Auckland: 15 June
Won 15-6
Dowling, Gary
Quinn
Cronin 1t, 3g
Brentnall
Anderson
Thompson
Raudonikis 1t
Young
*Peponis
Morris, R.
Boyd 1t
Reddy 1t
Price

1981 France
Sydney: 4 July
Won 43-3
Brentnall 1t
Ribot 1t
Cronin 8g
*Rogers 1t
Boustead 1t
Lewis
Mortimer, S. 2t
Hilditch
Masterman 1t
Young
Boyd
McCabe 2t
Price
Subs: Sigsworth
        Morris, R.

1981 France
Brisbane: 18 July
Won 17-2
Brentnall
Ribot
*Rogers
Cronin 4g
Fahey 2t
Lewis
Mortimer, S.
Hilditch
Masterman
Morris, R. 1t
McCabe
Boyd
Price
Sub: Ayliffe

1982 New Zealand
Brisbane: 3 July
Won 11-8
Brentnall
Ribot
Cronin 4g
Rogers
Boustead
Lewis
Mortimer, S.
Young
*Krilich
Morris, R.
Hancock, R.
Boyd
Vautin
Sub: Muggleton 1t

1982 New Zealand
Sydney: 17 July
Won 20-2
Brentnall 1t
Boustead 1t
Cronin 4g
Meninga
Ribot
Lewis 1t
Mortimer, S.
Young
*Krilich
Hancock, R.
Muggleton
Boyd
Price 1t
Subs: Rogers
        Morris, R.

1982 Papua New Guinea
Port Moresby: 2 Oct.
Won 38-2
Brentnall 2t
Boustead 1t
Rogers 1t
Meninga 1t, 4g
Ribot 4t
Kenny 1t
Mortimer, S.
Young
*Krilich
Hancock, R.
Muggleton
Reddy
Price
Subs: Murray
        Brown, R.

1982 Great Britain
Hull City FC: 30 Oct.
Won 40-4
Brentnall
Boustead 1t
Meninga 1t, 8g
Rogers
Grothe 1t
Kenny 1t
Sterling
Young
*Krilich
Boyd 1t
Pearce 1t
Reddy 1t
Price 1t

1982 Great Britain
Wigan: 20 Nov.
Won 27-6
Brentnall
Boustead
Meninga 1t, 6g
Rogers 1t
Grothe 1t
Kenny
Sterling 1t
Young
*Krilich
Boyd
Pearce
Reddy
Price 1t
Subs: Lewis
        Brown, R.

1982 Great Britain
Leeds: 28 Nov.
Won 32-8
Brentnall
Boustead 1t
Meninga 7g
Rogers 1t
Ribot 1t
Kenny 1t
Sterling
Boyd
*Krilich 1t
Morris, R.
McCabe
Reddy
Pearce 1t
Subs: Lewis
        Brown, R.

1982 France
Avignon: 5 Dec.
Won 15-4
Brentnall
Boustead
Rogers
Kenny
Meninga 3g
Lewis
Sterling
Young
*Krilich
Morris, R.
McCabe
Boyd
Pearce 1t
Subs: Grothe 2t
      Brown, R.

1982 France
Narbonne: 18 Dec.
Won 23-9
Brentnall
Boustead
Rogers
Meninga 1t, 4g
Grothe 2t
Kenny 1t
Sterling
Young
*Krilich
Boyd
McCabe
Reddy 1t
Pearce

1983 New Zealand
Auckland: 12 June
Won 16-4
Brentnall
Boustead
Meninga 4g
Rogers 1t
Grothe 1t
Lewis
Sterling
Brown, D.
*Krilich
Gerard
Fullerton-Smith
McCabe
Vautin
Subs: Murray
      Jarvis

1983 New Zealand
Brisbane: 9 July
Lost 12-19
Scott
Boustead
Meninga 2g
Miles
Grothe 1t
Lewis
Mortimer, S.
Tessman
*Krilich
Brown, D.
Fullerton-Smith
Vautin
Price
Subs: Ella 1t
      Brown, R.

1984 Great Britain
Sydney: 9 June
Won 25-8
Jack
Boustead 1t
Miles
Kenny
Conlon 4g
*Lewis 1t, 1dg
Murray 1t
Brown, D.
Conescu
Dowling, Greg
Niebling
Pearce
Price 1t
Sub: Young

1984 Great Britain
Brisbane: 26 June
Won 18-6
Jack
Boustead
Meninga 1t, 3g
Miles
Grothe 1t
*Lewis
Murray
Brown, D.
Conescu
Dowling, Greg
Niebling
Vautin
Pearce 1t
Subs: Mortimer, S.
      Fullerton-Smith

1984 Great Britain
Sydney: 7 July
Won 20-7
Jack 1t
Boustead
Meninga 4g
Miles
Grothe 1t
*Lewis
Mortimer, S.
Niebling
Conescu 1t
Dowling, Greg
Fullerton-Smith
Pearce
Price
Subs: Kenny
      Brown, D.

1985 New Zealand
Brisbane: 18 June
Won 26-20
Jack
Ribot 2t, 1g
Close 1t
Meninga 2g
Ferguson
*Lewis
Murray
Dowling, Greg
Conescu
Roach 1t
Cleal 1t
Wynn, P.
Pearce
Sub: Tunks

1985 New Zealand
Auckland: 30 June
Won 10-6
Jack
Ribot 1t, 1g
Close
Meninga 2g
Ferguson
*Lewis
Murray
Dowling, Greg
Conescu
Roach
Vautin
Wynn, P.
Pearce
Subs: Ella
      Cleal

1985 New Zealand (Also WC)
Auckland: 7 July
Lost 0-18
Jack
Ribot
Meninga
Ella
Ferguson
*Lewis
Hasler
Tunks
Elias
Roach
Vautin
Wynn, P.
Pearce
Subs: Close
    Dowling, Greg

1986 New Zealand
Auckland: 6 July
Won 22-8
Jack
O'Connor 3g
Kenny 2t
Miles
Shearer 1t
*Lewis
Sterling
Roach
Simmons
Tunks
Cleal
Folkes 1t
Pearce
Subs: Lamb
    Niebling

1986 New Zealand
Sydney: 19 July
Won 29-12
Jack 1t
O'Connor 4g
Kenny 1t
Miles 1t
Kiss
*Lewis 1t
Sterling 1dg
Roach
Simmons
Tunks
Cleal
Folkes
Pearce 1t
Sub: Niebling

1986 New Zealand (Also WC)
Brisbane: 29 July
Won 32-12
Jack
O'Connor 1t, 4g
Kenny 2t
Miles 1t
Kiss
*Lewis 1t
Sterling 1t
Roach
Simmons
Tunks
Cleal
Folkes
Pearce
Subs: Lamb
    Niebling

1986 Papua New Guinea (Also WC)
Port Moresby: 4 Oct.
Won 62-12
Jack 1t
Kiss 2t
Mortimer, C. 1t
Miles
O'Connor 2t, 7g
*Lewis 1t
Hasler 1t
Roach 1t
Simmons
Niebling
Dunn
Cleal 2t
Lindner 1t
Subs: Meninga
    Sironen

1986 Great Britain
Old Trafford: 25 Oct.
Won 38-16
Jack 1t
Kiss
Kenny
Miles 3t
O'Connor 3t, 5g
*Lewis
Sterling
Dowling, Greg
Simmons
Roach
Cleal
Niebling
Lindner
Subs: Lamb
    Meninga

1986 Great Britain
Elland Rd, Leeds: 8 Nov.
Won 34-4
Jack 2t
Shearer
Kenny 1t
Miles
O'Connor 1t, 5g
*Lewis 1t
Sterling
Dowling, Greg
Simmons
Dunn
Cleal
Niebling
Lindner 1t
Subs: Lamb
    Meninga

1986 Great Britain (Also WC)
Wigan: 22 Nov.
Won 24-15
Jack
Shearer 1t
Kenny
Miles 1t
O'Connor 4g
*Lewis 1t
Sterling
Dowling, Greg
Simmons
Dunn
Meninga
Niebling
Lindner 1t
Subs: Lamb
    Davidson

1986 France
Perpignan: 30 Nov.
Won 44-2
Jack 1t
Shearer
Kenny
Miles 2t
O'Connor 3t, 4g
*Lewis
Sterling 1t
Dowling, Greg
Simmons
Dunn
Davidson
Niebling
Lindner 2t
Subs: Lamb
    Sironen

1986 France
Carcassonne: 13 Dec.
Won 52-0
Jack 3t
Shearer 4t
Kenny
Miles
O'Connor 1t, 6g
*Lewis
Sterling
Dowling, Greg
Simmons
Dunn
Folkes 1t
Niebling 1t
Lindner
Subs: Lamb
   Davidson

1987 New Zealand
Brisbane: 21 July
Lost 6-13
Jack
Shearer
Miles
Kenny
O'Connor 1g
*Lewis
Sterling 1t
Dowling, Greg
Simmons
Tunks
Pearce
Niebling
Lindner
Subs: Johnston
   Davidson

1988 Great Britain
Sydney: 11 June
Won 17-6
Jack
Ettingshausen
O'Connor 2g
Jackson 2t
Currie
*Lewis 1dg
Sterling
Daley, P.
Conescu
Backo 1t
Fullerton-Smith
Vautin
Lindner
Subs: Belcher
   Folkes

1988 Great Britain
Brisbane: 28 June
Won 34-14
Jack
Ettingshausen 1t
O'Connor 1t, 5g
Jackson 1t
Currie
*Lewis 1t
Sterling
Daley, P.
Conescu
Backo 1t
Fullerton-Smith
Vautin
Pearce 1t
Subs: Belcher
   Lindner

1988 Great Britain (Also WC)
Sydney: 9 July
Lost 12-26
Jack
Ettingshausen
O'Connor 2g
Jackson
Currie
*Lewis 1t
Sterling
Bella
Conescu
Backo 1t
Fullerton-Smith
Vautin
Pearce
Subs: Belcher
   Lindner

1988 Papua New Guinea
Wagga: 20 July
Won 70-8
Jack 1t
O'Connor 4t, 7g
Meninga 2t
Jackson
Currie 1t
*Lewis 1t
Langer 2t
Dunn
Conescu 1t
Daley, P.
Fullerton-Smith 1t
Miller 1t
Pearce
Subs: Hasler
   Vautin

1988 New Zealand (WCF)
Auckland: 9 Oct.
Won 25-12
Jack
O'Connor 4g
Farrar
McGaw
Shearer 1t
*Lewis
Langer 2t
Dunn
Elias 1dg
Roach
Sironen
Miller 1t
Pearce
Subs: Lamb
   Gillespie

1989 New Zealand
Christchurch: 9 July
Won 26-6
Belcher
Shearer
Meninga 5g
Currie 1t
Hancock, M.
*Lewis 1t
Alexander
Backo
Walters, Kerrod 1t
Roach
Sironen 1t
Clyde
Vautin
Subs: O'Connor
   McGuire

1989 New Zealand
Rotorua: 16 July
Won 8-0
Belcher
Shearer
Meninga 2g
Currie
Hancock, M. 1t
*Lewis
Alexander
Backo
Walters, Kerrod
Roach
Sironen
Clyde
Vautin
Sub: Hasler

1989 New Zealand
Auckland: 23 July
Won 22-14
Belcher
Hancock, M.
Shearer 1t
Currie
O'Connor 1t, 2g
*Lewis
Hasler
Backo
Walters, Kerrod
Roach
Meninga 1t, 1g
Clyde 1t
Vautin
Sub: McGuire

1990 France (Also WC)
Parkes: 27 June
Won 34-2
Belcher 1g
O'Connor
*Meninga 1t
McGaw 2t
Shearer 1t
Daley, L. 1t
Langer
Bella
Walters, Kerrod
Roach
Sironen
Gillespie
Mackay, B. 3t
Subs: Carroll
      Ettingshausen

1990 New Zealand
Wellington: 19 Aug.
Won 24-6
Belcher
Hancock, M. 1t
*Meninga 4g
McGaw 1t
Shearer
Daley, L.
Langer 1t
Bella
Walters, Kerrod
Roach
Roberts
Sironen
Lindner
Subs: Ettingshausen
      Hasler
      Mackay, B. 1t
      Lazarus

1990 Great Britain
Wembley: 27 Oct.
Lost 12-19
Belcher
Hancock, M.
*Meninga 1t, 2g
McGaw 1t
Ettingshausen
Stuart
Langer
Bella
Walters, Kerrod
Roach
Cartwright
Sironen
Lindner
Subs: Shearer
      Hasler
      Alexander
      Lazarus

1990 Great Britain
Old Trafford: 10 Nov.
Won 14-10
Belcher
Ettingshausen
*Meninga 1t, 1g
Daley, L.
Shearer 1t
Lyons 1t
Stuart
Lazarus
Elias
Roach
Lindner
Sironen
Mackay, B.

1990 Great Britain (Also WC)
Elland Rd, Leeds: 24 Nov.
Won 14-0
Belcher
Ettingshausen 1t
*Meninga 1t, 1g
Daley, L.
Shearer
Lyons
Stuart
Lazarus
Elias 1t
Roach
Lindner
Sironen
Mackay, B.
Subs: Alexander
      Hasler
      Sargent
      Gillespie

1990 France
Avignon: 2 Dec.
Won 60-4
Belcher 2t
Ettingshausen 2t
*Meninga 1g
Daley, L.
Shearer 1t
Lyons
Stuart
Lazarus 1t
Elias
Roach
Gillespie 1t
Sironen 1t
Mackay, B.
Subs: Alexander 3t, 7g
      Hasler
      Geyer
      Sargent

1990 France (Also WC)
Perpignan: 9 Dec.
Won 34-10
Belcher
Alexander 1t, 3g
*Meninga 1t
Shearer 1t
Ettingshausen 1t
Lyons
Stuart
Lazarus
Elias
Roach 1t
Lindner
Sironen
Mackay, B. 2t
Subs: Johns
      Hasler
      Gillespie
      Sargent

1991 New Zealand
Melbourne: 3 July
Lost 8-24
Hauff
Ettingshausen
*Meninga 2g
Johns
Shearer
Lewis
Langer
Roach
Walters, S. 1t
Bella
Roberts
Lindner
Clyde
Subs: Gillespie
      Cartwright

287

1991 New Zealand
Sydney: 24 July
Won 44-0
Ettingshausen
Carne 1t
*Meninga 6g
Daley, L. 2t
Wishart 1t
Jackson
Langer
Salvatori
Walters, S.
Bella
Gillespie 1t
Geyer 1t
Clyde 1t
Subs: Johns
    Roberts
    Hasler 1t
    Cartwright

1991 New Zealand (Also WC)
Brisbane: 31 July
Won 40-12
Ettingshausen 1t
Carne 1t
*Meninga 1t, 6g
Daley, L. 1t
Wishart 1t
Jackson
Langer
Salvatori
Walters, S. 1t
Bella
Gillespie
Geyer
Clyde 1t
Subs: Johns
    Roberts
    Hasler
    Cartwright

1991 Papua New Guinea
Goroka: 6 Oct.
Won 58-2
Belcher 5g
Wishart 3t
*Meninga
Ettingshausen 2t
Carne 3t
Lyons 1t
Toovey
Lazarus
Walters, Kerrod
Bella
Roberts 1t
Clyde
Fittler 2t
Subs: Johns
    Coyne
    Walters, Kevin
    Gourley

1991 Papua New Guinea (Also WC)
Port Moresby: 13 Oct.
Won 40-6
Belcher 1t
Carne 3t
*Meninga 1t, 2g
Ettingshausen 1t
Wishart 1t
Jackson 1t
Toovey
Lazarus
Walters, Kerrod
Bella
Roberts
Clyde 1t
Fittler
Subs: Johns
    Coyne
    Walters, Kevin
    Lyons

1992 Great Britain
Sydney: 12 June
Won 22-6
Ettingshausen
Wishart 3g
*Meninga 2t
Daley, L.
Hancock, M. 1t
Jackson
Langer
Lazarus
Walters, S.
Harragon
Sironen 1t
Lindner
Clyde
Subs: Fittler
    Gillespie
    Walters, Kevin
    Mackay, B.

1992 Great Britain
Melbourne: 26 June
Lost 10-33
Ettingshausen
Wishart
*Meninga 1g
Daley, L.
Hancock, M.
Jackson
Langer
Gillespie
Walters, S.
Harragon
Sironen
Lindner 1t
Clyde
Subs: Johns 1t
    Lazarus
    Walters, Kevin
    Mackay, B.

1992 Great Britain (Also WC)
Brisbane: 3 July
Won 16-10
Ettingshausen
Carne
*Meninga 1t, 4g
Fittler
Hancock, M.
Daley, L. 1t
Langer
Lazarus
Walters, S.
Harragon
Sironen
Lindner
Clyde
Subs: Johns
    Cartwright
    Walters, Kevin
    Gillespie

1992 Papua New Guinea (Also WC)
Townsville: 17 July
Won 36-14
Carne 1t
Mackay, G. 2t
*Meninga 4g
Fittler 1t
Hancock, M.
Daley, L. 1t
Langer
Lazarus
Walters, S.
Gillespie
Sironen
Lindner
Mackay, B.
Subs: Walters, Kevin
    Johns 1t
    Cartwright
    Sargent 1t

1992 Great Britain (WCF)
Wembley: 24 Oct.
Won 10-6
Brasher
Carne
*Meninga 3g
Renouf 1t
Hancock, M.
Fittler
Langer
Lazarus
Walters, S.
Sargent
Sironen
Lindner
Clyde
Subs: Walters, Kevin
    Gillespie
    Cartwright

1993 New Zealand	**1993 New Zealand**	**1993 New Zealand**
Auckland: 20 June	Palmerston N: 25 June	Brisbane: 30 June
Drew 14-14	Won 16-8	Won 16-4
Shearer 1t, 2g	Shearer 2g	Shearer 2g
Carne	Carne 1t	Carne
*Daley, L. 2dg	*Meninga	*Meninga 1t
Fittler	Fittler	Fittler 1t
Hancock, M.	Hancock, M. 1t	Hancock, M. 1t
Walters, Kevin	Daley, L.	Daley, L.
Langer	Langer	Langer
Lazarus	Lazarus	Lazarus
Walters, S. 1t	Walters, S.	Walters, S.
Harragon	Harragon	Harragon
Sironen	Sironen	Sironen
Lindner	Lindner	Lindner
Clyde	Clyde 1t	Clyde
Subs: Roberts	Subs: Mackay, B.	Subs: Ettingshausen
Mackay, B.	Ettingshausen	Walters, Kevin
Renouf	Gillespie	Gillespie
	Walters, Kevin	Roberts

Australia celebrate the capture of the 1992 Stones Bitter World Cup after defeating Great Britain 10-6 at Wembley in front of a world record international crowd of 73,631.

AUSTRALIA REGISTER
1974-94

The following is an index of players who have appeared for Australia, toured or been members of a World Cup squad since 1974. Where a player began his international career before 1974 his preceding record is also given.

Appearances refer to Test and World Cup matches only. For matches in France the year given is for the first half of the season.

World Cup matches are in bold letters in the list of *Appearances* except when they doubled as Test matches. Substitute appearances are in lower case letters. In 1975 the World Cup was in two sections — 1 refers to the first part in Australia, 2 refers to the second part in Britain and France.

Key: B — Britain, E — England, F — France, NSW — New South Wales, NZ — New Zealand, PNG — Papua New Guinea, SA — South Africa, W — Wales.

ALEXANDER, Greg (NSW)
Tours: Britain 1986,1990; NZ 1989
Appearances: 1989 NZ2; 1990 b2,Ff
ANDERSON, Chris (NSW)
Tours: Britain 1978,1982; NZ 1980
World Cup: 1975 (1)
Appearances: **1975NZ,e;** 1978 B3,F2; 1979 B; 1980 NZ2
AYLIFFE, Royce (NSW)
Appearances: 1981 f

BACKO, Sam (Queensland)
Tours: 1989 NZ
Appearances: 1988 B3; 1989 NZ3
BEETSON, Arthur (NSW)
Tours: Britain 1973
World Cup: 1968,1972,1975(1&2),1977
Appearances: 1966 B; **1968 B,F2;** 1970 B3; 1972 NZ2,**B2,F;** 1973 B3,F2; 1974 B3; **1975 F2,E2, W; 1977 F,B2**
BELCHER, Gary (Queensland)
Tours: Britain 1986,1990; PNG 1991
Appearances: 1988 b3; 1989 NZ3; 1990 F,NZ,B3,F2; 1991 PNG2
BELLA, Martin (Queensland)
Tours: Britain 1986,1990; PNG 1991
Appearances: 1988 B; 1990 F,NZ,B; 1991 NZ3,PNG2
BOUSTEAD, Kerry (Queensland)
Tours: Britain 1978,1982; NZ 1980
Appearances: 1978 NZ3,B3,F2; 1979 B2; 1980 NZ; 1981 F; 1982 NZ2,PNG,B3,F2; 1983 NZ2; 1984 B3

BOYD, Les (NSW)
Tours: Britain 1978,1982; NZ 1980
Appearances: 1978 Bb,F; 1979 B3; 1980 NZ2; 1981 F2; 1982 NZ2,B3,F2
BRANIGHAN, Ray (NSW)
Tours: Britain 1973; NZ 1971
World Cup: 1970,1972,1975(1)
Appearances: 1970 NZ,Bb,F; 1971 NZ; **1972 B2,NZ,F;** 1973 B3,F2; 1974 Bb; **1975 nz**
BRASHER, Tim (Queensland)
World Cup: 1992
Appearances: **1992 B**
BRASS, John (NSW)
World Cup: 1975(2)
Appearances: 1970 B3; **1975 NZ,F,E**
BRENTNALL, Greg (NSW)
Tours: NZ 1980; Britain 1982
Appearances: 1980 NZ2; 1981 F2; 1982 NZ2,PNG,B3,F2; 1983 NZ
BROWN, Dave (NSW)
Appearances: 1983 NZ2; 1984 B2b
BROWN, Ray (NSW)
Tours: Britain 1982
Appearances: 1982 png,b2,f; 1983 nz

CARNE, Willie (Queensland)
Tours: PNG 1991
World Cup: 1992
Appearances: 1991 NZ2,PNG2; 1992 B,PNG,**B**; 1993 NZ3
CARROLL, Mark (NSW)
Tours: Britain 1990
Appearances: 1990 f
CARTWRIGHT, John (NSW)
Tours: Britain 1990
World Cup: 1992
Appearances: 1990 B; 1991 nz3; 1992 b,png,**b**
CLEAL, Noel (NSW)
Tours: NZ 1985; Britain 1986
Appearances: 1985 NZnz; 1986 NZ3,PNG,B2
CLOSE, Chris (Queensland)
Tours: NZ 1980,1985
Appearances: 1985 NZ2nz;
CLYDE, Bradley (NSW)
Tours: NZ 1989; PNG 1991
World Cup: 1992
Appearances: 1989 NZ3; 1991 NZ3,PNG2; 1992 B3,**B**; 1993 NZ3
CONESCU, Greg (Queensland)
Tours: Britain 1982; NZ 1985
Appearances: 1984 B3; 1985 NZ2; 1988 B3,PNG
CONLON, Ross (NSW)
Appearances: 1984 B
COOTE, Ron (NSW)
Tours: Britain 1967; NZ 1969
World Cup: 1968,1970,1975(1)
Appearances: 1967 B2,F3; **1968 B,NZ,F2;** 1969 NZ2; 1970 B3; **1970 NZ,F,B;** 1974 B3; **1975 NZ,F,E**
COROWA, Larry (NSW)
Tours: Britain 1978
Appearances: 1979 B2

COYNE, Gary (Queensland)
Tours: PNG 1991
Appearances: 1991 png2
CREAR, Steve (Queensland)
World Cup: 1977
CRONIN, Michael (NSW)
Tours: Britain 1973,1978; NZ 1980
World Cup: 1975(1&2),1977
Appearances: 1973 F2; 1974 B3; **1975 NZ2,W2,E2,F;1977
NZ,F,B2;** 1978 NZ3,B3,F2; 1979 B3; 1980 NZ2;
1981 F2; 1982 NZ2
CURRIE, Tony (Queensland)
Tours: NZ 1989
Appearances: 1988 B3,PNG; 1989 NZ3

DALEY, Laurie (NSW)
Tours: Britain 1990
Appearances: 1990 F,NZ,B2,F; 1991 NZ2; 1992 B3,PNG;
1993 NZ3
DALEY, Phil (NSW)
Tours: Britain 1986
Appearances: 1988 B2,PNG
DAVIDSON, Les (NSW)
Tours: Britain 1986
Appearances: 1986 b,Ff; 1987 nz
DONNELLY, John (NSW)
World Cup: 1975(1)
Appearances: **1975 F,e,w;** 1978 NZ
DORAHY, John (NSW)
Appearances: 1978 NZ2
DOWLING, Gary (NSW)
Tours: NZ 1980
Appearances: 1980 NZ2
DOWLING, Greg (Queensland)
Tours: NZ 1985; Britain 1986
Appearances: 1984 B3; 1985 NZ2nz; 1986 B3,F2;
1987 NZ
DUNN, Paul (NSW)
Tours: Britain 1986
Appearances: 1986 PNG,B2,F2; 1988 PNG,**NZ**

EADIE, Graham (NSW)
Tours: Britain 1973,1978
World Cup: 1975(2),1977
Appearances: 1973 B2; 1974 B; **1975 NZ,W,F,E; 1977
B2,NZ,F;** 1978 NZ,B3,F2; 1979 B3
ELIAS, Ben (NSW)
Tours: NZ 1985; Britain 1986,1990
Appearances: 1985 NZ; **1988 NZ;** 1990 B2,F2
ELLA, Steve (NSW)
Tours: Britain 1982; NZ 1985
Appearances: 1983 nz; 1985 NZnz
ETTINGSHAUSEN, Andrew (NSW)
Tours: Britain 1990; PNG 1991
Appearances: 1988 B3; 1990 f,nz,B3,F2; 1991 NZ3,
PNG2; 1992 B3; 1993 nz2

FAHEY, Terry (NSW)
World Cup: 1975(1),1977
Appearances: **1975 NZ: 1977 F,B;** 1978 NZ; 1979 B;
1981 F

FARRAR, Andrew (NSW)
Appearances: **1988 NZ**
FERGUSON, John (NSW)
Tours: NZ 1985
Appearances: 1985 NZ3
FITTLER, Brad (NSW)
Tours: Britain 1990; PNG 1991
World Cup: 1992
Appearances: 1991 PNG2; 1992 Bb,PNG,**B**; 1993 NZ3
FITZGERALD, Denis (NSW)
World Cup: 1975(1),1977
Appearances: **1975 NZ; 1977 NZ,F,Bb**
FOLKES, Steve (NSW)
Tours: Britain 1986
Appearances: 1986 NZ3,F; 1988 b
FULLERTON-SMITH, Wally (Queensland)
Tours: NZ 1985
Appearances: 1983 NZ2; 1984 Bb; 1988 B3,PNG
FULTON, Bobby (NSW)
Tours: NZ 1971; Britain 1973,1978
World Cup: 1968,1970,1972,1975(1)
Appearances: **1968nz,F2;** 1970 B; **1970 B2,NZ,F;**
1971 NZ; 1972 NZ2; **1972 B2,NZ,F;** 1973 B3,F2;
1974 B3; **1975 NZ,W,F,E;** 1978 NZ3,B3,F2

GARTNER, Russel (NSW)
World Cup: 1977
Appearances: **1977 B,f**
GEE, Andrew (Queensland)
Tours: 1991 PNG
GEIGER, Nick (Queensland)
World Cup: 1977
Appearances: **1977 B2,NZ,F**
GERARD, Geoff (NSW)
Tours: Britain 1978
Appearances: 1978 B3,F2; 1983 NZ
GEYER, Mark (NSW)
Tours: Britain 1990
Appearances: 1990 f; 1991 NZ2
GIBBS, Johnny (NSW)
Tours: Britain 1978
GILLESPIE, David (NSW)
Tours: Britain 1990
World Cup: 1992
Appearances: **1988 nz;** 1990 F,b,Ff; 1991 NZ2nz; 1992
Bb2,PNG,b; 1993 nz2
GLOVER, Neville (NSW)
Appearances: 1978 NZ2
GODDEN, Brad (NSW)
World Cup: 1992
GOURLEY, Scott (NSW)
Tours: PNG 1991
Appearances: 1991 png
GROTHE, Eric (NSW)
Tours: Britain 1982
Appearances: 1982 B2,Ff; 1983 NZ2; 1984 B2

HANCOCK, Michael (Queensland)
Tours: NZ 1989; Britain 1990
World Cup: 1992
Appearances: 1989 NZ3; 1990 NZ,B; 1992 B3,PNG,**B**;
1993 NZ3

HANCOCK, Rohan (Queensland)
Tours: NZ 1980; Britain 1982
Appearances: 1982 NZ2,PNG
HARRAGON, Paul (NSW)
World Cup: 1992
Appearances: 1992 B3; 1993 NZ3
HARRIS, Mark (NSW)
World Cup: 1970,1972,1975(l),1977
Appearances: **1970 B2;** 1972 NZ; **1972 B2,F; 1975 W,F,E;
1977 NZ,B**
HASLER, Des (NSW)
Tours: NZ 1985,1989; Britain 1986,1990
Appearances: 1985 NZ; 1986 PNG; 1988 png; 1989 Nznz;
1990 nz,b2,f2; 1991 nz2
HAUFF, Paul (Queensland)
Appearances: 1991 NZ
HIGGS, Ray (Queensland-NSW)
World Cup: 1975(2),1977
Appearances: 1974 B; **1975 NZ,W,F,E; 1977 NZ,f,bB**
HILDITCH, Ron (NSW)
Tours: Britain 1978
Appearances: 1978 F; 1981 F2

JACK, Garry (NSW)
Tours: NZ 1985; Britain 1986
Appearances: 1984 B3; 1985 NZ3; 1986 NZ3,PNG,B3,F2;
1987 NZ; 1988 B3,PNG,**NZ**
JACKSON, Peter (Queensland)
Tours: NZ 1989; PNG 1991
Appearances: 1988 B3,PNG; 1991 NZ2,PNG; 1992 B2
JARVIS, Pat (NSW)
Appearances: 1983 nz
JOHNS, Chris (NSW)
Tours: Britain 1990; PNG 1991
World Cup: 1992
Appearances: 1990 f; 1991 NZnz2,png2; 1992 b2,png
JOHNSTON, Brian (NSW)
Appearances: 1987 nz

KENNY, Brett (NSW)
Tours: Britain 1982,1986
Appearances: 1982 PNG,B3,F2; 1984 Bb; 1986 NZ3,
B3,F2; 1987 NZ
KISS, Les (Queensland)
Tours: Britain 1986
Appearances: 1986 NZ2,PNG,B
KNEEN, Steve (NSW)
Tours: Britain 1978
KOLC, John (NSW)
World Cup: 1977
Appearances: **1977 B**
KRILICH, Max (NSW)
Tours: Britain 1978,1982
Appearances: 1978 NZ,B2; 1982 NZ2,PNG,B3,F2;
1983 NZ2

LAMB, Terry (NSW)
Tours: Britain 1986
Appearances: 1986 nz2,b3,f2; **1988 nz**
LANG, John (Queensland-NSW)
Tours: Britain 1973; NZ 1980
World Cup: 1975(1&2)

292

Appearances: 1973 F; 1974 B; **1975 NZ,W,F2,E;** 1978 NZ
LANGER, Allan (Queensland)
Tours: Britain 1990
World Cup: 1992
Appearances: 1988 PNG,**NZ;** 1990 F,NZ,B; 1991 NZ3;
1992 B3,PNG,**B;** 1993 NZ3
LANGLANDS, Graeme (NSW)
Tours: Britain 1963,1967,1973; NZ 1965,1969,1971
World Cup: 1968,1972,1975(1)
Appearances: 1963 NZ3,SA2,B3,F2; 1964 F2; 1965 NZ2;
1966 B2; 1967 NZ3,B3,F3; **1968 F,B,NZ;** 1969
NZ2; 1970 B; 1971 NZ; 1972 NZ2; **1972 B2,NZ,F;**
1973 B; 1974 B2; **1975 NZ,W,F,E**
LANGMACK, Paul (NSW)
Tours: Britain 1986
LAZARUS, Glenn (NSW)
Tours: Britain 1990; PNG 1991
World Cup: 1992
Appearances: 1990 nz,B2b,F2; 1991 PNG2; 1992
B2b,PNG,**B;** 1993 NZ3
LEIS, Jim (NSW)
Tours: NZ 1980
LEWIS, Wally (Queensland)
Tours: Britain 1982,1986; NZ 1985,1989
Appearances: 1981 F2; 1982 NZ2,b2,F; 1983 NZ2;
1984 B3; 1985 NZ3; 1986 NZ3,PNG,B3,F2;
1987 NZ; 1988 B3,PNG,**NZ;** 1989 NZ3; 1991 NZ
LINDNER, Bob (Queensland)
Tours: Britain 1986,1990
World Cup: 1992
Appearances: 1986 PNG,B3,F2; 1987 NZ; 1988 Bb2;
1990 NZ,B3,F; 1991 NZ; 1992 B3,PNG,**B;**
1993 NZ3
LYONS, Cliff (NSW)
Tours: Britain 1990; PNG 1991
Appearances: 1990 B2,F2; 1991 PNGpng

MACKAY, Brad (NSW)
Tours: Britain 1990
Appearances: 1990, F,nz,B2,F2; 1992 b2,PNG; 1993 nz2
MACKAY, Graham (NSW)
World Cup: 1992
Appearances: 1992 PNG
MACKAY, Ian (NSW)
World Cup: 1975(2)
Appearances: **1975 NZ,E,w**
McCABE, Paul (NSW)
Tours: Britain 1982
Appearances: 1981 F2; 1982 B,F2; 1983 NZ
McCARTHY, Bob (NSW)
Tours: NZ 1969,1971; Britain 1973
World Cup: 1970,1972
Appearances: 1969 NZ2; 1970 B; **1970 NZ,B2,F;**
1971 NZ; 1972 NZ2; **1972 B;** 1973 B2; 1974 Bb
McGAW, Mark (NSW)
Tours: Britain 1990; PNG 1991
Appearances: **1988 NZ;** 1990 F,NZ,B
McGUIRE, Bruce (NSW)
Tours: NZ 1989; PNG 1991
Appearances: 1989 nz2
McKINNON, Don (NSW)
Tours: Britain 1982

McMAHON, Allan (NSW)
Tours: Britain 1978
World Cup: 1975(2),1977
Appearances: **1975 W: 1977 NZ,F,B2**
MARTIN, Steve (NSW)
Tours: Britain 1978; NZ 1980
Appearances: 1978 F
MASTERMAN, Jeff (NSW)
Appearances: 1981 F2
MAYES, Johnny (NSW)
World Cup: 1975(2)
Appearances: **1975 NZ,W,E**
MENINGA, Mal (Queensland)
Tours: Britain 1982,1986,1990; NZ 1985,1989; PNG
   1991
World Cup: 1992
Appearances: 1982 NZ,PNG,B3,F2; 1983 NZ2; 1984 B2;
   1985 NZ3; 1986 png,Bb2; 1988 PNG; 1989 NZ3;
   1990 F,NZ,B3,F2; 1991 NZ3,PNG2; 1992 B3,PNG,**B**;
   1993 NZ2
MILES, Gene (Queensland)
Tours: Britain 1982,1986
Appearances: 1983 NZ; 1984 B3; 1986 NZ3,PNG,B3,F2;
   1987 NZ
MILLER, Gavin (NSW)
Appearances: 1988 PNG,**NZ**
MORRIS, Rod (Queensland-NSW)
Tours: Britain 1978,1982; NZ 1980
Appearances: 1978 NZnz,B,F; 1979 B3; 1980 NZ2;
   1981 Ff; 1982 NZnz,B,F
MORRIS, Steve (NSW)
Appearances: 1978 NZ
MORTIMER, Chris (NSW)
Tours: Britain 1986
Appearances: 1986 PNG
MORTIMER, Steve (NSW)
Tours: Britain 1982
Appearances: 1981 F2; 1982 NZ2,PNG; 1983 NZ;
   1984 Bb
MUGGLETON, John (NSW)
Tours: Britain 1982
Appearances: 1982 NZnz,PNG
MURRAY, Mark (Queensland)
Tours: Britain 1982; NZ 1985
Appearances: 1982 png; 1983 nz; 1984 B2; 1985 NZ2

NIEBLING, Bryan (Queensland)
Tours: Britain 1986
Appearances: 1984 B3; 1986 nz3,PNG,B3,F2: 1987 NZ

O'CONNOR, Michael (NSW)
Tours: NZ 1985,1989; Britain 1986
Appearances: 1986 NZ3,PNG,B3,F2; 1987 NZ;
   1988 B3,PNG,**NZ:** 1989 nznZ; 1990 F
OLIPHANT, Greg (Queensland)
Tours: Britain 1978
Appearances: 1978 NZnz
OLLING, Graeme (NSW)
Tours: Britain 1978
Appearances: 1978 NZ2,B2

O'NEILL, John (NSW)
Tours: Britain 1973
World Cup: 1970,1972,1975(1)
Appearances: **1970 NZ,B2; 1972 B2,NZ,F;** 1973 F;
   1974 B; **1975 W**
O'REILLY, Bob (NSW)
Tours: NZ 1971; Britain 1973
World Cup: 1970,1972
Appearances: **1970 NZ,B2,F;** 1971 NZ; 1972 NZ2;
   1972 NZ,F,B; 1973 B3,F; 1974 B2
ORR, Warren (Queensland)
Tours: Britain 1973
Appearances: 1974 B2

PEARCE, Wayne (NSW)
Tours: Britain 1982; NZ 1985
Appearances: 1982 B3,F2; 1984 B3; 1985 NZ3; 1986 NZ3;
   1987 NZ; 1988 B2,PNG,**NZ**
PEARD, John (NSW)
World Cup: 1975(2),1977
Appearances: **1975 NZ,W,F,E; 1977 NZ,F,B2**
PEPONIS, George (NSW)
Tours: Britain 1978; NZ 1980
Appearances: 1978 NZ,B,F; 1979 B3; 1980 NZ2
PICKUP, Tim (NSW)
Tours: Britain 1973
World Cup: 1975(1)
Appearances: 1972 NZ2; 1973 Bb,F2; 1974 B;
   1975 NZ,W,F,E
PIERCE, Greg (NSW)
Tours: Britain 1973,1978
World Cup: 1975(2),1977
Appearances: 1973 F; **1975 F,E; 1977 NZ,B2;** 1978 NZ2
PIGGINS, George (NSW)
World Cup: 1975(2)
Appearances: **1975 NZ,W,E**
PLATZ, Greg (Queensland)
Appearances: 1978 NZ
PLATZ, Lew (Queensland)
World Cup: 1975(1&2)
Appearances: **1975 NZ2,F2,W,E**
PORTER, Jim (NSW)
World Cup: 1975(2)
Appearances: **1975 F,w**
PRICE, Ray (NSW)
Tours: Britain 1978,1982; NZ 1980
Appearances: 1978 NZ3,B3,F2; 1979 B3; 1980 NZ2;
   1981 F2; 1982 NZ,PNG,B2; 1983 NZ; 1984 B2

QUAYLE, John (NSW)
World Cup: 1975(2)
Appearances: **1975 NZ,W**
QUINN, Graham (NSW)
Tours: NZ 1980
Appearances: 1980 NZ

RANDALL, Terry (NSW)
Tours: Britain 1973
World Cup: 1975(1&2),1977
Appearances: **1975 NZ,W2,F2,E2; 1977 NZ,F,B2**

RAUDONIKIS, Tom (NSW)
Tours: Britain 1973,1978; NZ 1971,1980
World Cup: 1972,1975(1&2),1977
Appearances: 1972 NZ2; **1972 B;** 1973 B3,F; 1974 B3;
    1975 W,F2,E,nz; 1977 NZ,F,B; 1978 NZ,B3,F2;
    1979 B3; 1980 NZ2
REDDY, Rod (NSW)
Tours: Britain 1978,1982; NZ 1980
World Cup: 1977
Appearances: **1977 F;** 1978 NZ3,B2,F; 1979 B3;
    1980 NZ2; 1982 PNG,B3,F
RENOUF, Steve (Queensland)
World Cup: 1992
Appearances: **1992 B;** 1993 nz
RHODES, Johnny (Queensland)
World Cup: 1968,1975(1&2)
Appearances: **1968 B,NZ,F2; 1975 W,F2,E2,NZ**
RIBOT, John (Queensland)
Tours: Britain 1982; NZ 1985
Appearances: 1981 F2; 1982 NZ2,PNG,B; 1985 NZ3
RICHARDSON, Geoff (Queensland)
Appearances: 1974 B2
ROACH, Steve (NSW)
Tours: NZ 1985,1989; Britain 1986,1990; PNG 1991
Appearances: 1985 NZ3; 1986 NZ3,PNG,B; **1988 NZ;**
    1989 NZ3; 1990 F,NZ,B3,F2; 1991 NZ
ROBERTS, Ian (NSW)
Tours: PNG 1991
Appearances: 1990 NZ; 1991 NZnz2,PNG2; 1993 nz2
ROGERS, Steve (NSW)
Tours: Britain 1973,1978,1982
World Cup: 1975(2)
Appearances: **1975 NZ,F,e;** 1978 NZ3,B3,F; 1979 B3;
    1981 F2; 1982 NZnz,PNG,B3,F2; 1983 NZ

SAIT, Paul (NSW)
Tours: NZ 1971; Britain 1973
World Cup: 1970,1972,1975(1)
Appearances: **1970 NZ,B2,F;** 1971 NZ; **1972 b,NZ,F;**
    1973 B3,F; 1974 B2; **1975 nz,W**
SALVATORI, Craig (NSW)
Tours: PNG 1991
Appearances: 1991 NZ2
SARGENT, Mark (NSW)
Tours: Britain 1990
World Cup: 1992
Appearances: 1990 b,f2; 1992 png,**B**
SCHUBERT, Ian (NSW)
Tours: Britain 1978,1982
World Cup: 1975(2)
Appearances: **1975 NZ,W,f,E**
SCOTT, Colin (Queensland)
Appearances: 1983 NZ
SHEARER, Dale (Queensland)
Tours: Britain 1986,1990; NZ 1989
Appearances: 1986 NZ,B2,F2; 1987 NZ; **1988 NZ;**
    1989 NZ3; 1990 F,NZ,B2b,F2; 1991 NZ; 1993 NZ3
SIGSWORTH, Phil (NSW)
Appearances: 1981 f
SIMMONS, Royce (NSW)
Tours: Britain 1986
Appearances: 1986 NZ3,PNG,B3,F2; 1987 NZ

SIRONEN, Paul (NSW)
Tours: Britain 1986,1990; NZ 1989
World Cup: 1992
Appearances: 1986 png,f; 1988 **NZ;** 1989 NZ2;
    1990 F,NZ,B3,F2; 1992 B3,PNG,**B;** 1993 NZ3
STAINS, Dan (Queensland)
Tours: NZ 1989
STERLING, Peter (NSW)
Tours: Britain 1982,1986
Appearances: 1982 B3,F2; 1983 NZ; 1986 NZ3,B3,F2;
    1987 NZ; 1988 B3
STEVENS, Gary (NSW)
Tours: Britain 1973
World Cup: 1972,1975(1)
Appearances: **1972 nz,F,B;** 1973 B2,F; 1974 B2;
    1975 NZ,W,E
STRUDWICK, Ross (Queensland)
World Cup: 1975(1)
Appearances: **1975 NZ**
STUART, Ricky (NSW)
Tours: Britain 1990
World Cup: 1992
Appearances: 1990 B3,F2

TESSMAN, Brad (Queensland)
Appearances: 1983 NZ
THOMAS, Mark (Queensland)
World Cup: 1977
Appearances: **1977 NZ,F,B**
THOMPSON, Alan (NSW)
Tours: Britain 1978; NZ 1980
Appearances: 1978 b2; 1979 B3; 1980 NZ2
THOMSON, Ian (NSW)
Tours: Britain 1978
Appearances: 1978 NZ,b,F
TOOVEY, Geoff (NSW)
Tours: PNG 1991
Appearances: 1991 PNG2
TREWHELLA, David (NSW)
Tours: NZ 1989
TUNKS, Peter (NSW)
Tours: NZ 1985
Appearances: 1985 NZnz; 1986 NZ3; 1987 NZ
TURNER, Ron (NSW)
World Cup: 1970
Appearances: **1970 nz,f,B;** 1974 B

VAUTIN, Paul (NSW)
Tours: NZ 1985,1989
Appearances: 1982 NZ; 1983 NZ2; 1984 B; 1985 NZ2;
    1988 B3,PNG; 1989 NZ3
VEIVERS, Greg (Queensland)
World Cup: 1975(2), 1977
Appearances: **1975 NZ,W; 1977 NZ,F,B2**

WAITE, David (NSW)
Tours: Britain 1973
Appearances: 1973 B2,F2; 1974 B2
WALKER, Bruce (NSW)
Tours: Britain 1978
WALTERS, Elwyn (NSW)
Tours: 1967,1973: NZ 1969

World Cup: 1970,1972
Appearances: 1969 NZ2; 1970 B2; **1970 NZ,Bb,F;**
    1972 NZ2; **1972 B2,NZ,F;** 1973 B3,F2; 1974 B
WALTERS, Kerrod (Queensland)
Tours: NZ 1989; Britain 1990; PNG 1991
World Cup: 1992
Appearances: 1989 NZ3; 1990 F,NZ,B; 1991 PNG2
WALTERS, Kevin (Queensland)
Tours: Britain 1990; PNG 1991
World Cup: 1992
Appearances: 1991 png2; 1992 b3,png,**b**; 1993 nz2NZ
WALTERS, Steve (Queensland)
Tours: PNG 1991
World Cup: 1992
Appearances: 1991 NZ3; 1992 B3,PNG,**B**; 1993 NZ3
WILLIAMSON, Lionel (Queensland-NSW)
Tours: NZ 1971; Britain 1973
World Cup: 1968,1970
Appearances: **1968 F2; 1970 NZ,B2,F;** 1971 NZ;
    1973 B2,F; 1974 B

WISHART, Rod (NSW)
Tours: PNG 1991
Appearances: 1991 NZ2,PNG2; 1992 B2
WRIGHT, David (Queensland)
World Cup: 1975(1)
Appearances: **1975 NZ**
WYNN, Graeme (NSW)
Tours: NZ 1980
WYNN, Peter (NSW)
Tours: NZ 1985
Appearances: 1985 NZ3

YOUNG, Craig (NSW)
Tours: Britain 1978,1982; NZ 1980
Appearances: 1978 NZ,B3,F2; 1979 B3; 1980 NZ2;
    1981 F; 1982 NZ2,PNG,B2,F2; 1984 b

*Scrum half Allan Langer, a Test debutant in 1988 and
a 1990 Kangaroo.*

Centre Mal Meninga, Test skipper since 1990.

AUSTRALIA TOURS OF BRITAIN

1908-09 TOUR

MATCH RESULTS

Mid-Rhondda	won	20-6	7,500
Bradford N.	won	12-11	4,000
Rochdale H.	won	5-0	3,000
York	drew	5-5	3,000
Salford	drew	9-9	6,100
Runcorn	won	9-7	3,000
Cumberland League (W'haven)	**won**	**52-10**	**4,000**
Leigh	lost	11-14	6,000
Dewsbury	lost	0-15	2,000
Yorkshire (Hull)	**won**	**24-11**	**3,500**
Hunslet	won	12-11	6,000
Aberdare	won	37-10	5,000
Warrington	lost	3-10	5,000
Northern RL (Everton)	**won**	**10-9**	**6,000**
Hull K.R.	lost	16-21	7,000
Lancashire (Wigan)	**won**	**20-6**	**4,000**
Barrow	won	21-5	6,500
Halifax	lost	8-12	6,000
Swinton	won	10-9	1,500
BRITAIN (QPR, London)	**drew**	**22-22**	**2,000**
Treherbert	won	6-3	4,000
Wakefield T.	lost	13-20	3,000
Leeds	won	14-10	12,000
Oldham	lost	5-11	12,000
England (Huddersfield)	**lost**	**9-14**	**7,000**
Widnes	won	13-2	1,000
†Wigan	lost	7-10	4,000
Batley	lost	5-12	2,000
Welsh League (Merthyr Tydfil)	**lost**	**13-14**	**6,000**
Ebbw Vale	won	9-8	5,000
†Wigan	lost	8-16	8,000
BRITAIN (Newcastle)	**lost**	**5-15**	**22,000**
Keighley	drew	8-8	1,000
Hull	lost	8-9	10,000
England (Glasgow)	**drew**	**17-17**	**3,000**
Cumberland (Carlisle)	**lost**	**2-11**	**2,000**
Broughton R.	lost	12-14	12,000
St. Helens	lost	0-9	1,500
Warrington	drew	8-8	7,000
BRITAIN (Birmingham)	**lost**	**5-6**	**9,000**
Huddersfield	lost	3-5	9,677
Barrow	lost	3-11	6,000
Merthyr Tydfil	lost	13-15	4,000
England (Everton)	**lost**	**7-14**	**4,500**
Lancashire (Leigh)	**won**	**14-9**	**4,000**

● The tourists also played an exhibition match against Widnes at Southport on January 1, winning 55-3, but this is not included in tour records.

†There were two matches against Wigan because the first was marred by fog.

SUMMARY

Played 45   Won 17   Drew 6   Lost 22

For
Tries 113   Goals 87   Points 513
Against
Tries 106   Goals 78   Points 474

Lost Test series 2-0 with one drawn
Attendance total: 250,777

TOUR PARTY

Manager: J. Giltinan   Captain: D. Lutge

	App	Tries	Gls	Pts
Jim Abercrombie	31	2	6	18
Tommy Anderson	5	0	0	0
Arthur Anlezark	17	1	0	3
Bill Bailey	3	3	0	9
Mick Bolewski	33	2	0	6
Alex Burdon	25	3	0	9
Arthur Butler	23	4	1	14
Bill Cann	8	0	0	0
Frank Cheadle	7	0	0	0
Albert Conlon	7	3	2	13
Tedda Courtney	27	8	0	24
James Davis	6	0	0	0
Sid Deane	27	6	0	18
Jim Devereux	30	17	3	57
Alf Dobbs	5	0	0	0
Dan Frawley	22	10	0	30
Bob Graves	21	2	0	6
Arthur Halloway	29	5	0	15
Bill Hardcastle	6	1	0	3
Charlie Hedley	17	1	1	5
Bill Heidke	25	3	0	9
Arthur Hennessy	7	0	0	0
Lou Jones	5	1	0	3
Dinny Lutge	5	0	0	0
Tom McCabe	20	4	0	12
Herbert Messenger	32	10	65	160
Peter Moir	4	2	0	6
Andy Morton	23	4	9	30
Bill Noble	3	0	0	0
Larry O'Malley	35	5	0	15
Sid Pearce	32	2	0	6
Albert Rosenfeld	15	5	0	15
John Rosewell	1	0	0	0
Pat Walsh	29	9	0	27

MEMO

First match on 3 October, last match on 8 March.

All three Test matches were played on soccer grounds outside the Northern Union area in a move to expand the game, but it was not a success.

The party included Herbert "Dally" Messenger who had toured the previous season with New Zealand.

Among the players who were to sign for English clubs was Albert Rosenfeld, who scored a record 80 tries in a season while with Huddersfield.

1911-12 TOUR

MATCH RESULTS

Midlands — South (Coventry)	**won**	**20-11**	**3,000**
Yorkshire (Sheffield)	**won**	**33-13**	**4,000**
Broughton R.	won	18-8	12,000
Lancashire (Blackburn)	**won**	**25-12**	**5,000**
Wales (Ebbw Vale)	**won**	**28-20**	**7,000**
Widnes	won	23-0	5,000
St. Helens	won	16-5	12,000
England (Fulham)	**won**	**11-6**	**6,000**
Hunslet	drew	3-3	4,000
Northern RL (Everton)	**won**	**16-3**	**6,000**
Wigan	lost	2-7	25,000
Swinton	won	28-9	4,000
Hull	won	26-7	6,000
BRITAIN (Newcastle)	**won**	**19-10**	**6,500**
Oldham	lost	8-14	10,000
Leigh	won	13-12	6,000
Wakefield T.	won	24-10	5,000
Cumberland (Maryport)	**won**	**5-2**	**6,000**
Barrow	won	44-8	6,500
Runcorn	won	23-7	2,000
Huddersfield	lost	7-21	17,000
England (Nottingham)	**lost**	**3-5**	**3,000**
Salford	won	6-3	4,000
York	won	16-8	1,500
BRITAIN (Edinburgh)	**drew**	**11-11**	**6,000**
Wales and West of England (Bristol)	**won**	**23-3**	**1,000**
Rochdale H.	won	18-6	4,500
Halifax	won	23-5	10,000
Warrington	won	34-6	8,500
BRITAIN (Birmingham)	**won**	**33-8**	**4,000**
Leeds	won	8-6	1,000
Hull K.R.	won	5-2	7,000
Barrow	won	22-5	1,500
Batley	lost	5-13	4,000
Northern RL (Wigan)	**won**	**20-12**	**2,000**

SUMMARY

Played 35   Won 28   Drew 2   Lost 5

For
Tries 149   Goals 86   Points 619

Against
Tries 63   Goals 46   Points 281

Won Test series 2-0 with one drawn

Attendance total: 216,000

● The Australians also played an exhibition match against Runcorn at Southport on December 25, winning 54-6, but this is not included in tour records.

TOUR PARTY

Managers: J. Quinlan and C. Ford
Captain: C. McKivat

	App	Tries	Gls	Pts
Tom Berecry	12	12	0	36
Albert Broomham	19	5	0	15
Peter Burge	4	1	0	3
Bill Cann	21	10	3	36
Tedda Courtney	25	4	0	12
Robert Craig	30	8	2	28
Steve Darmody	6	0	9	18
Viv Farnsworth	28	18	0	54
Bill Farnsworth	14	1	0	3
Arthur Francis (NZ)	24	9	49	125
Charles Fraser	20	0	12	24
Dan Frawley	11	13	3	45
Herbert Gilbert	29	20	2	64
George Gillett (NZ)	4	0	0	0
Howard Hallett	29	12	1	38
Arthur Halloway	12	0	0	0
Paddy McCue	22	6	0	18
Chris McKivat	31	10	0	30
Charlie McMurtrie	8	3	0	9
Joe Murray	7	1	0	3
Wiliam Neill	7	0	0	0
Bill Noble	21	1	0	3
Charlie Russell	24	9	5	37
Charlie Savory (NZ)	4	1	0	3
Bob Stuart	2	0	0	0
Con Sullivan	16	1	0	3
Robert Williams	19	3	0	9
Frank Woodward (NZ)	6	1	0	3

MEMO

First match on September 23, last match on January 31.
The tour party included the following New Zealanders: Francis, Gillett, Savory and Woodward.
A star of the party was Herbert Gilbert who later signed for Hull and became the first overseas player to captain an RL Challenge Cup-winning side, in 1914.
Often regarded as the best-ever touring party, they were the first Australian squad to remain unbeaten in a Test series in this country.
The Tests were again played on soccer grounds outside the Northern Union area, again without success.

1921-22 **TOUR**

MATCH RESULTS

Salford	won	48-3	9,000
Keighley	won	29-0	5,500
Hull K.R.	won	26-6	13,000
Bradford N.	won	53-3	3,000
BRITAIN (Leeds)	lost	5-6	32,000
Widnes	won	28-4	11,000
Broughton R.	won	18-6	17,000
England (Arsenal)	lost	4-5	12,000
Wigan	won	14-6	24,308
Leeds	won	11-5	14,000
Wakefield T.	won	29-3	6,000
Batley	won	33-7	6,000
Warrington	lost	5-8	16,000
York	lost	3-9	5,000
BRITAIN (Hull)	**won**	**16-2**	**21,504**
Bramley	won	92-7	1,500
Rochdale H.	won	16-2	12,000
Swinton	lost	0-9	6,000
Huddersfield	won	36-2	12,000
St. Helens	won	16-8	6,000
Oldham	won	16-5	15,000
Lancashire League (Everton)	**won**	**29-6**	**17,000**
Barrow	won	24-15	8,000
Yorkshire (Wakefield)	**won**	**24-8**	**6,000**
Wales (Pontypridd)	**won**	**21-16**	**13,000**
Lancashire (Warrington)	lost	6-8	6,000
Dewsbury	lost	6-13	6,000
Leigh	won	17-4	5,000
Hull	won	21-10	12,000
Widnes	won	17-8	12,000
Halifax	won	35-6	12,000
Hunslet	won	19-10	3,174
Cumberland (Workington)	**won**	**25-12**	**5,000**
BRITAIN (Salford)	lost	0-6	21,000
Oldham	lost	5-15	6,000
St. Helens Recs	won	16-5	5,000

SUMMARY

Played 36   Won 27   Lost 9

For
Tries 187   Goals 101   Points 763

Against
Tries 44   Goals 58   Points 248

Lost Test series 2-1

Attendance total: 384,986

TOUR PARTY

Managers: S. Ball and W. Cann
Captain: L. Cubitt

	App	Tries	Gls	Pts
Cecil Blinkhorn	29	39	0	117
Neville Broadfoot	4	2	0	6
Edwin Brown	4	1	0	3
Frank Burge	23	33	6	111
Harry Caples	24	7	0	21
George Carstairs	17	7	2	25
Jimmy Craig	24	10	14	58
Les Cubitt	4	1	0	3
Charles Fraser	23	2	1	8
Bert Gray	5	2	0	6
Harold Horder	25	35	11	127
Clarrie Ives	6	1	0	3
Albert Johnston	12	3	1	11
Bert Laing (NZ)	10	4	0	12
Reg Latta	22	7	0	21
Ted McGrath	16	1	2	7
Rex Norman	21	2	13	32
Sid Pearce	21	0	0	0
Herman Peters	4	2	0	6
Norman Potter	10	1	0	3
Clarrie Prentice	25	3	2	13
Bill Richards	15	4	0	12
Felix Ryan	24	6	0	18
Bill Schultz	24	1	0	3
Duncan Thompson	26	3	49	107
Dick Townsend	13	2	0	6
Dick Vest	26	7	0	21
Jack Watkins	11	1	0	3

MEMO

First match on September 17, last match on January 21.
Three players dominated the tryscoring on this tour. Cecil Blinkhorn, a winger, scored a tour record 39 tries and Frank Burge's 33 tries were the most by a forward on tour. Harold Horder, another winger, scored 35 tries.
Blinkhorn's total included a tour record seven against Bramley, who were beaten 92-7 – another tour record. Horder also got five as the tourists ran in 24 tries despite being penalised 18 times to Bramley's three. The half-time score was 43-5.
Sid "Sandy" Pearce, a hooker, who was in the first tour party of 1908, returned at 41 years of age, to play 21 matches including two Tests.

1929-30 TOUR

MATCH RESULTS

Rochdale H.	won	36-3	6,521
York	won	32-11	4,729
Batley	won	27-5	6,000
Widnes	won	37-13	6,400
Broughton R.	won	21-8	6,514
Lancashire (Warrington)	**won**	**29-14**	**24,000**
Wakefield T.	lost	3-14	9,786
Keighley	won	15-9	3,000
BRITAIN (Hull K.R.)	**won**	**31-8**	**20,000**
Castleford	won	53-2	4,000
Huddersfield	won	18-8	18,560
Leigh	won	19-16	8,000
Barrow	won	13-10	10,000
Leeds	lost	7-8	10,000
Hull	won	35-2	10,000
Oldham	won	18-10	18,000
BRITAIN (Leeds)	**lost**	**3-9**	**31,402**
Bradford N.	won	26-17	7,000
St. Helens	drew	18-18	9,500
Yorkshire (Wakefield)	**won**	**25-12**	**7,011**
Halifax	won	58-9	8,440
Swinton	lost	5-9	9,000
Northern League (Wigan)	**lost**	**5-18**	**9,987**
Cumberland (Workington)	**lost**	**5-8**	**3,500**
Glamorgan and Monmouthshire	**won**	**39-9**	**3,000**
(White City, Cardiff)			
St. Helens Recs	won	22-8	9,000
Northern League (Newcastle)	**won**	**32-22**	**9,690**
Warrington	lost	8-17	12,826
Hunslet	lost	3-18	12,000
Hull K.R.	won	10-5	12,000
Wigan	won	10-9	8,000
(Abandoned after 65 mins — waterlogged)			
BRITAIN (Swinton)	**drew**	**0-0**	**34,709**
Salford	won	21-5	8,000
BRITAIN (Rochdale)	**lost**	**0-3**	**16,743**
Wales (Wembley)	**won**	**26-10**	**16,000**

SUMMARY

Played 35   Won 24   Drew 2   Lost 9

For
Tries 164   Goals 109   Points 710

Against
Tries 67   Goals 73   Points 347

Lost Test series 2-1 with one drawn

Attendance total: 393,318

TOUR PARTY

Managers: J. Dargan and H. Sunderland
Captain: T. Gorman   Coach: A. Hennessy

	App	Tries	Gls	Pts
Vic Armbruster	19	6	0	18
George Bishop	15	4	0	12
Bill Brogan	20	2	0	6
Joe Busch	19	2	0	6
Dan Dempsey	10	0	0	0
Arthur Edwards	9	3	0	9
Cec Fifield	22	8	0	24
Harry Finch	10	16	18	84
Tom Gorman	22	2	0	6
Arthur Henderson	7	0	0	0
Jack Holmes	12	5	0	15
Arthur Justice	13	2	0	6
Harry Kadwell	8	2	5	16
Jack Kingston	26	18	0	54
Fred Laws	15	2	5	16
Frank McMillan	26	0	4	8
Peter "Mick" Madsen	17	1	0	3
Pat Maher	12	4	0	12
Wally Prigg	16	4	0	12
Alan Ridley	7	11	0	33
Eddie Root	15	3	0	9
Les Sellars	8	1	0	3
Bill Shankland	23	24	17	106
Bill Spencer	22	23	0	69
Herb Steinohrt	21	0	0	0
George Treweek	22	6	0	18
Jack Upton	19	10	4	38
Eric Weissel	20	5	56	127

MEMO

First match on September 7, last match on January 18.
This was the tour that featured a fourth Test match. The unique extra Test followed a 0-0 draw in the third match after Britain had lost the first and won the second.
Demands for a deciding Test match were answered with a Wednesday afternoon fixture at Rochdale on January 15. A late try by Stan Smith snatched Britain a 3-0 victory.
This was also the first tour in which Australia appointed an official coach to join the party, the position going to Arthur Hennessy.

1933-34 TOUR

MATCH RESULTS

St. Helens Recs	won	13-9	8,880
Leigh	won	16-7	4,600
Hull K.R.	won	20-0	7,831
Bramley	won	53-6	1,902
Oldham	won	38-6	15,281
Yorkshire (Leeds)	**won**	**13-0**	**10,309**
Barrow	won	24-5	12,221
Lancashire (Warrington)	**won**	**33-7**	**16,576**
Wigan	won	10-4	15,712
Castleford	won	39-6	4,250
Halifax	won	16-5	10,358
BRITAIN (Belle Vue, Man'r)	**lost**	**0-4**	**34,000**
Bradford N.	lost	5-7	3,328
Warrington	lost	12-15	16,431
Hunslet	won	22-18	6,227
Salford	lost	9-16	15,761
Widnes	won	31-0	6,691
Wakefield T.	won	17-6	5,596
Bradford N.	won	10-7	9,937
Northern League (York)	**lost**	**5-7**	**3,158**
Swinton	lost	4-10	13,341
BRITAIN (Leeds)	**lost**	**5-7**	**29,618**
Keighley	won	14-7	3,800
Huddersfield	won	13-5	7,522
London Highfield	won	20-5	10,541
Broughton R.	won	19-0	5,527
Leeds	won	15-7	5,295
St. Helens	won	20-11	5,735
Rochdale H.	won	26-4	3,603
Cumberland (Whitehaven)	**lost**	**16-17**	**5,800**
BRITAIN (Swinton)	**lost**	**16-19**	**10,990**
York	won	15-7	6,500
Hull	won	19-5	16,341
Wales (Wembley)	**won**	**51-19**	**10,000**
England (Paris)	**won**	**63-13**	**5,000**
Oldham	won	38-5	4,000
England (Gateshead)	**lost**	**14-19**	**15,576**

SUMMARY

Played 37   Won 27   Lost 10

For
Tries 162   Goals 134   Points 754

Against
Tries 47   Goals 77   Points 295

Lost Test series 3-0

Attendance total: 368,238

TOUR PARTY

Managers: H. Sunderland and W. Webb
Captain: F. McMillan

	App	Tries	Gls	Pts
Dave Brown	32	19	114	285
Frank Curran	12	0	0	0
Dan Dempsey	12	1	0	3
Henry Denny	8	0	0	0
Frank Doonar	11	2	0	6
Joe Doyle	21	7	0	21
Arthur Folwell	21	2	0	6
Fred Gardner	20	13	2	43
Jimmy Gibbs	19	10	0	30
Fred Gilbert	4	2	0	6
Melville Glasheen	2	1	0	3
Vic Hey	26	14	0	42
Fred Laws	15	1	5	13
Jack Little	4	0	0	0
Frank McMillan	21	1	3	9
Peter "Mick" Madsen	25	2	0	6
Les Mead	15	2	5	16
Fred Neumann	9	1	0	3
Frank O'Connor	16	7	0	21
Cliff Pearce	27	6	1	20
Sid "Joe" Pearce	24	12	4	44
Wally Prigg	32	16	0	48
Alan Ridley	27	25	0	75
Bill Smith	16	3	0	9
Ray Stehr	26	4	0	12
Viv Thicknesse	18	3	0	9
Jack Why	17	8	0	24

● Ray Morris was taken ill en route to England and died in hospital in Malta.

MEMO

First match on August 26, last match on January 13.

Dave Brown scored 114 goals and 285 points on this tour, two records which still stand. The centre's points total, which included 19 tries, came from 32 matches.

The tourists helped launch the game in France by playing England in Paris on 31 December, winning 63-13.

Vic Hey was one of the tour's biggest successes, later returning to England and becoming a great favourite at Leeds.

An extra fixture to the official programme of matches was a seven-a-side match against England at Roundhay Park, Leeds.

1937 TOUR

MATCH RESULTS

Leigh	won	11-9	5,000
York	won	15-6	5,000
Newcastle	won	37-0	4,000
Lancashire (Warrington)	**lost**	**5-7**	**16,250**
Halifax	lost	2-12	14,500
Yorkshire (Bradford)	**won**	**8-4**	**7,570**
Wakefield T.	won	17-10	8,696
Rochdale H.	won	6-0	2,400
BRITAIN (Leeds)	**lost**	**4-5**	**31,949**
Widnes	drew	13-13	4,201
Hull	won	22-12	15,000
Bradford N.	won	19-6	5,748
Salford	lost	8-11	12,000
Wigan	won	25-23	9,800
Oldham	won	10-6	15,000
BRITAIN (Swinton)	**lost**	**3-13**	**31,724**
Liverpool S.	won	28-9	1,500
Huddersfield	lost	7-17	9,383
Swinton	lost	3-5	4,113
Warrington	lost	6-8	12,637
Leeds	lost	8-21	5,000
St. Helens XIII	won	15-7	2,000
Barrow	lost	8-12	8,153
BRITAIN (Huddersfield)	**won**	**13-3**	**9,093**
Broughton R.	lost	0-13	3,000

SUMMARY

Played 25   Won 13   Drew 1   Lost 11

For
Tries 67   Goals 46   Points 293

Against
Tries 40   Goals 56   Points 232

Lost Test series 2-1

Attendance total: 243,717

TOUR PARTY

Managers: H. Sunderland and R. Savage
Captain: W. Prigg

	App	Tries	Gls	Pts
Jack Beaton	18	3	28	65
Edward Collins	2	1	0	3
Frank Curran	11	4	0	12
Les Dawson	17	6	0	18
Percy Fairall	8	0	0	0
Jimmy Gibbs	12	0	0	0
Fred Gilbert	13	2	4	14
Frank Griffiths	6	0	0	0
Charlie Hazelton	8	3	0	9
Les Heidke	14	1	0	3
Eric Lewis	12	2	0	6
Ross McKinnon	19	3	6	21
Doug McLean	5	1	0	3
Gordon McLennan	11	1	0	3
Herb Narvo	15	5	0	15
Fred Nolan	5	0	0	0
Ernie Norman	16	3	0	9
Andy Norval	10	6	0	18
Harry Pierce	15	3	0	9
Wally Prigg	18	8	0	24
Jack Reardon	19	7	0	21
Harry Robison	9	2	0	6
Ray Stehr	12	0	0	0
Roy Thompson	5	1	2	7
Laurie Ward	18	1	0	3
Gordon Whittle	7	0	0	0
Bert Williams	11	4	0	12
Percy Williams	9	0	6	12

● Sid "Joe" Pearce was injured in New Zealand and although he continued the trip did not play in England. Herb Narvo replaced him.

MEMO
First match on September 18, last match on December 25.

This was Harry Sunderland's third trip as manager and Wally Prigg completed his hat-trick as a player, this time captaining the squad.

For the first time Australia made a brief tour of France, including two Tests which they won.

A reduced number of matches and a less adventurous style resulted in a drop in tryscoring with no player scoring more than 10 on the tour.

1948 TOUR

MATCH RESULTS

Huddersfield	lost	3-22	26,017
Belle Vue Rangers	won	14-9	7,535
Hull	won	13-3	16,616
Wakefield T.	won	26-19	20,040
Leigh	won	24-12	12,968
Salford	won	13-2	16,627
Castleford	won	10-8	14,004
BRITAIN (Leeds)	**lost**	**21-23**	**36,529**
Cumberland (Whitehaven)	**lost**	**4-5**	**8,818**
St. Helens	lost	8-10	20,175
Dewsbury	won	14-4	13,614
Hull K.R.	lost	12-17	7,614
Wigan	lost	11-16	28,554
Barrow	won	11-5	13,143
Leeds	won	15-2	13,542
Warrington	lost	7-16	26,879
BRITAIN (Swinton)	**lost**	**7-16**	**36,354**
Bradford N.	won	21-7	13,287
Workington T.	lost	7-10	13,253
Swinton	won	21-0	5,849
Wales (Swansea)	**won**	**12-5**	**9,161**
Yorkshire (Leeds)·	**lost**	**2-5**	**5,310**
Halifax	won	10-8	6,520
Oldham	won	27-7	14,798
Lancashire (Wigan)	**lost**	**8-13**	**11,788**
Widnes	won	18-8	10,761
BRITAIN (Bradford)	**lost**	**9-23**	**42,000**

SUMMARY

Played 27   Won 15   Lost 12

For
Tries 76   Goals 60   Points 348

Against
Tries 57   Goals 52   Points 275

Lost Test series 3-0

Attendance total: 451,756

First Kangaroo tour for full back Clive Churchill.

TOUR PARTY

Managers: W. Buckley and E. Simmonds
Captain: C. Maxwell

	App	Tries	Gls	Pts
Fred de Belin	10	1	0	3
Henry Benton	6	0	0	0
Eddie Brosnan	12	0	0	0
Vic Bulgin	11	0	1	2
Clive Churchill	16	0	1	2
Les Cowie	15	5	0	15
Bobby Dimond	9	2	0	6
Keith Froome	12	2	21	48
Alf Gibbs	13	1	0	3
Johnny Graves	15	6	24	66
Duncan Hall	15	5	0	15
Neville Hand	11	1	0	3
Johnny Hawke	17	7	0	21
Jack Holland	17	3	0	9
Bruce Hopkins	9	0	8	16
Jack Horrigan	16	13	5	49
Frank Johnson	3	0	0	0
Bobby Lulham	13	8	0	24
Pat McMahon	18	10	0	30
Doug McRitchie	8	1	0	3
Col Maxwell	9	2	0	6
Noel Mulligan	15	1	0	3
Wally O'Connell	15	1	0	3
Len Pegg	10	1	0	3
Jack Rayner	19	2	0	6
Kevin Schubert	17	1	0	3
Bill Thompson	11	1	0	3
Bill Tyquin	9	2	0	6

MEMO
First match on September 18, last match on January 29.

The final match was to have been the third Test at Bradford on December 18 but fog caused a postponement and the party left to tour France.

They lost only one of 10 matches in France and returned for the third Test against Britain on January 29. Although Britain had already retained the Ashes there was a then record crowd for a Test against Australia in this country of 42,000.

Britain won the Test series 3-0, but several of Australia's best players were playing for English clubs. Three different captains were used in the Tests, Wally O'Connell, Col Maxwell and Bill Tyquin.

A surprise omission from the party was Len Smith who had led Australia in the previous Test series against New Zealand. He was expected to be an automatic choice as centre and captain.

This was the first tour by Clive Churchill who was to become one of Australia's greatest full backs. He was on tour again as a player in 1952 and 1956, and also coached the 1959 squad.

1952 TOUR

MATCH RESULTS

Keighley	won	54-4	7,431
Hull	won	28-0	15,364
Barrow	won	26-2	16,045
Whitehaven	won	15-5	9,253
Oldham	drew	7-7	19,370
Halifax	won	39-7	18,773
Wigan	won	23-13	16,223
St. Helens	lost	8-26	17,205
Featherstone R.	won	50-15	3,700
BRITAIN (Leeds)	**lost**	**6-19**	**34,505**
Bradford N.	won	20-6	29,287
Warrington	won	34-10	21,478
Leigh	won	34-5	8,409
Swinton	won	31-8	10,269
Hunslet	won	49-2	3,273
Workington T.	won	27-15	11,341
Doncaster	won	41-13	2,452
Huddersfield	won	27-9	25,494
BRITAIN (Swinton)	**lost**	**5-21**	**32,421**
Wakefield T.	won	58-8	7,239
Hull K.R.	won	31-6	5,817
Lancashire (Warrington)	**won**	**36-11**	**5,863**
Leeds	won	45-4	20,335
Yorkshire (Huddersfield)	**won**	**55-11**	**3,737**
Dewsbury	won	22-7	2,485
Widnes	won	18-7	7,411
BRITAIN (Bradford)	**won**	**27-7**	**30,509**

SUMMARY

Played 27   Won 23   Drew 1   Lost 3

For
Tries 176   Goals 144   Points 816

Against
Tries 42   Goals 61   Points 248

Lost Test series 2-1

Attendance total: 385,689

Twelve appearances by Ken Kearney.

TOUR PARTY

Managers: D. McLean and N. Robinson
Captain: C. Churchill

	App	Tries	Gls	Pts
Ferris Ashton	14	7	0	21
Roy Bull	9	1	0	3
Brian Carlson	14	19	2	61
Clive Churchill	17	2	17	40
Arthur Collinson	17	9	0	27
Harold Crocker	11	2	0	6
Brian Davies	16	7	0	21
Col Donohoe	11	4	0	12
Rees Duncan	12	8	0	24
Denis Flannery	11	15	0	45
Col Geelan	15	8	0	24
Charlie Gill	14	1	0	3
Duncan Hall	17	2	0	6
Greg Hawick	9	4	0	12
Noel Hazzard	16	5	0	15
Keith Holman	10	8	7	38
Ken Kearney	12	0	0	0
Ken McCaffery	8	8	0	24
Des McGovern	6	10	0	30
Albert Paul	13	8	4	32
Noel Pidding	15	17	79	209
Jack Rooney	12	1	0	3
Tommy Ryan	13	16	0	48
Kevin Schubert	14	0	0	0
Frank Stanmore	15	3	0	9
Tom Tyrrell	13	7	0	21
Harry Wells	7	2	0	6
Ron Willey	10	2	35	76

MEMO
First match on September 6, last match on December 13.
This was the most free-scoring tour squad of all time. They opened with a 54-4 defeat of Keighley and went on to score a record 816 points from 27 matches.
They also scored half centuries against Featherstone Rovers, Wakefield Trinity and Yorkshire.
The only club side to beat them was St. Helens, Oldham forcing a draw.
After losing the first two Tests, Australia finished with a third Test victory in a brawling match which gained notoriety as "The Battle of Odsal".
For the first time an Australian tour match was televised, when the BBC covered the opening match at Keighley. The whole of the first Test match was also televised.
Australia used 23 players in the Test matches with only Clive Churchill, Brian Davies, Noel Hazzard and Duncan Hall playing in all three.
Captained by Willie Horne, Britain used 17 players in the Tests with nine playing in all three.

1956 TOUR

MATCH RESULTS

Liverpool C.	won	40-12	4,712
Leeds	lost	13-18	24,459
Hull-Hull K.R.	won	37-14	17,172
Barrow	won	25-11	9,988
Whitehaven	lost	11-14	10,840
Bradford N.	won	23-11	2,743
Warrington	lost	17-21	15,613
League XIII (Leigh)	**won**	**19-15**	**7,811**
York	won	20-18	6,842
Oldham	lost	2-21	8,458
Huddersfield	won	20-10	12,127
BRITAIN (Wigan)	**lost**	**10-21**	**22,473**
Hunslet	won	27-11	4,451
St. Helens	lost	2-44	15,579
BRITAIN (Bradford)	**won**	**22-9**	**23,634**
Halifax	lost	3-6	2,254
Wigan	won	32-4	15,854
Wakefield T.	lost	12-17	3,381
BRITAIN (Swinton)	**lost**	**0-19**	**17,542**

SUMMARY

Played 19   Won 10   Lost 9

For
Tries 69   Goals 64   Points 335

Against
Tries 58   Goals 61   Points 296

Lost Test series 2-1

Attendance total: 225,933

TOUR PARTY

Managers: C. Fahy and C. Connell
Captain: K. Kearney

	App	Tries	Gls	Pts
Don Adams	8	6	0	18
Bob Banks	13	3	0	9
Roy Bull	14	2	0	6
Clive Churchill	9	0	11	22
Gordon Clifford	9	1	34	71
Cyril Connell	9	6	1	20
Brian Davies	10	5	1	17
Ian Doyle	10	2	0	6
Denis Flannery	11	8	0	24
Don Furner	10	0	3	6
Ernie Hammerton	8	0	0	0
Keith Holman	10	5	2	19
Ian Johnston	6	3	0	9
Ken Kearney	11	0	0	0
Des McGovern	8	5	0	15
Bill Marsh	12	3	0	9
Ian Moir	10	7	0	21
Kevin O'Brien	7	2	0	6
Bryan Orrock	3	0	0	0
Kel O'Shea	11	2	0	6
Tom Payne	8	0	0	0
Dick Poole	12	6	0	18
Norm Provan	9	0	0	0
Bernie Purcell	6	0	12	24
Tom Tyquin	10	2	0	6
Alex Watson	13	1	0	3

MEMO

First match on October 10, last match on December 15.

A disappointing tour with no player totalling more than 10 tries during a programme reduced to fewer than 20 matches for the first time.

They were badly hit by a series of injuries to Norm Provan, one of their greatest-ever forwards, which caused him to miss all three Test matches.

Alan Prescott led Britain and was one of nine players to appear in all three Tests.

Clive Churchill, regarded as one of the legendary figures of Australian rugby, ended an illustrious international career against Britain after the first Test.

Ken Kearney returned as captain of the tour squad after having played for Leeds.

Norm Provan, ruled out of the three Tests through injury.

1959 TOUR

MATCH RESULTS

Leeds	won	44-20	14,629
Rochdale H.	won	27-14	10,155
Warrington	won	30-24	17,112
Lancashire (St. Helens)	**lost**	**22-30**	**15,743**
Salford	won	22-20	11,008
Yorkshire (York)	**lost**	**15-47**	**7,338**
Widnes	won	45-15	9,381
Oldham	won	25-14	17,630
Leigh	lost	17-18	11,932
St. Helens	won	15-2	29,156
BRITAIN (Swinton)	**won**	**22-14**	**35,224**
Whitehaven-Workington T.	won	13-8	7,463
Barrow	lost	9-12	8,488
Hull-Hull K.R.	won	29-9	15,944
Bradford N.	won	29-8	4,126
Halifax	won	17-5	8,274
Featherstone R.	lost	15-23	7,671
Wigan	lost	9-16	24,466
BRITAIN (Leeds)	**lost**	**10-11**	**30,184**
Swinton	won	25-24	5,021
Wakefield T.	lost	10-20	17,615
Huddersfield	won	21-7	2,349
Hunslet	won	12-11	8,061
BRITAIN (Wigan)	**lost**	**12-18**	**26,089**

SUMMARY

Played 24   Won 15   Lost 9

For
Tries 93   Goals 108   Points 495

Against
Tries 68   Goals 93   Points 390

Lost Test series 2-1

Attendance total: 345,059

TOUR PARTY

Managers: J. Argent and E. Keefer
Captain: K. Barnes   Coach: C. Churchill

	App	Tries	Gls	Pts
Keith Barnes	12	0	52	104
Dud Beattie	15	0	0	0
Ron Boden	11	4	0	12
Tony Brown	6	2	0	6
Bob Bugden	5	4	0	12
Peter Burke	8	4	0	12
Brian Carlson	15	10	39	108
Darrell Chapman	12	1	0	3
Brian Clay	14	2	0	6
Bill Delamere	11	2	0	6
Reg Gasnier	12	14	0	42
Brian Hambly	12	5	0	15
Ken Irvine	13	7	0	21
Noel Kelly	9	2	0	6
Eddie Lumsden	16	8	0	24
Reg Mossop	19	0	0	0
Barry Muir	13	1	0	3
Gary Parcell	12	1	0	3
Don Parish	9	3	16	41
Jim Paterson	12	2	0	6
Johnny Raper	8	7	0	21
Elton Rasmussen	13	3	1	11
John Riley	11	2	0	6
Ian Walsh	15	1	0	3
Harry Wells	16	6	0	18
Billy Wilson	13	2	0	6

MEMO

First match September 12, last match December 12.

Australia again flattered to deceive. After winning the first Test they went down in the other two, but only a late try and goal robbed them of the Ashes in the second Test.

Reg Gasnier made a sensational first tour and went on to become probably Australia's greatest centre of all time.

Gasnier scored three tries on his Test match debut and was a prominent figure in the other two.

Australia used only 15 players for the three Test matches, led each time by Keith Barnes.

The second Test was Neil Fox's first against Australia. In the third Test the big centre scored 15 of Britain's 18 points with six goals and a try.

Keith Barnes, scorer of 52 goals in 12 games.

1963 TOUR

MATCH RESULTS

Warrington	won	28-20	20,090
Huddersfield	won	6-5	13,398
Yorkshire (Hull K.R.)	**lost**	**5-11**	**10,324**
Leeds	won	13-10	16,641
Lancashire (Wigan)	**lost**	**11-13**	**15,068**
St. Helens	won	8-2	21,284
Featherstone R.	lost	17-23	7,898
Oldham	won	12-4	11,338
Leigh	won	33-7	9,625
Hull-Hull K.R. XIII	won	23-10	10,481
BRITAIN (Wembley)	**won**	**28-2**	**13,946**
Rochdale H.	won	3-0	8,637
Hunslet	won	17-13	4,400
Wakefield T.	won	29-14	15,821
Cumberland (Workington)	**won**	**21-0**	**8,229**
Barrow	won	18-5	10,130
BRITAIN (Swinton)	**won**	**50-12**	**30,833**
Castleford	lost	12-13	7,887
Wigan	won	18-10	11,746
Widnes	won	20-9	6,509
Swinton	drew	2-2	11,947
BRITAIN (Leeds)	**lost**	**5-16**	**20,497**

SUMMARY

Played 22   Won 16   Drew 1   Lost 5

For
Tries 75   Goals 77   Points 379

Against
Tries 31   Goals 54   Points 201

Won Test series 2-1

Attendance total: 286,729

TOUR PARTY

Managers: J. Lynch and A. Sparkes
Captain: A. Summons

	App	Tries	Gls	Pts
John Cleary	6+1	0	0	0
Mike Cleary	13	6	0	18
Ken Day	9	0	0	0
Peter Dimond	15	6	0	18
Peter Gallagher	12	0	0	0
Reg Gasnier	10	11	0	33
John Gleeson	5	0	0	0
Brian Hambly	13	1	0	3
Earl Harrison	11+1	3	0	9
Ken Irvine	17	17	2	55
Les Johns	10	2	24	54
Noel Kelly	14	1	0	3
Graeme Langlands	15	11	51	135
Jimmy Lisle	8	0	0	0
Barry Muir	13	1	0	3
Paul Quinn	15	1	0	3
Johnny Raper	13	2	0	6
Barry Rushworth	10+1	5	0	15
Kevin Ryan	4	0	0	0
Kevin Smyth	8	1	0	3
Frank Stanton	9+1	1	0	3
Arthur Summons	7	0	0	0
Ken Thornett	11	1	0	3
Dick Thornett	15	4	0	12
Ian Walsh	16	1	0	3
Graham Wilson	7	0	0	0

MEMO
  First match September 14, last match November 30.
  One of the most successful of all touring teams to Britain, the Australians returned home with the Ashes for the first time since 1911-12.
  They clinched the series in the second Test with a record victory over Britain of 50-12. Britain were reduced to 11 men during the match because of injuries, but Australia had already displayed their superiority.
  In the first Test at Wembley Australia won 28-2 with Reg Gasnier scoring another hat-trick of tries, the match watched by the Duke of Edinburgh.
  Britain made several changes for the third Test which they won 16-5. This was a brawling affair at Headingley with referee Eric Clay sending off Australia's Brian Hambly and Barry Muir, plus Britain's Cliff Watson.
  Although Arthur Summons was captain and coach of the squad, he did not play against Britain, Ian Walsh leading Australia in all three Tests.
  The only club teams to beat Australia were Castleford and Featherstone Rovers but the Kangaroos also lost to Lancashire and Yorkshire.

Frank Stanton, one try in 10 appearances.

1967 TOUR

MATCH RESULTS

Warrington	won	16-7	11,642
Yorkshire (Wakefield)	**lost**	**14-15**	**19,370**
Hull K.R.	lost	15-27	11,252
Lancashire (Salford)	**won**	**14-2**	**9,369**
Wigan	lost	6-12	22,770
Rochdale H.	won	25-2	2,676
BRITAIN (Leeds)	**lost**	**11-16**	**22,293**
St. Helens	lost	4-8	17,275
Wakefield T.	won	33-7	10,056
BRITAIN (W'City, London)	**won**	**17-11**	**17,445**
Castleford	lost	3-22	6,137
Oldham	won	18-8	3,174
Widnes	won	33-11	9,828
Barrow	drew	10-10	8,418
Cumberland (Workington)	**lost**	**15-17**	**7,545**
Swinton	won	12-9	5,640
Leeds	won	7-4	5,522
Halifax	won	22-2	5,285
Bradford N.	won	7-3	14,173
BRITAIN (Swinton)	**won**	**11-3**	**13,615**

SUMMARY

Played 20   Won 12   Drew 1   Lost 7

For
Tries 57   Goals 61   Points 293

Against
Tries 30   Goals 53   Points 196

Won Test series 2-1

Attendance total: 223,485

Noel Kelly, 12 appearances on a third Kangaroo tour.

TOUR PARTY

Managers: J. Drewes and H. Schmidt
Captain: R. Gasnier

	App	Tries	Gls	Pts
Tony Branson	11+1	3	0	9
Ron Coote	13	5	0	15
Noel Gallagher	10	0	0	0
Peter Gallagher	11+1	1	0	3
Reg Gasnier	5	1	0	3
John Gleeson	11	2	1	8
Kevin Goldspink	9	0	0	0
Johnny Greaves	10	2	0	6
Les Hanigan	8	2	0	6
Ken Irvine	13	8	5	34
Les Johns	9+1	1	5	13
Kevin Junee	6	2	1	8
Noel Kelly	12	0	0	0
Johnny King	13	8	0	24
Graeme Langlands	14	3	36	81
Ron Lynch	12	2	0	6
John McDonald	11	4	10	32
Dennis Manteit	10+1	2	0	6
Brian Moore	7	4	0	12
Johnny Raper	9	0	0	0
Elton Rasmussen	13	0	0	0
Ron Saddler	8	0	0	0
John Sattler	9+1	0	0	0
Billy Smith	11	3	3	15
Allan Thomson	8+1	2	0	6
Elwyn Walters	5	2	0	6

MEMO

First match September 30, last match December 9.

Australia retained the Ashes with victory in the third Test at a frostbound Swinton. Heavy snow fell during the match in which Arthur Keegan's tackling at full back kept Australia's winning margin down to 11-3.

Britain had won the first Test at Headingley, but lost the second at White City, London.

Reg Gasnier's great international career ended in the first Test when he received a broken leg, a match which was Roger Millward's first Test against Australia.

In Gasnier's absence, Peter Gallagher captained Australia in the second Test and Johnny Raper took over for the third.

Australia recovered after losing five of their first eight matches although they later crashed 22-3 at Castleford.

1973 TOUR

MATCH RESULTS

Salford	won	15-12	11,064
Wakefield T.	won	13-9	5,863
Dewsbury	won	17-3	5,685
Castleford	won	*18-10	2,419
Widnes	won	25-10	5,185
Oldham	won	44-10	2,895
Cumbria (Whitehaven)	**won**	**28-2**	**3,666**
Bradford N.	won	50-14	5,667
BRITAIN (Wembley)	**lost**	**12-21**	**9,874**
Hull K.R.	won	25-9	5,150
Huddersfield	won	32-2	1,333
Leigh	won	31-4	2,607
St. Helens	lost	7-11	10,013
Featherstone R.	won	18-13	5,659
BRITAIN (Leeds)	**won**	**14-6**	**16,674**
BRITAIN (Warrington)	**won**	**15-5**	**10,019**

*Australia's score includes penalty under 7-point try rule although this was not within International Rules.

SUMMARY

Played 16   Won 14   Lost 2

For
Tries 81   Goals 60   Drop goals 1   Points 364

Against
Tries 18   Goals 42   Drop goals 3   Points 141

Won Test series 2-1

Attendance total: 103,773

TOUR PARTY

Managers: C. Gibson and A. Bishop
Captain: G. Langlands

	App	Tries	Gls	Pts
Arthur Beetson	13	3	0	9
Ray Branighan	10+1	6	0	18
Mick Cronin	8+1	6	23	64
Graham Eadie	10	4	10	32
Bobby Fulton	10+1	16	1(1)	49
Ted Goodwin	6+1	5	0	15
Bill Hamilton	5+2	1	0	3
John Lang	6	1	0	3
Graeme Langlands	8	4	27	66
Bob McCarthy	8	4	0	12
Ken Maddison	11+1	5	0	15
John O'Neill	3+1	0	0	0
Bob O'Reilly	11+1	0	0	0
Warren Orr	5+1	2	0	6
Tim Pickup	8+1	2	0	6
Greg Pierce	6	0	0	0
Terry Randall	5	1	0	3
Tom Raudonikis	9	3	0	9
Steve Rogers	5+1	2	0	6
Paul Sait	10+1	2	0	6
Geoff Starling	10+1	7	0	21
Gary Stevens	7	1	0	3
David Waite	9+1	4	0	12
Elwyn Walters	11+1	2	0	6
Dennis Ward	7	0	0	0
Lionel Williamson	7+1	0	0	0

( ) Drop goal included in total

MEMO
First match September 30, last match December 1.
After losing the series Down Under in 1970, Australia returned to power despite being convincingly beaten in the first Test at Wembley.
They won the second Test at Headingley and regained the Ashes with a 15-5 victory at Warrington on a frostbound pitch. Australia scored five tries to one to win much more easily than the score suggests.
St. Helens were the only club side to beat the tourists, with Bradford Northern suffering the biggest defeat by 50-14.
A serious hand injury ruled out tour captain Graeme Langlands for the second and third Tests, giving the chance for Graham Eadie to emerge as a new Test star at full back.
Other stars of the tour were Bobby Fulton and Arthur Beetson, while centres Steve Rogers and Mick Cronin gained valuable experience as stars of the future.

Scrum half Tom Raudonikis, three tries in nine games.

1978 TOUR

MATCH RESULTS

Blackpool B.	won	39-1	2,700
Cumbria (Barrow)	**won**	**47-4**	**5,964**
Britain Under-24 (Hull K.R.)	**won**	**30-8**	**6,418**
Bradford N.	won	21-11	15,755
Warrington	lost	12-15	10,143
Wales (Swansea)	**won**	**8-3**	**4,250**
Leeds	won	25-19	9,781
BRITAIN (Wigan)	**won**	**15-9**	**17,644**
Widnes	lost	10-11	12,202
Hull	won	34-2	10,723
Salford	won	14-2	6,155
BRITAIN (Bradford)	**lost**	**14-18**	**26,447**
Wigan	won	28-2	10,645
St. Helens	won	26-4	16,352
York	won	29-2	5,155
BRITAIN (Leeds)	**won**	**23-6**	**29,627**

SUMMARY

Played 16   Won 13   Lost 3

For
Tries 79   Goals 68   Drop goals 2   Points 375

Against
Tries 12   Goals 39   Drop goals 3   Points 117

Won Test series 2-1

Attendance total: 189,961

Wingman Ian Schubert, three tries in eight matches.

TOUR PARTY

Managers: P. Moore and J. Caldwell
Captain: R. Fulton   Coach: F. Stanton

	App	Tries	Gls	Pts
Chris Anderson	9	3	0	9
Kerry Boustead	10	2	0	6
Les Boyd	7+1	3	0	9
Larry Corowa	5	4	0	12
Mick Cronin	10+1	2	46	98
Graham Eadie	9+1	4	0	12
Bobby Fulton	12	9	2(2)	29
Geoff Gerard	8+2	3	0	9
John Gibbs	2	1	0	3
Ron Hilditch	5	1	0	3
Steve Kneen	5	2	0	6
Max Krilich	6	0	0	0
Allan McMahon	8	6	1	20
Steve Martin	4+3	1	0	3
Rod Morris	7+2	2	0	6
Greg Oliphant	3	0	0	0
Graeme Olling	7	2	0	6
George Peponis	6	6	0	18
Greg Pierce	4	0	0	0
Ray Price	9+1	2	0	6
Tom Raudonikis	11	4	0	12
Rod Reddy	10	3	0	9
Steve Rogers	12	8	21	66
Ian Schubert	8	3	0	9
Alan Thompson	9+4	4	0	12
Ian Thomson	8+2	0	0	0
Bruce Walker	5	2	0	6
Craig Young	9+2	2	0	6

() Drop goal included in total

MEMO
First match September 30, last match November 18.

Australia's dominance continued despite going down to Britain's "Dad's Army" pack in the second Test at Odsal.

The Kangaroos had a narrow first Test win but retained the Ashes with a runaway success in the third Test at Headingley.

The only club teams to beat the tourists were Warrington and Widnes.

Defence was the tourists' strong point. They did not concede a try until their fourth match and finished with only 12 against them in 16 matches.

The tourists did much to revive interest in international rugby with attendances showing a big increase over the previous tour.

It was a magnificent farewell to touring for Australia's captain Bobby Fulton, but a sad end to the wonderful Test career of Britain's captain Roger Millward.

309

1982 TOUR

MATCH RESULTS

Hull K.R.	won	30-10	10,742
Wigan	won	13-9	12,158
Barrow	won	29-2	6,282
St. Helens	won	32-0	8,190
Leeds	won	31-4	11,570
Wales (Cardiff)	**won**	**37-7**	**5,617**
BRITAIN (Hull C. FC)	**won**	**40-4**	**26,771**
Leigh	won	44-4	7,680
Bradford N.	won	13-6	10,506
Cumbria (Carlisle)	**won**	**41-2**	**5,748**
Fulham	won	22-5	10,432
Hull	won	13-7	16,049
BRITAIN (Wigan)	**won**	**27-6**	**23,216**
Widnes	won	19-6	9,790
BRITAIN (Leeds)	**won**	**32-8**	**17,318**

SUMMARY

Played 15   Won 15   Lost 0

For
Tries 97   Goals 66   Points 423

Against
Tries 7   Goals 29   Drop goals 1   Points 80

Won Test series 3-0

Attendance total: 182,069

TOUR PARTY

Managers: F. Farrington and T. Drysdale
Captain: M. Krilich   Coach: F. Stanton

	App	Tries	Gls	Pts
Chris Anderson	7	3	0	9
Kerry Boustead	8+1	8	0	24
Les Boyd	10	3	0	9
Greg Brentnall	9	1	0	3
Ray Brown	5+4	0	0	0
Greg Conescu	2+2	1	0	3
Steve Ella	7+1	9	3	33
Eric Grothe	7	7	0	21
Rohan Hancock	4	0	0	0
Brett Kenny	8	2	0	6
Max Krilich	8	1	0	3
Wally Lewis	7+5	3	9	27
Paul McCabe	8	7	0	21
Don McKinnon	5	3	1	11
Mal Meninga	10	6	50	118
Gene Miles	6	1	0	3
Rod Morris	6+2	0	0	0
Steve Mortimer	5	2	0	6
John Muggleton	6+2	4	0	12
Mark Murray	4+1	3	0	9
Wayne Pearce	9	4	0	12
Ray Price	6+2	2	0	6
Rod Reddy	8	1	0	3
John Ribot	8	10	0	30
Steve Rogers	9+3	8	3	30
Ian Schubert	7	2	0	6
Peter Sterling	8	5	0	15
Craig Young	8	1	0	3

MEMO
First match October 10, last match November 28.

The young 28-man squad — only two players were over 30 — rewrote the record books by displaying a showcase of skill, strength and speed that was to thrill millions worldwide and alarm bells ringing throughout the British game.

The 1982 Kangaroos became the first touring party from any country to win all their matches in Britain and the first tourists to win all three Tests in Britain, their total of 99 points being the most scored in an Anglo-Aussie Test series in either country.

The tourists amassed 97 tries and conceded only seven in their 15-match programme in which they piled up 27 points or more on 10 occasions.

Tour stars such as triple record breaker Mal Meninga, inspiring captain Max Krilich, mercurial Peter Sterling, artistic Brett Kenny and rampaging Wayne Pearce captivated the British public, the average tour gate of 12,138 being the best for 20 years.

Scrum half Peter Sterling, five tries in eight games.

1986 TOUR

MATCH RESULTS

Wigan	won	26-18	30,622
Hull K.R.	won	46-10	6,868
Leeds	won	40-0	11,389
Cumbria (Barrow)	**won**	**48-12**	**4,233**
BRITAIN (Man U. FC)	**won**	**38-16**	**50,583**
Halifax	won	36-2	7,193
St. Helens	won	32-8	15,381
Oldham	won	22-16	5,678
BRITAIN (Elland Rd, Leeds)	**won**	**34-4**	**30,808**
Widnes	won	20-4	10,268
Hull	won	48-0	8,213
Bradford N.	won	38-0	10,663
BRITAIN (Wigan)	**won**	**24-15**	**20,169**

SUMMARY

Played 13   Won 13   Lost 0

For
Tries 85   Goals 56   Points 452

Against
Tries 14   Goals 24   Drop goals 1   Points 105

Won Test series 3-0

Attendance total: 212,068

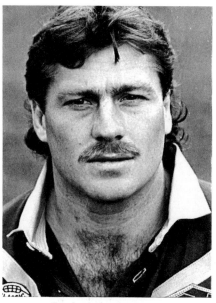

Terry Lamb, the only ever-present.

TOUR PARTY

Managers: J. Fleming and G. Treichel
Captain: W. Lewis   Coach: D. Furner

	App	Tries	Gls	Pts
Greg Alexander	5+1	8	5	42
Gary Belcher	6	2	0	8
Martin Bella	6	1	0	4
Noel Cleal	7	3	0	12
Phil Daley	3+1	0	0	0
Les Davidson	5+4	0	0	0
Greg Dowling	6+1	1	0	4
Paul Dunn	6+1	0	0	0
Ben Elias	6	3	0	12
Steve Folkes	3	0	0	0
Des Hasler	2+1	2	0	8
Garry Jack	7	5	0	20
Brett Kenny	8+1	4	0	16
Les Kiss	4	1	0	4
Terry Lamb	6+7	15	13	86
Paul Langmack	6	1	0	4
Wally Lewis	7	6	0	24
Bob Lindner	7	3	0	12
Mal Meninga	8+3	5	7	34
Gene Miles	8	6	0	24
Chris Mortimer	6	3	0	12
Bryan Niebling	7	1	0	4
Michael O'Connor	8+1	7	31	90
Steve Roach	4	0	0	0
Dale Shearer	9	6	0	24
Royce Simmons	7	0	0	0
Paul Sironen	5+2	0	0	0
Peter Sterling	7	2	0	8

MEMO

First match October 12, last match November 22.

The Kangaroos arrived with the added pressure of being compared with the 1982 *Invincibles* who won all their matches. They responded by equalling that feat and earning the tag of *Invincibles II*.

Their 13-match tour was the shortest-ever but they again made a lasting impression with the average attendance of 16,313, second only to the 16,732 of 1948.

It opened with an all-time record crowd for a club tour game of 30,622 at Wigan and the first Test attracted the then biggest-ever attendance for an international match in this country of 50,583 at Old Trafford, Manchester.

Captain Wally Lewis was elected the outstanding player, while Terry Lamb emerged as the busiest after playing in all 13 matches including seven as substitute.

The Kangaroos' 100 per cent success record meant they had not lost in Britain since the second Test of 1978, giving them a winning run of 32 matches.

They also went on to win all seven matches in France for the second successive trip.

1990 TOUR

MATCH RESULTS

St. Helens	won	34-4	15,219
Wakefield T.	won	36-18	7,724
Wigan	won	34-6	24,814
Cumbria (Workington)	**won**	**42-10**	**6,750**
Leeds	won	22-10	16,037
BRITAIN (Wembley)	**lost**	**12-19**	**54,569**
Warrington	won	26-6	10,200
Castleford	won	28-8	9,033
Halifax	won	36-18	8,730
BRITAIN (Man U. FC)	**won**	**14-10**	**46,615**
Hull	won	34-4	13,081
Widnes	won	15-8	14,666
BRITAIN (Elland Rd, Leeds)	**won**	**14-0**	**32,500**

SUMMARY

Played 13   Won 12   Lost 1

For
Tries 68   Goals 37   Drop goals 1   Points 347

Against
Tries 21   Goals 17   Drop goals 3   Points 121

Won Test series 2-1

Attendance total: 259,938

Brad Fittler, two tries in five games.

TOUR PARTY

Managers: K. Barnes and L. Stokes
Captain: M. Meninga   Coach: R. Fulton

	App	Tries	Gls	Pts
Greg Alexander	6+6	2	21	50
Gary Belcher	8	2	2(1)	11
Martin Bella	5+3	0	0	0
Mark Carroll	2+1	1	0	4
John Cartwright	5+2	0	0	0
Laurie Daley	5	0	0	0
Ben Elias	7+1	2	0	8
Andrew Ettingshausen	9	11	0	44
Brad Fittler	5	2	0	8
Mark Geyer	4+1	3	0	12
David Gillespie	5+3	0	0	0
Michael Hancock	5+1	4	0	16
Des Hasler	4+4	2	0	8
Chris Johns	5+2	3	0	12
Allan Langer	7+1	1	0	4
Glenn Lazarus	6+5	1	0	4
Bob Lindner	8+1	2	0	8
Cliff Lyons	6	3	0	12
Mark McGaw	5+1	1	0	4
Brad Mackay	7+3	2	0	8
Mal Meninga	9	7	15	58
Steve Roach	8	1	0	4
Mark Sargent	5+1	3	0	12
Dale Shearer	8+1	6	0	24
Paul Sironen	8	2	0	8
Ricky Stuart	6+1	1	0	4
Kerrod Walters	6	2	0	8
Kevin Walters	5	4	0	16

( ) Drop goal included in total

MEMO

First match October 7, last match November 24.

Australia's remarkable run of 37 tour victories in Britain, stretching back to 1978, ended when they lost the first Test at Wembley before a then record international crowd in this country of 54,569.

But Australia went on to clinch the series which attracted a record Test aggregate attendance of 133,684. The overall tour crowd average of 19,995 was another record as was Australia's tour share of £570,000.

Although the big improvement in British playing standards provided the Kangaroos with their toughest tour for 12 years they still maintained their record of not losing against club opposition since 1978.

Back row forward Bob Lindner was elected Australia's man of the Test series, with Ellery Hanley gaining the British award.

The Kangaroos' captain Mal Meninga became only the second Australian to score a try in each Test of a series in Britain.

These included the memorable last-minute matchwinner in the second Test at Old Trafford following a long-distance break by scrum half Ricky Stuart.

AUSTRALIA APPENDIX

In addition to full tours, World Cup parties made occasional appearances as follows, Australia score first:

1960	St. Helens	lost	12-15	12,750
1970	St. Helens	lost	10-37	15,570
1972	St. Helens	won	24-9	10,000
	Wigan	drew	18-18	6,000
	Bradford N.	won	29-16	2,820
1975	Salford	won	44-6	5,357
	St. Helens	won	32-7	10,170
	Oldham	won	20-10	3,575
	York	won	45-4	4,082
	England (Leeds)	won	25-0	7,680
1992	Huddersfield	won	66-2	4,716
	Sheffield E.	won	52-22	5,500
	Cumbria (Workington)	won	44-0	5,156

1992 WORLD CUP TOUR

TOUR PARTY

Managers: G. Carr and T. Weber
Captain: M. Meninga   Coach: R. Fulton

	App	Tries	Gls	Pts
Tim Brasher	4	4	6	28
Willie Carne	3	1	2	8
John Cartwright	2+2	0	0	0
Bradley Clyde	3	3	0	12
Brad Fittler	3+1	1	1	6
David Gillespie	2+2	2	0	8
Brad Godden	1+1	0	0	0
Michael Hancock	2+1	3	0	12
Paul Harragon	1+1	1	0	4
Chris Johns	1	0	0	0
Allan Langer	3	2	0	8
Glenn Lazarus	4	0	0	0
Bob Lindner	2+2	2	0	8
Graham Mackay	2	4	1	18
Mal Meninga	3	2	8	24
Steve Renouf	4	4	0	16
Mark Sargent	3+1	2	0	8
Paul Sironen	3+1	0	0	0
Ricky Stuart	1+1	0	0	0
Kerrod Walters	1	0	0	0
Kevin Walters	1+2	1	0	4
Steve Walters	3	2	0	8

RECORDS AGAINST CLUB SIDES

Highest score: 92-7 v. Bramley in 1921-22
(Also widest margin win)
Biggest defeat: 2-44 v. St. Helens in 1956. Also lost 15-47 to Yorkshire in 1959, the most points conceded in any tour match in Britain.

INDIVIDUAL RECORDS

Club and representative matches
Most tries on tour: 39 by Cecil Blinkhorn in 1921-22
Most goals and points on tour: 114g-285pts (19t) by Dave Brown in 1933-34
Most appearances on tour: 35 by Larry O'Malley in 1908-09
Most tries in a match: 7 by Cecil Blinkhorn v. Bramley in 1921-22
Most goals in a match: 11 by Eric Weissel v. Halifax in 1929-30
by Noel Pidding v. Wakefield T. in 1952-53
Most points in a match: 31 by Noel Pidding v. Wakefield T. in 1952-53

AUSTRALIA TOURS OF FRANCE

Each tour immediately followed trip to Britain	P	W	D	L	F	A
1937-38	10	9	—	1	267	80
Won Test series 2-0						
1948-49	10	9	—	1	279	71
Won Test series 2-0						
1952-53	13	10	—	3	301	125
Lost Test series 2-1						
1956-57	9	8	1	—	207	110
Won Test series 3-0						
1959-60	11	9	—	2	277	120
Won Test series 3-0						
1963-64	14	12	—	2	328	111
Won Test series 2-1						
1967-68	7	4	1	2	105	53
Lost Test series 2-0, one drawn						
1973-74	3	3	—	—	59	24
Won Test series 2-0						
1978-79	6	3	—	3	116	73
Lost Test series 2-0						
1982-83	7	7	—	—	291	20
Won Test series 2-0						
1986-87	7	7	—	—	286	21
Won Test series 2-0						
1990-91	5	5	—	—	256	47
Won Test series 2-0						

313

• During their tour of Britain in 1933-34 Australia beat England 63-13 in Paris in an exhibition game.

• The 1960 World Cup squad played an extra game against France, winning 37-12. The 1970 squad beat France 7-4 and France B 36-8. In 1975, Rouergue were beaten 35-4.

AUSTRALIA TOURS OF NEW ZEALAND

	P	W	D	L	F	A
1919 Won Test series 3-1	9	8	—	1	443	101
1935 Won Test series 2-1	6	5	—	1	173	95
1937	3	1	—	2	32	40

En route to Britain, the Australians played two Test matches against New Zealand recording a win and a loss. They also lost against the Maoris.

	P	W	D	L	F	A
1949 Drew Test series 1-1	10	9	—	1	299	123
1953 Lost Test series 2-1	9	7	—	2	366	98
1961 Drew Test series 1-1	9	7	—	2	215	68
1965 Drew Test series 1-1	8	7	—	1	159	58
1969 Drew Test series 1-1	6	4	—	2	137	78
1971 Lost Test series 1-0	3	1	—	2	52	53
1980 Won Test series 2-0	7	5	1	1	158	48
1985 Won Test series 2-1 including one Test win in Australia	6	5	—	1	192	44
1989 Won Test series 3-0	6	5	—	1	158	74

● World Cup squads also played extra games as follows:

1975 Beat Auckland 17-6.

1977 Beat South Island 68-5 and lost 19-15 to Auckland.

1988 Beat Wellington Invitation 24-12.

AUSTRALIA TOUR OF PAPUA NEW GUINEA

	P	W	D	L	F	A
1991 Won Test series 2-0	5	5	—	—	208	42

RECORDS IN TEST AND WORLD CUP MATCHES

For Australia

Highest score: 70-8 v. Papua New Guinea at Wagga 20 July, 1988 (also widest margin)

Most tries in a match: 4 by John Ribot v. Papua New Guinea at Port Moresby 2 Oct., 1982
4 by Dale Shearer v. France, Second Test at Carcassonne 13 Dec., 1986
4 by Michael O'Connor v. Papua New Guinea at Wagga 20 July, 1988

Most goals in a match: 10 by Keith Barnes v. France, Second Test at Brisbane 2 July 1960
10 by Eric Simms v. New Zealand, World Cup at Wigan 10 Oct., 1970
10 by Mick Cronin v. Britain, First Test at Brisbane 16 June, 1979

Most points in a match: 30 (4t,7g) by Michael O'Connor v. Papua New Guinea at Wagga 20 July, 1988

Most appearances: 45 by Graeme Langlands (1963-1975)

Most career tries: 33 by Ken Irvine (1959-1967)

Most career goals: 141 by Mick Cronin (1973-1982)

Most career points: 309 (9t,141g) by Mick Cronin (1973-1982)

Biggest attendance (home): 70,204 v. Britain, First Test at Sydney 6 June, 1932

Biggest attendance (away): 73,631 v. Britain, World Cup final at Wembley 24 Oct., 1992

Against Australia

Highest score: 49-25 v. New Zealand, Second Test at Brisbane 28 June, 1952 (also widest margin)

Most tries in a match: 4 by Jim Leytham (Britain) Second Test at Brisbane 2 July, 1910

Most goals in a match: 11 by Des White (New Zealand) Second Test at Brisbane 28 June, 1952

Most points in a match: 22 by Des White (as above)

Full back Morvin Edwards, scorer of two tries in eight games on the 1993 Kiwi tour of Europe.

1993 KIWIS

1993 TOUR REVIEW

Howie Tamati arrived in Britain for his first Kiwi tour as coach full of confidence. Six weeks later, the mood had turned to confusion as the New Zealanders crashed to their first Test series whitewash in Britain for 42 years.

The confidence came from Tamati's debutant series against the all-conquering Australians only four months earlier, the Kiwis gaining a draw and two creditable narrow defeats in a hard-fought Test series.

The confusion resulted from roller-coaster form which brought his John Smith's tour party six victories from eight non-Test fixtures and included the impressive scalps of Wales, Wigan, St. Helens, Leeds, Widnes and Great Britain Under-21s, performances which could not be transferred to the Test arena.

Extra confusion arose from Test selection options, with British-based Kiwis being available only for the three John Smith's Tests. Tamati, experienced on British soil with Wigan in 1983-84 and the Kiwi tourists in 1980 and 1985, put his faith largely in the touring party for the first John Smith's Test at Wembley with only three of the 17-man squad being from British clubs. As Britain gained a stranglehold on the Tests, however, he drafted in another five exiles.

The confusion, fuelled further by 15 of the 26-man squad playing in New Zealand and the other 11 with Australian clubs, turned to apparent panic as Tamati approached the third Test at Leeds bidding to avoid a 3-0 hammering, dropping experienced duo Gary Freeman, the skipper and scrum half, and ex-Warrington hooker Duane Mann in a bold move which did not pay off.

New Zealand lost the John Smith's Tests 17-0 at Wembley, 29-12 at Wigan and 29-10 at Leeds, conceding 10 tries while scoring only three. Tamati then lost his coaching job on his return home, ultimate proof of the theory that a touring side is measured in Test football regardless of results in other tour fixtures.

The principle of trying to combine a selection of touring squad members with the availability for Test matches only of Kiwis serving British clubs was a shadow which hung over the 11-match tour.

The extent of the dilemma was shown by the fact that a credible New Zealand Test side could have been chosen from Kiwis in British club football alone.

Tamati's trauma was further exacerbated by the tourists' form leading up to the first showpiece John Smith's Test at Wembley. His first choice tour side beat Wales 24-19 in the opening encounter at Swansea and a week later pulled off a morale-boosting victory against the mighty Wigan at Central Park by 25-18.

Despite two midweek defeats for his second string at Bradford Northern and Castleford, Tamati opted to back his tourists for the first Test and drafted in only three British-based players, centre duo Kevin Iro (Leeds) and Dave Watson (Bradford N.), plus Castleford loose forward Tawera Nikau.

Great Britain coach Malcolm Reilly produced a gameplan based on tactical kicking which was carried out to near perfection, Wigan winger Jason Robinson grabbing the headlines with a two-try Test debut.

Iro and Watson were retained for the rest of the series, with Wigan's Frano Botica, Castleford's Tony Kemp and Oldham's Se'e Solomona being brought in for the remaining two encounters. Nikau was dropped; Gary Mercer, of Leeds, featured in the second Test only, on the bench; and Castleford's Richard Blackmore was called up for the third meeting, also as a substitute.

But the Kiwis could not find a winning combination and British skipper Garry Schofield climbed the Headingley steps to receive the John Smith's Trophy after the Lions had adopted a more expansive game in the second and third Test victories.

Wigan loose forward Phil Clarke was chosen by the British management as the John Smith's

Player of the Series, ahead of Warrington's Jonathan Davies, who justified his controversial selection at full back with three outstanding performances featuring a tally of 26 points from a try, 10 goals and two drop goals.

Reilly continued his policy of selecting in-form players with the debut in the third Test of Wigan second row man Andrew Farrell, the youngest-ever British forward at 18 years five months.

The 13th Kiwi tour of Britain, the shortest-ever, was hit by two late withdrawals from the 26-man squad, both Australian-based key men. Canterbury-Bankstown and former St. Helens centre Jarrod McCracken and Gold Coast prop Brent Todd, the tour vice-captain, were ruled out by injury, being replaced by the inexperienced Canterbury duo Blair Harding and Paul Johnson.

The Kiwis were well served by the impressive back row of Stephen Kearney — who took over the captaincy in the third Test — Quentin Pongia and loose forward Jason Mackie, who opened the tour with a John Smith's Man of the Match performance against Wales.

Manly half back Gene Ngamu, recruited by newly formed Sydney Premiership side Auckland Warriors, was pushed into the spotlight at the start of the tour by being selected at stand off against both Wales and Wigan, the uncapped 19-year-old being retained for the Wembley Test in preference to experienced campaigners such as Watson, Botica and Kemp. The debutant failed to shine and was replaced for the rest of the series by Kemp.

Freeman, in mid-move between Australian clubs Balmain and Penrith, was the linchpin of the tour squad, having been an automatic choice for 34 successive Tests since his debut in 1986. The mercurial scrum half equalled the New Zealand Test record of 36 caps in the second Test at Wigan but was denied the new record until he went to France by being dropped for the final encounter in favour of former Chorley Borough Second Division player Aaron Whittaker, a gamble which did not pay off.

The Kiwis achieved only average success on the full tour, winning six matches and losing five, scoring 189 points and conceding 193.

New Zealand's first-ever appearance at Wembley produced the third best Anglo-Kiwi attendance in the 80th meeting, the 36,131 gate trailing only to the 42,680 at Bradford in 1947 and the 37,475, also at Odsal, in 1951.

The three-Test aggregate of 67,772 and average of 22,590 were the best attendance figures since the 1951 series.

Despite playing in only the first Test, utility back Daryl Halligan finished as top scorer in four categories — most goals and points on the tour and in a match, sharing the most points in a match record with scrum half Whittaker.

Loose forward Jason Mackie was the tour's top try scorer with a modest four from a total of 32. Most full tour appearances were made by Whittaker with seven, while Whetu Taewa and Jason Williams each made nine including four as substitute.

The Kiwis' disciplinary record was almost unblemished with just one dismissal — Quentin Pongia at Bradford — and one sin-bin, for hooker Denvour Johnston at St. Helens.

It was on the disciplinary front that the Kiwis made history. At the International Board meeting nearly four months earlier the principle of "trial by video" had been adopted. After the Wembley Test, the British League cited New Zealand second row man Kearney for a tackle on opposite number Denis Betts, who suffered a broken cheekbone. The Kiwi management retaliated by citing Lions' skipper Schofield for a tackle on Jason Williams.

At a special hearing at Rugby League Headquarters, it was decided that no further action be taken, mainly because of procedural matters in the calling of the hearing.

BRITISH TOUR RESULTS

Date	Result	Score	Opposition	Venue	Attendance
October 3	Won	24-19	Wales	Swansea C. FC	6,073
October 6	Lost	10-17	Bradford N.	Bradford	5,015
October 10	Won	25-18	Wigan	Wigan	13,669
October 12	Lost	4-16	Castleford	Castleford	4,927
October 16	Lost	0-17	GREAT BRITAIN	Wembley	36,131
October 20	Won	14-8	St. Helens	St. Helens	8,165
October 24	Won	35-6	Leeds	Leeds	6,898
October 26	Won	37-24	Great Britain Under-21s	Workington	3,099
October 30	Lost	12-29	GREAT BRITAIN	Wigan	16,502
November 2	Won	18-10	Widnes	Widnes	5,646
November 6	Lost	10-29	GREAT BRITAIN	Leeds	15,139

BRITISH TOUR SUMMARY

							FOR			AGAINST	
P	W	D	L	T	G	Dr	Pts	T	G	Dr	Pts
11	6	0	5	32	29	3	189	33	28	5	193

BRITISH TEST SUMMARY

P	W	D	L	T	G	Dr	Pts	T	G	Dr	Pts
3	0	0	3	3	5	0	22	13	10	3	75

FRENCH TOUR RESULTS

Date	Result	Score	Opposition	Venue	Attendance
Nov. 11	Won	24-22	**Roussillon Select**	Perpignan	5,000

T: Angell, P. Edwards, Taewa, Johnston
G: Halligan (4)

| Nov. 14 | Won | 45-4 | **French Select** | Carpentras | 2,000 |

T: Williams (2), Stuart, Mackie,
L. Edwards, Ropati, Whittaker, Halligan
G: Halligan (6), Whittaker (dg)

| Nov. 17 | Won | 30-2 | **Midi-Pyrenees Select** | St. Gaudens | 1,900 |

T: Mackie (2), Paul, Ropati, Halligan
G: Halligan (5)

| Nov. 21 | Won | 36-11 | **FRANCE** | Carcassonne | 3,500 |

France:
Frantz Martial; Claude Sirvent (1t), Pierre Chamorin (1g,1dg),
David Fraisse, Pascal Bomati; Jean-Marc Garcia, Patrick Entat
(Capt); Bernard Llong (1t), Mathieu Khedimi, Lilian Herbert,
Ezzedine Attia, Mark Bourneville, Daniel Divet.
Subs: Pascal Jampy, Thierry Valero, Jean Frison (played);
Lucien De Macedo (not used).

New Zealand:
Morvin Edwards; Daryl Halligan (1t,6g), Kevin Iro (2t), Whetu
Taewa (1t), Jason Williams; Tony Kemp, Gary Freeman
(Capt) (1t); John Lomax, Denvour Johnston, Brent Stuart,
Jason Lowrie, Quentin Pongia, Jason Mackie (1t).
Subs: David Lomax, Logan Edwards, Peter Edwards,
Iva Ropati (all played).
Referee: John Holdsworth (England).

FRENCH TOUR SUMMARY

							FOR			AGAINST	
P	W	D	L	T	G	Dr	Pts	T	G	Dr	Pts
4	4	0	0	23	21	1	135	7	5	1	39

BRITISH TOUR RECORDS

Biggest attendance: 36,131 first Test v. Great Britain at Wembley
Highest score: 37-24 v. Great Britain Under-21s at Workington
Widest margin: 35-6 v. Leeds
Highest score against: Lost to Great Britain 29-12, second Test at Wigan; and 29-10, third Test at Leeds *(also widest margin defeat)*
Most tries in a match: No player scored three or more
Most goals in a match: 6 by Daryl Halligan v. Wales at Swansea
Most points in a match: 12 by Daryl Halligan v. Wales at Swansea; by Aaron Whittaker v. Leeds

Most tries on tour: 4 by Jason Mackie
Most goals on tour: 13, including one drop goal, by Daryl Halligan
Most points on tour: 29 by Daryl Halligan
Most appearances: 9 by Whetu Taewa (including four as substitute); by Jason Williams (including four as substitute)
Most full appearances: 7 by Aaron Whittaker
Sent off: Quentin Pongia v. Bradford Northern
Sin-bin: Denvour Johnston v. St. Helens
Opponents sent off: Paul Medley (Bradford N.) Sonny Nickle (Great Britain), third Test
Opponents' sin-bin: Sonny Nickle (St. Helens)

New Zealand's three British-based players called up for the first John Smith's Test at Wembley, from the left, Tawera Nikau, Dave Watson and Kevin Iro.

TOUR PARTY
Manager: Richard Bolton
Coach: Howie Tamati
Physiotherapist: Peter Boyle

Assistant Manager: Laurie Stubbing
Doctors: Wayne Morris (Britain), Stephen Culpan (France)
Trainer: Willie Ford

Player	Club	IN BRITAIN					IN FRANCE					TOUR TOTALS				
		App	Sub	T	G	Pts	App	Sub	T	G	Pts	App	Sub	T	G	Pts
ANGELL, Simon	Canterbury, NZ	4	1	2	–	8	2	–	1	–	4	6	1	3	–	12
DONNELLY, Jason	St. George, Aus	6	1	1	–	4	–	2	–	–	–	6	1	1	–	4
EDWARDS, Logan	Canterbury, NZ	4	2	2	–	8	1	1	1	–	4	5	4	3	–	12
EDWARDS, Morvin	Balmain, Aus	5	1	–	–	–	3	1	1	–	4	8	2	1	–	4
EDWARDS, Peter	Wellington, NZ	6	–	2	2	12	2	1	1	–	4	8	1	3	2	16
FREEMAN, Gary	Penrith, Aus	5	1	1	13(1)	29	2	1	3	21	54	7	2	4	34(1)	83
HALLIGAN, Daryl	North Sydney, Aus	4	1	1	–	4	4	1	–	–	–	8	3	1	–	4
HARDING, Blair	Canterbury, NZ	3	2	–	–	–	2	1	–	–	–	5	3	–	–	–
HOPPE, Sean	Canberra, Aus	6	–	3	–	12	1	1	–	–	–	7	2	3	–	12
JOHNSON, Paul	Canterbury, NZ	3	1	1	–	4	1	1	–	–	–	4	2	1	–	4
JOHNSTON, Denvour	Canterbury, NZ	5	–	–	–	–	3	1	–	–	–	8	1	–	–	–
KEARNEY, Stephen	Western Suburbs, Aus	6	–	1	–	4	2	–	1	–	4	8	–	2	–	8
LOMAX, David	Wellington, NZ	4	4	–	–	–	1	2	–	–	–	5	6	–	–	–
LOMAX, John	Canberra, Aus	6	2	–	–	–	3	–	–	–	–	9	2	–	–	–
LOWRIE, Jason	Eastern Suburbs, Aus	3	4	1	–	4	3	2	–	–	–	6	4	1	–	4
MACKIE, Jason	Northland, NZ	6	2	4	–	16	3	–	4	–	16	6	2	8	–	32
MANN, Duane	Auckland, NZ	5	–	1	1(1)	5	1	1	–	–	–	7	–	1	1(1)	5
NGAMU, Gene	Manly-Warringah, Aus	6	–	2	3	14	–	–	–	–	–	6	2	2	3	14
NIXON, Mark	Canterbury, NZ	3	–	1	–	4	3	–	1	–	4	5	1	1	–	4
*PAUL, Henry	Auckland Warriors, NZ	5	3	–	–	–	2	–	1	–	4	8	2	1	–	4
PIVA, Robert	Wellington, NZ	6	2	–	–	–	–	2	–	–	–	8	3	–	–	–
PONGIA, Quentin	Canberra, Aus	6	2	–	–	–	2	1	–	–	–	6	3	–	–	–
ROPATI, Iva	Auckland, NZ	6	1	3	–	12	2	1	2	–	8	8	1	5	–	20
STUART, Brent	Canterbury, NZ	5	–	1	–	4	2	1	–	–	–	7	5	1	–	4
TAEWA, Whetu	Canterbury, NZ	7	4	2	8(1)	23	2	1	1	1(1)	5	9	5	3	9(2)	28
WHITTAKER, Aaron	Canterbury, NZ	5	2	3	–	12	2	2	2	–	8	7	5	5	–	20
WILLIAMS, Jason	Cant'bury-Bankstown, Aus	5	4	3	–	12	2	1	2	–	8	7	5	5	–	20
British-based																
BLACKMORE, Richard	Castleford	2	1	–	–	–	–	–	–	–	–	–	1	–	–	–
BOTICA, Frano	Wigan	2	–	–	5	10	–	–	–	–	–	2	–	–	5	10
IRO, Kevin	Leeds	3	–	–	–	–	1	–	2	–	8	4	2	2	–	8
KEMP, Tony	Castleford	2	1	–	–	–	1	1	–	–	–	3	1	–	–	–
MERCER, Gary	Leeds	–	1	1	–	4	–	–	–	–	–	–	–	1	–	–
NIKAU, Tawera	Castleford	1	–	–	–	–	–	–	–	–	–	1	–	–	–	–
SOLOMONA, Se'e	Oldham	2	1	–	–	–	–	–	–	–	–	2	1	–	–	–
WATSON, Dave	Bradford N.	3	–	1	–	4	–	–	–	–	–	3	1	1	–	4

(1) Indicates drop goal included in total
* Replacement on 1 November for Piva

1993 Kiwis
Left to right.
Back row: Denvour Johnston, Jason Mackie, Blair Harding, Brent Stuart, Sean Hoppe, Simon Angell, Stephen Kearney, Daryl Halligan,
Quentin Pongia, Robert Piva, Paul Johnson
Middle row: Peter Boyle (Physio), Gene Ngamu, Tea Ropati, Logan Edwards, Jason Lowrie, Jason Donnelly, Morvin Edwards, John Lomax,
Whetu Taewa, Dave Lomax, Jason Williams, Wayne Morris (Doctor)
Front row: Willie Ford (Conditioner), Peter Edwards, Mark Nixon, Howie Tamati (Coach), Gary Freeman (Captain), Richard Bolton (Manager),
Duane Mann, Aaron Whittaker, Laurie Stubbing (Manager).

JOHN SMITH'S TOUR... MATCH BY MATCH

WALES INTERNATIONAL

Wales justified their belated inclusion in the 1995 Centenary World Cup by making New Zealand battle for a 24-19 victory in the opening match of the Kiwi tour at Swansea City FC's Vetch Field.

With only 11 minutes left and trailing 17-22, the Dragons claimed a probable match-winning touchdown by John Devereux in a scramble behind the posts from skipper Jonathan Davies's high kick, only for British referee John Connolly to disallow it for offside by another Welsh player.

In a hectic finish, Davies and Kiwi Daryl Halligan exchanged penalty goals to complete an exciting John Smith's International which deserved a bigger crowd than the disappointing 6,073.

The nailbiting finish left Wales angry at Devereux's disallowed try but referee Connolly was proved correct on video analysis. It also provided Wales with their second defeat in the five outings since re-formation in 1991.

The New Zealanders' successful launch to their 13th tour of Britain ended the 3-3 stalemate in the six meetings between the two countries since 1908.

Davies, who missed both of the previous season's Welsh games due to injury, showed only occasional flashes of his attacking flair, though his accurate tactical kicking led to both of Wales's tries and he landed five goals, all from penalties.

Bradford Northern winger Gerald Cordle followed up the kicks each time to win the race to touch down in only his second match since breaking his jaw against England on the same ground a year earlier.

The most impressive aspect of a patchy performance by the Kiwis, fielding their strongest touring side, was the mobility and support play of their back three.

Uncapped loose forward Jason Mackie took the John Smith's Man of the Match award after scoring a vital try just before the interval and providing the pass for winger Sean Hoppe to score what turned out to be the match-clinching try in the 62nd minute.

Second row pair Steve Kearney and Quentin Pongia ran him close for match honours, linking in great style. Winger Halligan also stood out with six goals from seven attempts, including some colossal efforts.

The first 25 minutes was more of a goal-kicking duel with Halligan's early penalty being wiped out by a Jonathan Griffiths drop goal, followed by two penalties from Davies.

The boot continued to be predominant and it brought Wales the opening try when Davies kicked superbly for the corner from 40 metres. Cordle had a flying start on the Kiwi defence and the Bradford winger was able to slow up to make certain of touching down.

The touch judges disagreed over Davies's touchline kick and referee Connolly was left to decide it was no goal.

Halligan then showed his kicking power with two mighty penalties from near halfway to pull the visitors right back into the game, and the Kiwis' first try looked inevitable after several near misses. It came just before the interval as the impressive Pongia broke down the left and slipped the ball inside for Mackie to go in at the corner, Halligan's touchline goal giving New Zealand their 12-9 half-time lead.

The Kiwis surged further ahead within five minutes of the restart when captain Gary Freeman pulled off a series of dummies to give centre Iva Ropati a clear run to the line.

Wales refused to be fazed and Davies produced his second try-making kick which Cordle did well to collect to go over near the flag. Davies was off target with the goal kick, but two successful penalties put the Welshmen ahead on the hour, before Hoppe struck with his try two minutes later, Halligan adding another touchline goal.

JOHN SMITH'S INTERNATIONAL

3 October   **Vetch Field, Swansea**

WALES   19   **NEW ZEALAND   24**

Phil Ford (Salford)	1.	Morvin Edwards
Gerald Cordle (Bradford N.)	2.	Daryl Halligan
Allan Bateman (Warrington)	3.	Iva Ropati
John Devereux (Widnes)	4.	Whetu Taewa
Anthony Sullivan (St. Helens)	5.	Sean Hoppe
Jonathan Davies (Warrington), Capt.	6.	Gene Ngamu
Kevin Ellis (Warrington)	7.	Gary Freeman, Capt.
Mark Jones (Hull)	8.	John Lomax
Barry Williams (Carlisle)	9.	Duane Mann
David Young (Salford)	10.	Brent Stuart
Ian Marlow (Wakefield T.)	11.	Stephen Kearney
Rowland Phillips (Warrington)	12.	Quentin Pongia
Jonathan Griffiths (St. Helens)	13.	Jason Mackie
Adrian Hadley (Widnes)	14.	Mark Nixon
Gary Pearce (Ryedale-York)	15.	Logan Edwards
Peter Williams (Salford)	16.	Jason Williams
Rob Ackerman (Cardiff Inst. ARL)	17.	Robert Piva

T: Cordle (2)   T: Hoppe, Mackie, Ropati
G: Davies (5), Griffiths (dg)   G: Halligan (6)
Substitutions: Substitutions:
Ackerman for Marlow (41 min.)   Piva for Lomax (62 min.)
Hadley for B. Williams (67 min.)   Williams for M. Edwards (69 min.)
Half-time: 9-12   L. Edwards for Mackie (75 min.)
Referee: John Connolly (Wigan)   Attendance: 6,073

Kiwi centre Whetu Taewa weighs up Welsh opposite number John Devereux.

6 October

BRADFORD N.   17
NEW ZEALAND   10

1. P. Edwards (Halligan, 19 min.)
2. Donnelly
3. Harding
4. Williams
5. Taewa
6. Nixon
7. Whittaker (Freeman, 63 min.)
8. Piva (Johnson, 60 min.)
9. Johnston
10. Lowrie
11. Angell (Pongia, 63 min.)
12. D. Lomax
13. L. Edwards
T: Angell
G: Halligan (2), P. Edwards

Bradford N:
Watson; Cordle, McGowan (D. Powell), Shelford, Kebbie; Summers, Fox; Grayshon (Winterburn), Clark, Hamer, R. Powell, Medley (Greenwood), Fairbank (Mumby)
T: Cordle, Kebbie
G: Fox (4, 1dg)
Half-time: 14-6
Referee: Russell Smith (Castleford)
Attendance: 5,015

Bradford Northern's victory, based on sound defence, was overshadowed by a brawl involving several players eight minutes from time which resulted in Kiwi tourist Pongia and Northern forward Medley being sent off.

Pongia had only been on the field for nine minutes, while Medley entered the fray from the substitutes' bench having been taken off 12 minutes earlier.

The Kiwi second string were disappointing, even considering the relentless driving rain, and only prop Piva pushed Test claims in a Man of the Match performance. Scrum half Fox made the first of Northern's two tries, also kicking four goals and a drop goal.

10 October

WIGAN   18
NEW ZEALAND   25

1. Halligan (Donnelly, 46 min.)
2. Hoppe
3. Ropati
4. Taewa
5. Williams
6. Ngamu
7. Freeman
8. J. Lomax
9. Mann
10. Stuart (Lowrie, 52 min.)
11. Kearney
12. Piva (D. Lomax, 46 min.)
13. Mackie
T: Hoppe (2), Mackie, Ngamu, Taewa
G: Halligan (1, 1dg), Ngamu

Wigan:
Lydon; Robinson, Bell, Connolly, Panapa; Botica, Edwards; Cowie (Mather), Hall (Dermott), Gildart, Betts, Farrell, Clarke
T: Cowie, Edwards, Hall
G: Botica (3)
Half-time: 12-7
Referee: Robin Whitfield (Widnes)
Attendance: 13,669

The Kiwis came back from an 18-7 deficit to win what they classed as the "fourth Test", leaving it late with the deciding tries not coming until the last six minutes.

The well-earned victory came at the right time, a week before the opening John Smith's Test at Wembley, providing a boost in morale for the tourists and an upsurge in interest for ticket sales.

The conquering of Britain's top club left coach Howie Tamati with a selection headache for the first Test, prop John Lomax, winger Hoppe, centre Ropati and half back Ngamu all staking claims against the calling up of British-based Kiwis. The Kiwi performance was marred only by lapses of concentration either side of half-time when Wigan scored two of their three tries.

12 October

| **CASTLEFORD** | **16** |
| **NEW ZEALAND** | **4** |

1. P. Edwards
2. Donnelly
3. Harding
4. Ropati
5. M. Edwards (Williams, 75 min.)
6. Nixon
7. Whittaker
8. Piva
9. Johnston
10. Johnson (Lowrie, 36 min.)
11. Angell (Mackie, 50 min.)
12. Pongia (D. Lomax, 59 min.)
13. L. Edwards
T: L. Edwards

Castleford:
Steadman; Ellis, Blackmore (T. Smith), Anderson, Middleton; Kemp (Flowers), Ford; Crooks (Sampson), Russell, Ketteridge (England), Hay, Morrison, Smales
T: Ellis (3), Middleton
Half-time: 8-0
Referee: David Campbell (Widnes)
Attendance: 4,927

A hat-trick of tries from Castleford winger Ellis, his second in three days, shattered a lacklustre Kiwi second team, leaving them empty handed from their opening two midweek fixtures.

Ellis's tries were created by Kiwis Blackmore and Kemp, both disregarded by New Zealand for the opening John Smith's Test at Wembley four days later.

The only bright spots for the uninspired Kiwis were the injury-free appearances of Test men Morvin Edwards, showing full recovery from a thigh strain and influenza, and Pongia, who played 58 minutes after missing the previous Sunday's fixture through suspension.

Second row man Quentin Pongia, back in action against Castleford after suspension.

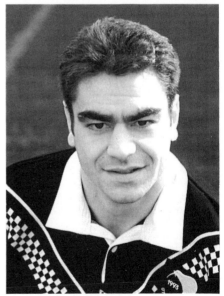

Wheldon Road try scorer Logan Edwards.

325

FIRST TEST

Great Britain served up a coach's dream performance in the first John Smith's Test at Wembley, their 17-0 success being achieved with clinical efficiency.

New Zealand were nilled for the first time in a Test in Britain, the Lions' kicking plan being near perfect with all three tries coming from the boot, and handling errors down to just four.

The immaculate transfer of the tactical plans from the drawing board to the sacred turf of Wembley even brought a smile to the face of hard-to-please British coach Malcolm Reilly.

The gameplan was never exuberant or expansionist, but was a triumph for their mastery of the 10-metre rule. Props Karl Fairbank and Karl Harrison gained the desired ground and a succession of kicks kept the tourists pinned well down in their own half.

New Zealand contributed to their downfall by committing a host of basic errors and putting their faith in the wholesale selection of tourists rather than British-based players, although Tawera Nikau (Castleford), Dave Watson (Bradford Northern) and Kevin Iro (Leeds) did little to undermine that selection policy.

Britain capitalised on the predetermined tactic of kicking to the wings, following the example of Wales in the opening tour match two weeks earlier, so that all five tries conceded by New Zealand in their opening two internationals had been to wingers chasing kicks, four of them on Sean Hoppe's flank.

In Swansea, veteran Gerald Cordle had grabbed two for Wales. Teenager Jason Robinson now repeated the feat on his Test debut, the youngster showing great pace and determination to beat the much bigger Hoppe to the ball.

Robinson's two tries were the result of the Wigan connection. Teammate Shaun Edwards set up the first in the 17th minute with a superbly-placed kick to the corner, followed 11 minutes later by Phil Clarke giving Gary Connolly the chance to slot the ball along the touchline for Robinson to pounce for the second time.

Britain's third touchdown went to left winger John Devereux – putting two Wembley nightmares behind him – who dived in when Jonathan Davies's towering kick divebombed out of the sun to have Kiwi full back Morvin Edwards in a tangle over his own line.

Shaun Edwards was totally involved throughout, being at the heart of Britain's kicking game with a variety that had the Kiwis twisting and turning in all directions. His defensive contribution of 20 tackles also went towards his official rating as John Smith's Man of the Match.

Despite Edwards's individual match award, New Zealand skipper Gary Freeman was the most dangerous of the four half backs on attack, going nearest to scoring a Kiwi try when teasing his way across the home defence before being bundled into touch near the corner flag.

Warrington's Welsh centre Jonathan Davies answered those who had doubts about his selection at full back with a splendid all-round display. In addition to his try-making kick and three goals, including a drop goal, he produced the game's most thrilling run with a late 60-metre dash.

Britain's victory, their first in an opening Test against New Zealand in Britain since 1965, owed a lot to a stonewall defence, Clarke heading the official tackle count with 34, followed by forward colleagues Harrison and Chris Joynt with 27 each. The most remarkable tackling figure was the 26 by Connolly, an astonishing tally for a centre. Britain's day of tactical glory was marred only by second row man Denis Betts suffering a cracked cheekbone.

FIRST JOHN SMITH'S TEST

16 October   **Wembley**

GREAT BRITAIN   17

Jonathan Davies (Warrington)	1.
Jason Robinson (Wigan)	2.
Paul Newlove (Bradford N.)	3.
Gary Connolly (Wigan)	4.
John Devereux (Widnes)	5.
Garry Schofield (Leeds), Capt.	6.
Shaun Edwards (Wigan)	7.
Karl Harrison (Halifax)	8.
Martin Dermott (Wigan)	9.
Karl Fairbank (Bradford N.)	10.
Denis Betts (Wigan)	11.
Chris Joynt (St. Helens)	12.
Phil Clarke (Wigan)	13.
Daryl Powell (Sheffield E.)	14.
Richie Eyres (Leeds)	15.
Alan Tait (Leeds)	16.
Sonny Nickle (St. Helens)	17.

NEW ZEALAND   0

Morvin Edwards
Daryl Halligan
Kevin Iro (Leeds)
Dave Watson (Bradford N.)
Sean Hoppe
Gene Ngamu
Gary Freeman, Capt.
John Lomax
Duane Mann
Brent Stuart
Stephen Kearney
Quentin Pongia
Tawera Nikau (Castleford)
Jason Williams
Jason Mackie
Whetu Taewa
Jason Lowrie

T: Robinson (2), Devereux
G: Davies (2, 1dg)
Substitutions:
Nickle for Fairbank (54 min.)
Eyres for Joynt (63 min.)
Powell for Newlove (68 min.)
Tait for Devereux (77 min.)
Half-time: 10-0
Referee: Greg McCallum (Australia)

Substitutions:
Lowrie for Lomax (58 min.)
Williams for Edwards (62 min.)
Mackie for Nikau (69 min.)
Taewa for Halligan (76 min.)
Attendance: 36,131

Scorechart

Minute	Score	GB	NZ
17:	Robinson (T)	4	0
28:	Robinson (T)	8	0
34:	Davies (P)	10	0
53:	Devereux (T)		
	Davies (G)	16	0
61:	Davies (DG)	17	0
	Scrums	14	10
	Penalties	3	9

New Zealand Test skipper Gary Freeman.

20 October

| ST. HELENS | 8 |
| NEW ZEALAND | 14 |

1. P. Edwards
2. Hoppe
3. Taewa (M. Edwards, 68 min.)
4. Williams
5. Donnelly
6. Ngamu (Nixon, 35 min.)
7. Whittaker
8. Piva
9. Johnston
10. J. Lomax
11. Kearney
12. Pongia (D. Lomax, 67 min.)
13. Mackie
T: P. Edwards, Mackie, Nixon
G: Ngamu

St. Helens:
Lyon; Riley, Veivers, Loughlin (Quirk), Hunte; Ropati, Griffiths; Neill (Fogerty), Dwyer, Mann, Joynt, Nickle (O'Donnell), Cooper
T: Hunte, Riley
Half-time: 4-6
Referee: John Connolly (Wigan)
Attendance: 8,165

As if to confirm their inconsistency, the Kiwis bounced back from the disaster of the first Test four days earlier to add the impressive scalp of St. Helens to those of Wigan and Wales.

The much needed competitive element spilled over on occasions, culminating in the sin-binning of Kiwi hooker Johnston and Saints' Test forward Nickle.

The St. Helens' Kiwi duo of George Mann and Tea Ropati were not outstanding enough to merit Test selection, but tryscoring tourist loose forward Mackie was an inspiration and a constant source of danger, further pushing his claim for upgrading from the Test substitutes' bench.

24 October

| LEEDS | 6 |
| NEW ZEALAND | 35 |

1. P. Edwards
2. Hoppe
3. Ropati
4. M. Edwards (Nixon, 58 min.)
5. Donnelly
6. Whittaker
7. Freeman
8. Lowrie
9. Mann
10. Stuart
11. Piva (Angell, 44 min.)
12. D. Lomax (Harding, 69 min.)
13. Mackie (L. Edwards, 63 min.)
T: Donnelly, P. Edwards, Mackie, Mann, Ropati, Whittaker
G: Whittaker (4), P. Edwards, Mann (dg)

Leeds:
Tait; Fallon, Iro, Irving (Holroyd), Scales; Schofield, Stephens (Gregory); Harmon, Lowes, Rose (Leatham), Scott (Cummins), Eyres, Mercer
T: Iro
G: Irving
Half-time: 6-10
Referee: John Holdsworth (Kippax)
Attendance: 6,898

New Zealand maintained their unbeaten record against Leeds in official tour matches to take their current tour tally to four wins in seven matches.

Leeds's generosity on defence allowed the Kiwis to play an expansive game, moving the ball about with purpose to run in six tries.

Several players took the opportunity to stake claims for second Test selection, particularly scrum half Whittaker, who kicked four goals from five attempts and scored a try. Ropati and Mackie also helped their cause, the former scoring one try and making two others.

Kiwi coach Tamati was also impressed by a New Zealander in the Leeds ranks, back row man Mercer standing out in a disappointing home side.

26 October

Workington

GREAT BRITAIN UNDER-21s	**24**
NEW ZEALAND	**37**

1. P. Edwards (Piva, 67 min.)
2. Donnelly
3. Harding
4. Nixon
5. Williams
6. Ngamu
7. Whittaker (Taewa, 54 min.)
8. J. Lomax (Lowrie, 41 min.)
9. Johnston
10. Johnson
11. Angell
12. D. Lomax
13. L. Edwards
T: Williams (2), Whittaker, Angell, Johnston, Ngamu, Harding
G: Whittaker (3, 1dg), Ngamu

Great Britain Under-21s:
Lee Penny (Warrington); Daio Powell (Bradford N.), Richard Goddard (Wakefield T.), Rob Danby (Hull), Iestyn Harris (Warrington); Francis Maloney (Featherstone R.), Gareth Stephens (Leeds); Alex Thompson (Sheffield E.), Steve McCurrie (Widnes), Mick Cassidy (Wigan), Barrie-Jon Mather (Wigan), Lee Harland (Halifax), Andrew Farrell (Wigan). Substitutes: Craig Makin (Widnes) for Thompson; Scott Martin (Leigh) for Makin; Nigel Wright (Wigan) for Powell; Jez Cassidy (Hull) for Harland.
T: Farrell (2), Danby, McCurrie
G: Harris (4)
Half-time: 12-13
Referee: Greg McCallum (Australia)
Attendance: 3,099

Hooker Johnston and scrum half Whittaker inspired the Kiwis' fourth successive victory, although Great Britain Under-21s provided a fright before fading away in an entertaining 61-point contest.

Johnston earned John Smith's Man of the Match rating, while Whittaker continued his scoring form with 11 points from a try, three goals and a drop goal before hobbling off in the 54th minute.

Whittaker's opening try and goal in the third minute gave the Kiwis a flying start, but the young Lions fought back with two tries in five minutes before the Kiwis were fortunate to grab a 13-12 interval lead, sealing victory with three tries in 15 minutes after the break and two tries from Williams in the dying stages.

A touchdown for second row man Simon Angell.

Two-try scorer, winger Jason Williams.

Man of the Match, hooker Denvour Johnston.

SECOND TEST

Great Britain clinched the John Smith's Test series by again inflicting a 17-point margin defeat on the New Zealanders, though the style of execution was in direct contrast with the Wembley win two weeks earlier.

The Lions' 29-12 triumph was exhilarating, a sheer delight for lovers of spontaneous, free-running action.

But pre-planned method was still evident, earning full credit for British coach Malcolm Reilly in his most impressive double since taking over as coach seven years earlier.

The Test victories over Australia in 1988, 1990 and 1992 would remain as Reilly's greatest single successes, but this Kiwi victory meant that he had followed up one outstanding win with an even better one.

Having masterminded the first Test success through a tightly controlled kicking game, Reilly changed course to introduce a far more expansive gameplan, allowing the backs, who had been kept on a short rein at Wembley, to cut loose with devastating effect as they swept in for all five tries.

No one enjoyed the extra freedom more than British skipper Garry Schofield, giving his most effective performance of the season. He played a key role in Britain's new plan of attack, while snapping up a try and sending over a drop goal to move into second place behind Neil Fox as Britain's most prolific pointscorer of all time with 149.

Britain's awesome strike power was best summed up by Martin Offiah's 70th-minute try. Schofield linked with substitute forward Daryl Powell whose imaginative long pass set centre Paul Newlove pounding down the left, looking all set to go for the line himself. Instead the Bradford Northern record signing made sure of the score by handing on for his winger to finish the attack in classical style with a touchdown in the corner.

When Newlove did decide to go on his own two minutes later, the result was the same with the threequarter confirming his status as one of the world's most powerful centres. With Jonathan Davies adding both goals from near the touchline, New Zealand looked a completely outclassed and demoralised side at 29-6.

But they made a token rally to finish as they began in the sixth minute with a try and a goal.

New Zealand's bright start put Great Britain's convincing victory even more into perspective. Having opened the scoring, the Kiwis were a little unlucky to be 12-6 behind at the interval, the score easily being reversed if loose forward Jason Mackie had been able to ground the ball as he dived between the posts and Bradford Northern's Dave Watson had not sent out the over-ambitious pass which John Devereux swooped on to go in for his and Britain's second try.

Watson's aberration was a typical extremity of form by the full back. In contrast, only minutes earlier his superb tackle had brought down the flying Offiah and he had opened the scoring with a lovely run to the posts.

With the Kiwi forwards driving deep down the middle, Britain looked to be in for a tough battle, before weathering the storm to dominate the second half completely.

John Smith's Man of the Match Devereux's contribution was immense. The Welsh winger charged through a mass of defenders with the power of a rampaging forward for the first try — his 100th career touchdown — and showed alertness for a second before being denied a hat-trick when obstructed, the referee's advantage ruling allowing Schofield to nip in for the touchdown. Fellow countryman Davies was the only other serious contender for the individual match award.

The convincing victory set the stage for Great Britain's first home whitewash of the Kiwis for 42 years.

SECOND JOHN SMITH'S TEST
30 October   Wigan

GREAT BRITAIN 29		NEW ZEALAND 12
Jonathan Davies (Warrington)	1.	Dave Watson (Bradford N.)
John Devereux (Widnes)	2.	Frano Botica (Wigan)
Gary Connolly (Wigan)	3.	Kevin Iro (Leeds)
Paul Newlove (Bradford N.)	4.	Iva Ropati
Martin Offiah (Wigan)	5.	Sean Hoppe
Garry Schofield (Leeds), Capt.	6.	Tony Kemp (Castleford)
Shaun Edwards (Wigan)	7.	Gary Freeman, Capt.
Karl Harrison (Halifax)	8.	Se'e Solomona (Oldham)
Lee Jackson (Sheffield E.)	9.	Duane Mann
Karl Fairbank (Bradford N.)	10.	Brent Stuart
Sonny Nickle (St. Helens)	11.	Stephen Kearney
Chris Joynt (St. Helens)	12.	Quentin Pongia
Philip Clarke (Wigan)	13.	Jason Mackie
Daryl Powell (Sheffield E.)	14.	Jason Williams
Richie Eyres (Leeds)	15.	John Lomax
Alan Tait (Leeds)	16.	Whetu Taewa
Michael Jackson (Halifax)	17.	Gary Mercer (Leeds)

T: Devereux (2), Schofield, Offiah, Newlove
G: Davies (4), Schofield (dg)
Substitutions:
M. Jackson for Fairbank (29 min.)
Eyres for Nickle (59 min.)
Powell for Harrison (67 min.)
Tait for Connolly (73 min.)
Referee: Greg McCallum (Australia)

T: Watson, Ropati
G: Botica (2)
Substitutions:
Mercer for Mackie (46 min.)
Williams for Hoppe (50 min.)
Lomax for Solomona (59 min.)
Taewa for Mann (73 min.)
Half-time: 12-6
Attendance: 16,502

Scorechart

Minute	Score	GB	NZ
6:	Watson (T)		
	Botica (G)	0	6
11:	Devereux (T)		
	Davies (G)	6	6
39:	Devereux (T)		
	Davies (G)	12	6
45:	Schofield (T)	16	6
52:	Schofield (DG)	17	6
70:	Offiah (T)		
	Davies (G)	23	6
72:	Newlove (T)		
	Davies (G)	29	6
79:	Ropati (T)		
	Botica (G)	29	12
	Scrums	6	7
	Penalties	7	9

Kiwi try scorer Iva Ropati, making his Test debut.

2 November

WIDNES   **10**
NEW ZEALAND   **18**

1. P. Edwards
2. Halligan
3. Taewa
4. M. Edwards
5. Donnelly
6. Ngamu
7. Whittaker (Nixon, 44 min.)
8. Lowrie
9. L. Edwards
10. Johnson (Harding, 69 min.)
11. Angell (Pongia, 49 min.) (Paul, 74 min.)
12. J. Lomax
13. D. Lomax
T: L. Edwards, Lowrie, Halligan
G: Halligan (3)
Widnes:
Spruce; Myers, D. Ruane, Hammond, Hadley (Hunter); Tyrer, Goulding; Ireland (Harris), McCurrie, Howe, Faimalo, Grieve (D. Smith), D. Hulme
T: Tyrer, Myers
G: Tyrer
Half-time: 6-0
Referee: Ian Ollerton (Wigan)
Attendance: 5,646

Winger Daryl Halligan, scorer of a try and three goals.

Scrum half Whittaker justified his shock call up for the third John Smith's Test by putting the Kiwis on route to a sixth tour victory before being taken off in the 44th minute.

Whittaker's darting run sent Logan Edwards in for an equalising try immediately after the break, though Widnes refused to lie down. Goulding's inch-perfect kick to the corner allowed Myers to win a close run for the touchdown to put the Chemics back in front.

But that sparked the tourists into life and they hit back with a couple of tries that swung the game. Prop Lowrie claimed the first before winger Halligan sealed victory with a contested try, adding his third goal for a personal tally of 10 points.

New Zealand introduced Junior Kiwis captain Henry Paul as a substitute for his senior international debut after being brought into the squad as a replacement for the injured Piva.

Scrum half Aaron Whittaker, substituted after 44 minutes, four days in advance of his Test debut.

THIRD TEST

Wigan's Andrew Farrell gave an extraordin- arily mature performance for a player making his debut as the youngest forward in British Test history as Great Britain completed the first home series whitewash of New Zealand for 42 years.

The Lions scored five tries to one in a con- vincing 29-10 victory in the third John Smith's Test at Headingley, Leeds, firmly establishing their ranking as number two side in the world and setting up the mouthwatering prospect of an autumn series with the current world champions Australia.

Teenager Farrell stole the individual spot- light as he took over the "youngest-ever" mantle from 1982 Test debutant packman Lee Crooks. At 18 years five months Farrell was more than a match for the Kiwis, his 6ft 4in frame providing the power for his rating as Britain's most penetrative forward.

He charged 50 metres on one occasion and was twice involved in the long distance raid which finished with him scoring Britain's last try.

Farrell's debut produced, arguably, Britain's youngest-ever back row, with 21-year-old St. Helens second row man Chris Joynt further improving on his fourth Test appearance and loose forward Phil Clarke, at 22, taking the John Smith's Man of the Match award for a show of pace and power on attack and defence.

Britain made the 15,000-plus crowd wait for an hour before unleashing the brand of ex- hilarating football which had been the hall- mark of the second Test success at Wigan.

After struggling to master the slippery conditions, three tries in a devastating 12- minute spell completed the ruination of a Kiwi tour squad that had arrived with such great expectations after giving Australia a closely-run series.

It followed a long siege of the home line which came to nothing as Britain defended in great style and ended with Jonathan Davies pulling off a lightning interception of Tony Kemp's pass. The Welshman held off all pur- suers over 90 metres for a spectacular touch- down which went close to snatching him the Man of the Match prize.

His candidature for the individual award was endorsed by four goals and a drop goal, plus his overall performance at full back in the first half and stand off after the interval.

Yet this was another impressive team per- formance where each member of the 17-man squad deserved praise, with the exception of St. Helens packman Sonny Nickle. The sub- stitute forward's late dismissal for an off-the- ball elbow blow on John Lomax spoiled Britain's otherwise highly commendable dis- ciplinary record over the three-match series.

Otherwise, the Kiwi whitewash was the sustained peak of Malcolm Reilly's seven-year reign as coach, a product of his club-style squad system and the resultant moulding of team spirit, so evident when injuries threat- ened to break up his gameplan.

Captain Garry Schofield was an early casualty with a rib injury and his stand off replacement Daryl Powell was unable to resume after the interval because of a damaged shoulder. The reshuffled side still found cohesion with some spectacular raids, most notably when Martin Offiah completed an 80- metre move instigated by Joynt.

Shaun Edwards provided the final pass and also the one that sent in prop forward Karl Fairbank for the opening try, confirming his overall authority in the series. He had seen off the vastly-experienced Kiwi skipper Gary Freeman in the first two Tests and now com- pletely overshadowed replacement scrum half Aaron Whittaker on his international debut.

Whittaker, formerly with Second Division Chorley Borough, was one of several contro- versial changes by coach Howie Tamati for the last match of the British leg of the tour, and these summed up the frustration and desper- ation in the New Zealand camp.

THIRD JOHN SMITH'S TEST

6 November   **Leeds**

GREAT BRITAIN 29		NEW ZEALAND 10
Jonathan Davies (Warrington)	1.	Dave Watson (Bradford N.)
John Devereux (Widnes)	2.	Frano Botica (Wigan)
Gary Connolly (Wigan)	3.	Kevin Iro (Leeds)
Paul Newlove (Bradford N.)	4.	Iva Ropati
Martin Offiah (Wigan)	5.	Jason Williams
Garry Schofield (Leeds), Capt.	6.	Tony Kemp (Castleford)
Shaun Edwards (Wigan)	7.	Aaron Whittaker
Kelvin Skerrett (Wigan)	8.	Se'e Solomona (Oldham)
Lee Jackson (Sheffield E.)	9.	Denvour Johnston
Karl Fairbank (Bradford N.)	10.	Brent Stuart
Andrew Farrell (Wigan)	11.	Stephen Kearney, Capt.
Chris Joynt (St. Helens)	12.	Quentin Pongia
Philip Clarke (Wigan)	13.	Jason Mackie
Daryl Powell (Sheffield E.)	14.	Richard Blackmore (Castleford)
Sonny Nickle (St. Helens)	15.	John Lomax
Alan Tait (Leeds)	16.	Whetu Taewa
Michael Jackson (Halifax)	17.	David Lomax

T: Fairbank, Clarke, Davies, Offiah, Farrell
G: Davies (4, 1dg)
Substitutions:
Powell for Schofield (11 min.)
Tait for Powell (Half-time)
Nickle for Fairbank (48 min.)
M. Jackson for Newlove (70 min.)
Referee: Greg McCallum (Australia)

T: Williams
G: Botica (3)
Substitutions:
Blackmore for Watson (48 min.)
J. Lomax for Solomona (48 min.)
Taewa for Ropati (70 min.)
D. Lomax for Mackie (70 min.)
Half-time: 12-4
Attendance: 15,139

Scorechart

Minute	Score	GB	NZ
10:	Fairbank (T)		
	Davies (G)	6	0
16:	Clarke (T)		
	Davies (G)	12	0
18:	Botica (P)	12	2
31:	Botica (P)	12	4
50:	Davies (P)	14	4
55:	Davies (DG)	15	4
60:	Davies (T)	19	4
69:	Offiah (T)		
	Davies (G)	25	4
72:	Farrell (T)	29	4
79:	Williams (T)		
	Botica (G)	29	10
	Scrums	12	7
	Penalties	6	8

*Kiwi second row man Stephen Kearney, promoted to Test
skipper for the first time.*

*Tony Kemp in action for Newcastle Knights, who finished ninth
in the 1993 Winfield Cup.*

DOWN UNDER

WINFIELD CUP
1993 Premiership Grand Final
Brisbane Broncos retained the Winfield Cup with a second successive final defeat of St. George. Although St. George improved on their 28–8 defeat the year before, they were still well beaten as Brisbane scored all the game's three tries in their 14–6 follow-up victory.

One consolation for the losers was that loose forward Brad Mackay won the Clive Churchill Medal as the Man of the Match.

Cause for all-round satisfaction was a Sydney Football Stadium record attendance of 42,239. The appearance of raunchy pop singer Tina Turner as guest and pre-match performer added to the day's entertainment.

Brisbane became the first side to win the final from fifth position, while St. George finished second.

It was the fourth successive final in which no British player was involved.

The victory completed a memorable first season at the ANZ Stadium for Brisbane, who drew a world-record average home crowd of 43,200. The next best-supported Winfield Cup club in 1993 were Canterbury-Bankstown with an average of 16,959.

Brisbane's crowds included a record for any "home" match in Australia, 58,593, ironically against St. George, who brought off a surprise 16–10 victory.

Hull full back Richard Gay making his sole appearance for St. George in the 1993 Winfield Cup.

Widnes threequarter John Devereux in the colours of Manly-Warringah, scoring two tries and two goals in 15 matches in the 1993 Winfield Cup.

WINFIELD CUP GRAND FINAL

26 September 1993   **Sydney Football Stadium**

BRISBANE BRONCOS 14   ST. GEORGE 6

Julian O'Neill	1.	Michael Potter, Capt.
Michael Hancock	2.	Ricky Walford
Steve Renouf	3.	Graeme Bradley
Chris Johns	4.	Mark Coyne
Willie Carne	5.	Ian Herron
Kevin Walters	6.	Tony Smith
Allan Langer, Capt.	7.	Noel Goldthorpe
Glenn Lazarus	8.	Tony Priddle
Kerrod Walters	9.	Wayne Collins
Mark Hohn	10.	Jason Stevens
Trevor Gillmeister	11.	David Barnhill
Alan Cann	12.	Scott Gourley
Terry Matterson	13.	Brad Mackay

T: Johns, Matterson, Carne   G: Herron 3
G: O'Neill
Substitutions: Substitutions:
Andrew Gee for Hohn   Jeff Hardy for Stevens
John Plath for Matterson   Gorden Tallis for Barnhill
Peter Ryan for Gee   Phil Blake for Smith
Coach: Wayne Bennett   Nathan Brown for Collins
Half-time: 10-2   Coach: Brian Smith
Referee: Greg McCallum   Clive Churchill Medal for Man of the
Scrums: 10-6   Match: Brad Mackay (St. George)
Penalties: 3-6   Attendance: 42,239

1993 WINFIELD CUP

	P.	W.	D.	L.	F.	A.	Pts
Canterbury-Bankstown	22	17	0	5	464	254	34
St. George	22	17	0	5	418	258	34
Canberra	22	16	1	5	587	272	33
Manly-Warringah	22	16	0	6	442	232	32
Brisbane Broncos	22	16	0	6	517	330	32
North Sydney	22	14	1	7	448	325	29
Illawarra	22	12	0	10	373	253	24
Eastern Suburbs	22	11	1	10	343	356	23
Newcastle	22	10	0	12	337	381	20
Cronulla-Sutherland	22	9	0	13	272	399	18
Parramatta	22	9	0	13	237	439	18
Penrith	22	7	0	15	314	428	14
Western Suburbs	22	7	0	15	319	475	14
South Sydney	22	6	0	16	319	560	12
Balmain	22	6	1	15	327	412	11*
Gold Coast	22	1	0	21	229	572	2

*Two points deducted for breaking the player replacement rule against Penrith.

WINFIELD CUP PLAY-OFF
Minor preliminary semi-final
Brisbane Broncos 36 v. Manly-Warringah 10
Major preliminary semi-final
St. George 31 v. Canberra 10
Minor semi-final
Brisbane Broncos 30 v. Canberra 12
Major semi-final
St. George 27 v. Canterbury-Bankstown 12
Preliminary final
Brisbane Broncos 23 v. Canterbury-Bankstown 16
Grand Final
Brisbane Broncos 14 v. St. George 6

• All matches played at the Sydney Football Stadium.

LEADING SCORERS
• Not including play-offs.

Tries
19 Noa Nadruku (Canberra)
Goals (inc. drop goals)
85 Daryl Halligan (North Sydney)
Points
180 Daryl Halligan (North Sydney)

BRITISH PLAYERS IN GRAND FINALS
British players who have appeared in the Sydney Grand Final are:
Dick Huddart (St. George) 1966 winners, 1 try
Dave Bolton (Balmain) 1966 losers; 1969 winners, 2 drop goals
Mervyn Hicks (Canterbury) 1967 losers
Ken Batty (St. George) 1971 losers
Malcolm Reilly (Manly) 1972 winners; 1973 winners
Tommy Bishop (Cronulla) 1973 losers
Bob Wear (Cronulla) 1973 losers
Cliff Watson (Cronulla) 1973 losers
Brian Lockwood (Canterbury) 1974 losers
Gary Stephens (Manly) 1976 winners
Steve Norton (Manly) 1976 winners
Phil Lowe (Manly) 1976 winners, 1 try
Kevin Ward (Manly) 1987 winners
Ellery Hanley (Balmain) 1988 losers
Andy Currier (Balmain) 1989 losers, 3 goals
Shaun Edwards (Balmain) 1989 losers, sub
Apart from Hicks, all the above also appeared in a Challenge Cup final at Wembley. In addition, Len Killeen, the South African winger who began his League career with St. Helens, also played at Wembley and got a Grand Final winners' medal with

Balmain in 1969 when he kicked two goals.
Australians who have achieved the big double since the Grand Final became mandatory in 1954 are: Chris Anderson, Harry Bath, Graham Eadie, Andrew Farrar, John Ferguson, Kerry Hemsley, Brett Kenny, John Muggleton, Michael O'Connor, Julian O'Neill, Peter Sterling and Paul Vautin.
There were a record four British players in the 1973 Grand Final. Reilly got a winners' medal with Manly, while Bishop, Watson and Wear were in the beaten Cronulla side.
Three British players — Stephens, Norton and Lowe — were also in the Manly side which won the final in 1976.
Ellery Hanley was the first player to appear in both major finals in the same year. In 1988 he led Wigan to success at Wembley and four months later was in Balmain's beaten Grand Final team.
Shaun Edwards is the only other British player to play in both finals in the same year. He was stand off when Wigan beat St. Helens at Wembley in 1989 and made a late substitute appearance for Balmain when they were beaten by Canberra at Sydney.
Julian O'Neill is the only Australian to have played in the Challenge Cup final at Wembley and the Grand Final in the same year. He made a substitute appearance for Widnes when they were beaten by Wigan in 1993 and was full back in the Brisbane Broncos side that beat St. George later that year.

BRITISH PLAYERS IN 1993 WINFIELD CUP
Five British players appeared in the 1993 Winfield Cup competition, but only Gary Connolly and John Devereux played more than a few matches.
Connolly made a big impression at Canterbury-Bankstown where he scored five tries in 15 appearances. During his spell in Australia, the centre was transferred from St. Helens to Wigan.
Devereux of Widnes also did well at Manly-Warringah, scoring two tries and two goals in 15 matches, including one substitute appearance.
Harvey Howard went to Eastern Suburbs in the middle of a dispute with Widnes and made four appearances, including one as a substitute.
Richard Gay of Hull joined St. George to gain experience and made only one senior appearance as substitute.
Martin Offiah played just 52 minutes for Eastern Suburbs before badly dislocating a shoulder, which ended the Wigan winger's summer spell in Australia.
Reported to have been on £2,000 a match for Easts, Offiah had himself paid the £11,000 insurance premium demanded by Wigan, who had handed a world record £440,000 transfer fee to Widnes over a year earlier.
The injury caused Offiah to miss Wigan's first seven matches of the new season and Great Britain's opening Test against New Zealand.

STATE OF ORIGIN

The State of Origin matches between New South Wales and Queensland began in 1980 and are now established as a major part of the Australian Rugby League scene.

Their introduction revived interest in the inter-state matches which had been dominated by New South Wales, who had won the last 15 matches by mainly wide margins.

Under the old system, players appeared for the state in which they were playing club rugby at the time, and this gave a big advantage to New South Wales because many of Queensland's best players were with Sydney clubs.

But in State of Origin matches players appear for the state in which they first played senior rugby, and this has resulted in the matches becoming more fiercely and evenly fought before increased attendances.

NEW SOUTH WALES v. QUEENSLAND RESULTS State of Origin only. *Not part of 1987 series.

Date	Winner	Score	Venue	Attendance
8 July 1980	Queensland	20-10	Brisbane	31,000
28 July 1981	Queensland	22-15	Brisbane	25,613
1 June 1982	New South Wales	20-16	Brisbane	27,326
8 June 1982	Queensland	11-7	Brisbane	19,435
22 June 1982	Queensland	10-5	Sydney	20,242
7 June 1983	Queensland	24-12	Brisbane	29,412
21 June 1983	New South Wales	10-6	Sydney	21,620
28 June 1983	Queensland	43-22	Brisbane	26,084
29 May 1984	Queensland	29-12	Brisbane	33,662
19 June 1984	Queensland	14-2	Sydney	29,088
17 July 1984	New South Wales	22-12	Brisbane	16,599
28 May 1985	New South Wales	18-2	Brisbane	33,011
11 June 1985	New South Wales	21-14	Sydney	39,068
23 July 1985	Queensland	20-6	Brisbane	18,825
27 May 1986	New South Wales	22-16	Brisbane	33,000
10 June 1986	New South Wales	24-20	Sydney	40,707
1 July 1986	New South Wales	18-16	Brisbane	21,097
2 June 1987	New South Wales	20-16	Brisbane	33,411
16 June 1987	Queensland	12-6	Sydney	42,048
15 July 1987	Queensland	10-8	Brisbane	33,000
*6 Aug. 1987	New South Wales	30-18	California	12,349
17 May 1988	Queensland	26-18	Sydney	26,441
31 May 1988	Queensland	16-6	Brisbane	31,817
21 June 1988	Queensland	38-22	Sydney	16,910
23 May 1989	Queensland	36-6	Brisbane	33,000
14 June 1989	Queensland	16-12	Sydney	40,000
28 June 1989	Queensland	36-16	Brisbane	33,000
9 May 1990	New South Wales	8-0	Sydney	41,235
30 May 1990	New South Wales	12-6	Melbourne	25,800
13 June 1990	Queensland	14-10	Brisbane	31,000
8 May 1991	Queensland	6-4	Brisbane	31,500
29 May 1991	New South Wales	14-12	Sydney	41,520
12 June 1991	Queensland	14-12	Brisbane	32,500
6 May 1992	New South Wales	14-6	Sydney	40,039
20 May 1992	Queensland	5-4	Brisbane	32,000
3 June 1992	New South Wales	16-4	Sydney	41,878
3 May 1993	New South Wales	14-10	Brisbane	33,000
17 May 1993	New South Wales	16-12	Sydney	41,895
31 May 1993	Queensland	24-12	Brisbane	31,500

SUMMARY New South Wales won 17; Queensland won 22. Since it became a three-match series in 1982, Queensland have won seven series to New South Wales's five.

ENGLISH REFEREES English referees who have taken charge of State of Origin matches are: Billy Thompson on 8 July 1980 and Robin Whitfield on 28 June 1983.

1993 STATE OF ORIGIN MATCHES *Denotes captain

3 May
Brisbane
New South Wales 14
Brasher (Balmain)
Wishart (Illawarra) 1t, 3g
Fittler (Penrith)
McGregor (Illawarra)
Ettingshausen (Cronulla)
*Daley (Canberra)
Stuart (Canberra) 1t
Lazarus (Brisbane B.)
Elias (Balmain)
Roberts (Manly)
Sironen (Balmain)
Harragon (Newcastle)
B. Mackay (St. George)

Subs: Fairleigh (Norths)
Salvatori (Easts)

17 May
Sydney
New South Wales 16
Brasher (Balmain)
Wishart (Illawarra) 1t, 2g
Fittler (Penrith)
McGregor (Illawarra)
Ettingshausen (Cronulla)
*Daley (Canberra) 1t
Stuart (Canberra)
Lazarus (Brisbane B.)
McCormack (Newcastle)
Roberts (Manly)
Sironen (Balmain)
Harragon (Newcastle)
B. Mackay (St. George) 1t

Subs: Fairleigh (Norths)
Croker (Canberra)
Taylor (Wests)
Gillespie (Wests)

31 May
Brisbane
New South Wales 12
Brasher (Balmain)
Wishart (Illawarra) 2g
Fittler (Penrith)
Ettingshausen (Cronulla) 1t
G. Mackay (Penrith)
*Daley (Canberra)
Stuart (Canberra)
Lazarus (Brisbane B.)
Elias (Balmain)
Fairleigh (Norths)
Sironen (Balmain)
Harragon (Newcastle) 1t
B. Mackay (St. George)

Subs: Gourley (St. George)
Gillespie (Wests)
Hill (Wests)
Taylor (Wests)

Queensland 10
Belcher (Canberra)
Hancock (Brisbane B.)
*Meninga (Canberra) 1g
Renouf (Brisbane B.)
Carne (Brisbane B.) 1t
Kevin Walters (Brisbane B.)
Langer (Brisbane B.)
S. Jackson (Gold Coast)
S. Walters (Canberra)
Bella (Canterbury)
Larson (Norths)
Lindner (Illawarra) 1t
Moore (Norths)

Subs: Shearer (Gold Coast)
M. Coyne (St. George)
Hohn (Brisbane B.)
Gee (Brisbane B.)

Referee: Greg McCallum
Man of the Match: Stuart

Queensland 12
Shearer (Gold Coast) 1g
Brunker (Newcastle) 1g
*Meninga (Canberra) 1t
M. Coyne (St. George)
Carne (Brisbane B.)
Kevin Walters (Brisbane B.) 1t
Langer (Brisbane B.)
Bella (Canterbury)
S. Walters (Canberra)
Hohn (Brisbane B.)
Gillmeister (Brisbane B.)
Larson (Norths)
Lindner (Illawarra)

Subs: Moore (Norths)
O'Neill (Brisbane B.)
D. Smith (Canterbury)
S. Jackson (Gold Coast)

Referee: Eddie Ward
Man of the Match: Brasher

Queensland 24
Shearer (Gold Coast)
Dallas (Canterbury)
*Meninga (Canberra) 2g
M. Coyne (St. George)
Carne (Brisbane B.) 2t
O'Neill (Brisbane B.) 2g
Langer (Brisbane B.)
Hohn (Brisbane B.)
S. Walters (Canberra) 1t
Bella (Canterbury)
Gillmeister (Brisbane B.)
Larson (Norths)
Lindner (Illawarra) 1t

Subs: Kevin Walters (Brisbane B.)
S. Jackson (Gold Coast)
Moore (Norths)
D. Smith (Canterbury)

Referee: Greg McCallum
Man of the Match: Shearer

NEW SOUTH WALES v. QUEENSLAND RECORDS
State of Origin only.

NEW SOUTH WALES
Highest score: 30-18 at California, 6 August 1987
Widest margin: 18-2 at Brisbane, 28 May 1985
Most full appearances: 19 by Michael O'Connor (St. George, Manly)
Most tries in a match: 3 by Chris Anderson (Canterbury), 28 June 1983
Most goals in a match: No player has kicked more than five
Most points in a match: 18 (2t,5g) Michael O'Connor (Manly), 28 May 1985
Biggest home attendance: 42,048, 16 June 1987

QUEENSLAND

Highest score:	43-22 at Brisbane, 28 June 1983
Widest margin:	36-6 at Brisbane, 23 May 1989
Most full appearances:	31 by Wally Lewis (Fortitude Valley, Wynnum Manly, Brisbane Broncos, Gold Coast)
Most tries in a match:	3 by Kerry Boustead (Manly), 29 May 1984
Most goals in a match:	7 by Mal Meninga (Souths, B), 8 July 1980
Most points in a match:	16 (2t,4g) by Mal Meninga (Canberra), 23 May 1989 and Dale Shearer (Manly), 28 June 1989
Biggest home attendance:	33,662, 29 May 1984

Coaches:

New South Wales:	Ted Glossop (1980, 1981, 1983); Frank Stanton (1982, 1984); Terry Fearnley (1985); Ron Willey (1986, 1987); John Peard (1988); Jack Gibson (1989, 1990); Tim Sheens (1991); Phil Gould (1992, 1993)
Queensland:	John McDonald (1980); Arthur Beetson (1981, 1982, 1983, 1984, 1989, 1990); Des Morris (1985); Wayne Bennett (1986, 1987, 1988); Graham Lowe (1991, 1992); Wally Lewis (1993)

NEW SOUTH WALES REGISTER

The following is a register of players who have appeared for New South Wales in the State of Origin series plus the match against Queensland in the United States of America, up to and including 1993. + indicates number of matches played as a substitute. B-Brisbane, S-Sydney.

ALEXANDER, Greg (4+2) Penrith
ANDERSON, Chris (4) Canterbury
AYLIFFE, Royce (1+2) Easts, S

BLAKE, Phil (+1) Souths, S
BOWDEN, Steve (1) Newtown
BOYD, Les (3) Manly
BOYLE, David (2+2) Souths, S
BRASHER, Tim (3+1) Balmain
BRENTNALL, Greg (4) Canterbury
BROOKS, David (1) Balmain
BROWN, Ray (1+2) Manly
BUGDEN, Geoff (2) Parramatta

CARTER, Steve (+1) Penrith
CARTWRIGHT, John (5+3) Penrith
CLEAL, Noel (11+1) Manly
CLYDE, Bradley (10) Canberra
CONLON, Ross (3) Canterbury
COOPER, Bob (1) Wests, S
COVENEY, John (2) Canterbury
CROKER, Jason (+1) Canberra
CRONIN, Mick (6) Parramatta

DALEY, Laurie (11) Canberra
DALEY, Phil (3) Manly
DAVIDSON, Les (5) Souths, S
DOCKING, Jonathan (2) Cronulla
DOWLING, Gary (+1) Parramatta
DUKE, Phillip (1) Moree
DUNN, Paul (2+1) Canterbury

EADIE, Graham (1) Manly
EDGE, Steve (1) Parramatta
ELIAS, Ben (16) Balmain
ELLA, Steve (3+4) Parramatta
ETTINGSHAUSEN, Andrew (18+1) Cronulla

FAHEY, Terry (2) Easts, S
FAIRLEIGH, David (1+3) Norths, S
FARRAR, Andrew (5+2) Canterbury
FENECH, Mario (2) Souths, S
FERGUSON, John (8) Easts, S 3; Canberra 5

FIELD, Paul (2) Cootamundra
FITTLER, Brad (7+2) Penrith
FLORIMO, Greg (+1) Norths, S
FOLKES, Steve (8+1) Canterbury

GERARD, Geoff (2) Manly
GEYER, Mark (3) Penrith
GILLESPIE, David (5+9) Canterbury 3+3; Wests 2+6
GOURLEY, Scott (+1) St. George
GROTHE, Eric (9) Parramatta
GURR, Marty (2) Easts, S

HAMBLY, Gary (1) Souths, S
HANSON, Steve (1) Norths, S
HARRAGON, Paul (6) Newcastle
HASLER, Des (6+6) Manly
HASTINGS, Kevin (+1) Easts, S
HETHERINGTON, Brian (1+1) Illawarra
HILDITCH, Ron (1) Parramatta
HILL, Terry (+1) Wests, S
HUNT, Neil (2) Parramatta

IZZARD, Brad (2+2) Penrith

JACK, Garry (17) Balmain
JARVIS, Pat (6+2) St. George 4+2; Canterbury 2
JENSEN, Barry (1) Newtown
JOHNS, Chris (7) Brisbane Broncos
JOHNSTON, Brian (8) St. George
JOHNSTON, Lindsay (2) Norths, S
JURD, Stan (1+1) Parramatta

KELLY, Peter (2) Penrith
KENNY, Brett (16+1) Parramatta
KRILICH, Max (5) Manly

LAMB, Terry (4+3) Canterbury 3+3; Wests, S 1
LANGMACK, Paul (3+1) Canterbury
LAZARUS, Glenn (7+4) Canberra 1+4; Brisbane Broncos 6
LEIS, Jim (1) Wests, S
LYONS, Cliff (6) Manly
LYONS, Graham (2+1) Souths, S

341

McCORMACK, Robbie (1+1) Newcastle
McGAW, Mark (10+3) Cronulla
McGREGOR, Paul (5) Illawarra
McGUIRE, Bruce (5) Balmain
MACKAY, Brad (7+4) St. George
MACKAY, Graham (3) Penrith
McKINNON, Don (1) Norths, S
MARTIN, Steve (+1) Manly
MATTERSON, Terry, (+1) Brisbane Broncos
MELROSE, Tony (1) Souths, S
MERLO, Paul (1) Wests, S
MILLER, Gavin (5) Cronulla
MORRIS, Steve (2) St. George
MORTIMER, Chris (8+1) Canterbury 7; Penrith 1+1
MORTIMER, Steve (8) Canterbury
MUGGLETON, John (2) Parramatta

NISZCZOT, Ziggy (2) Souths, S

O'CONNOR, Michael (19) St. George 6; Manly 13

PEARCE, Wayne (15) Balmain
POTTER, Michael (+1) Canterbury
PRICE, Ray (8) Parramatta

RAMPLING, Tony (2+1) Souths, S
RAUDONIKIS, Tom (1) Newtown
ROACH, Steve (17) Balmain

ROBERTS, Ian (7) Manly
ROGERS, Steve (4) Cronulla

SALVATORI, Craig (+5) Easts, S
SARGENT, Mark (+1) Newcastle
SIGSWORTH, Phil (3) Newtown 2; Manly 1
SIMMONS, Royce (10) Penrith
SIMON, John (1) Illawarra
SIRONEN, Paul (8+3) Balmain
STERLING, Peter (13) Parramatta
STONE, Robert (+1) St. George
STUART, Ricky (11) Canberra

TAYLOR, Jason (+2) Wests, S
THOMPSON, Alan (5+1) Manly
TOOVEY, Geoff (+1) Manly
TREWHELLA, David (1+1) Easts, S
TUNKS, Peter (7+1), Souths 1; Canterbury 6+1

WALFORD, Ricky (1) St. George
WALSH, Chris (1) St. George
WILSON, Alan (+2) Cronulla
WISHART, Rod (11) Illawarra
WRIGHT, Rex (1) N. Newcastle
WYNN, Graeme (1) St. George
WYNN, Peter (4) Parramatta

YOUNG, Craig (4+1) St. George

QUEENSLAND REGISTER

The following is a register of players who have appeared for Queensland in the State of Origin series plus the match against New South Wales in the United States of America, up to and including 1993. + indicates number of matches played as a substitute. B-Brisbane, S-Sydney.

ALLEN, Gavin (2+3) Brisbane Broncos
ASTILL, Bruce (+1) Souths, B

BACKER, Brad (3) Easts, B
BACKO, Sam (7) Canberra 3; Brisbane Broncos 4
BEETSON, Arthur (1) Parramatta
BELCHER, Gary (16) Canberra
BELLA, Martin (20) Norths, S 8; Manly 9;
    Canterbury 3
BOUSTEAD, Kerry (6) Easts, S 3; Manly 3
BRENNAN, Mitch (4) Souths, S 3; Redcliffe 1
BROHMAN, Darryl (2) Penrith
BROWN, Dave (9+1) Manly 5+1; Easts, S 4
BRUNKER, Adrian (3) Newcastle
BUTLER, Terry (1) Wynnum Manly

CARNE, Willie (8) Brisbane Broncos
CARR, Norm (2) Wests, B
CLOSE, Chris (9) Manly 7; Redcliffe 2
CONESCU, Greg (20) Norths, B 4; Redcliffe 10;
    Gladstone Brothers 3; Brisbane Broncos 3
COYNE, Gary (2+9) Canberra
COYNE, Mark (4+4) St. George
CURRIE, Tony (8+3) Wests, B +1; Redcliffe +1;
    Canterbury 5+1; Brisbane Broncos 3

DALLAS, Brett (1) Canterbury
DOWLING, Greg (11) Wynnum Manly 7; Norths, B 4
DOWLING, John (3) St. George

FRENCH, Brett (1+3) Wynnum Manly; Norths, S +3
FRENCH, Ian (3+6) Wynnum Manly 2+3;
    Norths, S 1+3

FULLERTON-SMITH, Wally (12) Redcliffe 8;
    St. George 4

GEE, Andrew (3+2) Brisbane Broncos
GILLMEISTER, Trevor (8+6) Easts, S 5+5;
    Brisbane Broncos 3+1

HAGAN, Michael (2+3) Newcastle
HANCOCK, Michael (10) Brisbane Broncos
HANCOCK, Rohan (5) Easts, B 1; Toowoomba
    Wattles 4
HAUFF, Paul (3) Brisbane Broncos
HENRICK, Ross (2) Norths, B 1; Fortitude Valley 1
HEUGH, Cavill (2+1) Easts, B
HOHN, Mark (2+1) Brisbane Broncos

JACKSON, Peter (14+2) Canberra 7; Souths, B +1;
    Brisbane Broncos 1+1; Norths, S 6
JACKSON, Steve (5+4) Wests, S 3+1; Gold Coast 2+3
JONES, Gavin (3) Norths, S

KELLAWAY, Bob (+1) Souths, B
KHAN, Paul (4) Easts, B 3; Cronulla 1
KILROY, Joe (2) Brisbane Broncos
KISS, Les (4) Norths, S

LANG, John (1) Easts, S
LANGER, Allan (21) Ipswich 4; Brisbane Broncos 17
LARSON, Gary (9) Norths, S
LEWIS, Wally (31) Wynnum Manly 13;
    Fortitude Valley 8; Brisbane Broncos 7;
    Gold Coast 3
LINDNER, Bob (22+3) Souths, B 1; Wynnum
    Manly 5; Parramatta 6; Gold Coast 2; Wests, S 5+1;
    Illawarra 3

McCABE, Paul (5) Easts, S 1; Manly 4
McINDOE, Alan (9) Illawarra 3; Penrith 6
McLEAN, Mike (4+1) Newcastle 3; Gold Coast 1+1
MENINGA, Mal (29) Souths, B 13; Canberra 16
MILES, Gene (19) Wynnum Manly 14;
  Brisbane Broncos 5
MOORE, Billy (3+2) Norths, S
MORRIS, Rod (4) Balmain 2; Wynnum Manly 2
MURRAY, Mark (14) Fortitude Valley 3; Redcliffe 11

NIEBLING, Bryan (9) Fortitude Valley 3; Redcliffe 6

OLIPHANT, Greg (1) Balmain
O'NEILL, Julian (1+1) Brisbane Broncos

PHELAN, Chris (2) Souths, B 1; Parramatta 1

QUINN, Graham (1) St. George

REDDY, Rod (1) St. George
RENOUF, Steve (1+2) Brisbane Broncos
RIBOT, John (8) Manly 5; Redcliffe 3

SCOTT, Colin (16+1) Wynnum Manly 15+1;
  Easts, B 1
SHEARER, Dale (19+5) Manly 11+2;
  Brisbane Broncos 3+2; Gold Coast 5+1
SMITH, Allan (1) Norths, S
SMITH, Darren (+4) Canterbury
SMITH, Gary (+1) Brothers
STACEY, Steve (2) Easts, B
STAINS, Danny (4) Cronulla

TESSMAN, Brad (4+1) Souths, B 3; Easts, S 1+1
TRONC, Scott (+1) Wests, S

VAUTIN, Paul (20+1) Manly 19+1; Easts, S 1

WALKER, Bruce (1) Manly
WALTERS, Kerrod (5) Brisbane Broncos
WALTERS, Kevin (3+8) Canberra +1;
  Brisbane Broncos 3+7
WALTERS, Steve (10) Canberra

NEW ZEALAND v AUSTRALIA TESTS IN 1993

Date		Venue	Attendance
20 June	**NEW ZEALAND 14 AUSTRALIA 14**	Auckland	22,994

New Zealand:
Morvin Edwards; Sean Hoppe (2t), Jarrod McCracken, Dave Watson, Daryl Halligan (3g); Tea Ropati, Gary Freeman (Capt); Se'e Solomona, Duane Mann, Brent Todd, Gary Mercer, Quentin Pongia, Tawera Nikau. Subs: Tony Kemp, Brendon Tuuta, Jason Donnelly, John Lomax (all played).
Australia:
Dale Shearer (1t,2g); Willie Carne, Laurie Daley (Capt) (2dg), Brad Fittler, Michael Hancock; Kevin Walters, Allan Langer; Glenn Lazarus, Steve Walters (1t), Paul Harragon, Paul Sironen, Bob Lindner, Bradley Clyde. Subs: Ian Roberts, Brad Mackay, Steve Renouf (all played); Andrew Ettingshausen (not used).
Referee: Russell Smith (England).

25 June	**NEW ZEALAND 8 AUSTRALIA 16**	Palmerston North 19,000

New Zealand:
Morvin Edwards; Sean Hoppe, Jarrod McCracken, Dave Watson, Daryl Halligan (2g); Tony Kemp, Gary Freeman (Capt) (1t); Se'e Solomona, Duane Mann, Brent Todd, Gavin Hill, Gary Mercer, Tawera Nikau. Subs: Tea Ropati, Brendon Tuuta, Jason Donnelly, John Lomax (all played).
Australia:
Dale Shearer (2g); Michael Hancock (1t), Brad Fittler, Mal Meninga (Capt), Willie Carne (1t); Laurie Daley, Allan Langer; Glenn Lazarus, Steve Walters, Paul Harragon, Paul Sironen, Bob Lindner, Bradley Clyde (1t). Subs: Brad Mackay, Andrew Ettingshausen, David Gillespie, Kevin Walters (all played).
Referee: Russell Smith (England).

30 June   **AUSTRALIA 16 NEW ZEALAND 4**   Brisbane   31,000

Australia:
Dale Shearer (2g); Willie Carne, Mal Meninga (Capt) (1t), Brad
Fittler (1t), Michael Hancock (1t); Laurie Daley, Allan Langer;
Glenn Lazarus, Steve Walters, Paul Harragon, Paul Sironen, Bob
Lindner, Bradley Clyde. Subs: Andrew Ettingshausen, Kevin
Walters, David Gillespie, Ian Roberts (all played).

New Zealand:
Morvin Edwards; Sean Hoppe, Jarrod McCracken, Dave Watson,
Jason Donnelly; Tony Kemp, Gary Freeman (Capt); Brent Todd,
Duane Mann, Gavin Hill (2g), Brendon Tuuta, Gary Mercer,
Tawera Nikau. Subs: Tea Ropati, John Lomax, Daryl Halligan,
Stephen Kearney (all played).
Referee: Russell Smith (England).

Great Britain second row man Denis Betts comes to grips with
New Zealand winger Daryl Halligan in the first John Smith's
Test at Wembley in October 1993.

26 Jun. 1984	L	6-18	Brisbane	26,534	27 Oct. 1990	W	19-12	Wembley	54,569
7 Jul. 1984	L	7-20	Sydney	18,756	10 Nov. 1990	L	10-14	Man U. FC	46,615
25 Oct. 1986	L	16-38	Man U. FC	50,583	* 24 Nov. 1990	L	0-14	Elland Rd,	
8 Nov. 1986	L	4-34	Elland Rd,					Leeds	32,500
			Leeds	30,808	12 Jun. 1992	L	6-22	Sydney	40,141
* 22 Nov. 1986	L	15-24	Wigan	20,169	26 Jun. 1992	W	33-10	Melbourne	30,257
11 Jun. 1988	L	6-17	Sydney	24,202	* 3 Jul. 1992	L	10-16	Brisbane	32,313
28 Jun. 1988	L	14-34	Brisbane	27,103	* Also World Cup match.				
* 9 Jul. 1988	W	26-12	Sydney	15,994					

	Played	Won	Drawn	Lost	Tries	Goals	Dr	Pts for
Great Britain	108	52	4	52	262	270	7	1362
Australia	108	52	4	52	309	333	6	1653

GREAT BRITAIN-AUSTRALIA TEST MATCH RECORDS

Britain

Highest score: 40-17 Third Test at Sydney, 19 July 1958

Widest margin win: As above and
33-10 Second Test at Melbourne, 26 June 1992

Most tries in a match: 4 by Jim Leytham (Wigan) Second Test at Brisbane, 2 July 1910

Most goals in a match: 10 by Lewis Jones (Leeds) Second Test at Brisbane, 3 July 1954

Most points in a match: 20 by Lewis Jones (as above)
20 (2t, 7g) by Roger Millward (Hull K.R.) Second Test at Sydney, 20 June 1970

Biggest attendance: 54,569 First Test at Wembley, London, 27 October 1990

● For the World Cup final at Wembley on 24 October 1992, there was an attendance of 73,631

Australia

Highest score: 50-12 Second Test at Swinton, 9 Nov 1963 (Also widest margin win)

Most tries in a match: 3 by Jimmy Devereux, First Test at QPR, London, 12 December 1908
3 by Reg Gasnier, First Test at Swinton, 17 October 1959
3 by Reg Gasnier, First Test at Wembley, 16 October 1963
3 by Ken Irvine, Second Test at Swinton, 9 November 1963
3 by Ken Irvine, Third Test at Sydney, 23 July 1966
3 by Gene Miles, First Test at Old Trafford, Manchester, 25 October 1986
3 by Michael O'Connor, First Test at Old Trafford, Manchester, 25 October 1986

Most goals in a match: 10 by Mick Cronin, First Test at Brisbane, 16 June 1979

Most points in a match: 22 (3t, 5g) by Michael O'Connor, First Test at Old Trafford, Manchester, 25 October 1986

Biggest attendance: 70,204 First Test at Sydney, 6 June 1932

● In a World Cup match at Perpignan, France, on 29 October 1972, Bobby Fulton scored 3 tries

GREAT BRITAIN v. NEW ZEALAND

25 Jan. 1908	W	14-6	Leeds	8,182
8 Feb. 1908	L	6-18	Chelsea	14,000
15 Feb. 1908	L	5-8	Cheltenham	4,000
30 Jul. 1910	W	52-20	Auckland	16,000
1 Aug. 1914	W	16-13	Auckland	15,000
31 Jul. 1920	W	31-7	Auckland	34,000
7 Aug. 1920	W	19-3	Christchurch	10,000
14 Aug. 1920	W	11-10	Wellington	4,000
2 Aug. 1924	L	8-16	Auckland	22,000
6 Aug. 1924	L	11-13	Wellington	6,000
9 Aug. 1924	W	31-18	Dunedin	14,000
2 Oct. 1926	W	28-20	Wigan	14,500
13 Nov. 1926	W	21-11	Hull	7,000
15 Jan. 1927	W	32-17	Leeds	6,000
4 Aug. 1928	L	13-17	Auckland	28,000
18 Aug. 1928	W	13-5	Dunedin	12,000
25 Aug. 1928	W	6-5	Christchurch	21,000
30 Jul. 1932	W	24-9	Auckland	25,000
13 Aug. 1932	W	25-14	Christchurch	5,000
20 Aug. 1932	W	20-18	Auckland	6,500
8 Aug. 1936	W	10-8	Auckland	25,000
15 Aug. 1936	W	23-11	Auckland	17,000
10 Aug. 1946	L	8-13	Auckland	10,000
4 Oct. 1947	W	11-10	Leeds	28,445
8 Nov. 1947	L	7-10	Swinton	29,031
20 Dec. 1947	W	25-9	Bradford	42,680
29 Jul. 1950	L	10-16	Christchurch	10,000
12 Aug. 1950	L	13-20	Auckland	20,000
6 Oct. 1951	W	21-15	Bradford	37,475
10 Nov. 1951	W	20-19	Swinton	29,938
15 Dec. 1951	W	16-12	Leeds	18,649
24 Jul. 1954	W	27-7	Auckland	22,097
31 Jul. 1954	L	14-20	Greymouth	4,240
14 Aug. 1954	W	12-6	Auckland	6,186
8 Oct. 1955	W	25-6	Swinton	21,937
12 Nov. 1955	W	27-12	Bradford	24,443
17 Dec. 1955	L	13-28	Leeds	10,438
26 Jul. 1958	L	10-15	Auckland	25,000
9 Aug. 1958	W	32-15	Auckland	25,000
30 Sep. 1961	L	11-29	Leeds	16,540
21 Oct. 1961	W	23-10	Bradford	19,980
4 Nov. 1961	W	35-19	Swinton	22,536
28 Jul. 1962	L	0-19	Auckland	14,976
11 Aug. 1962	L	8-27	Auckland	16,411
25 Sep. 1965	W	7-2	Swinton	8,541
23 Oct. 1965	W	15-9	Bradford	15,740
6 Nov. 1965	D	9-9	Wigan	7,919
6 Aug. 1966	W	25-8	Auckland	14,494
20 Aug. 1966	W	22-14	Auckland	10,657
11 Jul. 1970	W	19-15	Auckland	15,948
19 Jul. 1970	W	23-9	Christchurch	8,600
25 Jul. 1970	W	33-16	Auckland	13,137
25 Sep. 1971	L	13-18	Salford	3,764
16 Oct. 1971	L	14-17	Castleford	4,108
6 Nov. 1971	W	12-3	Leeds	5,479
27 Jul. 1974	L	8-13	Auckland	10,466
4 Aug. 1974	W	17-8	Christchurch	6,316
10 Aug. 1974	W	20-0	Auckland	11,574
21 Jul. 1979	W	16-8	Auckland	9,000
5 Aug. 1979	W	22-7	Christchurch	8,500
11 Aug. 1979	L	11-18	Auckland	7,000
18 Oct. 1980	D	14-14	Wigan	7,031
2 Nov. 1980	L	8-12	Bradford	10,946
15 Nov. 1980	W	10-2	Leeds	8,210
14 Jul. 1984	L	0-12	Auckland	10,238
22 Jul. 1984	L	12-28	Christchurch	3,824
28 Jul. 1984	L	16-32	Auckland	7,967
19 Oct. 1985	L	22-24	Leeds	12,591
2 Nov. 1985	W	25-8	Wigan	15,506
* 9 Nov. 1985	D	6-6	Elland Rd, Leeds	22,209
* 17 Jul. 1988	L	10-12	Christchurch	8,525
21 Oct. 1989	L	16-24	Man U. FC	18,273
28 Oct. 1989	W	26-6	Elland Rd, Leeds	13,073
* 11 Nov. 1989	W	10-6	Wigan	20,346
24 Jun. 1990	W	11-10	Palmerston N.	8,073
8 Jul. 1990	W	16-14	Auckland	7,843
* 15 Jul. 1990	L	18-21	Christchurch	3,133
12 Jul. 1992	L	14-15	Palmerston N.	11,548
19 Jul. 1992	W	19-16	Auckland	10,223
16 Oct. 1993	W	17-0	Wembley	36,131
30 Oct. 1993	W	29-12	Wigan	16,502
6 Nov. 1993	W	29-10	Leeds	15,139

* Also World Cup match.

	Played	Won	Drawn	Lost	Tries	Goals	Dr	Pts for
Great Britain	82	51	3	28	291	236	8	1401
New Zealand	82	28	3	51	185	232	2	1062

GREAT BRITAIN-NEW ZEALAND TEST MATCH RECORDS

Britain

Highest score:	52-20 First Test at Auckland, 30 July 1910 (Also widest margin win)
Most tries in a match:	4 by Billy Boston (Wigan) First Test at Auckland, 24 July 1954
	4 by Garry Schofield (Hull) Second Test at Wigan, 2 November 1985
Most goals in a match:	7 by Eric Fraser (Warrington) Second Test at Auckland, 9 August 1958
	7 by Neil Fox (Wakefield T.) Third Test at Swinton, 4 November 1961
Most points in a match:	16 (4t) by Garry Schofield (Hull) Second Test at Wigan, 2 November 1985
Biggest attendance:	42,680 Third Test at Bradford, 20 December 1947

● In a World Cup match at Pau, France, on 4 November 1972, Britain won 53-19 with John Holmes (Leeds) scoring 26 points from 10 goals and two tries.
In a World Cup match at Sydney on 8 June 1968, Bev Risman scored 7 goals.

New Zealand

Highest score:	32-16 Third Test at Auckland, 28 July 1984
Widest margin win:	19-0 First Test at Auckland, 28 July 1962
	27-8 Second Test at Auckland, 11 August 1962

No player has scored three tries or more in a Test.

Most goals and points:	7g-14pts by Des White, Second Test at Greymouth, 31 July 1954
	Jack Fagan, First Test at Headingley, 30 September 1961
	Ernie Wiggs, Second Test at Auckland, 20 August 1966
Biggest attendance:	34,000 First Test at Auckland, 31 July 1920

● In a World Cup match at Sydney, Australia, on 25 June 1957, Bill Sorensen also scored 7 goals, 14 points.

Great Britain prop Karl Harrison on the defensive in the first John Smith's Test against New Zealand at Wembley in October 1993.

GREAT BRITAIN v. FRANCE
● **Results since France were given Test match status.**

26 Jan. 1957	W	45-12	Leeds	20,221
3 Mar. 1957	D	19-19	Toulouse	16,000
10 Apr. 1957	W	29-14	St. Helens	23,250
3 Nov. 1957	W	25-14	Toulouse	15,000
23 Nov. 1957	W	44-15	Wigan	19,152
2 Mar. 1958	W	23-9	Grenoble	20,000
14 Mar. 1959	W	50-15	Leeds	22,000
5 Apr. 1959	L	15-24	Grenoble	8,500
6 Mar. 1960	L	18-20	Toulouse	15,308
26 Mar. 1960	D	17-17	St. Helens	14,000
11 Dec. 1960	W	21-10	Bordeaux	8,000
28 Jan. 1961	W	27-8	St. Helens	18,000
17 Feb. 1962	L	15-20	Wigan	17,277
11 Mar. 1962	L	13-23	Perpignan	14,000
2 Dec. 1962	L	12-17	Perpignan	5,000
3 Apr. 1963	W	42-4	Wigan	19,487
8 Mar. 1964	W	11-5	Perpignan	4,326
18 Mar. 1964	W	39-0	Leigh	4,750
6 Dec. 1964	L	8-18	Perpignan	15,000
23 Jan. 1965	W	17-7	Swinton	9,959
16 Jan. 1966	L	13-18	Perpignan	6,000
5 Mar. 1966	L	4-8	Wigan	14,004
22 Jan. 1967	W	16-13	Carcassonne	10,650
4 Mar. 1967	L	13-23	Wigan	7,448
11 Feb. 1968	W	22-13	Paris	8,000
2 Mar. 1968	W	19-8	Bradford	14,196
30 Nov. 1968	W	34-10	St. Helens	6,080
2 Feb. 1969	L	9-13	Toulouse	10,000
7 Feb. 1971	L	8-16	Toulouse	14,960
17 Mar. 1971	W	24-2	St. Helens	7,783
6 Feb. 1972	W	10-9	Toulouse	11,508
12 Mar. 1972	W	45-10	Bradford	7,313
20 Jan. 1974	W	24-5	Grenoble	5,500
17 Feb. 1974	W	29-0	Wigan	10,105
6 Dec. 1981	W	37-0	Hull	13,173
20 Dec. 1981	L	2-19	Marseilles	6,500
20 Feb. 1983	W	20-5	Carcassonne	3,826
6 Mar. 1983	W	17-5	Hull	6,055
29 Jan. 1984	W	12-0	Avignon	4,000
17 Feb. 1984	W	10-0	Leeds	7,646
1 Mar. 1985	W	50-4	Leeds	6,491
17 Mar. 1985	L	16-24	Perpignan	5,000
* 16 Feb. 1986	D	10-10	Avignon	4,000
1 Mar. 1986	W	24-10	Wigan	8,112
* 24 Jan. 1987	W	52-4	Leeds	6,567
8 Feb. 1987	W	20-10	Carcassonne	2,000
24 Jan. 1988	W	28-14	Avignon	6,500
6 Feb. 1988	W	30-12	Leeds	7,007
21 Jan. 1989	W	26-10	Wigan	8,266
5 Feb. 1989	W	30-8	Avignon	6,500
18 Mar. 1990	W	8-4	Perpignan	6,000
7 Apr. 1990	L	18-25	Leeds	6,554
* 27 Jan. 1991	W	45-10	Perpignan	3,965
16 Feb. 1991	W	60-4	Leeds	5,284
16 Feb. 1992	W	30-12	Perpignan	5,688
* 7 Mar. 1992	W	36-0	Hull	5,250
7 Mar. 1993	W	48-6	Carcassonne	5,500
2 Apr. 1993	W	72-6	Leeds	8,196
20 Mar. 1994	W	12-4	Carcassonne	7,000

*Also World Cup match.

	Played	Won	Drawn	Lost	Tries	Goals	Dr	Pts for
Great Britain	59	42	3	14	282	258	1	1473
France	59	14	3	42	106	137	4	625

GREAT BRITAIN-FRANCE TEST MATCH RECORDS

Britain

Highest score:	72-6 at Leeds, 2 April 1993 (Also widest margin win)
Most tries in a match:	5 by Martin Offiah (Widnes) at Leeds, 16 February 1991
Most goals in a match:	10 by Bernard Ganley (Oldham) at Wigan, 23 November 1957
	10 by Jonathan Davies (Widnes) at Leeds, 2 April 1993
Most points in a match:	21 (1t, 9g) by Lewis Jones (Leeds) at Leeds, 26 January 1957
	21 (1t, 9g) by Neil Fox (Wakefield T.) at Wigan, 3 April 1963
	21 (1t, 9g) by Neil Fox (Wakefield T.) at Leigh, 18 March 1964
Biggest attendance:	23,250 at St. Helens, 10 April 1957

France

Highest score:	25-18 at Leeds, 7 April 1990
Widest margin win:	19-2 at Marseilles, 20 December 1981
Most tries in a match:	3 by Didier Couston at Perpignan, 17 March 1985
Most goals in a match:	7 by Pierre Lacaze at Wigan, 4 March 1967
Most points in a match:	14 by Pierre Lacaze (as above)
	14 (2t, 4g) by Gilbert Benausse at Wigan, 17 February 1962
Biggest attendance:	20,000 at Grenoble, 2 March 1958

● In a World Cup match at Toulouse on 7 November 1954, there were 37,471

Additional Great Britain v. France

Pre-Test status

22 May 1952	L	12-22	Paris	16,466
24 May 1953	L	17-28	Lyons	
27 Apr. 1954	W	17-8	Bradford	14,153
11 Dec. 1955	L	5-17	Paris	18,000
11 Apr. 1956	W	18-10	Bradford	10,453

Other match

31 July 1982	L	7-8	Venice	1,500

GREAT BRITAIN v. PAPUA NEW GUINEA

5 Aug. 1984	W	38-20	Mt. Hagen	7,510
*24 Oct. 1987	W	42-0	Wigan	9,121
*22 May 1988	W	42-22	Port Moresby	12,107
27 May 1990	L	18-20	Goroka	11,598
*2 Jun. 1990	W	40-8	Port Moresby	5,969
*9 Nov. 1991	W	56-4	Wigan	4,193
31 May 1992	W	20-14	Port Moresby	7,294

*Also World Cup match.

	Played	Won	Lost	Tries	Goals	Dr	Pts for
Great Britain	7	6	1	45	38	0	256
Papua New Guinea	7	1	6	14	15	2	88

GREAT BRITAIN-PAPUA NEW GUINEA TEST MATCH RECORDS

Britain

Highest score:	56-4 at Wigan, 9 November 1991 (Also widest margin win)
Most tries in a match:	No player has scored 3 or more
Most goals in a match:	8 by Jonathan Davies (Widnes) at Wigan, 9 November 1991
Most points in a match:	16 by Jonathan Davies (Widnes) as above
Biggest attendance:	9,121 at Wigan, 24 October 1987

Papua New Guinea

Highest score:	22-42 at Port Moresby, 22 May 1988
Only win:	20-18 at Goroka, 27 May 1990
Most tries in a match:	No player has scored 3 or more
Most goals in a match:	6 by Bal Numapo at Goroka, 27 May 1990
Most points in a match:	11 (5g, 1dg) by Bal Numapo as above
Biggest attendance:	12,107 at Port Moresby, 22 May 1988

CLUB REPRESENTATION

Wigan hold the record for most players supplied by one club for a Test or World Cup match. They have had eight in Great Britain's starting line-up on three occasions as follows:

v. Papua New Guinea at Wigan on 24 October 1987. Won 42-0: Steve Hampson, David Stephenson, Joe Lydon, Shaun Edwards, Andy Gregory, Brian Case, Andy Goodway and Ellery Hanley (capt).

v. Australia at Melbourne on 26 June 1992. Won 33-10: Martin Offiah, Shaun Edwards, Kelvin Skerrett, Martin Dermott, Andy Platt, Denis Betts, Billy McGinty and Phil Clarke.

v. Australia at Brisbane on 3 July 1992. Lost 10-16: As above.

In the second and third Tests of 1992 Wigan became the first club to provide all six forwards.

Wigan had a record 10 players on duty for the first 1992 Test against Australia, seven in the starting line-up plus three substitutes, all of whom played. For a brief period, there were a record nine Wigan players in action.

Wigan also hold the record for the total of players selected from one club over the years with 85.

Only three of last season's clubs have not had a player selected for Great Britain — Bramley, Carlisle and Doncaster.

Of the extinct clubs only Broughton Rangers (later Belle Vue Rangers), Merthyr Tydfil, St. Helens Recs and Runcorn had players selected for Britain.

*A register of each club's representation for Great Britain is featured in the CLUBS section.

GREAT BRITAIN TEAMS
...A 20-year review

The following is a compendium of Great Britain Test and World Cup teams since the start of the 1974-75 season.

Initials are included where more than one celebrated player shared a surname in the same era. Only playing substitutes are included on the teamsheet.

(WC): World Cup t: try g: goal dg: drop goal * captain

Full back George Fairbairn, awarded 17 Great Britain caps between 1977 and 1982.

1977 France (WC)
Auckland: 5 June
Won 23-4
Fairbairn (Wigan) 7g
Fielding (Salford)
Holmes (Leeds)
Dyl (Leeds) 1t
Wright, S. (Widnes) 1t
*Millward (Hull K.R.) 1t
Nash (Salford)
Thompson, J. (Featherstone R.)
Ward, D. (Leeds)
Pitchford, S. (Leeds)
Bowman, E. (Workington T.)
Nicholls (St. Helens)
Hogan (Barrow)
Sub: Gill, K. (Salford)
Casey (Hull K.R.)

1977 New Zealand (WC)
Christchurch: 12 June
Won 30-12
Fairbairn (Wigan) 6g
Wright, S. (Widnes) 2t
Holmes (Leeds)
Dyl (Leeds)
Francis, W. (Wigan)
*Millward (Hull K.R.) 1t
Nash (Salford)
Thompson, J. (Featherstone R.)
Ward, D. (Leeds)
Pitchford, S. (Leeds)
Bowman, E. (Workington T.) 1t
Nicholls (St. Helens) 1t
Hogan (Barrow) 1t
Sub: Casey (Hull K.R.)

1977 Australia (WC)
Brisbane: 18 June
Lost 5-19
Fairbairn (Wigan) 1g
Wright, S. (Widnes)
Francis, W. (Wigan)
Dyl (Leeds)
Fielding (Salford)
*Millward (Hull K.R.) 1t
Nash (Salford)
Thompson, J. (Featherstone R.)
Ward, D. (Leeds)
Pitchford, S. (Leeds)
Bowman, E. (Workington T.)
Nicholls (St. Helens)
Hogan (Barrow)
Sub: Holmes (Leeds)
Smith, P. (Featherstone R.)

1977 Australia (WC)
Sydney: 25 June
Lost 12-13
Fairbairn (Wigan) 3g
Wright, S. (Widnes)
Holmes (Leeds)
Dyl (Leeds)
Francis, W. (Wigan)
*Millward (Hull K.R.)
Nash (Salford)
Thompson, J. (Featherstone R.)
Elwell (Widnes)
Pitchford, S. (Leeds) 1t
Bowman, E. (Workington T.)
Casey (Hull K.R.)
Hogan (Barrow)
Sub: Gill, K. (Salford) 1t
Smith, P. (Featherstone R.)

1978 Australia
Wigan: 21 Oct.
Lost 9-15
Fairbairn (Wigan) 3g
Wright, S. (Widnes)
Hughes (Widnes)
Cunningham (St. Helens)
Bevan, J. (Warrington) 1t
*Millward (Hull K.R.)
Nash (Salford)
Thompson, J. (Featherstone R.)
Ward, D. (Leeds)
Rose, P. (Hull K.R.)
Nicholls (St. Helens)
Casey (Hull K.R.)
Norton (Hull)
Sub: Holmes (Leeds)
Hogan (Barrow)

1978 Australia
Bradford: 5 Nov.
Won 18-14
Fairbairn (Wigan) 6g
Wright, S. (Widnes) 2t
Joyner (Castleford)
Dyl (Leeds)
Atkinson, J. (Leeds)
*Millward (Hull K.R.)
Nash (Salford)
Mills (Widnes)
Fisher (Bradford N.)
Lockwood (Hull K.R.)
Nicholls (St. Helens)
Lowe, P. (Hull K.R.)
Norton (Hull)
Sub: Holmes (Leeds)
Rose, P. (Hull K.R.)

1978 Australia
Leeds: 18 Nov.
Lost 6-23
Fairbairn (Wigan)
Wright, S. (Widnes)
Joyner (Castleford)
Bevan, J. (Warrington) 1t
Atkinson, J. (Leeds)
*Millward (Hull K.R.) 1t
Nash (Salford)
Mills (Widnes)
Fisher (Bradford N.)
Farrar (Hull)
Nicholls (St. Helens)
Lowe, P. (Hull K.R.)
Norton (Hull)
Sub: Holmes (Leeds)
Rose, P. (Hull K.R.)

1979 Australia
Brisbane: 16 June
Lost 0-35
Woods, J. (Leigh)
Barends (Bradford N.)
Joyner (Castleford)
Hughes (Widnes)
Mathias (St. Helens)
Holmes (Leeds)
Stephens (Castleford)
Mills (Widnes)
Ward, D. (Leeds)
Skerrett, T. (Wakefield T.)
Nicholls (St. Helens)
*Laughton (Widnes)
Norton (Hull)
Sub: Evans, S. (Featherstone R.)
Hogan (Hull K.R.)

1979 Australia
Sydney: 30 June
Lost 16-24
Fairbairn (Wigan)
Barends (Bradford N.)
Joyner (Castleford) 1t
Woods, J. (Leigh) 5g
Hughes (Widnes) 1t
Holmes (Leeds)
Stephens (Castleford)
*Nicholls (St. Helens)
Ward, D. (Leeds)
Skerrett, T. (Wakefield T.)
Casey (Bradford N.)
Grayshon (Bradford N.)
Adams, M. (Widnes)
Sub: Evans, S. (Featherstone R.)
Watkinson (Hull K.R.)

355

1979 Australia
Sydney: 14 July
Lost 2-28
Fairbairn (Wigan) 1g
Evans, S. (Featherstone R.)
Joyner (Castleford)
Woods, J. (Leigh)
Hughes (Widnes)
Topliss (Wakefield T.)
Redfearn, A. (Bradford N.)
*Nicholls (St. Helens)
Ward, D. (Leeds)
Casey (Bradford N.)
Hogan (Hull K.R.)
Grayshon (Bradford N.)
Norton (Hull)
Sub: Holmes (Leeds)
    Adams, M. (Widnes)

1979 New Zealand
Auckland: 21 July
Won 16-8
Fairbairn (Wigan) 1t, 2g
Evans, S. (Featherstone R.) 1t
Joyner (Castleford)
Smith, M. (Hull K.R.) 1t
Hughes (Widnes) 1t
Holmes (Leeds)
Stephens (Castleford)
Casey (Bradford N.)
Ward, D. (Leeds)
*Nicholls (St. Helens)
Hogan (Hull K.R.)
Grayshon (Bradford N.)
Adams, M. (Widnes)
Sub: Lockwood (Hull K.R.)

1979 New Zealand
Christchurch: 5 Aug.
Won 22-7
Fairbairn (Wigan) 5g
Evans, S. (Featherstone R.) 1t
Joyner (Castleford)
Smith, M. (Hull K.R.)
Hughes (Widnes) 1t
Holmes (Leeds)
Stephens (Castleford)
*Nicholls (St. Helens)
Ward, D. (Leeds)
Skerrett, T. (Wakefield T.)
Casey (Bradford N.) 1t
Grayshon (Bradford N.) 1t
Adams, M. (Widnes)

1979 New Zealand
Auckland: 11 Aug.
Lost 11-18
Fairbairn (Wigan) 1g
Evans, S. (Featherstone R.)
Joyner (Castleford)
Smith, M. (Hull K.R.) 1t
Hughes (Widnes) 1t
Holmes (Leeds)
Stephens (Castleford) 1t
Skerrett, T. (Wakefield T.)
Ward, D. (Leeds)
*Nicholls (St. Helens)
Casey (Bradford N.)
Grayshon (Bradford N.)
Adams, M. (Widnes)
Sub: Woods, J. (Leigh)
    Hogan (Hull K.R.)

1980 New Zealand
Wigan: 18 Oct.
Drew 14-14
*Fairbairn (Wigan) 4g
Camilleri (Barrow) 1t
Joyner (Castleford)
Smith, M. (Hull K.R.) 1t
Bentley, K. (Widnes)
Hartley, S. (Hull K.R.)
Dick (Leeds)
Holdstock (Hull K.R.)
Watkinson (Hull K.R.)
Skerrett, T. (Hull)
Gorley, L. (Widnes)
Grayshon (Bradford N.)
Casey (Hull K.R.)
Sub: Pinner (St. Helens)

1980 New Zealand
Bradford: 2 Nov.
Lost 8-12
*Fairbairn (Wigan) 4g
Drummond (Leigh)
Joyner (Castleford)
Smith, M. (Hull K.R.)
Camilleri (Barrow)
Kelly, K. (Warrington)
Dick (Leeds)
Holdstock (Hull K.R.)
Elwell (Widnes)
Shaw, G. (Widnes)
Casey (Hull K.R.)
Grayshon (Bradford N.)
Pinner (St. Helens)
Sub: Evans, S. (Featherstone R.)
    Gorley, L. (Widnes)

1980 New Zealand
Leeds: 15 Nov.
Won 10-2
Burke (Widnes) 2g
Drummond (Leigh) 2t
Joyner (Castleford)
Evans, S. (Featherstone R.)
Atkinson, J. (Leeds)
Woods, J. (Leigh)
Walker (Whitehaven)
Skerrett, T. (Hull)
Elwell (Widnes)
*Casey (Hull K.R.)
Gorley, P. (St. Helens)
Adams, M. (Widnes)
Norton (Hull)

1981 France
Hull: 6 Dec.
Won 37-0
Fairbairn (Hull K.R.) 1g
Drummond (Leigh) 2t
Smith, M. (Hull K.R.)
Woods, J. (Leigh) 1t, 7g
Gill, H. (Wigan) 3t
Hartley, S. (Hull K.R.) 1t
Gregory, A. (Widnes)
Grayshon (Bradford N.)
*Ward, D. (Leeds)
Skerrett, T. (Hull)
Gorley, L. (Widnes)
Gorley, P. (St. Helens)
Norton (Hull)
Sub: Burke (Widnes)
    Szymala (Barrow)

1981 France
Marseilles: 20 Dec.
Lost 2-19
Burke (Widnes)
Drummond (Leigh)
Smith, M. (Hull K.R.)
Woods, J. (Leigh) 1g
Gill, H. (Wigan)
Hartley, S. (Hull K.R.)
Gregory, A. (Widnes)
*Grayshon (Bradford N.)
Watkinson (Hull K.R.)
Skerrett, T. (Hull)
Gorley, L. (Widnes)
Szymala (Barrow)
Norton (Hull)
Sub: Gorley, P. (St. Helens)

1982 Australia
Hull City FC: 30 Oct.
Lost 4-40
Fairbairn (Hull K.R.)
Drummond (Leigh)
Hughes (Widnes)
Dyl (Leeds)
Evans, S. (Hull)
Woods, J. (Leigh)
*Nash (Salford)
Grayshon (Bradford N.)
Ward, D. (Leeds)
Skerrett, T. (Hull)
Gorley, L. (Widnes)
Crooks, L. (Hull) 2g
Norton (Hull)
Sub: Heron, D. (Leeds)

1982 Australia
Wigan: 20 Nov.
Lost 6-27
Mumby (Bradford N.) 3g
Drummond (Leigh)
Smith, M. (Hull K.R.)
Stephenson (Wigan)
Gill, H. (Wigan)
Holmes (Leeds)
Kelly, K. (Warrington)
*Grayshon (Bradford N.)
Dalgreen (Fulham)
Skerrett, T. (Hull)
Eccles (Warrington)
Burton (Hull K.R.)
Heron, D. (Leeds)
Sub: Woods, J. (Leigh)
　　　Rathbone (Bradford N.)

1982 Australia
Leeds: 28 Nov.
Lost 8-32
Fairbairn (Hull K.R.)
Drummond (Leigh)
Stephenson (Wigan)
Smith, M. (Hull K.R.)
Evans, S. (Hull) 1t
*Topliss (Hull)
Gregory, A. (Widnes)
O'Neill, M. (Widnes)
Noble (Bradford N.)
Rose, P. (Hull)
Smith, P. (Featherstone R.)
Crooks, L. (Hull) 2g, 1dg
Crane (Hull)
Sub: Courtney (Warrington)

1983 France
Carcassonne: 20 Feb.
Won 20-5
Burke (Widnes) 1g
Drummond (Leigh)
Joyner (Castleford) 1t
Duane, R. (Warrington)
Lydon (Widnes) 1t, 3g
Myler, A. (Widnes)
Gregory, A. (Widnes)
O'Neill, M. (Widnes)
Noble (Bradford N.) 1t
Goodway (Oldham) 1t
*Casey (Hull K.R.)
Rathbone (Bradford N.)
Flanagan (Oldham)
Sub: Woods, J. (Leigh)
　　　Smith, P. (Featherstone R.)

1983 France
Hull: 6 Mar.
Won 17-5
Mumby (Bradford N.) 4g
Drummond (Leigh)
Joyner (Castleford)
Duane, R. (Warrington) 1t
Lydon (Widnes)
Myler, A. (Widnes)
Gregory, A. (Widnes) 1t
O'Neill, M. (Widnes)
Noble (Bradford N.)
Goodway (Oldham)
*Casey (Hull K.R.)
Rathbone (Bradford N.)
Flanagan (Oldham)
Sub: Smith, P. (Featherstone R.) 1t

1984 France
Avignon: 29 Jan.
Won 12-0
*Mumby (Bradford N.)
Drummond (Leigh)
Duane, R. (Warrington)
Foy, D. (Oldham) 1t
Clark (Hull K.R.)
Lydon (Widnes)
Cairns (Barrow)
Rayne, Keith (Leeds)
Watkinson (Hull K.R.)
Goodway (Oldham) 1t
Worrall, M. (Oldham)
Hobbs, D. (Featherstone R.)
Hall (Hull K.R.)
Sub: Hanley (Bradford N.)
　　　Crooks, L. (Hull) 2g

1984 France
Leeds: 17 Feb.
Won 10-0
Mumby (Bradford N.)
Clark (Hull K.R.)
Joyner (Castleford)
Schofield (Hull)
Basnett (Widnes)
Hanley (Bradford N.)
Cairns (Barrow)
Rayne, Keith (Leeds)
*Noble (Bradford N.)
Ward, K. (Castleford)
Jasiewicz (Bradford N.)
Hobbs, D. (Featherstone R.) 5g
Hall (Hull K.R.)
Sub: Smith, M. (Hull K.R.)
　　　Smith, P. (Featherstone R.)

1984 Australia
Sydney: 9 June
Lost 8-25
Burke (Widnes) 2g
Drummond (Leigh)
Schofield (Hull) 1t
Mumby (Bradford N.)
Hanley (Bradford N.)
Foy, D. (Oldham)
Holding (St. Helens)
Crooks, L. (Hull)
*Noble (Bradford N.)
Goodway (Oldham)
Burton (Hull K.R.)
Worrall, M. (Oldham)
Adams, M. (Widnes)
Sub: Lydon (Widnes)
　　　Hobbs, D. (Featherstone R.)

1984 Australia
Brisbane: 26 June
Lost 6-18
Burke (Widnes) 1g
Drummond (Leigh)
Schofield (Hull) 1t
Mumby (Bradford N.)
Hanley (Bradford N.)
Myler, A. (Widnes)
Holding (St. Helens)
Rayne, Keith (Leeds)
*Noble (Bradford N.)
Crooks, L. (Hull)
Burton (Hull K.R.)
Goodway (Oldham)
Worrall, M. (Oldham)
Sub: Gregory, A. (Widnes)
　　　Adams, M. (Widnes)

1984 Australia
Sydney: 7 July
Lost 7-20
Burke (Widnes) 1g
Drummond (Leigh)
Schofield (Hull)
Mumby (Bradford N.)
Hanley (Bradford N.) 1t
Myler, A. (Widnes)
Holding (St. Helens) 1dg
Hobbs, D. (Featherstone R.)
*Noble (Bradford N.)
Case (Wigan)
Burton (Hull K.R.)
Goodway (Oldham)
Adams, M. (Widnes)

1984 New Zealand
Auckland: 14 July
Lost 0-12
Burke (Widnes)
Drummond (Leigh)
Schofield (Hull)
Mumby (Bradford N.)
Hanley (Bradford N.)
Smith, M. (Hull K.R.)
Holding (St. Helens)
Hobbs, D. (Featherstone R.)
*Noble (Bradford N.)
Case (Wigan)
Burton (Hull K.R.)
Goodway (Oldham)
Adams, M. (Widnes)

1984 New Zealand
Christchurch: 22 July
Lost 12-28
Burke (Widnes) 2g
Drummond (Leigh)
Hanley (Bradford N.) 1t
Mumby (Bradford N.)
Lydon (Widnes)
Myler, A. (Widnes) 1t
Gregory, A. (Widnes)
Hobbs, D. (Featherstone R.)
*Noble (Bradford N.)
Case (Wigan)
Burton (Hull K.R.)
Goodway (Oldham)
Adams, M. (Widnes)
Sub: Joyner (Castleford)
       Beardmore, K. (Castleford)

1984 New Zealand
Auckland: 28 July
Lost 16-32
Burke (Widnes) 4g
Drummond (Leigh)
Hanley (Bradford N.) 1t
Mumby (Bradford N.) 1t
Lydon (Widnes)
Myler, A. (Widnes)
Gregory, A. (Widnes)
Hobbs, D. (Featherstone R.)
*Noble (Bradford N.)
Case (Wigan)
Adams, M. (Widnes)
Goodway (Oldham)
Flanagan (Oldham)
Sub: Donlan (Leigh)
       Joyner (Castleford)

1984 Papua New Guinea
Mount Hagen: 5 Aug.
Won 38-20
Burke (Widnes) 1t, 5g
Drummond (Leigh) 2t
Hanley (Bradford N.) 1t
Mumby (Bradford N.) 1t
Lydon (Widnes)
Myler, A. (Widnes)
Gregory, A. (Widnes)
Rayne, Keith (Leeds) 1t
*Noble (Bradford N.)
Goodway (Oldham)
Flanagan (Oldham)
Hobbs, D. (Featherstone R.) 1t
Adams, M. (Widnes)
Sub: Donlan (Leigh)
       Proctor (Hull)

1985 France
Leeds: 1 Mar.
Won 50-4
Edwards (Wigan)
Ledger (St. Helens)
Creasser (Leeds) 8g
Gribbin (Whitehaven) 1t
Gill, H. (Wigan) 1t
Hanley (Bradford N.) 2t
Fox (Featherstone R.) 2t, 1g
Dickinson (Leeds)
Watkinson (Hull K.R.) 1t
Dannatt (Hull)
*Goodway (Oldham)
Rathbone (Bradford N.)
Divorty (Hull) 1t
Sub: Gibson (Batley)
       Platt (St. Helens)

1985 France
Perpignan: 17 Mar.
Lost 16-24
Johnson, C. (Leigh)
Clark (Hull K.R.)
Creasser (Leeds) 1g
Foy, D. (Oldham) 1t
Ford, P. (Wigan) 2t
*Hanley (Bradford N.)
Fox (Featherstone R.)
Dickinson (Leeds)
Kiss (Wigan)
Wane (Wigan)
Dannatt (Hull)
Rathbone (Bradford N.)
Divorty (Hull) 1g
Sub: Harkin, P. (Hull K.R.)
       Powell, R. (Leeds)

1985 New Zealand
Leeds: 19 Oct.
Lost 22-24
Burke (Widnes) 3g
Drummond (Leigh)
Schofield (Hull)
Hanley (Wigan) 1t
Lydon (Widnes) 1t, 2g
Myler, A. (Widnes)
Fox (Featherstone R.)
Crooks, L. (Hull)
Watkinson (Hull K.R.)
Fieldhouse (Widnes)
Goodway (Wigan) 1t
Potter (Wigan)
*Pinner (St. Helens)
Sub: Arkwright (St. Helens)

1985 New Zealand
Wigan: 2 Nov.
Won 25-8
Burke (Widnes)
Drummond (Leigh)
Schofield (Hull) 4t
Hanley (Wigan)
Lydon (Widnes) 4g
Myler, A. (Widnes)
Fox (Featherstone R.)
Grayshon (Leeds)
Watkinson (Hull K.R.)
Fieldhouse (Widnes)
Goodway (Wigan)
Potter (Wigan)
*Pinner (St. Helens) 1dg
Sub: Edwards (Wigan)
       Burton (Hull K.R.)

1985 New Zealand (Also WC)
Elland Rd, Leeds: 9 Nov.
Drew 6-6
Burke (Widnes)
Drummond (Leigh)
Schofield (Hull)
Edwards (Wigan)
Lydon (Widnes)
Hanley (Wigan)
Fox (Featherstone R.)
Grayshon (Leeds)
Watkinson (Hull K.R.)
Fieldhouse (Widnes)
Goodway (Wigan)
Potter (Wigan)
*Pinner (St. Helens)
Sub: Arkwright (St. Helens)
    Crooks, L. (Hull) 3g

1986 France (Also WC)
Avignon: 16 Feb.
Drew 10-10
Burke (Widnes)
Drummond (Leigh)
Schofield (Hull)
Hanley (Wigan) 1t
Gill, H. (Wigan)
Myler, A. (Widnes)
Fox (Featherstone R.)
Crooks, L. (Hull) 3g
Watkinson (Hull K.R.)
Wane (Wigan)
Potter (Wigan)
Fieldhouse (Widnes)
*Pinner (St. Helens)

1986 France
Wigan: 1 Mar.
Won 24-10
Lydon (Wigan)
Drummond (Leigh) 1t
Schofield (Hull) 1t, 2g
Marchant (Castleford) 1t
Laws (Hull K.R.)
Myler, A. (Widnes)
Fox (Featherstone R.)
Crooks, L. (Hull) 2g
*Watkinson (Hull K.R.)
Fieldhouse (Widnes)
Rayne, Kevin (Leeds)
James (Halifax) 1t
Potter (Wigan)
Sub: Platt (St. Helens)

1986 Australia
Man U. FC: 25 Oct.
Lost 16-38
Lydon (Wigan) 1t
Marchant (Castleford)
Schofield (Hull) 2t
Hanley (Wigan)
Gill, H. (Wigan) 1g
Myler, A. (Widnes)
Fox (Featherstone R.)
Ward, K. (Castleford)
*Watkinson (Hull K.R.)
Fieldhouse (Widnes)
Crooks, L. (Hull) 1g
Potter (Wigan)
Goodway (Wigan)

1986 Australia
Elland Rd, Leeds: 8 Nov.
Lost 4-34
Lydon (Wigan)
Ledger (St. Helens)
Schofield (Hull) 1t
Marchant (Castleford)
Gill, H. (Wigan)
Myler, A. (Widnes)
Fox (Featherstone R.)
Ward, K. (Castleford)
*Watkinson (Hull K.R.)
Fieldhouse (St. Helens)
Crooks, L. (Hull)
Potter (Wigan)
Goodway (Wigan)
Sub: Edwards (Wigan)
    Platt (St. Helens)

1986 Australia (Also WC)
Wigan: 22 Nov.
Lost 15-24
Lydon (Wigan) 2g
Gill, H. (Wigan) 1g
Schofield (Hull) 2t, 1dg
Stephenson (Wigan)
Basnett (Widnes)
Myler, A. (Widnes)
Gregory, A. (Warrington)
Ward, K. (Castleford)
*Watkinson (Hull K.R.)
Crooks, L. (Hull)
Burton (Hull K.R.)
Goodway (Wigan)
Pinner (Widnes)
Sub: Potter (Wigan)

1987 France (Also WC)
Leeds: 24 Jan.
Won 52-4
Lydon (Wigan) 1t, 8g
Forster (Warrington) 1t
Schofield (Hull)
Stephenson (Wigan)
Gill, H. (Wigan)
*Hanley (Wigan) 2t
Edwards (Wigan) 2t
Hobbs, D. (Oldham)
Beardmore, K. (Castleford)
Crooks, L. (Hull)
Goodway (Wigan) 1t
Haggerty (St. Helens)
Gregory, M. (Warrington) 2t
Sub: Creasser (Leeds)
    England (Castleford)

1987 France
Carcassonne: 8 Feb.
Won 20-10
Lydon (Wigan) 4g
Forster (Warrington)
Schofield (Hull)
*Hanley (Wigan) 1t
Gill, H. (Wigan) 1t
Edwards (Wigan)
Gregory, A. (Wigan)
Hobbs, D. (Oldham)
Beardmore, K. (Castleford) 1t
England (Castleford)
Burton (Hull K.R.)
Haggerty (St. Helens)
Gregory, M. (Warrington)
Sub: Dixon (Halifax)

1987 Papua New Guinea (Also WC)
Wigan: 24 Oct.
Won 42-0
Hampson (Wigan)
Drummond (Warrington)
Stephenson (Wigan) 7g
Lydon (Wigan) 1t
Ford, P. (Bradford N.) 1t
Edwards (Wigan) 2t
Gregory, A. (Wigan) 1t
Ward, K. (Castleford)
Groves (St. Helens)
Case (Wigan)
Medley (Leeds) 1t
Goodway (Wigan)
*Hanley (Wigan) 1t
Sub: Woods, J. (Warrington)
    Fairbank (Bradford N.)

1988 France
Avignon: 24 Jan.
Won 28-14
Hampson (Wigan)
Drummond (Warrington) 1t
Schofield (Leeds) 2t
Loughlin (St. Helens) 3g
Offiah (Widnes) 1t
*Hanley (Wigan) 1t
Edwards (Wigan)
Ward, K. (Castleford)
Beardmore, K. (Castleford)
Waddell (Oldham)
Powell, R. (Leeds)
Medley (Leeds)
Platt (St. Helens)
Sub: Creasser (Leeds) 1g
    Dixon (Halifax)

1988 Australia
Sydney: 11 June
Lost 6-17
Loughlin (St. Helens) 1g
Ford, P. (Bradford N.)
Schofield (Leeds)
Stephenson (Leeds)
Offiah (Widnes)
Hulme, D. (Widnes)
Gregory, A. (Wigan)
Ward, K. (Castleford)
Beardmore, K. (Castleford)
Dixon (Halifax)
Gregory, M. (Warrington)
Platt (St. Helens)
*Hanley (Wigan) 1t
Sub: Gill, H. (Wigan)
    Powell, R. (Leeds)

1988 New Zealand (Also WC)
Christchurch: 17 July
Lost 10-12
Ford, P. (Bradford N.)
Gill, H. (Wigan)
Stephenson (Leeds)
Loughlin (St. Helens) 1t, 1g
Offiah (Widnes)
Hulme, D. (Widnes) 1t
Gregory, A. (Wigan)
Ward, K. (Castleford)
Beardmore, K. (Castleford)
Waddell (Oldham)
Gregory, M. (Warrington)
Powell, R. (Leeds)
*Hanley (Wigan)
Sub: Hulme, P. (Widnes)

1988 France
Leeds: 6 Feb.
Won 30-12
Hampson (Wigan)
Plange (Castleford) 1t
Schofield (Leeds) 1t, 5g
*Hanley (Wigan) 2t
Ford, P. (Bradford N.)
Edwards (Wigan)
Gregory, A. (Wigan) 1t
Ward, K. (Castleford)
Beardmore, K. (Castleford)
Waddell (Oldham)
Powell, R. (Leeds)
Dixon (Halifax)
Platt (St. Helens)
Sub: Stephenson (Leeds)
    Medley (Leeds)

1988 Australia
Brisbane: 28 June
Lost 14-34
Loughlin (St. Helens) 3g
Gill, H. (Wigan)
Ford, P. (Bradford N.) 1t
*Hanley (Wigan)
Offiah (Widnes) 1t
Hulme, D. (Widnes)
Gregory, A. (Wigan)
Ward, K. (Castleford)
Beardmore, K. (Castleford)
Powell, R. (Leeds)
Dixon (Halifax)
Platt (St. Helens)
Gregory, M. (Warrington)
Sub: Wright, D. (Widnes)
    Hulme, P. (Widnes)

1989 France
Wigan: 21 Jan.
Won 26-10
Tait (Widnes)
Ford, P. (Leeds) 1t
Loughlin (St. Helens) 3g
Lydon (Wigan) 1t
Offiah (Widnes) 1t
Edwards (Wigan) 1t
Gregory, A. (Wigan)
Ward, K. (Castleford)
Beardmore, K. (Castleford)
Waddell (Leeds)
Gregory, M. (Warrington)
Powell, R. (Leeds)
*Hanley (Wigan) 1t
Sub: Williams, P. (Salford)
    Eyres (Widnes)

1988 Papua New Guinea (Also WC)
Port Moresby: 22 May
Won 42-22
Loughlin (St. Helens) 7g
Ford, P. (Bradford N.)
Schofield (Leeds) 2t
Stephenson (Leeds) 1t
Gill, H. (Wigan) 2t
Edwards (Wigan)
Gregory, A. (Wigan)
Ward, K. (Castleford)
Beardmore, K. (Castleford)
Case (Wigan)
Medley (Leeds) 1t
Gregory, M. (Warrington) 1t
*Hanley (Wigan)
Sub: Hulme, D. (Widnes)
    Dixon (Halifax)

1988 Australia (Also WC)
Sydney: 9 July
Won 26-12
Ford, P. (Bradford N.) 1t
Gill, H. (Wigan) 2t
Stephenson (Leeds)
Loughlin (St. Helens) 3g
Offiah (Widnes) 1t
Hulme, D. (Widnes)
Gregory, A. (Wigan)
Ward, K. (Castleford)
Hulme, P. (Widnes)
Waddell (Oldham)
Gregory, M. (Warrington) 1t
Powell, R. (Leeds)
*Hanley (Wigan)
Sub: Case (Wigan)

1989 France
Avignon: 5 Feb.
Won 30-8
Tait (Widnes) 1t
Ford, P. (Leeds) 2t
Williams, P. (Salford) 1t
Lydon (Wigan) 3g
Offiah (Widnes)
Edwards (Wigan) 1t
Gregory, A. (Wigan)
Ward, K. (Castleford)
Beardmore, K. (Castleford)
Crooks, L. (Leeds)
Gregory, M. (Warrington)
Powell, R. (Leeds)
*Hanley (Wigan) 1t
Sub: Hampson (Wigan)
    England (Castleford)

1989 New Zealand
Man U. FC: 21 Oct.
Lost 16-24
Tait (Widnes) 1t
Ford, P. (Leeds) 1t
Currier (Widnes)
Loughlin (St. Helens) 2g
Offiah (Widnes) 1t
Hulme, D. (Widnes)
Gregory, A. (Wigan)
Skerrett, K. (Bradford N.)
Beardmore, K. (Castleford)
Hobbs, D. (Bradford N.)
Goodway (Wigan)
Platt (Wigan)
*Gregory, M. (Warrington)
Sub: Edwards (Wigan)
    Newlove (Featherstone R.)

1989 New Zealand
Elland Rd, Leeds: 28 Oct.
Won 26-6
Hampson (Wigan)
Ford, P. (Leeds)
Newlove (Featherstone R.)
Loughlin (St. Helens) 5g
Offiah (Widnes) 1t
Edwards (Wigan) 1t
Hulme, D. (Widnes)
Skerrett, K. (Bradford N.)
Hulme, P. (Widnes)
Platt (Wigan)
Goodway (Wigan) 2t
Powell, R. (Leeds)
*Gregory, M. (Warrington)
Sub: Hobbs, D. (Bradford N.)
    Fox (Featherstone R.)

1989 New Zealand (Also WC)
Wigan: 11 Nov.
Won 10-6
Tait (Widnes) 1t
Ford, P. (Leeds)
Newlove (Featherstone R.)
Loughlin (St. Helens) 1g
Offiah (Widnes) 1t
Edwards (Wigan)
Hulme, D. (Widnes)
Skerrett, K. (Bradford N.)
Hulme, P. (Widnes)
Platt (Wigan)
Goodway (Wigan)
Powell, R. (Leeds)
*Gregory, M. (Warrington)
Sub: Lydon (Wigan)
    England (Castleford)

1990 France
Perpignan: 18 Mar.
Won 8-4
Tait (Widnes)
Lydon (Wigan)
Schofield (Leeds) 2g
Loughlin (St. Helens)
Offiah (Widnes) 1t
Edwards (Wigan)
Gregory, A. (Wigan)
Skerrett, K. (Bradford N.)
Beardmore, K. (Castleford)
Platt (Wigan)
Gregory, M. (Warrington)
Goodway (Wigan)
*Hanley (Wigan)
Sub: Powell, D. (Sheffield E.)
    Betts (Wigan)

1990 France
Leeds: 7 Apr.
Lost 18-25
Tait (Widnes) 1t
Cordle (Bradford N.) 1t
Schofield (Leeds)
Gibson (Leeds)
Offiah (Widnes) 1t
Steadman (Castleford) 3g
*Edwards (Wigan)
Skerrett, K. (Bradford N.)
Beardmore, K. (Castleford)
England (Castleford)
Betts (Wigan)
Fairbank (Bradford N.)
Gregory, M. (Warrington)
Sub: Irwin (Castleford)
    Bishop (Hull K.R.)

1990 Papua New Guinea
Goroka: 27 May
Lost 18-20
Tait (Widnes)
Eastwood (Hull) 1t
Powell, D. (Sheffield E.)
Davies (Widnes) 1t, 3g
Gibson (Leeds)
Schofield (Leeds)
Goulding (Wigan) 1t
Powell, R. (Leeds)
Jackson, L. (Hull)
Dixon (Leeds)
Betts (Wigan)
Fairbank (Bradford N.)
*Gregory, M. (Warrington)
Sub: Irwin (Castleford)
    England (Castleford)

1990 Papua New Guinea (Also WC)
Port Moresby: 2 June
Won 40-8
Tait (Widnes)
Eastwood (Hull) 1t
Davies (Widnes) 6g
Powell, D. (Sheffield E.) 1t
Gibson (Leeds) 2t
Schofield (Leeds) 1t
Goulding (Wigan) 1t
Powell, R. (Leeds)
Jackson, L. (Hull)
England (Castleford)
Betts (Wigan)
Dixon (Leeds) 1t
*Gregory, M. (Warrington)
Sub: Fox (Featherstone R.)
    Clarke (Wigan)

1990 New Zealand
Palmerston North: 24 June
Won 11-10
Bibb (Featherstone R.)
Davies (Widnes) 1t, 1g
Lydon (Wigan)
Gibson (Leeds) 1t
Offiah (Widnes)
Schofield (Leeds) 1dg
Goulding (Wigan)
Skerrett, K. (Bradford N.)
Dermott (Wigan)
England (Castleford)
Betts (Wigan)
Dixon (Leeds)
*Gregory, M. (Warrington)
Sub: Powell, D. (Sheffield E.)
    Powell, R. (Leeds)

1990 New Zealand
Auckland: 8 July
Won 16-14
Lydon (Wigan)
Davies (Widnes) 2g
Powell, D. (Sheffield E.)
Gibson (Leeds)
Offiah (Widnes) 1t
Schofield (Leeds) 1t
Goulding (Wigan)
Skerrett, K. (Bradford N.)
Jackson, L. (Hull)
England (Castleford)
Betts (Wigan) 1t
Dixon (Leeds)
*Gregory, M. (Warrington)
Sub: Irwin (Castleford)
    Powell, R (Leeds)

1990 New Zealand (Also WC)
Christchurch: 15 July
Lost 18-21
Lydon (Wigan)
Davies (Widnes) 3g
Gibson (Leeds)
Powell, D. (Sheffield E.)
Offiah (Widnes) 1t
Schofield (Leeds) 1t
Goulding (Wigan)
Skerrett, K. (Bradford N.)
Dermott (Wigan)
England (Castleford)
Betts (Wigan)
Powell, R. (Leeds) 1t
*Gregory, M. (Warrington)
Sub: Irwin (Castleford)
  Dixon (Leeds)

1990 Australia (Also WC)
Elland Rd, Leeds: 24 Nov.
Lost 0-14
Hampson (Wigan)
Eastwood (Hull)
Powell, D. (Sheffield E.)
Gibson (Leeds)
Offiah (Widnes)
Schofield (Leeds)
Gregory, A. (Wigan)
Harrison (Hull)
Jackson, L. (Hull)
Platt (Wigan)
Betts (Wigan)
Dixon (Leeds)
*Hanley (Wigan)
Sub: Davies (Widnes)
  Gregory, M. (Warrington)
  Powell, R. (Leeds)

1991 Papua New Guinea (Also WC)
Wigan: 9 Nov.
Won 56-4
Hampson (Wigan)
Newlove (Featherstone R.) 1t
Powell, D. (Sheffield E.) 1t
Davies (Widnes) 8g
Sullivan, A. (St. Helens) 1t
*Schofield (Leeds) 1t
Edwards (Wigan)
Harrison (Halifax)
Dermott (Wigan)
Platt (Wigan)
Betts (Wigan) 1t
Moriarty (Widnes) 2t
Jackson, M. (Wakefield T.) 2t
Sub: Connolly (St. Helens)
  Fox (Featherstone R.)
  Fairbank (Bradford N.) 1t
  Price, G. H. (Wakefield T.)

1990 Australia
Wembley: 27 Oct.
Won 19-12
Hampson (Wigan)
Eastwood (Hull) 2t, 3g
Powell, D. (Sheffield E.)
Gibson (Leeds)
Offiah (Widnes) 1t
Schofield (Leeds) 1dg
Gregory, A. (Wigan)
Harrison (Hull)
Jackson, L. (Hull)
Dixon (Leeds)
Betts (Wigan)
Powell, R. (Leeds)
*Hanley (Wigan)
Sub: Fairbank (Bradford N.)
  Ward, K. (St. Helens)

1991 France (Also WC)
Perpignan: 27 Jan.
Won 45-10
Hampson (Wigan)
Eastwood (Hull) 6g
Powell, D. (Sheffield E.)
Gibson (Leeds)
Offiah (Widnes) 2t
Schofield (Leeds) 2t, 1dg
Edwards (Wigan) 2t
Lucas (Wigan)
Jackson, L. (Hull)
Platt (Wigan) 1t
Betts (Wigan) 1t
Holliday (Widnes)
*Hanley (Wigan)
Sub: Aston (Sheffield E.)
  Ellis, S. (Castleford)
  Fairbank (Bradford N.)

1992 France
Perpignan: 16 Feb.
Won 30-12
Tait (Widnes)
Devereux (Widnes) 1t
Connolly (St. Helens)
*Davies (Widnes) 3g
Bentley, J. (Leeds) 1t
Griffiths (St. Helens) 1t
Goulding (Leeds)
Crooks, L. (Castleford)
Jackson, L. (Hull)
Dixon (Leeds)
Fairbank (Bradford N.)
Jackson, M. (Wakefield T.)
Holliday (Widnes)
Sub: Powell, D. (Sheffield E.)
  Steadman (Castleford) 2t
  Jones, M. (Hull)
  Eyres (Widnes) 1t

1990 Australia
Man U. FC: 10 Nov.
Lost 10-14
Hampson (Wigan)
Eastwood (Hull) 1g
Powell, D. (Sheffield E.)
Gibson (Leeds)
Offiah (Widnes)
Schofield (Leeds)
Gregory, A. (Wigan)
Harrison (Hull)
Jackson, L. (Hull)
Platt (Wigan)
Betts (Wigan)
Dixon (Leeds) 1t
*Hanley (Wigan)
Sub: Loughlin (St. Helens) 1t
  Ward, K. (St. Helens)

1991 France
Leeds: 16 Feb.
Won 60-4
Hampson (Wigan) 1t
Eastwood (Hull) 1t, 8g
Powell, D. (Sheffield E.)
Loughlin (St. Helens)
Offiah (Widnes) 5t
Schofield (Leeds) 3t
Edwards (Wigan) 1t
Dannatt (Hull)
Jackson, L. (Hull)
Platt (Wigan)
Eyres (Widnes)
Fairbank (Bradford N.)
*Hanley (Wigan)
Sub: Ellis, K. (Warrington)
  Ellis, S. (Castleford)
  England (Castleford)
  Powell, R. (Leeds)

1992 France (Also WC)
Hull: 7 Mar.
Won 36-0
Steadman (Castleford)
Eastwood (Hull) 1t, 6g
Connolly (St. Helens)
Bateman (Warrington)
Hunte (St. Helens) 1t
Powell, D. (Sheffield E.)
*Edwards (Wigan)
Crooks, L. (Castleford)
Dermott (Wigan) 1t
Skerrett, K. (Wigan)
Betts (Wigan)
Fairbank (Bradford N.)
Holliday (Widnes)
Sub: Fox (Featherstone R.) 1t
  Platt (Wigan) 1t
  McNamara (Hull)

1992 Papua New Guinea
Port Moresby: 31 May
Won 20-14
Hampson (Wigan)
Eastwood (Hull) 1t
*Schofield (Leeds)
Loughlin (St. Helens) 2g
Offiah (Wigan) 2t
Powell, D. (Sheffield E.)
Edwards (Wigan)
Crooks, L. (Castleford)
Dermott (Wigan)
Platt (Wigan)
Betts (Wigan)
Fairbank (Bradford N.)
Clarke (Wigan) 1t
Sub: Lydon (Wigan)
    Skerrett, K. (Wigan)
    Newlove (Featherstone R.)
    Nickle (St. Helens)

1992 Australia
Brisbane: 3 July
Lost 10-16
Steadman (Castleford)
Eastwood (Hull) 3g
Powell, D. (Sheffield E.)
Newlove (Featherstone R.)
Offiah (Wigan) 1t
*Schofield (Leeds)
Edwards (Wigan)
Skerrett, K. (Wigan)
Dermott (Wigan)
Platt (Wigan)
Betts (Wigan)
McGinty (Wigan)
Clarke (Wigan)
Sub: Connolly (St. Helens)
    Hulme, P. (Widnes)
    Lydon (Wigan)
    Harrison (Halifax)

1992 Australia (WC Final)
Wembley: 24 Oct.
Lost 6-10
Lydon (Wigan)
Hunte (St. Helens)
Connolly (St. Helens)
*Schofield (Leeds)
Offiah (Wigan)
Edwards (Wigan)
Fox (Bradford N.) 3g
Ward, K. (St. Helens)
Dermott (Wigan)
Platt (Wigan)
Betts (Wigan)
Clarke (Wigan)
Hanley (Leeds)
Sub: Devereux (Widnes)
    Tait (Leeds)
    Skerrett, K. (Wigan)
    Eyres (Widnes)

1992 Australia
Sydney: 12 June
Lost 6-22
Steadman (Castleford)
Newlove (Featherstone R.)
Powell, D. (Sheffield E.)
Loughlin (St. Helens)
Offiah (Wigan)
*Schofield (Leeds)
Gregory, A. (Wigan)
Skerrett, K. (Wigan)
Dermott (Wigan)
Crooks, L. (Castleford) 1g
Betts (Wigan)
Platt (Wigan)
Clarke (Wigan)
Sub: Edwards (Wigan)
    Jackson, M. (Wakefield T.)
    Lydon (Wigan) 1t
    Lucas (Wigan)

1992 New Zealand
Palmerston North: 12 July
Lost 14-15
Steadman (Castleford)
Eastwood (Hull) 3g
Powell, D. (Sheffield E.)
Connolly (St. Helens)
Offiah (Wigan)
*Schofield (Leeds)
Edwards (Wigan) 1t
Skerrett, K. (Wigan)
Jackson, L. (Hull)
Platt (Wigan)
Betts (Wigan)
McGinty (Wigan)
Clarke (Wigan) 1t
Sub: Lydon (Wigan)
    Hulme, P. (Widnes)
    Harrison (Halifax)

1993 France
Carcassonne: 7 Mar.
Won 48-6
Spruce (Widnes)
Devereux (Widnes) 1t
Currier (Widnes) 6g
Connolly (St. Helens)
Hunte (St. Helens)
*Schofield (Leeds) 3t
Edwards (Wigan) 1t
Cowie (Wigan)
McCurrie (Widnes)
Molloy (Leeds)
Eyres (Widnes) 1t
Clarke (Wigan)
Hanley (Leeds) 2t
Sub: Ford, M. (Castleford) 1t
    Joynt (St. Helens)
    Bateman (Warrington)
    McNamara (Hull)

1992 Australia
Melbourne: 26 June
Won 33-10
Steadman (Castleford) 1t
Eastwood (Hull) 6g
Newlove (Featherstone R.) 1t
Powell, D. (Sheffield E.)
Offiah (Wigan) 1t
*Schofield (Leeds) 1t, 1dg
Edwards (Wigan)
Skerrett, K. (Wigan)
Dermott (Wigan)
Platt (Wigan)
Betts (Wigan)
McGinty (Wigan)
Clarke (Wigan) 1t
Sub: Connolly (St. Helens)
    Hulme, P. (Widnes)
    Lydon (Wigan)
    Harrison (Halifax)

1992 New Zealand
Auckland: 19 July
Won 19-16
Steadman (Castleford)
Eastwood (Hull) 3g
Powell, D. (Sheffield E.)
Connolly (St. Helens)
Offiah (Wigan) 1t
*Schofield (Leeds) 1dg
Edwards (Wigan)
Harrison (Halifax)
Jackson, L. (Hull) 1t
Platt (Wigan)
Betts (Wigan) 1t
McGinty (Wigan)
Clarke (Wigan)
Sub: Newlove (Featherstone R.)
    Jackson, M. (Wakefield T.)
    Devereux (Widnes)
    Fairbank (Bradford N.)

1993 France
Leeds: 2 Apr.
Won 72-6
Tait (Leeds) 2t
Devereux (Widnes) 1t
Newlove (Featherstone R.) 3t
Connolly (St. Helens)
Hunte (St. Helens) 2t
Davies (Widnes) 10g
Edwards (Wigan) 2t
Harrison (Halifax)
Dermott (Wigan)
*Platt (Wigan)
Betts (Wigan) 1t
Eyres (Widnes)
Clarke (Wigan)
Sub: Ford, M. (Castleford) 1t
    Fairbank (Bradford N.)
    Powell, D. (Sheffield E.) 1t
    Nickle (St. Helens)

1993 New Zealand
Wembley: 16 Oct.
Won 17-0
Davies (Warrington) 2g, 1dg
Robinson (Wigan) 2t
Newlove (Bradford N.)
Connolly (Wigan)
Devereux (Widnes) 1t
*Schofield (Leeds)
Edwards (Wigan)
Harrison (Halifax)
Dermott (Wigan)
Fairbank (Bradford N.)
Betts (Wigan)
Joynt (St. Helens)
Clarke (Wigan)
Sub: Powell, D. (Sheffield E.)
  Eyres (Leeds)
  Tait (Leeds)
  Nickle (St. Helens)

1994 France
Carcassonne: 20 Mar.
Won 12-4
Steadman (Castleford)
Bentley, J. (Halifax)
Connolly (Wigan)
Newlove (Bradford N.) 1t
Offiah (Wigan)
*Schofield (Leeds)
Edwards (Wigan) 1t
Crooks, L. (Castleford) 1g
Jackson, L. (Sheffield E.)
Molloy (Featherstone R.)
Farrell (Wigan) 1g
Fairbank (Bradford N.)
Joynt (St. Helens)
Sub: Ellis, S. (Castleford)
  Moriarty (Widnes)
  Powell, D. (Sheffield E.)
  Mather (Wigan)

1993 New Zealand
Wigan: 30 Oct.
Won 29-12
Davies (Warrington) 4g
Devereux (Widnes) 2t
Connolly (Wigan)
Newlove (Bradford N.) 1t
Offiah (Wigan) 1t
*Schofield (Leeds) 1t, 1dg
Edwards (Wigan)
Harrison (Halifax)
Jackson, L. (Sheffield E.)
Fairbank (Bradford N.)
Nickle (St. Helens)
Joynt (St. Helens)
Clarke (Wigan)
Sub: Powell, D. (Sheffield E.)
  Eyres (Leeds)
  Tait (Leeds)
  Jackson, M. (Halifax)

1993 New Zealand
Leeds: 6 Nov.
Won 29-10
Davies (Warrington) 1t, 4g, 1dg
Devereux (Widnes)
Connolly (Wigan)
Newlove (Bradford N.)
Offiah (Wigan) 1t
*Schofield (Leeds)
Edwards (Wigan)
Skerrett, K. (Wigan)
Jackson, L. (Sheffield E.)
Fairbank (Bradford N.) 1t
Farrell (Wigan) 1t
Joynt (St. Helens)
Clarke (Wigan) 1t
Sub: Powell, D. (Sheffield E.)
  Nickle (St. Helens)
  Tait (Leeds)
  Jackson, M. (Halifax)

Great Britain's half back pairing for the 1993-94 season, skipper Garry Schofield (left) and scrum half Shaun Edwards.

GREAT BRITAIN REGISTER

The following is a record of the 615 players who have appeared for Great Britain in 282 Test and World Cup matches.

It does not include matches against France before 1957, the year they were given official Test match status.

Figures in brackets are the total of appearances, with the plus sign indicating substitute appearances, e.g. (7+3).

For matches against touring teams, the year given is for the first half of the season.

World Cup matches are in bold letters except when also classified as Test matches. Substitute appearances are in lower case letters.

A - Australia, F - France, NZ - New Zealand, P - Papua New Guinea.

ACKERLEY, Alvin (2) Halifax: 1952 A; 1958 NZ
ADAMS, Les (1) Leeds: 1932 A
ADAMS, Mick (11+2) Widnes: 1979 Aa,NZ3;
    1980 NZ; 1984 A2a,NZ3,P
ARKWRIGHT, Chris (+2) St. Helens: 1985 nz2
ARKWRIGHT, Jack (6) Warrington: 1936 A2,NZ;
    1937 A3
ARMITT, Tom (8) Swinton: 1933 A; 1936 A2,NZ2;
    1937 A3
ASHBY, Ray (2) Liverpool: 1964 F; Wigan: 1965 F
ASHCROFT, Ernest (11) Wigan: 1947 NZ2; 1950
    A3,NZ; 1954 A3,NZ2
ASHCROFT, Kevin (5+1) Leigh: **1968 A**; 1968 F;
    1969 F; **1970 F,NZ**; Warrington: 1974 nz
ASHTON, Eric (26) Wigan: **1957 A,NZ**; 1958
    A2,NZ2; 1959 F, A3; 1960 F2; **1960 NZ,A**;
    1961 NZ3; 1962 F3,A3; 1963 F,A2
ASHURST, Bill (3) Wigan: 1971 NZ; 1972 F2
ASKIN, Tom (6) Featherstone R: 1928 A3,NZ3
ASPINALL, Willie (1) Warrington: 1966 NZ
ASTON, Len (3) St. Helens: 1947 NZ3
ASTON, Mark (+1) Sheffield E: 1991 f
ATKINSON, Arthur (11) Castleford: 1929 A3; 1932
    A3,NZ3; 1933 A; 1936 A
ATKINSON, John (26) Leeds: **1968 F,NZ**; 1970
    A3,NZ3; **1970 A2,F,NZ**; 1971 F2,NZ; 1972
    F2; **1972 A2,F,NZ**; 1973 A2; 1978 A2; 1980 NZ
AVERY, Albert (4) Oldham: 1910 A,NZ; 1911 A2

BACON, Jim (11) Leeds: 1920 A3,NZ3; 1921 A3;
    1924 A; 1926 NZ
BARENDS, David (2) Bradford N: 1979 A2
BARTON, Frank (1) Wigan: 1951 NZ
BARTON, John (2) Wigan: 1960 F; 1961 NZ
BASNETT, John (2) Widnes: 1984 F; 1986 A
BASSETT, Arthur (2) Halifax: 1946 A2
BATEMAN, Allan (1+1) Warrington: 1992 F; 1993 f
BATES, Alan (2+2) Dewsbury: 1974 F2,nz2
BATTEN, Billy (10) Hunslet: 1907 NZ; 1908 A3;
    1910 A2,NZ; 1911 A2; Hull: 1921 A
BATTEN, Eric (4) Bradford N: 1946 A2,NZ; 1947 NZ
BATTEN, Ray (3) Leeds: 1969 F; 1973 A2
BAXTER, Johnnie (1) Rochdale H: 1907 NZ
BEAMES, Jack (2) Halifax: 1921 A2
BEARDMORE, Kevin (13+1) Castleford: 1984 nz;
    1987 F; 1988 F2,P,A2,NZ; 1989 F2,NZ;
    1990 F2
BELSHAW, Billy (8) Liverpool S: 1936 A3,NZ2;
    1937 A; Warrington: 1937 A2
BENNETT, Jack (7) Rochdale H: 1924 A3,NZ3;
    Wigan: 1926 NZ
BENTHAM, Billy (2) Broughton R: 1924 NZ2
BENTHAM, Nat (10) Wigan H: 1928 A3,NZ3;
    Halifax: 1929 A2; Warrington: 1929 A2
BENTLEY, John (2) Leeds: 1992 F; Halifax: 1994 F
BENTLEY, Keith (1) Widnes: 1980 NZ
BENYON, Billy (5+1) St. Helens: 1971 F2,NZnz;
    1972 F2

BETTS, Denis (21+1) Wigan: 1990 fF,P2,NZ3,A3;
    1991 F,P; 1992 F,P,A3,NZ2, **A**; 1993F,NZ
BEVAN, Dai (1) Wigan: 1952 A
BEVAN, John (6) Warrington: 1974 A2,NZ2;
    1978 A2
BEVERLEY, Harry (6) Hunslet: 1936 A3; 1937 A;
    Halifax: 1937 A2
BIBB, Chris (1) Featherstone R: 1990 NZ
BIRCH, Jim (1) Leeds: 1907 NZ
BISHOP, David (+1) Hull KR: 1990 f
BISHOP, Tommy (15) St. Helens: 1966 A3,NZ2;
    1967 A3; 1968 F3; **1968 A,F,NZ**; 1969 F
BLAN, Billy (3) Wigan: 1951 NZ3
BLINKHORN, Tom (1) Warrington: 1929 A
BOLTON, Dave (23) Wigan: 1957 F3; 1958 F,A2;
    1959 F,A3; 1960 F2; 1961 NZ3; 1962 F2,A,NZ2;
    1963 F,A2
BOSTON, Billy (31) Wigan: 1954 A2,NZ3; 1955
    NZ; 1956 A3; 1957 F5; **1957 F,A**; 1958 F; 1959
    A; 1960 F; **1960 A**; 1961 F,NZ3; 1962
    F2,A3,NZ; 1963 F
BOTT, Charlie (1) Oldham: 1966 F
BOWDEN, Jim (3) Huddersfield: 1954 A2,NZ
BOWEN, Frank (3) St. Helens Recs: 1928 NZ3
BOWERS, Joe (1) Rochdale H: 1920 NZ
BOWMAN, Eddie (4) Workington T: **1977 F,NZ,A2**
BOWMAN, Harold (8) Hull: 1924 NZ2; 1926 NZ2;
    1928 A2,NZ; 1929 A
BOWMAN, Ken (3) Huddersfield: 1962 F;
    1963 F,A
BOYLEN, Frank (1) Hull: 1908 A
BRADSHAW, Tommy (6) Wigan: 1947 NZ2;
    1950 A3,NZ
BRIDGES, John "Keith" (3) Featherstone R:
    1974 F2,A
BRIGGS, Brian (1) Huddersfield: 1954 NZ
BROGDEN, Stan (16) Huddersfield: 1929 A;
    1932 A3,NZ3; 1933 A2; Leeds: 1936 A3,NZ2;
    1937 A2
BROOKE, Ian (13) Bradford N: 1966 A3,NZ2;
    Wakefield T: 1967 A3; 1968 F2; **1968 A,F,NZ**
BROOKS, Ernie (3) Warrington: 1908 A3
BROUGH, Albert (2) Oldham: 1924 A,NZ
BROUGH, Jim (5) Leeds: 1928 A2,NZ2; 1936 A
BROWN, Gordon (6) Leeds: **1954 F2,NZ,A**;
    1955 NZ2
BRYANT, Bill (4+1) Castleford: 1964 F2; 1966 Aa;
    1967 F
BUCKLEY, Alan (7) Swinton: 1963 A; 1964 F;
    1965 NZ; 1966 F,A2,NZ
BURGESS, Bill (16) Barrow: 1924 A3,NZ3;
    1926 NZ3; 1928 A3,NZ2; 1929 A2
BURGESS, Bill (14) Barrow: 1962 F; 1963 A; 1965
    NZ2; 1966 F,A3,NZ2; 1967 F,A; 1968 F; Salford:
    1969 F
BURGHAM, Oliver (1) Halifax: 1911 A
BURKE, Mick (14+1) Widnes: 1980 NZ; 1981 fF;
    1983 F; 1984 A3,NZ3,P; 1985 NZ3; 1986 F

BURNELL, Alf (3) Hunslet: 1951 NZ2; 1954 NZ
BURTON, Chris (8+1) Hull KR: 1982 A; 1984
A3,NZ2; 1985 nz; 1986 A; 1987 F
BURWELL, Alan (7+1) Hull KR: 1967 a; 1968 F3;
1968 A,F,NZ; 1969 F
BUTTERS, Fred (2) Swinton: 1929 A2

CAIRNS, David (2) Barrow: 1984 F2
CAMILLERI, Chris (2) Barrow: 1980 NZ2
CARLTON, Frank (2) St. Helens: 1958 NZ; Wigan:
1962 NZ
CARR, Charlie (7) Barrow: 1924 A2,NZ2;
1926 NZ3
CARTWRIGHT, Joe (7) Leigh: 1920 A,NZ3;
1921 A3
CASE, Brian (6+1) Wigan: 1984 A,NZ3; 1987 P;
1988 P,a
CASEY, Len (12+2) Hull KR: **1977 f,nz,A**; 1978 A;
Bradford N: 1979 A2,NZ3; Hull KR: 1980 NZ3;
1983 F2
CASTLE, Frank (4) Barrow: 1952 A3; 1954 A
CHALLINOR, Jim (3) Warrington: 1958 A,NZ;
1960 F
CHARLTON, Paul (18+1) Workington T: 1965
NZ; **1970 nz**; 1972 F2; **1972 A2,F,NZ**;
1973 A3; 1974 F2,A3,NZ3
CHERRINGTON, Norman (1) Wigan: 1960 F
CHILCOTT, Jack (3) Huddersfield: 1914 A3
CHISNALL, Dave (2) Leigh: 1970 A; **1970 NZ**
CHISNALL, Eric (4) St. Helens: 1974 A2,NZ2
CLAMPITT, Jim (3) Broughton R: 1907 NZ;
1911 A; 1914 NZ
CLARK, Doug (11) Huddersfield: 1911 A2; 1914
A3; 1920 A3,NZ3
CLARK, Garry (3) Hull KR: 1984 F2; 1985 F
CLARK, Mick (5) Leeds: 1968 F2; **1968 A,F,NZ**
CLARKE, Colin (7) Wigan: 1965 NZ; 1966 F,NZ;
1967 F; 1973 A3
CLARKE, Phil (12+1) Wigan: 1990 p; 1992
P,A3,NZ2, **A**; 1993 F2,NZ3
CLAWSON, Terry (14) Featherstone R: 1962 F2;
Leeds: **1972 A2,F**; Oldham: 1973 A3; 1974
F2,A2,NZ2
CLOSE, Don (1) Huddersfield: 1967 F
COLDRICK, Percy (4) Wigan: 1914 A3,NZ
COLLIER, Frank (2) Wigan: 1963 A; Widnes: 1964 F
CONNOLLY, Gary (11+3) St. Helens: 1991 p; 1992
F2,a2,NZ2,**A**; 1993 F2; Wigan: 1993 NZ3; 1994 F
CORDLE, Gerald (1) Bradford N: 1990 F
COULMAN, Mike (2+1) Salford: 1971 f,NZ2
COURTNEY, Neil (+1) Warrington: 1982 a
COVERDALE, Bob (4) Hull: **1954 F2,NZ,A**
COWIE, Neil (1) Wigan: 1993 F
CRACKNELL, Dick (2) Huddersfield: 1951 NZ2
CRANE, Mick (1) Hull: 1982 A
CREASSER, David (2+2) Leeds: 1985 F2; 1987 f;
1988 f

CROOKS, Lee (17+2) Hull: 1982 A2; 1984 f,A2;
1985 NZnz; 1986 F2,A3; 1987 F; Leeds: 1989 F;
Castleford: 1992 F2,P,A; 1994 F
CROSTON, Jim (1) Castleford: 1937 A
CROWTHER, Hector (1) Hunslet: 1929 A
CUNLIFFE, Billy (11) Warrington: 1920 A,NZ2;
1921 A3; 1924 A3,NZ; 1926 NZ
CUNLIFFE, Jack (4) Wigan: 1950 A,NZ; 1951
NZ; 1954 A
CUNNIFFE, Bernard (1) Castleford: 1937 A
CUNNINGHAM, Eddie (1) St. Helens: 1978 A
CURRAN, George (6) Salford: 1946 A,NZ; 1947
NZ; 1948 A3
CURRIER, Andy (2) Widnes: 1989 NZ; 1993 F
CURZON, Ephraim (1) Salford: 1910 A

DAGNALL, Bob (4) St. Helens: 1961 NZ2; 1964 F;
1965 F
DALGREEN, John (1) Fulham: 1982 A
DANBY, Tom (3) Salford: 1950 A2,NZ
DANIELS, Arthur (3) Halifax: 1952 A2; 1955 NZ
DANNATT, Andy (3) Hull: 1985 F2; 1991 F
DARWELL, Joe (5) Leigh: 1924 A3,NZ2
DAVIES, Alan (20) Oldham: 1955 NZ; 1956 A3;
1957 F,A; 1957 F2; 1958 F,A2,NZ2; 1959 F2,A;
1960 NZ,F,A; 1960 F
DAVIES, Billy (1) Swinton: 1968 F
DAVIES, Billy J (1) Castleford: 1933 A
DAVIES, Evan (3) Oldham: 1920 NZ3
DAVIES, Jim (2) Huddersfield: 1911 A2
DAVIES, Jonathan (11+1) Widnes: 1990 P2,NZ3,a;
1991 P; 1992 F; 1993 F; Warrington: 1993 NZ3
DAVIES, Will T (1) Halifax: 1911 A
DAVIES, Willie A (2) Leeds: 1914 A,NZ
DAVIES, Willie T.H (3) Bradford N: 1946 NZ;
1947 NZ2
DAWSON, Edgar (1) York: 1956 A
DERMOTT, Martin (11) Wigan: 1990 NZ2; 1991 P;
1992 F,P,A3,**A**; 1993 F,NZ
DEVEREUX, John (6+2) Widnes: 1992 F,nz,a;
1993 F2,NZ3
DICK, Kevin (2) Leeds: 1980 NZ2
DICKENSON, George (1) Warrington: 1908 A
DICKINSON, Roy (2) Leeds: 1985 F2
DINGSDALE, Billy (3) Warrington: 1929 A2;
1933 A
DIVORTY, Gary (2) Hull: 1985 F2
DIXON, Colin (12+2) Halifax: 1968 F; Salford:
1969 F; 1971 NZ; **1972 F**; 1973 a2; 1974
F2,A3,NZ3
DIXON, Malcolm (2) Featherstone R: 1962 F;
1964 F
DIXON, Paul (11+4) Halifax: 1987 f; 1988
fF,p,A2; Leeds: 1990 P2,NZ2nz,A3; 1992 F
DOCKAR, Alec (1) Hull KR: 1947 NZ
DONLAN, Steve (+2) Leigh: 1984 nz,p
DRAKE, Bill (1) Hull: 1962 F
DRAKE, Jim (1) Hull: 1960 F

DRUMMOND, Des (24) Leigh: 1980 NZ2; 1981
F2; 1982 A3; 1983 F2; 1984 F,A3,NZ3,P; 1985
NZ3; 1986 F2; Warrington: 1987 P; 1988 F
DUANE, Ronnie (3) Warrington: 1983 F2; 1984 F
DUTTON, Ray (6) Widnes: 1970 NZ2; **1970
A2,F,NZ**
DYL, Les (11) Leeds: 1974 A2,NZ3; **1977 F,NZ,A2;**
1978 A; 1982 A
DYSON, Frank (1) Huddersfield: 1959 A

EASTWOOD, Paul (13) Hull: 1990 P2,A3; 1991
F2; 1992 F,P,A2,NZ2
ECCLES, Bob (1) Warrington: 1982 A
ECCLES, Percy (1) Halifax: 1907 NZ
ECKERSLEY, David (2+2) St. Helens: 1973 Aa;
1974 Aa
EDGAR, Brian (11) Workington T: 1958 A,NZ;
1961 NZ; 1962 A3,NZ; 1965 NZ; 1966 A3
EDWARDS, Alan (7) Salford: 1936 A3,NZ2;
1937 A2
EDWARDS, Derek (3+2) Castleford: 1968 f; 1970
A; 1971 NZ2nz
EDWARDS, Shaun (30+4) Wigan: 1985 F,nzNZ;
1986 a; 1987 F2,P; 1988 F2,P; 1989 F2,nzNZ2;
1990 F2; 1991 F2,P; 1992 F,P,aA2,NZ2,**A;**
1993 F2,NZ3; 1994 F
EGAN, Joe (14) Wigan: 1946 A3; 1947 NZ3; 1948
A3; 1950 A3,NZ2
ELLABY, Alf (13) St. Helens: 1928 A3,NZ2; 1929
A2; 1932 A3,NZ2; 1933 A
ELLIS, Kevin (+1) Warrington: 1991 f
ELLIS, St. John (+3) Castleford: 1991 f2; 1994 f
ELWELL, Keith (3) Widnes: **1977 A;** 1980 NZ2
ENGLAND, Keith (6+5) Castleford: 1987 fF; 1989
f,nz; 1990 F,pP,NZ3; 1991 f
EVANS, Bryn (10) Swinton: 1926 NZ; 1928 NZ;
1929 A; 1932 A2,NZ3; 1933 A2
EVANS, Frank (4) Swinton: 1924 A2,NZ2
EVANS, Jack (4) Hunslet: 1951 NZ; 1952 A3
EVANS, Jack (3) Swinton: 1926 NZ3
EVANS, Roy (4) Wigan: 1961 NZ2; 1962 F,NZ
EVANS, Steve (7+3) Featherstone R: 1979 Aa2,NZ3;
1980 NZnz; Hull: 1982 A2
EYRE, Ken (1) Hunslet: 1965 NZ
EYRES, Richard (3+6) Widnes: 1989 f; 1991 fF;
1992 f,**a**; 1993 F2; Leeds: 1993 nz2

FAIRBAIRN, George (17) Wigan: **1977 F,NZ,A2;**
1978 A3; 1979 A2,NZ3; 1980 NZ2; Hull KR:
1981 F; 1982 A2
FAIRBANK, Karl (10+6) Bradford N: 1987 p; 1990
F,P,a; 1991 fF,p; 1992 F2,P,nz; 1993 f,NZ3; 1994 F
FAIRCLOUGH, Les (6) St. Helens: 1926 NZ; 1928
A2,NZ2; 1929 A
FARRAR, Vince (1) Hull: 1978 A
FARRELL, Andrew (2) Wigan: 1993 NZ; 1994 F
FEATHERSTONE, Jim (6) Warrington: 1948 A;
1950 NZ2; 1952 A3

FEETHAM, Jack (8) Hull KR: 1929 A; Salford:
1932 A2,NZ2; 1933 A3
FIELD, Harry (3) York: 1936 A,NZ2
FIELD, Norman (1) Batley: 1963 A
FIELDHOUSE, John (7) Widnes: 1985 NZ3; 1986
F2,A; St. Helens: 1986 A
FIELDING, Keith (3) Salford: 1974 F2; **1977 F**
FILDES, Alec (15) St. Helens Recs: 1926 NZ2;
1928 A3,NZ3; 1929 A3; St. Helens: 1932 A,NZ3
FISHER, Tony (11) Bradford N: 1970 A2,NZ3;
1970 A; Leeds: **1970 A;** 1971 F2; Bradford N:
1978 A2
FLANAGAN, Peter (14) Hull KR: 1962 F; 1963 F;
1966 A3,NZ; 1967 A3; 1968 F2; **1968 F,NZ;**
1970 A
FLANAGAN, Terry (4) Oldham: 1983 F2; 1984 NZ,P
FOGERTY, Terry (2+1) Halifax: 1966 nz; Wigan:
1967 F; Rochdale H: 1974 F
FORD, Mike (+2) Castleford: 1993 f2
FORD, Phil (13) Wigan: 1985 F; Bradford N: 1987
P; 1988 F,P,A3,NZ; Leeds: 1989 F2,NZ3
FORSTER, Mark (2) Warrington: 1987 F2
FOSTER, Frank (1) Hull KR: 1967 A
FOSTER, Peter (3) Leigh: 1955 NZ3
FOSTER, Trevor (3) Bradford N: 1946 NZ;
1948 A2
FOX, Deryck (10+4) Featherstone R: 1985 F2,
NZ3; 1986 F2,A2; 1989 nz; 1990 p; 1991 p;
1992 f; Bradford N: 1992 **A**
FOX, Don (1) Featherstone R: 1963 A
FOX, Neil (29) Wakefield T: 1959 F,A2; 1960 F3;
1961 NZ2; 1962 F3,A3,NZ2; 1963 A2,F; 1964
F; 1965 F; 1966 F; 1967 F2,A; 1968 F3; 1969 F
FOY, Des (3) Oldham: 1984 F,A; 1985 F
FRANCIS, Bill (4) Wigan: 1967 A; **1977 NZ,A2**
FRANCIS, Roy (1) Barrow: 1947 NZ
FRASER, Eric (16) Warrington: 1958 A3,NZ2;
1959 F2,A; 1960 F3; **1960 F,NZ;** 1961 F,NZ2
FRENCH, Ray (4) Widnes: 1968 F2; **1968 A,NZ**
FRODSHAM, Alf (3) St. Helens: 1928 NZ2; 1929 A

GABBITAS, Brian (1) Hunslet: 1959 F
GALLAGHER, Frank (12) Dewsbury: 1920 A3;
1921 A; Batley: 1924 A3,NZ3; 1926 NZ2
GANLEY, Bernard (3) Oldham: 1957 F2; 1958 F
GARDINER, Danny (1) Wigan: 1965 NZ
GEE, Ken (17) Wigan: 1946 A3,NZ; 1947 NZ3;
1948 A3; 1950 A3,NZ2; 1951 NZ2
GEMMELL, Dick (3) Leeds: 1964 F; Hull: 1968 F;
1969 F
GIBSON, Carl (10+1) Batley: 1985 f; Leeds: 1990
F,P2,NZ3,A3; 1991 F
GIFFORD, Harry (2) Barrow: 1908 A2
GILFEDDER, Laurie (5) Warrington: 1962 A,NZ2,F;
1963 F
GILL, Henderson (14+1) Wigan: 1981 F2; 1982 A;
1985 F; 1986 F,A3; 1987 F2; 1988 P,A2a,NZ
GILL, Ken (5+2) Salford: 1974 F2,A2,NZ; **1977 f,a**

GOODWAY, Andy (23) Oldham: 1983 F2; 1984 F,A3,NZ3,P; 1985 F; Wigan: 1985 NZ3; 1986 A3; 1987 F,P; 1989 NZ3; 1990 F
GOODWIN, Dennis (5) Barrow: 1957 F2; 1958 F,NZ2
GORE, Jack (1) Salford: 1926 NZ
GORLEY, Les (4+1) Widnes: 1980 NZnz; 1981 F2; 1982 A
GORLEY, Peter (2+1) St. Helens: 1980 NZ; 1981 Ff
GOULDING, Bobby (6) Wigan: 1990 P2,NZ3; Leeds: 1992 F
GOWERS, Ken (14) Swinton: 1962 F; 1963 F,A3; 1964 F2; 1965 NZ2; 1966 F2,A,NZ2
GRAY, John (5+3) Wigan: 1974 f2,A2a,NZ3
GRAYSHON, Jeff (13) Bradford N: 1979 A2,NZ3; 1980 NZ2; 1981 F2; 1982 A2; Leeds: 1985 NZ2
GREENALL, Doug (6) St. Helens: 1951 NZ3; 1952 A2; 1954 NZ
GREENALL, Johnny (1) St. Helens Recs: 1921 A
GREENOUGH, Bobby (1) Warrington: **1960 NZ**
GREGORY, Andy (25+1) Widnes: 1981 F2; 1982 A; 1983 F2; 1984 a,NZ2,P; Warrington: 1986 A; Wigan: 1987 F,P; 1988 F,P,A3,NZ; 1989 F2,NZ; 1990 F,A3; 1992 A
GREGORY, Mike (19+1) Warrington: 1987 F2; 1988 P,A3,NZ; 1989 F2,NZ3; 1990 F2,P2,NZ3,a
GRIBBIN, Vince (1) Whitehaven: 1985 F
GRIFFITHS, Jonathan (1) St. Helens: 1992 F
GRONOW, Ben (7) Huddersfield: 1911 A2; 1920 A2,NZ3
GROVES, Paul (1) St. Helens: 1987 P
GRUNDY, Jack (12) Barrow: 1955 NZ3; 1956 A3; 1957 F3; **1957 F,A,NZ**
GUNNEY, Geoff (11) Hunslet: 1954 NZ3; 1956 A; 1957 F3; **1957 F,NZ**; 1964 F; 1965 F
GWYNNE, Emlyn (3) Hull: 1928 A,NZ; 1929 A
GWYTHER, Elwyn (6) Belle Vue R: 1947 NZ2; 1950 A3; 1951 NZ

HAGGERTY, Roy (2) St. Helens: 1987 F2
HAIGH, Bob (5+1) Wakefield T: **1968 A,F**; Leeds: **1970 NZ,a**; 1971 F,NZ
HALL, Billy (4) Oldham: 1914 A3,NZ
HALL, Dave (2) Hull KR: 1984 F2
HALLAS, Derek (2) Leeds: 1961 F,NZ
HALMSHAW, Tony (1) Halifax: 1971 NZ
HALSALL, Hector (1) Swinton: 1929 A
HAMPSON, Steve (11+1) Wigan: 1987 P; 1988 F2; 1989 f,NZ; 1990 A3; 1991 F2,P; 1992 P
HANLEY, Ellery (35+1) Bradford N: 1984 fF,A3,NZ3,P; 1985 F2; Wigan: 1985 NZ3; 1986 F,A; 1987 F2,P; 1988 F2,P,A3,NZ; 1989 F2; 1990 F,A3; 1991 F2; Leeds: 1992 A; 1993 F
HARDISTY, Alan (12) Castleford: 1964 F3; 1965 F,NZ; 1966 A3,NZ; 1967 F2; 1970 A
HARE, Ian (1) Widnes: 1967 F
HARKIN, Paul (+1) Hull KR: 1985 f

HARRIS, Tommy (25) Hull: 1954 NZ2; 1956 A3; 1957 F5; **1957 F,A**; 1958 A3,NZ,F; 1959 F2,A3; 1960 F2; **1960 NZ**
HARRISON, Fred (3) Leeds: 1911 A3
HARRISON, Karl (8+3) Hull: 1990 A3; Halifax: 1991 P; 1992 a2,nzNZ; 1993 F,NZ2
HARRISON, Mick (7) Hull: 1967 F2; 1971 NZ2; 1972 F2; 1973 A
HARTLEY, Dennis (11) Hunslet: 1964 F2; Castleford: 1968 F; 1969 F; 1970 A2,NZ2; **1970 A2,F**
HARTLEY, Steve (3) Hull KR: 1980 NZ; 1981 F2
HELME, Gerry (12) Warrington: 1948 A3; 1954 A3,NZ2; **1954 F2,A,NZ**
HEPWORTH, Keith (11) Castleford: 1967 F2; 1970 A3,NZ2; **1970 A2,F,NZ**
HERBERT, Norman (6) Workington T: 1961 NZ; 1962 F,A3,NZ
HERON, David (1+1) Leeds: 1982 aA
HESKETH, Chris (21+2) Salford: 1970 NZ; **1970 NZ,a**; 1971 Ff,NZ3; **1972 A2,F,NZ**; 1973 A3; 1974 F2,A3,NZ3
HICKS, Mervyn (1) St. Helens: 1965 NZ
HIGGINS, Fred (6) Widnes: 1950 A3,NZ2; 1951 NZ
HIGGINS, Harold (2) Widnes: 1937 A2
HIGSON, John (2) Hunslet: 1908 A2
HILL, Cliff (1) Wigan: 1966 F
HILL, David (1) Wigan: 1971 F
HILTON, Herman (7) Oldham: 1920 A3,NZ3; 1921 A
HILTON, Jack (4) Wigan: 1950 A2,NZ2
HOBBS, David (10+2) Featherstone R: 1984 F2,Aa,NZ3,P; Oldham: 1987 F2; Bradford N: 1989 NZnz
HODGSON, Martin (16) Swinton: 1929 A2; 1932 A3,NZ3; 1933 A3; 1936 A3,NZ; 1937 A
HOGAN, Phil (6+3) Barrow: **1977 F,NZ,A2**; 1978 a; Hull KR: 1979 Aa,NZnz
HOGG, Andrew (1) Broughton R: 1907 NZ
HOLDEN, Keith (1) Warrington: 1963 A
HOLDER, Billy (1) Hull: 1907 NZ
HOLDING, Neil (4) St. Helens: 1984 A3,NZ
HOLDSTOCK, Roy (2) Hull KR: 1980 NZ2
HOLLAND, Dave (4) Oldham: 1914 A3,NZ
HOLLIDAY, Bill (9+1) Whitehaven: 1964 F; Hull KR: 1965 F,NZ3; 1966 Ff; 1967 A3
HOLLIDAY, Les (3) Widnes: 1991 F; 1992 F2
HOLLINDRAKE, Terry (1) Keighley: 1955 NZ
HOLMES, John (14+6) Leeds: 1971 NZ; 1972 F2; **1972 Aa,NZ**; **1977 F,NZ,Aa**; 1978 a3; 1979 A2a,NZ3; 1982 A
HORNE, Willie (8) Barrow: 1946 A3; 1947 NZ; 1948 A; 1952 A3
HORTON, Bill (14) Wakefield T: 1928 A3,NZ3; 1929 A; 1932 A3,NZ; 1933 A3
HOWLEY, Tommy (6) Wigan: 1924 A3,NZ3

HUDDART, Dick (16) Whitehaven: 1958 A2,NZ2; St. Helens: 1959 A; 1961 NZ3; 1962 F2,A3,NZ2; 1963 A

HUDSON, Barney (8) Salford: 1932 NZ; 1933 A2; 1936 A,NZ2; 1937 A2

HUDSON, Bill (1) Wigan: 1948 A

HUGHES, Eric (8) Widnes: 1978 A; 1979 A3,NZ3; 1982 A

HULME, David (7+1) Widnes: 1988 p,A3,NZ; 1989 NZ3

HULME, Paul (3+5) Widnes: 1988 aA,nz; 1989 NZ2; 1992 a2,nz

HUNTE, Alan (4) St. Helens: 1992 F,**A**; 1993 F2

HURCOMBE, Danny (8) Wigan: 1920 A2,NZ; 1921 A; 1924 A2,NZ2

HYNES, Syd (12+1) Leeds: 1970 A2,NZ2nz; **1970 A2,F,NZ**; 1971 F; 1973 A3

IRVING, Bob (8+3) Oldham: 1967 F2,A3; 1970 a,NZ; 1971 NZ; 1972 f; **1972 NZ,a**

IRWIN, Shaun (+4) Castleford: 1990 f,p,nz2

JACKSON, Ken (2) Oldham: 1957 F2

JACKSON, Lee (14) Hull: 1990 P2,NZ,A3; 1991 F2; 1992 F,NZ2; Sheffield E: 1993 NZ2; 1994 F

JACKSON, Michael (2+4) Wakefield T: 1991 P; 1992 F,a,nz; Halifax: 1993 nz2

JACKSON, Phil (27) Barrow: 1954 A3,NZ3; **1954 F2,A,NZ**; 1955 NZ3; 1956 A3; **1957 F,NZ**; 1957 F5; 1958 F,A2,NZ

JAMES, Neil (1) Halifax: 1986 F

JARMAN, Billy (2) Leeds: 1914 A2

JASIEWICZ, Dick (1) Bradford N: 1984 F

JEANES, David (8) Wakefield T: 1971 F,NZ2; 1972 F2; Leeds: **1972 A2,NZ**

JENKINS, Bert (12) Wigan: 1907 NZ3; 1908 A3; 1910 A,NZ; 1911 A2; 1914 A,NZ

JENKINS, Dai (1) Hunslet: 1929 A

JENKINS, Dai (1) Leeds: 1947 NZ

JENKINS, Emlyn (9) Salford: 1933 A; 1936 A3,NZ2; 1937 A3

JENKINSON, Albert (2) Hunslet: 1911 A2

JOHNSON, Albert (4) Widnes: 1914 A,NZ; 1920 A2

JOHNSON, Albert (6) Warrington: 1946 A2,NZ; 1947 NZ3

JOHNSON, Chris (1) Leigh: 1985 F

JOLLEY, Jim (3) Runcorn: 1907 NZ3

JONES, Berwyn (3) Wakefield T: 1964 F; 1965 F; 1966 F

JONES, Dai (2) Merthyr: 1907 NZ2

JONES, Ernest (4) Rochdale H: 1920 A,NZ3

JONES, Joe (1) Barrow: 1946 NZ

JONES, Keri (2) Wigan: **1970 F,NZ**

JONES, Les (1) St. Helens: 1971 NZ

JONES, Lewis (15) Leeds: 1954 A3,NZ3; 1955 NZ3; 1957 F3; **1957 F,A,NZ**

JONES, Mark (+1) Hull: 1992 f

JORDAN, Gary (2) Featherstone R: 1964 F; 1967 A

JOYNER, John (14+2) Castleford: 1978 A2; 1979 A3,NZ3; 1980 NZ3; 1983 F2; 1984 F,nz2

JOYNT, Chris (4+1) St. Helens: 1993 f,NZ3; 1994 F

JUBB, Ken (2) Leeds: 1937 A2

JUKES, Bill (6) Hunslet: 1908 A3; 1910 A2,NZ

KARALIUS, Tony (4+1) St. Helens: 1971 NZ3; 1972 F; **1972 nz**

KARALIUS, Vince (12) St. Helens: 1958 A2,NZ2; 1959 F; **1960 NZ,F,A**; 1960 F; 1961 F; Widnes: 1963 A2

KEEGAN, Arthur (9) Hull: 1966 A2; 1967 F2,A3; 1968 F; 1969 F

KELLY, Ken (4) St. Helens: 1972 F2; Warrington: 1980 NZ; 1982 A

KEMEL, George (2) Widnes: 1965 NZ2

KERSHAW, Herbert (2) Wakefield T: 1910 A,NZ

KINNEAR, Roy (1) Wigan: 1929 A

KISS, Nicky (1) Wigan: 1985 F

KITCHEN, Frank (2) Leigh: **1954 A,NZ**

KITCHIN, Phil (1) Whitehaven: 1965 NZ

KITCHING, Jack (1) Bradford N: 1946 A

KNAPMAN, Ernest (1) Oldham: 1924 NZ

KNOWELDEN, Bryn (1) Barrow: 1946 NZ

LAUGHTON, Doug (15) Wigan: 1970 A3,NZ2; **1970 A2,F,NZ**; 1971 F2; Widnes: 1973 A; 1974 F2; 1979 A

LAWRENSON, John (3) Wigan: 1948 A3

LAWS, David (1) Hull KR: 1986 F

LEDGARD, Jim (11) Dewsbury: 1947 NZ2; Leigh: 1948 A; 1950 A2,NZ; 1951 NZ; **1954 F2,A,NZ**

LEDGER, Barry (2) St. Helens: 1985 F; 1986 A

LEWIS, Gordon (1) Leigh: 1965 NZ

LEYTHAM, Jim (5) Wigan: 1907 NZ2; 1910 A2,NZ

LITTLE, Syd (10) Oldham: 1956 A; 1957 F5; **1957 F,A,NZ**; 1958 F

LLEWELLYN, Tom (2) Oldham: 1907 NZ2

LLOYD, Robbie (1) Halifax: 1920 A

LOCKWOOD, Brian (8+1) Castleford: **1972 A2,F,NZ**; 1973 A2; 1974 F; Hull KR: 1978 A; 1979 nz

LOMAS, Jim (7) Salford: 1908 A2; 1910 A2,NZ; Oldham: 1911 A2

LONGSTAFF, Fred (2) Huddersfield: 1914 A,NZ

LONGWORTH, Bill (3) Oldham: 1908 A3

LOUGHLIN, Paul (14+1) St. Helens: 1988 F,P,A3,NZ; 1989 F,NZ3; 1990 F,a; 1991 F; 1992 P,A

LOWE, John (1) Leeds: 1932 NZ

LOWE, Phil (12) Hull KR: 1970 NZ; 1972 F2; **1972 A2,F,NZ**; 1973 A3; 1978 A2

LOXTON, Ken (1) Huddersfield: 1971 NZ

LUCAS, Ian (1+1) Wigan: 1991 F; 1992 a

LYDON, Joe (23+7) Widnes: 1983 F2; 1984 F,a,NZ2,P; 1985 NZ3; Wigan: 1986 F,A3; 1987 F2,P; 1989 F2,nz; 1990 F,NZ3; 1992 p,a3,nz,**A**

McCORMICK, Stan (3) Belle Vue R: 1948 A2; St. Helens: 1948 A
McCUE, Tommy (6) Widnes: 1936 A; 1937 A; 1946 A3,NZ
McCURRIE, Steve (1) Widnes: 1993 F
McGINTY, Billy (4) Wigan: 1992 A2,NZ2
McINTYRE, Len (1) Oldham: 1963 A
McKEATING, Vince (2) Workington T: 1951 NZ2
McKINNEY, Tom (11) Salford: 1951 NZ; 1952 A2; 1954 A3,NZ; Warrington: 1955 NZ3; St. Helens: **1957 NZ**
McNAMARA, Steve (+2) Hull: 1992 f; 1993 f
McTIGUE, Brian (25) Wigan: 1958 A2,NZ2; 1959 F2,A3; 1960 F2; **1960 NZ,F,A**; 1961 F,NZ3; 1962 F,A3,NZ2; 1963 F
MANN, Arthur (2) Bradford N: 1908 A2
MANTLE, John (13) St. Helens: 1966 F2,A3; 1967 A2; 1969 F; 1971 F2,NZ2; 1973 A
MARCHANT, Tony (3) Castleford: 1986 F,A2
MARTIN, Billy (1) Workington T: 1962 F
MARTYN, Mick (2) Leigh: 1958 A; 1959 A
MATHER, Barrie-Jon (+1) Wigan: 1994 f
MATHIAS, Roy (1) St. Helens: 1979 A
MEASURES, Jim (2) Widnes: 1963 A2
MEDLEY, Paul (3+1) Leeds: 1987 P; 1988 Ff,P
MIDDLETON, Alf (1) Salford: 1929 A
MILLER, Joe (1) Wigan: 1911 A
MILLER, Joe (6) Warrington: 1933 A3; 1936 A,NZ2
MILLS, Jim (6) Widnes: 1974 A2,NZ; 1978 A2; 1979 A
MILLWARD, Roger (28+1) Castleford: 1966 F; Hull KR: 1967 A3; 1968 F2; **1968 A,F,NZ**; 1970 A2,NZ3; 1971 F,NZ3; 1973 A; 1974 A2a; **1977 F,NZ,A2**; 1978 A3
MILNES, Alf (2) Halifax: 1920 A2
MOLLOY, Steve (2) Leeds: 1993 F; Featherstone R: 1994 F
MOONEY, Walter (2) Leigh: 1924 NZ2
MOORHOUSE, Stan (2) Huddersfield: 1914 A,NZ
MORGAN, Arnold (4) Featherstone R: 1968 F2; **1968 F,NZ**
MORGAN, Edgar (2) Hull: 1921 A2
MORGAN, Ron (2) Swinton: 1963 F,A
MORIARTY, Paul (1+1) Widnes: 1991 P; 1994 f
MORLEY, Jack (2) Wigan: 1936 A; 1937 A
MORTIMER, Frank (2) Wakefield T: 1956 A2
MOSES, Glyn (9) St. Helens: 1955 NZ2; 1956 A; 1957 F3; **1957 F,A,NZ**
MUMBY, Keith (11) Bradford N: 1982 A; 1983 F; 1984 F2,A3,NZ3,P
MURPHY, Alex (27) St. Helens: 1958 A3,NZ; 1959 F2,A; **1960 NZ,F,A**; 1960 F; 1961 F,NZ3; 1962 F,A3; 1963 A2; 1964 F; 1965 F,NZ; 1966 F2; Warrington: 1971 NZ
MURPHY, Harry (1) Wakefield T: 1950 A

MYLER, Frank (23+1) Widnes: **1960 NZ,F,A;** 1960 F; 1961 F; 1962 F; 1963 A; 1964 F; 1965 F,NZ; 1966 A,NZnz; 1967 F2; St. Helens: 1970 A3,NZ3; **1970 A2,F**
MYLER, Tony (14) Widnes: 1983 F2; 1984 A2,NZ2,P; 1985 NZ2; 1986 F2,A3

NASH, Steve (24) Featherstone R: 1971 F,NZ; 1972 F2; **1972 A2,F,NZ**; 1973 A2; 1974 A3,NZ3; Salford: **1977 F,NZ,A2**; 1978 A3; 1982 A
NAUGHTON, Albert (2) Warrington: **1954 F2**
NEWBOULD, Tommy (1) Wakefield T: 1910 A
NEWLOVE, Paul (11+3) Featherstone R: 1989 nzNZ2; 1991 P; 1992 p,A3,nz; 1993 F; Bradford N: 1993 NZ3; 1994 F
NICHOLLS, George (29) Widnes: 1971 NZ; 1972 F2; St. Helens: 1973 A2; 1974 F2,A3,NZ3; **1977 F,NZ,A**; 1978 A3; 1979 A3,NZ3
NICHOLSON, Bob (3) Huddersfield: 1946 NZ 1948 A2
NICKLE, Sonny (1+4) St. Helens: 1992 p; 1993 f,NZnz2
NOBLE, Brian (11) Bradford N: 1982 A; 1983 F2; 1984 F,A3,NZ3,P
NORTON, Steve (11+1) Castleford: 1974 a,NZ2; Hull: 1978 A3; 1979 A2; 1980 NZ; 1981 F2; 1982 A

OFFIAH, Martin (30) Widnes: 1988 F,A3,NZ; 1989 F2,NZ3; 1990 F2,NZ3,A3; 1991 F2; Wigan: 1992 P,A3,NZ2,**A**; 1993 NZ2; 1994 F
O'GRADY, Terry (6) Oldham: 1954 A2,NZ3; Warrington: 1961 NZ
OLIVER, Joe (4) Batley: 1928 A3,NZ
O'NEILL, Dennis (2+1) Widnes: 1971 nz; **1972 A,F**
O'NEILL, Mike (3) Widnes: 1982 A; 1983 F2
OSTER, Jack (1) Oldham: 1929 A
OWEN, Jim (1) St. Helens Recs: 1921 A
OWEN, Stan (1) Leigh: 1958 F
OWENS, Ike (4) Leeds: 1946 A3,NZ

PADBURY, Dick (1) Runcorn: 1908 A
PALIN, Harold (2) Warrington: 1947 NZ2
PARKER, Dave (2) Oldham: 1964 F2
PARKIN, Jonty (17) Wakefield T: 1920 A2,NZ3; 1921 A2; 1924 A3,NZ; 1926 NZ2; 1928 A,NZ; 1929 A2
PARR, Ken (1) Warrington: 1968 F
PAWSEY, Charlie (7) Leigh: 1952 A3; 1954 A2,NZ2
PEPPERELL, Albert (2) Workington T: 1950 NZ; 1951 NZ
PHILLIPS, Doug (4) Oldham: 1946 A3; Belle Vue R: 1950 A
PIMBLETT, Albert (3) Warrington: 1948 A3
PINNER, Harry (6+1) St. Helens: 1980 nzNZ; 1985 NZ3; 1986 F; Widnes: 1986 A
PITCHFORD, Frank (2) Oldham: 1958 NZ; 1962 F
PITCHFORD, Steve (4) Leeds: **1977 F,NZ,A2**

PLANGE, David (1) Castleford: 1988 F
PLATT, Andy (21+4) St. Helens: 1985 f; 1986 f,a;
1988 F2,A2; Wigan: 1989 NZ3; 1990 F,A2;
1991 F2,P; 1992 f,P,A3,NZ2,**A**; 1993 F
POLLARD, Charlie (1) Wakefield T: 1924 NZ
POLLARD, Ernest (2) Wakefield T: 1932 A2
POLLARD, Roy (1) Dewsbury: 1950 NZ
POOLE, Harry (3) Hull KR: 1964 F; Leeds:
1966 NZ2
POTTER, Ian (7+1) Wigan: 1985 NZ3;
1986 F2,A2a
POWELL, Daryl (17+8) Sheffield E: 1990
f,P2,nzNZ2,A3; 1991 F2,P; 1992 fF,P,A3,NZ2;
1993 f,nz3; 1994 f
POWELL, Roy (13+6) Leeds: 1985 f; 1988
F2,A2a,NZ; 1989 F2,NZ2; 1990 P2,nz2NZ,Aa;
1991 f
POYNTON, Harold (3) Wakefield T: 1962 A2,NZ
PRESCOTT, Alan (28) St. Helens: 1951 NZ2; 1952
A3; 1954 A3,NZ3; 1955 NZ3; 1956 A3; 1957
F5; **1957 F,A,NZ**; 1958 F,A2
PRICE, Gary H (+1) Wakefield T: 1991 p
PRICE, Jack (6) Broughton R: 1921 A2; Wigan:
1924 A2,NZ2
PRICE, Malcolm (2) Rochdale H: 1967 A2
PRICE, Ray (9) Warrington: 1954 A,NZ2; 1955
NZ; 1956 A3; 1957 F2
PRICE, Terry (1) Bradford N: 1970 A
PRIOR, Bernard (1) Hunslet: 1966 F
PROCTOR, Wayne (+1) Hull: 1984 p
PROSSER, Dai (1) Leeds: 1937 A
PROSSER, Stuart (1) Halifax: 1914 A

RAE, Johnny (1) Bradford N: 1965 NZ
RAMSDALE, Dick (8) Wigan: 1910 A2; 1911 A2;
1914 A3,NZ
RAMSEY, Bill (7+1) Hunslet: 1965 NZ2; 1966
F,A2,NZ2; Bradford N; 1974 nz
RATCLIFFE, Gordon (3) Wigan: 1947 NZ;
1950 A2
RATHBONE, Alan (4+1) Bradford N: 1982 a;
1983 F2; 1985 F2
RAYNE, Keith (4) Leeds: 1984 F2,A,P
RAYNE, Kevin (1) Leeds: 1986 F
REDFEARN, Alan (1) Bradford N: 1979 A
REDFEARN, David (6+1) Bradford N: **1972 nz**;
1974 F2,A,NZ3
REES, Billo (11) Swinton: 1926 NZ2; 1928
A3,NZ3; 1929 A3
REES, Dai (1) Halifax: 1926 NZ
REES, Tom (1) Oldham: 1929 A
REILLY, Malcolm (9) Castleford: 1970 A3,NZ3;
1970 A2,F
RENILSON, Charlie (7+1) Halifax: 1965 NZ; 1967
a; 1968 F3; **1968 A,F,NZ**
RHODES, Austin (4) St. Helens: **1957 NZ; 1960
F,A**; 1961 NZ
RICHARDS, Maurice (2) Salford: 1974 A,NZ

RILEY, Joe (1) Halifax: 1910 A
RING, Johnny (2) Wigan: 1924 A; 1926 NZ
RISMAN, Gus (17) Salford: 1932 A,NZ3; 1933 A3;
1936 A2,NZ2; 1937 A3; 1946 A3
RISMAN, Bev (5) Leeds: 1968 F2; **1968 A,F,NZ**
RIX, Sid (9) Oldham: 1924 A3,NZ3; 1926 NZ3
ROBERTS, Ken (10) Halifax: 1963 A; 1964 F2;
1965 F,NZ3; 1966 F,NZ2
ROBINSON, Asa (3) Halifax: 1907 NZ; 1908 A2
ROBINSON, Bill (2) Leigh: 1963 F,A
ROBINSON, Dave (13) Swinton: 1965 NZ; 1966
F2,A3,NZ2; 1967 F2,A2; Wigan: 1970 A
ROBINSON, Don (10) Wakefield T: **1954 F2,NZ,A**;
1955 NZ; Leeds: 1956 A2; 1959 A2; 1960 F
ROBINSON, Jack (2) Rochdale H: 1914 A2
ROBINSON, Jason (1) Wigan: 1993 NZ
ROGERS, Johnny (7) Huddersfield: 1914 A; 1920
A3; 1921 A3
ROSE, David (4) Leeds: **1954 F2,A,NZ**
ROSE, Paul (2+3) Hull KR: 1974 a; 1978 Aa2;
Hull: 1982 A
ROUND, Gerry (8) Wakefield T: 1959 A; 1962
F2,A3,NZ2
RUDDICK, George (3) Broughton R: 1907 NZ2;
1910 A
RYAN, Bob (5) Warrington: 1950 A,NZ2; 1951 NZ;
1952 A
RYAN, Martin (4) Wigan: 1947 NZ; 1948 A2;
1950 A
RYDER, Ron (1) Warrington: 1952 A

SAYER, Bill (7) Wigan: 1961 NZ; 1962 F,A3,NZ;
1963 A
SCHOFIELD, Derrick (1) Halifax: 1955 NZ
SCHOFIELD, Garry (44) Hull: 1984 F,A3,NZ;
1985 NZ3; 1986 F2,A3; 1987 F2; Leeds: 1988
F2,P,A; 1990 F2,P2,NZ3,A3; 1991 F2,P; 1992
P,A3,NZ2,**A**; 1993 F,NZ3; 1994 F
SEABOURNE, Barry (1) Leeds: 1970 NZ
SENIOR, Ken (2) Huddersfield: 1965 NZ; 1967 F
SHARROCK, Jim (4) Wigan: 1910 A2,NZ; 1911 A
SHAW, Brian (6) Hunslet: 1956 A2; **1960 F,A**; 1960
F; Leeds: 1961 F
SHAW, Glyn (1) Widnes: 1980 NZ
SHAW, John (5) Halifax: **1960 F,A**; 1960 F; 1961 F;
1962 NZ
SHELTON, Geoff (7) Hunslet: 1964 F2; 1965 NZ3;
1966 F2
SHOEBOTTOM, Mick (10+2) Leeds: **1968 A,nz**;
1969 F; 1970 A2a,NZ; **1970 A2,F,NZ**; 1971 F
SHUGARS, Frank (1) Warrington: 1910 NZ
SILCOCK, Dick (1) Wigan: 1908 A
SILCOCK, Nat (12) Widnes: 1932 A2,NZ2; 1933
A3; 1936 A3; 1937 A2
SILCOCK, Nat (3) Wigan: 1954 A3
SIMMS, Barry (1) Leeds: 1962 F
SKELHORNE, George (7) Warrington: 1920 A,NZ3;
1921 A3

SKERRETT, Kelvin (14+2) Bradford N: 1989 NZ3; 1990 F2,NZ3; Wigan: 1992 F,p,A3,NZ,a; 1993 NZ

SKERRETT, Trevor (10) Wakefield T: 1979 A2,NZ2; Hull: 1980 NZ2; 1981 F2; 1982 A2

SLOMAN, Bob (5) Oldham: 1928 A3,NZ2

SMALES, Tommy (8) Huddersfield: 1962 F; 1963 F,A; 1964 F2; Bradford N: 1965 NZ3

SMALL, Peter (1) Castleford: 1962 NZ

SMITH, Alan (10) Leeds: 1970 A2,NZ3; **1970 A2**; 1971 F2; 1973 A

SMITH, Arthur (6) Oldham: 1907 NZ3; 1908 A3

SMITH, Bert (2) Bradford N: 1926 NZ2

SMITH, Fred (9) Hunslet: 1910 A,NZ; 1911 A3; 1914 A3,NZ

SMITH, Geoff (3) York: 1963 A; 1964 F2

SMITH, Mike (10+1) Hull KR: 1979 NZ3; 1980 NZ2; 1981 F2; 1982 A2; 1984 f,NZ

SMITH, Peter (1+5) Featherstone R: **1977 a2**; 1982 A; 1983 f2; 1984 f

SMITH, Sam (4) Hunslet: **1954 A,NZ,F2**

SMITH, Stanley (11) Wakefield T: 1929 A; Leeds: 1929 A2; 1932 A3,NZ3; 1933 A2

SOUTHWARD, Ike (11) Workington T: 1958 A3,NZ; Oldham: 1959 F2,A2; 1960 F2; 1962 NZ

SPENCER, Jack (1) Salford: 1907 NZ

SPRUCE, Stuart (1) Widnes: 1993 F

STACEY, Cyril (1) Halifax: 1920 NZ

STEADMAN, Graham (8+1) Castleford: 1990 F; 1992 fF,A3,NZ2; 1994 F

STEPHENS, Gary (5) Castleford: 1979 A2,NZ3

STEPHENSON, David (9+1) Wigan: 1982 A2; 1986 A; 1987 F,P; Leeds: 1988 f,P,A2,NZ

STEPHENSON, Mick (5+1) Dewsbury: 1971 nz; 1972 F; **1972 A2,F,NZ**

STEVENSON, Jeff (19) Leeds: 1955 NZ3; 1956 A3; 1957 F5; **1957 F,A,NZ**; 1958 F; York: 1959 A2; 1960 F2

STOCKWELL, Squire (3) Leeds: 1920 A; 1921 A2

STONE, Billy (8) Hull: 1920 A3,NZ3; 1921 A2

STOPFORD, John (12) Swinton: 1961 F; 1963 F,A2; 1964 F2; 1965 F,NZ2; 1966 F2,A

STOTT, Jim (1) St. Helens: 1947 NZ

STREET, Harry (4) Dewsbury: 1950 A3,NZ

SULLIVAN, Anthony (1) St. Helens: 1991 P

SULLIVAN, Clive (17) Hull: 1967 F; **1968 A,F,NZ**; 1970 A; 1971 NZ3; 1972 F2; **1972 A2,F,NZ**; 1973 A3

SULLIVAN, Jim (25) Wigan: 1924 A3,NZ; 1926 NZ3; 1928 A3,NZ3; 1929 A3; 1932 A3,NZ3; 1933 A3

SULLIVAN, Mick (46) Huddersfield: **1954 F2,NZ,A**; 1955 NZ3; 1956 A3; 1957 F3; **1957 F,A,NZ**; Wigan: 1957 F2; 1958 F,A3,NZ2; 1959 F2,A3; 1960 F3; **1960 F,NZ,A**; St. Helens: 1961 F,NZ2; 1962 F3,A3,NZ; York: 1963 A

SZYMALA, Eddie (1+1) Barrow: 1981 fF

TAIT, Alan (10+4) Widnes: 1989 F2,NZ2; 1990 F2,P2; 1992 F; Leeds: 1992 a; 1993 F,nz3

TAYLOR, Bob (2) Hull: 1921 A; 1926 NZ

TAYLOR, Harry (3) Hull: 1907 NZ3

TEMBEY, John (2) St. Helens: 1963 A; 1964 F

TERRY, Abe (11) St. Helens: 1958 A2; 1959 F2,A3; 1960 F; 1961 F,NZ; Leeds: 1962 F

THOMAS, Arthur "Ginger" (4) Leeds: 1926 NZ2; 1929 A2

THOMAS, George (1) Warrington: 1907 NZ

THOMAS, Gwyn (9) Wigan: 1914 A; Huddersfield: 1920 A3,NZ2; 1921 A3

THOMAS, Johnny (8) Wigan: 1907 NZ; 1908 A3; 1910 A2,NZ; 1911 A

THOMAS, Les (1) Oldham: 1947 NZ

THOMAS, Phil (1) Leeds: 1907 NZ

THOMPSON, Cecil (2) Hunslet: 1951 NZ2

THOMPSON, Jim (20+1) Featherstone R: 1970 A2,NZ2; **1970 A2,F,NZ**; 1971 Ff; 1974 A3,NZ3; **1977 F,NZ,A2**; Bradford N: 1978 A

THOMPSON, Joe (12) Leeds: 1924 A,NZ2; 1928 A,NZ; 1929 A; 1932 A3,NZ3

THORLEY, John (4) Halifax: **1954 F2,NZ,A**

TOOHEY, Ted (3) Barrow: 1952 A3

TOPLISS, David (4) Wakefield T: 1973 A2; 1979 A; Hull: 1982 A

TRAILL, Ken (8) Bradford N: 1950 NZ2; 1951 NZ; 1952 A3; 1954 A,NZ

TROUP, Alec (2) Barrow: 1936 NZ2

TURNBULL, Andrew (1) Leeds: 1951 NZ

TURNER, Derek (24) Oldham: 1956 A2; 1957 F5; **1957 F,A,NZ**; 1958 F; Wakefield T: 1959 A; 1960 F3; **1960 NZ,A**; 1961 F,NZ; 1962 A2,NZ2,F

TYSON, Brian (3) Hull KR: 1963 A; 1965 F; 1967 F

TYSON, George (4) Oldham: 1907 NZ; 1908 A3

VALENTINE, Bob (1) Huddersfield: 1967 A

VALENTINE, Dave (15) Huddersfield: 1948 A3; 1951 NZ; 1952 A2; 1954 A3,NZ2; **1954 F2,NZ,A**

VINES, Don (3) Wakefield T: 1959 F2,A

WADDELL, Hugh (5) Oldham: 1988 F2,A,NZ; Leeds: 1989 F

WAGSTAFF, Harold (12) Huddersfield: 1911 A2; 1914 A3,NZ; 1920 A2,NZ2; 1921 A2

WALKER, Arnold (1) Whitehaven: 1980 NZ

WALLACE, Jim (1) St. Helens Recs: 1926 NZ

WALSH, Joe (1) Leigh: 1971 NZ

WALSH, John (4+1) St. Helens: 1972 f; **1972 A2,F,NZ**

WALTON, Doug (1) Castleford: 1965 F

WANE, Shaun (2) Wigan: 1985 F; 1986 F

WARD, Billy (1) Leeds: 1910 A

WARD, David (12) Leeds: **1977 F,NZ,A**; 1978 A; 1979 A3,NZ3; 1981 F; 1982 A

WARD, Edward (3) Wigan: 1946 A2; 1947 NZ

WARD, Ernest (20) Bradford N: 1946 A3,NZ; 1947 NZ2; 1948 A3; 1950 A3,NZ2; 1951 NZ3; 1952 A3

WARD, Johnny (4) Castleford: 1963 A; 1964 F2; Salford: 1970 NZ

WARD, Kevin (15+2) Castleford: 1984 F; 1986 A3; 1987 P; 1988 F2,P,A3,NZ; 1989 F2; St. Helens: 1990 a2; 1992 **A**

WARLOW, John (6+1) St. Helens: 1964 F; **1968 f,NZ**; 1968 F; Widnes: 1971 F2,NZ

WARWICK, Silas (2) Salford: 1907 NZ2

WATKINS, Billy (7) Salford: 1933 A; 1936 A2,NZ2; 1937 A2

WATKINS, David (2+4) Salford: 1971 f,NZ; 1973 a; 1974 f2,A

WATKINSON, David (12+1) Hull KR: 1979 a; 1980 NZ; 1981 F; 1984 F; 1985 F,NZ3; 1986 F2,A3

WATSON, Cliff (29+1) St. Helens: 1963 A2; 1966 F2,A3,NZ2; 1967 F,A3; 1968 F2; **1968 A,F,nz**; 1969 F; 1970 A3,NZ3; **1970 A2,F,NZ**; 1971 F

WATTS, Basil (5) York: **1954 F2,NZ,A**; 1955 NZ

WEBSTER, Fred (3) Leeds: 1910 A2,NZ

WHITCOMBE, Frank (2) Bradford N: 1946 A2

WHITE, Les (7) Hunslet: 1932 A3,NZ2; 1933 A2

WHITE, Les (6) York: 1946 A3,NZ; Wigan: 1947 NZ2

WHITE, Tommy (1) Oldham: 1907 NZ

WHITEHEAD, Derek (3) Warrington: 1971 F2,NZ

WHITELEY, Johnny (15) Hull: **1957 A**; 1958 A3,NZ; 1959 F2,A2; 1960 F; **1960 NZ,F**; 1961 NZ2; 1962 F

WILKINSON, Jack (13) Halifax: 1954 A,NZ2;

1955 NZ3; Wakefield T: 1959 A; 1960 F2; **1960 NZ,F,A**; 1962 NZ

WILLIAMS, Billy (2) Salford: 1929 A; 1932 A

WILLIAMS, Dickie (12) Leeds: 1948 A2; 1950 A2,NZ2; 1951 NZ3; Hunslet: 1954 A2,NZ

WILLIAMS, Frank (2) Halifax: 1914 A2

WILLIAMS, Peter (1+1) Salford: 1989 fF

WILLICOMBE, David (3) Halifax: 1974 F; Wigan: 1974 F,NZ

WILSON, George (3) Workington T: 1951 NZ3

WILSON, Harry (3) Hunslet: 1907 NZ3

WINSLADE, Charlie (1) Oldham: 1959 F

WINSTANLEY, Billy (5) Leigh: 1910 A,NZ; Wigan: 1911 A3

WOOD, Alf (4) Oldham: 1911 A2; 1914 A,NZ

WOODS, Harry (6) Liverpool S: 1936 A3,NZ2; Leeds: 1937 A

WOODS, Jack (1) Barrow: 1933 A

WOODS, John (7+4) Leigh: 1979 A3,nz; 1980 NZ; 1981 F2; 1982 Aa; 1983 f; Warrington: 1987 p

WOODS, Tommy (2) Rochdale H: 1911 A2

WORRALL, Mick (3) Oldham: 1984 F,A2

WRIGHT, Darren (+1) Widnes: 1988 a

WRIGHT, Joe (1) Swinton: 1932 NZ

WRIGHT, Stuart (7) Widnes: **1977 F,NZ,A2**; 1978 A3

WRIGLESWORTH, Geoff (5) Leeds: 1965 NZ; 1966 A2,NZ2

YOUNG, Chris (5) Hull KR: 1967 A3; 1968 F2

YOUNG, Frank (1) Leeds: 1908 A

YOUNG, Harold (1) Huddersfield: 1929 A

Kevin Ward, holder of 17 Great Britain caps, on the rampage against Australia in July 1988, the double Kangaroo tackle being made by hooker Greg Conescu and skipper Wally Lewis (upper).

GREAT BRITAIN TOUR SUMMARIES

	P	W	D	L	T	G	For Pts	T	G	Against Pts
1910										
In Australia	14	9	1	4	76	56	340	51	47	247
In New Zealand	4	4	0	0	43	29	187	11	7	47
TOTAL	18	13	1	4	119	85	527	62	54	294
1914	P	W	D	L	T	G	Pts	T	G	Pts
In Australia	12	9	0	3	77	55	341	24	31	134
In New Zealand	6	6	0	0	46	28	194	12	13	62
TOTAL	18	15	0	3	123	83	535	36	44	196
1920	P	W	D	L	T	G	Pts	T	G	Pts
In Australia	15	12	0	3	83	64	377	48	42	228
In New Zealand	10	9	0	1	89	47	361	24	16	104
TOTAL	25	21	0	4	172	111	738	72	58	332
1924	P	W	D	L	T	G	Pts	T	G	Pts
In Australia	18	14	0	4	104	77	466	56	45	258
In New Zealand	9	7	0	2	64	40	272	25	21	117
TOTAL	27	21	0	6	168	117	738	81	66	375
1928	P	W	D	L	T	G	Pts	T	G	Pts
In Australia	16	11	1	4	67	60	321	43	45	219
In New Zealand	8	7	0	1	55	36	237	16	12	72
TOTAL	24	18	1	5	122	96	558	59	57	291
1932	P	W	D	L	T	G	Pts	T	G	Pts
In Australia	18	15	1	2	105	84	483	32	38	172
In New Zealand	8	8	0	0	65	52	299	17	18	87
TOTAL	26	23	1	2	170	136	782	49	56	259
1936	P	W	D	L	T	G	Pts	T	G	Pts
In Australia	17	14	0	3	79	82	401	38	45	204
In New Zealand	8	8	0	0	52	27	210	8	16	56
TOTAL	25	22	0	3	131	109	611	46	61	260
1946	P	W	D	L	T	G	Pts	T	G	Pts
In Australia	20	16	1	3	146	100	638	36	45	198
In New Zealand	7	5	0	2	35	20	145	12	21	78
TOTAL	27	21	1	5	181	120	783	48	66	276
1950	P	W	D	L	T	G	Pts	T	G	Pts
In Australia	19	15	0	4	133	102	603	22	56	178
In New Zealand	6	4	0	2	37	25	161	16	20	88
TOTAL	25	19	0	6	170	127	764	38	76	266

1954	P	W	D	L	T	G	**For** Pts	T	G	**Against** Pts
In Australia	*22	13	1	7	133	114	627	78	96	426
In New Zealand	10	8	0	2	60	56	292	14	32	106
TOTAL	*32	21	1	9	193	170	919	92	128	532

*One match abandoned. Scores included in points total.

1958	P	W	D	L	T	G	Pts	T	G	Pts
In Australia	21	19	1	1	184	129	810	64	93	378
In New Zealand	9	8	0	1	88	61	386	18	27	108
TOTAL	30	27	1	2	272	190	1,196	82	120	486

1962	P	W	D	L	T	G	Pts	T	G	Pts
In Australia	21	18	0	3	151	113	679	61	60	303
In New Zealand	9	6	0	3	73	50	319	35	28	161
TOTAL	30	24	0	6	224	163	998	96	88	464

1966	P	W	D	L	T	G	Pts	T	G	Pts
In Australia	22	13	0	9	112	85	506	47	83	307
In New Zealand	8	8	0	0	57	47	265	10	24	78
TOTAL	30	21	0	9	169	132	771	57	107	385

1970	P	W	D	L	T	G	Pts	T	G	Pts
In Australia	17	15	1	1	104	92	496	27	66	213
In New Zealand	7	7	0	0	61	37	257	9	24	75
TOTAL	24	22	1	1	165	129	753	36	90	288

1974	P	W	D	L	T	G	DG	Pts	T	G	DG	Pts
In Australia	20	15	0	5	104	93	2	500	38	59	3	235
In New Zealand	8	6	0	2	37	32	0	175	8	27	0	78
TOTAL	28	21	0	7	141	125	2	675	46	86	3	313

1979	P	W	D	L	T	G	DG	Pts	T	G	Pts
In Australia	18	13	1	4	66	73	3	347	39	68	253
In New Zealand	9	8	0	1	48	34	0	212	15	12	69
TOTAL	27	21	1	5	114	107	3	559	54	80	332

1984	P	W	D	L	T	G	DG	Pts	T	G	DG	Pts
In Australia	15	11	0	4	70	59	1	399	40	46	2	254
In New Zealand	8	4	0	4	32	25	1	179	21	21	0	126
In Papua New Guinea	1	1	0	0	7	5	0	38	4	2	0	20
TOTAL	24	16	0	8	109	89	2	616	65	69	2	400

1988	P	W	D	L	T	G	DG	Pts	T	G	DG	Pts
In Papua New Guinea	2	2	0	0	13	13	0	78	7	6	0	40
In Australia	13	8	0	5	59	47	0	330	42	36	1	241
In New Zealand	3	1	0	2	8	8	0	48	10	10	0	60
TOTAL	18	11	0	7	80	68	0	456	59	52	1	341

								For			**Against**	
1990	P	W	D	L	T	G	DG	Pts	T	G	DG	Pts
In Papua New Guinea	5	4	0	1	31	24	0	172	7	15	2	60
In New Zealand	10	6	0	4	30	28	3	179	24	32	1	161
TOTAL	15	10	0	5	61	52	3	351	31	47	3	221
1992	P	W	D	L	T	G	DG	Pts	T	G	DG	Pts
In Papua New Guinea	3	3	0	0	15	11	0	82	8	8	1	49
In Australia	10	7	0	3	32	29	2	188	20	19	0	118
In New Zealand	4	3	0	1	10	11	2	64	7	8	1	45
TOTAL	17	13	0	4	57	51	4	334	35	35	2	212

GREAT BRITAIN TOUR SQUADS TO AUSTRALIA AND NEW ZEALAND

Captains in bold

1910 Tour

J. Lomas (Salford)
A. Avery (Oldham)
J. Bartholomew (Huddersfield)
W. Batten (Hunslet)
F. Boylen (Hull)
E. Curzon (Salford)
J. Davies (Huddersfield)
F. Farrar (Hunslet)
T. Helm (Oldham)
B. Jenkins (Wigan)
T. Jenkins (Ebbw Vale)
W. Jukes (Hunslet)
H. Kershaw (Wakefield T.)
J. Leytham (Wigan)
T. Newbould (Wakefield T.)
R. Ramsdale (Wigan)
J. Riley (Halifax)
G. Ruddick (Broughton R.)
J. Sharrock (Wigan)
F. Shugars (Warrington)
F. Smith (Hunslet)
J. Thomas (Wigan)
W. Ward (Leeds)
F. Webster (Leeds)
W. Winstanley (Leigh)
F. Young (Leeds)

Managers: J. Clifford
(Huddersfield) and J.
Houghton (St. Helens)

1914 Tour

H. Wagstaff (Huddersfield)
J. Chilcott (Huddersfield)
J. Clampitt (Broughton R.)
D. Clark (Huddersfield)
A. Coldrick (Wigan)
W. A. Davies (Leeds)
A. Francis (Hull)
J. Guerin (Hunslet)
W. Hall (Oldham)
D. Holland (Oldham)
J. Jarman (Leeds)
B. Jenkins (Wigan)
A. Johnson (Widnes)
F. Longstaff (Huddersfield)
S. Moorhouse (Huddersfield)
J. O'Garra (Widnes)
W. Prosser (Halifax)
R. Ramsdale (Wigan)
J. Robinson (Rochdale H.)
J. Rogers (Huddersfield)
W. Roman (Rochdale H.)
J. Smales (Hunslet)
F. Smith (Hunslet)
G. Thomas (Wigan)
F. Williams (Halifax)
A. Wood (Oldham)

Managers: J. Clifford
(Huddersfield) and J.
Houghton (St. Helens)

1920 Tour

H. Wagstaff (Huddersfield)
J. Bacon (Leeds)
J. Bowers (Rochdale H.)
J. Cartwright (Leigh)
D. Clark (Huddersfield)
W. Cunliffe (Warrington)
E. Davies (Oldham)
J. Doyle (Barrow)
F. Gallagher (Dewsbury)
B. Gronow (Huddersfield)
H. Hilton (Oldham)
D. Hurcombe (Wigan)
A. Johnson (Widnes)
E. Jones (Rochdale H.)
R. Lloyd (Halifax)
A. Milnes (Halifax)
J. Parkin (Wakefield T.)
G. Rees (Leeds)
W. Reid (Widnes)
J. Rogers (Huddersfield)
G. Skelhorne (Warrington)
J. Stacey (Halifax)
S. Stockwell (Leeds)
W. Stone (Hull)
G. Thomas (Huddersfield)
A. Wood (Oldham)

Managers: S. Foster (Halifax)
and J. Wilson (Hull K.R.)

1924 Tour

J. Parkin (Wakefield T.)
J. Bacon (Leeds)
J. Bennett (Rochdale H.)
W. Bentham (Broughton R.)
H. Bowman (Hull)
A. Brough (Oldham)
W. Burgess (Barrow)
C. Carr (Barrow)
W. Cunliffe (Warrington)
J. Darwell (Leigh)
F. Evans (Swinton)
F. Gallagher (Batley)
B. Gronow (Huddersfield)
T. Howley (Wigan)
D. Hurcombe (Wigan)
E. Knapman (Oldham)
W. Mooney (Leigh)
C. Pollard (Wakefield T.)
J. Price (Wigan)
D. Rees (Halifax)
J. Ring (Wigan)
S. Rix (Oldham)
R. Sloman (Oldham)
J. Sullivan (Wigan)
J. Thompson (Leeds)
S. Whitty (Hull)

Managers: J.H. Dannatt
(Hull) and E. Osborne
(Warrington)

1928 Tour

J. Parkin (Wakefield T.)
T. Askin (Featherstone R.)
N. Bentham (Wigan Highfield)
F. Bowen (St. Helens Recs)
H. Bowman (Hull)
J. Brough (Leeds)
W. Burgess (Barrow)
O. Dolan (St. Helens Recs)
A. Ellaby (St. Helens)
B. Evans (Swinton)
J. Evans (Swinton)
L. Fairclough (St. Helens)
A. Fildes (St. Helens Recs)
A. Frodsham (St. Helens)
W. Gowers (Rochdale H.)
E. Gwynne (Hull)
B. Halfpenny (St. Helens)
W. Horton (Wakefield T.)
J. Oliver (Batley)
W. Rees (Swinton)
M. Rosser (Leeds)
R. Sloman (Oldham)
J. Sullivan (Wigan)
J. Thompson (Leeds)
W. Williams (Salford)
H. Young (Bradford N.)

Managers: G. Hutchins
(Oldham) and E. Osborne
(Warrington)

1932 Tour

J. Sullivan (Wigan)
L. Adams (Leeds)
A. Atkinson (Castleford)
S. Brogden (Huddersfield)
F. Butters (Swinton)
I. Davies (Halifax)
W. Dingsdale (Warrington)
A. Ellaby (St. Helens)
B. Evans (Swinton)
J. Feetham (Salford)
N. Fender (York)
A. Fildes (St. Helens)
M. Hodgson (Swinton)
W. Horton (Wakefield T.)
B. Hudson (Salford)
J. Lowe (Leeds)
E. Pollard (Wakefield T.)
A. Risman (Salford)
G. Robinson (Wakefield T.)
N. Silcock (Widnes)
S. Smith (Leeds)
J. Thompson (Leeds)
L. White (Hunslet)
W. Williams (Salford)
J. Woods (Barrow)
J. Wright (Swinton)

Managers: R. Anderton
(Warrington) and G. Hutchins
(Oldham)

1936 Tour

J. Brough (Leeds)
J. Arkwright (Warrington)
T. Armitt (Swinton)
A. Atkinson (Castleford)
W. Belshaw (Liverpool S.)
H. Beverley (Hunslet)
S. Brogden (Leeds)
E. Davies (Wigan)
A. Edwards (Salford)
H. Ellerington (Hull)
G. Exley (Wakefield T.)
H. Field (York)
F. Harris (Leeds)
M. Hodgson (Swinton)

B. Hudson (Salford)
E. Jenkins (Salford)
H. Jones (Keighley)
T. McCue (Widnes)
J. Miller (Warrington)
J. Morley (Wigan)
A. Risman (Salford)
N. Silcock (Widnes)
S. Smith (Leeds)
L. Troup (Barrow)
W. Watkins (Salford)
H. Woods (Liverpool S.)

Managers: R. Anderton
(Warrington) and
W. Popplewell (Bramley)

1946 Tour

A. Risman (Salford)
A. Bassett (Halifax)
E. Batten (Bradford N.)
G. Curran (Salford)
W.T.H. Davies (Bradford N.)
J. Egan (Wigan)
T. Foster (Bradford N.)
K. Gee (Wigan)
W. Horne (Barrow)
F. Hughes (Workington T.)
D. Jenkins (Leeds)
A. Johnson (Warrington)

J. Jones (Barrow)
J. Kitching (Bradford N.)
B. Knowelden (Barrow)
J. Lewthwaite (Barrow)
T. McCue (Widnes)
H. Murphy (Wakefield T.)
R. Nicholson (Huddersfield)
I. Owens (Leeds)
D. Phillips (Oldham)
M. Ryan (Wigan)
Edward Ward (Wigan)
Ernest Ward (Bradford N.)
F. Whitcombe (Bradford N.)
L. White (York)

Managers: W. Popplewell
(Bramley) and W. Gabbatt
(Barrow)

1950 Tour

E. Ward (Bradford N.)
E. Ashcroft (Wigan)
T. Bradshaw (Wigan)
J. Cunliffe (Wigan)
T. Danby (Salford)
A. Daniels (Halifax)
J. Egan (Wigan)
J. Featherstone (Warrington)
K. Gee (Wigan)
E. Gwyther (Belle Vue R.)
F. Higgins (Widnes)
J. Hilton (Wigan)
W. Horne (Barrow)
J. Ledgard (Leigh)
H. Murphy (Wakefield T.)
D. Naughton (Widnes)
F. Osmond (Swinton)
A. Pepperell (Workington T.)
D. Phillips (Belle Vue R.)
R. Pollard (Dewsbury)
G. Ratcliffe (Wigan)
M. Ryan (Wigan)
R. Ryan (Warrington)
H. Street (Dewsbury)
K. Traill (Bradford N.)
R. Williams (Leeds)

Managers: G. Oldroyd
(Dewsbury) and T. Spedding
(Belle Vue R.)

1954 Tour

R. Williams (Hunslet)
E. Ashcroft (Wigan)
W. Boston (Wigan)
J. Bowden (Huddersfield)
B. Briggs (Huddersfield)
A. Burnell (Hunslet)
E. Cahill (Rochdale H.)
F. Castle (Barrow)
J. Cunliffe (Wigan)
D. Greenall (St. Helens)
G. Gunney (Hunslet)
T. Harris (Hull)
G. Helme (Warrington)
J. Henderson (Workington T.)
P. Jackson (Barrow)
B. L. Jones (Leeds)
T. McKinney (Salford)
T. O'Grady (Oldham)
C. Pawsey (Leigh)
A. Prescott (St. Helens)
R. Price (Warrington)
N. Silcock (Wigan)
K. Traill (Bradford N.)
A. Turnbull (Leeds)
D. Valentine (Huddersfield)
J. Wilkinson (Halifax)

Managers: T. Hesketh
(Wigan) and H. Rawson
(Hunslet)

1958 Tour

A. Prescott (St. Helens)
A. Ackerley (Halifax)
H. Archer (Workington T.)
E. Ashton (Wigan)
D. Bolton (Wigan)
F. Carlton (St. Helens)
J. Challinor (Warrington)
A. Davies (Oldham)
B. Edgar (Workington T.)
E. Fraser (Warrington)
D. Goodwin (Barrow)
T. Harris (Hull)
R. Huddart (Whitehaven)
K. Jackson (Oldham)
P. Jackson (Barrow)
V. Karalius (St. Helens)

B. McTigue (Wigan)
M. Martyn (Leigh)
G. Moses (St. Helens)
A. Murphy (St. Helens)
F. Pitchford (Oldham)
I. Southward (Workington T.)
M. Sullivan (Wigan)
A. Terry (St. Helens)
J. Whiteley (Hull)
W. Wookey (Workington T.)

Managers: B. Manson
(Swinton) and T. Mitchell
(Workington T.)
Coach: J. Brough
(Workington T.)

1962 Tour

E. Ashton (Wigan)
D. Bolton (Wigan)
W. Boston (Wigan)
F. Carlton (Wigan)
G. Cooper (Featherstone R.)
B. Edgar (Workington T.)
R. Evans (Wigan)
D. Fox (Featherstone R.)
N. Fox (Wakefield T.)
E. Fraser (Warrington)
L. Gilfedder (Warrington)
N. Herbert (Workington T.)
R. Huddart (St. Helens)
B. McTigue (Wigan)
A. Murphy (St. Helens)
K. Noble (Huddersfield)
H. Poynton (Wakefield T.)
G. Round (Wakefield T.)
W. Sayer (Wigan)
J. Shaw (Halifax)
P. Small (Castleford)
I. Southward (Workington T.)
M. Sullivan (St. Helens)
J. Taylor (Hull K.R.)
D. Turner (Wakefield T.)
J. Wilkinson (Wakefield T.)

Managers: S. Hadfield
(Wakefield T.) and A. Walker
(Rochdale H.)
Coach: C. Hutton (Hull K.R.)

1966 Tour

H. Poole (Leeds)
W. Aspinall (Warrington)
T. Bishop (St. Helens)
I. Brooke (Bradford N.)
W. Bryant (Castleford)
A. Buckley (Swinton)
W. Burgess (Barrow)
C. Clarke (Wigan)
G. Crewdson (Keighley)
C. Dooler (Featherstone R.)
B. Edgar (Workington T.)
P. Flanagan (Hull K.R.)
T. Fogerty (Halifax)
K. Gowers (Swinton)
A. Hardisty (Castleford)
B. Jones (Wakefield T.)
A. Keegan (Hull)
J. Mantle (St. Helens)
F. Myler (Widnes)
W. Ramsey (Hunslet)
K. Roberts (Halifax)
D. Robinson (Swinton)
G. Shelton (Hunslet)
J. Stopford (Swinton)
C. Watson (St. Helens)
G. Wriglesworth (Leeds)

Managers: W. Spaven (Hull
K.R.) and J. Errock (Oldham)

1970 Tour

F. Myler (St. Helens)
J. Atkinson (Leeds)
D. Chisnall (Leigh)
R. Dutton (Widnes)
D. Edwards (Castleford)
A. Fisher (Bradford N.)
P. Flanagan (Hull K.R.)
A. Hardisty (Castleford)
D. Hartley (Castleford)
K. Hepworth (Castleford)
C. Hesketh (Salford)
S. Hynes (Leeds)
R. Irving (Oldham)
D. Laughton (Wigan)
P. Lowe (Hull K.R.)
R. Millward (Hull K.R.)
T. Price (Bradford N.)

M. Reilly (Castleford)
D. Robinson (Wigan)
B. Seabourne (Leeds)
M. Shoebottom (Leeds)
A. Smith (Leeds)
C. Sullivan (Hull)
J. Thompson (Featherstone R.)
J. Ward (Salford)
C. Watson (St. Helens)

Manager: J. Harding (Leigh)
Coach: J. Whiteley (Hull)

1974 Tour

C. Hesketh (Salford)
K. Ashcroft (Warrington)
J. Atkinson (Leeds)
A. Bates (Dewsbury)
J. Bates (Dewsbury)
J. Bevan (Warrington)
J. Bridges (Featherstone R.)
J. Butler (Rochdale H.)
P. Charlton (Salford)
E. Chisnall (St. Helens)
T. Clawson (Oldham)
C. Dixon (Salford)
L. Dyl (Leeds)
D. Eckersley (St. Helens)
K. Gill (Salford)
J. Gray (Wigan)
J. Mills (Widnes)
R. Millward (Hull K.R.)
S. Nash (Featherstone R.)
G. Nicholls (St. Helens)
S. Norton (Castleford)
D. Redfearn (Bradford N.)
P. Rose (Hull K.R.)
J. Thompson (Featherstone R.)
D. Watkins (Salford)
D. Willicombe (Wigan)

Replacements during tour
W. Ramsey (Bradford N.) for
J. Bates; M. Richards
(Salford) for Atkinson

Manager: R. Parker
(Blackpool B.)
Coach: J. Challinor
(St. Helens)

1979 Tour

D. Laughton (Widnes)
M. Adams (Widnes)
D. Barends (Bradford N.)
L. Casey (Bradford N.)
S. Evans (Featherstone R.)
P. Glynn (St. Helens)
J. Grayshon (Bradford N.)
P. Hogan (Hull K.R.)
J. Holmes (Leeds)
E. Hughes (Widnes)
M. James (St. Helens)
J. Joyner (Castleford)
G. Liptrot (St. Helens)
B. Lockwood (Hull K.R.)
T. Martyn (Warrington)
R. Mathias (St. Helens)
J. Mills (Widnes)
R. Millward (Hull K.R.)
K. Mumby (Bradford N.)
S. Nash (Salford)
G. Nicholls (St. Helens)
S. Norton (Hull)
A. Redfearn (Bradford N.)
T. Skerrett (Wakefield T.)
M. Smith (Hull K.R.)
G. Stephens (Castleford)
C. Stone (Hull)
D. Ward (Leeds)
D. Watkinson (Hull K.R.)
J. Woods (Leigh)

Replacements during tour
J. Burke (Wakefield T.) for
Mills; G. Fairbairn (Wigan)
for Martyn; D. Topliss
(Wakefield T.) for Millward

Managers: H. Womersley
(Bradford N.) and
R. Gemmell (Hull)
Coach: E. Ashton (St. Helens)

1984 Tour*

B. Noble (Bradford N.)
M. Adams (Widnes)
R. Ashton (Oldham)
K. Beardmore (Castleford)
M. Burke (Widnes)
C. Burton (Hull K.R.)
B. Case (Wigan)
G. Clark (Hull K.R.)
L. Crooks (Hull)
S. Donlan (Leigh)
D. Drummond (Leigh)
R. Duane (Warrington)
T. Flanagan (Oldham)
D. Foy (Oldham)
A. Goodway (Oldham)
A. Gregory (Widnes)
E. Hanley (Bradford N.)
D. Hobbs (Featherstone R.)
N. Holding (St. Helens)
J. Joyner (Castleford)
J. Lydon (Widnes)
K. Mumby (Bradford N.)
A. Myler (Widnes)
M. O'Neill (Widnes)
H. Pinner (St. Helens)
W. Proctor (Hull)
Keith Rayne (Leeds)
G. Schofield (Hull)
M. Smith (Hull K.R.)
M. Worrall (Oldham)

Replacement during tour
J. Basnett (Widnes) for Duane

Managers: R. Gemmell (Hull)
and R. Davis (RLHQ)
Coach: Frank Myler (Oldham)

*One match in Papua New
 Guinea

1988 Tour*

E. Hanley (Wigan)
K. Beardmore (Castleford)
B. Case (Wigan)
L. Crooks (Leeds)
P. Dixon (Halifax)
S. Edwards (Wigan)
K. Fairbank (Bradford N.)
M. Ford (Oldham)
P. Ford (Bradford N.)
C. Gibson (Leeds)
H. Gill (Wigan)
A. Gregory (Wigan)
M. Gregory (Warrington)
P. Groves (St. Helens)
R. Haggerty (St. Helens)
D. Hulme (Widnes)
P. Loughlin (St. Helens)
P. Medley (Leeds)
M. Offiah (Widnes)
A. Platt (St. Helens)
R. Powell (Leeds)
G. Schofield (Leeds)
D. Stephenson (Leeds)
H. Waddell (Oldham)
K. Ward (Castleford)
I. Wilkinson (Halifax)

Replacements during tour
D. Wright (Widnes) for
Edwards; A. Currier (Widnes)
and P. Hulme (Widnes) for
Schofield and Medley; R.
Eyres (Widnes) and J. Joyner
(Castleford) for Crooks, Dixon
and Platt

Managers: L. Bettinson
(Salford) and D. Howes
(RLHQ)
Coach: M. Reilly

*Including Papua New Guinea

1990 Tour*

M. Gregory (Warrington)
D. Betts (Wigan)
C. Bibb (Featherstone R.)
D. Bishop (Hull K.R.)
P. Clarke (Wigan)
J. Davies (Widnes)
M. Dermott (Wigan)
P. Dixon (Leeds)
P. Eastwood (Hull)
K. England (Castleford)
K. Fairbank (Bradford N.)
D. Fox (Featherstone R.)
C. Gibson (Leeds)
R. Goulding (Wigan)
S. Irwin (Castleford)
L. Jackson (Hull)
I. Lucas (Wigan)
J. Lydon (Wigan)
M. Offiah (Widnes)
D. Powell (Sheffield E.)
R. Powell (Leeds)
G. H. Price (Wakefield T.)
G. Schofield (Leeds)
R. Simpson (Bradford N.)
K. Skerrett (Bradford N.)
I. Smales (Featherstone R.)
G. Steadman (Castleford)
A. Sullivan (Hull K.R.)
A. Tait (Widnes)

Replacements during tour
J. Devereux (Widnes) for
Sullivan; D. Lyon
(Warrington) for Tait

Manager: M. Lindsay (Wigan)
Coach: M. Reilly

*Papua New Guinea and
 New Zealand only

1992 Tour*

E. Hanley (Leeds)
D. Betts (Wigan)
P. Clarke (Wigan)
G. Connolly (St. Helens)
N. Cowie (Wigan)
L. Crooks (Castleford)
M. Dermott (Wigan)
J. Devereux (Widnes)
P. Eastwood (Hull)
S. Edwards (Wigan)
K. Ellis (Warrington)
K. Fairbank (Bradford N.)
D. Fox (Featherstone R.)
A. Gregory (Wigan)
G. Hallas (Hull K.R.)
S. Hampson (Wigan)
L. Holliday (Widnes)
A. Hunte (St. Helens)
L. Jackson (Hull)
M. Jackson (Wakefield T.)
P. Loughlin (St. Helens)
I. Lucas (Wigan)
J. Lydon (Wigan)

W. McGinty (Wigan)
P. Newlove (Featherstone R.)
S. Nickle (St. Helens)
M. Offiah (Wigan)
A. Platt (Wigan)
D. Powell (Sheffield E.)
G. Schofield (Leeds)
K. Skerrett (Wigan)
G. Steadman (Castleford)

Replacements during tour
P. Hulme (Widnes) for Nickle
K. Harrison (Halifax),
S. McNamara (Hull), D. Myers
(Wigan), M. Aston (Sheffield E.)
and P. Broadbent (Sheffield E.)
for Gregory, Holliday, Loughlin,
Hanley and Lucas; D. Sampson
(Castlford) for Cowie

Manager: M. Lindsay (Wigan)
Coach: M. Reilly

*Including Papua New Guinea

The Great Britain side on duty against France at Toulouse in February 1969, from left to right.
Back row: Colin Dixon, John Mantle, Dennis Hartley, Cliff Watson, Dick Gemmell, Neil Fox.
Front row: Bill Burgess, Mick Shoebottom, Alan Burwell, Tommy Bishop, Ray Batten, Kevin Ashcroft, Arthur Keegan.

ALL TIME TOUR RECORDS

IN AUSTRALIA
Highest score: 101-0 v. South Australia in 1914

Biggest defeat: 42-6 v. New South Wales in 1920
(Also *widest margin*)

Fewest defeats: 1 (and 1 draw) from 21 matches in 1958 and from 17 matches in 1970

Most defeats: 9 from 22 matches in 1966

Biggest attendances: 70,419 v. New South Wales (Sydney) in 1950

IN NEW ZEALAND
Highest score: 81-14 v. Bay of Plenty in 1962

Widest margin win: 72-3 v. Buller in 1928
72-3 v. North Island in 1958

Biggest defeat: 46-13 v. Auckland in 1962 (Also *widest margin*)

Fewest defeats: The tourists have won all their matches in the following years: 1910 (4 matches), 1914 (6), 1932 (8), 1936 (8), 1966 (8), 1970 (7).

Most defeats: 4 from 8 matches in 1984

Biggest attendance: 35,000 v. Auckland in 1920

PLAYERS' FULL TOUR RECORDS
Most full appearances: 24 by Dick Huddart in 1958

Most tries: 38 by Mick Sullivan in 1958

Most goals and points: 127g, 278 pts by Lewis Jones in 1954

Most tours: 4 by Garry Schofield (1984, 1988, 1990, 1992)

Biggest club representation: 13+1 replacement by Wigan in 1992 — Denis Betts, Phil Clarke, Neil Cowie, Martin Dermott, Shaun Edwards, Andy Gregory, Steve Hampson, Ian Lucas, Joe Lydon, Billy McGinty, Martin Offiah, Andy Platt, Kelvin Skerrett, plus David Myers as a replacement

Brothers touring together: Bryn and Jack Evans (1928), Don and Neil Fox (1962), Alan and John Bates (1974), David and Paul Hulme (1988, Paul as replacement)

GREAT BRITAIN IN THE WORLD CUP

A — Australia, Fr — France, GB — Great Britain, NZ — New Zealand, PNG — Papua New Guinea

1954 in France   *Winners:* Great Britain

30 Oct.	Fr	22	NZ	13	Paris	13,240
31 Oct.	GB	28	A	13	Lyons	10,250
7 Nov.	GB	13	Fr	13	Toulouse	37,471
7 Nov.	A	34	NZ	15	Marseilles	20,000
11 Nov.	GB	26	NZ	6	Bordeaux	14,000
11 Nov.	A	5	Fr	15	Nantes	13,000

Play-off

13 Nov.	GB	16	Fr	12	Paris	30,368

Final Table

	P.	W.	D.	L.	F.	A.	Pts.
Great Britain	3	2	1	0	67	32	5
France	3	2	1	0	50	31	5
Australia	3	1	0	2	52	58	2
New Zealand	3	0	0	3	34	82	0

1957 in Australia   *Winners:* Australia

15 June	GB	23	Fr	5	Sydney	50,007
15 June	A	25	NZ	5	Brisbane	29,636
17 June	GB	6	A	31	Sydney	57,955
17 June	NZ	10	Fr	14	Brisbane	28,000
22 June	A	26	Fr	9	Sydney	35,158
25 June	GB	21	NZ	29	Sydney	14,263

Final Table

	P.	W.	D.	L.	F.	A.	Pts.
Australia	3	3	0	0	82	20	6
Great Britain	3	1	0	2	50	65	2
New Zealand	3	1	0	2	44	60	2
France	3	1	0	2	28	59	2

1960 in England   *Winners:* Great Britain

24 Sep.	GB	23	NZ	8	Bradford	20,577
24 Sep.	A	13	Fr	12	Wigan	20,278
1 Oct.	A	21	NZ	15	Leeds	10,773
1 Oct.	GB	33	Fr	7	Swinton	22,923
8 Oct.	A	3	GB	10	Bradford	32,773
8 Oct.	NZ	9	Fr	0	Wigan	2,876

Final Table

	P.	W.	D.	L.	F.	A.	Pts.
Great Britain	3	3	0	0	66	18	6
Australia	3	2	0	1	37	37	4
New Zealand	3	1	0	2	32	44	2
France	3	0	0	3	19	55	0

1968 in Australia   *Winners:* Australia
and New Zealand

25 May	A	25	GB	10	Sydney	62,256
25 May	Fr	15	NZ	10	Auckland	18,000
1 June	A	31	NZ	12	Brisbane	23,608
2 June	Fr	7	GB	2	Auckland	15,760
8 June	A	37	Fr	4	Brisbane	32,600
8 June	GB	38	NZ	14	Sydney	14,105

Final Table

	P.	W.	D.	L.	F.	A.	Pts.
Australia	3	3	0	0	93	26	6
France	3	2	0	1	26	49	4
Great Britain	3	1	0	2	50	46	2
New Zealand	3	0	0	3	36	84	0

Play-off final

| 10 June | A | 20 | Fr | 2 | Sydney | 54,290 |

Featherstone Rovers prop forward Arnie Morgan, a member of the 1968 Great Britain World Cup squad.

1970 in England   *Winners:* Australia

21 Oct.	A	47	NZ	11	Wigan	9,586
24 Oct.	GB	11	A	4	Leeds	15,084
25 Oct.	NZ	16	Fr	15	Hull	3,824
28 Oct.	GB	6	Fr	0	Castleford	8,958
31 Oct.	GB	27	NZ	17	Swinton	5,609
1 Nov.	Fr	17	A	15	Bradford	6,215

Final Table

	P.	W.	D.	L.	F.	A.	Pts.
Great Britain	3	3	0	0	44	21	6
Australia	3	1	0	2	66	39	2
France	3	1	0	2	32	37	2
New Zealand	3	1	0	2	44	89	2

Play-off final

| 7 Nov. | A | 12 | GB | 7 | Leeds | 18,776 |

1972 in France   *Winners:* Great Britain

28 Oct.	Fr	20	NZ	9	Marseilles	20,748
29 Oct.	GB	27	A	21	Perpignan	6,324
1 Nov.	A	9	NZ	5	Paris	8,000
1 Nov.	GB	13	Fr	4	Grenoble	5,321
4 Nov.	GB	53	NZ	19	Pau	7,500
5 Nov.	A	31	Fr	9	Toulouse	10,332

Final Table

	P.	W.	D.	L.	F.	A.	Pts.
Great Britain	3	3	0	0	93	44	6
Australia	3	2	0	1	61	41	4
France	3	1	0	2	33	53	2
New Zealand	3	0	0	3	33	82	0

Play-off final

| 11 Nov. | GB | 10 | A | 10 | Lyons | 4,231 |

No further score after extra-time so Great Britain took the championship because they had scored the greatest number of points in the qualifying League table.

1977 in Australia   *Winners:* Australia
and New Zealand

29 May	A	27	NZ	12	Auckland	18,000
5 June	GB	23	Fr	4	Auckland	10,000
11 June	A	21	Fr	9	Sydney	13,231
12 June	GB	30	NZ	12	C'church	7,000
18 June	A	19	GB	5	Brisbane	27,000
19 June	NZ	28	Fr	20	Auckland	8,000

Final Table

	P.	W.	D.	L.	F.	A.	Pts.
Australia	3	3	0	0	67	26	6
Great Britain	3	2	0	1	58	35	4
New Zealand	3	1	0	2	52	77	2
France	3	0	0	3	33	72	0

Play-off final

25 June A   13 GB 12 Sydney   24,457

1985-88 Series   *Winners:* Australia

1985

7 July	NZ	18	A	0	Auckland	19,000
9 Nov.	GB	6	NZ	6	Leeds	22,209
7 Dec.	Fr	0	NZ	22	Perpignan	5,000

1986

16 Feb.	Fr	10	GB	10	Avignon	4,000
29 July	A	32	NZ	12	Brisbane	22,811
17 Aug.	PNG	24	NZ	22	Port Moresby	15,000
4 Oct.	PNG	12	A	62	Port Moresby	17,000
22 Nov.	GB	15	A	24	Wigan	20,169
13 Dec.	Fr	0	A	52	Carcassonne	3,000

1987

24 Jan.	GB	52	Fr	4	Leeds	6,567
24 Oct.	GB	42	PNG	0	Wigan	9,121
15 Nov.	Fr	21	PNG	4	Carcassonne	5,000

1988

22 May	PNG	22	GB	42	Port Moresby	12,077
9 July	A	12	GB	26	Sydney	15,994
10 July	NZ	66	PNG	14	Auckland	8,392
17 July	NZ	12	GB	10	Christchurch	8,525
20 July	A	70	PNG	8	Wagga Wagga	11,685

Final Table

	P.	W.	D.	L.	F.	A.	Pts.
Australia	7	5	0	2	252	91	12★
New Zealand	7	4	1	2	158	86	11★
Great Britain	8	4	2	2	203	90	10
P. N. Guinea	7	1	0	6	84	325	4★
France	5	1	1	3	35	140	3

★Awarded two points in lieu of France's non-fulfilment of fixtures Down Under.

Play-off final

1988

9 Oct.   A   25 NZ 12 Auckland   47,363

GREAT BRITAIN WORLD CUP SQUADS

Captains in bold

1954 IN FRANCE

D. Valentine (Huddersfield)
W. Banks (Huddersfield)
H. Bradshaw (Huddersfield)
G. Brown (Leeds)
R. Coverdale (Hull)
G. Helme (Warrington)
P. Jackson (Barrow)
F. Kitchen (Leigh)
J. Ledgard (Leigh)

A. Naughton (Warrington)
D. Robinson (Wakefield T.)
D. Rose (Leeds)
R. Rylance (Huddersfield)
S. Smith (Hunslet)
M. Sullivan (Huddersfield)
J. Thorley (Halifax)
B. Watts (York)
J. Whiteley (Hull)

Manager: G. Shaw (Castleford)

1957 IN AUSTRALIA

A. Prescott (St. Helens)
E. Ashton (Wigan)
W. Boston (Wigan)
A. Davies (Oldham)
J. Grundy (Barrow)
G. Gunney (Hunslet)
T. Harris (Hull)
P. Jackson (Barrow)
B.L. Jones (Leeds)

S. Little (Oldham)
T. McKinney (St. Helens)
G. Moses (St. Helens)
R. Price (Warrington)
A. Rhodes (St. Helens)
J. Stevenson (Leeds)
M. Sullivan (Huddersfield)
D. Turner (Oldham)
J. Whiteley (Hull)

Managers: W. Fallowfield (RL Secretary) and H. Rawson (Hunslet)

1960 IN ENGLAND

E. Ashton (Wigan)
W. Boston (Wigan)
J. Challinor (Warrington)
A. Davies (Oldham)
E. Fraser (Warrington)
R. Greenough (Warrington)
T. Harris (Hull)
V. Karalius (St. Helens)
B. McTigue (Wigan)

A. Murphy (St. Helens)
F. Myler (Widnes)
A. Rhodes (St. Helens)
B. Shaw (Hunslet)
J. Shaw (Halifax)
M. Sullivan (Wigan)
D. Turner (Wakefield T.)
J. Whiteley (Hull)
J. Wilkinson (Wakefield T.)

Manager: W. Fallowfield (RL Secretary)

1968 IN AUSTRALIA AND NEW ZEALAND

B. Risman (Leeds)
K. Ashcroft (Leigh)
J. Atkinson (Leeds)
T. Bishop (St. Helens)
I. Brooke (Wakefield T.)
A. Burwell (Hull K.R.)
M. Clark (Leeds)

D. Edwards (Castleford)
P. Flanagan (Hull K.R.)
R. French (Widnes)
R. Haigh (Wakefield T.)
R. Millward (Hull K.R.)
A. Morgan (Featherstone R.)
C. Renilson (Halifax)

M. Shoebottom (Leeds)
C. Sullivan (Hull)
J. Warlow (St. Helens)
C. Watson (St. Helens)
C. Young (Hull K.R.)

Manager: W. Fallowfield (RL Secretary)   Coach: C. Hutton (Hull K.R.)

1970 IN ENGLAND

F. Myler (St. Helens)
K. Ashcroft (Leigh)
J. Atkinson (Leeds)
P. Charlton (Salford)
D. Chisnall (Leigh)
R. Dutton (Widnes)
A. Fisher (Bradford N. & Leeds)

R. Haigh (Leeds)
D. Hartley (Castleford)
K. Hepworth (Castleford)
C. Hesketh (Salford)
S. Hynes (Leeds)
K. Jones (Wigan)
D. Laughton (Wigan)

M. Reilly (Castleford)
M. Shoebottom (Leeds)
A. Smith (Leeds)
J. Thompson (Featherstone R.)
C. Watson (St. Helens)

Manager: J. Harding (Leigh)   Coach: J. Whiteley (Hull K.R.)

1972 IN FRANCE

C. Sullivan (Hull)
J. Atkinson (Leeds)
P. Charlton (Salford)
T. Clawson (Leeds)
C. Dixon (Salford)
C. Hesketh (Salford)
J. Holmes (Leeds)

R. Irving (Oldham)
D. Jeanes (Leeds)
A. Karalius (St. Helens)
B. Lockwood (Castleford)
P. Lowe (Hull K.R.)
S. Nash (Featherstone R.)
G. Nicholls (Widnes)

D. O'Neill (Widnes)
D. Redfearn (Bradford N.)
M. Stephenson (Dewsbury)
D. Topliss (Wakefield T.)
John Walsh (St. Helens)

Manager: W. Spaven (Hull K.R.)   Coach: J. Challinor (St. Helens)

385

1977 IN AUSTRALIA AND NEW ZEALAND

R. Millward (Hull K.R.)
E. Bowman (Workington T.)
L. Casey (Hull K.R.)
L. Dyl (Leeds)
K. Elwell (Widnes)
G. Fairbairn (Wigan)
K. Fielding (Salford)

W. Francis (Wigan)
K. Gill (Salford)
A. Hodkinson (Rochdale H.)
P. Hogan (Barrow)
J. Holmes (Leeds)
G. Lloyd (Castleford)
S. Nash (Salford)

G. Nicholls (St. Helens)
S. Pitchford (Leeds)
P. Smith (Featherstone R.)
J. Thompson (Featherstone R.)
D. Ward (Leeds)
S. Wright (Widnes)

Manager: R. Parker (Blackpool B.)   Coach: D. Watkins (Salford)

GREAT BRITAIN RECORDS

● In Test and World Cup matches.

MOST TRIES IN CAREER

*41 Mick Sullivan (Huddersfield, Wigan,
   St. Helens, York)................................. 1954-63
31 Garry Schofield (Hull, Leeds) 1984-
26 Martin Offiah (Widnes, Wigan) 1988-
24 Billy Boston (Wigan) 1954-63
20 Ellery Hanley (Bradford N., Wigan, Leeds) . 1984-
17 Roger Millward (Cas'd, Hull K.R.) 1966-78
16 Alex Murphy (St. Helens, Warrington)...... 1958-71
15 Shaun Edwards (Wigan) 1985-
14 Eric Ashton (Wigan)............................. 1957-63
14 Neil Fox (Wakefield T.)......................... 1959-69
13 Clive Sullivan (Hull) 1967-73
12 John Atkinson (Leeds) 1968-80
10 Jim Leytham (Wigan) 1907-10
*Mick Sullivan also scored two tries for Great Britain
against France before the matches were given Test
status.
●Most tries by a forward is eight by Derek Turner
(Oldham, Wakefield T.) 1956-62; and Phil Lowe (Hull
K.R.) 1970-78.

MOST GOALS IN CAREER

93 Neil Fox (Wakefield T.) 1959-69
66 Lewis Jones (Leeds)............................. 1954-57
64 Jim Sullivan (Wigan)............................ 1924-33
53 Eric Fraser (Warrington) 1958-61
48 Jonathan Davies (Widnes, Warrington) 1990-
44 George Fairbairn (Wigan, Hull K.R.) 1977-82
39 Paul Eastwood (Hull) 1990-
31 Paul Loughlin (St. Helens) 1988-
26 Joe Lydon (Widnes, Wigan).................... 1983-
25 Terry Clawson
   (Featherstone R., Leeds, Oldham) 1962-74
22 Ray Dutton (Widnes) 1970
22 John Holmes (Leeds) 1971-82
22 Ernest Ward (Bradford N.)..................... 1946-52
21 Mick Burke (Widnes)........................... 1980-86
21 Ken Gowers (Swinton)........................... 1962-66

MOST POINTS IN CAREER

228 Neil Fox (Wakefield T.)......................... 1959-69
149 Garry Schofield (Hull, Leeds) 1984-
147 Lewis Jones (Leeds) 1954-57
128 Jim Sullivan (Wigan) 1924-33
123 Mick Sullivan (Huddersfield, Wigan,
   St. Helens, York)................................. 1954-63
109 Eric Fraser (Warrington)....................... 1958-61
106 Paul Eastwood (Hull)........................... 1990-
106 Jonathan Davies (Widnes, Warrington) 1990-
104 Martin Offiah (Widnes, Wigan) 1988-
91 George Fairbairn (Wigan, Hull K.R.)........ 1977-82
81 Roger Millward (Castleford, Hull K.R.)..... 1966-78
80 Ellery Hanley (Bradford N., Wigan, Leeds)... 1984-
79 Joe Lydon (Widnes, Wigan) 1983-

MOST TRIES IN A MATCH

5 by Martin Offiah (Widnes) v. France at Leeds
   16 February, 1991
4 by Jim Leytham (Wigan) v. Australia at Brisbane
   2 July, 1910
   Billy Boston (Wigan) v. New Zealand at Auckland
   24 July, 1954
   Alex Murphy (St. Helens) v. France at Leeds
   14 March, 1959
   Garry Schofield (Hull) v. New Zealand at Wigan
   2 November, 1985
3 by Bill Jukes (Hunslet) v. Australia at Sydney
   18 June, 1910
   Bert Avery (Oldham) v. New Zealand at Auckland
   30 July, 1910
   Billy Stone (Hull) v. New Zealand at Auckland
   31 July, 1920
   Jonty Parkin (Wakefield T.) v. New Zealand at
   Auckland 31 July, 1920
   Charlie Carr (Barrow) v. New Zealand at Leeds
   15 January, 1927
   Stan Smith (Leeds) v. Australia at Sydney
   16 July, 1932
   Arthur Bassett (Halifax) v. Australia at Brisbane
   6 July, 1946
   George Wilson (Workington T.) v. New Zealand at
   Bradford 6 October, 1951

Mick Sullivan (Huddersfield) v. New Zealand at
Bradford 12 November, 1955
Dave Bolton (Wigan) v. France at Wigan
23 November, 1957
Mick Sullivan (Wigan) v. Australia at Sydney
19 July, 1958
Mick Sullivan (Wigan) v. New Zealand at
Auckland 9 August, 1958
Mick Sullivan (Wigan) v. France at Leeds
14 March, 1959
Clive Sullivan (Hull) v. New Zealand at Sydney
(World Cup) 8 June, 1968
Bill Burgess (Barrow) v. France at St. Helens
30 November, 1968
Keith Fielding (Salford) v. France at Grenoble
20 January, 1974
Henderson Gill (Wigan) v. France at Hull
6 December, 1981
Garry Schofield (Leeds) v. France at Leeds
16 February, 1991
Garry Schofield (Leeds) v. France at Carcassonne
7 March, 1993
Paul Newlove (Featherstone R.) v. France at Leeds
2 April, 1993

●Bill Jukes and Bert Avery are the only forwards to have
scored hat-tricks for Great Britain, both on tour in 1910.

MOST GOALS IN A MATCH

10 by Lewis Jones (Leeds) v. Australia at Brisbane
3 July, 1954
Bernard Ganley (Oldham) v. France at Wigan
23 November, 1957
John Holmes (Leeds) v. New Zealand at Pau
(World Cup) 4 November, 1972
Jonathan Davies (Widnes) v. France at Leeds
2 April, 1993
9 by Lewis Jones (Leeds) v. France at Leeds
26 January, 1957
Neil Fox (Wakefield T.) v. France at Wigan
3 April, 1963
Neil Fox (Wakefield T.) v. France at Leigh
18 March, 1964
8 by Eric Fraser (Warrington) v. Australia at Sydney
19 July, 1958
David Creasser (Leeds) v. France at Leeds
1 March, 1985
Joe Lydon (Wigan) v. France at Leeds
24 January, 1987
Paul Eastwood (Hull) v. France at Leeds
16 February, 1991
Jonathan Davies (Widnes) v. Papua New Guinea
at Wigan 9 November, 1991

7 by Lewis Jones (Leeds) v. France at St. Helens
10 April, 1957
Eric Fraser (Warrington) v. New Zealand at
Auckland 9 August, 1958
Eric Fraser (Warrington) v. France at Leeds
14 March, 1959
Neil Fox (Wakefield T.) v. New Zealand at
Swinton 4 November, 1961
Neil Fox (Wakefield T.) v. France at Swinton
23 January, 1965
Bev Risman (Leeds) v. New Zealand at Sydney
(World Cup) 8 June, 1968
Roger Millward (Hull K.R.) v. Australia at
Sydney 20 June, 1970
George Fairbairn (Wigan) v. France at Auckland
(World Cup) 5 June, 1977
John Woods (Leigh) v. France at Hull
6 December, 1981
David Stephenson (Wigan) v. Papua New Guinea
at Wigan 24 October, 1987
Paul Loughlin (St. Helens) v. Papua New Guinea
at Port Moresby 22 May, 1988

MOST POINTS IN A MATCH

26 (2t, 10g) by John Holmes (Leeds) v. New Zealand
at Pau (World Cup)
4 November, 1972
21 (1t, 9g) by Lewis Jones (Leeds) v. France at
Leeds 26 January, 1957
Neil Fox (Wakefield T.) v. France at
Wigan 3 April, 1963
Neil Fox (Wakefield T.) v. France at
Leigh 18 March, 1964
20 (10g) by Lewis Jones (Leeds) v. Australia at
Brisbane 3 July, 1954
(10g) Bernard Ganley (Oldham) v. France at
Wigan 23 November, 1957
(2t, 7g) Roger Millward (Hull K.R.) v.
Australia at Sydney 20 June, 1970
(1t, 8g) Joe Lydon (Wigan) v. France at Leeds
24 February, 1987
(5t) Martin Offiah (Widnes) v. France at
Leeds 16 February, 1991
(1t, 8g) Paul Eastwood (Hull) v. France at
Leeds 16 February, 1991
(10g) Jonathan Davies (Widnes) v. France at
Leeds 2 April, 1993

MOST APPEARANCES

46	Mick Sullivan*
44	Garry Schofield
36(1)	Ellery Hanley
34(4)	Shaun Edwards
31	Billy Boston
30(1)	Cliff Watson
30(7)	Joe Lydon
30	Martin Offiah
29	George Nicholls
29	Neil Fox
29(1)	Roger Millward
28	Alan Prescott
27	Phil Jackson
27	Alex Murphy
26	Eric Ashton
26	John Atkinson
26(1)	Andy Gregory
25	Brian McTigue
25	Jim Sullivan
25	Tommy Harris
25(4)	Andy Platt
25(8)	Daryl Powell
( )	Indicates substitute appearance included in total

* Mick Sullivan's record number of appearances includes a record run of 36 successive matches. In addition he played in two matches against France before they were given Test status.

LONGEST TEST CAREERS

14 years — Gus Risman
1932 to 1946 (17 appearances)
13 years 9 months — Billy Batten
1908 to 1921 (10 appearances)
13 years 6 months — Alex Murphy
1958 to 1971 (27 appearances)
12 years 9 months — Roger Millward
1966 to 1978 (28+1 appearances)
12 years 6 months — John Atkinson
1968 to 1980 (26 appearances)
12 years 6 months — Terry Clawson
1962 to 1974 (14 appearances)

YOUNGEST TEST PLAYER

Paul Newlove was 18 years 72 days old when he made his Great Britain Test debut as a 76th-minute substitute in the first Test against New Zealand at Old Trafford, Manchester, on 21 October 1989, making his full debut a week later. Born on 10 August 1971, he beat the previous record held by Shaun Edwards (born 17 October 1966) who was 18 years 135 days old when capped against France at Leeds on 1 March 1985.

Roger Millward (born 16 September 1947) was 18 years 37 days old when he was a non-playing substitute for the second Test against New Zealand at Bradford on 23 October 1965.

OLDEST TEST PLAYER

Jeff Grayshon (born 4 March 1949) was 36 years 8 months when he played in his last Test for Britain, against New Zealand at Elland Road, Leeds, on 9 November 1985.

RECORD TEAM CHANGES

The record number of team changes made by the Great Britain selectors is 10, on three occasions, all against Australia.

In 1929, Britain crashed 31-8 to Australia in the first Test at Hull KR and retained only three players for the second Test at Leeds, where they won 9-3.

After their biggest ever defeat of 50-12 in the 1963 second Test at Swinton, Britain dropped nine players and were forced to make another change when Vince Karalius was injured and replaced by Don Fox. Britain stopped Australia making a clean sweep of the series by winning 16-5 at Leeds in the last Test.

Following the 40-4 first Test defeat at Hull City's soccer ground in 1982, the selectors again made 10 changes, not including substitutes, Britain going down 27-6 in the second Test at Wigan.

Britain have never fielded the same team for three or more successive Tests.

Hull centre Rob Danby in action for Great Britain Under-21s against France at Warrington in December 1993.

UNDER-21s

Great Britain Under-21s followed up a creditable 37–24 defeat by the New Zealand tourists with a convincing 28–14 triumph in the John Smith's International against France Under-21s at Warrington.

The young Lions gave the Kiwis a fright in the October tour fixture at Workington, holding the visitors to a slender 13–12 lead at half-time and contributing four excellent tries in a 61-point encounter. Full details of the tour match are featured in the section 1993 KIWIS.

Just over a month later, the British youngsters capitalised on a huge advantage in power and defensive technique to run in five tries against the French.

Most of the damage was done from half back by Francis Maloney and Gareth Stephens, who learned each other's styles in the reserves at Leeds before Maloney left for Featherstone Rovers. There were also telling contributions from Wigan duo Barrie-Jon Mather and Mick Cassidy, plus threequarters Daio Powell, of Bradford Northern, and Hull's Rob Danby.

France were a delight on brief occasions with some spectacular handling, as they showed in the final 15 minutes when two tries from winger Pierre Jammes brought them some respectability.

But the visitors were overstretched to contain the British, who were always prepared to play an expansive game. The only criticism of the home team was a bout of complacency towards the end, making the final score closer than it should have been.

JOHN SMITH'S INTERNATIONAL
2 December 1993   **Warrington**

GREAT BRITAIN 28		FRANCE 16
Lee Penny (Warrington)	1.	Laurent Lucchese (Huddersfield)
Daio Powell (Bradford N.)	2.	Pierre Jammes (Limoux)
Richard Goddard (Wakefield T.)	3.	Pascal Bomati (XIII Catalan)
Rob Danby (Hull)	4.	Arnaud Dulac (St. Gaudens)
Iestyn Harris (Warrington)	5.	Philippe Ricard (Albi)
Francis Maloney (Featherstone R.)	6.	Lilian Tiburcio (St. Esteve)
Gareth Stephens (Leeds)	7.	Vincent Banet (XIII Catalan)
Nathan Sykes (Castleford)	8.	Frederic Teixido (Limoux)
Richard Chamberlain (Hull K.R.)	9.	Stephane Tena (XIII Catalan)
Mick Cassidy (Wigan)	10.	Cyril Baudouin (Carpentras)
Barrie-Jon Mather (Wigan)	11.	Regis Jean (La Reole)
Mark Perrett (Halifax)	12.	Pascal Jampy (XIII Catalan)
Steve McCurrie (Widnes), Capt.	13.	Stephane Chamorin (St. Esteve)
Graham Holroyd (Leeds)	14.	Patrice Satge (Carcassonne)
Jez Cassidy (Hull)	15.	Frederic Banquet (Carcassonne)
Scott Martin (Leigh)	16.	Laurent Garnier (Cabestany)
Lee Harland (Halifax)	17.	David Gagliazzo (Carcassonne)

T: Mather, Powell, Maloney, McCurrie, Harris
G: Harris (4)
Substitutions:
Harland for Mather (64 min.)
Holroyd for Maloney (66 min.)
J. Cassidy for M. Cassidy (66 min.)
Martin for Powell (70 min.)
Referee: Marcel Chanfreau (France)
Attendance: 1,744

T: Jammes (2), Baudouin
G: Chamorin, Tiburcio
Substitutions:
Satge for Tiburcio (47 min.)
Garnier for Tena (58 min.)
Banquet for Ricard (62 min.)
Gagliazzo for Jean (66 min.)
Half-time: 20-8

GREAT BRITAIN
UNDER-21s RESULTS

25 Nov.	1984	W 24-8	v. F	Castleford
16 Dec.	1984	W 8-2	v. F	Albi
9 Oct.	1985	L 12-16	v. NZ	Bradford
19 Jan.	1986	L 6-19	v. F	St. Esteve
2 Feb.	1986	W 6-2	v. F	Whitehaven
8 Mar.	1987	W 40-7	v. F	St. Jean de Luz
21 Mar.	1987	W 54-6	v. F	St. Helens
6 Mar.	1988	L 13-14	v. F	Ausillon
19 Mar.	1988	L 4-8	v. F	St. Helens
20 Jan.	1989	W 30-0	v. F	Leeds
4 Feb.	1989	L 8-16	v. F	Carpentras
20 Jan.	1990	W 22-0	v. F	Villeneuve
16 Feb.	1990	W 20-6	v. F	Doncaster
26 Jan.	1991	W 48-2	v. F	Limoux
15 Feb.	1991	L 6-16	v. F	Wigan
30 Oct.	1991	W 58-0	v. P	Leeds
6 Mar.	1992	W 56-2	v. F	Halifax
20 Mar.	1992	W 34-2	v. F	Albi
17 Feb.	1993	W 46-10	v. F	Rochdale
26 Oct.	1993	L 24-37	v. NZ	Workington
2 Dec.	1993	W 28-16	v. F	Warrington

Key: F — France   NZ — New Zealand
P — Papua New Guinea

GREAT BRITAIN UNDER-21s
REGISTER

The following is a register of appearances for Great Britain Under-21s since this classification of match was introduced in 1984.

Figures in brackets are the total appearances, with the plus sign indicating substitute appearances, e.g. (3+1).

Away matches are in bold letters. Substitute appearances are in lower case letters.

ALLEN, Shaun (1) St. Helens: 1984 F
ANDERSON, Grant (4) Castleford: 1989 F, **F**; 1990 **F**, F
ANDERSON, Paul (2) Leeds: 1992 **F**; 1993 F
ATCHESON, Paul (1) Wigan: 1993 F

BECKWITH, Mark (1+1) Whitehaven: 1986 f, **F**
BETTS, Denis (4) Wigan: 1989 F, **F**; 1990 **F**, F
BIBB, Chris (5) Featherstone R.: 1987 **F**, F; 1988 F; 1989 F, **F**
BISHOP, Paul (1+1) Warrington: 1987 **F**, f
BONSON, Paul (2) Featherstone R.: 1992 F, **F**
BOOTHROYD, Giles (1) Castleford: 1989 F
BURGESS, Andy (+1) Salford: 1991 f
BUSBY, Dean (2+1) Hull: 1991 P; 1992 F, f

CARBERT, Brian (3) Warrington: 1985 NZ; 1986 **F**, F
CASSIDY, Frank (1+1) Swinton: 1988 f, **F**
CASSIDY, Jez (+2) Hull: 1993 nz, f
CASSIDY, Mick (2+1) Wigan: 1993 f, NZ, F
CHAMBERLAIN, Richard (1+1) Hull K.R.: 1993 f, F
CHAMBERS, Gary (2) Warrington: 1991 **F**, F
CHRISTIE, Gary (1) Oldham: 1993 F
CLARK, Garry (2) Hull K.R.: 1984 F, **F**
CLARKE, Phil (5) Wigan: 1990 **F**; 1991 **F**, F; 1992 F, **F**
CONNOLLY, Gary (4) St. Helens: 1990 **F**; 1991 F, P; 1992 **F**
CONWAY, Mark (1) Leeds: 1984 F
CREASSER, David (5) Leeds: 1984 F, **F**; 1985 NZ; 1986 **F**, F
CRITCHLEY, Jason (+1) Widnes: 1990 f
CROOKS, Lee (2) Hull: 1984 F, **F**
CURRIER, Andy (2) Widnes: 1984 F, **F**

DALTON, James (3) Whitehaven: 1985 NZ; 1986 **F**, F
DANBY, Rob (2) Hull: 1993 NZ, F
DANNATT, Andy (6) Hull: 1984 F, **F**; 1985 NZ; 1986 **F**; 1987 **F**, F
DARBYSHIRE, Paul (1+1) Warrington: 1991 f, F
DELANEY, Paul (+2) Leeds: 1990 f, f
DERMOTT, Martin (5) Wigan: 1987 **F**, **F**; 1988 **F**, **F**; 1989 F
DISLEY, Gary (+1) Salford: 1987 f
DIVORTY, Gary (6) Hull: 1984 **F**; 1985 NZ; 1986 **F**, **F**; 1987 **F**, F
DIXON, Mike (1) Hull: 1991 P
DONOHUE, Jason (+2) Leigh: 1992 f; 1993 f

EASTWOOD, Paul (2) Hull: 1987 **F**, F
EDWARDS, Shaun (4) Wigan: 1984 **F**; 1985 NZ; 1987 **F**, F

FARRELL, Andrew (1) Wigan: 1993 NZ
FARRELL, Anthony (1+1) Huddersfield: 1989 f, **F**
FAWCETT, Vince (3) Leeds: 1990 **F**, F; 1991 **F**
FLETCHER, Mike (2) Hull K.R.: 1988 **F**, F
FORD, Mike (3+1) Wigan: 1985 NZ; 1986 **F**; Leigh: 1987 f, F
FORSHAW, Michael (+2) Wigan: 1991 f, f
FORSTER, Mark (3) Warrington: 1985 NZ; 1986 **F**, F
FOX, Deryck (1) Featherstone R.: 1984 **F**

391

Bradford Northern winger Daio Powell, a try scorer against France in December 1993.

Hull K.R. hooker Richard Chamberlain, capped twice for the Under-21s.

GILDART, Ian (6) Wigan: 1988 **F**, F; 1989 F, **F**; 1990 **F**, F
GODDARD, Richard (2) Wakefield T.: 1993 NZ, F
GOULDING, Bobby (5) Wigan: 1990 **F**, F; 1991 **F**, F;
   Leeds: 1991 P
GREGORY, Mike (1) Warrington: 1984 **F**
GRIBBIN, Vince (1+1) Whitehaven: 1984 f, **F**
GROVES, Paul (3) Salford: 1984 F, **F**; 1985 NZ

HALLAS, Graeme (1+2) Hull K.R.: 1991 P; 1992 f, f
HARCOMBE, Kevin (1) Rochdale H.: 1986 F
HARLAND, Lee (1+1) Halifax: 1993 NZ, f
HARMON, Neil (1+3) Warrington: 1988 f, F; 1989 f, f
HARRIS, Iestyn (2) Warrington: 1993 NZ, F
HILL, Brendan (+1) Leeds: 1986 f
HILL, Kenny (3) Castleford: 1988 **F**, F; 1989 **F**
HOLROYD, Graham (+1) Leeds: 1993 f
HUGHES, Gary (1) Leigh: 1986 F
HUGHES, Ian (1) Sheffield E.: 1993 F
HULME, David (2+1) Widnes: 1985 nz; 1986 **F**, F
HUNTE, Alan (2) St. Helens: 1990 **F**; 1991 F

IRWIN, Shaun (4) Castleford: 1988 **F**; 1989 F, **F**; 1990 **F**

JACKSON, Michael (+1) Hunslet: 1991 f
JOHNSON, Errol (2) Leeds: 1988 **F**, F
JOYNT, Chris (4) Oldham: 1991 P; 1992 F, **F**; St. Helens:
   1993 F

LAY, Steve (+1) Hunslet: 1989 f
LORD, Gary (1) Castleford: 1988 **F**
LOUGHLIN, Paul (2) St. Helens: 1987 **F**, F
LUCAS, Ian (4) Wigan: 1988 **F**, F; 1989 F, **F**
LUMB, Tim (+1) Hunslet: 1991 f
LYMAN, Paul (3) Featherstone R.: 1985 NZ; 1986 **F**, F
LYON, David (2) Widnes: 1985 NZ; 1986 **F**

McCORMACK, Kevin (2) St. Helens: 1987 **F**, F
McCURRIE, Steve (4+1) Widnes: 1991 P; 1992 f; 1993 F,
   NZ, F
McNAMARA, Steve (5) Hull: 1991 **F**, F, P; 1992 **F**; 1993 F
MAKIN, Craig (+1) Widnes: 1993 nz
MALONEY, Francis (2) Featherstone R.: 1993 NZ, F
MARTIN, Scott (+2) Leigh: 1993 nz, f
MARTYN, Tommy (1+3) Oldham: 1991 **F**, f, p; 1992 f
MATHER, Barrie-Jon (3+1) Wigan: 1992 f; 1993 F, NZ, F
MEDLEY, Paul (2) Leeds: 1987 **F**, F
MOLLOY, Steve (2) Warrington: 1990 **F**, F
MOSLEY, James (1) Wakefield T.: 1993 F
MOUNTAIN, Dean (+1) Castleford: 1987 f
MOXON, Darren (1) Bradford N.: 1991 **F**
MYCOE, David (4) Sheffield E.: 1990 **F**; 1991 P; 1992 F, **F**
MYERS, David (5) Wigan: 1991 **F**, F, P; 1992 F, **F**

NEWLOVE, Paul (8) Featherstone R.: 1989 F, **F**; 1990 **F**, F;
   1991 **F**, P; 1992 F, **F**
NICKLE, Sonny (1) Sheffield E.: 1990 **F**

O'DONNELL, Gus (2) Wigan: 1992 F, **F**

PARKER, Wayne (2) Hull K.R.: 1988 **F**, F
PARR, Chris (1) Huddersfield: 1991 P
PEARSON, Martin (4) Featherstone R.: 1991 P; 1992 F, **F**;
   1993 F
PENNY, Lee (3) Warrington: 1993 F, NZ, F
PERRETT, Mark (1) Halifax: 1993 F
PICKSLEY, Richard (1) Sheffield E.: 1992 F
PINKNEY, Nick (+1) Ryedale-York: 1991 p
POWELL, Daio (2) Bradford N.: 1993 NZ, F
POWELL, Roy (5) Leeds: 1984 F, **F**; 1985 NZ; 1986 **F**, F
PRATT, Richard (2) Leeds: 1988 **F**, F
PRECIOUS, Andy (+1) Hunslet: 1991 p
PRICE, Gary H. (5+1) Wakefield T.: 1988 f; 1989 F, **F**;
   1990 F; 1991 **F**, F
PRICE, Richard (2) Hull: 1989 F, F
PROCTOR, Wayne (+1) Hull: 1984 f
PUCKERING, Neil (4) Hull: 1986 **F**, F; 1987 **F**, F

RICHARDS, Craig (2) Bradford N.: 1991 **F**, F
RILEY, Mike (2) St. Helens: 1992 F, **F**
RIPPON, Andy (1) Swinton: 1984 **F**
ROBINSON, Jason (1) Wigan: 1993 F
ROBINSON, Steve (1) Halifax: 1988 F
ROEBUCK, Neil (+1) Castleford: 1990 f
ROUND, Paul (1+1) St. Helens: 1984 F, f
RUDD, Chris (2) Warrington: 1991 **F**, F
RUSSELL, Richard (1+1) Wigan: 1987 F; 1988 f

SAMPSON, Dean (1) Castleford: 1988 **F**
SANDERSON, Gary (4) Warrington: 1987 **F**, F; 1988 **F**, F
SCHOFIELD, Garry (2) Hull: 1984 **F**, F
SLATER, Richard (+1) Wakefield T.: 1992 f
SMITH, Tony (1) Castleford: 1991 F
SOUTHERNWOOD, Graham (6) Castleford: 1990 **F**, F;
   1991 **F**, F; 1992 F, **F**
SOUTHERNWOOD, Roy (2) Castleford: 1989 F, **F**
SPRUCE, Stuart (+1) Widnes: 1991 f
STEPHENS, Gareth (2+1) Leeds: 1993 f, NZ, F
STREET, Tim (2) Leigh: 1989 F, **F**
SULLIVAN, Anthony (1) Hull K.R.: 1990 F
SUMNER, Phil (3) Warrington: 1990 F; 1991 P; 1992 F
SYKES, Nathan (1) Castleford: 1993 F

THOMPSON, Alex (1) Sheffield E.: 1993 NZ
TURNER, Robert (1) Warrington: 1990 F

WANE, Shaun (3) Wigan: 1984 **F**; 1985 NZ; 1986 **F**
WESTHEAD, John (1+2) Leigh: 1985 nz; 1986 f, F
WRIGHT, Darren (2) Widnes: 1987 F; 1988 **F**
WRIGHT, Nigel (1+1) Wakefield T.: 1993 F; Wigan:
   1993 nz

UNDER-21s RECORDS

Highest score: 58-0 v. Papua New Guinea at
         Leeds, 30 October 1991

Highest against: 6-19 v. France at St. Esteve,
         19 January 1986

Most tries in a match: 3 by Neil Puckering (Hull)
         v. France at St. Helens,
         21 March 1987
         David Myers (Wigan) v. PNG
         at Leeds, 30 October 1991
         David Myers (Wigan) v. France
         at Halifax, 6 March 1992
         Martin Pearson (Featherstone
         R.) v. France at Halifax,
         6 March 1992
         David Myers (Wigan) v. France
         at Albi, 20 March 1992

Most goals in a match: 8 by Chris Rudd (Warrington)
         v. France at Limoux,
         26 January 1991
         Martin Pearson (Featherstone
         R.) v. PNG at Leeds,
         30 October 1991

Most points in a match: 24 (3t,6g) by Martin Pearson
         (Featherstone R.) v. France
         at Halifax, 6 March 1992

Biggest attendance: 4,596 v. France at Doncaster,
         16 February 1990

UNDER-24s RESULTS

3 Apr.	1965	W 17-9	v.	F	Toulouse
20 Oct.	1965	W 12-5	v.	F	Oldham
26 Nov.	1966	L 4-7	v.	F	Bayonne
17 Apr.	1969	W 42-2	v.	F	Castleford
14 Nov.	1976	W 19-2	v.	F	Hull K.R.
5 Dec.	1976	W 11-9	v.	F	Albi
12 Nov.	1977	W 27-9	v.	F	Hull
18 Dec.	1977	W 8-4	v.	F	Tonneins
4 Oct.	1978	L 8-30	v.	A	Hull K.R.
14 Jan.	1979	W 15-3	v.	F	Limoux
24 Nov.	1979	W 14-2	v.	F	Leigh
13 Jan.	1980	W 11-7	v.	F	Carcassonne
5 Nov.	1980	L 14-18	v.	NZ	Fulham
10 Jan.	1981	W 9-2	v.	F	Villeneuve
16 Jan.	1982	W 19-16	v.	F	Leeds
21 Feb.	1982	W 24-12	v.	F	Tonneins
16 Jan.	1983	W 19-5	v.	F	Carpentras
11 Nov.	1983	W 28-23	v.	F	Villeneuve
4 Dec.	1983	W 48-1	v.	F	Oldham

GREAT BRITAIN UNDER-24s REGISTER
Since reintroduction in 1976

The following is a register of appearances by current players, who played at least one club game in 1993-94, for Great Britain Under-24s since this classification of match was reintroduced in 1976, until it was replaced by the new Under-21 level in 1984.

Figures in brackets are the total appearances, with the plus sign indicating substitute appearances, e.g. (7+3).

Away matches are in bold letters. Substitute appearances are in lower case letters.

ASHTON, Ray (3) Oldham: 1983 **F**, **F**, F

CROOKS, Lee (1) Hull: 1983 F

DRUMMOND, Des (5) Leigh: 1979 F; 1980 **F**; 1981 **F**; 1982 F, **F**

ECCLES, Bob (2) Warrington: 1978 A; 1979 F
ENGLAND, Keith (+1) Castleford: 1983 f

FIELDHOUSE, John (1+1) Warrington: 1983 **F**, f
FORD, Phil (1) Warrington: 1982 **F**

GOODWAY, Andy (2) Oldham: 1983 **F**, F
GREGORY, Andy (1) Widnes: 1982 F

HANLEY, Ellery (2) Bradford N.: 1982 F; 1983 F
HARKIN, Paul (1) Hull K.R.: 1981 **F**
HOBBS, David (2) Featherstone R.: 1982 F, **F**

LEDGER, Barry (2) St. Helens: 1983 **F**, F
LYDON, Joe (3) Widnes: 1983 **F**, **F**, F

MASKILL, Colin (1) Wakefield T.: 1983 **F**
MUMBY, Keith (6) Bradford N.: 1976 F, **F**; 1977 F, **F**; 1978 A; 1981 **F**

NOBLE, Brian (4) Bradford N.: 1982 F, **F**; 1983 F, **F**

O'NEILL, Mike (3+2) Widnes: 1980 nz; 1982 F, f; 1983 **F**, **F**

POTTER, Ian (4) Warrington: 1979 **F**; 1981 **F**; Leigh: 1982 F, **F**

SCHOFIELD, Garry (+2) Hull: 1983 f, f

WORRALL, Mick (3) Oldham: 1983 **F**, **F**, F

Wales winger Anthony Sullivan in action against New Zealand at Swansea in October 1993.

ENGLAND AND WALES

ENGLAND AND WALES

1993-94 WALES REVIEW

The 1993-94 campaign was one of mixed fortunes for Wales in their third successive season after being re-formed in 1991 following a seven-year absence from the international scene.

The good news was belated confirmation of their inclusion in the line-up for the Centenary World Cup in 1995, having been omitted from the original plans; the unearthing of new young talent into an ageing squad; and a last-minute, one-point victory over the French at Cardiff.

The less pleasing aspects were a 24–19 defeat by the New Zealand tourists at Swansea; crowds of around only 6,000 at each of the John Smith's internationals; and the poor quality of performance in the last-gasp victory over a revitalised France.

The addition of Wales to the already named eight countries in the Centenary World Cup was announced only days before the Dragons hosted the opening fixture of the Kiwis' 11-match programme. Wales were denied a try with only 11 minutes left, although referee John Connolly's decision was justified by television replays, which could have set up a hard-earned victory as they trailed 17–22. Full details of the tour fixture are chronicled in the section 1993 KIWIS.

Five months later Wales entertained France at Ninian Park, Cardiff, only the second Rugby League international to be staged at the soccer club after a 12-year break.

Former British Lion and Wales Rugby Union forward Richard Webster came off the substitutes' bench for his Wales Rugby League debut with only six minutes left and the home side trailing 12-7. The Salford forward sank the superb French challenge with only his second touch of the ball, driving over for a try at the start of injury time.

Wales's other hero, skipper Jonathan Davies, defied a painful leg injury to step forward to add the goal to secure the slenderest of victories. It took the Warrington centre's match tally to four goals and a drop goal and

killed off a brave French side which had looked like clinching success only minutes earlier.

Recalled loose forward Thierry Valero created the gap for winger Jean-Marc Garcia, his high speed break leaving the limping Davies stranded. Immediately after the touchdown, France allowed their discipline to slip for the first time and gave away two penalties in quick succession to take Wales upfield for Webster to crash over the line.

The French transition from the two record defeats by Great Britain during the previous campaign was led by the two best players on view, skipper and scrum half Patrick Entat and Hull second row man Daniel Divet, both absent from the twin rout a year earlier.

Divet invariably broke the first tackle and managed to keep the ball alive when held, while former Hull player Entat was the epitome of a League half back, incessantly prompting his pack, scuttling through the half gap and supplying constant support for his runners.

It was the inspirational Entat who broke the deadlock in the 20th minute, scooping up a loose Kevin Ellis pass on the halfway line to beat the cover and slip out of full back Phil Ford's tackle to go under the posts, Patrick Torreilles adding the easy kick.

Ford did not have an enjoyable return to his native Cardiff, spilling the ball on numerous occasions, especially in the second half, before being replaced by debutant Daio Powell.

Wales battled into driving rain in a first half which could have seen the resurgent French extend a 6-0 lead if Pascal Fages's kick through for the chasing Garcia had bounced more kindly and winger Claude Sirvent had not dropped a David Fraisse pass with the line at his mercy.

Second row man Rowland Phillips, out of favour at Warrington, was the most penetrative forward as Wales began to claw back into the game after the interval. Phillips took the ball up tirelessly, swatting off the tiring French defenders as the Welsh began to gnaw away at the six-point deficit.

Davies opened their account after 55 minutes with a penalty goal after Torreilles was sin-binned for holding down Ellis. A superb Davies break and kick almost brought a try for Ellis before Davies added a second penalty when Didier Cabestany was penalised for holding down.

From the restart, Fages kicked the ball directly into touch and Davies hit a 50-metre penalty goal to level the scores, putting Wales ahead for the first time with a drop goal.

The one-pointer promised to be enough to snatch victory. But Garcia's try, plus Torreilles's second goal, gave the French hope before being dashed by Webster's last-gasp effort.

Webster was one of three Welsh debutants, the Swansea-born packman being joined by Great Britain Under-21 products Powell and loose forward Mark Perrett, both qualifying by Welsh parentage.

Wales half back Kevin Ellis, an ever present since re-formation in October 1991.

JOHN SMITH'S INTERNATIONAL

4 March   **Ninian Park, Cardiff**

WALES 13   FRANCE 12

Phil Ford (Salford)	1.	Jean Frison (Villefranche)
Gerald Cordle (Bradford N.)	2.	Jean-Marc Garcia (St. Esteve)
Allan Bateman (Warrington)	3.	David Despin (Villeneuve)
Jonathan Davies (Warrington), Capt.	4.	David Fraisse (Sheffield E.)
Anthony Sullivan (St. Helens)	5.	Claude Sirvent (St. Gaudens)
Jonathan Griffiths (St. Helens)	6.	Pascal Fages (Pia)
Kevin Ellis (Warrington)	7.	Patrick Entat (Avignon), Capt.
Mark Jones (Hull)	8.	Frederic Teixido (Limoux)
Barry Williams (Carlisle)	9.	Patrick Torreilles (Pia)
David Young (Salford)	10.	Bernard Llong (XIII Catalan)
Paul Moriarty (Widnes)	11.	Daniel Divet (Hull)
Rowland Phillips (Warrington)	12.	Didier Cabestany (XIII Catalan)
Mark Perrett (Halifax)	13.	Thierry Valero (Lezignan)
Daio Powell (Bradford N.)	14.	Ezzedine Attia (Carpentras)
Ian Marlow (Wakefield T.)	15.	Pascal Jampy (XIII Catalan)
Adrian Hadley (Widnes)	16.	Christophe Martinez (St. Gaudens)
Richard Webster (Salford)	17.	Alexander Couttet (Carcassonne)

T: Webster

G: Davies (4, 1dg)

Substitutions:

Powell for Ford (68 min.)

Marlow for Jones (74 min.)

Webster for Young (74 min.)

Referee: David Campbell (Widnes)

T: Entat, Garcia

G: Torreilles (2)

Substitutions:

Martinez for Despin (24 min.)

Attia for Teixido (Half-time)

Jampy for Llong (72 min.)

Half-time: 0-6

Attendance: 6,287

EUROPEAN CHAMPIONSHIP

● The following is a list of European Championship matches since the tournament was introduced in 1935, the year that France emerged as an international competitor.
E — England, Fr — France, ON — Other Nationalities, W — Wales

1934-35   *Winners:* England on points average

1 Jan.	Fr	18	W	11	Bordeaux
28 Mar.	Fr	15	E	15	Paris
10 Apr.	E	24	W	11	Liverpool

1935-36   *Winners:* Wales

23 Nov.	W	41	Fr	7	Llanelli
1 Feb.	E	14	W	17	Hull K.R.
16 Feb.	Fr	7	E	25	Paris

1936-37   *Winners:* Wales

7 Nov.	W	3	E	2	Pontypridd
6 Dec.	Fr	3	W	9	Paris
10 Apr.	E	23	Fr	9	Halifax

1937-38   *Winners:* Wales

29 Jan.	E	6	W	7	Bradford
20 Mar.	Fr	15	E	17	Paris
2 Apr.	W	18	Fr	2	Llanelli

1938-39   *Winners:* France

5 Nov.	W	17	E	9	Llanelli
25 Feb.	E	9	Fr	12	St. Helens
16 Apr.	Fr	16	W	10	Bordeaux

1945-46   *Winners:* England on points average

24 Nov.	W	11	E	3	Swansea
23 Feb.	E	16	Fr	6	Swinton
24 Mar.	Fr	19	W	7	Bordeaux

1946-47   *Winners:* England

12 Oct.	E	10	W	13	Swinton
16 Nov.	W	5	E	19	Swansea
8 Dec.	Fr	0	E	3	Bordeaux
18 Jan.	Fr	14	W	5	Marseilles
12 Apr.	W	17	Fr	15	Swansea
17 May	E	5	Fr	2	Leeds

1947-48   *Winners:* England

20 Sep.	E	8	W	10	Wigan
25 Oct.	E	20	Fr	15	Huddersfield
23 Nov.	Fr	29	W	21	Bordeaux
6 Dec.	W	7	E	18	Swansea
20 Mar.	W	12	Fr	20	Swansea
11 Apr.	Fr	10	E	25	Marseilles

1948-49   *Winners:* France

22 Sep.	E	11	W	5	Wigan
23 Oct.	W	9	Fr	12	Swansea
28 Nov.	Fr	5	E	12	Bordeaux
5 Feb.	W	14	E	10	Swansea
12 Mar.	E	5	Fr	12	Wembley
10 Apr.	Fr	11	W	0	Marseilles

1949-50   *Winners:* England on points average

19 Sep.	E	7	ON	13	Workington
22 Oct.	W	5	ON	6	Abertillery
12 Nov.	W	16	Fr	8	Swansea
4 Dec.	Fr	5	E	13	Bordeaux
15 Jan.	Fr	8	ON	3	Marseilles
1 Mar.	E	11	W	6	Wigan

1950-51   *Winners:* France on points average

14 Oct.	W	4	E	22	Abertillery
11 Nov.	E	14	Fr	9	Leeds
10 Dec.	Fr	16	ON	3	Bordeaux
31 Mar.	W	21	ON	27	Swansea
11 Apr.	E	10	ON	35	Wigan
15 Apr.	Fr	28	W	13	Marseilles

1951-52   *Winners:* France on points average

19 Sep.	E	35	W	11	St. Helens
3 Nov.	ON	17	Fr	14	Hull
25 Nov.	Fr	42	E	13	Marseilles
1 Dec.	W	11	ON	22	Abertillery
6 Apr.	Fr	20	W	12	Bordeaux
23 Apr.	E	31	ON	18	Wigan

1952-53   *Winners:* Other Nats on points average

17 Sep.	E	19	W	8	Wigan
18 Oct.	E	12	ON	31	Huddersfield
25 Oct.	W	22	Fr	16	Leeds
23 Nov.	Fr	10	ON	29	Marseilles
11 Apr.	Fr	13	E	15	Paris
15 Apr.	W	18	ON	16	Warrington

1953-54   *Winners:* England

16 Sep.	E	24	W	5	St. Helens
7 Oct.	ON	30	W	5	Bradford
18 Oct.	Fr	10	ON	15	Bordeaux
7 Nov.	E	7	Fr	5	Bradford
28 Nov.	E	30	ON	22	Wigan
13 Dec.	Fr	23	W	22	Marseilles

● Championship suspended in 1954-55 because of World Cup

1955-56   *Winners:* Other Nationalities

12 Sep.	E	16	ON	33	Wigan
19 Oct.	ON	32	Fr	19	Leigh
10 May	Fr	23	E	9	Lyons

1969-70   *Winners:* England on points average

18 Oct.	E	40	W	23	Leeds
23 Oct.	W	2	Fr	8	Salford
25 Oct.	E	11	Fr	11	Wigan
25 Jan.	Fr	11	W	15	Perpignan
24 Feb.	E	26	W	7	Leeds
15 Mar.	Fr	14	E	9	Toulouse

1974-75   *Winners:* England

19 Jan.	Fr	9	E	11	Perpignan
16 Feb.	W	21	Fr	8	Swansea
25 Feb.	E	12	W	8	Salford

● Championship suspended in 1975-76 because of World Cup

1976-77   *Winners:* France

29 Jan.	E	2	W	6	Leeds
20 Feb.	Fr	13	W	2	Toulouse
20 Mar.	Fr	28	E	15	Carcassonne

1977-78   *Winners:* England

15 Jan.	W	29	Fr	7	Widnes
5 Mar.	Fr	11	E	13	Toulouse
28 May	E	60	W	13	St. Helens

1978-79   *Winners:* England

4 Feb.	Fr	15	W	8	Narbonne
16 Mar.	E	15	W	7	Widnes
24 Mar.	E	12	Fr	6	Warrington

1979-80   *Winners:* England

26 Jan.	W	7	Fr	21	Widnes
29 Feb.	E	26	W	9	Hull K.R.
16 Mar.	Fr	2	E	4	Narbonne

1980-81   *Winners:* France

31 Jan.	Fr	23	W	5	Narbonne
21 Feb.	E	1	Fr	5	Leeds
18 Mar.	E	17	W	4	Hull K.R.

1975 WORLD CHAMPIONSHIP

Winners: Australia (home and away basis)

Date	Match and Result				Venue	Attendance
2 Mar.	France	14	Wales	7	Toulouse	7,563
16 Mar.	England	20	France	2	Leeds	10,842
1 June	Australia	36	New Zealand	8	Brisbane	10,000
10 June	Wales	12	England	7	Brisbane	6,000
14 June	Australia	30	Wales	13	Sydney	25,386
15 June	New Zealand	27	France	0	Christchurch	2,500
21 June	New Zealand	17	England	17	Auckland	12,000
22 June	Australia	26	France	6	Brisbane	9,000
28 June	New Zealand	13	Wales	8	Auckland	18,000
28 June	Australia	10	England	10	Sydney	33,858
20 Sep.	England	22	Wales	16	Warrington	5,034
27 Sep.	New Zealand	8	Australia	24	Auckland	18,000
11 Oct.	France	2	England	48	Bordeaux	1,581
17 Oct.	France	12	New Zealand	12	Marseilles	18,000
19 Oct.	Wales	6	Australia	18	Swansea	11,112
25 Oct.	England	27	New Zealand	12	Bradford	5,507
26 Oct.	France	2	Australia	41	Perpignan	10,440
1 Nov.	England	16	Australia	13	Wigan	9,393
2 Nov.	Wales	25	New Zealand	24	Swansea	2,645
6 Nov.	Wales	23	France	2	Salford	2,247

Final Table

	P.	W.	D.	L.	F.	A.	Pts
Australia	8	6	1	1	198	69	13
England	8	5	2	1	167	84	12
Wales	8	3	0	5	110	130	6
New Zealand	8	2	2	4	121	149	6
France	8	1	1	6	40	204	3

1975 World Championship squads for Australasian section

ENGLAND	WALES
R. Millward (Hull K.R.)	**D. Watkins (Salford)**
J. Atkinson (Leeds)	P. Banner (Salford)
J. Bridges (Featherstone R.)	B. Butler (Swinton)
D. Chisnall (Warrington)	K. Coslett (St. Helens)
E. Chisnall (St. Helens)	E. Cunningham (St. Helens)
P. Cookson (Leeds)	C. Dixon (Salford)
M. Coulman (Salford)	R. Evans (Swinton)
G. Dunn (Hull K.R.)	T. Fisher (Leeds)
L. Dyl (Leeds)	W. Francis (Wigan)
G. Fairbairn (Wigan)	J. Mantle (St. Helens)
K. Fielding (Salford)	R. Mathias (St. Helens)
K. Gill (Salford)	J. Mills (Widnes)
P. Gordon (Warrington)	M. Nicholas (Warrington)
T. Martyn (Warrington)	P. Rowe (Blackpool B.)
M. Morgan (Wakefield T.)	C. Sullivan (Hull K.R.)
S. Nash (Featherstone R.)	D. Treasure (Oldham)
G. Nicholls (St. Helens)	G. Turner (Hull K.R.)
D. Noonan (Warrington)	R. Wanbon (Warrington)
S. Norton (Castleford)	D. Willicombe (Wigan)
J. Walsh (St. Helens)	F. Wilson (St. Helens)
Manager: W. Oxley (Barrow)	Manager: R. Simpson (Castleford)
Coach: A.J. Murphy (Warrington)	Coach: L. Pearce (Halifax)

ENGLAND — OTHER INTERNATIONAL MATCHES

● W-Won, D-Drawn, L-Lost refer to England.

v. WALES

20 Apr. 1908	L	18-35	Tonypandy
28 Dec. 1908	W	31-7	Broughton
4 Dec. 1909	W	19-13	Wakefield
9 Apr. 1910	L	18-39	Ebbw Vale
10 Dec. 1910	W	39-13	Coventry
1 Apr. 1911	W	27-8	Ebbw Vale
20 Jan. 1912	W	31-5	Oldham
15 Feb. 1913	W	40-16	Plymouth
14 Feb. 1914	W	16-12	St. Helens

v. FRANCE

*15 Apr. 1934	W	32-21	Paris
17 Nov. 1962	W	18-6	Leeds

*Included Welsh players.

v. OTHER NATIONALITIES

5 Apr. 1904	L	3-9	Wigan
2 Jan. 1905	W	26-11	Bradford (Park Avenue)
1 Jan. 1906	D	3-3	Wigan

v. WALES (cont.)			
21 Jan. 1921	W	35-9	Leeds
11 Dec. 1922	W	12-7	London, Herne Hill
7 Feb. 1923	L	2-13	Wigan
1 Oct. 1923	W	18-11	Huddersfield
7 Feb. 1925	W	27-22	Workington
30 Sep. 1925	W	18-14	Wigan
12 Apr. 1926	W	30-22	Pontypridd
6 Apr. 1927	W	11-8	Broughton
11 Jan. 1928	W	20-12	Wigan
14 Nov. 1928	W	39-15	Cardiff
18 Mar. 1931	W	23-18	Huddersfield
27 Jan. 1932	W	19-2	Salford
30 Nov. 1932	W	14-13	Leeds
23 Dec. 1939	L	3-16	Bradford
9 Nov. 1940	W	8-5	Oldham
18 Oct. 1941	D	9-9	Bradford
27 Feb. 1943	W	15-9	Wigan
26 Feb. 1944	D	9-9	Wigan
10 Mar. 1945	W	18-8	Wigan
7 Nov. 1968	L	17-24	Salford
8 Nov. 1981	W	20-15	Cardiff
14 Oct. 1984	W	28-9	Ebbw Vale
27 Nov. 1992	W	36-11	Swansea C. FC

v. OTHER NATIONALITIES (cont.)			
*5 Feb. 1921	W	33-16	Workington
15 Oct. 1924	L	17-23	Leeds
4 Feb. 1926	W	37-11	Whitehaven
20 Mar. 1929	W	27-20	Leeds
7 Apr. 1930	L	19-35	Halifax
1 Oct. 1930	W	31-18	St. Helens
30 Mar. 1933	W	34-27	Workington

*Other Nationalities side all-Welsh.

v. AUSTRALIA			
2 Jan. 1909	W	14-9	Huddersfield
3 Feb. 1909	D	17-17	Glasgow
3 Mar. 1909	W	14-7	Everton
18 Oct. 1911	L	6-11	Fulham
6 Dec. 1911	W	5-3	Nottingham
10 Oct. 1921	W	5-4	Arsenal
*31 Dec. 1933	L	13-63	Paris
*13 Jan. 1934	W	19-14	Gateshead
12 Nov. 1975	L	0-25	Leeds

*Included Welsh players.

v. NEW ZEALAND			
11 Jan. 1908	W	18-16	Wigan

v. PAPUA NEW GUINEA			
16 July 1975	W	40-12	Port Moresby

ENGLAND RECORDS

Highest score: 60-13 v. Wales at St. Helens, 28 May 1978
(Also widest margin win)
Highest score against: 63-13* v. Australia at Paris, 31 December 1933
*England included Welshmen. Highest score against All-England side 42-13 v. France at Marseilles, 25 November 1951 (Also widest margin defeat)
Most tries in a match: 4 by J. Leytham (Wigan) v. Other Nationalities
at Bradford, 2 January 1905
4 by S. Moorhouse (Huddersfield) v. Wales
at Plymouth, 15 February 1913
4 by P. Norburn (Swinton) v. Other Nationalities
at Wigan, 28 November 1953
4 by K. Fielding (Salford) v. France
at Bordeaux, 11 October 1975
4 by S. Wright (Widnes) v. Wales
at St. Helens, 28 May 1978
Most goals and points 9g-21pts by G. Pimblett (St. Helens) v. Wales
in a match: at St. Helens, 28 May 1978
Biggest home attendance: 27,500 v. Wales at Wigan, 1 March 1950

WALES — OTHER INTERNATIONAL MATCHES

● W-Won, D-Drawn,
L-Lost refer to Wales.

v. FRANCE
*19 May 1955	L	11-24	Nantes
1 Mar. 1959	L	8-25	Toulouse
17 Feb. 1963	L	3-23	Toulouse
9 Mar. 1969	L	13-17	Paris
22 Mar. 1992	W	35-6	Swansea C. FC
13 Dec. 1992	W	19-18	Perpignan
4 Mar. 1994	W	13-12	Cardiff C. FC

*v. France 'B'

v. NEW ZEALAND
1 Jan. 1908	W	9-8	Aberdare
4 Dec. 1926	W	34-8	Pontypridd
18 Oct. 1947	L	20-28	Swansea
7 Dec. 1951	L	3-15	Bradford
3 Oct. 1993	L	19-24	Swansea C. FC

v. AUSTRALIA
7 Oct. 1911	L	20-28	Ebbw Vale
10 Dec. 1921	L	16-21	Pontypridd
18 Jan. 1930	L	10-26	Wembley
30 Dec. 1933	L	19-51	Wembley
20 Nov. 1948	L	5-12	Swansea
15 Oct. 1978	L	3-8	Swansea
24 Oct. 1982	L	7-37	Cardiff C. FC

A Welsh League XIII beat Australia 14-13 at Merthyr on 16 January 1909.

v. PAPUA NEW GUINEA
27 Oct. 1991	W	68-0	Swansea C. FC

v. NORTHERN RL
17 Apr. 1937	W	15-12	Newcastle

v. EMPIRE XIII
19 May 1951	L	16-29	Llanelli

Wales hooker Barry Williams, capped four times between 1981 and 1984.

WALES RECORDS

Highest score:	68-0 v. Papua New Guinea at Swansea C. FC, 27 October 1991 (Also widest margin win)
Highest score against:	60-13 v. England at St. Helens, 28 May 1978 (Also widest margin defeat)
Most tries in a match:	4 by W. T. Davies (Halifax) v. Australia at Ebbw Vale, 7 October 1911
Most goals and points in a match:	8g-24pts by Jonathan Davies (Widnes) v. Papua New Guinea at Swansea C. FC, 27 October 1991
Biggest home attendance:	30,000 v. England at Swansea, 24 November 1945

MISCELLANEOUS

1908	November	18	Northern RL	9	v.	Australia	10	Everton
1909	January	16	Welsh League	14	v.	Australia	13	Merthyr Tydfil
1910	September	17	Wales & the West	27	v.	England	25	Plymouth
1910	September	19	Tourists	15	v.	Colonials	31	Leeds
1910	December	27	Tourists	40	v.	Colonials	22	Wigan
1911	September	23	Midlands & South	11	v.	Australia	20	Coventry
1911	October	25	Northern RL	3	v.	Australia	16	Everton
1911	December	20	Wales & the West	3	v.	Australia	23	Bristol
1912	January	31	Northern RL	12	v.	Australia	20	Wigan
1929	December	4	Northern RL	18	v.	Australia	5	Wigan
1929	December	18	Northern RL	22	v.	Australia	32	Newcastle
1933	November	1	Northern RL	7	v.	Australia	5	York
1934	March	17	Northern RL	32	v.	France	16	Warrington
1935	April	28	French XIII	12	v.	Northern RL	32	Paris
1935	May	6	Northern RL	25	v.	France	18	Leeds
1936	April	26	France	8	v.	Dominions XIII	5	Paris
1937	March	21	France	3	v.	Dominions XIII	6	Lyons
1937	November	1	France	0	v.	Empire XIII	15	Paris
1938	April	28	French XIII	13	v.	Northern RL	25	Pau
1940	March	23	Lancs League	10	v.	Yorks League	13	Barrow
1940	May	4	Tour Probables	29	v.	1936 Tourists	21	Salford
1942	March	21	RL XIII	18	v.	N. Command	22	Halifax
1942	October	10	RL XIII	10	v.	N. Command	14	Hull
1943	December	18	RL XIII	11	v.	Army XIII	4	Halifax
1944	October	7	RL XIII	27	v.	N. Command	23	Huddersfield
1946	January	6	French XIII	6	v.	British XIII	19	Paris
1946	April	28	Paris XIII	19	v.	RL XIII	36	Paris
1949	May	26	French XIII	23	v.	Empire XIII	10	Bordeaux
1949	May	29	French XIII	12	v.	Empire XIII	38	Albi
1950	October	4	Tourists	23	v.	Rest of League	16	Wigan
1951	May	3	French XIII	10	v.	UK XIII	13	Paris
1951	May	19	Great Britain	20	v.	Australasia	23	Leeds
1952	January	23	Empire XIII	26	v.	New Zealand	2	Chelsea
1954	January	3	France	19	v.	Internat. XIII	15	Lyons
1954	November	17	RL XIII	13	v.	Australasia	25	Bradford
1955	December	7	RL XIII	24	v.	New Zealand	11	Bradford
1956	October	3	Great Britain	26	v.	Rest of League	23	Bradford
1956	October	21	France	17	v.	RL XIII	18	Marseilles
1956	October	29	RL XIII	15	v.	Australia	19	Leigh
1957	July	6	British XIII	26	v.	French XIII	12	Auckland
1957	July	20	British XIII	61	v.	French XIII	41	Benoni (S. Africa)
1957	July	24	British XIII	32	v.	French XIII	11	Durban (S. Africa)
1957	July	27	British XIII	69	v.	French XIII	11	East London (S. Africa)
1958	April	16	RL XIII	19	v.	France	8	Leeds
1958	November	22	RL XIII	8	v.	France	26	St. Helens
1960	September	12	Great Britain	21	v.	Rest of League	16	St. Helens
1960	October	10	Great Britain	33	v.	Rest of World	27	Bradford
1961	September	20	RL XIII	22	v.	New Zealand	20	White City, Manchester
1961	October	12	French XIII	21	v.	RL XIII	20	Paris
1962	August	23	South Africa	30	v.	Great Britain	49	Pretoria (S. Africa)
1962	August	26	South Africa	35	v.	Great Britain	39	Durban (S. Africa)
1962	August	28	South Africa	23	v.	Great Britain	45	Johannesburg (S. Africa)
1962	November	1	France	16	v.	Eastern Div.	23	Carcassonne
1965	August	18	Other Nats.	7	v.	New Zealand	15	Crystal Palace
1966	May	5	Paris XIII	20	v.	RL XIII	0	Paris
1966	November	6	Tourists	31	v.	Rest of League	38	Leeds

ENGLAND TEAMS ● From 1975 to 1982, revived in 1984 for one game and reintroduced in 1992.

1975 France
Perpignan: 19 Jan.
Won 11-9
Murphy (Oldham) 1t
Fielding (Salford) 1t
Walsh (St. Helens)
Dyl (Leeds) 1t
Redfearn, D. (Bradford N.)
Topliss (Wakefield T.)
*Millward (Hull K.R.)
Coulman (Salford)
Gray (Wigan) 1g
Millington (Hull K.R.)
Cunningham (Barrow)
Chisnall, E. (St. Helens)
Nicholls (St. Helens)
Sub: Eckersley (St. Helens)
　　　Morgan (Wakefield T.)

1975 Wales
Salford: 25 Feb.
Won 12-8
Sheard (Wakefield T.)
Dunn (Hull K.R.)
Noonan (Warrington) 1t
Dyl (Leeds)
Atkinson (Leeds) 1t
Gill, K. (Salford)
*Millward (Hull K.R.)
Coulman (Salford)
Gray (Wigan) 3g
Jackson, P. (Bradford N.)
Martyn (Warrington)
Cunningham (Barrow)
Morgan (Wakefield T.)
Sub: Chisnall, D. (Warrington)

1975 France (WC)
Leeds: 16 Mar.
Won 20-2
Charlton (Salford)
Fielding (Salford) 2t
Noonan (Warrington)
Dyl (Leeds)
Atkinson (Leeds)
Gill, K. (Salford)
*Millward (Hull K.R.) 1t
Chisnall, D. (Warrington)
Gray (Wigan) 4g
Jackson, P. (Bradford N.)
Martyn (Warrington)
Nicholls (St. Helens)
Philbin (Warrington)
Sub: Morgan (Wakefield T.) 1t

1975 Wales (WC)
Brisbane: 10 June
Lost 7-12
Fairbairn (Wigan) 2g
Fielding (Salford)
Noonan (Warrington)
Dyl (Leeds)
Atkinson (Leeds)
*Millward (Hull K.R.)
Nash (Featherstone R.)
Chisnall, D. (Warrington)
Morgan (Wakefield T.)
Coulman (Salford)
Chisnall, E. (St. Helens)
Nicholls (St. Helens)
Norton (Castleford)
Sub: Gill, K. (Salford)
　　　Martyn (Warrington) 1t

1975 New Zealand (WC)
Auckland: 21 June
Drew 17-17
Fairbairn (Wigan) 2t,4g
Fielding (Salford)
Walsh (St. Helens)
Dyl (Leeds)
Atkinson (Leeds) 1t
Gill, K. (Salford)
Nash (Featherstone R.)
Chisnall, D. (Warrington)
Bridges (Featherstone R.)
Chisnall, E. (St. Helens)
*Nicholls (St. Helens)
Cookson (Leeds)
Norton (Castleford)
Sub: Morgan (Wakefield T.)

1975 Australia (WC)
Sydney: 28 June
Drew 10-10
Fairbairn (Wigan) 2g
Fielding (Salford)
Walsh (St. Helens)
Dyl (Leeds)
Dunn (Hull K.R.) 1t
*Millward (Hull K.R.)
Nash (Featherstone R.)
Coulman (Salford)
Bridges (Featherstone R.)
Morgan (Wakefield T.)
Nicholls (St. Helens)
Cookson (Leeds)
Norton (Castleford)
Sub: Gill, K. (Salford) 1t
　　　Chisnall, E. (St. Helens)

1975 Wales (WC)
Warrington: 20 Sep.
Won 22-16
Fairbairn (Wigan) 6g
Fielding (Salford) 1t
Hughes (Widnes) 1t
Holmes (Leeds) 1t
Atkinson (Leeds)
Gill, K. (Salford)
*Millward (Hull K.R.)
Hogan, B. (Wigan)
Bridges (Featherstone R.) 1dg
Forsyth (Bradford N.)
Grayshon (Dewsbury)
Irving (Wigan)
Norton (Castleford)
Sub: Eckersley (St. Helens)
　　　Nicholls (St. Helens)

1975 France (WC)
Bordeaux: 11 Oct.
Won 48-2
Fairbairn (Wigan) 4g
Fielding (Salford) 4t
Hughes (Widnes) 1t
Holmes (Leeds) 2t
Dunn (Hull K.R.) 2t
Gill, K. (Salford) 1t
*Millward (Hull K.R.) 2g
Hogan, B. (Wigan) 1t
Bridges (Featherstone R.)
Forsyth (Bradford N.) 1t
Grayshon (Dewsbury)
Irving (Wigan)
Norton (Castleford)
Sub: Eckersley (St. Helens)
　　　Nicholls (St. Helens)

1975 New Zealand (WC)
Bradford: 25 Oct.
Won 27-12
Fairbairn (Wigan) 3g
Wright (Wigan) 1t
Hughes (Widnes) 1t
Holmes (Leeds)
Dunn (Hull K.R.) 1t
Gill, K. (Salford) 3t
*Millward (Hull K.R.)
Hogan, B. (Wigan)
Bridges (Featherstone R.)
Forsyth (Bradford N.)
Grayshon (Dewsbury)
Adams (Widnes)
Norton (Castleford) 1t
Sub: Dyl (Leeds)
　　　Nicholls (St. Helens)

1975 Australia (WC)
Wigan: 1 Nov.
Won 16-13
Fairbairn (Wigan) 5g
Dunn (Hull K.R.)
Holmes (Leeds) 1t
Dyl (Leeds)
Redfearn, D. (Bradford N.)
Gill, K. (Salford)
*Millward (Hull K.R.)
Hogan, B. (Wigan)
Bridges (Featherstone R.)
Thompson (Featherstone R.)
Grayshon (Dewsbury) 1t
Irving (Wigan)
Norton (Castleford)
Sub: Hughes (Widnes)
    Adams (Widnes)

1977 Wales
Leeds: 29 Jan.
Lost 2-6
Fairbairn (Wigan) 1g
Wright (Widnes)
Holmes (Leeds)
Dyl (Leeds)
Jones (St. Helens)
Gill, K. (Salford)
*Millward (Hull K.R.)
Hogan, B. (Wigan)
Bridges (Featherstone R.)
Thompson (Featherstone R.)
Grayshon (Dewsbury)
Gorley, L. (Workington T.)
Laughton (Widnes)
Sub: Eckersley (St. Helens)
    Reilly (Castleford)

1977 France
Carcassonne: 20 Mar.
Lost 15-28
Fairbairn (Wigan) 3g
Dunn (Hull K.R.)
Hughes (Widnes)
Dyl (Leeds)
Smith, D. (Leeds) 1t
Gill, K. (Salford)
*Millward (Hull K.R.)
Coulman (Salford)
Ward (Leeds)
Farrar (Featherstone R.)
Lowe (Hull K.R.) 1t
Rose (Hull K.R.)
Norton (Castleford)
Sub: Holmes (Leeds)
    Nicholls (St. Helens) 1t

1978 France
Toulouse: 5 Mar.
Won 13-11
Fairbairn (Wigan) 2g
Wright (Widnes)
Hughes (Widnes) 2t
Dyl (Leeds)
Atkinson (Leeds)
*Millward (Hull K.R.)
Nash (Salford)
Harrison (Leeds)
Elwell (Widnes)
Nicholls (St. Helens)
Lowe (Hull K.R.)
Adams (Widnes)
Casey (Hull K.R.)
Sub: Holmes (Leeds) 1t
    Thompson (Bradford N.)

1978 Wales
St. Helens: 28 May
Won 60-13
Pimblett (St. Helens) 1t,9g
Wright (Widnes) 4t
Hughes (Widnes) 2t
Dyl (Leeds) 1t
Atkinson (Leeds) 2t
*Millward (Hull K.R.) 1t
Nash (Salford) 1t
Harrison (Leeds)
Elwell (Widnes)
Nicholls (St. Helens)
Rose (Hull K.R.)
Casey (Hull K.R.) 1t
Norton (Hull) 1t
Sub: Eckersley (St. Helens)
    Thompson (Bradford N.)

1979 Wales
Widnes: 16 Mar.
Won 15-7
Mumby (Bradford N.) 1t,1g
Wright (Widnes)
Glynn (St. Helens)
Smith, K. (Wakefield T.) 1t
Hughes (Widnes)
Kelly, K. (Warrington)
Stephens (Castleford)
Beverley (Workington T.)
Liptrot (St. Helens)
*Lockwood (Hull K.R.)
Martyn (Warrington)
Grayshon (Bradford N.)
Adams (Widnes)
Sub: Woods (Leigh) 1t,2g
    Watkinson (Hull K.R.)

1979 France
Warrington: 24 Mar.
Won 12-6
Mumby (Bradford N.)
Wright (Widnes)
Glynn (St. Helens)
Woods (Leigh) 3g
Hughes (Widnes) 1t
Evans (Featherstone R.)
Redfearn, A. (Bradford N.)
Tindall (Hull)
Liptrot (St. Helens)
*Lockwood (Hull K.R.)
Martyn (Warrington) 1t
Grayshon (Bradford N.)
Hogan, P. (Hull K.R.)
Sub: Banks (York)
    Szymala (Barrow)

1980 Wales
Hull K.R.: 29 Feb.
Won 26-9
Fairbairn (Wigan) 1t,6g
Wright (Widnes)
Joyner (Castleford) 1t
Smith, M. (Hull K.R.)
Drummond (Leigh)
Evans (Featherstone R.)
Holding (St. Helens)
Holdstock (Hull K.R.) 1t
*Ward (Leeds)
Rayne, Keith (Wakefield T.) 1t
Casey (Hull K.R.)
Gorley, P. (St. Helens)
Pinner (St. Helens) 2dg
Sub: Woods (Leigh)
    Grayshon (Bradford N.)

1980 France
Narbonne: 16 Mar.
Won 4-2
Fairbairn (Wigan)
Drummond (Leigh)
Smith, M. (Hull K.R.)
Joyner (Castleford)
Evans (Featherstone R.) 1t
Woods (Leigh)
Redfearn, A. (Bradford N.) 1dg
Holdstock (Hull K.R.)
*Ward (Leeds)
Rayne, Keith (Wakefield T.)
Grayshon (Bradford N.)
Smith, P. (Featherstone R.)
Pinner (St. Helens)
Sub: Gorley, P. (St. Helens)

1981 France

Leeds: 21 Feb.

Lost 1-5

*Fairbairn (Wigan) 1dg
Drummond (Leigh)
Joyner (Castleford)
Smith, M. (Hull K.R.)
Fenton (Castleford)
Kelly, K. (Warrington)
Walker (Whitehaven)
O'Neill (Wigan)
Ward (Leeds)
Case (Warrington)
Casey (Hull K.R.)
Potter (Warrington)
Pinner (St. Helens)
Sub: Woods (Leigh)
      Pattinson (Workington T.)

1984 Wales

Ebbw Vale: 14 Oct.

Won 28-9

Burke (Widnes) 1t,4g
Drummond (Leigh)
Schofield (Hull)
Hanley (Bradford N.) 1t
Clark (Hull K.R.) 3t
*Donlan (Leigh)
Cairns (Barrow)
Hobbs (Featherstone R.)
Beardmore, K. (Castleford)
Waddell (Blackpool B.)
Kelly, A. (Hull K.R.)
Goodway (Oldham)
Huddart (Whitehaven)
Sub: Ledger (St. Helens)
      Arkwright (St. Helens)

1981 Wales

Hull K.R.: 18 Mar.

Won 17-4

*Fairbairn (Wigan) 4g
Richardson (Castleford)
Joyner (Castleford) 1t
Smith, M. (Hull K.R.)
Fenton (Castleford)
Kelly, K. (Warrington) 1t
Nash (Salford)
Holdstock (Hull K.R.)
Ward (Leeds)
Casey (Hull K.R.)
Potter (Warrington)
Pattinson (Workington T.)
Norton (Hull)
Sub: Woods (Leigh) 1t
      Adams (Widnes)

1992 Wales

Swansea C. FC: 27 Nov.

Won 36-11

Spruce (Widnes) 1t
Hunte (St. Helens)
Connolly (St. Helens)
Newlove (Featherstone R.) 1t
Offiah (Wigan) 2t
*Schofield (Leeds) 1t
Ford (Castleford)
Crooks (Castleford) 1t,4g
Jackson, L. (Hull)
Molloy (Leeds)
Eyres (Widnes)
Clarke (Wigan)
Hanley (Leeds) 1t
Sub: Powell, D. (Sheffield E.)
      Joynt (St. Helens)
      Critchley (Salford)
      Busby (Hull)

1981 Wales

Cardiff: 8 Nov.

Won 20-15

Fairbairn (Hull K.R.) 1g
Drummond (Leigh) 1t
Smith, M. (Hull K.R.)
Dyl (Leeds)
Gill, H. (Wigan) 1t
Woods (Leigh) 3g
Nash (Salford)
Grayshon (Bradford N.) 1t
*Ward (Leeds)
Millington (Hull K.R.)
Lowe (Hull K.R.)
Gorley, P. (St. Helens) 1t
Norton (Hull)
Sub: Gorley, L. (Widnes)

Back row forward Phil Clarke, an England debutant at the Vetch Field, Swansea, in November 1992.

ENGLAND REGISTER
● Since reintroduction in 1975

The following is a register of England appearances since the reintroduction of European and World Championship matches in 1975, but does not include the challenge match against Australia played after the 1975 World Championship.

Figures in brackets are the total appearances for England since 1975, with the plus sign indicating substitute appearances, e.g. (7+3).

A few players also played in the 1969-70 European Championship and this is shown as an additional total outside bracket, e.g. (11)2.

World Championship matches are in bold letters. Substitute appearances are in lower case letters.

A - Australia, F - France,
NZ - New Zealand, W - Wales.

ADAMS, Mick (3+2) Widnes: 1975 **NZ, a**; 1978 F; 1979 W; 1981 w
ARKWRIGHT, Chris (+1) St. Helens: 1984 w
ATKINSON, John (7)4 Leeds: 1975 W, **F, W, NZ, W**; 1978 F, W

BANKS, Barry (+1) York: 1979 f
BEARDMORE, Kevin (1) Castleford: 1984 W
BEVERLEY, Harry (1) Workington T: 1979 W
BRIDGES, John "Keith" (7) Featherstone R: 1975 **NZ, A, W, F, NZ, A**; 1977 W
BURKE, Mick (1) Widnes: 1984 W
BUSBY, Dean (+1) Hull: 1992 w

CAIRNS, David (1) Barrow: 1984 W
CASE, Brian (1) Warrington: 1981 F
CASEY, Len (5) Hull KR: 1978 F, W; 1980 W; 1981 F, W
CHARLTON, Paul (1) Salford: 1975 **F**
CHISNALL, Dave (3+1) Warrington: 1975 w, **F, W, NZ**
CHISNALL, Eric (3+1) St. Helens: 1975 F, **W, NZ, a**
CLARK, Garry (1) Hull KR: 1984 W
CLARKE, Phil (1) Wigan: 1984 W
CONNOLLY, Gary (1) St. Helens: 1992 W
COOKSON, Phil (2) Leeds: 1975 **NZ, A**
COULMAN, Mike (5) Salford: 1975 F, W, **W, A**; 1977 F
CRITCHLEY, Jason (+1) Salford: 1992 w
CROOKS, Lee (1) Castleford: 1992 W
CUNNINGHAM, John (2) Barrow: 1975 F, W

DONLAN, Steve (1) Leigh: 1984 W
DRUMMOND, Des (5) Leigh: 1980 W, F; 1981 F, W; 1984 W
DUNN, Ged (6) Hull KR: 1975 W, **A, F, NZ, A**; 1977 F
DYL, Les (12+1) Leeds: 1975 F, W, **F, W, NZ, A, nz, A**; 1977 W, F; 1978 F, W; 1981 W
ECKERSLEY, Dave (+5) St. Helens: 1975 f, **w, f**; Widnes: 1977 w; 1978 w
ELWELL, Keith (2) Widnes: 1978 F, W
EVANS, Steve (3) Featherstone R: 1979 F; 1980 W, F

EYRES, Richard (1) Widnes: 1992 W
FAIRBAIRN, George (15) Wigan: 1975 **W, NZ, A, W, F, NZ, A**; 1977 W, F; 1978 F; 1980 W, F; 1981 F, W; Hull KR: 1981 W
FARRAR, Vince (1) Featherstone R: 1977 F
FENTON, Steve (2) Castleford: 1981 F, W
FIELDING, Keith (7) Salford: 1975 F, **F, W, NZ, A, W, F**
FORD, Mike (1) Castleford: 1992 W
FORSYTH, Colin (3) Bradford N: 1975 **W, F, NZ**

GILL, Henderson (1) Wigan: 1981 W
GILL, Ken (9+2) Salford: 1975 W, **F, w, NZ, a, W, F, NZ, A**; 1977 W, F
GLYNN, Peter (2) St. Helens: 1979 W, F
GOODWAY, Andy (1) Oldham: 1984 W
GORLEY, Les (1+1) Workington T: 1977 W; Widnes: 1981 w
GORLEY, Peter (2+1) St. Helens: 1980 W, f; 1981 W
GRAY, John (3) Wigan: 1975 F, W, **F**
GRAYSHON, Jeff (9+1) Dewsbury: 1975 **W, F, NZ, A**; 1977 W; Bradford N: 1979 W, F; 1980 w, F; 1981 W

HANLEY, Ellery (2) Bradford N: 1984 W; Leeds: 1992 W
HARRISON, Mick (2) Leeds: 1978 F, W
HOBBS, David (1) Featherstone R: 1984 W
HOGAN, Brian (5) Wigan: 1975 **W, F, NZ, A**; 1977 W
HOGAN, Phil (1) Hull KR: 1979 F
HOLDING, Neil (1) St. Helens: 1980 W
HOLDSTOCK, Roy (3) Hull KR: 1980 W, F; 1981 W
HOLMES, John (5+2) Leeds: 1975 **W, F, NZ, A**; 1977 W, f; 1978 f
HUDDART, Milton (1) Whitehaven: 1984 W
HUGHES, Eric (8+1) Widnes: 1975 **W, F, NZ, a**; 1977 F; 1978 F, W; 1979 W, F
HUNTE, Alan (1) St. Helens: 1992 W

IRVING, Bob (3) Wigan: 1975 **W, F, A**

JACKSON, Lee (1) Hull: 1992 W
JACKSON, Phil (2) Bradford N: 1975 W, **F**

JONES, Les (1) St. Helens: 1977 W
JOYNER, John (4) Castleford: 1980 W, F; 1981 F, W
JOYNT, Chris (+1) St. Helens: 1992 w

KELLY, Andy (1) Hull KR: 1984 W
KELLY, Ken (3) Warrington: 1979 W; 1981 F, W

LAUGHTON, Doug (1) Widnes: 1977 W
LEDGER, Barry (+1) St. Helens: 1984 w
LIPTROT, Graham (2) St. Helens: 1979 W, F
LOCKWOOD, Brian (2)+1 Hull KR: 1979 W, F
LOWE, Phil (3)2 Hull KR: 1977 F; 1978 F; 1981 W

MARTYN, Tommy (4+1) Warrington: 1975 W, **F**, w;
    1979 W, F
MILLINGTON, John (2) Hull KR: 1975 F; 1981 W
MILLWARD, Roger (13)3+1 Hull KR: 1975 F, W,
    F, W, A, W, F, NZ, A; 1977 W, F; 1978 F, W
MOLLOY, Steve (1) Leeds: 1992 W
MORGAN, Mick (3+3) Wakefield T: 1975 f, W, f, **W,
    nz, A**
MUMBY, Keith (2) Bradford N: 1979 W, F
MURPHY, Martin (1) Oldham: 1975 F

NASH, Steve (7) Featherstone R: 1975 **W, NZ, A**;
    Salford: 1978 F, W; 1981 W, W
NEWLOVE, Paul (1) Featherstone R: 1992 W
NICHOLLS, George (7+4) St. Helens: 1975 F, **F, W,
    NZ, A, w, nz, f**; 1977 f; 1978 F, W
NOONAN, Derek (3) Warrington: 1975 W, **F, W**
NORTON, Steve (11) Castleford: 1975 **W, NZ, A, W, F,
    NZ, A**; 1977 F; Hull: 1978 W; 1981 W, W

OFFIAH, Martin (1) Wigan: 1992 W
O'NEILL, Steve (1) Wigan: 1981 F

PATTINSON, Bill (1+1) Workington T: 1981 f, W
PHILBIN, Barry (1) Warrington: 1975 **F**
PIMBLETT, Geoff (1) St. Helens: 1978 W
PINNER, Harry (3) St. Helens: 1980 W, F; 1981 F
POTTER, Ian (2) Warrington: 1981 F, W
POWELL, Daryl (+1) Sheffield E: 1992 w

RAYNE, Keith (2) Wakefield T: 1980 W, F
REDFEARN, Alan (2) Bradford N: 1979 F; 1980 F
REDFEARN, Dave (2) Bradford N: 1975 F, **A**
REILLY, Malcolm (+1)2 Castleford: 1977 w
RICHARDSON, Terry (1) Castleford: 1981 W
ROSE, Paul (2) Hull KR: 1977 F; 1978 W

SCHOFIELD, Garry (2) Hull: 1984 W; Leeds: 1992 W
SHEARD, Les (1) Wakefield T: 1975 W
SMITH, David (1) Leeds: 1977 F
SMITH, Keith (1) Wakefield T: 1979 W
SMITH, Mike (5) Hull KR: 1980 W, F; 1981 F, W, W
SMITH, Peter (1) Featherstone R: 1980 F
SPRUCE, Stuart (1) Widnes: 1992 W
STEPHENS, Gary (1) Castleford: 1979 W
SZYMALA, Eddie (+1) Barrow: 1979 f

THOMPSON, Jimmy (2+1)1 Featherstone R: 1975 **A**;
    1977 W; Bradford N: 1978 w
TINDALL, Keith (1) Hull: 1979 F
TOPLISS, David (1) Wakefield T: 1975 F

WADDELL, Hugh (1) Blackpool B: 1984 W
WALKER, Arnold (1) Whitehaven: 1981 F
WALSH, John (3) St. Helens: 1975 F, **NZ, A**
WARD, David (6) Leeds: 1977 F; 1980 W, F;
    1981 F, W, **W**
WATKINSON, David (+1) Hull KR: 1977 w
WOODS, John (3+4) Leigh: 1979 w, F; 1980 w, F;
    1981 f, w, W
WRIGHT, Stuart (7) Wigan: 1975 **NZ**; Widnes: 1977 W;
    1978 F, W; 1979 W, F; 1980 W

*England debutant Dean Busby attracts the attention of a quartet of Welshmen, left to right, David Young, Ian Marlow, David
Bishop and Kevin Ellis, in the Swansea encounter of November 1992.*

WALES TEAMS ● From 1975, when it revived after a gap of five years and continued until 1984, before folding again. Revived in 1991.

1975 France
Swansea: 16 Feb.

Won 21-8

Francis (Wigan)
Mathias (St. Helens) 1t
Willicombe (Wigan)
Wilson, F. (St. Helens)
Bevan (Warrington) 2t
*Watkins (Salford) 1dg
Banner (Salford)
Mills (Widnes) 1t
Fisher (Leeds)
Mantle (St. Helens)
Nicholas (Warrington)
Dixon (Salford)
Coslett (St. Helens) 4g
Sub: Gallacher (Keighley)

1975 England (WC)
Brisbane: 10 June

Won 12-7

Francis (Wigan)
Sullivan, C. (Hull K.R.) 1t
*Watkins (Salford) 3g
Willicombe (Wigan)
Mathias (St. Helens)
Treasure (Oldham) 1t
Banner (Salford)
Mills (Widnes)
Fisher (Leeds)
Wanbon (Warrington)
Dixon (Salford)
Cunningham, E. (St. Helens)
Coslett (St. Helens)
Sub: Wilson, F. (St. Helens)
    Mantle (St. Helens)

1975 England (WC)
Warrington: 20 Sep.

Lost 16-22

Francis (Wigan)
Sullivan, C. (Hull K.R.)
*Watkins (Salford) 5g
Wilson, F. (St. Helens)
Bevan (Warrington)
Treasure (Oldham)
Banner (Salford) 1t
Mantle (St. Helens)
Fisher (Castleford)
James (St. Helens)
Cunningham, E. (St. Helens)
Gregory (Wigan)
Coslett (St. Helens) 1t
Sub: Turner (Hull K.R.)
    Rowe (Blackpool B.)

1975 England
Salford: 25 Feb.

Lost 8-12

Francis (Wigan)
Mathias (St. Helens)
Willicombe (Wigan)
Wilson, F. (St. Helens)
Bevan (Warrington)
*Watkins (Salford) 1t,1g,1dg
Banner (Salford)
Mills (Widnes)
Evans (Swinton)
Mantle (St. Helens)
Dixon (Salford)
Gallacher (Keighley)
Coslett (St. Helens) 1g
Sub: Turner (Hull K.R.)
    Nicholas (Warrington)

1975 Australia (WC)
Sydney: 14 June

Lost 13-30

Francis (Wigan)
Sullivan, C. (Hull K.R.)
*Watkins (Salford) 5g
Willicombe (Wigan)
Mathias (St. Helens)
Turner (Hull K.R.)
Treasure (Oldham)
Mills (Widnes)
Fisher (Leeds) 1t
Wanbon (Warrington)
Mantle (St. Helens)
Cunningham, E. (St. Helens)
Coslett (St. Helens)
Sub: Wilson, F. (St. Helens)
    Rowe (Blackpool B.)

1975 Australia (WC)
Swansea: 19 Oct.

Lost 6-18

*Watkins (Salford) 3g
Mathias (St. Helens)
Francis (Wigan)
Wilson, F. (St. Helens)
Bevan (Warrington)
Turner (Hull K.R.)
Banner (Featherstone R.)
Mills (Widnes)
Fisher (Castleford)
Mantle (St. Helens)
Cunningham, E. (St. Helens)
Dixon (Salford)
Coslett (St. Helens)
Sub: Rowe (Blackpool B.)

1975 France (WC)
Toulouse: 2 Mar.

Lost 7-14

Francis (Wigan)
Mathias (St. Helens)
Willicombe (Wigan)
Wilson, F. (St. Helens) 1t
Richards (Salford)
*Watkins (Salford)
Banner (Salford)
Murphy (Bradford N.)
Evans (Swinton)
Butler (Swinton)
Dixon (Salford)
Mantle (St. Helens)
Coslett (St. Helens) 2g
Sub: Wallace (York)

1975 New Zealand (WC)
Auckland: 28 June

Lost 8-13

Francis (Wigan) 1t
Sullivan, C. (Hull K.R.)
*Watkins (Salford) 1g
Willicombe (Wigan)
Mathias (St. Helens)
Treasure (Oldham)
Banner (Salford)
Mills (Widnes) 1t
Fisher (Leeds)
Wanbon (Warrington)
Mantle (St. Helens)
Dixon (Salford)
Coslett (St. Helens)
Sub: Butler (Swinton)

1975 New Zealand (WC)
Swansea: 2 Nov.

Won 25-24

*Watkins (Salford) 5g
Mathias (St. Helens)
Wilson, F. (St. Helens)
Willicombe (Wigan) 1t
Bevan (Warrington) 1t
Francis (Wigan) 2t
Banner (Featherstone R.)
Mills (Widnes)
Fisher (Castleford)
Murphy (Bradford N.)
Mantle (St. Helens) 1t
Gallacher (Keighley)
Gregory (Wigan)
Sub: Jones, C. (Leigh)

1975 France (WC)
Salford: 6 Nov.
Won 23-2
*Watkins (Salford) 4g
Mathias (St. Helens)
Wilson, F. (St. Helens)
Willicombe (Wigan) 1t
Bevan (Warrington) 1t
Francis (Wigan) 1t
Banner (Featherstone R.) 1t
Mantle (St. Helens)
Evans (Swinton)
Murphy (Bradford N.)
Gregory (Wigan) 1t
Gallacher (Keighley)
Jones, C. (Leigh)
Sub: Turner (Hull K.R.)
    Butler (Warrington)

1978 France
Widnes: 15 Jan.
Won 29-7
Risman (Workington T.)
Mathias (St. Helens) 1t
Willicombe (Wigan)
Cunningham, E. (St. Helens) 1t
Sullivan, C. (Hull K.R.) 1t
*Francis (St. Helens) 1t
Woods (Widnes) 7g
Mills (Widnes) 1t
Evans (Salford)
James (St. Helens)
Nicholas (Warrington)
Shaw (Widnes)
Dixon (Salford)
Sub: Pritchard (Barrow)
    Jones, C. (Leigh)

1979 France
Narbonne: 4 Feb.
Lost 8-15
Box (Featherstone R.)
Sullivan, C. (Hull K.R.)
*Watkins (Salford) 2g,1dg
Bevan (Warrington)
Juliff (Wakefield T.)
Francis (St. Helens)
Woods (Rochdale H.)
Murphy (St. Jacques)
Cunningham, T. (Warrington)
James (St. Helens)
Skerrett (Wakefield T.)
Rowe (Huddersfield) 1t
Mathias (St. Helens)
Sub: Johns (Salford)
    Risman (Workington T.)

1977 England
Leeds: 29 Jan.
Won 6-2
*Watkins (Salford)
Mathias (St. Helens)
Bevan (Warrington)
Cunningham, E. (St. Helens) 1t
Richards (Salford)
Francis (Wigan)
Woods (Widnes) 1g
Mills (Workington T.)
Fisher (Castleford)
Mantle (Salford)
Nicholas (Warrington)
Dixon (Salford)
Rowe (Huddersfield) 1dg
Sub: Wilkins (Workington T.)

1978 England
St. Helens: 28 May
Lost 13-60
Watkins (Salford) 1g
Mathias (St. Helens)
Turner (Hull)
Willicombe (Wigan) 1t
Sullivan, C. (Hull K.R.) 1t
*Francis (St. Helens)
Woods (Widnes) 1g
Mills (Widnes)
Evans (Salford)
James (St. Helens) 1t
Davies, F. (New Hunslet)
Mantle (Leigh)
Cunningham, E. (St. Helens)
Sub: Pritchard (Barrow)
    Jones, C. (Leigh)

1979 England
Widnes: 16 Mar.
Lost 7-15
Box (Featherstone R.) 1t,2g
Sullivan, C. (Hull K.R.)
Risman (Workington T.)
Bevan (Warrington)
Juliff (Wakefield T.)
*Francis (St. Helens)
Woods (Rochdale H.)
Mills (Widnes)
Cunningham, T. (Warrington)
James (St. Helens)
Skerrett (Wakefield T.)
Rowe (Huddersfield)
Mathias (St. Helens)
Sub: Prendiville (Hull)
    Nicholas (Warrington)

1977 France
Toulouse: 20 Feb.
Lost 2-13
Wilkins (Workington T.)
Mathias (St. Helens)
Bevan (Warrington)
Treasure (Oldham)
Sullivan, C. (Hull K.R.)
*Francis (Wigan)
Woods (Widnes) 1g
Mills (Widnes)
Fisher (Castleford)
Butler (Warrington)
Nicholas (Warrington)
Dixon (Salford)
Rowe (Huddersfield)
Sub: Curling (Warrington)
    Murphy (Bradford N.)

1978 Australia
Swansea: 15 Oct.
Lost 3-8
*Watkins (Salford) 1g,1dg
Sullivan, C. (Hull K.R.)
Willicombe (Wigan)
Cunningham, E. (St. Helens)
Bevan (Warrington)
Francis (St. Helens)
Woods (Widnes)
Mills (Widnes)
Fisher (Bradford N.)
James (St. Helens)
Shaw (Widnes)
Skerrett (Wakefield T.)
Mathias (St. Helens)

1980 France
Widnes: 26 Jan.
Lost 7-21
Box (Featherstone R.)
Juliff (Wakefield T.)
Diamond (Wakefield T.) 2g
Bevan (Warrington) 1t
Camilleri (Barrow)
*Francis (Oldham)
Flowers (Wigan)
James (St. Helens)
Parry (Blackpool B.)
Shaw (Widnes)
McJennett (Barrow)
Skerrett (Wakefield T.)
Mathias (St. Helens)
Sub: Griffiths, C. (St. Helens)
    Seldon (St. Helens)

1980 England
Hull K.R.: 29 Feb.

Lost 9-26

Box (Featherstone R.)
Prendiville (Hull)
Walters (Hull)
*Francis (Oldham)
Juliff (Wakefield T.) 1t
Woods (Hull) 3g
Flowers (Wigan)
James (St. Helens)
Parry (Blackpool B.)
Shaw (Widnes)
Seldon (St. Helens)
Bevan (Warrington)
Mathias (St. Helens)
Sub: Diamond (Wakefield T.)

1981 England
Cardiff: 8 Nov.

Lost 15-20

Pritchard (Cardiff C.)
Cambriani (Fulham)
Bayliss (St. Helens)
Fenwick (Cardiff C.) 4g
*Bevan (Warrington)
Wilson, D. (Swinton) 1dg
Flowers (Wigan) 1t
James (St. Helens)
Parry (Blackpool B.)
David (Cardiff C.)
Shaw (Widnes)
Herdman (Fulham)
Ringer (Cardiff C.)
Sub: Prendiville (Hull) 1t
     Owen, R. (St. Helens)

1991 Papua New Guinea
Swansea C. FC: 27 Oct.

Won 68-0

Ford (Leeds) 3t
Devereux (Widnes)
Bateman (Warrington) 1t
*Davies, J. (Widnes) 2t,8g
Sullivan, A. (St. Helens) 2t
Griffiths, J. (St. Helens) 1t
Ellis (Warrington) 1t
Jones, M. (Hull)
Williams, Barry (Carlisle)
Young (Salford)
Ackerman (Carlisle) 1t
Moriarty (Widnes)
Bishop (Hull R.R.) 1t
Sub: Hadley (Salford) 1t
     Phillips (Warrington)
     Silva (Halifax)
     Pearce (Scarborough P.)

1981 France
Narbonne: 31 Jan.

Lost 5-23

Box (Wakefield T.)
Cambriani (Fulham)
Diamond (Wakefield T.)
*Bevan (Warrington)
Prendiville (Hull)
Wilson, D. (Swinton) 1g
Woods (Hull)
James (St. Helens)
Parry (Blackpool B.) 1t
Owen, G. (Oldham)
Skerrett (Hull)
Juliff (Wakefield T.)
Mathias (St. Helens)
Sub: Griffiths, C. (St. Helens)
     Owen, R. (St. Helens)

1982 Australia
Cardiff: 24 Oct.

Lost 7-37

Hopkins (Workington T.) 1g
Camilleri (Widnes)
Fenwick (Cardiff C.) 1g
*Bevan (Warrington)
Prendiville (Hull)
Hallett (Cardiff C.)
Williams, Brynmor (Cardiff C.) 1t
Shaw (Warrington)
Parry (Blackpool B.)
David (Cardiff C.)
Herdman (Fulham)
Juliff (Wigan)
Ringer (Cardiff C.)
Sub: McJennett (Barrow)

1992 France
Swansea C. FC: 22 Mar.

Won 35-6

Ford (Leeds) 1t
Devereux (Widnes) 1t
Bateman (Warrington) 1t
*Davies, J. (Widnes) 1t,5g,1dg
Sullivan, A. (St. Helens)
Griffiths, J. (St. Helens)
Ellis (Warrington)
Jones, M. (Hull)
Williams, Barry (Carlisle) 1t
Young (Salford)
Ackerman (Carlisle)
Marlow (Hull)
Bishop (Hull K.R.)
Sub: Hadley (Salford)
     Phillips (Warrington) 1t
     Cordle (Bradford N.)
     Pearce (Ryedale-York)

1981 England
Hull K.R.: 18 Mar.

Lost 4-17

Rule (Salford) 2g
Cambriani (Fulham)
Walters (Hull)
*Bevan (Warrington)
Juliff (Wakefield T.)
Wilson, D. (Swinton)
Woods (Hull)
James (St. Helens)
Parry (Blackpool B.)
Owen, G. (Oldham)
Skerrett (Hull)
Dixon (Hull K.R.)
Mathias (St. Helens)
Sub: Herdman (Fulham)

1984 England
Ebbw Vale: 14 Oct.

Lost 9-28

Hallett (Bridgend) 2g
Camilleri (Bridgend)
Prendiville (Hull)
Davies, M. (Bridgend)
Ford (Warrington)
Wilson, D. (Swinton) 1t,1dg
Flowers (Bridgend)
*Skerrett (Hull)
Preece (Bradford N.)
Shaw (Wigan)
McJennett (Barrow)
O'Brien (Bridgend)
Juliff (Wigan)
Sub: Johns (Blackpool B.)
     Walters (Bridgend)

1992 England
Swansea C. FC: 27 Nov.

Lost 11-36

Ford (Salford)
Cordle (Bradford N.)
Bateman (Warrington)
Devereux (Widnes) 1g
Sullivan, A. (St. Helens)
Griffiths, J. (St. Helens) 1t
Ellis (Warrington) 1dg
Jones, M. (Hull) 1t
Bishop (London C.)
*Young (Salford)
Moriarty (Widnes)
Marlow (Hull)
Ackerman (Salford)
Sub: Hadley (Widnes)
     Phillips (Warrington)
     Pearce (Ryedale-York)
     Moran (Leigh)

1992 France
Perpignan: 13 Dec.
Won 19-18
Ford (Salford)
Hadley (Widnes)
Bateman (Warrington) 1t
Devereux (Widnes) 1t
Sullivan, A. (St. Helens)
Pearce (Ryedale-York) 3g, 1dg
Ellis (Warrington)
Marlow (Hull)
Bishop (London C.)
*Young (Salford)
Moriarty (Widnes)
Phillips (Warrington)
Ackerman (Salford) 1t
Sub: Stevens (Hull)
     Moran (Leigh)
     Kennett (Swinton)
     Williams, P. (Salford)

1993 New Zealand
Swansea C. FC: 3 Oct.
Lost 19-24
Ford (Salford)
Cordle (Bradford N.) 2t
Bateman (Warrington)
Devereux (Widnes)
Sullivan, A. (St. Helens)
*Davies, J. (Warrington) 5g
Ellis (Warrington)
Jones, M. (Hull)
Williams, Barry (Carlisle)
Young (Salford)
Marlow (Wakefield T.)
Phillips (Warrington)
Griffiths, J. (St. Helens) 1dg
Sub: Hadley (Widnes)
     Ackerman (Cardiff I. ARL)

1994 France
Cardiff C. FC: 4 Mar.
Won 13-12
Ford (Salford)
Cordle (Bradford N.)
Bateman (Warrington)
*Davies, J. (Warrington) 4g, 1dg
Sullivan, A. (St. Helens)
Griffiths, J. (St. Helens)
Ellis (Warrington)
Jones, M. (Hull)
Williams, Barry (Carlisle)
Young (Salford)
Moriarty (Widnes)
Phillips (Warrington)
Perrett (Halifax)
Sub: Powell, D. (Bradford N.)
     Marlow (Wakefield T.)
     Webster (Salford) 1t

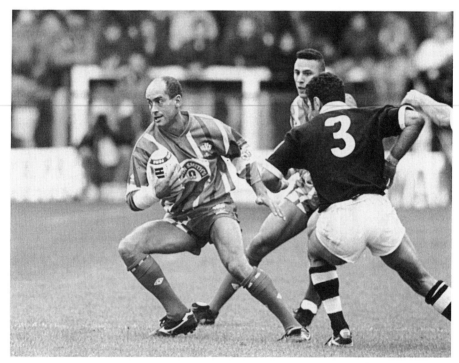

Phil Ford, Wales' ever present full back since reintroduction in 1991, evades Kiwi centre Iva Ropati in the John Smith's international at Swansea in October 1993.

WALES REGISTER
● Since 1975

Figures in brackets are the total appearances for Wales since 1975, with the plus sign indicating substitute appearances, e.g. (7+3).

A few players also played in the 1969-70 European Championship and this is shown as an additional total outside bracket, e.g. (11)2.

World Championship matches are in bold letters. Substitute appearances are in lower case letters. A - Australia, E - England, F - France, NZ - New Zealand, P - Papua New Guinea.

ACKERMAN, Rob (4+1) Carlisle: 1991 P; 1992 F; Salford: 1992 E, F; Cardiff I. ARL: 1993 nz

BANNER, Peter (9) Salford: 1975 F, E, **F, E, NZ**; Featherstone R: 1975 **E, A, NZ, F**

BATEMAN, Allan (6) Warrington: 1991 P; 1992 F, E, F; 1993 NZ; 1994 F

BAYLISS, Steve (1) St. Helens: 1981 E

BEVAN, John (17) Warrington: 1975 F, E, **E, A, NZ, F**; 1977 E, F; 1978 A; 1979 F, E; 1980 F, E; 1981 F, E, E; 1982 A

BISHOP, David (4) Hull KR: 1991 P; 1992 F; London C: 1992 E, F

BOX, Harold (5) Featherstone R: 1979 F, E; 1980 F, E; Wakefield T: 1981 F

BUTLER, Brian (2+2) Swinton: 1975 **F, nz**; Warrington: 1975 f; 1977 F

CAMBRIANI, Adrian (3) Fulham: 1981 F, E, E

CAMILLERI, Chris (3) Barrow: 1980 F; Widnes: 1982 A; Bridgend: 1984 E

CORDLE, Gerald (3+1) Bradford N: 1991 p; 1992 E; 1993 NZ; 1994 F

COSLETT, Kel (8)2 St. Helens: 1975 F, E, **F, E, A, NZ, E, A**

CUNNINGHAM, Eddie (8) St. Helens: 1975 **E, A, E, A**; 1977 E; 1978 F, E, A

CUNNINGHAM, Tommy (2) Warrington: 1979 F, E

CURLING, Dennis (+1) Warrington: 1977 f

DAVID, Tommy (2) Cardiff C: 1981 E; 1982 A

DAVIES, Frank (1) New Hunslet: 1978 E

DAVIES, Jonathan (4) Widnes: 1991 P; 1992 F; Warrington: 1993 NZ; 1994 F

DAVIES, Mike (1) Bridgend: 1984 E

DEVEREUX, John (5) Widnes: 1991 P; 1992 F, E, F; 1993 NZ

DIAMOND, Steve (2+1) Wakefield T: 1980 F, e; 1981 F

DIXON, Colin (10)3 Salford: 1975 F, E, **F, E, NZ, A**; 1977 E, F; 1978 F; Hull KR: 1981 E

ELLIS, Kevin (6) Warrington: 1991 P; 1992 F, E, F; 1993 NZ; 1994 F

EVANS, Richard (5) Swinton: 1975 E, **F, F**; 1978 F; Salford: 1978 E

FENWICK, Steve (2) Cardiff C: 1981 E; 1982 A

FISHER, Tony (10)4 Leeds: 1975 F, **E, A, NZ**; Castleford: 1975 **E, A, NZ**; 1977 E, F; Bradford N: 1978 A

FLOWERS, Ness (4) Wigan: 1980 F, E; 1981 E; Bridgend: 1984 E

FORD, Phil (7) Warrington: 1984 E; Leeds: 1991 P; 1992 F; Salford: 1992 E, F; 1993 NZ; 1994 F

FRANCIS, Bill (19) Wigan: 1975 F, E, **F, E, A, NZ, E, A, NZ, F**; 1977 E, F; St. Helens: 1978 F, E, A; 1979 F, E; Oldham: 1980 F, E

GALLACHER, Stuart (3+1) Keighley: 1975 f, E, **NZ, F**

GREGORY, Brian (3) Wigan: 1975 **E, NZ, F**

GRIFFITHS, Clive (+2) St. Helens: 1980 f; 1981 f

GRIFFITHS, Jonathan (5) St. Helens: 1991 P; 1992 F, E; 1993 NZ; 1994 F

HADLEY, Adrian (1+4) Salford: 1991 p; 1992 f; Widnes: 1992 e, F; 1993 nz

HALLETT, Lynn (2) Cardiff C: 1982 A; Bridgend: 1984 E

HERDMAN, Martin (2+1) Fulham: 1981 e, E; 1982 A

HOPKINS, Lyn (1) Workington T: 1982 A

JAMES, Mel (11) St. Helens: 1975 **E**; 1978 F, E, A; 1979 F, E; 1980 F, E; 1981 F, E, E

JOHNS, Graeme (+2) Salford: 1979 f; Blackpool B: 1984 E

JONES, Clive (1+3) Leigh: 1975 **nz, F**; 1978 f, e

JONES, Mark (5) Hull: 1991 P; 1992 F, E; 1993 NZ; 1994 F

JULIFF, Brian (8) Wakefield T: 1979 F, E; 1980 F, E; 1981 F, E; Wigan: 1982 A; 1984 E

KENNETT, Paul (+1) Swinton: 1992 f

McJENNETT, Mark (2+1) Barrow: 1980 F; 1982 a; 1984 E

MANTLE, John (11+1)3 St. Helens: 1975 F, E, **F, e, A, NZ, E, A, NZ, F**; 1977 E; 1978 E

MARLOW, Ian (4+1) Hull: 1992 F, E, F; Wakefield T: 1993 NZ; 1994 f

MATHIAS, Roy (20) St. Helens: 1975 F, E, **F, E, A, NZ, A, NZ, F**; 1977 E, F; 1978 F, E, A; 1979 F, E; 1980 F, E; 1981 F, E

MILLS, Jim (13)4 Widnes: 1975 F, E, **E, A, NZ, A, NZ**; 1977 E, F; 1978 F, E, A; 1979 E

MORAN, Mark (+2) Leigh: 1992 e, f

MORIARTY, Paul (4) Widnes: 1991 P; 1992 E, F; 1994 F

413

MURPHY, Mick (4+1) Bradford N: 1975 **F, NZ, F**; 1977 f; St. Jacques, France: 1979 F

NICHOLAS, Mike (4+2) Warrington: 1975 F, e; 1977 E, F; 1978 F; 1979 e

O'BRIEN, Chris (1) Bridgend: 1984 E

OWEN, Gareth (2) Oldham: 1981 E, F

OWEN, Roger (+2) St. Helens: 1981 f, e

PARRY, Donald (6) Blackpool B: 1980 F, E; 1981 F, E; 1982 A

PEARCE, Gary (1+3) Scarborough P: 1991 p; Ryedale-York: 1992 f, e, F

PERRETT, Mark (1) Halifax: 1994 F

PHILLIPS, Rowland (3+3) Warrington: 1991 p; 1992 f, e, F; 1993 NZ; 1994 F

POWELL, Daio (+1) Bradford N: 1994 f

PREECE, Chris (1) Bradford N: 1984 E

PRENDIVILLE, Paul (4+2) Hull: 1979 e; 1980 E; 1981 F, e; 1982 A; 1984 E

PRITCHARD, Gordon (1+2) Barrow: 1978 f, e; Cardiff C: 1981 E

RICHARDS, Maurice (2)1 Salford: 1975 **F**; 1977 E

RINGER, Paul (2) Cardiff C: 1981 E; 1982 A

RISMAN, John (2+1) Workington T: 1978 F; 1979 f, E

ROWE, Peter (4+3)2 Blackpool B: 1975 a, e, a; Huddersfield: 1977 E, F; 1979 F, E

RULE, Steve (1) Salford: 1981 E

SELDON, Chris (1+1) St. Helens: 1980 f, E

SHAW, Glyn (7) Widnes: 1978 F, A; 1980 F, E; 1981 E; Wigan: 1982 A; 1984 E

SILVA, Matthew (+1) Halifax: 1991 p

SKERRETT, Trevor (7) Wakefield T: 1978 A; 1979 F, E; 1980 F; Hull: 1981 F, E; 1984 E

STEVENS, Ian (+1) Hull: 1992 f

SULLIVAN, Anthony (6) St. Helens: 1991 P; 1992 F, E, F; 1993 NZ; 1994 F

SULLIVAN, Clive (10)4 Hull KR: 1975 **E, A, NZ, E**; 1977 F; 1978 F, E, A; 1979 F, E

TREASURE, David (5) Oldham: 1975 **E, A, NZ, E**; 1977 F

TURNER, Glyn (3+3) Hull KR: 1975 e, **A, e, A, f**; Hull: 1978 E

WALLACE, Richard (+1) York: 1975 f

WALTERS, Graham (2+1) Hull: 1980 E; 1981 E; Bridgend 1984 e

WANBON, Bobby (3)3+1 Warrington: 1975 **E, A, NZ**

WATKINS, David (14) Salford: 1975 F, E, **F, E, A, NZ, E, A, NZ, F**; 1977 E; 1978 E, A; 1979 F

WEBSTER, Richard (+1) Salford: 1994 f

WILKINS, Ray (1+1) Workington T: 1977 e, F

WILLIAMS, Barry (4) Carlisle: 1991 P; 1992 F; 1993 NZ; 1994 F

WILLIAMS, Brynmor (1) Cardiff C: 1982 A

WILLIAMS, Peter (+1) Salford: 1992 f

WILLICOMBE, David (11)+2 Wigan: 1975 F, E, **F, E, A, NZ, NZ, F**; 1978 F, E, A

WILSON, Danny (4) Swinton: 1981 F, E, E; 1984 E

WILSON, Frank (7+2)4 St. Helens: 1975 F, E, **F, e, a, E, A, NZ, F**

WOODS, Paul (10) Widnes: 1977 E, F; 1978 F, E, A; Rochdale H: 1979 F, E; Hull: 1980 E; 1981 F, E

YOUNG, David (6) Salford: 1991 P; 1992 F, E, F; 1993 NZ; 1994 F

Paul Newlove in action for Bradford Northern after his summer 1993 move from Featherstone Rovers, the League's Tribunal fixing a fee of £245,000.

TRANSFERS

TRANSFERS

TRANSFER REVIEW
1 June 1993 to 31 May 1994

Great Britain centres Gary Connolly and Paul Newlove were involved in the two biggest transfer deals in the period, both moving before the season kicked off.

Connolly went from St. Helens to Wigan for £250,000, while Bradford Northern signed Newlove from Featherstone Rovers for a Tribunal record fee of £245,000. The Tribunal decided on the amount after Featherstone had listed Newlove at a world record £750,000 and Bradford offered £150,000.

Another Test centre to move was Andy Currier, who joined Featherstone from Widnes for £150,000 but injured a knee in a pre-season game and was ruled out for the whole of the new campaign.

Nigel Wright, 19, was transferred from Wakefield Trinity to Wigan for £140,000 — a record fee for a teenager.

Leeds made two major forward signings from Widnes, recruiting Harvey Howard for £110,000 and Richie Eyres for a Tribunal-decided fee of £135,000. The Loiners also transferred prop Steve Molloy to Featherstone, with the Tribunal deciding on a £95,000 fee plus another £5,000 if the player made a second appearance for Great Britain, which he did.

Sonny Nickle's transfer fee also finally reached six figures after the forward played in the John Smith's Test series against New Zealand. The Tribunal had decided back in 1991 that St. Helens should pay Sheffield Eagles £80,000 plus £25,000 after Nickle had played in two Test matches against Australia and/or New Zealand.

Other six-figure transfers were: £115,000 Ian Smales (Featherstone to Castleford), and £100,000 Michael Jackson (Wakefield to Halifax).

The number of £100,000-plus transfers was a big increase on the previous season's two.

There was a total of 150 transfers between clubs, plus 87 loan transactions.

RUGBY UNION SIGNINGS

The most sensational signing of the year — and one of the most highly-publicised of all time — was Wigan's capture of All Black superstar Va'aiga Tuigamala.

Perhaps the best known Rugby Union player in the world, the big Western Samoan winger was the focal personality of the sport's promotional campaign in New Zealand.

Speculation that Wigan were to sign Tuigamala, 24, after the All Blacks' tour of England late in 1993 became fact when his signing hit the headlines on 23 December. It was reported that Tuigamala had signed a four-year contract worth £350,000, equalling the world record five-year sum that John Gallagher — another All Black — received from Leeds in May 1990.

Tuigamala made a belated debut for Wigan and scored a last-minute try in the 27-12 Stones Bitter Championship win at Widnes on 4 February.

Two British Lions Rugby Union internationals changed codes, Swansea and Wales stars Scott Gibbs signing for St. Helens and Richard Webster going to Salford.

Gibbs, 23, was a major capture, having played 20 times for Wales and twice for the British Lions. He had been close to signing for Wigan and Hull in recent years before having a late change of mind each time.

The strong-running centre signed a five-year deal for St. Helens on 19 April, reported to be worth about £250,000 despite Gibbs not having played any rugby for several months because of a knee injury. His debut for St. Helens was delayed until the new season.

Gibbs's switch to Rugby League brought strong criticism from the Union ranks, with officials claiming he had promised to stay an "amateur" in return for lucrative employment and other deals.

Webster, 26, signed for Salford in September after gaining 13 caps for Wales and touring New Zealand with the British Lions in 1993. The international flanker's five-year contract was reported variously between £150,000 and £250,000.

But he made little immediate impact and started only one match for Salford, in addition to making four substitute appearances. His greatest moment came with Wales in a John Smith's international, when he scored the late matchwinning try against France just a few minutes after going on as a substitute.

Two other overseas Rugby Union internationals also switched codes. Kenyan winger Bramwell Mwololo joined Hunslet in September, and Western Samoan forward Apollo Perelini signed for St. Helens at the end of the season.

The total of 26 Rugby Union signings was up from 17 in the previous 12 months.

AMATEUR SIGNINGS

A total of 254 players was signed from amateur Rugby League clubs, including recruits from Academy teams, compared with 196 in the previous period.

A controversial trend was the securing of young schoolboys on professional contracts. It reached the headlines when Wigan signed 12-year-old Daryl Lacey, who became the youngest player to be contracted to a professional club.

A loose forward with St. Helens junior club Blackbrook Under-13s, young Daryl can only be registered with the League as an amateur when he is 16, and as a professional at 17.

OVERSEAS SIGNINGS

The number of overseas players making first team appearances during 1993-94 dropped from the previous season's 162 to 141.

Australia continued to be the major source of overseas recruitment with 74 players, but only four were Test men, while 25 New Zealand internationals played for British clubs. France also provided two Test players as the steadily increasing number of Frenchmen in this country reached five.

The question of transfer fees involving Australian players reached the High Court when Sheffield Eagles forward Bruce McGuire won an injunction against the Rugby Football League withdrawing his registration.

The League's move followed an International Board ruling that Sheffield must pay Australian club Canterbury-Bankstown a retrospective transfer fee of £15,000 for McGuire.

Sheffield protested that no fee had been mentioned when they signed McGuire 18 months earlier after he had left Canterbury. The International Board agreement on transfer fees followed some time after McGuire's move. Warrington signed McGuire at the end of the season and agreed to pay Canterbury £15,000.

The following is a list of overseas players who made at least one first team appearance during 1993-94:

OVERSEAS REGISTER 1993-94
*Test players as at 1 June 1994
AUSTRALIA (74)

Darren Appleby	(Keighley C.)
Greg Austin	(Keighley C., Salford)
Geoff Bagnall	(Wakefield T.)
Paul Beath	(Hunslet)
Mike Bennett	(Hunslet)
Adam Bertoli	(Carlisle)
Michael Booth	(Batley)
David Boyd	(Halifax)
Mick Cameron	(Batley)
Glen Cannon	(Rochdale H.)
Paul Carr	(Sheffield E.)
Brett Clark	(Hunslet)
Troy Clarke	(Leigh)
Anthony Coffey	(Carlisle)
Glen Coughlan	(Dewsbury)
Brett Cullen	(Rochdale H.)
David Danes	(Bramley)
Paul Danes	(Swinton)
Brett Daunt	(Featherstone R.)
Bradley Davis	(Huddersfield)
Jeff Doyle	(Hull)
Leo Dynevor	(London C.)
Matthew Fuller	(Wakefield T.)
Ian Gately	(Keighley C.)
Steve Gibson	(Rochdale H.)
Wally Gibson	(Oldham)

James Grant	(Hull)	Logan Campbell	(London C.)
Jon Grieve	(Widnes)	*Dean Clark	(Hull K.R.)
Michael Hagan	(Halifax)	Trevor Clark	(Bradford N.)
Dean Hanger	(Leigh)	*Shane Cooper	(St. Helens)
David Harmer	(Rochdale H.)	Reg Dunn	(Whitehaven)
*Des Hasler	(Hull)	*Mark Elia	(Widnes)
Brad Hayes	(Doncaster, Ryedale-York, Sheffield E.)	*Esene Faimalo	(Widnes)
		*Clayton Friend	(Whitehaven)
Cavill Heugh	(Rochdale H.)	Joe Grima	(Keighley C.)
David Hosking	(Hull K.R.)	Carl Hall	(Doncaster, Bradford N.)
Rod Howe	(Widnes)	Shane Hansen	(Salford, Swinton)
*Garry Jack	(Salford)	Arnold Hema	(Bramley)
Bob Jackson	(Warrington)	Brad Hepi	(Workington T.)
Trent Jordan	(Highfield, Dewsbury)	*Gavin Hill	(Featherstone R.)
David King	(Huddersfield)	Craig Innes	(Leeds)
Jason Laurence	(Huddersfield)	*Kevin Iro	(Leeds)
David Liddiard	(Hull K.R.)	*Tony Kemp	(Castleford)
Glen Liddiard	(Oldham)	*Mike Kuiti	(Oldham)
*Bob Lindner	(Oldham)	Charlie McAlister	(Oldham)
Mark Lyons	(Ryedale-York)	Dixon McIvor	(London C.)
*Bruce McGuire	(Sheffield E.)	*George Mann	(St. Helens)
Danny McKelvie	(Hunslet)	*Gary Mercer	(Leeds)
Chris McKenna	(Sheffield E.)	*Tawera Nikau	(Castleford)
Phil McKenzie	(Workington T.)	*Sam Panapa	(Wigan)
Greg Mackey	(Warrington)	Henry Paul	(Wakefield T.)
Kevin Marr	(Keighley C.)	Neville Ramsey	(London C.)
David Marsh	(Hunslet)	Mark Riley	(London C.)
Darren Michalski	(London C.)	*Iva Ropati	(Featherstone R.)
Dean Morris	(Bramley)	*Tea Ropati	(St. Helens)
Danny Mulkerin	(London C.)	Joe Ryan	(Bramley)
Mark Mulligan	(Workington T.)	Darrall Shelford	(Bradford N.)
Michael Neil	(Salford)	*Kelly Shelford	(Warrington)
Shaun O'Bryan	(Swinton)	*Maseesee Solomona	(Oldham)
Greg Pearce	(Dewsbury, Huddersfield)	*Kurt Sorensen	(Whitehaven)
Michael Pechey	(Whitehaven)	*Sam Stewart	(London C.)
Scott Roskell	(London C.)	Shane Tupaea	(Oldham)
Steve Rosolen	(London C.)	*Brendon Tuuta	(Featherstone R.)
Troy Rugless	(London C.)	Jason Walker	(London C.)
Danny Russell	(Carlisle)	*Dave Watson	(Bradford N.)
Tim Russell	(Widnes)	Sonny Whakarau	(Doncaster)
Gary Schubert	(Workington T.)		
Anthony Singleton	(Barrow)		
Chris Tauro	(Salford)		
Craig Teitzel	(Warrington)		
Victor Timms	(London C.)		
Glen Tomlinson	(Batley)		
Phil Veivers	(St. Helens)		
Cameron Wade	(Ryedale-York)		
David Woods	(Wakefield T.)		

FIJI (1)

James Pickering	(Workington T.)

NEW ZEALAND (46)

*Dean Bell	(Wigan)
Glen Bell	(Dewsbury)
*Richard Blackmore	(Castleford)
*Frano Botica	(Wigan)
Mark Brooke-Cowden	(Keighley C.)

FRANCE (5)

*Daniel Divet	(Hull)
*David Fraisse	(Sheffield E.)
Pierre Jammes	(Huddersfield)
Laurent Lucchese	(Huddersfield)
Regis Pastre	(Batley)

KENYA (3)

Eric Kibe	(Hunslet)
Bramwell Mwololo	(Hunslet)
Eddie Rombo	(Dewsbury)

SOUTH AFRICA (3)
Jamie Bloem	(Doncaster)
Mark Johnson	(London C.)
Andre Stoop	(London C.)

TONGA (4)
Liuaki "Lee" Hansen	(Leigh)
Sam Hansen	(Barrow)
*[1]Emosi Koloto	(Widnes)
Peaufai Leuila	(St. Helens)
*[1]New Zealand Test player

WESTERN SAMOA (5)
Faausu Afoa	(Bradford N.)
Ben Matautia	(London C.)
Vila Matautia	(Doncaster)
John Schuster	(Halifax)
Va'aiga Tuigamala	(Wigan)

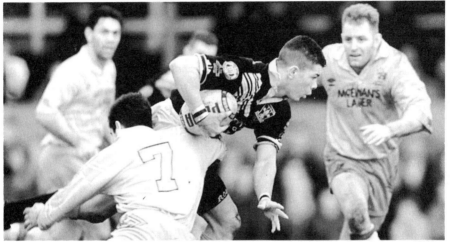

New Zealander Henry Paul, who skippered the Junior Kiwis and was a replacement Kiwi tourist in the autumn of 1993 before joining Wakefield Trinity for the rest of the season.

RECORD TRANSFERS
The first £1,000 transfer came in 1921 when Harold Buck joined Leeds from Hunslet, although there were reports at the time that another player was involved in the deal to make up the four-figure transfer. Other claims for the first £1,000 transfer are attached to Stan Brogden's move from Bradford Northern to Huddersfield in 1929. The following list shows how transfer fees have grown this century in straight cash deals only:

Season	Player	Position	From	To	Fee
1901-02	Jim Lomas	Centre	Bramley	Salford	£100
1910-11	Jim Lomas	Centre	Salford	Oldham	£300
1912-13	Billy Batten	Centre	Hunslet	Hull	£600
1921-22	Harold Buck	Wing	Hunslet	Leeds	£1,000
1929-30	Stanley Smith	Wing	Wakefield T.	Leeds	£1,075
1933-34	Stanley Brogden	Wing/centre	Huddersfield	Leeds	£1,200
1937-38	Billy Belshaw	Full back	Liverpool S.	Warrington	£1,450
1946-47	Bill Davies	Full back/centre	Huddersfield	Dewsbury	£1,650

1947-48	Bill Hudson	Forward	Batley	Wigan	£2,000
1947-48	Jim Ledgard	Full back	Dewsbury	Leigh	£2,650
1948-49	Ike Owens	Forward	Leeds	Castleford	£2,750
1948-49	Ike Owens	Forward	Castleford	Huddersfield	£2,750
1948-49	Stan McCormick	Wing	Belle Vue R.	St. Helens	£4,000
1949-50	Albert Naughton	Centre	Widnes	Warrington	£4,600
1950-51	Bruce Ryan	Wing	Hull	Leeds	£4,750
1950-51	Joe Egan	Hooker	Wigan	Leigh	£5,000
1950-51	Harry Street	Forward	Dewsbury	Wigan	£5,000
1957-58	Mick Sullivan	Wing	Huddersfield	Wigan	£9,500
1958-59	Ike Southward	Wing	Workington T.	Oldham	£10,650
1960-61	Mick Sullivan	Wing	Wigan	St. Helens	£11,000
1960-61	Ike Southward	Wing	Oldham	Workington T.	£11,002 10s
1968-69	Colin Dixon	Forward	Halifax	Salford	£12,000
1969-70	Paul Charlton	Full back	Workington T.	Salford	£12,500
1972-73	Eric Prescott	Forward	St. Helens	Salford	£13,500
1975-76	Steve Nash	Scrum half	Featherstone R.	Salford	£15,000
1977-78	Bill Ashurst	Forward	Wigan	Wakefield T.	£18,000
1978-79	Clive Pickerill	Scrum half	Castleford	Hull	£20,000
1978-79	Phil Hogan	Forward	Barrow	Hull K.R.	£35,000
1979-80	Len Casey	Forward	Bradford N.	Hull K.R.	£38,000
1980-81	Trevor Skerrett	Forward	Wakefield T.	Hull	£40,000
1980-81	George Fairbairn	Full back	Wigan	Hull K.R.	£72,500
1985-86	Ellery Hanley	Centre/stand off	Bradford N.	Wigan	£85,000
1985-86	Joe Lydon	Centre	Widnes	Wigan	£100,000
1986-87	Andy Gregory	Scrum half	Warrington	Wigan	£130,000
1987-88	Lee Crooks	Forward	Hull	Leeds	£150,000
1987-88	Garry Schofield	Centre	Hull	Leeds	£155,000
1989-90	Graham Steadman	Stand off	Featherstone R.	Castleford	£170,000
1991-92	Ellery Hanley	Forward	Wigan	Leeds	£250,000
1991-92	Martin Offiah	Winger	Widnes	Wigan	£440,000

MOST MOVES

Geoff Clarkson extended his record number of transfers to 12 when he left Leigh for Featherstone Rovers on 27 October 1983. He played for 10 different English clubs and had a brief spell in Australia.

Clarkson, born on 12 August 1943, was 40 years old when he finished playing regular first team rugby in 1983-84. He turned professional with Wakefield Trinity in 1966 after gaining Yorkshire County forward honours with Wakefield Rugby Union Club. Clarkson's club career in England was as follows:

1966 — Wakefield T.
1968 — Bradford N.
1970 — Leigh
1971 — Warrington
1972 — Leeds
1975 — York
1976 — Bramley
1978 — Wakefield T. and Hull K.R.
1980 — Bradford N. and Oldham
1981 — Leigh
1983 — Featherstone R.

Jonathan Davies, the first Welshman to receive the coveted title, Stones Bitter Man of Steel 1994.

	Man of Steel	1st Division Player	2nd Division Player	Young Player	Coach	Referee
1977	David Ward (Leeds)	Malcolm Reilly (Castleford)	Ged Marsh (Blackpool B.)	David Ward (Leeds)	Eric Ashton (St. Helens)	Billy Thompson (Huddersfield)
1978	George Nicholls (St. Helens)	George Nicholls (St. Helens)	John Woods (Leigh)	John Woods (Leigh)	Frank Myler (Widnes)	Billy Thompson (Huddersfield)
1979	Doug Laughton (Widnes)	Mick Adams (Widnes)	Steve Norton (Hull)	Steve Evans (Featherstone R.)	Doug Laughton (Widnes)	Mick Naughton (Widnes)
1980	George Fairbairn (Wigan)	Mick Adams (Widnes)	Steve Quinn (Featherstone R.)	Roy Holdstock (Hull K.R.)	Peter Fox (Bradford N.)	Fred Lindop (Wakefield)
1981	Ken Kelly (Warrington)	Ken Kelly (Warrington)	John Crossley (York)	Des Drummond (Leigh)	Billy Benyon (Warrington)	John Holdsworth (Kippax)
1982	Mick Morgan (Carlisle)	Steve Norton (Hull)	Mick Morgan (Carlisle)	Des Drummond (Leigh)	Arthur Bunting (Hull)	Fred Lindop (Wakefield)
1983	Allan Agar (Featherstone R.)	Keith Mumby (Bradford N.)	Steve Nash (Salford)	Brian Noble (Bradford N.)	Arthur Bunting (Hull)	Robin Whitfield (Widnes)
1984	Joe Lydon (Widnes)	Joe Lydon (Widnes)	David Cairns (Barrow)	Joe Lydon (Widnes)	Tommy Dawes (Barrow)	Billy Thompson (Huddersfield)
1985	Ellery Hanley (Bradford N.)	Ellery Hanley (Bradford N.)	Graham Steadman (York)	Lee Crooks (Hull)	Roger Millward (Hull K.R.)	Ron Campbell (Widnes)
1986	Gavin Miller (Hull K.R.)	Gavin Miller (Hull K.R.)	Derek Pyke (Leigh)	Shaun Edwards (Wigan)	Chris Anderson (Halifax)	Fred Lindop (Wakefield)
1987	Ellery Hanley (Wigan)	Andy Gregory (Wigan)	John Cogger (Runcorn H.)	Shaun Edwards (Wigan)	Graham Lowe (Wigan)	John Holdsworth (Kippax)
1988	Martin Offiah (Widnes)	Steve Hampson (Wigan)	Peter Smith (Featherstone R.)	Shaun Edwards (Wigan)	Doug Laughton (Widnes)	Fred Lindop (Wakefield)
1989	Ellery Hanley (Wigan)	David Hulme (Widnes)	Daryl Powell (Sheffield E.)	Paul Newlove (Featherstone R.)	Graham Lowe (Wigan)	John Holdsworth (Kippax)
1990	Shaun Edwards (Wigan)	Andy Goodway (Wigan)	John Woods (Rochdale H.)	Bobby Goulding (Wigan)	John Monie (Wigan)	Robin Whitfield (Widnes)

	Man of Steel	1st Division Player	2nd Division Player	3rd Division Player	Young Player	Coach	Referee
1991	Garry Schofield (Leeds)	Jonathan Davies (Widnes)	Tawera Nikau (Ryedale-York)	—	Denis Betts (Wigan)	John Monie (Wigan)	John Holdsworth (Kippax)
1992	Dean Bell (Wigan)	Graham Steadman (Castleford)	Iva Ropati (Oldham)	Wally Gibson (Huddersfield)	Gary Connolly (St. Helens)	John Monie (Wigan)	Robin Whitfield (Widnes)
1993	Andy Platt (Wigan)	Tea Ropati (St. Helens)	Paul Newlove (Featherstone R.)	Martin Wood (Keighley C.)	Jason Robinson (Wigan)	John Monie (Wigan)	John Connolly (Wigan)
1994	Jonathan Davies (Warrington)	Jonathan Davies (Warrington)	Martin Oglanby (Workington T.)	—	Andrew Farrell (Wigan)	John Joyner (Castleford)	John Connolly (Wigan)

NOMINEES:

1977 *1st Division Player*: Bruce Burton (Castleford), Vince Farrar (Featherstone R.), Jimmy Crampton (Hull), Harry Pinner (St. Helens). *Coach*: Keith Cotton (Featherstone R.), Mal Reilly (Castleford). *Referee*: Joe Jackson (Pudsey), Mick Naughton (Widnes).

1978 *1st Division Player*: Roger Millward (Hull K.R.), Harry Pinner (St. Helens). *2nd Division Player*: Phil Hogan (Barrow), Mick Morgan (York). *Young Player*: Neil Hague (Leeds), Keith Mumby (Bradford N.). *Coach*: Eric Ashton MBE (St. Helens), John Mantle (Leigh). *Referee*: Ron Campbell (Widnes), Fred Lindop (Wakefield).

1979 *1st Division Player*: Brian Lockwood (Hull K.R.), Tommy Martyn (Warrington). *2nd Division Player*: Barry Banks (York), John Wolford (Dewsbury). *Young Player*: Mick Burke (Widnes), John Woods (Leigh). *Coach*: Billy Benyon (Warrington), Arthur Bunting (Hull). *Referee*: Fred Lindop (Wakefield), Billy Thompson (Huddersfield).

1980 *1st Division Player*: Len Casey (Hull K.R.), George Fairbairn (Wigan). *2nd Division Player*: Mick Blacker (Halifax), John Wolford (Dewsbury). *Young Player*: Steve Hubbard (Hull K.R.), Harry Pinner (St. Helens). *Coach*: Maurice Bamford (Halifax), Arthur Bunting (Hull). *Referee*: Ron Campbell (Widnes), Billy Thompson (Huddersfield).

1981 *1st Division Player*: Mick Adams (Widnes), Tommy Martyn (Warrington). *2nd Division Player*: Arnie Walker (Whitehaven), Danny Wilson (Swinton). *Young Player*: Paul Harkin (Hull K.R.), Keith Mumby (Bradford N.). *Coach*: Reg Bowden (Fulham), Peter Fox (Bradford N.). *Referee*: Ron Campbell (Widnes), Fred Lindop (Wakefield).

1982 *1st Division Player*: Jeff Grayshon (Bradford N.), Andy Gregory (Widnes). *2nd Division Player*: Denis Boyd (Carlisle), Alan Fairhurst (Swinton). *Young Player*: Lee Crooks (Hull), Andy Gregory (Widnes). *Coach*: Doug Laughton (Widnes), Alex Murphy/Colin Clarke (Leigh). *Referee*: Gerry Kershaw (York), Billy Thompson (Huddersfield).

1983 *1st Division Player*: Bob Eccles (Warrington), David Topliss (Hull). *2nd Division Player*: Tommy David (Cardiff C.), Mike Lampkowski (Wakefield T.). *Young Player*: Ronnie Duane (Warrington), Andy Goodway (Oldham). *Coach*: Alex Murphy (Wigan), Frank Myler (Oldham). *Referee*: John Holdsworth (Leeds), Fred Lindop (Wakefield).

1984 *1st Division Player*: Garry Schofield (Hull), John Woods (Leigh). *2nd Division Player*: Lyn Hopkins (Workington T.), John Wolford (Hunslet). *Young Player*: Gary Divorty (Hull), Garry Schofield (Hull). *Coach*: Arthur Bunting (Hull), Roger Millward (Hull K.R.). *Referee*: Derek Fox (Wakefield), Fred Lindop (Wakefield).

1985 *1st Division Player*: Harry Pinner (St. Helens), Gary Prohm (Hull K.R.). *2nd Division Player*: Terry Langton (Mansfield M.), Peter Wood (Runcorn H.). *Young Player*: Deryck Fox (Featherstone R.), Andy Platt (St. Helens). *Coach*: Arthur Bunting (Hull), Colin Clarke/Alan McInnes (Wigan). *Referee*: Fred Lindop (Wakefield), Stan Wall (Leigh).

1986 *1st Division Player*: Steve Ella (Wigan), John Fieldhouse (Widnes). *2nd Division Player*: John Henderson (Leigh), Graham King (Hunslet). *Young Player*: Paul Lyman (Featherstone R.), Roy Powell (Leeds). *Coach*: Roger Millward (Hull K.R.), John Sheridan (Doncaster). *Referee*: John Holdsworth (Kippax), Robin Whitfield (Widnes).

1987 *1st Division Player:* Lee Crooks (Hull), Ellery Hanley (Wigan). *2nd Division Player:* Andy Bateman (Hunslet), Les Holliday (Swinton). *Young Player:* Paul Loughlin (St. Helens), Kevin McCormack (St. Helens). *Coach:* Chris Anderson (Halifax), Alex Murphy (St. Helens). *Referee:* Kevin Allatt (Southport), Fred Lindop (Wakefield).

1988 *1st Division Player:* Martin Offiah (Widnes), Kurt Sorensen (Widnes). *2nd Division Player:* Deryck Fox (Featherstone R.), Hugh Waddell (Oldham). *Young Player:* Paul Medley (Leeds), Steve Robinson (Halifax). *Coach:* Alex Murphy (St. Helens), Barry Seabourne (Bradford N.). *Referee:* John Holdsworth (Kippax), Ray Tennant (Castleford).

1989 *1st Division Player:* Andy Gregory (Wigan), Kelvin Skerrett (Bradford N.). *2nd Division Player:* Cavill Heugh (Barrow), Chris Johnson (Leigh). *Young Player:* Grant Anderson (Castleford), Denis Betts (Wigan). *Coach:* Peter Fox (Featherstone R.), Brian Smith (Hull). *Referee:* Ray Tennant (Castleford), Robin Whitfield (Widnes).

1990 *1st Division Player:* Deryck Fox (Featherstone R.), Andy Platt (Wigan). *2nd Division Player:* David Bishop (Hull K.R.), John Cogger (Oldham). *Young Player:* Denis Betts (Wigan), Anthony Sullivan (Hull K.R.). *Coach:* Tony Barrow (Oldham), Brian Johnson (Warrington). *Referee:* John Holdsworth (Kippax), Colin Morris (Huddersfield).

1991 *1st Division Player:* Andy Gregory (Wigan), George Mann (St. Helens). *2nd Division Player:* Steve Kerry (Salford), Peter Ropati (Leigh). *Young Player:* Phil Clarke (Wigan), Craig Richards (Bradford N.). *Coach:* Ray Ashton (Workington T.), Doug Laughton (Widnes). *Referee:* Brian Galtress (Bradford), Jim Smith (Halifax).

1992 *1st Division Player:* Dean Bell (Wigan), John Devereux (Widnes). *2nd Division Player:* Clayton Friend (Carlisle), Paul Topping (Leigh). *3rd Division Player:* Steve Carroll (Bramley), Paul Delaney (Dewsbury). *Young Player:* Paul Newlove (Featherstone R.), David Myers (Wigan). *Coach:* Alex Murphy (Huddersfield), Darryl Van de Velde (Castleford). *Referee:* Stuart Cummings (Widnes), John Holdsworth (Kippax).

1993 *1st Division Player:* Phil Clarke (Wigan), Andy Platt (Wigan). *2nd Division Player:* Neil Flanagan (Huddersfield), Brendon Tuuta (Featherstone R.). *3rd Division Player:* Clayton Friend (Whitehaven), Brad Hepi (Workington T.). *Young Player:* Chris Joynt (St. Helens), Nigel Wright (Wakefield T.). *Coach:* Peter Fox (Bradford N.), Mike McClennan (St. Helens). *Referee:* John Holdsworth (Kippax), Russell Smith (Castleford).

1994 *1st Division Player:* Lee Crooks (Castleford). *2nd Division Player:* Glen Tomlinson (Batley).

Wigan's Kiwi international Frano Botica, top goal scorer in 1993-94 with a tally of 184 including two John Smith's Tests against Great Britain.

425

STONES BITTER TEAM OF THE MONTH AWARDS 1993-94

Introduced in the 1979-80 season, the scheme acknowledges the adjudged Team of the Month in either division.

A panel of judges representing Stones Bitter and the Rugby League selected the two monthly winners, the First Division winners receiving £500 and the Second Division £350, plus a framed citation.

The awards were sponsored for the first four seasons by Shopacheck before Lada Cars took over in the 1983-84 season and introduced the first-ever Team of the Year title. Stones Bitter took over the sponsorship in 1987-88, the 1994 Team of the Year, **Wigan**, receiving £1,500.

	First Division	Second Division
Aug./Sept.	Bradford N.	Huddersfield
Oct.	Castleford	Keighley C.
Nov.	Warrington	London C.
Dec.	Wigan	Workington T.
Jan.	Castleford	Doncaster
Feb.	St. Helens	Dewsbury
Mar.	Sheffield E.	Doncaster
Apr./May	Wigan	Workington T.

Team of the Year
1983-84: Widnes
1984-85: Hull K.R.
1985-86: Halifax
1986-87: Wigan
1987-88: Widnes
1988-89: Wigan
1989-90: Wigan
1990-91: Wigan
1991-92: Wigan
1992-93: Wigan
1993-94: Wigan

WALLACE ARNOLD – SUNDAY MIRROR ENTERTAINER AWARDS 1993-94

Introduced in 1986-87, the scheme was sponsored by Wallace Arnold and promoted by the *Sunday Mirror.*

Each month a player was chosen as Entertainer of the Month to receive a Wallace Arnold holiday voucher for £400. The Entertainer of the Year was awarded a £1,500 holiday voucher, the 1994 winner being Warrington's Welsh centre **Jonathan Davies.**

Entertainer of the Month
Sept.	Jonathan Davies (Warrington)
Oct.	St. John Ellis (Castleford)
Nov.	Mark Conway (Dewsbury)
Dec.	Andy Gregory (Salford)
Jan.	Lee Crooks (Castleford)
Feb.	Martin Pearson (Featherstone R.)
Mar.	Shaun Edwards (Wigan)
Apr./May	Martin Offiah (Wigan)

Entertainer of the Year
1987:	Ellery Hanley (Wigan)
1988:	Martin Offiah (Widnes)
1989:	Martin Offiah (Widnes)
1990:	Deryck Fox (Featherstone R.)
1991:	Garry Schofield (Leeds)
1992:	Shaun Edwards (Wigan)
1993:	Frano Botica (Wigan)
1994:	Jonathan Davies (Warrington)

STONES BITTER TOP SCORERS AWARDS 1993-94

Launched in the 1976-77 season, the scheme was designed to reward the top try and goal scorers in the League. Sponsored by Stones Bitter, the 1994 awards were worth £500 to each player.

The top try merchant was London Crusaders' South African winger Mark Johnson who touched down 43 times.

The top marksman was Wigan stand off Frano Botica who hit the target 184 times for Wigan and New Zealand, not including the World Club Challenge.

REFEREES

REFEREES' HONOURS 1993-94

Silk Cut Challenge Cup final:
David Campbell

Regal Trophy final:
David Campbell

Stones Bitter Premiership final:
Stuart Cummings

Second Division Premiership final:
John Connolly

New Zealand v Australia (3):
Russell Smith

France v New Zealand:
John Holdsworth

France v Great Britain:
John Connolly

Wales v New Zealand:
John Connolly

Wales v France:
David Campbell

SENIOR REFEREES 1994-95

DAVID ASQUITH (York)
Date of birth: 20.6.53
Grade One: 1989-90

DAVID ATKIN (Hull)
Date of birth: 19.12.64
Grade One: 1992-93

ALAN BURKE (Oldham)
Date of birth: 21.1.57
Grade One: 1987-88
Lancashire Cup 1990-91

DAVID CAMPBELL (St. Helens)
Date of birth: 9.10.54
Grade One: 1989-90
Challenge Cup 1993-94
Regal Trophy 1993-94
Lancashire Cup 1991-92
Wales v France 1993-94

DAVE CARTER (Widnes)
Date of birth: 29.11.55
Grade One: 1984-85
France v Great Britain Under-21s 1988-89

JOHN CONNOLLY (Wigan)
Date of birth: 30.9.59
Grade One: 1990-91
Second Division Premiership 1992-93, 1993-94
France v Great Britain 1993-94
Wales v New Zealand 1993-94

ROBERT CONNOLLY (Wigan)
Date of birth: 30.9.59
Grade One: 1990-91

STEVE CROSS (Hull)
Date of birth: 23.3.50
Grade One: 1986-87

STUART CUMMINGS (Widnes)
Date of birth: 17.11.60
Grade One: 1991-92
Premiership Trophy 1993-94
Divisional Premiership 1991-92
Lancashire Cup 1992-93
Charity Shield 1992-93

BRIAN GALTRESS (Bradford)
Date of birth: 8.10.51
Grade One: 1988-89
Regal Trophy 1991-92
Second Division Premiership 1990-91
France v Great Britain Under-21s 1990-91

JOHN HOLDSWORTH (Kippax)
Date of birth: 25.1.47
Grade Two: 1979-80
Grade One: 1980-81
Challenge Cup 1986-87, 1989-90
Regal Trophy 1985-86, 1986-87, 1988-89, 1992-93
Premiership Trophy 1980-81, 1987-88, 1988-89,
    1990-91, 1991-92, 1992-93
Lancashire Cup 1982-83, 1985-86
Yorkshire Cup 1991-92
World Club Challenge 1987-88
Australia v New Zealand (3) 1991
France v Australia (2) 1990-91
France v New Zealand 1993-94
Wales v England 1980-81
Great Britain v Rest of World 1988-89
RL Chairman's XIII v Papua New Guinea 1987-88
Cumbria v Yorkshire 1981-82
France v Great Britain Under-24s 1982-83
War of the Roses 1987-88
Charity Shield 1987-88, 1989-90

KARL KIRKPATRICK (Warrington)
Date of birth: 3.12.64
Grade One: 1994-95

PAUL LEE (Leigh)
Date of birth: 28.7.57
Grade One: 1994-95

IAN McGREGOR (Huddersfield)
Date of birth: 27.12.53
Grade One: 1993-94

COLIN MORRIS (Huddersfield)
Date of birth: 11.3.57
Grade One: 1989-90
Premiership Trophy 1989-90
Papua New Guinea v France 1991
France v Papua New Guinea 1991-92
Wales v France 1991-92
Russia v France 1992
France v Great Britain Under-21s 1989-90
Charity Shield 1990-91
Cumbria v Papua New Guinea 1991-92
Cumbria v Australia 1992-93
War of the Roses 1991-92

STEVE NICHOLSON (Whitehaven)
Date of birth: 5.4.61
Grade One: 1992-93

NICK ODDY (Halifax)
Date of birth: 16.4.62
Grade One: 1994-95

IAN OLLERTON (Wigan)
Date of birth: 31.3.53
Grade One: 1990-91

STEVE PRESLEY (Castleford)
Date of birth: 4.4.57
Grade One: 1993-94

RUSSELL SMITH (Castleford)
Date of birth: 24.1.64
Grade One: 1991-92
Challenge Cup 1992-93
Yorkshire Cup 1992-93
New Zealand v Australia (3) 1993
France v Great Britain Under-21s 1991-92

NEIL WOOD (Keighley)
Date of birth: 12.7.62
Grade One: 1992-93

Whistle blowing Connolly twins, Bob (left) and John, named Stones Bitter Referee of the Year for the second successive season.

THE ALLIANCE

YOUNGER'S ALLIANCE 1993-94

FIRST DIVISION

	P.	W.	D.	L.	Dg.	Gls.	Trs.	Pts.	Dg.	Gls.	Trs.	Pts.	Pts.
						FOR				AGAINST			
Warrington	26	21	0	5	13	130	142	841	1	51	70	383	42
Wigan	26	20	0	6	3	91	144	761	5	63	73	423	40
St. Helens	26	20	0	6	10	117	146	828	5	74	88	505	40
Salford	26	17	0	9	3	96	148	787	4	74	86	496	34
Bradford N.	26	17	0	9	6	78	111	606	5	70	92	513	34
Castleford	26	16	0	10	2	77	104	572	5	52	74	405	32
Halifax	26	14	0	12	2	73	109	584	3	93	106	613	28
Wakefield T.	26	11	0	15	2	70	108	574	6	85	119	652	22
Hull	26	10	0	16	0	68	75	436	5	81	111	611	20
Featherstone R.	26	10	0	16	4	75	75	454	6	105	117	684	20
Leeds	26	8	1	17	4	79	89	518	6	90	109	622	17
Ryedale-York	26	8	1	17	4	81	93	538	5	96	124	693	17
Batley	26	5	0	21	8	55	60	358	2	107	152	824	10
Widnes	26	4	0	22	0	53	70	386	3	102	153	819	8

SECOND DIVISION

	P.	W.	D.	L.	Dg.	Gls.	Trs.	Pts.	Dg.	Gls.	Trs.	Pts.	Pts.
						FOR				AGAINST			
Oldham	22	21	1	0	2	117	152	844	3	44	49	287	43
Dewsbury	22	18	1	3	1	82	122	653	8	42	52	300	37
Doncaster	22	16	0	6	4	83	121	654	2	48	59	334	32
Hull K.R.	22	16	0	6	8	94	104	612	6	42	58	322	32
Rochdale H.	22	14	0	8	3	88	105	599	3	65	77	441	28
Keighley C.	22	13	1	8	5	66	106	561	4	58	63	372	27
Workington T.	22	12	1	9	0	85	118	642	1	55	73	403	25
Leigh	22	11	0	11	2	79	94	536	4	64	77	440	22
Swinton	22	11	0	11	4	64	85	472	1	92	113	637	22
Huddersfield	22	9	1	12	3	56	78	427	4	64	82	460	19
Bramley	22	9	0	13	1	55	84	447	3	84	118	643	18
Sheffield E.	22	8	0	14	8	64	72	424	4	60	67	392	16
Hunslet	22	7	0	15	2	76	84	490	9	77	120	643	14
Carlisle	22	4	1	17	5	54	70	393	0	102	144	780	9
London C.	22	3	0	19	1	38	61	321	1	117	162	883	6
Barrow	22	1	0	21	5	41	53	299	1	128	195	1037	2

YOUNGER'S ALLIANCE CHALLENGE CUP 1994

First Round

Barrow	8	Featherstone R.	44	Leigh	14	Ryedale-York	24
Batley	12	Leeds	23	London C.	18	Sheffield E.	10
Bradford N.	28	Workington T.	8	Rochdale H.	12	Warrington	34
Bramley	0	Doncaster	32	St. Helens	96	Carlisle	14
Dewsbury	0	Salford	52	Wakefield T.	12	Halifax	26
Huddersfield	0	Castleford	32	Widnes	16	Keighley C.	22
Hunslet	18	Hull K.R.	26	Wigan	84	Swinton	6

Second Round

*Bradford N.	25	Oldham	27
Castleford	34	St. Helens	10
Doncaster	16	Halifax	0
Hull	14	Salford	18
Leeds	60	Keighley C.	14
Ryedale-York	30	Hull K.R.	40
Warrington	48	London C.	6
*Wigan	12	Featherstone R.	12

Replay

Wigan	14	Featherstone R.	18

*After extra time

Third Round

Doncaster	12	Warrington	25
Hull K.R.	14	Castleford	10
Oldham	46	Featherstone R.	4
Salford	54	Leeds	14

Semi-Finals

Oldham	44	Hull K.R.	6
Salford	14	Warrington	10

Final

Oldham	14	Salford	8

YOUNGER'S ALLIANCE SECOND DIVISION CUP 1994

First Round

Doncaster	16	Workington T.	6
Hunslet	40	Carlisle	14
Leigh	32	Huddersfield	6
London C.	6	Oldham	16
Rochdale H.	20	Hull K.R.	4
Sheffield E.	9	Dewsbury	13
Swinton	10	Bramley	16

Second Round

Barrow	10	Rochdale H.	44
Bramley	20	Dewsbury	32
Hunslet	10	Oldham	36
Leigh	10	Doncaster	14

Semi-Finals

Dewsbury	10	Oldham	32
Rochdale H.	12	Doncaster	18

Final

Doncaster	14	Oldham	20

YOUNGER'S LANCASHIRE COUNTY CHALLENGE SHIELD 1993-94

First Round

Oldham	38	Workington T.	10
Rochdale H.	36	Barrow	7
Salford	28	St. Helens	19
Warrington	86	Carlisle	0
Widnes	34	Swinton	18
Widnes St. Bedes	12	Simms Cross	15
Wigan	26	Thatto Heath	14
Wigan St. Judes	22	Leigh	30

Second Round

Leigh	26	Widnes	18
Simms Cross	12	Rochdale H.	34
Warrington	31	Salford	22
Wigan	22	Oldham	26

Semi-Finals

Oldham	12	Warrington	6
Rochdale H.	28	Leigh	12

Final

Rochdale H.	20	Oldham	32

YOUNGER'S YORKSHIRE SENIOR COMPETITION CHALLENGE CUP 1993-94

Preliminary Round

Leeds	12	Hull	42

First Round

Bramley	38	Hunslet	10
Castleford	44	Huddersfield	12
Dewsbury	27	Sheffield E.	18
Doncaster	18	Bradford N.	28
Featherstone R.	18	Batley	4
Halifax	22	Hull	26
Hull K.R.	28	Wakefield T.	14
Ryedale-York	18	Keighley C.	8

Second Round

Bramley	6	Featherstone R.	22
Castleford	34	Bradford N.	6
Dewsbury	22	Hull	10
Hull K.R.	10	Ryedale-York	19

Semi-Finals

Castleford	26	Dewsbury	8
Ryedale-York	56	Featherstone R.	10

Final

Ryedale-York	4	Castleford	24

YOUNGER'S ALLIANCE PLAYER OF THE YEAR
1994: Chris Kelly (Widnes)

POT POURRI

DIARY OF LANDMARKS

1895 August 29... the beginning. The Northern Rugby Football Union formed at The George Hotel, Huddersfield, following the breakaway from the English RU by 21 clubs who wanted to pay players for taking time off work to play.

September 7... season opens with 22 clubs.

Joseph Platt appointed Rugby League Secretary.

1897 April 24... Batley won the first Northern Union — later Rugby League — Challenge Cup final.

Line-out abolished and replaced by punt from touch.

All goals to be worth two points.

1898 Professionalism allowed but players must be in full-time employment.

1899 Scrum if player cannot release the ball after a tackle.

1901 Punt from touch replaced by 10-yard scrum when ball is carried into touch.

1902 Two divisions introduced.

Punt from touch abolished completely. Touch-finding rule introduced with the ball having to bounce before entering touch.

1905 Two divisions scrapped.

Lancashire and Yorkshire County Cup competitions inaugurated.

1906 Thirteen-a-side introduced, from traditional 15.

Play-the-ball introduced.

1907 First tour — New Zealand to England. The tour party were RU "rebels".

First Top Four play-off for championship.

1908 Australia and New Zealand launch Rugby League.

First Australian tour of England.

1910 First British tour of Australia and New Zealand.

1915 Competitive rugby suspended for duration of First World War.

1919 Competitive rugby resumed in January.

1920 John Wilson appointed Rugby League Secretary.

1922 Title of Northern Rugby Football Union changed to Rugby Football League.

Goal from a mark abolished.

1927 First radio broadcast of Challenge Cup final — Oldham v. Swinton at Wigan.

1929 Wembley staged its first RL Challenge Cup final — Wigan v. Dewsbury.

1932 London exhibition match under floodlights at White City — Leeds v. Wigan.

1933 France staged its first Rugby League match — an exhibition between England and Australia in Paris.

London Highfield, formerly Wigan Highfield, became capital's first Rugby League team, also first to play regularly under floodlights.

1934 A French squad made a short tour of England before Rugby League was officially launched in France.

1935 European Championship introduced, contested by England, France and Wales.

1939 Second World War. Emergency war-time competitions introduced.

1945 War-time emergencies over.

Bill Fallowfield appointed Rugby League Secretary.

1946 First all-ticket match — Hull v. Hull K.R.

1948 King George VI became first reigning monarch to attend Rugby League match — Wigan v. Bradford Northern Cup final at Wembley.

First televised match — at Wembley — but shown only in London area.

Wembley's first all-ticket final.

International Board formed.

1949 Welsh League formed.

1950 Italian squad made brief tour of England.

1951 First televised match in the North — Britain v. New Zealand at Swinton.

First floodlights installation by Northern club, Bradford Northern.

1952 First nationally televised Challenge Cup final — Workington Town v. Featherstone Rovers.

1954 First World Cup, staged in France.

1955	London staged series of televised floodlit matches for the Independent Television Association Trophy.
	Welsh League disbanded.
1956	Sunday rugby for amateurs permitted by the Rugby Football League.
1962	Two divisions reintroduced, with Eastern and Western Divisions also formed.
1964	Substitutes allowed for injuries, but only up to half-time.
	Two divisions and regional leagues scrapped. One league system with Top 16 play-off for championship.
1965	BBC-2 Floodlit Trophy competition began with regular Tuesday night series.
	Substitutes allowed for any reason up to and including half-time.
	English Schools Rugby League formed.
1966	Four-tackle rule introduced for Floodlit Trophy competition in October, then for all games from December.
1967	First Sunday fixtures played, two matches on December 17.
1969	Substitutes allowed at any time.
	Universities and Colleges Rugby League

	Association formed.
1971	John Player Trophy competition launched.
1972	Six-tackle rule introduced.
	Timekeepers with hooter system to signal end of match introduced.
	Colts League formed.
1973	Two divisions reintroduced.
	March 4... British Amateur Rugby League Association formed.
1974	Drop goal value halved to one point. Had been reduced earlier in international matches.
	David Oxley appointed Rugby League Secretary.
	David Howes appointed first full-time Public Relations Officer to the Rugby Football League.
	National Coaching Scheme launched.
1975	Premiership Trophy competition launched.
1976	Differential penalty introduced for technical scrum offences.
1977	County Championship not held for first time since 1895, excluding war years.
	Anglo-Australian transfer ban agreed.
1978	Papua New Guinea admitted as full members of International Board.

Former Wigan chairman Maurice Lindsay, appointed Rugby League Chief Executive in November 1992.

1981	Rugby League Professional Players' Association formed.
1982	County Championship scrapped.
1983	January 1... Sin bin introduced.
	Try value increased to four points.
	Handover after sixth tackle introduced, among several other new or amended laws following meeting of International Board.
	Anglo-Australian transfer ban lifted.
1984	Alliance League introduced in reserve grade reorganisation.
1985	First Charity Shield match played in Isle of Man.
	War of the Roses launched on Lancashire v. Yorkshire county of origin basis.
	Relegation-promotion reduced to three down, three up.
1986	Relegation-promotion altered for one year only to four down, two up to provide a 14-strong First Division for the 1987-88 season.
1987	Division Two Premiership Trophy competition launched.
	New players' contracts system introduced.
	Random drug testing introduced.
1988	Colts scrapped for new youth scheme.
	Six-man League Board of Directors appointed.
1990	Russia introduced Rugby League and sent 90-man squad on three-match tour to Britain.
1991	Russian eight-club league launched.
	Three divisions introduced for 1991-92 season.
	Academy Under-18 league formed.
	Blood bin introduced.
1992	Maurice Lindsay appointed Rugby League Chief Executive on retirement of David Oxley.
	Ten-metre play-the-ball rule introduced.
1993	Two divisions reintroduced with three bottom clubs demoted to non-League status.
	National pro-am Conference League launched.
	County Cups scrapped.
1994	Broadcaster Harry Gration appointed Rugby League Public Affairs Executive on resignation of David Howes.

DISCIPLINARY RECORDS

This sub-section is a compilation of sendings off and disciplinary verdicts for first team players.

The following information is based on the workings of the League's Disciplinary Committee which meets weekly during a season.

– club not in existence	1993-94	1992-93	1991-92	1990-91	1989-90
Barrow	2	3	6	5	5
Batley	3	4	7	4	1
Blackpool G.	–	0	6	2	9
Bradford N.	2	0	4	3	5
Bramley	3	4	2	5	4
Carlisle	9	6	2	4	0
Castleford	1	3	3	4	6
Chorley B.	–	0	5	7	3
Dewsbury	4	1	1	5	3
Doncaster	3	2	3	4	2
Featherstone R.	3	3	7	1	4
Halifax	1	1	2	3	8
Highfield	3	7	7	3	3
Huddersfield	3	6	2	1	7
Hull	1	3	2	1	3
Hull K.R.	0	0	1	3	3
Hunslet	5	3	2	6	6
Keighley C.	3	2	4	5	10
Leeds	2	1	2	5	3
Leigh	3	1	3	1	7
London C.	1	5	2	1	4
Nottingham C.	–	2	2	2	5
Oldham	2	6	5	3	6
Rochdale H.	1	2	4	5	3
Ryedale-York	4	2	1	3	7
St. Helens	3	1	6	1	6
Salford	1	0	0	5	4
Scarborough P.	–	–	1	–	–
Sheffield E.	1	4	7	2	3
Swinton	2	3	4	1	4
Wakefield T.	3	1	3	2	6
Warrington	0	2	6	2	4
Whitehaven	4	1	5	3	6
Widnes	0	5	2	2	6
Wigan	1	2	2	7	8
Workington T.	2	4	6	4	8
Totals	**76**	**90**	**127**	**115**	**172**

DISCIPLINARY ANALYSIS 1993-94

The following is a club-by-club disciplinary record for last season, showing the players sent off in first team matches and the findings of the League's Disciplinary Committee.

The committee's verdict is featured in the brackets after the player's name, each number indicating the match ban imposed. SOS stands for sending off sufficient and NG for not guilty. A suspension reduced or increased on appeal is shown as follows, 6 to 4.

During 1988-89 the totting-up system for sin-bin suspensions was abandoned. Previously two points were issued for a 10-minute temporary dismissal, a one-match ban being imposed when the total reached six. Instead, the sin bins were recorded and taken into account when considering a full dismissal.

The 1984-85 season was the first time video action other than official BBC or ITV tapes could be offered in evidence. Seven cases were considered by the committee after viewing a video, the player not having been dismissed.

Four-match ban for Alan Hunte, one of three St. Helens players to be sent off during the 1993-94 season.

Club	Total sent off	Dismissed Player	Number of sin bins
Barrow	2	Stuart Rhodes (2), Sam Hansen (NG)	9
Batley	3	Jeff Grayshon (SOS), Jimmy Irvine (2, SOS)	17
Bradford N.	2	Dave Watson (5), Paul Medley (1)	6
Bramley	3	Ray Ashton (SOS), Kevin Bell (3), Dean Hall (10)	16
Carlisle	9	Ian Armstrong (1), Gary Murdock (4, SOS), Barry Williams (4,3), Gary Charlton (6 to 4), Duncan McCartney (2), Anthony Coffey (5), Adam Bertoli (2)	19
Castleford	1	Andy Fisher (2)	16
Dewsbury	4	Neil Kelly (SOS, NG), Mark Conway (2,1)	10
Doncaster	3	Andy Clarke (6), Sonny Whakarau (2), Vila Matautia (2)	16
Featherstone R.	3	Neil Roebuck (3), Gary H. Price (SOS), Steve Molloy (1)	13
Halifax	1	Michael Wilson (1)	11
Highfield	3	David Hine (1), David Brown (1), Tony Pemberton (2)	3

Huddersfield	3	Gary Senior (4), Gary Coulter (2), Andy Pucill (1)	9
Hull	1	Tim Street (2)	16
Hull K.R.	0		3
Hunslet	5	David Croft (4, 2), Roy Sampson (SOS), Mark Ellis (2, 1)	10
Keighley C.	3	Brendan Hill (4), Andy Eyres (2 to SOS), Robert Reeves (3)	7
Leeds	2	Simon Irving (2), Harvey Howard (SOS)	11
Leigh	3	Mark Meadows (2), Mark Sarsfield (6), Liuaki Hansen (6)	9
London C.	1	Sam Stewart (1)	8
Oldham	2	Barrie McDermott (4,2)	14
Rochdale H.	1	Carl Partington (6)	10
Ryedale-York	4	Lee Marsden (SOS), Dean Thomas (NG), Mark Lyons (NG, NG)	4
St. Helens	3	Tommy Martyn (1), Alan Hunte (4), Sonny Nickle (2)	11
Salford	1	Andy Gregory (4)	11
Sheffield E.	1	Lee Jackson (1)	4
Swinton	2	Tony Humphries (4), Danny Whittle (4)	12
Wakefield T.	3	Paul Round (2), Matt Fuller (SOS), David Woods (1)	10
Warrington	0		7
Whitehaven	4	David Lightfoot (4), Billy Fisher (6), John Routledge (4), Clayton Friend (1)	6
Widnes	0		14
Wigan	1	Andy Platt (1)	13
Workington T.	2	Martin Oglanby (3), James Pickering (2)	8

In addition, the Disciplinary Committee carried out seven trials by video, calling up after viewing a video tape players who had not been dismissed by the referee. The following match bans were imposed: Gary Coulter of Huddersfield (4); Wally Gibson of Oldham (2); John Fieldhouse of Halifax (1 to SOS); Andy Clarke of Doncaster (4); Martin Rowse of Doncaster (5); Neil Cowie of Wigan (NG); Dean Sampson of Castleford (4).

SPONSORSHIP
This updated sub-section is a record of the sponsorship programme under the control of the Rugby Football League.

1993-94 COMPETITIONS:

Silk Cut Challenge Cup	£360,000
Regal Trophy	£360,000
Stones Bitter Championship and Premiership	£335,000
John Smith's Tests	£250,000
GRAND TOTAL	£1,305,000

QUEEN'S HONOURS

Nine Rugby League players have been awarded the MBE by Her Majesty the Queen for their services to the game. Former Castleford player-coach Malcolm Reilly was awarded the OBE in June 1991, while Great Britain's full-time coach.

Player	Awarded MBE	GB Caps	Career	Clubs
Eric Ashton	June 1966	26	1955-69	Wigan
Geoff Gunney	June 1970	11	1951-73	Hunslet
Clive Sullivan	January 1974	17	1961-85	Hull, Hull K.R., Oldham, Doncaster
Chris Hesketh	January 1976	21+2	1963-79	Wigan, Salford
Roger Millward	January 1983	28+1	1963-80	Castleford, Hull K.R.
Neil Fox	June 1983	29	1956-79	Wakefield T., Bradford N., Hull K.R., York, Bramley, Huddersfield
David Watkins	January 1986	2+4	1967-82	Salford, Swinton, Cardiff C.
Ellery Hanley	January 1990	33+1	1978-	Bradford N., Wigan, Leeds
Jeff Grayshon	June 1992	13	1970-	Dewsbury, Bradford N., Leeds, Featherstone R., Batley
	Awarded OBE			
Malcolm Reilly	June 1991	9	1967-87	Castleford

ATTENDANCES

CLUB ATTENDANCE REVIEW

The following is a review of clubs' home attendances for League matches from 1985-86.

The main figure is the individual club's average gate for League games during that season. The figure in brackets indicates an upward or downward trend compared with the previous season.

Also indicated is the division the club competed in that season, i.e.,

1 — First Division, 2 — Second Division, 3 — Third Division.

Club	85-86	86-87	87-88	88-89	89-90	90-91	91-92	92-93	93-94
Barrow	2 1926 (−802)	1 2664 (+738)	2 1624 (−1040)	2 1594 (−30)	1 1997 (+403)	2 962 (−1035)	3 1003 (+41)	3 786 (−217)	2 1318 (+532)
Batley	2 930 (−85)	2 744 (−186)	2 859 (+115)	2 924 (+65)	2 1506 (+582)	2 1188 (−318)	3 1145 (−43)	3 925 (−220)	2 1227 (+302)
Blackpool G.	2 534 (−21)	2 475 (−59)	2 922 (+447)	2 512 (−410)	2 780 (+258)	2 638 (−142)	3 309 (−329)	3 475 (+166)	—
Bradford N.	1 3975 (−276)	1 4312 (+377)	1 4723 (+411)	1 4969 (+246)	1 5584 (+615)	1 5274 (−310)	1 4725 (−549)	1 5082 (+357)	1 6513 (+1431)
Bramley	2 831 (−27)	2 737 (−94)	2 858 (+121)	2 1004 (+146)	2 982 (−22)	2 805 (−177)	3 870 (+65)	2 980 (+110)	2 729 (−251)
Carlisle	2 618 (−368)	2 789 (+171)	2 763 (−26)	2 678 (−85)	2 574 (−104)	2 781 (+207)	2 800 (+19)	2 648 (−152)	2 603 (−45)
Castleford	1 3701 (+484)	1 4758 (+1057)	1 4520 (−238)	1 6580 (+2060)	1 6428 (−152)	1 6019 (−409)	1 6465 (+446)	1 5658 (−807)	1 5555 (−103)
Chorley B.	—	—	—	—	2 806 (−)	2 690 (−116)	3 394 (−296)	3 434 (+40)	—
Dewsbury	1 1819 (+824)	2 669 (−1150)	2 658 (−11)	2 772 (+114)	2 1227 (+455)	2 955 (−272)	3 1140 (+185)	3 1108 (−32)	2 1366 (+258)
Doncaster	2 689 (+423)	2 1543 (+854)	2 1450 (−93)	2 1906 (+456)	2 1965 (+59)	2 1458 (−507)	3 1158 (−300)	3 997 (−161)	2 1648 (+651)
Featherstone R.	1 2320 (−221)	1 2606 (+286)	2 1879 (−727)	1 4379 (+2500)	1 4269 (−110)	1 4722 (+453)	1 4001 (−721)	2 2670 (−1331)	1 4030 (+1360)
Halifax	1 4944 (+1447)	1 4891 (−53)	1 6521 (+1630)	1 8022 (+1501)	2 5921 (−2101)	2 4458 (−1463)	1 7181 (+2723)	1 6452 (−729)	1 6608 (+156)
Highfield	2 363 (−146)	2 331 (−32)	2 515 (+184)	2 298 (−217)	2 453 (+155)	2 632 (+179)	3 319 (−313)	3 378 (+59)	2 403 (+25)
Huddersfield	2 678 (−227)	2 524 (−154)	2 601 (+77)	2 1114 (+513)	2 1634 (+520)	2 1306 (−328)	3 2271 (+965)	2 1985 (−286)	2 2227 (+242)
Hull	1 6245 (−2280)	1 5538 (−707)	1 5111 (−427)	1 6804 (+1693)	1 6218 (−586)	1 6699 (+481)	1 5892 (−807)	1 4860 (−1032)	1 4314 (−546)
Hull K.R.	1 4855 (−1860)	1 4651 (−204)	1 4186 (−465)	1 5298 (+1112)	2 4851 (−447)	1 4952 (+101)	1 4752 (−200)	1 3609 (−1143)	1 3403 (−206)
Hunslet	2 722 (−1524)	1 1050 (+328)	1 2678 (+1628)	2 947 (−1731)	2 1046 (+99)	2 767 (−279)	3 770 (+3)	3 724 (−46)	2 740 (+16)

Keighley C.	2 685 (−137)	2 445 (−240)	2 958 (+513)	2 961 (+3)	2 936 (−25)	2 985 (+49)	3 1196 (+211)	3 2060 (+864)	2 3032 (+972)
Leeds	1 6928 (−402)	1 6393 (−535)	1 9911 (+3518)	1 12060 (+2149)	1 12251 (+191)	1 11102 (−1149)	1 12164 (+1062)	1 11527 (−637)	1 9545 (−1982)
Leigh	2 2710 (−1112)	1 4232 (+1522)	1 4516 (+284)	2 2346 (−2170)	1 4568 (+2222)	2 1719 (−2849)	2 3014 (+1295)	1 3967 (+953)	1 3385 (−582)
London C.	2 817 (−132)	2 684 (−133)	2 615 (−69)	2 588 (−27)	2 841 (+253)	2 557 (−284)	2 724 (+167)	2 554 (−170)	2 734 (+180)
Nottingham C.	2 487 (−533)	2 368 (−119)	2 368 (−)	2 560 (+192)	2 577 (+17)	2 255 (−322)	3 270 (+15)	3 270 (−)	—
Oldham	1 4333 (−229)	1 3915 (−418)	2 3790 (−125)	1 5759 (+1969)	2 4401 (−1358)	1 5094 (+693)	2 3149 (−1945)	2 2809 (−340)	1 4062 (+1253)
Rochdale H.	2 1267 (+725)	2 877 (−390)	2 1106 (+229)	2 1027 (−79)	2 2510 (+1483)	1 2542 (+32)	2 1415 (−1127)	2 1308 (−107)	2 1063 (−245)
Ryedale-York	1 2828 (+1300)	2 1520 (−1308)	2 1406 (−114)	2 2021 (+615)	2 2495 (+474)	2 1857 (−638)	2 1181 (−676)	3 1701 (+520)	2 1311 (−390)
St. Helens	1 6022 (−1314)	1 7341 (+1319)	1 8417 (+1076)	1 9514 (+1097)	1 8555 (−959)	1 7391 (−1164)	1 8456 (+1065)	1 8908 (+452)	1 7264 (−1644)
Salford	1 2520 (+725)	1 2826 (+306)	1 3747 (+921)	1 5470 (+1723)	1 3720 (−1750)	2 2314 (−1406)	1 3785 (+1471)	1 4098 (+313)	1 4106 (+8)
Scarborough P.	—	—	—	—	—	—	3 777 (−)	—	—
Sheffield E.	2 698 (−187)	2 708 (+10)	2 847 (+139)	2 838 (−9)	1 4038 (+3200)	1 4031 (−7)	2 2435 (−1596)	1 3069 (+634)	1 3050 (−19)
Swinton	1 2706 (+1116)	2 1622 (−1084)	1 2987 (+1365)	2 1435 (−1552)	2 1678 (+243)	2 1737 (+59)	1 2702 (+965)	2 1051 (−1651)	2 788 (−263)
Wakefield T.	2 1714 (+146)	1 2637 (+923)	2 2416 (−221)	1 5151 (+2735)	1 5428 (+277)	1 4848 (−580)	1 5022 (+174)	1 4505 (−517)	1 3822 (−683)
Warrington	1 3618 (−183)	1 4172 (+554)	1 4974 (+802)	1 4893 (−81)	1 5412 (+519)	1 5915 (+503)	1 5204 (−711)	1 4550 (−754)	1 6188 (+1638)
Whitehaven	2 1878 (+338)	2 1800 (−78)	2 1772 (−28)	2 1310 (−462)	2 961 (−349)	2 1035 (+74)	3 632 (−403)	3 1462 (+830)	2 1257 (−205)
Widnes	1 4019 (−247)	1 3840 (−179)	1 6262 (+2422)	1 8648 (+2386)	1 7858 (−790)	1 6793 (−1065)	1 6291 (−502)	1 5540 (−751)	1 4525 (−1015)
Wigan	1 12515 (+2459)	1 12732 (+217)	1 13021 (+289)	1 14543 (+1522)	1 13973 (−570)	1 14493 (+520)	1 14040 (−453)	1 14553 (+513)	1 14561 (+8)
Workington T.	2 702 (−218)	2 653 (−49)	2 737 (+84)	2 774 (+37)	2 691 (−83)	2 1426 (+735)	2 1884 (+458)	3 2040 (+156)	2 2603 (+563)

COMPETITION ATTENDANCE REVIEW

		85-86	86-87	87-88	88-89	89-90	90-91	91-92	92-93	93-94
FIRST	Total	1,100,329	1,162,666	1,060,296	1,327,192	1,173,815	1,168,407	1,185,117	1,122,955	1,364,056
DIVISION	Av.	4,585	4,844	5,826	7,292	6,450	6,420	6,511	6,170	5,683
SECOND	Total	310,311	217,552	381,825	298,776	515,687	371,398	204,304	168,069	315,841
DIVISION	Av.	1,014	863	1,364	1,067	1,754	1,263	1,824	1,501	1,316
THIRD	Total	—	—	—	—	—	—	159,209	160,348	—
DIVISION	Av.							875	1,027	
LEAGUE TOTALS (1st & 2nd) *plus 3rd	Total	1,410,640	1,380,218	1,442,121	1,625,968	1,689,502	1,539,805	1,548,630*	1,451,372*	1,679,897
	Av.	2,584	2,805	3,121	3,519	3,549	3,235	3,253*	3,225*	3,499
R.L. CUP	Av.	8,280	6,965	8,764	8,666	7,339	6,748	6,899	7,771	5,907
REGAL	Av.	4,232	4,122	3,570	4,987	4,876	3,515	4,007	3,624	2,690
PREMIER	Av.	9,273	15,154	13,462	15,856	16,796	12,483	13,513	12,788	13,165
10,000+ (No. of)		36	43	46	59	54	43	49	38	41

20,000-plus crowds .... A 10-year review

All matches except the Rugby League Challenge Cup final at Wembley

25,237	Hull v. Hull K.R.	Yorks Cup final	Hull C. FC	27 Oct. 1984
26,074	St. Helens v. Wigan	Lancs Cup final	Wigan	28 Oct. 1984
25,326	Hull v. Hull K.R.	John Player final	Hull C. FC	26 Jan. 1985
20,982	Hull v. Castleford	RL Cup semi-final	Leeds	6 Apr. 1985
20,968	Hull v. Castleford	RL Cup semi-final replay	Leeds	10 Apr. 1985
22,209	Britain v. New Zealand	Third Test	Elland Rd, Leeds	9 Nov. 1985
21,813	Wigan v. St. Helens	Division One	Wigan	26 Dec. 1985
23,866	Hull K.R. v. Leeds	RL Cup semi-final	Elland Rd, Leeds	29 Mar. 1986
32,485	Hull K.R. v. Leeds	RL Cup semi-final replay	Elland Rd, Leeds	3 Apr. 1986
28,252	Wigan v. St. Helens	Lancs Cup semi-final	Wigan	1 Oct. 1986
30,622	Wigan v. Australia	Tour	Wigan	12 Oct. 1986
20,180	Oldham v. Wigan	Lancs Cup final	St. Helens	19 Oct. 1986
50,583	Britain v. Australia	First Test	Manchester U. FC	25 Oct. 1986
30,808	Britain v. Australia	Second Test	Elland Rd, Leeds	8 Nov. 1986
20,169	Britain v. Australia	Third Test	Wigan	22 Nov. 1986
21,214	St. Helens v. Wigan	Division One	St. Helens	26 Dec. 1986
21,144	Warrington v. Wigan	John Player final	Bolton W. FC	10 Jan. 1987
20,355	Wigan v. St. Helens	Division One	Wigan	17 Apr. 1987
22,457	Wigan v. Halifax	Premiership semi-final	Wigan	10 May 1987
38,756	Warrington v. Wigan	Premiership final	Manchester U. FC	17 May 1987
36,895	Wigan v. Manly	World Club Challenge	Wigan	7 Oct. 1987
20,234	Wigan v. Warrington	Lancs Cup final	St. Helens	11 Oct. 1987
23,809	Wigan v. St. Helens	Division One	Wigan	27 Dec. 1987
25,110	Wigan v. Leeds	RL Cup round 2	Wigan	14 Feb. 1988
20,783	Salford v. Wigan	RL Cup semi-final	Bolton W. FC	12 Mar. 1988

(continued)

439

20,534	Halifax v. Hull	RL Cup semi-final	Leeds	26 Mar. 1988
25,117	Halifax v. Hull	RL Cup semi-final replay	Elland Rd, Leeds	30 Mar. 1988
21,812	St. Helens v. Wigan	Division One	St. Helens	1 Apr. 1988
35,252	St. Helens v. Widnes	Premiership final	Manchester U. FC	15 May 1988
22,968	Castleford v. Leeds	Yorks Cup final	Elland Rd, Leeds	16 Oct. 1988
20,709	Widnes v. Wigan	John Player final	Bolton W. FC	7 Jan. 1989
26,080	Leeds v. Widnes	RL Cup round 2	Leeds	26 Feb. 1989
26,529	Warrington v. Wigan	RL Cup semi-final	Manchester C. FC	25 Mar. 1989
21,076	Wigan v. St. Helens	Division One	Wigan	12 Apr. 1989
40,194	Hull v. Widnes	Premiership final	Manchester U. FC	14 May 1989
30,786	Widnes v. Canberra	World Club Challenge	Manchester U. FC	4 Oct. 1989
20,346	Britain v. New Zealand	Third Test	Wigan	11 Nov. 1989
27,075	Wigan v. St. Helens	Division One	Wigan	26 Dec. 1989
23,570	Leeds v. Wigan	Division One	Leeds	4 Mar. 1990
26,489	St. Helens v. Wigan	RL Cup semi-final	Manchester U. FC	10 Mar. 1990
24,462	Wigan v. Leeds	Division One	Wigan	10 Apr. 1990
40,796	Bradford N. v. Widnes	Premiership final	Manchester U. FC	13 May 1990
24,814	Wigan v. Australia	Tour	Wigan	14 Oct. 1990
54,569	Britain v. Australia	First Test	Wembley	27 Oct. 1990
46,615	Britain v. Australia	Second Test	Manchester U. FC	10 Nov. 1990
32,500	Britain v. Australia	Third Test	Elland Rd, Leeds	24 Nov. 1990
29,763	Wigan v. Widnes	Division One	Wigan	9 Apr. 1991
42,043	Hull v. Widnes	Premiership final	Manchester U. FC	12 May 1991
20,152	Wigan v. Penrith	World Club Challenge	Liverpool FC	2 Oct. 1991
26,307	Wigan v. St. Helens	Division One	Wigan	26 Dec. 1991
21,736	Wigan v. Warrington	RL Cup round 2	Wigan	16 Feb. 1992
20,821	Leeds v. Wigan	Division One	Leeds	15 Mar. 1992
33,157	St. Helens v. Wigan	Premiership final	Manchester U. FC	17 May 1992
20,534	St. Helens v. Wigan	Lancs Cup final	St. Helens	18 Oct. 1992
73,631	Britain v. Australia	World Cup final	Wembley	24 Oct. 1992
20,258	Leeds v. Castleford	Division One	Leeds	26 Dec. 1992
21,191	Wigan v. St. Helens	RL Cup round 2	Wigan	13 Feb. 1993
20,057	Leeds v. Wigan	Division One	Leeds	3 Mar. 1993
20,085	Bradford N. v. Wigan	RL Cup semi-final	Elland Rd, Leeds	27 Mar. 1993
29,839	Wigan v. St. Helens	Division One	Wigan	9 Apr. 1993
36,598	St. Helens v. Wigan	Premiership final	Manchester U. FC	16 May 1993
36,131	Britain v. New Zealand	First Test	Wembley	16 Oct. 1993
29,100	Wigan v. St. Helens	Division One	Wigan	26 Dec. 1993
22,615	Leeds v. Bradford N.	RL Cup quarter-final	Leeds	27 Feb. 1994
20,771	St. Helens v. Leeds	RL Cup semi-final	Wigan	26 Mar. 1994
35,644	Castleford v. Wigan	Premiership final	Manchester U. FC	22 May 1994

1993-94 ATTENDANCE ANALYSIS
FIRST DIVISION

Total 1,364,056

Average 5,683

Wigan extended their own divisional record for the highest average gate to 14,561, topping the attendance chart for the 10th successive season. Seven of the 16 clubs registered increases in gates, including Salford and Wigan who both added just eight per match. Joint table-toppers Warrington attracted the biggest increase with 1,638 per match. The return to a 16-club First Division format brought in an extra 241,101 spectators, but the average gate for the 240 fixtures fell from 6,170 in 1992-93 to 5,683, a 7.9 per cent annual decrease.

SECOND DIVISION

Total 315,841
Average 1,316

The scrapping of the Third Division and the return to a 16-club Second Division resulted in 10 clubs registering an annual increase in gates. Keighley Cougars, the previous season's Third Division champions, led the way by topping the chart with an average gate of over 3,000, an annual increase of nearly 50 per cent. The annual difference between the 112 games in the previous season's eight-club Second Division and the 240 matches in the 1993-94 16-club format was a decrease of 9.3 per cent.

LEAGUE CHAMPIONSHIP

Aggregate 1,679,897
Average 3,499

The demotion of three clubs and a return to two divisions of 16 brought about the best average League gates for four years. The 480 fixtures in both divisions attracted over 200,000 extra attendees to boost the annual average to 3,499, an increase of 8.5 per cent.

SILK CUT CHALLENGE CUP

The introduction of a new format for the 1993-94 Silk Cut Challenge Cup, with the Second Division clubs entertaining non-League opposition in the third round and the First Division clubs entering in the fourth round, brought an inevitable decrease in the average gate, although the experiment did increase awareness. The 47 ties from the third round onwards attracted an aggregate of 277,671 fans, an average of 5,907, an annual decrease of 24 per cent compared with the previous season's figure of 7,771.

REGAL TROPHY

A new Regal Trophy formula welcomed 16 non-League sides into a first round, playing away to Second Division clubs, the 16 First Division sides being exempt until the second round. Accordingly, the extra fixtures forced a decrease in the average gates, the 47-tie competition attracting 126,476 spectators, for an average of 2,690, a 26 per cent decrease compared with the 1992-93 figure of 3,624.

STONES BITTER PREMIERSHIP

A total of 92,157 spectators watched the 1994 seven-tie end-of-season tournament, the average gate of 13,165 being a three per cent increase on the 1993 figure of 12,788.

SECOND DIVISION PREMIERSHIP

The scrapping of the Third Division after two years brought about a return to the old seven-tie Second Division Premiership, which attracted a total turnout of 15,600 – excluding the Old Trafford final – for an average gate of 2,600 from six games. This was an annual increase of seven per cent compared with the 1993 figure of 2,428 from 10 matches.

FIVE-FIGURE CROWDS

There was a total of 41 five-figure crowds in 1993-94, compared with 38 in the previous campaign. The Silk Cut Challenge Cup final was again the biggest attraction, with a sell-out crowd of 78,348. Of the 25 five-figure crowds in the Stones Bitter Championship, 14 were at Wigan with a further four being at grounds where the Riversiders were visitors. Five matches exceeded 20,000, including over 36,000 for the first John Smith's Test between Great Britain and New Zealand at Wembley.

The 10,000-plus gates were divided into the following categories:

League....................................25
Challenge Cup 7
Premiership Trophy.................... 4
New Zealand Tour 4
Regal Trophy........................... 1

STONES BITTER CHAMPIONSHIP	1993-94 Average	Annual Difference
Wigan	14561	(+8)
Leeds	9545	(−1982)
St. Helens	7264	(−1644)
Halifax	6608	(+156)
Bradford N.	6513	(+1431)
Warrington	6188	(+1638)
Castleford	5555	(−103)
Widnes	4525	(−1015)
Hull	4314	(−546)
Salford	4106	(+8)
*Oldham	4062	(+1253)
*Featherstone R.	4030	(+1360)
Wakefield T.	3822	(−683)
Hull K.R.	3403	(−206)
Leigh	3385	(−582)
Sheffield E.	3050	(−19)

*Promoted 1992-93

SECOND DIVISION	1993-94 Average	Annual Difference
Keighley C.	3032	(+972)
Workington T.	2603	(+563)
Huddersfield	2227	(+242)
Doncaster	1648	(+651)
Dewsbury	1366	(+258)
Barrow	1318	(+532)
Ryedale-York	1311	(−390)
Whitehaven	1257	(−205)
Batley	1227	(+302)
Rochdale H.	1063	(−245)
Swinton	788	(−263)
Hunslet	740	(+16)
London C.	734	(+180)
Bramley	729	(−251)
Carlisle	603	(−45)
Highfield	403	(+25)

FIXTURES

STONES BITTER CHAMPIONSHIP 1994-95

FRIDAY, 19 AUGUST 1994

Workington T.	v.	Leeds	7.30

SUNDAY, 21 AUGUST 1994

Featherstone R.	v.	Wigan	3.30
Hull	v.	Warrington	3.15
Oldham	v.	Halifax	3.00
St. Helens	v.	Doncaster	3.00
Wakefield T.	v.	Salford	3.30
Widnes	v.	Castleford	3.00

TUESDAY, 23 AUGUST 1994

Sheffield E.	v.	Bradford N.	7.45

WEDNESDAY, 24 AUGUST 1994

Warrington	v.	St. Helens	7.30

FRIDAY, 26 AUGUST 1994

Doncaster	v.	Widnes	7.30

SUNDAY, 28 AUGUST 1994

Bradford N.	v.	Oldham	3.00
Castleford	v.	Workington T.	3.30
Halifax	v.	St. Helens	3.00
Leeds	v.	Featherstone R.	3.00
Salford	v.	Hull	3.00
Warrington	v.	Wakefield T.	3.00
Wigan	v.	Sheffield E.	3.00

WEDNESDAY, 31 AUGUST 1994

Widnes	v.	Salford	7.30

FRIDAY, 2 SEPTEMBER 1994

Wakefield T.	v.	Bradford N.	7.30

SUNDAY, 4 SEPTEMBER 1994

Doncaster	v.	Leeds	3.00
Featherstone R.	v.	Warrington	3.30
Hull	v.	Castleford	3.15
Oldham	v.	Wigan	3.00
St. Helens	v.	Salford	3.00
Widnes	v.	Halifax	3.00
Workington T.	v.	Sheffield E.	3.00

WEDNESDAY, 7 SEPTEMBER 1994

Bradford N.	v.	Warrington	7.30

FRIDAY, 9 SEPTEMBER 1994

Wigan	v.	Leeds	7.30

SUNDAY, 11 SEPTEMBER 1994

Bradford N.	v.	Widnes	3.00
Castleford	v.	Sheffield E.	3.30
Doncaster	v.	Wakefield T.	3.00
Halifax	v.	Hull	3.00
Salford	v.	Featherstone R.	3.00
Warrington	v.	Oldham	3.00
Workington T.	v.	St. Helens	3.00

FRIDAY, 16 SEPTEMBER 1994

Featherstone R.	v.	Bradford N.	7.30

SUNDAY, 18 SEPTEMBER 1994

Halifax	v.	Wakefield T.	3.00
Leeds	v.	Salford	3.00
Oldham	v.	Doncaster	3.00
Sheffield E.	v.	Warrington	3.15
St. Helens	v.	Castleford	3.00
Wigan	v.	Widnes	3.00
Workington T.	v.	Hull	3.00

FRIDAY, 23 SEPTEMBER 1994

Castleford	v.	Wigan	7.30

SUNDAY, 25 SEPTEMBER 1994

Bradford N.	v.	Workington T.	3.00
Doncaster	v.	Warrington	3.00
Hull	v.	Oldham	3.15
St. Helens	v.	Sheffield E.	3.00
Salford	v.	Halifax	3.00
Wakefield T.	v.	Featherstone R.	3.30
Widnes	v.	Leeds	3.00

FRIDAY, 30 SEPTEMBER 1994

Leeds	v.	Castleford	7.30

SUNDAY, 2 OCTOBER 1994

Featherstone R.	v.	Workington T.	3.30
Halifax	v.	Warrington	3.00
Hull	v.	Bradford N.	3.15
Oldham	v.	St. Helens	3.00
Salford	v.	Doncaster	3.00
Sheffield E.	v.	Widnes	3.15
Wigan	v.	Wakefield T.	3.00

FRIDAY, 7 OCTOBER 1994

Warrington	v.	Bradford N.	7.30

SUNDAY, 9 OCTOBER 1994

Castleford	v.	Salford	3.30
Doncaster	v.	Halifax	3.00
St. Helens	v.	Leeds	3.00
Sheffield E.	v.	Hull	3.15
Wakefield T.	v.	Oldham	3.30
Widnes	v.	Featherstone R.	3.00

WEDNESDAY, 12 OCTOBER 1994

Workington T.	v.	Wigan	7.30

FRIDAY, 14 OCTOBER 1994

Oldham	v.	Widnes	7.30

SUNDAY, 16 OCTOBER 1994

Bradford N.	v.	St. Helens	3.00
Doncaster	v.	Castleford	3.00
Leeds	v.	Sheffield E.	3.00
Wakefield T.	v.	Hull	3.30
Warrington	v.	Workington T.	3.00
Wigan	v.	Salford	3.00

TUESDAY, 25 OCTOBER 1994

Featherstone R.	v.	Halifax	7.30

FRIDAY, 28 OCTOBER 1994

Hull	v.	Wigan	7.30

SUNDAY, 30 OCTOBER 1994

Castleford	v.	Bradford N.	3.30
Halifax	v.	Sheffield E.	3.00
Leeds	v.	Wakefield T.	3.00
Oldham	v.	Featherstone R.	3.00
Workington T.	v.	Doncaster	3.00

FRIDAY, 4 NOVEMBER 1994

Salford	v.	Wakefield T.	7.30

SUNDAY, 6 NOVEMBER 1994

Bradford N.	v.	Sheffield E.	3.00
Castleford	v.	Widnes	3.30
Doncaster	v.	St. Helens	3.00
Halifax	v.	Oldham	3.00
Leeds	v.	Workington T.	3.00
Warrington	v.	Hull	3.00
Wigan	v.	Featherstone R.	3.00

FRIDAY, 11 NOVEMBER 1994

Sheffield E.	v.	Wigan	7.30

SUNDAY, 13 NOVEMBER 1994

Featherstone R.	v.	Leeds	3.30
Hull	v.	Salford	3.15
St. Helens	v.	Halifax	3.00
Wakefield T.	v.	Warrington	3.30
Widnes	v.	Doncaster	3.00
Workington T.	v.	Castleford	3.00

TUESDAY, 22 NOVEMBER 1994

Oldham	v.	Bradford N.	7.30

FRIDAY, 25 NOVEMBER 1994

Halifax	v.	Widnes	7.30

SUNDAY, 27 NOVEMBER 1994

Bradford N.	v.	Wakefield T.	3.00
Castleford	v.	Hull	3.30
Leeds	v.	Doncaster	3.00
Salford	v.	St. Helens	3.00
Sheffield E.	v.	Workington T.	3.15
Warrington	v.	Featherstone R.	3.00
Wigan	v.	Oldham	3.00

FRIDAY, 9 DECEMBER 1994

Sheffield E.	v.	Castleford	7.30

SUNDAY, 11 DECEMBER 1994

Featherstone R.	v.	Salford	3.30
Hull	v.	Halifax	3.15
Leeds	v.	Wigan	3.00
Oldham	v.	Warrington	3.00
St. Helens	v.	Workington T.	3.00
Wakefield T.	v.	Doncaster	3.30
Widnes	v.	Bradford N.	3.00

MONDAY, 26 DECEMBER 1994

Castleford	v.	Featherstone R.	3.30
Halifax	v.	Bradford N.	3.00
Hull	v.	Leeds	3.15
St. Helens	v.	Wigan	3.00
Salford	v.	Oldham	3.00
Sheffield E.	v.	Doncaster	3.15
Warrington	v.	Widnes	3.00
Workington T.	v.	Wakefield T.	3.00

SUNDAY, 1 JANUARY 1995

Bradford N.	v.	Salford	3.00
Doncaster	v.	Hull	3.00
Featherstone R.	v.	Sheffield E.	3.30
Leeds	v.	Halifax	3.00
Oldham	v.	Workington T.	3.00
Wakefield T.	v.	Castleford	3.30
Widnes	v.	St. Helens	3.00
Wigan	v.	Warrington	3.00

FRIDAY, 6 JANUARY 1995

Widnes	v.	Workington T.	7.30

SUNDAY, 8 JANUARY 1995

Doncaster	v.	Bradford N.	3.00
Featherstone R.	v.	Hull	3.30
Halifax	v.	Wigan	3.00
Oldham	v.	Leeds	3.00
Salford	v.	Sheffield E.	3.00
Wakefield T.	v.	St. Helens	3.30
Warrington	v.	Castleford	3.00

FRIDAY, 13 JANUARY 1995

Salford	v.	Warrington	7.30

SUNDAY, 15 JANUARY 1995

Castleford	v.	Oldham	3.30
Hull	v.	Widnes	3.15
Leeds	v.	Bradford N.	3.00
St. Helens	v.	Featherstone R.	3.00
Sheffield E.	v.	Wakefield T.	3.15
Wigan	v.	Doncaster	3.00
Workington T.	v.	Halifax	3.00

FRIDAY, 20 JANUARY 1995

Bradford N.	v.	Wigan	7.30

SUNDAY, 22 JANUARY 1995

Featherstone R.	v.	Doncaster	3.30
Halifax	v.	Castleford	3.00
Leeds	v.	Warrington	3.00
Oldham	v.	Sheffield E.	3.00
St. Helens	v.	Hull	3.00
Widnes	v.	Wakefield T.	3.00
Workington T.	v.	Salford	3.00

FRIDAY, 27 JANUARY 1995

Warrington	v.	Sheffield E.	7.30

SUNDAY, 29 JANUARY 1995

Bradford N.	v.	Featherstone R.	3.00
Castleford	v.	St. Helens	3.30
Doncaster	v.	Oldham	3.00
Hull	v.	Workington T.	3.15
Salford	v.	Leeds	3.00
Wakefield T.	v.	Halifax	3.30
Widnes	v.	Wigan	3.00

FRIDAY, 3 FEBRUARY 1995

Leeds	v.	Widnes	7.30

SUNDAY, 5 FEBRUARY 1995

Featherstone R.	v.	Wakefield T.	3.30
Halifax	v.	Salford	3.00
Oldham	v.	Hull	3.00
Sheffield E.	v.	St. Helens	3.15
Warrington	v.	Doncaster	3.00
Wigan	v.	Castleford	3.00
Workington T.	v.	Bradford N.	3.00

FRIDAY, 17 FEBRUARY 1995

Castleford	v.	Leeds	7.30

SUNDAY, 19 FEBRUARY 1995

Bradford N.	v.	Hull	3.00
Doncaster	v.	Salford	3.00
St. Helens	v.	Oldham	3.00
Wakefield T.	v.	Wigan	3.30
Warrington	v.	Halifax	3.00
Widnes	v.	Sheffield E.	3.00
Workington T.	v.	Featherstone R.	3.00

FRIDAY, 3 MARCH 1995

Hull	v.	Sheffield E.	7.30

SUNDAY, 5 MARCH 1995

Featherstone R.	v.	Widnes	3.30
Halifax	v.	Doncaster	3.00
Leeds	v.	St. Helens	3.00
Oldham	v.	Wakefield T.	3.00
Salford	v.	Castleford	3.00
Wigan	v.	Workington T.	3.00

FRIDAY, 17 MARCH 1995

St. Helens	v.	Bradford N.	7.30

SUNDAY, 19 MARCH 1995

Castleford	v.	Halifax	3.30
Doncaster	v.	Featherstone R.	3.00
Hull	v.	Wakefield T.	3.15
Salford	v.	Wigan	3.00
Sheffield E.	v.	Leeds	3.15
Widnes	v.	Oldham	3.00
Workington T.	v.	Warrington	3.00

SUNDAY, 26 MARCH 1995

Bradford N.	v.	Leeds	3.00
Doncaster	v.	Wigan	3.00
Featherstone R.	v.	St. Helens	3.30
Halifax	v.	Workington T.	3.00
Oldham	v.	Castleford	3.00
Wakefield T.	v.	Sheffield E.	3.30
Warrington	v.	Salford	3.00
Widnes	v.	Hull	3.00

SUNDAY, 2 APRIL 1995

Bradford N.	v.	Doncaster	3.00
Castleford	v.	Warrington	3.30
Hull	v.	Featherstone R.	3.15
Leeds	v.	Oldham	3.00
St. Helens	v.	Wakefield T.	3.00
Sheffield E.	v.	Salford	3.15
Wigan	v.	Halifax	3.00
Workington T.	v.	Widnes	3.00

SUNDAY, 9 APRIL 1995

Castleford	v.	Doncaster	3.30
Halifax	v.	Featherstone R.	3.00
Hull	v.	St. Helens	3.15
Salford	v.	Workington T.	3.00
Sheffield E.	v.	Oldham	3.15
Wakefield T.	v.	Widnes	3.30
Warrington	v.	Leeds	3.00
Wigan	v.	Bradford N.	3.00

FRIDAY, 14 APRIL 1995

Bradford N.	v.	Halifax	7.30
Doncaster	v.	Sheffield E.	7.30
Featherstone R.	v.	Castleford	7.30
Leeds	v.	Hull	7.30
Oldham	v.	Salford	3.00
Wakefield T.	v.	Workington T.	7.30
Widnes	v.	Warrington	3.00
Wigan	v.	St. Helens	3.00

MONDAY, 17 APRIL 1995

Castleford	v.	Wakefield T.	3.00
Halifax	v.	Leeds	3.00
Hull	v.	Doncaster	3.15
St. Helens	v.	Widnes	3.00
Salford	v.	Bradford N.	3.00
Sheffield E.	v.	Featherstone R.	3.15
Warrington	v.	Wigan	3.00
Workington T.	v.	Oldham	3.00

SUNDAY, 23 APRIL 1995

Bradford N.	v.	Castleford	3.00
Doncaster	v.	Workington T.	3.00
Featherstone R.	v.	Oldham	3.30
St. Helens	v.	Warrington	3.00
Salford	v.	Widnes	3.00
Sheffield E.	v.	Halifax	3.15
Wakefield T.	v.	Leeds	3.30
Wigan	v.	Hull	3.00

SECOND DIVISION

SUNDAY, 21 AUGUST 1994

Barrow	v.	Rochdale H.	2.30
Batley	v.	Huddersfield	3.15
Bramley	v.	Dewsbury	3.00
Highfield	v.	Hull K.R.	3.00
Keighley C.	v.	Whitehaven	3.15
Leigh	v.	Hunslet	3.00
London B.	v.	Carlisle	3.00
Swinton	v.	Ryedale-York	3.00

SUNDAY, 28 AUGUST 1994

Carlisle	v.	Batley	3.00
Huddersfield	v.	Barrow	3.30
Hull K.R.	v.	Bramley	3.15
Hunslet	v.	London B.	3.30
Rochdale H.	v.	Keighley C.	3.00
Ryedale-York	v.	Highfield	3.15
Whitehaven	v.	Leigh	3.00

SUNDAY, 4 SEPTEMBER 1994

Barrow	v.	London B.	2.30
Batley	v.	Highfield	3.15
Carlisle	v.	Bramley	3.00
Hunslet	v.	Hull K.R.	3.30
Keighley C.	v.	Ryedale-York	3.15
Leigh	v.	Dewsbury	3.00
Swinton	v.	Huddersfield	3.00
Whitehaven	v.	Rochdale H.	3.00

SUNDAY, 11 SEPTEMBER 1994

Bramley	v.	Whitehaven	2.15
Dewsbury	v.	Barrow	3.00
Highfield	v.	Leigh	3.00
Huddersfield	v.	Hunslet	3.30
Hull K.R.	v.	Swinton	3.15
London B.	v.	Keighley C.	3.00
Rochdale H.	v.	Carlisle	3.00
Ryedale-York	v.	Batley	3.15

SUNDAY, 18 SEPTEMBER 1994

Barrow	v.	Ryedale-York	2.30
Batley	v.	Whitehaven	3.15
Highfield	v.	London B.	3.00
Hull K.R.	v.	Rochdale H.	3.15
Hunslet	v.	Carlisle	3.30
Keighley C.	v.	Dewsbury	3.15
Leigh	v.	Huddersfield	3.00
Swinton	v.	Bramley	3.00

SUNDAY, 25 SEPTEMBER 1994

Bramley	v.	Keighley C.	3.00
Carlisle	v.	Swinton	3.00
Dewsbury	v.	Highfield	3.00
Huddersfield	v.	Hull K.R.	3.30
London B.	v.	Batley	3.00
Rochdale H.	v.	Hunslet	3.00
Ryedale-York	v.	Leigh	3.15
Whitehaven	v.	Barrow	3.00

SUNDAY, 2 OCTOBER 1994

Barrow	v.	Keighley C.	2.30
Batley	v.	Rochdale H.	3.15
Carlisle	v.	Dewsbury	3.00
Highfield	v.	Huddersfield	3.00
Hunslet	v.	Ryedale-York	3.30
Leigh	v.	Bramley	3.00
London B.	v.	Swinton	3.00
Whitehaven	v.	Hull K.R.	3.00

SUNDAY, 9 OCTOBER 1994

Barrow	v.	Leigh	2.30
Bramley	v.	Highfield	3.00
Dewsbury	v.	London B.	3.00
Huddersfield	v.	Rochdale H.	3.30
Hull K.R.	v.	Carlisle	3.15
Keighley C.	v.	Batley	3.15
Ryedale-York	v.	Whitehaven	3.15
Swinton	v.	Hunslet	3.00

SUNDAY, 16 OCTOBER 1994

Batley	v.	Swinton	3.15
Carlisle	v.	Highfield	3.00
Hull K.R.	v.	Barrow	3.15
Hunslet	v.	Keighley C.	3.30
London B.	v.	Bramley	3.00
Rochdale H.	v.	Leigh	3.00
Ryedale-York	v.	Dewsbury	3.15
Whitehaven	v.	Huddersfield	3.00

TUESDAY, 25 OCTOBER 1994

Dewsbury	v.	Swinton	7.30

SUNDAY, 30 OCTOBER 1994

Barrow	v.	Hunslet	2.30
Bramley	v.	Huddersfield	3.00
Dewsbury	v.	Hull K.R.	3.00
Highfield	v.	Rochdale H.	3.00
Keighley C.	v.	Carlisle	3.15
Leigh	v.	Batley	3.00
London B.	v.	Ryedale-York	3.00
Swinton	v.	Whitehaven	3.00

SUNDAY, 6 NOVEMBER 1994

Carlisle	v.	London B.	3.00
Dewsbury	v.	Bramley	3.00
Huddersfield	v.	Batley	3.30
Hull K.R.	v.	Highfield	3.15
Hunslet	v.	Leigh	3.30
Rochdale H.	v.	Barrow	3.00
Ryedale-York	v.	Swinton	3.15
Whitehaven	v.	Keighley C.	3.00

SUNDAY, 13 NOVEMBER 1994

Barrow	v.	Huddersfield	2.30
Batley	v.	Carlisle	3.15
Bramley	v.	Hull K.R.	3.00
Highfield	v.	Ryedale-York	3.00
Keighley C.	v.	Rochdale H.	3.15
Leigh	v.	Whitehaven	3.00
London B.	v.	Hunslet	3.00
Swinton	v.	Dewsbury	3.00

SUNDAY, 11 DECEMBER 1994

Bramley	v.	Carlisle	3.00
Dewsbury	v.	Leigh	3.00
Highfield	v.	Batley	3.00
Huddersfield	v.	Swinton	3.30
Hull K.R.	v.	Hunslet	3.15
London B.	v.	Barrow	3.00
Rochdale H.	v.	Whitehaven	3.00
Ryedale-York	v.	Keighley C.	3.15

SUNDAY, 18 DECEMBER 1994

Barrow	v.	Dewsbury	2.30
Batley	v.	Ryedale-York	3.15
Carlisle	v.	Rochdale H.	3.00
Hunslet	v.	Huddersfield	3.30
Keighley C.	v.	London B.	3.15
Leigh	v.	Highfield	3.00
Swinton	v.	Hull K.R.	3.00
Whitehaven	v.	Bramley	3.00

MONDAY, 26 DECEMBER 1994

Bramley	v.	Hunslet	3.00
Carlisle	v.	Barrow	3.00
Dewsbury	v.	Batley	11.30
Highfield	v.	Whitehaven	3.00
Keighley C.	v.	Hull K.R.	3.15
Leigh	v.	London B.	3.00
Rochdale H.	v.	Swinton	3.00
Ryedale-York	v.	Huddersfield	3.15

SUNDAY, 1 JANUARY 1995

Barrow	v.	Highfield	2.30
Huddersfield	v.	Keighley C.	3.30
Hull K.R.	v.	Ryedale-York	3.15
Hunslet	v.	Dewsbury	3.30
London B.	v.	Rochdale H.	3.00
Swinton	v.	Leigh	3.00
Whitehaven	v.	Carlisle	3.00

MONDAY, 2 JANUARY 1995

Batley	v.	Bramley	3.15

SUNDAY, 8 JANUARY 1995

Batley	v.	Barrow	3.15
Bramley	v.	Ryedale-York	3.00
Carlisle	v.	Huddersfield	3.00
Highfield	v.	Swinton	3.00
Hull K.R.	v.	London B.	3.15
Keighley C.	v.	Leigh	3.15
Rochdale H.	v.	Dewsbury	3.00
Whitehaven	v.	Hunslet	3.00

SUNDAY, 15 JANUARY 1995

Barrow	v.	Bramley	2.30
Batley	v.	Hull K.R.	3.15
Dewsbury	v.	Whitehaven	3.00
Huddersfield	v.	London B.	3.30
Hunslet	v.	Highfield	3.30
Leigh	v.	Carlisle	3.00
Ryedale-York	v.	Rochdale H.	3.15
Swinton	v.	Keighley C.	3.00

SUNDAY, 29 JANUARY 1995

Bramley	v.	Swinton	3.00
Carlisle	v.	Hunslet	3.00
Dewsbury	v.	Keighley C.	3.00
Huddersfield	v.	Leigh	3.30
London B.	v.	Highfield	3.00
Rochdale H.	v.	Hull K.R.	3.00
Ryedale-York	v.	Barrow	3.15
Whitehaven	v.	Batley	3.00

SUNDAY, 5 FEBRUARY 1995

Barrow	v.	Whitehaven	2.30
Batley	v.	London B.	3.15
Highfield	v.	Dewsbury	3.00
Hull K.R.	v.	Huddersfield	3.15
Hunslet	v.	Rochdale H.	3.30
Keighley C.	v.	Bramley	3.15
Leigh	v.	Ryedale-York	3.00
Swinton	v.	Carlisle	3.00

SUNDAY, 19 FEBRUARY 1995

Bramley	v.	Leigh	3.00
Dewsbury	v.	Carlisle	3.00
Huddersfield	v.	Highfield	3.30
Hull K.R.	v.	Whitehaven	3.15
Keighley C.	v.	Barrow	3.15
Rochdale H.	v.	Batley	3.00
Ryedale-York	v.	Hunslet	3.15
Swinton	v.	London B.	3.00

SUNDAY, 5 MARCH 1995

Batley	v.	Keighley C.	3.15
Carlisle	v.	Hull K.R.	3.00
Highfield	v.	Bramley	3.00
Hunslet	v.	Swinton	3.30
Leigh	v.	Barrow	3.00
London B.	v.	Dewsbury	3.00
Rochdale H.	v.	Huddersfield	3.00
Whitehaven	v.	Ryedale-York	3.00

SUNDAY, 12 MARCH 1995

Barrow	v.	Swinton	2.30
Dewsbury	v.	Huddersfield	3.00
Hull K.R.	v.	Leigh	3.15
Hunslet	v.	Batley	3.30
Keighley C.	v.	Highfield	3.15
London B.	v.	Whitehaven	3.00
Rochdale H.	v.	Bramley	3.00
Ryedale-York	v.	Carlisle	3.15

SUNDAY, 19 MARCH 1995

Barrow	v.	Hull K.R.	2.30
Bramley	v.	London B.	3.00
Dewsbury	v.	Ryedale-York	3.00
Highfield	v.	Carlisle	3.00
Huddersfield	v.	Whitehaven	3.30
Keighley C.	v.	Hunslet	3.15
Leigh	v.	Rochdale H.	3.00
Swinton	v.	Batley	3.00

SUNDAY, 26 MARCH 1995

Batley	v.	Leigh	3.15
Carlisle	v.	Keighley C.	3.00
Huddersfield	v.	Bramley	3.30
Hull K.R.	v.	Dewsbury	3.15
Hunslet	v.	Barrow	3.30
Rochdale H.	v.	Highfield	3.00
Ryedale-York	v.	London B.	3.15
Whitehaven	v.	Swinton	3.00

SUNDAY, 2 APRIL 1995

Barrow	v.	Batley	2.30
Dewsbury	v.	Rochdale H.	3.00
Huddersfield	v.	Carlisle	3.30
Hunslet	v.	Whitehaven	3.30
Leigh	v.	Keighley C.	3.00
London B.	v.	Hull K.R.	3.00
Ryedale-York	v.	Bramley	3.15
Swinton	v.	Highfield	3.00

FRIDAY, 7 APRIL 1995

Hull K.R.	v.	Batley	7.30

SUNDAY, 9 APRIL 1995

Bramley	v.	Barrow	3.00
Carlisle	v.	Leigh	3.00
Highfield	v.	Hunslet	3.00
Keighley C.	v.	Swinton	3.15
London B.	v.	Huddersfield	3.00
Rochdale H.	v.	Ryedale-York	3.00
Whitehaven	v.	Dewsbury	3.00

FRIDAY, 14 APRIL 1995

Barrow	v.	Carlisle	2.30
Batley	v.	Dewsbury	7.30
Huddersfield	v.	Ryedale-York	7.30
Hull K.R.	v.	Keighley C.	3.15
Hunslet	v.	Bramley	7.30
London B.	v.	Leigh	3.00
Swinton	v.	Rochdale H.	3.00
Whitehaven	v.	Highfield	3.00

MONDAY, 17 APRIL 1995

Bramley	v.	Batley	3.00
Carlisle	v.	Whitehaven	3.00
Dewsbury	v.	Hunslet	3.00
Highfield	v.	Barrow	3.00
Keighley C.	v.	Huddersfield	3.15
Leigh	v.	Swinton	3.00
Rochdale H.	v.	London B.	3.00
Ryedale-York	v.	Hull K.R.	3.15

SUNDAY, 23 APRIL 1995

Batley	v.	Hunslet	3.15
Bramley	v.	Rochdale H.	3.00
Carlisle	v.	Ryedale-York	3.00
Highfield	v.	Keighley C.	3.00
Huddersfield	v.	Dewsbury	3.30
Leigh	v.	Hull K.R.	3.00
Swinton	v.	Barrow	3.00
Whitehaven	v.	London B.	3.00

PRINCIPAL DATES 1994-95

1994

19/21 August	Stones Bitter Championship campaign opens
22 October	GREAT BRITAIN v. AUSTRALIA (1) at Wembley
30 October	WALES v. AUSTRALIA at Cardiff
5 November	GREAT BRITAIN v. AUSTRALIA (2) at Old Trafford, Manchester
15 November	Great Britain U21 v. Australia at Gateshead
20 November	GREAT BRITAIN v. AUSTRALIA (3) at Elland Road, Leeds
3/4 December	Regal Trophy (Round 2)
17/18 December	Regal Trophy (Round 3)

1995

7/8 January	Regal Trophy (Round 4)
14/15 January	Regal Trophy (Semi-finals)
28 January	Regal Trophy Final
1 February	WALES v. ENGLAND
11/12 February	Silk Cut Challenge Cup (Round 4)
15 February	ENGLAND v. FRANCE
25/26 February	Silk Cut Challenge Cup (Round 5)
4 March	FRANCE v. WALES
	France U21 v. Great Britain U21
	France Academy v. Great Britain Academy
11/12 March	Silk Cut Challenge Cup (Round 6)
15 March	Great Britain Academy v. France Academy
25 March	Silk Cut Challenge Cup (Semi-final 1)
1 April	Silk Cut Challenge Cup (Semi-final 2)
29 April	Silk Cut Challenge Cup Final at Wembley
7 May	Stones Bitter Premiership (Round 1)
	Second Division Premiership (Round 1)
14 May	Stones Bitter Premiership (Semi-finals)
	Second Division Premiership (Semi-finals)
21 May	Stones Bitter Premiership Finals at Old Trafford, Manchester

1994 JOHN SMITH'S AUSTRALIA TOUR ITINERARY

5 October	Leeds
8 October	Wigan
12 October	Castleford
16 October	Halifax
22 October	FIRST JOHN SMITH'S TEST at Wembley
26 October	Sheffield Eagles
30 October	WALES at Cardiff
1 November	St. Helens
5 November	SECOND JOHN SMITH'S TEST at Old Trafford, Manchester
9 November	Warrington
13 November	Bradford Northern
15 November	Great Britain U21 at Gateshead
20 November	THIRD JOHN SMITH'S TEST at Elland Road, Leeds

448